THE
TINKER
AND
TALISMAN

Written by Alan Hudson

First published in Great Britain in 2004
by Welcome To Life UK, Chelsea, London SW10 0EP

All pictures supplied by The Press Association

ISBN 0-9548337-0-8

To my mate Huddy:

Great stuff pal, it brings back many wonderful memories and none better than the goal I scored at Old Trafford in the League Cup when Chopper tried to catapult me out of the ground. I buckled but unlike today's 'divers' stayed on my feet to score one of my all time favourite goals in a red shirt. However, it is no secret that I wanted to wear the royal blue one when Charlie Cooke, Peter Osgood and yourself were strutting your stuff. Can you just imagine the looks on the opposition's faces when reading our team sheet just half an hour before we left the dressing room. Goodness gracious!

Back to you my friend, we have both had our demons to fight against and after reading your latest masterpiece I guess you have rid yourself of yours, but all I can do is carry on fighting like you did after that horrendous car accident. I send my best wishes and hope the 'Tinker' becomes a roaring success for you, for you deserve some luck in a world that had not always been good to both you and I.

I look forward to seeing you again and, as I once wrote to you, you were the best of your era in the position you played. You, like I was never fortunate to reach the finals of the World Cup and show the world our talents, so we really have been down the same path in our lifetimes.

God bless, and congratulations.

Your pal,
George Best

Many people have a lot to thank Alan Hudson for and I am no exception. In the summer of 2001 I was facing the biggest decision of my career. I was leaving West Ham United having spent my whole life at Upton Park and had received offers from both Chelsea and Leeds United among others. I met with David O'Leary who was manager at Elland Road at the time and I have to admit that I was very impressed. At that time, Leeds was a very exciting place to be – they were riding high in the Premiership, had just lost a Champions League semi-final and were very much the up and coming team in England. Apart from that, I knew a few of the lads there including Rio Ferdinand and after speaking a lot to my dad about it we were definitely leaning towards Leeds. I was also worried about the rivalry between the London clubs and moving across the city to Chelsea brought with it problems which I thought I didn't need. It was getting close to the time when I had to make my mind up when my dad got a phone call from Alan whom he has known for many, many years. They talked about what was going on and my dad explained to him that while Chelsea was an attractive option it looked like we would go the other way. Alan, whose opinion I respect, as does my dad, was absolutely certain that turning down a move to Stamford Bridge would be a mistake. If Frank wants to become a star he should go to Chelsea he told him, he would just be another number at Leeds. That advice began a chain of events, which saw me sign for the Blues, and I don't think I have to say how happy I am with how things have worked out. Because it's there for everyone to see each time I pull on that Chelsea shirt and play a game for the club. One of the first things I did was choose my squad number and it is no coincidence that I wear the number eight. Jimmy Greaves wore it as well and while I am a bit too young to claim that I saw Alan wear it before me that does not mean to say I am unaware of the act I am following. When I speak to Chelsea fans they mention Alan's name and the number eight and you can tell just by the way they talk about him that he was worshipped as a very special player. I've seen videos of some of the games from the seventies when he played for Chelsea and England and it's clear that he possessed the kind of skill which very few were blessed with. There was an element of the maverick about him as well which made the fans love him even more and while I don't think I have that rebellious streak I am honoured when people make comparisons between the two of us because it tells me that I must be doing something right. Though his England career could have been more extensive it was eventful – none more so than when he dismantled the mighty West Germany at Wembley almost single-handedly and that is the kind of performance that any professional who loves playing the game for his country dreams of. I hope I am helping to maintain the proud history of England players who have come from Chelsea, which Alan was so much a part of during his career. Alan's son was in the youth team at West Ham during my first season in the first team and he would often be around the training ground. I remember he would pull me aside during a quiet moment after training to give me advice about my game. He understands what it takes to play in central midfield and his was a voice, which I have always paid attention to. What struck me most about him was that he was always honest with you – brutally honest on some occasions and when you are a young player trying to make your way and improve, you need that kind of input to help you develop. During his playing career he was an inspiration to those around him but, tragically, he was involved in a road accident a few years ago, which nearly claimed his life. The fact that he has fought back to health from such a horrific experience shows a character that never knows when to give up and deserves a huge amount of admiration. It's a privilege to be asked to be a part of Alan Hudson's new book. He is someone we should all be thankful for.

Frank Lampard

I am delighted to have read your new book and congratulate you on a rather different – as usual – and brilliantly constructed piece of work. It is a must read for every football lover, not just Chelsea Football Club, for you are still revered here in the Potteries and I am sure Highbury. You have grown in many ways since first writing for us, and you should be – apart from writing books of such taste – be working for one of the big nationals. Your ability to put the game across still astounds me, just like when you played the game. You are a one-off. I, along with all the staff at the *Sentinel*, hope your health is good after that incredible accident, and wish you every success on a wonderfully written account of the past football season. Like in your accident you have bounced back and shown once again – in your life – that you are definitely a winner, I think you have one here.

Sean Dooley
Editor of the *Sentinel* S.O.T. Staffs

I DEDICATE THE FOLLOWING PAGES TO:

John Westwood, Gary the Blue, Tommy Mason junior and senior, Graham Bell, Michael Henry, Tony Millard, Tony Banks, Gary Shepherd and of course my son Allen. This is also for Leslie May, Matthew Harding and Billy Lampton who are although not with us, always a big part of our lives. Last but not least all you Blues out there who have been so patient with that sleeping giant in SW6.

I thank the following people for assisting me on not only this book, but also my rehabilitation and reminding me that the world is not that bad a place when I am in their company. Tommy Nicholson, Martin Knight, George, Charlie and Anthony Mason, Stephen August, David Rodwell, Tony Davis, Michael Carter, Peter May, Tommy Cook, Dean Powell, Brian Shenton, Tommy Wisbey, Malcolm Molineux, Gary Trowsdale, Alan Brazil, Sean Dooley, Michael Bloomfield, Simon Boynton, Jeremy Hancock.

Then I am very grateful for all the help Paul Miller has given me through my toughest of times. Also my best friend in the world of football, Harry Redknapp.

Harry is so very fortunate to have a wonderful family and I am honoured to be their great friend.

Also Michael Segen introduced to me by Paul Miller.

INSPIRATION

Behind every great story there must be an inspiration and mine has been Frank Sinatra, Bocelli, Phil Collins and the latest sensation Michael Buble.

LIFE SAVERS

This book would not have been possible to write if not for all of those wonderful doctors and nurses in both the Royal London and St Bartholomew's Hospitals, especially Frank Cross, David Goodier, Claire Strickland, Otto Chan, David Badenoch, Sue Clarke, Professor Mundy and Professor Norman Williams. Claire for her great ability to make me feel like a fully paid up invalid, which made me fight harder.

David Goodier, Frank Cross, Sue Clarke whilst on the Operating table whether alone or assisting the two Professors. I cannot thank you all enough.

DEE EUROPEAN HOTEL
'CONGRATULATIONS'

Congratulations and well done, Alan, from all of us at the Dee European Hotel here in Famagusta – the place where you have spent so many wonderful times writing beside our pool and bar area. We are chuffed that you have finished your 'masterpiece' and hope it gets the recognition it deserves. We are delighted that we are a part of your latest success.

We all know exactly how you feel after overcoming that horrific accident way back in 1997. You have not only survived but, shown just what a fighter you are and continue to live to fight another day. We know you love visiting us, and have not only been inspiring, but so vital in your rehabilitation. We hope this wonderful read sells as well as it should and look forward to your next visit where and when we can join you in your celebrations.

We are working on having a celebratory 'Dinner' for you on your next visit and if any of your fans and friends would like to join us they can contact us by E-Mail at europeanestaste@hotmail or by telephone (0392) 366 3010 or fax: (0392) 366 3010.

We wait in great anticipation – with our best wishes for both you and the 'Tinkerman'.

With love from Dee and Dogan.

THE BEST OF ENEMIES

West Germany's visit to Wembley in March 1975 bore striking parallels to the visit just over twenty years before. Once again they were arriving as World Champions and once again they were bringing a team much weaker than that which had actually won the crown. As in 1954, the hosts had much more to prove than the guests.

Interest in the game was certainly high. Wembley sold out and fourteen cinemas had contracted to show the match live, adding another 40,000 to the audience. Ramsey and the once glorious past had been swept aside during the twelve months prior to the match, and the footballing public were hoping to see a brighter future emerge against the old enemy.

Revie had inherited a side which had already undergone transformations during Ramsey's last few months in charge and Joe Mercer's caretaker period, and made no dramatic changes of his own in his first few months in charge. Only Bell and Ball remained of Ramsey's old guard, the latter surprisingly recalled for this match, more than a little controversially, given the captaincy to boot. Sunderland's Dave Watson and Derby's Colin Todd were a year into establishing themselves at the heart of the team's defence, and the partnership of Southampton's Mick Channon and Liverpool's Kevin Keegan was becoming a solid fixture in attack.

A Leeds-Ipswich Cup replay had deprived Revie of probable first choice fullbacks Paul Madeley and Kevin Beattie, and new caps were awarded to Leicester's Steve Whitworth and QPR's Ian Gillard. Up front, Malcolm MacDonald was offered another chance to prove he could perform at this level, and, most exciting of all, Stoke City's extravagantly gifted Alan Hudson was given a debut alongside Ball and Bell in midfield.

Hudson's inclusion was some compensation for the absence of other flair players, such as Trevor Brooking, Frank Worthington and Duncan McKenzie, though one of the most talented players of his generation was never selected to play for England and often had trouble even making the first team at his various League clubs.

If England were relatively short on flair, so – rather less intentionally – were their West German opponents. Now in his eleventh year as a coach, Helmet Schon had lost Grabowski and four Bayern players – Muller, Breitner, Schwarzenbeck and Hoeness – since the World Cup, and their replacements, as soon became apparent, were lacking the same level of inspiration. Players like Bernard Cullman, Heinz Flohe and Bernd Holzenbein, all of whom eventually won a respectable forty or so caps, were technically efficient, excellent 'runners' who would never let anyone down, but they were light years away from Netzer, Hoeness and Grabowski. And, of course, Muller was irreplaceable. The most golden of golden periods for West Germany national team was coming to an end.

There was still Beckenbauer, though, and as he shook hands with Alan Ball in the centre circle it was hard to believe that the two of them had first faced each other at Wembley in February 1966. Then, they had been winning their fourth and sixth caps respectively; now, they were winning their eighty-ninth and sixty-seventh.

The match proved a happier one for Ball than for Beckenbauer. England looked more positive, more incisive, right from the beginning, and the German sweeper found few opportunities for going forward in support of his lacklustre attack. On this occasion it was England midfield players and forwards who caught the eye, and none more so than Alan Hudson. As early as the fifth minute he brilliantly made space for himself in the penalty area only to find his forwards badly placed, and in the twenty-sixth minute it was his beautifully flighted free-kick which was volleyed in by Bell. Later in the half, Hudson's pass sent MacDonald clean through to shoot over the bar, and throughout the first forty-five minutes his overall orchestration of the game, his comfort on the ball, his changes of pace and wide range of accurate passes were reminiscent of a Netzer or a Charlton.

It was a measure of his success that Schon felt obliged to take off the attack minded Wimmer at half time and replace him with the more prosaic Kremers. With Cullman and Flohe also working themselves into the ground, Hudson and his colleagues in midfield certainly had a harder second half. Nonetheless the West Germans looked no more likely to score. They didn't win their first corner until an hour had been played, and at the other end Bell almost punished them for their temerity, by just failing to find the net after MacDonald's shot had been blocked. Five minutes later the Newcastle man did score, heading in after Channon's quickly taken free kick sent Ball to the by-line for a far post cross.

While the Germans did finally manage to exert a little pressure, they never looked like scoring. The two most memorable incidents of the final quarter featured Beckenbauer inelegantly diving to cut out a through ball with his hand, and Keegan finding the underside of the bar with a glorious chip. The crowd went home wondering whether England had been as good as they looked. Had they just witnessed the first stages of a resurrection?

The papers thought so. **ENGLAND COME GOOD AGAIN** headlined *The Times,* speaking for them all.

The hero of the hour was **Alan Hudson,** whom the same paper hoped and believed was 'the man England had been looking for since 1970'. In the *Daily Mirror* Frank McGhee thought that **Hudson** had strolled through his debut 'with the assurance, the elegance and the efficiency of someone who was born to play at this level'.

He was 'Here to stay – all the way to the 1978 World Cup'.

Even the Germans were impressed. Schon thought the Stoke City player had 'good vision', and that with Ball and Todd he could form 'the basis of a very fine England team'.

The watching **Gunter Netzer** wondered out loud where the English had been hiding him: Hudson had been 'magnificent' and had all it took to be 'a world class player'.

There were caveats. David Lacey qualified his praise with thought that 'not so long ago skills of this sort were accepted as the norm in an England team', and Brian Glanville cautioned against reading too much into one performance against weak opposition.

All that aside, the West Germans had been beaten for the first time since 1966, England had looked good for the first time in many moons, and for a few weeks it was hard to resist a rare and heady sort of optimism.

Alan Hudson played one more match for his country after that?

This was taken from a book written by David Downing about all matches between England and their forever enemies West Germany.

Total Football said that, "You'll find no better insight into the history of the Anglo-German football rivalry."

THE SUN

Just over twenty years later the *Sun* newspaper put out this statement and I appreciate the way they published it for the *Star* newspaper – who I was going to sue – had headlines of 'SMASHED' trying to be funny – by assuming I was boozed up – at a time my family were going through quite a devastating time just outside my room in the Intensive Trauma Unit. Such a heading was disgusting and upset several of my friends and family: Alan Hudson lies unconscious and heavily sedated at the Royal London Hospital in the East Ends Whitechapel.

The surgery he has undergone would have been enough to see off most people who had not kept themselves as fit as the former Chelsea, Stoke City, Arsenal and England star.

The incident left him with a blood clot on the brain, a shattered pelvis, a fractured sternum, broken ribs and several other internal injuries.

He underwent a fourteen-hour operation to remove a blood clot and another four hours of surgery to piece his pelvis back together again.

He had his legs cut open to prevent gangrene and to drain the fluid from his lungs. Then there was the internal bleeding. He may yet have to have his spleen removed. Despite all of this he is still with us. He battles on winning one medical skirmish after another. But then Alan Hudson, probably the most gifted player of his generation and a man who Alf Ramsey once said that, "There is no limit to what this player can achieve", has been a fighter.

His most prized possession is a framed letter from George Best on his mantelpiece. It reads You are the most gifted player in the country, don't let anyone tell you any different.

Like Best, Hudson was a maverick, a one-off. At the same time, the stars never really worked for him. If he had been born on another day, he could well have achieved so much more.

Let us remember this as he continues his fight of his life, and let us hope he continues to amaze his surgeons as he once astounded football fans.

The *Sun* newspaper on the 9th of January 1998

The one and only Bobby Moore said that Alan Hudson could have conquered the world. Perhaps for a while he did. King of the Kings Road and arguably the finest footballer London ever produced, Alan was the genius at the heart of Chelsea's dream team of the 1970's.

He is more than just alive now and the following you are about to read comes from a man who has defied death and beat all of his demons. The Tinker and Talisman is his latest project in a life that keeps him behind his PC when not in his local watering hole in Chelsea. He cannot run – even jog – for his right leg is permanently damaged, his balance, one his greatest strengths, is no more and kills the rest of his life in a continual battle in the gymnasium in a rehabilitation that is now life long. He welcomes you to join him in one of the most fantastic journeys in our lifetime – a cat and dog fight of power with several twists and turns and right up until the last page nobody knows or knew just what was going on behind the closed doors of a football ground where he was born just a David Beckham free-kick away. Not ever forgetting Ian Hutchinson's incredible long throw.

A TURBULENT YEAR

1969 was a turbulent year as the Kray twins have received thirty years apiece and the lid has been lifted off a murderous London underworld. Brian Jones has been found floating face down in his swimming pool – rather like the Michael Barrymore case of not too long ago – which led to Mick Jagger and the boys performing a surreal free concert in Hyde Park where two prevalent youth 'cults' of the summer – the skinheads and Hells Angels – flex their muscles, reminiscent of a Chelsea and Leeds match that was to be played in the FA Cup Final come May of the following year, for the watching millions. In Northern Ireland there has been a kick-off of a rather different nature as British troops are deployed in Belfast to quell the violence between the Catholics and the Protestants. Everyone seems to be demonstrating about one thing or another, and it was quite appropriate that 'Something In The Air' was an unlikely 'smash' for Thunderclap Newman and knocks the Beatles off the number one spot and captures the mood. Meanwhile down at the Dell – the home of Southampton Football Club – an 18-year-old Alan Hudson – was making his Chelsea debut.

THE BEGINNING

I thought initially that I had stolen a march on all others when coming up with this brilliant idea about what you are about to read, but alas, I hadn't. But having said that nobody – apart from the rest of that Chelsea team of the seventies could do so – or any player since because I am the original and one and only Kings Road kid. Having said that, though, there is nobody as interested in writing as much as yours truly in fact that is what I class myself as nowadays, simply a writer. I wrote 'The Working Mans Ballet' and the upcoming 'Spectacular', which is now being put to bed – tidied up – by my pal Malcolm Molineux. You can be the greatest writer in the world but you cannot express such times that led us into this latest bombshell unless you have been theire and worn the t-shirt. We experienced all those glory days, although there were not enough of them, as our manager – Dave Sexton – chose to break up our team very similar to the way Alex Ferguson broke up his team of ardent drinkers, yeah Manchester United had their very own 'Rat Pack' the same as our Chelsea team. In fact it would have been interesting to have taken on Bryan Robson, Paul McGrath and Norman Whiteside, the three main wise guys in the United pack. Whilst ours were Peter Osgood, Charlie Cooke, Ian Hutchinson, Tommy Baldwin, Eddie McCreadie and yours truly. In the late sixties and early seventies I was breaking into the Chelsea first team squad – as you've already read – and in no time had played against players of such calibre of the awesome Pele, the incredible Johan Cruyff, the absolute genius of George Best and a genius of another kind – the fabulous Jimmy Greaves. Quite a baptism for one so young, wouldn't you say?

This was around the time the late Matthew Harding was beginning his love affair with Chelsea Football Club, a man we sadly lost way back in '96' a man who would have been an integral part of the goings-on, leading up to this new beginning. These other writers had never worked under Docherty or Sexton and the two chairman Brian Mears and Ken Bates so that too is something else I have experienced. Tommy Docherty signed me as an Apprentice and after leaving I found myself under the management of Dave Sexton who firstly signed me as a Professional and secondly kicked me through the exit door into the back alley as quickly as I had made a name for myself. You know the back alley I mean, like in those movies in the States where a drunk is tossed into the garbage cans outside the back door of some sleazy bar!

I was to become the most 'local boy made good' to have played for Chelsea Football Club and that still stands today, and always will, have no doubt!

What you are about to read is a story within a story and a man who has beaten off his demons to bring this to you first hand. This football club are one of the great underachievers in the history of the game, winning only one paltry League Championship since they were founded in the year of 1905 as Chelsea Football Club, Stamford Bridge, Fulham Road, London, SW6.

'NEVER LIVED THE DREAM'

This all came about on my favourite day of the year, July 4th – Independence Day in the United States of America – where I once lived in what seems now another lifetime – but still celebrate along with my friends over the Atlantic as I owe them for allowing me to live my life to the full amongst them. As they say, only in America!

As a player for this club playing at Stamford Bridge on nights like those in the European Cup Winners Cup matches against Bruges and Manchester City and also in that unforgettable FA Cup winning year of 1970 where we broke all goal scoring records and if we had not had a replay at Burnley in the fourth round we would have been the only club to have won the FA Cup without leaving London. We began by hitting Birmingham for three, Burnley for five – over two matches – Queens Park Rangers for four, Crystal Palace for five and gave the same treatment to Watford in the semi-final at White Hart Lane. All along the way we took an army called the 'Shed', the kind of supporters who in our hour of need at the Bridge pulled us through, especially on that famous evening when we had to fight back from a two-goal deficit against one of the finest teams in Europe that season, Bruges of Belgium. It is with these experiences I have the advantage over all other writers who are mainly jumping on the Russian Revolution's Bandwagon. The Russian you will hear about very soon. It is with all of these experiences and emotions – once pulling that royal blue shirt over ones head I share the story with you. If you were going to buy a book about thoroughbred horse racing you would not look for Delia Smith, you would scan the shelves for Lester Piggott, the Aga Khan, Henry Cecil or today, Michael Tabor; if writing about music would you pick up a book by Ant and Dec or Lennon and McCartney, Rodgers and Hart or Quincy Jones!

When I hear football clubs of today moaning and groaning about money I have absolutely no sympathy, for as a young kid growing up and signing for Chelsea my family should have been looked after, for they were the ones that made me a player. Look at it this way; My father worked all hours god sent to buy my brother John and I our boots, trainers, shirts, shorts, socks and footballs etc, etc, etc.

My mother – without a washing machine – would turn us out looking 'ace' for all our training sessions and matches leading up to our Apprenticeships. So although Chelsea sold me for a record £240,000 part of that money should have gone to my family. I have always said that and I still believe so to this day. Why should the club earn all that money after my father educated me at the beginning of my football journey through life?

I thought this introduction important to explain that there are so many books written about a certain subject where the author has not got the real 'feel' for the story, or should I say, never 'lived the dream'. It is rather like if someone 'big time' took over the Actors Guild and I decided to write about Drama Classes – it would be absolute nonsense, wouldn't you say?

That job would have been given to my second wife, who walked away when I was at my lowest ebb, whilst hospitalised for those eleven months. Okay I couldn't dance no more and our marriage vows just six months before such an accident were as useless as our marriage and counted for nothing. She most certainly would have stayed around if I had had what Ray Parlour had today, especially as I was on my deathbed. He has just been raped by his ex-wife and her lawyers – in what they call a court of law – some justice!

My upbringing in Chelsea is not the most important factor but having grown in those times leading up to the 'Swinging Sixties' was quite something special and became a part of that – at times – brilliant team even more so. I know there is already a book along the same lines written by a friend Harry Harris, but again I have breathed the air within on some of the most incredible nights in the history of Chelsea Football Club. The Russians have finally arrived at Stamford Bridge and taken over the club lock stock and barrel and in doing so have opened the door to a whole new world for the many thousands of the Chelsea faithful and former players. We will not have to be body searched anymore like under the Chairmanship of Mr Ken Bates. Roman Abramovich and his entourage have made the most amazing and dramatic entrance to a club, which was just about to go into administration, under thirty-six hours in fact, with the timing as perfect of a Sinatra song. The once cock sure bookmakers have now met their match and will have to keep on the lookout for any more moves once Roman gets comfortable in his new owners chair?

My bookmaker of great reliance is a fantastic man named Mervyn Wilson – of Wilson Sports and Racing who will allow me to keep my finger on the pulse of odds that will no doubt swing to and fro as Manchester United,

Arsenal and the new Chelsea go full steam ahead for a brand new Premiership season. I am going to enjoy writing this book for all of you young, middle and old age Chelsea Pensioners and of course each and every other football lover who follow our game with the kind of passion that carried me through my darkest hour. I can remember sitting on my father's shoulders as Chelsea beat Tottenham in the FA Cup amongst a packed house of 72,000 people, then again at White Hart Lane as Spurs beat Crewe 13-2 after escaping a real banana skin of a cup-tie at Gresty Road, where with the scores level the home side missed a 'sitter' with the very last kick of an incredible first match. Then there was that night where I can still hear another massive crowd singing 'Arrivederci Roma' as Terry Venable ripped the hearts out of a different Roman with a magnificent hat-trick in the Inter Cities Fairs Cup – the equivalent of today's UEFA Cup – really quite an experience for a youngster like me standing under the North Stand where Matthew Harding started his love affair with his beloved Chelsea Football Club!

Out with the old and in with the new and it is for that I thank Mr Roman Abramovich and also in the fashion and style in which he has done so far. This has also given me the opportunity to possibly go back to a club with my hand on my heart; something I have not always been allowed to do since the day I walked through those old Chelsea gates and made my way to the Potteries. I never knew at that particular time that this move – to Tony Waddington – who you'll read a lot more of later – would take me on the greatest football journey I could have ever asked for. This transfer – a mere £240,000 – would lead me into a new world where a man became more than just a 'boss' he was my mentor, great friend, and second father. Had this man been alive today and allowed to run the new Chelsea under the ownership of Mr Abramovich the whole football world would have had to run for cover and very quickly at that. What he did at the Victoria Ground in Stoke-on-Trent was like in the 'Ten Commandments' with my new boss taking over the role of Charlton Heston!

You remember the scene where he divided the ocean waves for his people to walk through.

He is now above us with my father Bill, my mother – who has left us whilst in writing – and my best friend Leslie May who left this earth far too early and in such a brutalised fashion. But this book is not about doom and gloom as for those of you who are close to Alan Anthony Hudson will know that is not my style. My father taught me the game before allowing Tony to take over from him and I could not have asked for anything more as my education of how to play the game I love so much, was completed by these two men. I just hope – and know – they will be keeping an eye on this situation and on me of course. I would not have swapped my playing career for all the Russian's billions because 'Money Can't Buy Me Love' – there you are Lennon and McCartney once again. Football was and always will be my first love where in between I had other loves but nothing as fulfilling and rewarding as coming off a football field knowing you have been taught well by your masters and preformed admirably.

How I miss the camaraderie in the dressing rooms I have been involved with which led to bars, clubs and restaurants from London to New York to Seattle to Jamaica and Tampa Bay which will always be inside of me. These times were so special simply a joy to wake up in the morning as Saturday afternoon got closer, a buzz that – not even cocaine – that players now take – can give you. This book is all about the very first season in the life of Roman Abramovich's ownership of Chelsea Football Club, his manager Claudio Ranieri better known as the Tinkerman, with Stamford Bridge being the cathedral that has brought an Italian and Russian united as one. A three-way marriage if you want to include the chief executive to be Peter Kenyon. But would it be a happy one?

The year just gone had been one of extraordinary happenings, and this one we have just entered promises to be even more so, as the horses swing away after the first circuit and next time round will be the real 'nail-biting' stuff, through Easter when they get to the Elbow before entering the longest uphill run-in, in sport. Yeah, football is a Grand National and Gold Cup all rolled into one with no place for early birds and sprinters, where and when the going gets tough Manchester United are usually the ones that get tougher!

Our country's finest hour was when the English rugby team returned home glorious and victorious from their World Cup win against – and in – Australia, the David Beckham and Real Madrid transfer sensation, the Rio Ferdinand drug scandal, the downfall of Leeds United and the new Chelsea boasting five young players in the England squad. Then of course there are still so many fireworks still to come between Sir Alex Ferguson and John Magnier of the Coolmore Stud, better known in Ireland as the 'Coolmore Mafia'. Magnier along with his partner JP McManus have close to majority share holdings at Old Trafford, which has led to the United boss's signing a new contract on the back burner. The Manchester United manager has also got a date with the authorities over having his son's Elite Management Agency handling transfers to and from Old Trafford. He has been previously warned but good old Alex just keeps going along making and breaking rules for fun, although this year the fun might just halt if Arsenal continue their unbeaten run and the Irish win a case where they must be odds on favourites to do so. They rarely lose!

I will be bringing you this and more, but overall the book title alone tells you what and why I decided to make this my number one project from last July to the upcoming Champions League Final almost a year later, just hoping that our teams can hang in there all the way for it will be great for all concerned and for me – bringing it to you first hand – even more exciting!

This book is mainly for all of you Chelsea diehards and the rest of you – who just like me – are simply football lovers, holding the kind of fire and passion that wins matches when all seems lost. Having said that, there are moments for both you Stoke City and Arsenal fans who shared the seventies and eighties with me. I will be bringing you my views on what is going on all around us in the football world. This is yet another Alan Hudson roller-coaster ride so pour yourself your favourite tipple, sit right back and enjoy the Tinker and Talisman, and if you enjoy reading it as much as I have writing it, you will have enjoyed it immensely!

This is just something I wrote without the book in mind, but decided – at the last minute – to include it and as you reads on you'll understand the reason why!

TIME TO DIE

My time here was almost over, as I drift slowly away
When all of a sudden – like lightning – my world turned and I was back
    to stay
My body lies in bloodstained ruins, my chances simply pie in the sky
Then along came my angels just as me and mine were asking why?
Slowly pieced together I began to recover with no time to sigh
There is time to weep, time to laugh and cry, and then time to die!

With time running out and the morphine disguising such almighty pain
A cry for help was heard, and from nowhere a strange voice came
In the melee a crucifix, c-clamp and many helping hands were there
This was all I needed to come out of this ongoing nightmare
Fifty-nine days in darkness is lonely no matter how hard you try
There is time to weep, to laugh and cry and then time to die!

I arrived back slowly into an entirely different world in a deeply traumatic
    time
My first love had flown, my second too, both acts of crime
With those two loves gone behind me I edge scarily into my third
My angels will return dancing to my Robins song, and I will fly like a bird
Looking down I see a beaten body from the skies above so high
There is time to weep time to laugh and cry and then time to die!

My life was handed back to me, but far from the once Yellow Brick Road
While the suffering became less thanks to my angels sharing my load
They sing they dance to my cherubs, who are in the shape of a heart
My heart keeps strong and together we head for a brand new start
For love is here again and my aim, as before, is to reach for the sky
There is time to weep, to laugh and cry and then time to die!

My passion for life returns after many endless days of torment
An inmate I do not recommend after not knowing where my time went
Time is time and life is life and throughout I was in a heap
But after two loves and wedding rings they were now so cheap
Being alone in such darkness is some sentence no matter how hard you try
There is time to weep to laugh and cry and lastly time to die!

Alan Hudson 22nd April 2003

15th DECEMBER 1997
'November L, Unknown, age 99'

The Resuscitation Room of any Accident and Emergency Department is a fairly daunting place at the best of times and on the evening of the 15th of December1997 the one at the Royal London Hospital was no exception. It had been a quiet day and the main trauma bay was tidy and in semi-darkness lit only by the subdued light filtering through the door windows and the eerie glow of the red dot-matrix resuscitation timer, which was set on zero. At around a quarter past nine the red phone rang and was answered by the A&E staff nurse, a trauma case was on its way in, by ambulance a 47-year-old male pedestrian knocked over by a car. The resuscitation room slowly came to life as the accident staff opened up, turning on the lights and checking the equipment – the Propac vitals signs monitor, the oxygen and the anaesthetic machine. At twenty past nine the hospital switchboard put out the trauma call, activating both the internal bleeps of the resident trauma team and the radio pagers of the consultants at home. The hospital fields a resident A&E consultant and other specialties have a consultant at home who can come in at a moment's notice. Over the next few minutes the room was slowly filled with doctors, mostly in blue theatre garb, pulling on their bright yellow x-ray proof lead tabards and engaging in the normal pre-trauma banter, which occupies doctors at such a time. Everyone is slightly nervous since the resuscitation of a severely injured patience can have an uncertain outcome and the correct decisions need to be made swiftly and in the right order for the patient to have the best chance of survival.

At nine twenty-five the sounds of a siren heralds the arrival of the London Ambulance Service and a few moments later the trauma patient is wheeled in and the team swing into action. The front sheet, the computer-generated piece of paper, which records the details of the patient, had a section for 'complaint' and the word 'Trauma' is entered into the box. At this stage no-one knows the extent of the injuries or even the name or age of the patient and these details are entered as "November L, Unknown, age 99".

It is not very long before we find out that this is Alan Hudson, and his injuries are probably mortal. The trauma resuscitation clock is started.

The resuscitation of a trauma patient follows a carefully worked out plan where the most severe life-threatening injuries are sought and corrected, where possible, and the extent and nature of the injuries are logged so that the correct specialties can be called in. Under the direction of the team leader a speedy primary survey is started. The airway is secured first, since if it is blocked the patient could die in three minutes. Any breathing difficulties are then dealt with followed by problems with the circulation, such as bleeding either from the wounds or into the body cavities. The initial treatment thus follows an easily remembered 'ABC' format, which at the same time ensures that no major life-threatening injury is missed. X-rays of the neck, chest and pelvis, the three areas most likely to give problems, are taken, and the patient is then subjected to a slower secondary survey, which is the complete and thorough examination of the patient from head to toe, including the back and the genitals.

Alan went through the primary survey rapidly and the details were entered on the sheet. An impressive catalogue of injuries was quickly compiled. The most obvious injuries were to the head, chest and pelvis, the three most critical areas. Alan had clearly suffered a severe head injury and although not in a coma he was quickly anaesthetised and put on a ventilator to make sure the oxygen supply to the brain was secured. The chest x-ray showed a fractured breastbone and multiple rib fractures on the left. There was obviously a severe fracture of the pelvis leading to the major haemorrhage and severed damage to the soft tissues in the groin area. Drips were inserted into his arms and he was quickly given six litres of fluid and blood to maintain his blood pressure. First aid to a pelvic fracture is essential to slow blood loss by bringing the fractured bones together; the pelvis is a ring of bone which is associated with a lot of major blood vessels and these are often torn as well as when the ring is broken, usually in more than one place. In Alan's case an external fixator was applied almost immediately; this is a metal support, which is drilled into the pelvic bones and tightened, bringing the bone ends together.

The secondary survey revealed further serious injuries: the skeleton of the face was broken in several places and the bone supporting the left eye was broken, a condition known as orbital floor blowout, which can lead to a loss of sight in the affected eye. There was obviously internal damage to the abdomen and a catheter inserted into the bladder through the abdominal wall revealed bleeding either from the kidneys or direct trauma to the bladder. There was so much damage to the genitals that the insertion of a catheter through the normal route was not even attempted. Blood loss from the pelvic fracture was clearly devastating.

Frank W Cross MS FRCS

THE C-CLAMP

Chest: He had a fractured sternum with multiple rib fractures on the left side of bilateral haemoneumothoraces .

Abdomen; He had ruptured left a kidney with massive retroperitoneal and pelvic haematoma. His pelvis displayed multiple pelvic ring fractures with complete separate of the right hemipelvis. His bladder had been severely lacerated.

The most immediate problem was the bleeding from the pelvic injury. There is a complex network of blood vessels at the back of the pelvis, which had all been shredded by the fracture and could not clot off as the hemipelvis wax completely unrestrained. In an attempt to provide some stability an external fixator was applied to the front of the pelvis with pins driven into the iliac bone connected by two bars running across from one side of the pelvis to the other. It was, however, impossible to control the posterior elements of the injury and the bleeding continued. He went to theatre where the blood clot was evacuated from his brain but he continued losing blood and by the morning of the 16th of December had had more than thirty units of blood transfusion.

By a bizarre coincidence some three days earlier I had been shown a special external fixation clamp by a company representative that was designed to combat the blood loss in precisely this sort of pelvic fracture. The principle was that by applying a force at the back of his pelvis the blood loss could be contained and active bleeding could be stopped. Unfortunately such pieces of equipment are expensive (this one was a cheap version at £3,500) and even at the Royal London Hospital where we have a helicopter service would probably not be used more than two or three times a year.

When I arrived at 0800 hours on the morning of the sixteenth of December I learned about Alan in our Trauma Meeting. Out of interest I went round to the operating theatre, which was being set-up to try and block the bleeding vessels by arteriography. I realised immediately that Alan had already lost masses of blood and was no longer clotting properly because of it and decided to use the demonstration model clamp that we had available to try to help. There was immediate concern as the frame itself said 'sample only' on it but rapid consultation with the manufacturers confirmed that it was a working model. We applied the 'C-Clamp' in the theatres under image intensifier control with dramatic effect so that the bleeding appeared to stop and he was able to maintain a blood pressure without pouring blood into him. After consultation with the Urologists and Vascular Surgeons, it was felt that his urological injuries should be treated by a catheter.

Alan was then admitted onto the Intensive Care Unit at 12 o'clock on the 16th. He continued severely unwell and his legs swelled due to deep venous thrombosis. The pressures in the compartments of his legs rose dramatically jeopardising his circulation further and it was obvious he would need to return to theatre for decompression of the swollen legs by faciotomies (slitting the entire length of the upper thigh and both sides of the calf of both legs to allow the muscles to swell). I had a long conversation with his wife on the 17/12/97 where I explained what would be necessary. I recorded in the notes 'I have spoken to his wife and said the head injury may cause brain damage but it is too early to tell. The chest is very likely to get infection with adult respiratory distress syndrome. The kidneys are damaged, will need dialysis. May require laparotomy. Will need internal fixation of the face and will need further surgery to the scrotum.' I explained the procedure necessary to relieve the pressure on his legs and told her that, "he may die if he gets sepsis or multi-organ failure". It was felt by all involved in his care that this was highly likely at this point but that we should continue doing everything to try to prevent this. The only positive side was that the monitoring bolt left in his brain to keep an eye on his intracerebral pressure was not showing signs of severe brain injury.

David Goodier MBBS FRCS Orth
Consultation Orthopaedic Surgeon

Once Alan's condition was stabilised by bringing the blood pressure up he was quickly transferred to the CT scanner in order to define his injuries more clearly.

The Computerised Tomography scanner is a sophisticated device, which takes a series of x-ray photographs through the body, which appear on the computer screens as sections, which reveal all the internal organs and any damage they have suffered. This used to take hours and was dangerous because the patient could deteriorate whilst being scanned and further attempts at resuscitation interrupted the process, thus making it take even longer. The latest spiral CT scanners take a continuous spiral series of photographs as the patient is shredded through the scanner in an effortless ballet of technology and the entire body can be can be scanned in about fifteen minutes.

The results made grim viewing. The head scan showed bleeding into the skull, which was going to require immediate surgery to stop the bleeding and remove the clot in order to prevent brain damage. Fortunately there was no sign of a broken neck, which could otherwise have lead to paralysis. The chest part of the scan confirmed the fractured ribs but there was no obvious damage to the heart or lungs. There was clearly damage to the left kidney as shown by a lot of blood surrounding it, and the pelvic fracture was confirmed as a major one with a large amount of blood leaking into the surrounding tissues. Things could have been worse, but not much.

Blood loss from the pelvis continued but the situation in the head made urgent brain surgery a necessity and Alan was quickly transferred to the emergency operating theatre where his skull was opened and the blood clot removed. There was a depressed skull fracture, which had to be sorted out at the same time. The pelvic fixation was revised but the bleeding remained torrential and the radiologists were called to carry out angiography. This is a procedure where a major vessel at the top of the leg is entered with a needle and a catheter is run up into the main blood vessel in the abdomen, the aorta. An injection of contrast medium, which shows up on x-ray, is then made; the object of the procedure is to identify any uncontrolled bleeding vessel, which can be blocked by injecting superglue into it via the catheter. The procedure sounds bizarre but can be lifesaving. Unfortunately, no bleeding vessel suitable for this procedure could be seen on the x-ray screen. The position was accepted and Alan was transferred to the intensive care unit. He had been in theatre continuously from 2 o'clock in the morning until midday. During this time he had received 38 units of blood and 21 units of other fluids, an amount equivalent to five times his circulating blood volume.

The next twenty-four hours were fraught with difficulty. Alan was visited on the intensive care unit by a large collection of consultants. Responsibility for his head injury was taken by the neurosurgeons, the fasciomaxillary surgeons were looking after his facial fractures, the orthopaedic surgeons were dealing with his pelvic fracture, the urologists advised on his bladder, kidney and genital injuries, and the intensive care anaesthetists were looking after his fluid management and general resuscitation – in other words keeping him alive. I was in overall charge of his surgical care and responsible for co-ordinating everyone and in addition for looking after the injuries to the blood vessels in the pelvis; I am by trade a vascular and trauma surgeon. Alan's management was thus, by a conservative estimate, involving ten consultants, twenty junior doctors and a similar number of theatre and ITU nurses, not to mention the radiographers taking the x-rays and the radiologists interpreting them, and the laboratory technicians dealing with crossmatching blood and providing the results of numerous other blood tests.

By mid-afternoon on the 16th of December the bleeding from the pelvis came under control and Alan started down a well-worn pathway, which involved high-intensity care on the ITU with active management of further problems as they arose.

Deaths from trauma occur in three peaks. The first of these, accounting for 25% of trauma deaths, occurs at the scene of the accident and is due to severe head and chest injury. The second peak occurs at 24 hours, usually after extensive reparative surgery has failed, and the third occurs after about ten days of intensive care and is due to the failure of the vital organs of the body. It was beginning to look as if Alan had survived the first two peaks and it was now our job to see him through the third.

The first two setbacks were identified over the next 24 hours. Alan's urine output stopped, a common occurrence after massive transfusion with a low blood pressure, and due to shutdown of the kidneys. Renal replacement therapy, the use of an artificial kidney can be used to overcome this and the kidneys usually start to work again after about ten days, but the problem lays the patient open to further complications, especially if infection sets in, which might lead to failure of other organs such as the lungs and liver.

The second problem was massive swelling of the legs leading to obstruction of the circulation and this was clearly happening by December the 17th. Alan was taken back to theatre and fasciotomies were carried out on the legs. Fasciotomy is an operation where skin and underlying tissue surrounding the muscles in the legs are opened with wide incision to relieve the pressure in the legs and allow circulation to return to the muscles. The orthopaedic surgeons took the opportunity to carry out an internal fixation operation on the bones of the pelvis at the same time, a procedure that involves repairing the pelvic fracture using metal plates screwed into the bones. This was second of the several return visits to the theatre for Alan, all of which were critical to his survival.

Massive blood transfusion carries problems of its own, the most serious of which is poor blood clotting. Stored blood loses much of the proteins required to make the blood clot properly over a number of days in the fridge and the frozen blood plasma has to be given to counteract this. In addition, tiny cells in the blood called placelets are also essential to seal leaks in the circulation and stored blood contains none of these since they die off very quickly after blood is drawn from donors. Replacement platelets can and were given, but restoring proper clotting function is very difficult and Alan bled heavily from his fasciotomy wounds over the next couple of days, leading to further large transfusions which kept the circulation going but did not help his clotting. This is a sort of vicious circle, which can only be broken by stopping the bleeding.

By the 18th of December it was clear that Alan was going into a nutritional decline and intravenous feeding was started. His condition remained on a knife-edge over Christmas; he continued on a ventilator, unconscious, and a number of tubes going into and out of his body assumed alarming proportions. These included drips, a tube down the nose into the stomach, various drains into the pelvis, the artificial kidney tubes leading directly into the circulation, his urinary catheter, various tubes measuring the arterial and venous pressure, and a number of pumps attached to the drips feeding small amounts of drugs into him to keep his blood pressure up. The area around his bed resembled a small forest of devices and pumps keeping his vital functions going.

Talking to relatives at this point is a tricky business, to say the least. I had a number of sombre conversations with his wife, Ann, in common with the other consultants looking after him, and she managed to maintain a stoical optimism in relation to the eventual outcome, which I was finding difficult to share. I lost count of the number of times we told her that Alan was quite likely to die, and his persistent hold on life surprised me. I suppose that all those years of physical training combined with the psychological determination of the professional footballer had a bearing here, even though he was unconscious and on a ventilator.

By the 30th of December it was obvious that Alan had a major infection of the clotted blood in his pelvic cavity and that this was hampering his recovery by pouring poisons into his blood and preventing his major organs from recovery. A tear in the rectum was the most likely cause for this and physical examination the same day confirmed that there was a hole through which faeces were contaminating the pelvis. This was probably now the most severe complication that he had developed and I did not think that there was much chance of recovery. He was returned to theatre on News Years Eve for a defunctioning colostomy. The abdomen was opened and the large bowel was brought out onto the surface so that the faeces would be diverted into a bag instead of entering the pelvis through the tear. A tracheostomy was carried out in order to make it easier for us to manage his breathing.

Alan showed signs of improvement over the next two weeks and during this time the skin of his genitals began to die off, leading to wide areas of gangrene, which needed to be removed. We took him back to theatre on the 13th of January and revised the colostomy, washed out the bowel and removed huge quantities of dead tissue and infected clot from his pelvis and genital area. A similar procedure was carried out again on the 20th of January and again on the 28th of January when he had to return to theatre urgently to control further bleeding which was a result of infection, and remove more dead tissue. The bad news was at this point was that it had become clear that there was further damage to the bladder and urethra, and that Alan's genitals had become completely detached from the pelvic bone. There was a large hole in the back of the bladder, which resulted in a leak of urine through the pelvic fracture. The pelvic fracture was completely open to the outside world and was being dressed with large swabs, which had to be changed daily. I did not think that he would ever pass urine properly again, but I was happily wrong. I am sometimes amazed by the ability of the body to heal after the most horrific injuries. On February the 2nd another return visit was made to the theatre when, with the urology team, we removed the last of the infected tissue and repaired the hole in the bladder.

Once all the infected tissue had been removed Alan made a swift recovery. His kidney function was still poor and the artificial kidney was still needed, but all his other problems appeared to be slowly resolving. On the 9th of February Alan woke up and came off the ventilator. He was unable to talk properly because of the tracheostomy but it was obvious that he could communicate and had suffered no brain damage from his head injury – a minor miracle in itself. The tracheostomy tube and feeding tube were removed on the 16th of February and Alan began to talk normally and eat normally for the first time for two months. The next day he left the Intensive Care Unit for a normal ward and his recovery began in earnest. By the 25th of February his kidneys had recovered and he no longer needed an artificial kidney.

For the first time in ten weeks Alan was out of danger. All that remained now was to make an assessment of his residual disabilities, make a treatment plan to overcome these and provide intensive physiotherapy support to maintain his recovery and rehabilitation until it was time for him to go home. His injuries remained extensive and he had serious disabilities, not the least of which were a continued leak of urine from the bladder, an open pelvic wound and paralysis of the left leg from the nerve damage in the pelvis. Happily, and due in no small measure to the careful attentions of the specialists involved, his head and facial injuries appeared to have recovered remarkably well.

FW Cross Consultant Surgeon

I last saw him in outpatients on the 14th November 1998. His memory of the accident and his time on ITU was understandably virtually non-existent but despite some weakness and particularly loss of nerve function in the right foot, he managed to walk into clinic.

I doubt he will ever get complete nerve recovery on the right and will probably have an area of numbness affecting this side of the calf and the big toe with inability to lift up the foot on the right. The left side is recovering but may take another year before it does so completely and he is left with stiffness of his hips, knees, ankles and feet will require a lot of physiotherapy to overcome and also will probably not recover completely. He has ahead of him further surgery to his rectum and bladder but overall his recovery thus far has been nothing less than '**SPECTACULAR**' but in no small amount this is due to the dedicated team of Anaesthetic and ITU Consultants, Registrars, Senior House Officers, Nurses, Physiotherapists, Speech Therapists, Dieticians, Urologists, General Surgeons, Colorectal Surgeons, Orthopaedic Surgeons, Microbiologists, Renal Physicians and many other specialists of all grades and qualifications who had an active part in his management.

Mr W D Goodier RFCS (Orth)
Consultant Orthopaedic Surgeon

So there you have it, and this is only the opening of a book that does not really change too much, in a way that there are far too many downs, but my pleasure by far outweighs my downfalls, I promise you!

I really have made the most of what would have finished the majority of people. That is not tongue in cheek or disrespectful – just telling you how it is. After going out of your front door two weeks before Christmas and waking up mid-March is something that does not happen too often in one's lifetime. I have been out on benders with the boys but never this long but the amazing thing is that when I finally woke up I thought it was some kind of celebration, not knowing that I could not move a muscle in any part of my body. I was drugged wonderfully well and saw things in my hospital bed no one else did. My father was a coat hanging on a peg by the door and my water was the best tasting wine, but I am not a connoisseur of such luxuries. I had lost quite a bit of time – and weight – never thinking that I'd get it back. If you have ever faced the devil you are in my team!

The only difference is I was on the winning team especially with my uncle George – Mason – who led me through all the corridors, pavements in a wheelchair and once being able to walk with crutches he scraped me off the floor a few times. In the Working Mans Ballet, my autobiography, I labelled him as the 'Rock' and he certainly proved me right as he was always there for me when I needed him, nothing changes when it comes to great people, as my uncle and great friend is. Anyhow this is just a story about the beginning of the rest of my life since, and the most incredible happening of the Russians coming to rescue Chelsea Football Club, where I began my career, the place I was born and had so many memorable times both on and off the field!

I thank the wonderful doctors such as Cross, Goodier, Otto Chan, Sue Clarke, Marion and Claire Strickland my physiotherapist. Then, of course my two Professors Williams and Mundy. I always say that life is a team game and what a team I had working on a body that was once a machine, but by the time I got to them one completely wrecked!

Plus the memory of the late and very lovely Betty Shine!

This was the lady who contacted my family in those early days whilst I was out cold in the Intensive Trauma Unit telling them that I had spoken to her through the *Daily Mail* as she looked at the news of my accident. Betty was a wonderful woman who helped so many thousands of people through her wonderful ability to heal many different misfortunes.

BOBBY MOORE

They say that things happen in threes and in my case with the great Bobby Moore this seems to have touched reality through my knowing him. Firstly as a young member of the Chelsea team of 1970, quite memorable, Bobby made me feel so welcome in my first full international gathering at the end of the season – when we held the Home Internationals – and told me that I would be making my debut against Northern Ireland that evening. Alf Ramsey had changed his mind after telling Bobby his original team. I did not even get on the bench. Bobby, being the great man he was, apologised after that training session and looked after me that night at Wembley, introducing me to the Long Bar where it seemed was just one more step closer to the moon, Bobby was known as god amongst his peers!

This first disappointment led to a three-year ban from playing international football, after I refused to go on an Under-23 Tour. I was at Stamford Bridge one day after he had received my letter, and was told he was calling me about such a decision. He made it very clear in his very own words that, "If you are not at the Airport you will have to take the circumstances." I replied, "So be it."

The second big change in my life, involving Bobby, was when walking out of Arsenal and being out of work. I was hosting a hospitality box at Stamford Bridge for the season's home matches along with a couple of friends, Tony Davis and Michael Carter – and a near resident Dennis Waterman. Anyhow, I walked through the restaurant area one Saturday and bumped into the man who should have had it all, but in this country, no!

I asked Bobby to come into the box for a quick 'lager' and he arrived after the final whistle to the delight of every person in there. Moore was the best of the lot!

Can you imagine what you could charge in today's climate for the greatest England captain ever and the only man who will pick up the Jules Rimet Trophy in mine, if not your lifetime, I am fifty-two years of age!

On this afternoon Bobby asked me what I was doing serving drinks in a box at Chelsea Football Club when I – at twenty-seven years of age – should not be abusing my talent. I knew that this was a footballer's prime time, and thanks to Bobby I was given a chance to prove it to myself. Bobby then gave me his second piece of advice by saying that Jimmy Gabriel – the head coach of the Seattle Sounders – was having lunch in the restaurant and he was over here looking for players, and also that that he – Bobby himself – had been to Seattle to play in the Kingdome. "If you cannot get a job here, go speak to Jimmy, I recommend both Jimmy and Seattle very strongly" were the words of the great one. But, I thought inwardly that your first recommendation had badly backfired on me, in terms of Alf Ramsey and his change of mind, but I had absolutely nothing to lose, and was missing training every day and my Saturday afternoon socialising would never take the place of actually keeping all my dreams alive?

It, at that moment, was like a love affair without sex!

Anyhow, with nothing to lose and everything to gain I went to the table of Jimmy, a man I knew from an after-season tour of Jamaica that both his Southampton team and my Chelsea team were on. We had a drinking contest where nobody to this day knows just who won! Jimmy was a great man!

After speaking at the Bridge we arranged to meet on the Monday in a West London hotel, and once doing the business frequented our drinking club in Harrington Gardens called the Town House, the kind of club you had to be normal to join.

As I said we met in a hotel along with my friend Michael accompanying me, did the deal and the rest is history. The last thing I heard of that day was that Harry Redknapp – his then assistant coach – receiving the call from Jimmy who could hardly talk, I suppose with both excitement and the heavy duty social surroundings of one of the last memorable afternoon drinking holes before public houses began all day opening, what a crying shame for us duckers and divers of those days.

In the days following our discussion I became the captain of the Seattle Sounders with the great help of Ken Friar the General Manager of Arsenal Football Club. Ken Friar is one of those people behind the scenes that make good football clubs great, and I can never thank him enough for his assistance in sorting my new contract out!

THE INFINITE MIND

But we are on the Bobby Moore three-timer. This time it was out of my hands and Bobby and I had no idea that what you are about to read ever happened. Not until you read what Miss Betty Shine wrote in her – yet another – brilliant book, 'The Infinite Mind'. It was not until going through my notes for this book that I realised that Betty was a big part of everything I did since my departing the Royal London and St Bartholomew's Hospitals.

This chapter is the second one of that book labelled 'The Message' by Miss Shine:

Whilst reading the *Daily Mail* one morning in January 1998, my eye was drawn to a small photograph of a man. The words underneath told me that the photograph was of Alan Hudson, an ex-footballer.

Apparently, he had been left severely injured and in a coma after a car had knocked him down having mounted the pavement where he had been walking. Just then, a very strong male voice said to me, "Please help me". Then he said, "I want you to contact my wife and tell her not to give up on me, that I'm still here".

He then went on to tell me of intimate details of his private life. I must admit I had to smile and wondered, "Where do I go from here?"

I had never heard of Alan Hudson, although he was obviously well known in the football world.

Then my friend Kevin Keegan came to mind. Perhaps he could point me in the right direction?

As I have been friends with Kevin's family for some time, especially with his wife Jean, he did not seem to be too fazed by what I had to say and he promised to help.

For those of you, like me, who know nothing about football, Alan Hudson had a long and distinguished football career with Chelsea, Stoke City, Arsenal and Seattle Sounders in the United States of America. He was capped at Under 23 and senior level and won many honours in the game, including FA Cup and European Cup Winners Cup medals. Since retiring as a player he has been involved with coaching and journalism.

Later that same day, I was able to have a conversation with David Connolly, a friend of Alan Hudson. He told me that he had always been a sceptic where psychic matters were concerned, but that he was conscious that something very extraordinary was taking place, especially once I was able to pass on to him the private information that Alan had given me about his family.

David and I talked for some time, and I was able to help him with some problems of his own, which made it easier for him to pass on Alan's messages to his wife, Ann. I was able to tell him that Alan told me that that Bobby Moore had met him and was helping him.

I was naturally concerned about whether the messages I had received from Alan would be welcome to Ann, as one never knows how such communications will be received by the family. After all, they did not know me, and although they could check me out through my books, they might want to dismiss this as fantasy. Who could blame them?

The evidence Ann was going to receive from David was very specific. All that mattered was that she could accept that it was correct.

The following day I received a call from David who told me although Ann had been shocked, to say the least, she had confirmed everything that Alan had said about his family. She asked David to tell me that she would be contacting me.

From that time on, David rang me every day, and I would pass on messages to Ann from Alan. He was extremely positive, and was constantly reassuring us of his eventual recovery.

I was able to tell David that Alan's dead father was in the dimension, helping him.

NO USE ON THE DANCE FLOOR ANYMORE

Betty goes on to tell about her conversations with my ex-wife Ann, but I feel this is not worth the paper it is printed on, so forgive me, for as Betty said I am positive and do not like things that are untrue and most of all negative, especially as I had been given no hope of surviving this and believe to this day that was the way my wife wanted it. You might find that very difficult to understand but I can say this with my hand on my heart. What would have been the biggest injustice here is that she would have been seen as the loving daughter-in-law and that would have been a life of living a lie. I knew she would be leaving me and told a couple of my family members long before it happened but they said that could not be further from the truth, because I had not seen her through all of this ordeal, that is why I mentioned the acting earlier on. I was proved right despite whatever went on in the Intensive Trauma Unit. My family probably thought that the bang on my head had me thinking wonky, but I know her too well and I was no use to her on the dance floor anymore!

Betty continues by saying that: for four months I was able to give Ann information about her husband's injuries and about how they were progress-ing. I had to explain, because this information was so detailed, that I had a superb team of spirit doctors who were helping me. After all, this was all very new to her. At one point, I was able to alleviate Ann's worst fears by telling her that the swelling in Alan's brain had reduced, which was later confirmed by the medical team.

There were other strange things happening in Alan's family at this time. When his sister Julie was told about his accident she became desperately upset, screaming for her father. As she did so, a gold cross appeared on the wall behind her. It stayed for two days, and was seen by five other people. I believe that when she screamed for her dead father, who was helping Alan, he activated this symbol to give his daughter peace of mind. Julie told Ann that this cross had no shadow – which is quite normal with such phenomena – for spirits do not have shadows, they are the shadows!

Some time later, Julie redecorated the room, but the incredible energy impact needed to form the cross in the first place had left an indelible mark. The cross remains on the wall.

The role that David took on as middleman, passing messages from Alan and myself to Ann, was truly an act of a loyal and loving friend. He kept a diary, and it was only when reading his transcript that I realised just how awful those dark months of December and January had been for Alan's wife, family and friends. Eventually however, Alan came out of his coma and begun his long journey to recovery.

Whilst speaking to David on the phone one day, Alan's paternal grandfather appeared to me and told me has was helping Alan. I could see him so clearly that I was able to give David a detailed description of him. When this was passed on to Alan he was surprised, because he had never really had much contact with his paternal grandfather. So you see, when people are in trouble, everyone will gather round to help.

David and Ann have since visited me at my home, and we have all become close friends. I have spoken to Alan over the phone and am very excited about his recovery, although he obviously still has a lot of work to do to get back to a hundred per-cent. But the fact that he started working again from his hospital bed gives one an insight into the power and personality, which enabled him to contact me in the first place.

While he was still in hospital, I told Ann, via David, that one of the medical staff would, when Alan recovered, turn around and say, "This is nothing short of a miracle." As time passed, doctors and nurses alike would make remarks about his "incredible recovery", but Ann told me that she wanted to hear the exact words I had given to her. One day, as the sister was about to leave the room after speaking with Ann for some time, she reached the door, then turned around and said, "This is nothing short of a miracle." These words convinced Ann that a 'miracle' had taken place, because every word I had passed onto her, even about family matters, which at that time had not taken place, had come true.

When Alan came out of the coma, he said that he had actually seen his father.

He also told me, when I had my first telephone conversation with him, that he had always believed in psychic matters, and thought that he had certain gifts in this direction. He said something wonderful had happened to him and that he had seen the most beautiful of places, and he knew instinctively that these were not hallucinations, that they were real. In a letter he sent to me he wrote that, when he was travelling at high speed in the energy dimension, he passed both his father and a very dear friend who had died. Those of you who have never had a psychic experience may find it difficult to come to terms with the fact that the mind is infinite, that it survives death, and that it can take over when the brain has been damaged. But if we did not have a mind that is totally separate from the brain, none of us would exist, because it is the mind that creates the link between the Universal Mind and the brain. We are all children of the Universe, we came from the source, and to the source we will return. For the moment, let me assure you that nothing is what it seems, and that anything is possible. Because of the swelling in Alan's brain, he was reduced to a comatose state. This happens when the messages from brain to body are disrupted, and the mind seeks alternative communication.

Alan's story is typical of the stress that the personality endures when it feels it can no longer communicate through the brain. The patient does not suffer, because they are in a peaceful and loving environment. Their wish to communicate is driven by desire to ease the suffering of their friends and family, and, in Alan's case, to pass on to them the knowledge that he was going to survive. As I mentioned earlier, others in the spirit dimension can come forward to ease tension and give proof of surviving through these trying times.

The family has asked me to thank all the medical staff at the Royal London and at St Bartholomew's Hospital for all the loving care that Alan received from them during his long stay with them. As a medium, it was a great honour for me to bring two worlds together, easing the grief of the family as they waited for their loved one to recover from such terrible trauma. For me, this is just one of many hundreds of similar stories that are being played out every day, each one as remarkable as the last. I therefore hope that Alan's story will bring hope and comfort to the families of all those who are currently in a coma.

MUNICH AIR DISASTER

Miss Betty Shine, as you can read between the lines is a lady of great stature always being positive, which is maybe why I chose to 'scream' at her whilst she was reading her favourite newspaper. I had the great pleasure to have lunch with her and although it lifted me onto a higher plain I was so very disappointed that we could not sit and talk forever, maybe one day we will. The beginning of chapter three of her book read like this: I was first introduced to Bobby Moore through my contact with Bobby Keetch, and then again through Alan Hudson. There was an interval of twenty months between these messages. But the first contact I had from the Manchester United team was over twenty years ago.

Betty goes on to talk about the Munich Air crash which is also very interesting, but unless you believe don't bother putting your reading glasses on.

I do, and as she points out in my case I was very positive of how things were going to turn out. The reasons I cut my second wife, Ann, out of this was simply that I don't feel she should really be accepted in a book so positive and that I am very excited about. I like to put the bad times and people behind me, more so since that incredible accident, but I felt it necessary to give you an insight into how my mind works, so when I am critical of someone I mention in between the lines of these pages. You will find I cut in here and there whilst trying to keep tabs on both the Tinker and Talisman, but it is also very important that I mention the fantastic times that we had without the kind of good fortune or the kind of money that today's players have in their bank accounts. The Resuscitation Room was a very interesting place to visit after I had left hospital, at a time I was on crutches and had to return to see Mr David Goodier, the man responsible for saving my pelvis and in the end the keeping of my legs. My uncle George and I thought we would go and say hello to Mr Frank Cross who was the overseer of my case from the first minute the alarm bells began ringing on that tragic night of the 15th of December 1997.

Frank was absolutely delighted to see my uncle and I, knowing very few people return to such a daunting place – as is the Resuscitation Room – the one they first wheel you into after such an accident. It is here they put you on every machine available to see what they have to work on first to keep you alive. I returned both to there and the incredibly bleak Intensive Trauma Unit to say 'thanks' for looking after me in my darkest hour. The day George and I visited the ITU was incredible for it was a little like being Joseph Merrick again – the Elephant Man – as slowly the hallway filled with doctors and nurses coming out of each room as if summoned to see what had come through the door. Like Merrick, he ended up in a circus, but one for all the wrong reasons. One grew slowly to around a dozen as they looked me up and down in sheer amazement, as I stood there firmly leaning on my crutches. I asked one nurse if I could donate some money to buy the hospital the C-Clamp in which she replied "Alan every penny you get, you go out and enjoy it." I was disappointed and overjoyed at the same time, if that makes sense – but that's me being me, totally in a world of my own. The kind of world that keeps you alive when the odds are stacked against you – just as it proved. It was also strange to hear that people never return to the Intensive Trauma Unit, which made me feel good, for I told them I had come back to thank each and every one of those great souls who helped pull me through. Just a simple 'thank you!'

THE TINKERMAN

It was the nineteenth day of July 2000 that the headlines of my column in the Sentinel read like this; **Alan Hudson reckons there must be an English revolution – now**.

THREE YEARS ON

My day started as usual, if not sitting writing at my desk, making my way to the gymnasium for yet another day of gruelling rehabilitation. It gets no easier. The days of me going jogging around Greenwich Park, or along the Chelsea Embankment whenever I was in town are gone since that near fatal car accident in the December of 1997. It was through that I returned to my hometown of Chelsea where my football dream began back in 1966, the year I signed Apprentice forms for Chelsea Football Club. The year, of course, we witnessed England carry off the Jules Rimet Trophy for the first and only time in their history. This town Chelsea was once mine, as I became the most local lad to play for this club, although as a schoolboy I was a Fulham supporter and adored the one and only Johnny Haynes, whilst Chelsea boasted the incredible Jimmy Greaves whose number eight shirt I went on to wear as does Frank Lampard today. These two teamed up together in England shirts and were simply magnificent. Throughout my career, one of many twist and turns, I thought I had seen almost everything but today was one of the biggest bombshells ever to drop on the game of football. In a nutshell the Russians were not only coming, but had taken over. My handset rang whilst casually walking towards my daily workout, these days more important than ever before. My knees were still giving me grief, my right foot useless, my head still aching whilst my mind was still wondering why?

The voice on the other end was just another I needed not to hear but being me I fell into the trap one more time. It was from Sky TV and no fee involved, but Alan Hudson being Alan Hudson obliged to be interviewed about the most sensational news that has ever broke in the entire world of football, and that included David and his wife Victoria in Madrid, or should I say Victoria and her husband David?

This was to become quite astonishing!

The reason I agreed to be in front of the camera was purely and simply intrigue, plus I still hade my part time job of writing for the *Sentinel,* the newspaper that has won many awards under the leadership of Sean Dooley, the Editor of the Stoke-on-Trent based newspaper. I value my work and my friendship with Mr Dooley and have shared many a fine lunch with him when he comes into the capital. He is a Manchester United follower but has an open mind to most of the Premiership, obviously!

Back to the Bridge and the buying and selling of this sleeping giant, one that has underachieved more than any other club in the country, winning the old First Division championship only once and the Premiership, never before. This is why I value my European Cup Winners Cup and the FA Cup Winners medals – won the year prior – in my first season, although I sat through two matches of thunder against that incredible Leeds United machine. Getting to the FA Cup Final in my first full season for the team in royal blue and gold was something else and that season saw me also included in the squad that would be leaving London Heathrow for Mexico going to defend the World Cup, a match that was the most controversial of matches leaving the West Germans totally blitzed by the wonderful Bobby Moore and the class of '66'. But my luck was out when going down a hole at the Hawthorns the home of West Bromwich Albion on the Easter before that May final. My ankle ligaments were completely torn, never to recover. But here we were in the July of 2003 and a Roman at Stamford Bridge, do me a favour, this could not be true?!

But it happened and it just goes to prove that if ever you are facing a time in hell, heaven can, by believing it, be around the next corner!

No, this is not a reincarnation of Matthew Harding but a real live Russian who not only possesses oil wells but also has the ability to have say in the team selection of who plays whenever that same television station decide when they actually take the field. This is going to be quite brilliant because nobody around these parts had a clue what was going on here. I was the first on the scene of this extraordinary time in the history of Chelsea Football Club!

Yeah you guessed – I am a Chelsea boy born just off the Kings Road and the Fulham Road too, in fact Elm Park Gardens – a place where now Roman could afford to buy number 75 and all the houses running alongside. It was a wonderful big home where we could play our football safely on those lovely green pastures at such a young age.

The garden was shared by all but that was no problem in those days, the ones when you could leave your front and back door unlocked without the kind of fears of today.

Anyhow getting back to the 4th of July, the most wonderful time to be in the United States of America, 'Independence Day', though this began the previous day, it hit the news on this one. You will come to learn how much I love the USA and I will eventually write my next book from there, as my intention is to move there on a permanent basis. It is the most wonderful country, a place where the owners of the likes of the New York Jets and Yankees, Seattle Seahawks or the Tampa Bay Buccaneers would compare to this latest mind-blowing manoeuvre. George Steinbrenner the owner of the Yankees owns the Radisson Bay Harbour Inn, a hotel where me and mine have spent many terrific moments. But the Russians were taking over my hometown and all of Chelsea filled with the most incredible reactions, the first one being that 'this guy is a money launderer'.

DAVID BECKHAM FREE KICK

That's fickle football fans and fans wherever you watch football most, and along the way I might just repeat that if he has to tell the world where he got his money then so does all of Parliament and all the other rogues who have cheated there way through life without ever being questioned. I find it rather insulting and downright rude. I have met many rich and powerful men through my path of life and if I could put a percentage on 'straightness' the Russian would look pretty clean. To me it is great news and also I might just get some more work, purely selfish reasons although that really does make a change. I always like people before not liking them so this new entourage raiding Stamford Bridge were right up my street, no not Elm Park Gardens, my path of life again. Who is this man? What does he do? Where did he get his billions? Can he be trusted? Well these are the kind of things spoken by the biggest lot of two-time losers you would ever meet in your life. "Can he be trusted", Fagan asks about Oliver Twist?

Anyhow I was looking forward to watching just how these people were going about making this Chelsea a team – who have been a sleeping giant for so long – a real force in both the Premiership and the Champions League. The newspapers are going to have Christmas 365 days a year here in Chelsea and I am living just about a David Beckham free-kick away from where it all started for me in our prefab in Upcerne Road, about a three minute run to the front gates of Stamford Bridge itself. However these days after my accident running was a part of my last life for my new one has left me half crippled having my balance taken away, something that was a great asset in playing the game the way I played it.

Firstly Roman bought this football club less than thirty-six hours before the receivers were about to take over. Secondly, the questions about if several of the staff would be safe in their jobs. Thirdly the names that were being linked to my first club were quite astonishing, beginning with Vieri – from Inter Milan – at an asking price of £25million, Henry from Arsenal at £70million and a host of others that the media were throwing around like confetti at an Italian wedding. Then the ball starting rolling, but before it does here is a piece in the *Daily Express* written by Bill Pierce with the headline being the obvious **RUSSIAN ROULETTE:** He was born in the same year as Tony Adams Gianfranco Zola and Geoff Hurst's famous World Cup winning hat-trick. And without even kicking a ball, Roman Abramovich and his Russian revolution at Chelsea look like having at least twice as much impact on English football as any of the above. There is one certainty and that is all the gold in the world could not buy this country a World Cup!

The 36-year-old billionaire's £160million take over at Stamford Bridge is about to signal the end of a football life as we have recently come to know it. Already Chelsea are under a new kind of pressure – to live up to all the hype of the new owner's arrival – to knock both Manchester United and Arsenal off their Premiership perches. They also are trying to 'do a Blackburn' and buy the title. The late Jack Walker used his wad to boost the club he loved. But unlike him, Abramovich has no history with Chelsea. That is why the questions have been asked about the newcomer who threatens to transform the game and has quickly stated his ambition is to see Chelsea lifted to the same level as the mighty Real Madrid.

Politician Tony Banks, a Chelsea fan, and a good friend was the first to query Abramovich's football motivation and seek details of the background to his wealth. Abramovich is still intriguing, an almost shadowy figure, and fame is not something he has ever actively pursued. Rich and powerful, he was famous until recently only for keeping the lowest of profiles. Money and influence have always been regarded as his buzz-words in Russia, where pictures of him were so rare one Moscow newspaper offered cash for the first one sent in. He rides around in a bullet proof Mercedes, flanked by bodyguards, owns several luxury homes, a spectacular yacht and is the governor of a region in the far reaches of Siberia, towards Alaska. *Forbes Magazine* lists him as the second richest man in Russia with a personal fortune of around £3.2billion – and rising every day since his Sibnet oil company announced to make to merge and become the fourth biggest of its kind in the world.

SPURS, ARSENAL OR UNITED

And the *Sunday Times* recently named him as the 19th richest man in Europe, ahead of Formula One boss Bernie Ecclestone, whose business the Russian is said to covert.

A father of four, Abramovich already co-owns an ice hockey club in Russia and was believed to have tried to buy the football club CSKA Moscow this year.

He is said to have monitored Manchester United, Arsenal and Tottenham, before eventually being steered towards Chelsea, heading for the Champions League, but with liabilities of around £80million.

A little later he was supposed to be flying over the Stamford Bridge and to ask, "What club is that" a moment Ken Bates can count his lucky stars?

Abramovich – who was orphaned as a child and brought up by an uncle in Moscow (some circles say that this uncle was one of power in the Kremlin) – always knew the best route to riches was through taking sound expert advice and possessing the shrewdness to wield the power where it would do him most good. He rose to prominence in Russia during the days of Boris Yeltsin. He has formed a circle of alliance – soon known as 'The Family' – under his mentor, oil dealer Boris Berezovsky, which bankrolled Yeltsin's power campaign.

And his personal political influence was said to be so great he became known as the 'Kremlin Puppetmaster'.

Inevitably, Saratov-born Abramovich's brilliant career has not been without controversy.

He was implicated in the hijack of a freight train, 55 carriages laden with fuel – although the case was eventually dropped. His former mentor Berezovsky currently awaits extradition charges in London over a fraud case.

We may know before too long what Ambramovich has in store at Chelsea – but beyond question is that his arrival will instigate a shake-up in the game on a scale rarely seen before.

FIRST SIGNINGS

It did not take long for the new owner to bring fresh blood into the West London club and he did so by buying a young left back from West Ham United. Glen Johnson was pretty much an unknown quantity and it is still a little mystifying about who recommended this raw talented young defender. Was it manager Claudio Ranieri or Sven Goran Eriksson the Swedish-born England manager – who will be named quite often in this book. There were rumblings about the Swede visiting Abromovich's Knightsbridge home and all the Nationals had photographs of him entering the Chelsea owner's home on that occasion. Rumours were rife about Roman wanting to replace the Italian with the Swede but a ball had not been kicked and the Italians, record the season prior to this one was good enough to win them a place in the Champions League. Also if they had given him his P45 and the Swede left the England job to get on the Russian Roundabout it would not have been the smartest move for the jury is still out in the Swedes' case whilst the Tinkerman was becoming more and more popular with the Chelsea faithful.

I don't know if Frank Lampard junior had anything to do with the transfer of Johnson, for he would have known this very gifted young defender from his West Ham playing days. I asked my good friend – Millwall supporter – Michael Bloomfield if he had known of Johnson on his loan period at the New Den and he shook his head in disbelief saying that, "Do you know whilst he was on loan, if we had offered West Ham money for him, say between a quarter and a half a million pounds they would have bit our hands off. Then what a player we would have had and if we needed to sell him look at the fee and the kind of profit we would have made!"

My initial response was that after watching Johnson play in a couple of pre-season matches that he was going to become a very shrewd buy as he showed that a step up in class held no fears for him. Graham Le Saux was sold to Southampton to make way for both Johnson and Wayne Bridge the new boy who has already played for England and the swap that made sense, definitely looking like it was a move for the better of the team. Then came Damien Duff for £17million from Blackburn, a player with lorry loads of talent and one who impressed the watching millions as he strutted his stuff for his homeland Southern Ireland – or as they call it now the Republic – in the last World Cup. Another player shipped in was Rumanian International Adrian Mutu a player highly rated by ex-Chelsea blue Dan Petrescu, a player himself idolised around Chelsea's now impressive stadium. He says of Mutu, a player unheard of around the streets of Chelsea, that "Mutu is a winner and he will succeed, I am sure of that. And for the moment he can stay in my house in London. If he likes it he can stay for the full five years of his contract." My first thought was that the older Romanian was looking for something in return or maybe a thank you from the billionaire owner. Dan went on that "I have a lot of Romanian friends in London and I will ask them to help Adrian and Chelsea settle in together and speed up the time it takes for him to feel at home in the city and the English style of life".

Mutu 24, and Chelsea are hoping he receives a work permit before the opening day of the season at Anfield. The new Chelsea striker said, "I am ready to start a new period of my life and I am not afraid. It's a challenge and I like challenges and new experiences. I will be playing in the mother country of football, in a very strong competition with big clubs. I hope I will receive my work permit in time to be on the pitch in the opening game against Liverpool. What a big game that will be".

Mutu said that it was Chelsea's ambition, which brought him to this club not forgetting the millions being thrown at the club by Abramovich. And the Russian is set to splash out another £20million – on Auxerre hit-man Djibril Cisse.

Mutu goes on, "It was never an obsession for me to leave Parma. I was quite happy there. I decided to go only after I saw the Chelsea offer. It was impossible to say no.

"Dan Petrescu advised me many times to go to Chelsea because he spent a wonderful time there and said also that London was a great city. For me the choice wasn't anything to do with money but for the sporting opportunity to play in a great team with great ambitions and great players. There is also the sure fact they will play in the Champions League." Mutu is not eligible for Chelsea's opening match in the Champions League Qualifier against Slovakian champions ZK Zilina tomorrow.

Mutu went on, saying that, "I know in England the emphasis is on force and the play is more free, there are not so many tactics, but I am not afraid for the coach is Italian which is great, for I know we will have a good relationship and be able to produce some wonderful football. I am not afraid about the weather. Somebody said it was cold and always raining but these are only excuses. London is not Greenland and I'm sure the pitches will be better than the ones I had in Verona, for example." I believe that Mutu will take over the role of Gianfranco Zola as the favourite of the fans just as Peter Osgood and Charlie Cooke were back in those exciting days in the late sixties and early seventies. If Osgood was the 'King' then Charlie was the 'Prince' of Stamford Bridge and lets not forget Jimmy Greaves before them and going back further Roy Bentley who was probably Chelsea's equivalent to the great John Charles, the Welsh giant who played, just like Bentley, as both centre-half and centre forward. Then even one step further to the incredible Hughie Gallagher. That was just a little nostalgic history for you before we go into mid-August in 2003. They were great players indeed!

DOUBLE DEALING DESAILLY

Wednesday the 13th of August and the Blues skipper Marcel Desailly was now ready to talk about a one-year extension to his contract yesterday – but insists they are not expecting to win the title this season. Desailly, 34, said that, "Our objective is to do the best we can, to be consistent at the top level. But it is certainly not to win the Premiership. France were equally well equipped to have a great World Cup but were knocked out in the first round."

One of my few old friends in Fleet Street wrote this about the new owner:

Chelsea owner Roman Abramovich has dismissed suggestions he is about to leave his native Russia to live in England. The billionaire entrepreneur said: "We are selling some things and buying other things but I don't feel like doing business outside Russia". Reports suggested that he was on the verge of selling his myriad Russian interests, from oil to pig farming, following the arrest of another of the country's billionaires. Police have detained Piston Lebedev, a key business ally of Russia's richest man Mikhail Khodorkovsky, head of the oil company Yukos Leberdev, was charged with theft of state property in a 1994 Privatisation deal. Investors have also carried out a series of raids on offices of Yukos and its subsidiaries. The affair prompted concerns among business leaders that the authorities might revisit the massive 1990s sell off of state property.

A handful of magnates such as Khodorkovsky and Abramovich made overnight fortunes in state asset sales at the time. Yukos is due to merge with Sibnet, Abramovich's company in a deal worth £7 to 9million.

Abramovich was worried the Yukos affair was undermining the confidence of investors and this prompted analysis to suggest he might sell his interest to Chevron/Texaco from the United States.

Abramovich increased his shareholding in Chelsea Village plc to 95.22per cent yesterday. He can now make a compulsory purchase of the remaining shares before removing Chelsea Village from the Alternative Investment Market. This would enable Abramovich to buy any player he chooses without having to announce it to the Stock Market, wrote Steve Curry.

As I gave my interviews to SKY and about a half a dozen other TV and radio stations I looked around me and thought of all those years ago that we would play some of our greatest matches in that old forecourt area – in our Friday morning five-a-sides – and dug even deeper by thinking, why could this not be the late sixties and early seventies when our team were the talk of this incredible town. We had better individuals in Peter Osgood, Charlie Cooke, Eddie McCreadie, Marvin Hinton and yours truly, not forgetting our 'cat' the wonderful Peter Bonetti. Yeah Chelsea have a brilliant goalkeeper of their own, Carlo Cudicini, and he probably cost less than any player on their forty man roster, but our one defied logic with his frame more like one of an Ethiopian marathon runner. He would come for crosses in crowded penalty areas and whip the ball of the heads of players like Joe Jordan, Allan Clarke,

Mick Jones, Jackie Charlton, Joe Royle, John Radford, Ron and Wyn Davies and John Toshack. Peter was crucified for all the wrong reasons in Mexico 1970 – the World Cup I missed through the same ankle that cost me those two FA Cup Finals against Leeds United just a few weeks prior. This was my greatest heartache to date, never imagining that that would be surpassed so dramatically some years later. Bill Shankly once said that "football is more important than life" and as much as I admired such a man, I tend to disagree, and please believe me when I say that nobody loves this game more than I do!

BRIAN MEARS

I pass the ground very seldom but when I do I never really reminisce, just feeling the warmth in knowing we had so many wonderful moments both on and off the field playing for the great old club. I had a few photographs taken by young Michael Fresco the nephew of his famous uncle Monty. He snapped away and then said, "Fancy a quick one before I get these pictures back Al?"

A suggestion I never answered "no" to unless I was doing something more important, like cycling in the gymnasium for an hour and a half. We walked into the Blue Room opposite the main gates, a pub my good friend Danny Gillen ran before it became the Stamford Bridge Arms, then later on a lady called Greta was our hostess, a real lovely Irish lady. Yeah times pass, and yesterday goes with it whilst the only sad story of our times around then was the tragic death of Peter and Sally Houseman. They were passengers in the back seat of a car that hit another automobile head on just near London Airport on the M4. 'Nobby' was one of the straighter lads like John Hollins and Peter Bonetti but that was never a problem as I found out to my delight whilst touring Jamaica. I spent a good couple of hours up front of our fishing vessel, drinking punch with the man who provided all our crosses for Osgood and Hutchinson. Yeah the seventies are really a massive part of the history of Chelsea Football Club and of course as I said earlier there was Greaves and Bentley before us. Then of course the fantastic Hughie Gallagher the man who broke many scoring records and another who defied logic as a five feet five inch centre-forward, Gallagher still remains the only 'Jock' to score five goals in a Scotland shirt. He also scored at a rate of almost a goal a game for Newcastle United when they won their only League Championship.

Then there was the real 'chaps', Venables, Graham, Fascione, Murray and Tambling those who sewed the seeds for us to take onto another level of socialising. The then chairman Brian Mears was a nice chap, Bates not so and now Roman the man who could at last bring the Championship to the long suffering supporters of this grand old Football Club.

The first match of the season was nearly upon this new look Chelsea side and soon they would be joined by two other of today's superstars Crespo and Makelele to add to Geremi, Joe Cole, Johnson, Veron and Duff at a cost of an estimated £110million.

The team had returned from their pre-season tour and were preparing for a match at Liverpool – funnily enough the team they beat on the last day of last season to qualify for the Champions League – but they are no longer the force they were under both Bill Shankly and Bob Paisley. Similar to our side, the red half of the Mersey boasted the likes of Peter Thompson, one player who epitomised the wingers of that day with a spearhead of Hunt and St John, Dalglish and Rush followed those in quite a devastating fashion with Kenny the orchestra leader and Ian that phenomenal finisher.

John Aldridge came a little later when the immaculate Graeme Souness was pulling the strings in the heart of a typical Liverpool machine. I felt that the Dalglish/Rush partnership was far more potent than the Toshack and Keegan spearhead.

Today's Liverpool side in comparison boasted just one world-class player and that being the truly brilliant Michael Owen. Owen would be every parent's dream son with his childish good looks, the looks you had better not fall for if on the opposition team sheet. Michael has pace to spare, a good reader of the game and when it comes to scoring goals the kid is 'mustard'. He is pretty much a one-man band in a Liverpool side that frightened you no longer, so the Blues should beat them if they are going to be serious Championship material!

Chelsea should have bought Harry Kewell from Leeds United for when he gets into his stride he is a world-class performer, but I don't think he will reach the heights he is capable of with his new club!

I think Chelsea meet Liverpool at the right time having watched their performances in the Amsterdam tournament where Ajax looked a class apart, although they hosted this four team pre-season warm up.

WADDINGTON AND MICHELS

Chelsea needed to impose themselves on this match as early as possible for I saw the team who scored first would win this match as Liverpool even play on the counter attack on their home patch, something the 'Kop' of old would never had stood for, but it is new rules, coaching methods, systems and of course a host of players whose names most supporters can hardly pronounce. As they went into this match my column for the *Sentinel* read like this; **Claudio Ranieri does not just have the best job in football today but the greatest job any football manager or head coach has ever enjoyed in the history of our great game:** Some managers come across the ultimate job, such as leading the great Real Madrid sides of the fifties featuring Alfedo di Stefano and Ferenc Puskas or the crack Hungarians of that same era. Then there were the mighty sides of the Brazil in the fifties and early seventies. That side possibly had the best front line in the business to date with Jarzinho, Gerson Tostao, Pele and Rivelino. Then there was the Dutch playing 'total football', which they boasted and some years later Ruud Gullit called it 'sexy football'. It was the Cruyff led team who were bosses in the period once England faltered and only West Germany could stand up to them. Led By

Franz 'The Keizer' Beckenbauer the Germans beat the Dutch to win the World Cup but they had the advantage of home soil just as England did in '66. It was Cruyff who captured the eyes of world football with his lazy looking long stride and a movement that reminded me of my autobiography 'The Working Mans Ballet' a title picked out for me by the late great Tony Waddington a man of great footballing knowledge and vision much like the Dutch supreme Rinus Michels. Waddington was my second father and mentor and I miss him now just as much as I do my mother and father. He was a man of great insight and wonderful knowledge of the game. A man who in fact put the attendances up at The Victoria Ground from 4,000 to 36,000 by signing Sir Stanley Matthews. Then followed that by bringing George Eastham, Roy Vernon, Peter Dobing, Denis Violett, Jimmy Greenhoff to the Potteries, and last of all, but not least, yours truly who is proud to be amongst such royalty of our game. Let us not forget the 'stealing' of Gordon Banks who was rated the 'World's Best' who could have picked any green jumper he wanted, anywhere on this planet, Gordon was simply the best, and I played with both Peter Bonetti and the mighty Pat Jennings, two keepers who would come into the reckoning of such an accolade. My column followed on the influence of Graeme Souness in the red corner of the Mersey: leading a team that ploughed through Europe like tanks going through Baghdad. Before Souness over in the blue corner was a completely different type of team influenced and run by the marvellous Alan Ball with aid from his two sidekicks Howard Kendall and Colin Harvey. I am a great believer that the most important part of any business is the heart of the team and that includes on the playing field also. The engine room is another word for such jewels in any crown. Who knows just how great the 'Busby Babes' would have become if it were not for that dreadful night in Munich when their aeroplane came down into the freezing ice. But they bounced back and with the big three Denis Law, Bobby Charlton and George Best they became the first English team to boast winning the European Cup. George Best of course was the leader of this 'gang' and went on to become a player on the same planet as Pele. George, as I write, is having trouble with a donated liver and is trying to recapture his 'playboy' image that set him apart from the rest of the football world in those heady days of the 'swinging sixties' and before retiring at an age a footballer peaks, but I wonder if this would have been the same for George for it is near impossible to think he had improvement in his game. Don Revie had a 'mean team' in more ways than one with their 'win at all cost' approach to the game and had a Sicilian type scheme who would go to any lengths bar leaving their opponents' heads under those silk sheets at the bottom of the bed. Let's not forget Bill Nicholson who built a Tottenham Hotspurs side that captured the imagination of the football world with a team they called the 'push and run' team. Dave Mackay and Danny Blanchflower, the two most important players of that side, then there were the World Cup Trio of Bobby Moore, Martin Peters and Geoff Hurst players who were such a vital part of the class of '66. The best since the present day must swing back to Holland with the sensational Van Basten, the awesome Ruud Gullit and side kick Rickjaard. One of the greatest matches this country has seen was at Wembley not long after England had carried off or 'stole' the Jules Rimet Trophy from the West Germans at Wembley. It was the day the 'Jocks' hit town and they figured if they beat England at Wembley that would make them World Champions if only for that one day. That was enough!

With the elegance and brilliance of 'Slim' Jim Baxter they pulled off a truly remarkable victory with Denis Law amongst the goals and my great pal Eddie McCreadie putting the shackles on Alan Ball and everyone else who thought they might attack down Scotland's left side. My pal was having none of it!

But it was Baxter who teased and taunted the white shirted England and there was no way of stopping the great man on a day like this day.

JUAN SEBASTIAN VERON

Back to Ranieri, a manager now possessing the financial clout to chuck all of today's greatest players and pick them at random, rather like buying all the lottery tickets available for the Saturday night draw. On days gone by I have failed to mention Diego Maradona. Then there were Bruno Conti and Paulo Rossi, both World Cup winners for their Italian homeland. Before them there was another great Italian, the Rivera of AC Milan, and Suarez of Inter Milan and Spain. Never before has a manager had such wealth to buy the Premiership and the Champions League but now we have Roman Abramovich and all of his gold, roubles or oil in whatever order you would want to put them in!

One signing strikes me as the best and that is Juan Sebastian Veron, the man that Alex Ferguson bought thinking that the Argentine would be his 'jewel' in the crown but he let the real 'jewel' go to Real Madrid!

Now he wears the blue and white of Chelsea and has the opportunity to put one over on his old club by masterminding Chelsea's latest assault on both the Premiership and the Champions League. He is a player of immense talent but at times gets lost amongst the hustle and bustle of our game because he is an old time inside forward who plays the way they did back in the fifties, sixties and seventies. I am expecting a big season from the Argentine International, if not, it will be his last!

Ranieri had by now been called the 'Tinkerman' for the way he tinkers with his players much like playing a game of chess and this chess match is every bit as important as the one Bobby Fisher made famous.

It was column time again and my *Sentinel* headlines of August the 8th and what odds would Ladbrokes have given the ex-England manager being the first Premiership boss to leave the scene of what promises to be the best Premiership yet!

GLENN IN FIRING LINE
"First to go"

Glenn Hoddle made his first team debut against me at the Victoria Ground and I said to him after the game if he keeps playing like that he will go on to achieve great things in our game!

He most certainly did with his wonderful ability to see things early and put his ammunition to good use whether it was a raking crisp forty-yard pass or a 'chip' here and a 'dink' there – so delicate for a man standing over of six feet tall. Glenn Hoddle was undoubtedly one of this country's all-time great players who was clearly a class act but his management skills didn't follow suit. He is my bet for the first sacking of management this 2003/4 Premiership season. I say this with the ending of last season still very clear in mind when they lost by four goals to nil against Middlesborough at White Hart Lane and before that I criticized him for once leaving Southampton to manage Spurs where he signed their centre half Dean Richards for £7million, when he could and should have bought the new goal-scoring machine James Beattie for under half of that price. Spurs have continued to fail to impress and have had a torrid time of late whereas Beattie has since played for his country and last season ended up in a pack with van Nistelroy, Henry and Shearer looking to win the Golden Boot.

On Saturday the 9th of August – four days prior – the *Sport* newspaper gave out a statistic that Eidur Gudjohnsen was not as potent last season compared to the season before, but this may have been because of the brilliance of the now departed Gianfranco Zola. The Icelander scored 10 goals in twenty starts, but more will be expected of him if he is not ousted by one of the new signings. He has the talent to make a huge impact when his chance arrives. All players go through a sticky patch or two, but Eidur has the skill, stamina and determination to fight his way back into the £20million player bracket at Chelsea.

It was no surprise that Marcel Desailly has signed up for another season. This was noted in the *Evening Standard* with the headline reading:

DESAILLY IN U TURN ABOUT HIS PLANS TO RETIRE

The 34-yea-old defender was expected to retire from the game when his original contract expired but the news of Roman coming to town must have changed his mind seeing the euro sign much more clearer than he does the ball. He signed a contract that will go into 2005. The France International explained how the rebuilding under Abramovich had persuaded him to stay on. He says, "The new people running the club have shown that they are building for the long term. This means that I will be able to finish my career in Europe with a big club." One player set to join him is Rumania striker Mutu after the talks finally came to the ink being dried on his new contract. Mutu was definitely now a Chelsea blue costing the club another big fee over

£15.8million from Parma. His arrival will take Abramovich's spending to £74.3million.

On the following Monday the headline for Brian Glanville's *Evening Standard* piece was headlined **A Russian History Lesson:** Ken Bates, still chairman of Chelsea, and Roman Abramovich, the Russian billionaire who now owns the club have been making cautionary noises; don't expect success too soon, despite the endless influx of stars to Stamford Bridge. For all their expenditure on famous players over the generations, the only time Chelsea ever won the League Championship, in the 1954-55 season, it was largely with a job a lot of footballers in a predominantly Third Division-inspired forward line. Until then, the club had been something of a joke, renown for its inconsistency.

In the late 1930's, a comedian even recorded a satirical ditty, The Day Chelsea Won the Cup.

As it transpired, winning the FA Cup took them 65 years from foundation in 1905, when an ecstatic journalist proclaimed; "Chelsea will stagger humanity".

Things began to get more down to earth when Ted Drake became the manager in 1952, though in fact the first major transformation was of Drake himself.

As Arsenal and England centre forward he was famously robust, but constantly injured, then as manager of Reading, where a heavy fall brought his playing days to an end, he was ribald, noisy and jocular.

Taking charge at Chelsea, he immediately put on a pin stripe suit and grew strangely subdued. But he knew what he wanted, to have Chelsea taken seriously.

One of the things he did was to have the image of a Chelsea Pensioner taken off the clubs match programme; they would be known as The Pensioners no longer.

Then he set about rebuilding the side with players from the lower leagues. The Championship winning team had two inside-forwards bought from the Third Division South; John McNichol signed from Brighton in August 1952 for £15,000 and Les Stubbs from Southend United, who also cost five figures in the following December.

Probably the most inspired acquisition of all was of the 18-year-old left-winger from Crewe Alexandra of the Third Division North, who in no time at all would be playing for England.

He arrived in February 1953, the same year Derek Saunders, red-haired and reliable, a quietly effective left half and captain, came from Amateurs Walthamstow Avenue for nothing. He didn't miss a match in the Championship winning season. The same club provided the British Olympic international winger, Jim Lewis Junior; Seamus O'Connell, a blond inside left, like Lewis, still an Amateur, had played for Bishop Aukland.

There were veterans such as Ron Greenwood, the future West Ham and England manager, who had twenty-one league games that season at centre half and John Harris, a right back who had been centre half before him. Ken Armstrong, a Yorkshire born right half, had once filled the centre forward position. But now the position was splendidly taken by Roy Bentley, the one outstanding talent in the team, and England's striker in the ill fated 1950 World Cup Finals, scorer of 22 of Chelsea's 81 league goals in that celebrated season. He came in 1948 from Newcastle United for £11,000.

After a hectic start to that season, a match one still remembers is when Chelsea lost 6-5 at home to Manchester United, they settled down to take the title with 52 points, four ahead of Wolves, Portsmouth and Sunderland.

They should have gone on to contest the first ever European Cup, but their Chairman Joe Mears, also President of the Football League, was bullied out of it by the League's xenophobic secretary Alan Hardaker.

THE GREAT GALLAGHER

The Championship triumph was quite a contrast with the immediate post-war years. When football officially restarted in the 1946/47 season, when Chelsea fielded the glittering inside forward trio of Walker/Lawton/Goulden, which looked likely to win trophies galore.

Tommy Lawton, signed from Everton for eleven grand in 1945, was the prolific England centre forward, unrivalled in the air. Tommy Walker was a Scottish legend. Len Goulden from West Ham United scored a spectacular goal for England when they thrashed Germany 6-3 in Berlin in 1938.

But a law of diminishing returns seemed not to be in operation. The famous trio had their great days, but not a title was won.

Nor was it between the wars, despite the array of costly stars who came to Stamford Bridge.

Two of them, Alex Jackson and Hughie Gallagher had been members of the rampant Wembley Wizards, in the Scotland team, which thrashed England 5-1 in 1928. Jackson, the tallest member of that attack at five feet seven inches scored three of the goals.

Gallagher, a hugely skilful little centre forward, frequently provoked by opposing centre-halves was previously the idol at Newcastle United.

He was a notorious drinker. The story goes that the players of a team due to play Chelsea the next day at the Bridge were walking along the nearby Kings Road on a Friday evening when a man was thrown out of a pub which they were passing and a drunk lay throne on the pavement.

To their amazement they saw it was Gallagher. The following afternoon, he ran them ragged.

In more recent times, the tendency has been to import expensive players from abroad: Ruud Gullit, Jimmy Floyd Hasselbaink and Gianfranco Zola.

Yet go back some thirty years and you find that two of the most famous players in the club's history, Peter Osgood and Alan Hudson came through the system and were developed at Stamford Bridge as subsequently was Ray Wilkins.

There might be a moral there.

WHAT FOOTBALL CLUBS WERE

That was Brian Glanville's summation and one that I don't really agree with for my father Bill Hudson developed me, and Peter Osgood, although a raw Windsor born builder, was plucked and thrown straight into the Chelsea team by Tommy Docherty. There was quite an uproar from the Chelsea faithful when the 'Doc' left out the very popular Barry Bridges and told the *Evening News* and *Standard* that Osgood was being given a dozen matches – no less – to prove himself as the player that he thought he would become. Tommy 'The Tyke' Docherty was spot on in his predicting that Osgood would become one of the all-time Chelsea greats.

CHAMPIONS LEAGUE

On the eve of Chelsea's opening match in the Champions League, against SL Zilina the Slovakian champions Marcel Desailly was quoted as saying that "We can join the greats. We have the quality and opportunity to do some great things. This is a new beginning. Roman Abramovich has taken some intelligent decisions. He has put in place the means of making Chelsea one of the big clubs in Europe." Chelsea had been on the back pages of the National press from the day the deal was clinched by the Russian and John Terry was the first one to speak up on the Claudio Ranieri front.

The headlines of the *Sun* read **WE'LL SAVE RANIERI:** John Terry made it very clear how he feels about the present Chelsea manager who has been under pressure by media who were trying to tie the English manager Sven Goran Eriksson with the new Russian regime. Terry says that "Claudio is the man who gave me my chance and I want him to stay. There has been a lot of speculation about Sven but the manager here has done a superb job to get us where we are before he got any money". It is interesting listening to Terry because he will be the backbone of the Chelsea side for years to come. He has already made his mark in the International team and if he had behaved himself before the last World Cup would have had that experience under his belt also. He goes on "Now he has some money, he has brought in new faces and is looking to take us further. It is all down to us now. We must look forward to this match knowing we must reach the Champions League proper by winning this qualifier". At this moment in time Abramovich is in Alaska but has arranged for BBC TV pictures to be specially beamed to his yacht. Terry has just signed an extension to his current contract and admitted he was as shocked as everyone else at the speed of the Russian Revolution. He added that, "When I signed my new contract I asked Trevor Birch whether there would be any new players coming in and were William Gallas and Eidur Gudjohnsen staying. He replied that they were staying and with a grin said there would be new players coming in. The takeover came out of nowhere and is great for the club. The money has created some great excitement but the new signings and speculation have not affected the players. We have all had a chance and realise that are going to be a lot of games ahead of us this season.

'SHOOT MYSELF'

If we have a good cup run we could have to play sixty-odd matches and it is difficult to play that many matches. If the manager thinks a player needs a rest he can bring in someone who is just as good. We have all clicked straight away. I thought it would take a few months but the new lads have settled in quickly. Now we are all looking forward to the Champions League". The Blues chief will field almost £50million of new talent against Zilina in this Champions League third round first-leg qualifier. Wayne Bridge, Jan Veron, Damien Duff and Geremi are all set to start in Chelsea's first real competitive match since Roman Abramovich splashed his cash to buy the club. But Ranieri knows his men must stay in control at the tiny 6,500-seater Pod Dubnom Stadium if they are to avoid repeat embarrassments of the past in Europe. Ranieri says, "This is our first game of our season and it important to do well. But I am sure the players will not be nervous. If they are I will shoot myself. For everybody at Chelsea, our life has changed. This is a new Chelsea".

The Blues have come unstuck against Viking Stavanger, Hapoel Tel Aviv and St Gallen recently. My worst memory was being knocked out as the holders in the 1971/72 season by a Swedish team on the away goals rule. After being held in Sweden by their Cup Winners Advitaberg – a game that should seen us score at least five – I scored the first goal at the Bridge with a sizzling volley from about thirty yards out and then after missing a hatful which included a John Hollins penalty they somehow got through in the last minute and stole an equaliser. We went out at a time when things were going wrong on the field and lost in three cup matches that included the League Cup Final at Wembley against the club I would play for some six months later. The other horrid affair was at Leyton Orient where we led, again this time by two goals – and like out of a story book for Orient – they stormed back and got three to knock us out of the FA Cup Fifth Round. Our draw in the following round would have been a plum one against Arsenal at Stamford Bridge. This was all in a short spell and set the alarm bells ringing and Dave Sexton decided to break up the team with initially getting both Peter Osgood and myself out of the club. The most bizarre thing happened, for Sexton himself was sacked not long afterwards after the team were relegated. That was just simply ridiculous, letting your best two players go, something I told the Chairman – Brian Mears – some years later, for the fans pay to watch the best players. This was the downfall of Chelsea in the early seventies for just a short period after they were relegated and Sexton left the same way as Osgood and I had.

But this is a new Chelsea and the football world were buzzing about a Russian buying the club where with the signings he had made along with the sale of the club it came to over £200million. There was every chance that after seeing Abramovich at work that Alex Ferguson would be looking to keep up with the 'Jones's' so to speak. He still had the money from the departure of David Beckham, the player who gave United fantastic service. Whilst on service, he made the lion's share of their goals and also chipped in with some memorable free-kicks, however the one against Greece was possibly one of his most important goals ever!

With just a few seconds on the clock he put the ball down with his usual grace, looking up at the wall, he stepped back two or three paces, never taking his eyes off the Greek goalkeeper and the wall that was there to hide one side of his goal. The crowd at Old Trafford went totally berserk as David fired an unstoppable right footer into the right hand side of the goalkeeper's goal. England had qualified the moment that Beckham put his wonderful right foot in contact to the football, and England were to fight for another day.
England 2 Greece 2

UNITED LAND THEIR WONDER BOY

This was the headline of the *Daily Mail* on the same day as Chelsea were preparing for their opening match in Europe. It read that United had signed Portuguese teenage sensation Cristiano Ronaldo and that has ended speculation of taking West Ham's brilliant young Jermaine Defoe. I had not seen Ronaldo play but have been very impressed with the West Ham youngster, a player of immense talent though he only stands at around five feet six or seven, he plays that 'lone' role up front with such confidence and assurance. He is quick on the turn, sees situations early and has the instincts great goal-scorers need to be top notch. Defoe will be an England player in a few short months but playing in the Nationwide First Division will not help his chances, although he has impressed enough when being thrown in the deep end last season as his club were falling into a relegation battle, which ended in tears for the Hammers and their so-called Academy. That really does make me laugh!

The Premiership champions have almost agreed a fee for Ronaldo with their sister club Sporting Lisbon and hope to unveil the 18 year-old at Old Trafford later this week. And with World Cup Winning Brazilian Kleberson being granted a work permit yesterday United have already spent the money from the sale of David Beckham.

Matt Lawton of the *Daily Mail* wrote:

MOMENT OF TRUTH FOR THE ROMAN LEGION
'WHAT ABOUT ME'

If Roman Abramovich was even a tad reluctant to be here this evening for what could prove a perilous Champions League encounter for his new team, he appears to have done a fine job of avoiding any anxiety.

The new owner of Stamford Bridge is on business in Alaska, and will watch the match on a live feed to his yacht once again.

Spending £75million on a football team and then travelling to a remote corner of Slovakia yet still watching his team is really something new in our game. Tonight is the banana skin of banana skins, a journey into the uncharted territory of Zilina's 6,500-seat stadium with an untried team.

Claudio Ranieri seemed remarkably relaxed before boarding the flight at Gatwick yesterday but even he could be forgiven for wanting to duck this battle. After spending much of the summer big-game fishing, a little R and R with his new boss much have been appealing.

As it is, Ranieri has no choice but to come here to face the Slovakian Champions. He has been entrusted with the company chequebook and it is now up to him to mould a side from the players he already had and the seven he has just recruited. "My priority is to win" he said. "But also to start building a team".

The Tinkerman Claudio Ranieri still reflects on the news of Chelsea's Russian Revolution with a sense of bewilderment. "The whole club has changed in a single day" he said after a Chelsea fan working at the airport suggested he now put Brazil's Ronaldo at the top of his shopping list, "for the interest in us is just unbelievable."

As amazed as the Italian is, he is only too aware of just how precarious his own position has become.

"I remember when I first heard" he said. "I was driving back from Rome with my family and two dogs when somewhere in France I received a phone call. It must have been 11.20 in the evening and someone from the club said we'd been taken over. They said everything was okay" and I said "Great, but what about me".

August 15th...Duff inspires great start to Abramovih era – but now Hasselbaink is refusing to play ball. **ROMAN EMPIRES DAWNS** From David Hytna in Zilina;

The Roman Abramovich revolution finally burst into action last night, as Damien Duff inspired Chelsea to a 2-0 win over MSK Zilina, taking them one step closer to the group stage of the Champions League. The Russian billionaire has lavished £75million on fresh talent so far – he is still looking for more and has Real Madrid's Claude Makelele in his sights – and would be delighted with their immediate impact here in Slovakia, which left them one small step from a £20million windfall.

Only striker Jimmy Floyd Hasselbaink looked like upsetting the Chelsea party. Left on the bench, he insisted that he would not be forced out and would stay to fight for his place at Stamford Bridge. Abramovich wasn't at the match to see Eidur Gudjohnsen and a Zilina own goal give Chelsea victory because of other commitments, but must have enjoyed watching the live television feed of this third-round tie on his yacht off Alaska.

There were a host of impressive debuts, but £17million signing Damien Duff topped the lot. Defender John Terry who was outstanding predicts that this new signing from Blackburn will set the Premiership alive for Chelsea this season.

He said, "Damien will be a major threat to defenders, he played very well, made some great turns and put some great balls in". Manager Claudio Ranieri added that, "Duff was the best. Every ball he put in was very dangerous".

Zilina 0 Chelsea 2 Gudjohnsen and own goal: 6,512

It is believed that he wants to off load Dutch striker Hasselbaink and didn't want to cup-tie him in Europe by playing him against Zilina. Spanish club Real Betis head the list of suitors.

While all of this was going on Claude Makelele has gone on strike to persuade Real Madrid to double his wages or let him move to Chelsea. The French International midfielder is furious that David Beckham's arrival at Real means he is doing even more work on the pitch as the only defensive midfielder – but earns only a fifth of the England captain's wages. Makelele stormed into the office of coach Carlos Queiroz and told him in no uncertain terms that he would refuse to train until the situation was sorted out with a massive wage hike, or a money-spinning move to Chelsea. Then the 30-year-old refused to train yesterday and was immediately fined £100,000 by the club.

Makelele's agent said that "Claude is totally furious that he has been saying these things for two years about being underpaid and the club has ignored him. The whole world knows it is wrong, even the Real players know it. It just can't be right that he has to play next to someone who is earning five times as much."

Up in the North East Newcastle winger Roberto Solano was boasting that:

'THE TOON ARMY ARE BETTER BET THAN CHELSEA'

Newcastle United winger Roberto Solano last night claimed that the Geordies were better equipped than mega-rich Chelsea to conquer Europe. "Everyone is talking about Chelsea but we have a great squad here too. They have bought some very good players and what has happened puts pressure on all of us. But you have to build a team and that takes time. Look at Manchester United a few years ago. They had to wait before they started winning. At Newcastle most of these players have been together for a while, not like Chelsea. That is why I think we are a better bet in the Champions League. We are better equipped because our squad has gelled. It doesn't happen just like that. And we have learned from our experiences in the competition last season. That should help us. For Chelsea, it is all new – the team and the Champions League."

In the same newspaper, the *Daily Star*, other headlines were that:

SHEARER PLANS PARTY

Birthday boy Alan Shearer has his eyes on a Champions League ticket as the perfect present. The Newcastle skipper, 33 today, would love to celebrate with his 12th Euro goal for the club – but he's more interested in the winner's prize than individual glory.

That very same evening Lothar Matthaus's Partizan Belgrade lost 1-0 at home to Newcastle United. But the second leg did not go to plan for Solano and Shearer for they were knocked out by penalties at St James's Park.

KEEP STUM

I find it quite intriguing when players shout about what they are going to do and what they are not going to do. In Roberto Solano's case he should have worried more about what his team were going to do and leave Chelsea out of the equation, for it can leave a nasty stain for the rest of the season. I remember vividly one Friday morning at Stamford Bridge we were preparing for the following days match against the toughest opponents in the game then, Leeds United!

Before we began training Dave Sexton, quite correctly, touched on a certain player 'slagging' them off in a national newspaper. He pointed out the obvious, that Leeds "will be fired up enough for this visit without firing them up any more". Now this is only common sense and in those days the media loved creating a monster out of a pussycat. We hated Leeds and they loved us just as much so there was no need for such statements. It was ironical that Leeds' then boss, chose me for my England debut against reigning World Champions West Germany. Before the match he used the war as the main target of attack just as we left the home Wembley Dressing Room saying "Remember what these bastards did to our houses and shops during the war, remember that as you go up the tunnel." That did nothing to fire me up for I needed no more motivation than to simply see the fantastic Franz Beckenbauer stroll out of the other dressing room looking immaculate in his green shirt and the ball under his arm as if it was his personal belongings. That was all I needed and it worked fine for me, I made the first goal for Colin Bell and went on to enjoy myself thoroughly in a tremendous international debut, alongside our brilliant captain Alan Ball, in a wonderful 2-0 victory.

OPENING DAY 2003/4 SEASON

It was the first match of the Premiership season and Chelsea travelled to Liverpool for what was the last match of the last season – which decided which one of the two teams went into the Champions League Qualifying Round – this time around. However that was an easy win for Chelsea at Stamford Bridge which saw Steven Gerrard foolishly sent off for a mistimed tackle, one more of frustration than malicious, but Gerrard must learn to keep his cool if he is going to fulfil his early promise as a marauding midfielder for both club and country. So the scene was set at Anfield and I'll let Steve Curry carry you through the melee both on and off the playing field with the headlines in the *Daily Mail* as follows: **ROMAN HOLIDAY**: New owner shows he aims to be a winner. The only Chelsea man felt lost in Liverpool early on Sunday evening was Roman Abramovich, the billionaire who financed a revolution, which seems destined not to be confined to the football pitch.

It is the first season that Wilsonsports and Racing had a three horse race in the Premiership. Chelsea had now been backed from 20s 16s 14s – a friend of mine has had a big each way bet at 14's – right down to joint second favourites alongside Arsenal. Mainly because Arsene Wenger has not gone into the transfer market, relying on his faithful French troops that he said about last season would "go through the season undefeated." Quite a stupid statement, from a man who should know better, they obviously didn't!

His expensively assembled side had cast an intimidating shadow over Anfield and long after the crowd had dispersed, Abramovich appeared from one of its darker recesses, clearly lost and seeking the platoon of minders waiting in the foyer.

In an instant, the convoy of silver Mercedes was on its way to John Lennon Airport in Speke where six hours earlier he and his entourage had landed to enjoy a first Premiership victory with his new plaything.

The personally owned Boeing 767 which carries Abramovich from his homes in Moscow, London, France and Chukotcha, the outpost region of north-east Russia where he acts as proud governor of an ethnic community, had dipped through the scattered northern clouds at around two o'clock.

It joined the Global Express business jet that landed, bringing a group of Abramovich associates and friends from Russia for the game, And the helicopter that had whisked the Russian's security team from London.

Leading the posse of comrades was Eugene Shvidler, his closest business partner and friend, who was to make a real impact during the game with his repertoire of expressive gestures – all clenched fists and high fives. The pair met at Gubkin Russian State University of Oil and Gas, where many bright young Jewish boys were educated for a life of success and riches. Abramovich installed Shvidler as managing director of his oil company Sibnet.

The boardroom steward with his LFC blazer and clipboard was nonplussed when fourteen men in open necked shirts, speaking a strange language, descended on him. As he nervously searched his guest list, he was assured by a more familiar man with a white beard, that all were welcome!

Ken Bates enjoys a cordial relationship with Rick Parry and David Moores of the Liverpool hierarchy and although the number of guests accompanying Abamovich had changed almost hourly through the week, there would be no international incident. Not at Anfield, anyway.

The rules on young children were also waived, allowing 10-year-old Arkady, the second eldest of Abramovich's five children to join the grown-ups, including his mother Irina, whose English is much better than her husbands.

Abramovich, however is not without a smattering of English.

CREEPING BATES

He speaks it in familiar phrases and when a guest at his table stood up and was about to catch his head on a chandelier, he shouted, "Be careful". But conversation was helped along by Richard Creitzman – who with Bates – had formed an advance guard at the ground, awaiting news of Abramovich's landing.

A north Londoner, and Barnet fan, Creitzman left school with O-level Russian but is now fluent after working for ten years in Moscow as

Abramovich's head of corporate finance at Sibnet.

He is the new master's voice on the Chelsea board. But there was a problem. Abramovich is from Adam Crozier school of attire and had arrived without a tie.

One was quickly produced by an aide when his boss realised he would be breaking an Anfield edict.

Ties must be worn in the directors' box. Don't expect the same at Chelsea.

A brief appearance on the touchline with Creitzman, chief executive Trevor Birch and the inevitable cluster of minders brought him into the proximity of the London fans who showed their approval and in return got an almost embarrassed wave. Meanwhile wife Irina was showing off a £10,000 diamond-encrusted, gold brooch. It was a gift from Bates – one for her and one for her husband, the new owner of Chelsea Football Club.

The Chelsea chairman had them specially made the day after Abramovich bought the club, but he had trouble pinning his to his jacket so allowed Arkady to wear it proudly for the day.

When the game began, it was quickly evident that Abramovich meant what he said when he suggested he was not buying a business venture but was indulging his love of the game. He seems to love it, all right, but not quite so expressively as his friends.

They are not used to high fives from visiting hierarchy at Anfield. And certainly not used to looking up to see associates of the club owner standing with their fists punching the air when Michael Owen misses a penalty. Not that it happens often. But their antics proved a magnet for TV cameras.

There were nods of approval from the winners and muttered words of condolence to the losers. But there is no doubt the winner takes all philosophy will rule. Roman Abramovich, as he has already demonstrated, intends to be a winner.

In a match in which Chelsea had the lion's share of the ball turned out to be decisive. Michael Owen scored a controversial twice taken penalty and as Veron – who was freed by Frank Lampard and Geremi hunted the ball whenever Liverpool had possession – scored the equaliser. Then in it was Jimmy Floyd Hasselbaink who scored a sweetly struck winner to send the Russian contingent back to their private aeroplane very happy about their first sight of their team in the Premiership!

Anfield was no longer the fortress it once was and Chelsea won quite cosily in the end

And will be quietly confident that they can get a run going after such a bright start in one of the four competitions in this season's campaign. Liverpool on the other hand will be hard pressed to gain that fourth place that brings Champions League football to your club. If anything were to happen to Michael Owen or Steve Gerrard they would be in big danger of sliding slowly into the lower depths, which would be not acceptable by the faithful army of great support they have.

Liverpool 1 Chelsea 2 goalscorers: Veron and Jimmy Floyd; 44,802

Whilst all this was going on David Beckham was breaking new ground over in Spain and his initial sightings were all joyous as he found his feet firmly on the floor to win over both the players and fans after his move from Manchester United to Real Madrid. The frenzy that he caused both privately and on the Far East tour with his team mates was over and the real business was to begin for the most famous footballer on the planet

A packed Stamford Bridge, some 40,000, watched last season's promoted Leicester City come for what could only been said as a mere walk in the park for the new Chelsea and it was important that they tried to begin the home season well whilst working on making it their fortress. But they did not have it all there own way as at times you would have wondered just which team had just shelled out all those millions!

My friend Jeff Powell of the *Mail* was not impressed with Chelsea's performance calling them just the better of two ordinary looking teams. Chelsea needed the help of a fluke own-goal then Adrian Mutu lashed a spectacular winner, which had the opponent's manager saying, "That's what you get for £15.8million". The latest transfer news was of Argentina front man Hernan Crespo deal going through. It is pretty clear that Chelsea are building a situation where they have two teams which in many ways can work out against you, that is if the manager remembers who is who. The first two matches were played in a warm climate, which suited Chelsea, but they will find that teams will come and soak up pressure, but pressure is no good without the guile of a Paul Scholes or a Teddy Sherringham somewhere along the middle of the team. This was something quite new in the English game as coaches called it the 'man in the hole', a player playing between the front two and in touch with the midfield, a position where nine times out of ten the opposition found it very difficult to pick him up. English football in general is and has been for quite some years short of an old style inside football and the best in the business is Zinedene Zidane, the Frenchman strutting his stuff for Real Madrid, a player of immense power yet velvet when in possession of the football. He plays the game like we did as kids with so much time and space making the game look so easy. The sign of a real footballer, and he was possibly the only player in the world that is not told to play in any particular position as the coach trusts his football mind to take him wherever he is needed.

When you look at the likes of Zidane, Ronaldo, Rivaldo, Figo, and David Beckham you will see the difference between a bunch of superstars and a real football unit.

I select a Jeff Powell piece for he is a man who has wonderful knowledge of our game and a man I have known since my days as an apprentice at Stamford Bridge. These were his remarks after Chelsea's first home match of the 2003/4 season:

RANIERI NEEDS TO BUY A TEAM
NOT JUST A HOST OF PLAYERS

The rich and famous are flooding into the stands as well as onto the pitch at Chelsea. One football celebrity who began his football career as a £5 a week apprentice at Stamford Bridge returned there on Saturday with a £5,000 pair of newly purchased season tickets burning a hole in his pocket.

Terry Venables has caught the buzz generated by all the big spending.

At the end of an odyssey, which led him into all manner of adventures with Tottenham, Crystal Palace, Queens Park Rangers, Barcelona, England, Middlesbrough and Leeds United, El Tel has come home.

He can always go to matches as a VIP guest but Chelsea was his first love and he prefers to go back as a fully paid-up supporter. The second ticket is for his grandson Sam, a natural-born blues fan and a budding public school golfer.

Where once he swept the terraces while learning his football trade, Venables sits now in judgement on the Russian Revolution at the Bridge.

Thus he is asking the question which is on every supporters' lips; Can Roman Abramovich's millions buy the Premiership title and the Champions League?

"Of course money can buy success" says Venables. "Any manager worth his salt would love to be in the position to bring the best players in the world. But the key to it is not just signing great players but buying the component parts of a team".

On that count, the jury of more than 40,000 men, women and children were unable to return a verdict at the end of Chelsea's first home match of a new era.

Ladbrokes had it right by laying Chelsea at 2/5 on the fixed odds but there were plenty of Chelsea punters sweating before the final whistle, I can assure you!

The score-line – Roman Empire 2 Ancient Britons 1 – told the story. "Chelsea were just about the better, individually, of two pretty ordinary teams on the day", as visiting manager Micky Adams said after Mutu had lashed a spectacular winner.

Yet to acquire their early lead against Leicester's largely home-grown bunch of battlers, Chelsea's team of £75million imported talents had needed the help of an own-goal so crass that you wondered for a moment if Abramovich might be buying the opposition as well.

Despite all the jubilant Cossack cavorting in the directors box!

Nor as he himself conceded, is this the level of performance, which Claudio Ranieri needs from Chelsea if he is to keep his job very long.

Ranieri enjoys such an embarrassment of riches now that he could field two Premiership teams on any given day. His problem is that only eleven of those players can be on the field at one time so he has to identify his most effective team.

The doubt is whether the manager is shaping the transfer policy. This is not the Harlem Globetrotters. Yet, the appearance of Hernan Crespo in Saturday's star spangled crowd suggests that Ranieri's billionaire boss is buying big names rather than the specialist men for the jobs.

Ranieri made a clever joke of admitting that he had no idea how negotiations for Argentina goal-scorer Crespo were progressing. But what he must know is that Chelsea needs another striker like George Best needs his next vodka. With Desailly's powers waning, John Terry suffering as a consequence, a new centre-half would bring much more to the Premiership table.

Not that a scatter gun manner of Abramovich spending spree excuses Ranieri for omitting Billy Gallas from his defence or failing to recognise Joe Cole as the heir apparent to Gianfranco Zola.

Cole's ten-minute cameo as a substitute came as a reminder to the faithful that, despite all the exotic foreign signings, they still miss their favourite little Italian.

These are early days. It will take time to blend so many new players into a balanced unit. Meanwhile, so many virtuosos should be able to keep picking up points.

Even so, if Ranieri and his stalking horse as manager, Sven Goran Eriksson, really believe Juan Sebastian Veron is the best midfield player on the planet, we can only assume they have never seen Zinedine Zidane in full flow. Or for that matter, Roy Keane in the form which inspired Manchester United to put down a more emphatic marker at Newcastle earlier in the day.

Still, there is an atmosphere of genuine expectation in west London. These are exciting days for Chelsea. The throng rose to salute their Roman benefactor as he went on to the pitch before Saturday's kick-off.

Chelsea 2 Leicester City 1 goalscorers; Mutu and an own goal: 41,073l

So it is the maximum six points from their first two matches in the Premiership, with the next two matches also at Stamford Bridge, hosting both Blackburn Rovers and Tottenham Hotspurs who have a 'wicked' record against Chelsea over the last decade or so and don't forget what I wrote about their manager!

Still the bookies were no wiser but I am sure Arsene Wenger will not be worried about what they have to say!

KENYON IS BLUE BUT SO IS BIRCH

The Bridge is alive to the sound of money. The trick is to spend it wisely!

I was introduced to Trevor Birch over lunch at the House of Commons, a place where I get invited by Tony Banks MP from time to time and can happily say a good friend of mine. I found Trevor a really nice chap and was totally shocked that on the news, within forty-eight hours, was of Peter Kenyon, coming down from Manchester United to join the Russian Revolution. Kenyon a man so instrumental in many big business moves at his old club and a "big signing" for the Blues, maybe the most important one to date. Trevor was given two choices by the Directors and that was he could take a back seat to Kenyon or collect his outstanding contract which was around two and a quarter million pounds, and after giving it some thought Birch took the money which was now reported to be £2.9 million.

It was mid September and the headlines in the *Daily Mail* read that Chelsea had taken £144,000 from merchandise last weekend but their wage bill is £80 million and rising, the chief executive has been given a £2.9 million pay-off and Emperor Roman is ordering in sushi meals from a trendy Mayfair Restaurant.

It was Blackburn Rovers who came to town and they were a team who impressed me more times than not but with Chelsea winning their first two Premiership matches and one in Europe they had the winning feeling, a feeling that only breeds confidence and becomes a 'good habit' no matter just how well – or not – you are playing. Goal-machine Andy Cole has no time for reputations and put them one goal in front after a hash by Desailly out on the left touchline down at the end of the ground where the old north stand once stood. The French centre back overran a ball going out of play.

But once stopping it from going out could not stop himself and left it for Matt Jantzen – a player I like a lot – to whisk it away and crossed into the path of the old Arsenal, Newcastle United, and Manchester United goal getter, and the director's box with the new regime sitting comfortably saw their latest toy deflate for the second time in three matches. Cole scored again to put them 2-1 in front stunning the crowd into silence, but through Mutu, Chelsea grabbed a point whilst dropping two points for the first time.
Chelsea 2 Jimmy Floyd and Mutu Blackburn 2 Andy Cole 2: 41,006

Tottenham Hotspurs were next visitors at the Bridge and how Glenn Hoddle needed a result to stop the talk of his departure which I had predicted only days ago. The song goes by those Chelsea bluenose fans "Can we play you every week" such was their dominance over the north Londoners for so long now. They had a super result over Chelsea in the Worthington Cup only eighteen months ago but in the league Chelsea toyed with the formbook and this time was no different. Chelsea ran out 4-2 winners in a canter, although Hoddle said he thought his team played well but let silly goals in. What Glenn, and many other managers today seem to forget is that defending is all a part of the game and the signing of Dean Richards from Southampton was a move I believe justified his sacking only a few days later. Seven million pounds for a centre-half is nonsense when you could have bought James Beattie – a twenty goal a season man – more my kind of signing, especially when you are short of firepower. Glenn had a bird's eye view of both Beattie and Richards whilst managing Southampton before his move to his old club Spurs and for me got his homework wrong in buying the coloured ex-Wolves centre back.

Chelsea just rolled Spurs over and goals look like they are going to fly in thick and fast for this new Chelsea outfit. Jimmy Floyd was on the score sheet again and is beginning to regain the form that made him one of the most dangerous of Premiership hit men Chelsea have ever seen. It still amazes me how this player scores so many goals yet takes all the corners. I think he is not a genuine header of the ball and prefers to 'bullet' in crosses for others who do enjoy the glory of scoring headers from a corner kick, but like Henry it astounds me that they are not in amongst the bodies from dead ball kicks.

The headlines in the *Daily Mail* on Monday September 15th was that:

HODDLE'S LOVE AFFAIR IS NEARLY OVER

If football managers shared a common weakness it is that remarkable inability to anticipate their own demise.

Lost in romantic notion that they are never beaten, they possess a blinkered outlook – which is also, perhaps, what gives them their strength.

Take Claudio Ranieri and Glenn Hoddle, the two managers whose sides met at Stamford Bridge on Saturday. While one emerged in victory and the other defeat, they were united, it seems, in that they are both existing on borrowed time, but neither of them would admit this, but football men rarely do!

If Tottenham lose at home to Southampton next weekend it will take as long as it takes for his chairman, Daniel Levy, to return home from his honeymoon for the axe to fall. When Levy gets back, those in the know predict that Hoddle will be sacked.

However, in this particular match Freddie Kanoute scored a sublime opener for Spurs but at half time a little 'tinkering' once again from Ranieri brought great results with goals from Adrian Mutu who possesses pace, skill and a wonderful eye for the target that predators count on. He scored two fine goals to take his Premiership tally to four in three games. The Rumanian might have the distraction of private life turmoil, with a divorce and a custody battle under way, and the physical nature of the Premiership has left him nursing cuts and bruises, but on the pitch he retains his focus as well as his eye for goal.

ONE DAY WITHOUT A SMILE IS ONE DAY LOST

Mutu, who has an Italian tattoo that, translated, reads that, "One day without a smile is one day lost". I like that and the player and hope he keeps on knocking the ball past the goalkeeper for his tattoo says he brings a smile to the faces of the spectators whilst always likely to do something out of the ordinary. While Ranieri will be concerned about the ease with which Kanoute scored his goal he would have been delighted with the clinical finishing of Mutu and Jimmy Floyd to add to Frank Lampard's headed equaliser. After the game Abramovich stopped briefly in the Chelsea dressing room to congratulate both the players and their manager. They deserved such praise but what good it does for Ranieri in the long term is something Trevor Birch the chief executive who attended the match to say his farewells, would probably question. Football has become a ruthless business and nowhere more so than Chelsea Football Club!

Chelsea 4 Mutu 2, Jimmy Floyd and Lampard: Tottenham Hotspurs 2 Att: full house.

INSIDE THE WORLD OF CHELSKI

The Russian revolution at Stamford Bridge has entered its second stage with Roman Abramovich seeking to consolidate his multi-million pound investment in Chelsea.

The tills are ringing at Chelsea Village. Records are tumbling. Blue is still the colour. But there is a price to pay for the stampede for success down the Fulham Road.

Last Saturday there were record takings in the Chelsea megastore, more than £120,000 going over the counter, with a further £24,000 the following day.

For the game against Tottenham last Saturday, 25,000 programmes were sold and 4,000 people sat down to a silver-service lunch, not to mention the thousands of pounds that were taken at the fast-food outlets and over the bars. Records elsewhere.

The street traders outside Stamford Bridge are enjoying their own boost in trade, with baseball caps displaying a hammer and sickle above the CFC badge and Chelski embroidered on the front particularly popular.

Although the Abramovich entourage point out that Chelskov would have been more correct in Russian, they recognise that it's now too late.

In any event, it did not prevent one prominent member of the Russian contingent from buying sixty caps in one hit. They could have become the essential fashion item in Red Square.

Abramovich, the billionaire who has made it all possible, insists that he wants Chelsea run as a business so these revenues streams are important. But it will be a long time before he recovers his investment and you do wonder if he cares about that.

The £111million he has spent on new players this summer has increased the wage bill by over£30m and £80m is now needed just to keep the players happy. And that's before he pays a penny of the £1.5million-plus salary and £3million 'golden hello' for Manchester United defector Peter Kenyon.

The facilitator is Pini Zahavi, the former Te Aviv sports writer who has made friends and enemies out of just about everybody else at Chelsea. His job appears to be done for the time being. He cut a lonely figure at the Bridge on Saturday, but why should he worry?

He has trousered £6million in commission. For the time being he can get on with his wheeling and dealing elsewhere.

No doubt he will get another call sooner rather than later – expect to see him busy in the January sales – when Abramovich decides to complete his personal jigsaw by appointing a new manager. Send for Sven and Pini will be chauffeur.

In the meantime it is a back-row seat in the directors box for Zahavi, ostracised by chairman Ken Bates, snubbed by celebrity Chelsea fan David Mellor and not quite one of the inner circle who sit above the centre circle in their newly commandeered Millenium Suite.

It once belonged to the clubs kit manufacturers Umbro. When Abramovich recognised that it had the best view of his galaxy of stars, Umbro were politely asked to move along. They did, of course, agree. Ambramovich closed shop coterie is from the very top Russian politics and society. President Vladmir Putin has yet to climb abroad the private Boeing 767 for a Saturday afternoon at the Bridge but it has been suggested that Tatyana Dyachenko, daughter of former President Boris Yeltsin, has seen her first Chelsea match. But we must not forget that President Clinton named his daughter after this club, for I believe he supported them whilst studying at Oxford University.

The wind of change has blown quickly through Chelsea Village. Out of the door has gone Trevor Birch, the club's deposed chief executive, to make way for Kenyon, his departure cushioned by a £2.9million handshake personally sanctioned by Abramovich when the cohorts wanted to haggle downward. It was the least he could do for the man who had spent the summer piecing together the new owner's ambitious plans, negotiating fees and fixing salaries. His departure is a blow to morale down at the Village and was a mistake. He was a popular man.

This is how Ken Dyer of the **London England Standard** saw things beginning with the headline

DEVASTATED BIRCH
**Chelsea supreme considers his future
after Kenyon swoop**

Chelsea group chief executive Trevor Birch was said to be 'devastated' today by the news that Peter Kenyon is joining the club from Manchester United. Birch has been asked to stay at the club in a senior role, possibly as managing director, but was today thinking over his position. It looks likely Birch will decide that, with much of his responsibility severely reduced, his job is untenable. He could be in line for a £2.25million pay-off for the rest of his contract, which runs until December of 2007.

Birch, the former Liverpool footballer and finance expert, who saved the club from administration by bringing in new owner Roman Abramovich, had built himself a growing reputation at Stamford Bridge. But he looked to have little future at Chelsea following Abramovich's decision to headhunt the United chief executive.

The appointment of Kenyon, a United fan, stunned most people including Birch, who was apparently informed yesterday morning. Birch, who was in the Liverpool squad for their European Cup Final triumph over FC Brugge in 1978, was regarded as doing an impressive job in difficult circumstances.

He was appointed to help reduce an £80million debt but things changed dramatically during the summer when he made the call that brought in the Russian billionaire.

For his first eight months at the club Birch, his wife and three children, were based in the hotel at the stadium as he worked to alleviate what was potentially a perilous position. Then, after Abramovich's arrival, Birch was suddenly involved in multi-million pound transfers but he held his nerve and emerged from a tumultuous few months with his reputation enhanced.

It is difficult to see how Birch, a good friend of new FA chief executive Mark Palios, could continue in his present position with the imminent arrival of Kenyon. It is thought Kenyon will not be able to join Chelsea until the end of the next transfer window on the 1st of February. He is on gardening leave as negotiations continue with United.

Like many other employees of Chelsea, however, Birch perhaps failed to grasp the fact that Abramovich has brought his sweet shop and if he wants to mix the pear drops with the caramels then he will do it, and if you don't like the mix, then too bad.

The problem is that Birch's departure has left the club in turmoil – some say rudderless. Bates remains chairman and is there to be consulted. But he doesn't interfere – he needs to be asked. He has had his money and already dispensed a large sum to worthy causes his detractors wouldn't begin to know about it.

Maybe Bates would like to be consulted a little more. As far as the fans are concerned he is still Mr Chelsea and if the Russians hope to retain good will, there are those who suggest he should be left in his seat in front of the directors' box until the summer of 2005, when he plans to step down anyway.

By then the personable Richard Creitzman, a son of north London in his early thirties and Abramovich's ear on the ground, will have learned the ropes. He has stepped off the terraces at Barnet to join the board and his style is good. But he is young and has to learn.

He speaks Russian but gets his leg pulled by Abramovich when he makes a slip, but is trusted.

By the time the new suite of offices on the fifth floor at Chelsea Village have been converted and furnished for the Russian task force (they had to be reminded of very English necessities like planning permission) Chelsea will be de-listed from the Stock Market.

The club will no longer be a plc but it will need some tic, Abramovich wants success but surely he doesn't want soulless success. The club was built on teamwork and at the moment the workforce are nervous and unsure, from the manager to the waitresses.

The new owner is used to getting his own way, including having his match day sushi delivered from swanky Mayfair restaurant Nobu. The clubs loyal and very able in house caterers look on aghast.

Incidentals to Roman, important to staff!

Conventional collar and ties are out (shades of a former FA chief Adam Crozier). This is a hobby, time to relax.

But Roman may do well to remember that the bottom line is that the constituency of any club are the fans. He mustn't neglect them while he indulges his mates. If he needs gentle direction then the man to provide it is still his chairman.

In the middle of this article was a boxed ad saying:

SO YOU FANCY A TAKEAWAY?

If you want to join Roman at Nobu's takeaway counter you might want to think about taking out a second mortgage – there's not much change out of £100 a head for the ultra-modern Japanese cuisine. Plus you'd better wear your best designer outfit, as it is a cooler-than-cool celeb-haunt. PS – Ever wondered where Boris Becker's famous broom closet is?

Well that was the world of Chelski written by Steve Curry which I find good reading, however, although we all want to know more about this extraordinary man I much prefer to read about how the players are taking to the training leading up to matches etc.

As for the current chairman getting involved with looking after the fans, I'd like to ask Steve when he did this before?

Chelsea fans have been ripped off for so long and have not even got a championship to go with all of their hard earned cash, even close would ease the blow?

It was back to the football and thanks to the brilliant football coverage of SKY TV we are having a ball watching the matches from either the Crown pub in Dovehouse Street – the kind of house ran superbly by a quite charming Irishman named Alan. If we are not there we are in the Grosvenor Club in Bourne Street where the crack is second to none, company terrific and bar and food charges a little less than the extortionate prices the Chelsea chairman has running through the club. It may be alright for Steve Curry because his bill is down to the newspaper expense sheet but for all the hardworking Joes around the Chelsea area, who have had the blood sweat and many tears out of Stamford Bridge I think they have gone a 'Bridge Too Far'.

Give me a Russian vodka and orange juice and bag of dry roasted peanuts, and with my feet up either in the Crown or the Grosvenor are for me and mine.

A WHOLE NEW BALL GAME
Selling blue shirts in Beijing will be a lot harder than red ones.

Harry Harris of the Express tells his story; Peter Kenyon has defected from the world's richest club for perennial pretenders Chelsea and the football world wants to know why – outside of the salary that has doubled at a stroke – and how was the deal done?

The reason is simple, power. He could see that the balance of power was shifting quicker than anyone imagined from Old Trafford to Stamford Bridge!

Chelsea chairman Ken Bates, the former owner, always said he wanted to make Chelsea the Manchester United of the south. But soon it might be David Gill, left to fill the breach, who might be saying he wants United to become the Chelsea of the north.

Make no mistake, Kenyon will now be overlord of the Bridge, overseeing the commercial and marketing side and interpreting owner Roman Abramovich's vision to wrestle domestic and global domination from Manchester United and even Real Madrid. Kenyon will report to just one man – Abramovich – whereas United remain a plc, answerable to shareholders and fans alike.

So, if Kenyon and his United board would have awarded a high dividend to shareholders, it might appease and please the City but anger the fans who want the cash invested in more players.

If he spent heavily in the transfer market, as Sir Alex is omnipotent at Old Trafford, Claudio Ranieri has a mere fraction of that power at Stamford Bridge.

Furthermore, United have been susceptible to a takeover for a year, while Abramovich is the sole owner and shareholder, erasing any vulnerability Kenyon may have felt had someone taken over at United.

How the deal happened is almost as straightforward.

From the moment Abramovich stunned football with his £150million takeover on July the first, Kenyon was kept informed, at times daily, through his close relationship with Israeli football agent Pini Zahavi, who just happens to be the Russian's closest football adviser.

Almost from day one Zahavi was in touch with Kenyon.

The pair, who normally talk three or four times a week anyway, were in regular contact during United's attempt to buy Ronaldinho.

Zahavi had a 'finger in the pie' on the proposed transfer although eventually it fell through. Then, when Chelsea wanted to sign Juan Sebastian Veron the two friends went head to head again. Chelsea no doubt came up when they dined together occasionally as the summer progressed.

Then, when the transfer window closed at the beginning of last week and transfer business could be put to one side, the soundings that Zahavi had taken were used as the springboard for a firm and lucrative offer.

Kenyon can now fashion Chelsea just the way he – and his Russian boss – wants.

If, along the way, he is protecting his family for life with a five-year contract worth nearly £10million with bonuses and perks then it would not make much sense to reject it. These are the men Kenyon will have to deal with at Chelsea.

ZAHAVI known as the 'Fixer' has emerged as the most powerful mover and shaker in world football. He masterminded Abramovich's takeover, was the behind the scenes wheeler and dealer in the acquisition of a world record influx of new stars, and has now recruited Kenyon.

Add to that his role in the Presidential campaign of Joan Laporte at Barcelona and setting up the £30million deal for David Beckham that sparked the first tangible interest from Madrid. When the Russian billionaire wanted a top chief executive, Zahavi was the man to identify the prime candidate – Kenyon.

They had plenty of time to get to know one another when Zahavi represented Rio Ferdinand's move from Leeds United.

When Sven Goran Eriksson entered Abramovich's London flat, Zahavi was by his side. He has become the special envoy of the Roman Empire at the Bridge.

RANIERI Eriksson's shadow will continue to hang over him with Kenyon's appointment. It was Kenyon who had instigated the third party talks with the English coach and set up the deal for Eriksson to abandon the FA for Old Trafford. Until Sir Alex changed his mind.

TREVOR BIRCH Hired by Ken Bates because of his expertise in the survival of financially stretched companies. That is now defunct and Abramovich wants commercial and marketing expertise. Birch is fortunate to have been handed a new contract by Bates only six months ago for a four and a half years at £500,000 a year.

The contract stipulates a £2 million pay-off but he stressed yesterday he wants to stay – even if that means in a subordinate role. That is likely to depend on Kenyon.

BATES Events have confirmed that he no longer has any role in hiring and firing people over the last twenty-one years. Not consulted over the appointment of Kenyon, the once powerful owner is now left as a figurehead.

The logic of Bates staying on after pocketing £17.5million in the sale of his shares to Abramovich is that the new owner might want to tap into his vast experience.

While Bates will be invaluable inside the FA and at Premier League meetings, the arrival of Kenyon will dilute even those attributes. It might be a question of when he wants to go!

GWYN WILLIAMS The general manager, has served a raft of different bosses over the years.

Throughout he has given unswerving loyalty to Bates and is football's number one survivor.

But surely he will struggle to hold onto his time.

EUR IN FOR A TOUGH FIGHT CHELSEA

Another column reads that Chelsea want new chief executive Peter Kenyon to get them a place on European's top table.

At Manchester United, Kenyon was a key figure in the influential G14 group of Europe's clubs and is on first name terms with the leaders of big guns like Real Madrid, Barcelona and AC Milan.

Chelsea want to join the G14 and there have been suggestions their application will be looked at favourably. Kenyon is a well-respected figure within UEFA, whereas the man he replaced at Stamford Bridge, Trevor Birch, did not carry the clout Blues supremo Roman Abramovich wanted.

Birch, bitterly upset at his treatment has been offered the job as director of Chelsea Village but is expected to take a pay-off believed to be worth £2.5million.

A senior Chelsea source said, "We don't want to lose him but there are many emotional issues to consider".

But Kenyon will need to use all his diplomatic skills to get Chelsea in – especially as the election of a new member has to be unanimous and United still feel sore at his departure. And, last night, he was replaced as G14 vice-chairman by his Old Trafford successor David Gill.

'BEING SUB GIVES ME THE HUMP'

Says Frank Lampard in the *Sun* newspaper: Chelsea duo Frank Lampard and Jimmy Hasselbaink have revealed the growing unease as the reality of Roman Abramovich's spend, spend, spend policy hits home. Both players were shocked to be relegated to the substitutes bench for Tuesday's European match in Prague.

And, although they came on in the second half as subs to make vital contribution over Czech champs Sparta, the fear they are no longer part of Claudio Ranieri's strongest eleven is all too obvious. And Lampard said that, "I was hurt and disappointed by the manager's decision as the Champions League is a big thing for me and I want to play in it". And Hasselbaink, axed in favour of £16.8million Hernan Crespo, snapped when telling the *Sun* that, "I don't want to comment at it all. The manager hasn't spoken to me about it so you should direct your question to him."

For Lampard it was the first time since Boxing Day last year that he was not in the starting line-up. The £11million midfielder admitted that "You have to be grown up and professional about it because some times when you're not playing you'll get the hump. The important thing is the players who aren't in the team don't sulk or don't train badly because that really is going to be detrimental to the team. I was disappointed to be on the bench on Tuesday night and this is a new experience for me because for the last five years I have played week in week out for both West Ham and Chelsea. I cannot put a finger on how many games I expect to play this season but I have to look at the bigger picture with Chelsea now. We are not like any other club at the moment. In terms of the depth of the squad, we're probably up there with Real Madrid. I respect the manager and know it's very hard for him, so I'm not going to be banging on his door if I am not chosen. I worked hard last season to help the club qualify and I feel playing in that level of competition can only help me to improve as a player. It is the closest thing you can get to international football and I'm sure the England manager understands the situation at Chelsea".

Sven Goran Eriksson's assistant Tord Grip was in Prague only to discover England candidates Lampard, John Terry and Joe Cole were all on the bench.

FROM PRAGUE TO THE BLACK COUNTRY

Lampard went on by saying that "It is also tough for Joe Cole but he knew the situation when he signed here. He's showed a lot of good things when he's come on as sub and he has to keep doing just that".

Tuesday's 1-0 victory in their opening Group C match leaves Chelsea ideally placed to press on for the knockout stages of the competition. And goalkeeper Carlo Cudicin, probably the only certain starter in Chelsea's squad these days, believes the victory in Prague more than justified Ranieri's rotation policy. He insisted that everyone knows the manager very well and is aware he likes to change his team and his players. Therefore aptly named the Tinkerman. There are 23/24 players in our squad now and he has a lot of options. But on Tuesday night, we won the game so he obviously did the right thing and so did the players, and that is all you can ask for".

Next up was a trip to the midlands in the Black Country and that wonderful old football club Wolverhampton Wanderers. I have many great memories of the old ground having played there on several occasions. I remember one game for Stoke City in particular and the debut of Peter Shilton who was bought by Tony Waddington to replace John Farmer who had taken over from Gordon Banks who retired after that incredibly unlucky car smash on one of those tricky roads leading out of Newcastle-under-Lyme, where I once lived. I believe had Gordon not had that freak accident both he and I would now be proud owners of a first division – the old one – championship winner's medal. Isn't life crazy when you think any other injury to Gordon would probably not have stopped his magnificent career but an eye makes it seem very weird. Gordon is one of life's great people, terribly modest and always tries to smile over such a tragedy, but – although it's no consolation – I went one further for I can only just walk now and my balance is dodgy – even more so when sober. That is just one more important factor in getting through your rehabilitation – you must never lose your sense of humour. There is always someone worse off than yourself so you must cherish the great times you had, and you Gordon – my friend – had many, many of those times.

I have said to this day it was the biggest mistake of Tony's managerial career. Like Hoddle with Richards our problem was not with the goalkeeping for Farmer had been performing heroics when called upon and apart from my debut when he dropped the ball at Tommy Smith's feet only a couple of yards out he had played magnificently, and I repeat we did not need Peter Shilton. Funny thing though is that Peter's best ever game for us was that day at Wolves, flying around in a mud heap making the kind of saves that were his hallmark. Instinctive goalkeeping!

I truly believe to this day that had our manager not signed Shilton we would have won the Football League Championship that same season. We were having a great time rolling over all the fat cats to find ourselves top of the League just after Christmas and in doing so, played our way to the top. The back four of Marsh, Smith, Bloor and Pejic were as formidable as any in the country whilst Josh Mahoney, Geoff Salmons and I had the right chemistry in the engine room. Both vastly under-rated players with 'Josh' covering every blade of grass becoming my first lieutenant whilst on the left side of the field Geoff Salmons was running the line as good as anybody around, in fact only

John Barnes at Liverpool springs to mind when we talk about gifted left sided players. Yeah 'Sammy' gave us that 'perfect' balance and had a wonderful 'left peg' with the oncoming Greenhoff, Ritchie or Hurst knowing that he hit in lovely crosses into the most dangerous of areas. Greenhoff was the player for me who oozed the kind of class that made truly great players. Then, of course there was a young Alan Dodd, a local lad who found the game too easy, which affected him in a way that he wanted to do something more difficult, like climbing his ladder to fix his roof in his home at Endon in the heart of Staffordshire. 'Doddy' was a manager's dream for he would do his job perfectly against all kinds of centre-forwards such as Keegan, Jordan, Latchford and Allan Clarke, those just examples of players that would not bother him one iota. Whether it be for pace or high balls you could just get in position to receive the ball once he had dispossessed his man, sometimes like taking candy!

Back to Greenhoff, the kind of player we always lacked in this country, and I believe ninety-nine times out of a hundred we could read each other's minds. We most definitely got the best out of each other and how he was not in every England squad is just another case of 'diabolical' football management!

WOLVES MOLINEUX MISERY

But back to Molineux, the home of Wolves, a ground I attended on its opening and had the opportunity to shake hands with the great Ferenc Puskas. It was a match which brought back the memories of that wonderful night of football with the great Hungarian displaying his marvellous talents for Moscow Dynamo.

But no such stars like those were present on this particular day. And just what would have happened if there were to face the Premiership newcomers, poor old Wolves. Chelsea turned the screw early on and in as one sided a match as you'll get this season or any other come to that!

Chelsea hit them five times and had a perfectly good goal from John Terry disallowed. Chelsea could have easily have scored double figures as the country watched a team slowly progressing into one of strength and character – the kind you need to win championships, although do not get over excited about beating this Wolves team for they surely will return to the Nationwide for the next season. This is absolutely no fault of manager David Jones for he only has so many cards to deal whereas Chelsea have many full packs.

David Wragg of the Daily Express saw it this way, very much like me. "This whitewash took them to the top of the Premiership – until yesterday afternoon – and they are very, very good. Besides the five they scored, Chelsea had a John Terry goal wrongfully disallowed, Jesper Gronkjaer and Frank Lampard missed open goals, Eider Gudjohnsen failed with a one on one and Jimmy Floyd fired wide. Ten-one. That would have been a fairer score here – both Butler and Steffen Iverson headed the ball onto the bar for Wolves – and football would have stood up and acknowledged that an epoch in history is being bought at Chelsea. Lampard and Duff scored as well as Jimmy Floyd and Crespo who fired home two. Crespo only played twenty-four minutes. This was as convincing as any of the Arsenal and Manchester United's championship winning performances!

Wolverhampton Wanderers 0 Chelsea 5 Crespo 2 Lampard, Duff and Jimmy Floyd 29,208

This cannot be left out, as I think Claudio Ranieri's elevator just don't go to the top floor. In a national newspaper he was quoted as saying that "I get goose-bumps as I'm in charge of a footballing Ferrari. Never have I had so many world-class players. Once upon a time, Chelsea was destined to make only an isolated appearance in the Champions League. This time we are going to be the surprise of the tournament". I am sure that he cannot see the game from the touchline for if he can he is watching a match so very different than I am. You don't have to be a genius to sit down and watch a Chelsea team who better start performing like contenders before Manchester United start pulling away from them. But they play both Arsenal and United in the upcoming weeks after the England match in Turkey, a match that I cannot see England winning at any cost.

In the same paper the headlines read, '**I WON'T GET THE SACK'**.

On Monday the 22nd of September 2003 the Chelsea manager said that, "There was a time before I met the new owner of Chelsea, he might have been looking for another manager". Going on he added that "But once I met him and told him my plans, that was not the case any longer. I do not think that Mr Abramovich would have allowed me to spend so much money on new players to then sack me". Speculation remains that Sven Goran Eriksson has been lined up by Abramovich to take his job, but Ranieri said that, "I found that the owner had researched me very well when I met him. He knew what I had done at Chelsea and he knew what I done before at other clubs. Mr Abramovich knows me. He asked me what I wanted to do at Chelsea and I told him that I wanted two good players for every position, some young some experienced champions. He listened to this and said, 'go' this is what we have tried to do, to bring in the best".

Ranieri ended up by saying that, "Mr Abramovich has given me the opportunity to sign my dream team. I have done this and now we are making it work. It is obvious we are making progress".

BECKHAMANIA

Whilst all of this was going on David Beckham last night rifled in a magnificent free kick for Real Madrid in a 3-1 victory over Malaga on the Costa del Sol. His man-of-the-match performance included Real's second goal from a well-worked dead-ball routine with Portuguese team-mate Luis Figo in the 72nd minute. He said afterwards that, "It's always nice when you work on things in training and they come off."

Five thousand British fans paid up to £140 pounds to see Real earn their first away win of the new season. The England captain also supplied the corner, which led to Zinedine Zidane putting them in front. After Beckham had made it 2-0, Portugal striker Edgar pulled one back for Malaga but Guti put the game out of their reach with five minutes remaining.

The following week David Beckham was voted the best player in the Spanish La Liga.

La Liga stattos have confirmed the England captain has taken the country by storm following his £25million switch to the best League in the world. And Beckham has told Spanish media that playing for Spanish giants Real made him "The happiest man in the world." Real President Florentino Perez is delighted by the sensational impact his latest 'superstar' has had both on and off the pitch. Football boffins have analysed every single move made by the player to confirm that he is tops. After three league games he has touched the ball more times than any other player, made more passes and started more attacks. Perez beamed that "Beckham has conquered the Bernabeu.

"With his strength, his quality and integration he has gained the adulation of the Bernabeu public so very quickly. Real have plundered eleven goals in two games since Beckham was brought inside from his usual role with Manchester United."

And he underlined his leading role with another sizzling display as Real romped to a 4-2 win over Marseille on Tuesday. After the traumas suffered as a result of his bitter feud with Sir Alex Ferguson he has recovered his appetite for the game he plays so very well. Perez also says that, "He is happy. A great testament to that is his mother said to me that her son was the happiest man in the world. I spoke with him and he confirmed this. In addition he is playing with such incredible desire". Beckham is loving the Spanish way of life and has struck a friendship with Roberto Carlos the Brazilian left back, although he speaks little English. That is no surprise because my moles tell me that he was the same with Steve MacManaman who has left for the blue side of Manchester, City of course.

WASTE OF SPACE

The *Sun* newspaper ran an exclusive on Hernan Crespo, which was quite funny as he tells us that "the last time I had a fight I was in the seventh grade. I waited in the corner and when the person I was fighting was preparing his guard, I hit him. It wasn't pretty". He carries on to say, "As a boy I was a terrible loser. I would go to dances and not do anything. One night at a party, I got together with a girl called Fernanda. We began kissing but it seemed that she had less experience than me because she kept biting my tongue. I kept kissing her and she kept biting me. The next day I was very happy but my tongue hurt." Now Crespo is looking to inflict pain on Premiership defences. He said that, "This is a new football challenge — a new challenge. Everything is different for me but I cannot give you an honest opinion because we recently played against Blackburn and I had trained on the Friday only. It is nice that Juan Veron is here. We know each other well. I'm settling in well and looking forward to the challenge for this is a great opportunity to prove myself. And of course thanks to Abramovich's many millions, a great opportunity to set the Premiership all of a quiver."

MY MATE HARRY

That was not the best of interviews I must say, but that is not the fault of Chelsea's newest superstar. This player looks the business and with the pace of Mutu, silky skills of Gudjohnsen and power of Jimmy Floyd, Chelsea have four top strikers who will be needed this season at all times. Only Sir Alex Ferguson had such luxuries knowing that goal-scorers in the modern game are the difference between success and failure. He boasted having Beckham, Scholes, Yorke, Cole, Giggs and then of course, his latest 'gem' Ruud van Nistelrooy. Teddy Sherringham has been gone a while now and 'Steady Teddy' is doing his thing at my mate's club, Portsmouth. Harry Redknapp is my best friend in the modern day game of football, a man I worked with whilst playing for Seattle Sounders in the North American Soccer League. We became close again whilst my son Anthony was playing under Harry in the West Ham United's Youth Team. Harry had done miracles taking his new club from the Nationwide to the Premiership and his new team have began their new campaign in fine style with Teddy having scored six goals already. It will be a long season for them but they have showed a lot of promise in the opening five matches of the season, one match drawn at Highbury was their best performance. They had my old club on the edge of defeat, which will give them great confidence for the months ahead and knowing Harry like I do, the window opening on transfers in January will see him delving into market one more time at least.

LUCK AGAINST VILLA

Aston Villa came to the Bridge a team of no-hopers under the guidance of David O'Leary an old colleague of mine at Arsenal. But Chelsea huffed and puffed around for quite a while before Lampard hit a firm shot across the keeper, who could only parry it, and the typical following up by Jimmy Floyd had the easiest of tap-ins.

Jimmy Floyd doesn't miss those opportunities. So we expected to see Chelsea spring to life, but no, it was Villa who created the best chances, and in the main it was Angel who squandered three great chances. Only Frank Lampard was keeping his good form up and the team's performance left a lot to be desired and it was not the kind of display that would have either Manchester or Arsenal quaking in their very expensive boots. So Chelsea were lucky which once again kept the Chelsea faithful shaking their heads coming out of another packed house. Chelsea for my money are not showing me enough to be serious contenders to the title Manchester United hold. But they have a big match on Wednesday when the Turks arrive for the Champions League match.

Headlines said it all **WE'VE A RIGHT JUAN HERE.**

This match really was a turn off and Chelsea struggled to get the three points and can only thank Juan Pablo Angel for missing three sitters. The summing up of the two managers for a change, nearly spot on. Ranieri saying, that, "Aston Villa deserved a point. But the team are happy and I am happy because we know on days like this it is important to take the three points". His opposite number David O'Leary summed it up by saying "Chelsea were the luckiest team in the world. We deserved at least a draw and should have won. They were hanging on".

I will not bore you with a bad write up and go through reliving the match again is like a bad dream. Chelsea were awful and they were there for the taking but O'Leary cannot complain for had his team had any more about them they could, should and would have won the match. Chelsea will look back at the end of the season and thank their lucky stars, for these points could be very crucial on the run-in for the Premiership title.

Chelsea 1 Jimmy Floyd Aston Villa 0: 41,182

Off the field there was still much going on and this time it was Peter Kenyon who has neatly sidestepped restrictions imposed upon him by installing a 'take over boss' at Stamford Bridge. Sports Marketing Paul Smith will stand-in for Kenyon until he is free to get into the driving seat. Smith worked with sports marketing agency ISL before running IMG's football department. He has a long professional history with Kenyon, working in Asia and the Far East on United's commercial business. Meanwhile, Smith's former ISL colleague Andrew Craig was appointed as a consultant to the London Olympic bid. Veteran sports journalist Steve Parry was made director of media. Parry covered 16 Olympics over three decades at news agency Reuters. He has been a media consultant for the International Committee for three years.

NO THANKS ROMAN

In the *Daily Mail* Sir Alex underlined his commitment to Manchester United last night following confirmation that he had received an offer to move to Chelsea in the summer.

Sir Alex Ferguson reaffirmed his loyalty and commitment to Manchester United last night as it emerged that he was top of the list for the management at Chelsea Football Club. Russian billionaire sounded out the United boss via a third party immediately after becoming the new owner of the London cub. It is also said that his name remains top of Abramovich's manager shopping list. Alongside that is Sven Goran Eriksson but that name we already knew of. David Gill the man replacing Kenyon in Manchester said that "We are delighted to have Sir Alex as our manager and we want it to remain that way. It is early days regarding the manager s contract. All I will say, as Peter Kenyon had said – and he was talking on behalf of the board – is that we are positive about it and we won't get into a situation like last time. That will move ahead soon. Sir Alex has been the most successful manager ever here. He has been here for seventeen years and has another two on his contract".

Gill also revealed that part of Kenyon's severance agreement is that he is not allowed to 'tap up' Ferguson or any other United employees.

"Peter Kenyon is precluded in his contract against deliberate or blatant poaching. But knowing the man the way I do, I don't think there will be a lot of that".

19th September. Three days after Glenn Hoddle was quoted as saying that "I am working extremely hard with all my players and staff. I don't focus on the pressure" going on that "When I was at Chelsea we went to Southampton on Boxing Day 1993, six months into my reign as manager there and the fans were not happy. We were second from bottom. We lost 3-1 but the next game, two days later, we beat top of the table Newcastle 1-0, with Mark Stein scoring the goal, and that was the turning point. We went on and got to the FA Cup Final and into Europe."

22nd September 2003
SACKED Hoddle goes as Spurs patience finally run out:

Glenn Hoddle was finally sacked as Tottenham manager last night when the club admitted they had lost confidence in him. Martin O'Neill was top of the list to succeed him but Glasgow Celtic are still very much in the Champions League, a trophy the Irishman would love to win before he moved away from Glasgow. Others mentioned were Alan Curbishley of Charlton and Graeme Souness at Blackburn. There was a little in the news about Harry Redknapp and we know he was being considered but he made it quite clear he still had "unfinished business with my Portsmouth team."

CUT DOWN TO SIZE
Ranieri's side can't find way past ten men

Two moments of madness and by players who were there before Roman Times were enough to bring a touch of reality to all of the hype and hysteria that has surrounded Stamford Bridge over the last three months. Turkish champions Besikta's two goals in the opening half hour was enough to see off a Chelsea team who were very short of ideas on how to break down well organised defensive methods. This was not a great Turkish team by any stretch of the imagination but Chelsea started huffing and puffing once again and it seemed that it was something that set in the previous weekend when struggling badly to make any impact at all on a very ordinary Villa defence, winning by a goalkeeping error. The 'Tinkerman' was at it again as he made ten changes in his last two matches. He changed the system too, employing three at the back with Celestine Babayaro and Geremi supposed to be making forward runs from both flanks but this did not work out. It wasn't the Italian coach's evening having lost Babayaro with injury in the first half he then used his two remaining substitutes and found that he could not replace Billy Gallas once he was injured. The Chelsea coach could not have fielded a team with more experience as between them Desailly, Makelele, Crespo, and Veron had played 271 Champions League matches before this one. Veron once again looks struggling and plays in snatches reminding me of Doctor Jekyll after taking his medicine. He looks absolutely brilliant at times but other times he looks like he has never played the game before. So it was an awful result and performance from the Blues and a match they'll want to forget quickly and no better time and place as at Middlesbrough on Sunday afternoon. Chelsea's best player once more was the industrious Frank Lampard though it was he who missed a marvellous opportunity to put his team ahead. Within five minutes of that miss the Turks took advantage of a hesitant John Terry and the young centre-half will not be happy with such an error. Only four minutes later a ball hit long by keeper Oscar Cordoba saw Marcel Desailly slip as Cuducini came out looking like a 'Bat out of Hell' missing the ball to let Yalcin in for his second goal. Chelsea got a lifeline when Mansiz was sent off for ignoring the referee's whistle and putting the ball into the back of the net something that players should be able to do. We were taught as young apprentices to put the ball away first before stopping the play. This kind of refereeing really bugs me as to how long can it take off the watch and anyhow the fourth official has the time machine. Once again you ask if would the referee have given the same decision in Turkey. I say no!

The only luck the lady gave them on this torrid night of football was that Lazio could only draw against Sparta Prague after being – like the Blues – two goals down at half time. This kept Lazio top of Group G and the pressure will be on Chelsea when Roberto Mancini's team visit Stamford Bridge from Ranieri's native home Rome.

In Group E where we await the 'Battle of Britain' as Glasgow Rangers and Manchester United go head to head but on this particular evening of European Football Rangers drew in Athens and led right up till the last minute before Panathinaikos equalised. Alex McLeish is fast becoming a manager to be reckoned with!

Chelsea 0 Besiktas 2 32,957

'NOT MY FAULT'
Chelsea are £110m flops but Ranieri shifts blame

Claudio Ranieri last night defended his decision to chop and change his Chelsea side after their 2-0 defeat to Besiktas at Stamford Bridge. The Tinkerman refused to accept any blame for Chelsea's first loss under the ownership of Roman Abramovich, while Sir Alex Ferguson criticised his players after Manchester United went down 2-1 in Stuttgart.

Ranieri made another five changes to the side, which beat Aston Villa on

Saturday. But his tactics backfired as Sergen Yalcin scored twice inside half an hour and the Turkish champions never looked back, even after having a player sent-off early in the second half. Ranieri who spent £110million on players over the summer, said that, "After the game it is very easy to say we should have done one thing and not the other. When you make mistakes in the Premier League it is one thing but when you make them in the Champions League it costs you a goal 99 per cent of the time. I watched Bekitas against Lazio and they had 10 to 15 shots in that match. Even though Lazio beat them 2-0, they played very well. Tonight I did not see Besiktas create that many chances against us". John Terry was more critical, saying that, "Besiktas seemed to be in control from the start and both goals were sloppy. We have to look at that on the training pitch and put it right. It was not the only fault. When we went forward our final ball was poor." Besiktas manager Mercie Lucescu said that, "Ranieri did some very good work here last year but it's difficult for the players to come in at this level. You can see they are not integrated yet as a team. They were missing passes and making the wrong passes all night." Ferguson criticised his players' defending after United were beaten by the German league leaders. He said that "We had defended terribly for the two goals and if you defend badly in games of this nature you deserve to get beat". Rio Ferdinand picked up a slight injury but is expected to be ready for Saturday's crucial Euro 2004 match in Turkey.

On the Rio Ferdinand front, it was revealed today that he left the ground early dodging a random drug test and has been left out of the squad heading for Turkey's very difficult encounter. This has come on top of the recent trouble of several English players who gang raped a young girl in London's Grosvenor Hotel in the early hours of the morning. the *Sun* newspaper had the headlines as: **CHELSEA PLAYER LINKED TO RAPE QUIZ:** This was an exclusive by Mike Sullivan who reported that, "The footballer at the centre of the 'gang rape' investigation is a Chelsea player. He was the one a 17-year-old girl says she agreed to have sex with – before seven stars from another club entered the room.

This was not something I like putting in this book but it has to be said and cannot be ignored. The one thing that always staggers me is these players who are on such incredible pay packets are out in Night Clubs and if they are not fighting Asians at three o'clock in the morning they are gang raping seventeen-year-old girls. Back to the lighter side of the story of the Russians and I turn to the racing page to see that Red Rom is going to become a horse owner just like Sir Alex Ferguson. Although I go onto the more pleasant things in life this gang rape will return with more harrowing stories to be press released.

On a more light hearted note it is reported that Roman Abramovich is following Sir Alex into the world of thoroughbred horse racing.

CHELSEA GURU MOVES INTO HORSE RACING:

Shift over Sheikh Mohammed – Roman Abramovich is moving into racing. The Russian billionaire has transformed Chelsea, lavishing an incredible £110million on new players this season. Now the *News of the World* can exclusively reveal Abramovich plans to make a killing in the Sport of Kings where his staggering wealth would make him a major player. A source close to the Abramovich camp said last night that "I can confirm that Roman will be in a private box at Longchamp on Arc de Triomphe day next month. He will be guest of top French-based trainer Richard Gibson and will be discussing possible plans to put some horses in training. Roman has always been a gambler at heart. His entire business was a huge gamble that paid off in spades. He is testing the horse racing water by becoming an owner in France. He may decide to get involved in British racing as he is spending more and more time over there due to his commitments at Chelsea". Abramovich is believed to have caught the racing bug from a pal who is already a successful owner with Gibson.

And the turf is buzzing with the news that the Russian may have already have bought his first horse at the recent Deauville sales. Blood stock agent Charlie Gordon-Watson, himself an avid Chelsea fan, went to a cool £145,000 for a colt named Le Tigre D'Or for an unnamed client of Gibson. That sum pales the huge fees Abramovich has splashed out to secure some of the biggest names in football, with Damien Duff, Hernen Crespo, Adrian Mutu and Juan Sebastian Veron all brought in to the west London club for more than £15million each. Racing already enjoys a huge crossover with footballs biggest stars. Manchester United manager Sir Alex Ferguson had a huge hit with his first venture into the Sport of Kings as part-owner of the legendary Rock of Gibraltar who won a record seven Group One races in a row, earning almost £3million. Former England striker Mick Channon has become a top ten trainer under the patronage of the Maktoum family, while Manchester City boss Kevin Keegan is a successful owner and breeder.

BACK TO THE BALLPARK

Chelsea would have to pick themselves off the floor after a nightmare against the Turks and for quite some time it looked like they were struggling to get the better of Middlesbrough then a clever piece of play by Damien Duff in the seventeenth minute saw his feed into Gudjohnsen's path taken superbly before the talented youngster took it in his stride before coolly slipping the ball into the keeper's near post. Chelsea still could not take over completely and only a minute into the second half they conceded the equaliser. Nemeth, being fed nicely by the ex-Valencia skipper Gaizka Mendieta – a big favourite of mine – hit a cracking shot into the top corner of the net. That gave the home side just the lift they needed and they began to worry the Chelsea back four and a shock looked on the cards until Crespo came on as substitute once more and took the pressure of the 'Tinkerman' by heading Duff's cross at the far post into the corner of the net. Crespo was the hero again after his entrance last weekend saw him hitting two past Wolves. Chelsea will play a lot better and not win unless it is a simple case of 'From Russia with Luck' with Roman not only bringing his wallet but also a lucky charm or could it be the brooches bought for them by the ex-chairman of Chelsea Football Club. Whoever or whatever the cause for this latest rush of charmed life the Chelsea faithful were enjoying every minute of it and were getting on with the job at hand although not impressive enough for me to think they could win the Premiership, even when the new players were settled in. Manchester United are still the team to beat and the red army are just flexing their muscles as we know they start their real challenge just after the Christmas holidays, although with no Beckham this time around the jury is still well and truly out, in my eyes the verdict would be a verdict of guilty on the part of the manager of Manchester United!

Chelsea were now about to face their first match after a defeat and it was crucial to their Championship dreams to put in a solid performance and this was reflected by Jimmy Floyd the day after their disappointing display against the Turks. He says that "People have been waiting all season for us to slip up and now you are going to see how we react to this defeat. We are going to be looking to the characters that are going to get back up and fight. It is very important we bounce back immediately, so Sunday's match at Middlesbrough has become vital."

Middlesbrough 1 Mendieta Chelsea 2 Gudjohnsen and Crespo: 29,170

"We are all very, very disappointed because we had been on a very good run and weren't expecting that. We knew Besiktas were well organised. But we definitely did not think they would beat us, especially at home. We made a couple of mistakes but we are not blaming anyone for that. You play with eleven men and seven more on the bench. We are one big team and we win and lose together. I don't know if the changes unsettled us on Wednesday. It is not up to me to say. I am one of the pioneers of the team and with the other twenty-two players I'm trying very hard to make things work here. I always want to play from the start but there are 22 others who want the same thing. I don't see that as pressure, I regard it as a challenge. I like a challenge". Carlo Cudicini was one of the players blamed for errors that led to the second goal and he insisted that "Sometimes it is good to have a wake-up call and this defeat will only make us stronger. Hernen Crespo is very good in the air so we needed to play down the wings. That happened in the second half but it was too late for we only had Jimmy up on his own". His team-mate and co-offender for that goal says "United were beaten and Arsenal drew so that shows how difficult it is in this competition. The season is very long and we need to be positive".

On the Friday before Chelsea's trip to the North East Steve Curry claimed that

"RANIERI'S LIKE A KID WITH FAR TOO MANY TOYS"

'NO ONE CAN MAKE YOU FEEL INFERIOR WITHOUT YOUR CONSENT'

Eleanor Roosevelt

I thought that appropriate with the Arsenal match only four days away.

After that welcome win at Boro the Blues needed to come out of this match with three points which would have picked them up for the next two big ones – at Highbury and then at home to Lazio – the crunch match for the leadership of both the Premiership and Group G in the Champions League. So this is the confidence booster, for if they could pull something out of all these three matches it would put an entirely different picture on the rest of the season. Especially getting the Arsenal hoodoo put to rest before steaming into the Italians. This match at Birmingham was tough but the Blues should have won the match for having the best of scoring opportunities and when in control must put teams away if they are going to push both Manchester United and Arsenal – who they play next – all the way to the wire. For a team who have spent so much money on strikers they had better start earning their wages or next summer will see another 'Sale of the Century'.

Plus we ask the question again, could the Blues do with Mikael Forssell back from the Midlands where he has been magnificent so far this season?

Birmingham City 0 Chelsea 0: 29,460

Equally, Arsenal need to avoid defeat in Kiev tomorrow for the knockout stages to be within reach in the wake of their 3-0 defeat at home to Inter Milan last month.

Yet how well the Gunners have recovered from that setback, having superbly negotiated a sequence of fixtures which threatened to tear their season apart. "Mentally the players were very down after that Inter match, then they had to contend with what went on after our draw at Old Trafford," said the Arsenal manager. "But it's a tribute to their strength of character that they remained so focused."

The obvious difference between Arsenal and Chelsea at the moment, as Ranieri conceded, is that Arsenal are a team. "When Robert Pires has the ball Ashley Cole, Thierry Henry, Sylvain Wiltord, they all know what is going to happen", he said.

"When Damien Duff has it, Adrian Mutu and Hernan Crespo don't know where to go yet. That will take time, how long? I don't know."

It was almost too frank an assessment of where Chelsea are, but for all that, the result came down to Cudicini's extraordinary blunder, which was right up there with the all time great goalkeepers gaffes, such as when Gary Sprake threw the ball into his own net, Ray Clemence let a shot through his legs at

Hampden Park, Manchester United's Massimo Taibo allowed a dolly drive to pass under his body. Then in the final minute of a match at the Victoria Ground Malcolm McDonald hit a hopeful ball into our half, and as Alan Gowling gave chase Peter Shilton beat him to the ball and trying to send it down the Trent kicked the bloody floor and laid there whilst the rest of us walked off as there was not time enough to kick-off. I have to throw that one in for old time's sake, Pete! Now if it had not hit our championship hopes so badly I would have said it was one of the funniest things I have ever seen on a football field. And finally Thierry Henry being given a golden opportunity to send United reeling at Highbury last season. What made me laugh was that United were in front to a Paul Scholes goal at half-time and on the way out of the tunnel at half-time Barthez and Henry were seen 'French kissing'. Then with the match on a knife-edge the French keeper simply rolled the ball to his international team-mate to put into an empty net. All I can say if Bruce Grobbellar is bent there had better be a steward's inquiry into some other tricks that have gone on over the years! So it's back to Highbury once again and things had looked good for Chelsea when Argentina striker Crespo produced a superb 30-yard equaliser three minutes after Edu had given Arsenal the lead with a deflected free-kick.

If Chelsea made a mistake, it was that after half-time they seemed content to hold out for a draw, a dangerous thing to do against the Gunners, because the home side love coming forward and are an absolutely different side going towards their own goal. Arsenal on the other hand, were rewarded for going for the win as Pires drove forward from a quick 75th minute free-kick. Cuducini seemed to have comfortably beaten Henry to the cross, but as he attempted to dive on the ball he inexplicably thrust it back through his legs. Henry, who had given up chase, suddenly discovered the ball had hit his leg and rolled in.

"It is the luckiest goal I have ever scored" continuing with "I feel sorry for Cudicini because a few minutes earlier he had made a brilliant save from me. In fact, he made plenty of saves". Indeed he did. The fact is even most reliable keepers – and Cudicini has been one for two seasons – suffer embarrassing moments. But on the back of similar, if not quite so outrageous, errors of judgement, which have cost goals against Blackburn and Besiktas this season, he now faces a crisis in confidence.

"I will speak to him about that, but I have faith in him" said Ranieri.
Arsenal 2 Edu and Henry Chelsea 1 Crespo: 38,170

Rob Shepherd is one of the most reliable and best judges on the journalistic roundabout and gave a good report on Saturday's crunch match. However I think that he, and all the others in fact, do not give an in depth look at the strengths and weaknesses in two of the top teams in the country. In the match at Old Trafford where Arsenal acted like a gang of yobs who had just left the pub late Saturday night before their battle over Hackney Marshes for their

Sunday melee while suffering with several hefty hangovers. That childish affair following that van Nistelrooy penalty miss is dead but not buried for the two teams who will come face to face once again at Highbury and you can be sure that there will be some pretty hefty challenges going on. And there are several match-ups all over the field, not forgetting the match of the season between Keown and the 'Flying Dutchman' Ruud van Nistelrooy. Chelsea's failure to overcome a Patrick Vieira-less Arsenal will become very costly when all the points are totted up at the end of the most interesting ever Premiership season. The Tinkerman may be under pressure after this first big 'Premiership' defeat of their season but I would not mind being in his place for the shop window will soon be open and the Russian Roubles will go into overdrive once it is here. The men in the well-tailored suits got their first sight of just how tough it is going to be to wrestle the championship off of Manchester United!

With just under a quarter of matches gone the picture looks pretty clear as there is a five point gap between Chelsea in third and Manchester City in fourth. There is no shortage of football on television this coming week with four Premiership matches playing today, Sunday the 18th, one on Monday and plenty of European matches including a must-win match for Chelsea who host Italian giants Lazio. I will be flying to the United States of America for this season's Breeders Cup at Santa Anita but I will not be taking my finger off the pulse of the English game. I will be tuned in for the Chelsea and Manchester City match next weekend, one that should bring lots of goals as these are the two highest scorers in the Premiership and Kevin Keegan's boys are flying high and will be looking to close that five point gap between him and the Tinkerman. The latest rumblings from Stamford Bridge over the last couple of days is that Abramovich now wants Brazilian 'superstar' Ronaldo where they are willing to buy out his contract of £180million and he would probably cost them at least another £10million in wages. The massive buy-out clause is normal practice in Real Madrid's contracts – to ward off hungry predators like Chelsea and his Russian revolution. This is apart from Wayne Rooney and a surprise move for Rio Ferdinand who is still in the dock over the failed drug test.

On the morning of the Arsenal match there was a strange article in the *Daily Star* with the headlines:

WE ARE SECOND BEST

Chelsea manager Claudio Ranieri has amazingly tipped his table-toppers to play second fiddle to Arsenal today.

The moneybags Blues have spent £111million assembling the greatest squad in their history!

But as the league leaders go up against 'bogey' side Arsenal at Highbury this afternoon. Ranieri was insisting they are still poor relations. The Italian was yesterday named 'Manager of the Month' as his team put together three wins in September. Frank Lampard was the 'Player of the Month'. But the Italian continued to play down the chances of his star-spangled squad's title chances yesterday despite the huge outlay on new talent thanks to billionaire owner Roman Abramovich. On the day of Chelsea's match at Arsenal the Tinkerman was tinkering with the media by saying in no uncertain terms that his new Chelsea were "Not up with them yet. They are a strong team even without Vieira. We'll try to beat them and it will be a big test for us. Sometimes we have played well at Highbury but they have still won. This is reality. We want to get to the same level as them but we aren't ready yet. We are working to close the gap, but it's difficult to say just how long it will take". The Tinkerman carried on that, "Being top of the league after two months is good for the Premiership and football fans everywhere, because all they usually see is a two horse race". Ranieri spoke after he and Frank Lampard picked up their trophies for both Manager and Player of the Month, that month being September.

For such a shrewd man, I just cannot work out whose eyes the Tinkerman is trying to pull the wool over!

He does not tinker with my mind and my mind tells me that a huge performance was needed at Highbury and we never got one. I don't buy all this fuss about rotation systems taking time, for if that was the situation how would International teams like West Germany, Brazil and our '66' team had succeeded after getting together once every pancake day. Chelsea and their Tinkerman had better get their act together pretty soon because if the wheels fall off that would put them behind where they began the season, as fourth best.

ALL OUR YESTERDAYS

I found it interesting looking at this week, forty years ago, no I did not play, thank you!

The north London Derby is always a chaotic affair, but few Arsenal and Spurs encounters have been as dramatic as the Highbury clash of the 15th of October 1963.

A crowd of 67,000 watched a thrilling eight goal draw and there were 10,000 locked outside. Some of the younger spectators inside the ground were passed overhead to the ambulance men as hundreds of fans forced their way outside at half time because of the pressure inside. One young man was knocked out by a shot from Jimmy Greaves as he sat alongside the goal. He was a very unfortunate young man because Jimmy hardly ever missed the onion bag. Those who remained were treated to an absolutely brilliant feast of football as the home side, behind as early as the second minute fought back from 4-2 down to level the scores in the dying seconds.

The draw kept Spurs at the top of the Division One table – at Arsenal's expense, while Everton's 4-1 win over Sheffield United meant that with almost a third of the season over the top eleven teams were separated by just three points, seven of them sharing second place.

In Europe Manchester United completed a 7-2 aggregate trouncing of part time Dutch side Willen II. A 5-2 home victory included a Denis Law hat-trick and they were drawn against Tottenham in the next round of the European Cup Winners Cup.

On the back pages that week read that in the Olympics South African are banned from the forthcoming Tokyo Olympics Games in protest at their government's apartheid regime

Tuesday evening's results were Arsenal 4 Spurs 4 with George Eastham getting two with Joe Baker and Geoff Strong the others. Whilst Spurs goal-getters were Bobby Smith two, Greaves and Mackay. Everton 4 Sheffield United 1 Alex Young getting two with Stevens and Temple the other scorers, Wagstaff scoring for the visitors. European Cup Winners Cup as I told you Manchester United 5 Willen II 1 Denis Law three, Bobby Charlton and Chisnall for United with a Noel Cantwell own goal putting Willen II on the score-sheet.

The top five were Spurs, Manchester United, Blackburn, Forest and West Bromwich Albion. The eventual winners however were Liverpool with Manchester United runners-up. Relegated were Bolton and Ipswich.

HENRY AND ANELKA

Back to this October and a time when Alex Ferguson will be delighted with the weekend's results although a goalless draw would have been a better result for him and his team. But all you can do in this business is stay strong, build up slowly and keep picking up points no matter what everyone else does. A 1-0 win at Leeds would have him delighted and next week it is Fulham who visit the 'Theatre of Dreams'. The day after Arsenal play a tough derby match at Charlton whilst, as I said, Chelsea host Manchester City in what I would call my 'Match of the Day'. I like the way Keegan's teams always try to play the game, going all out attack no matter whether at home or on their travels. This is the only way to play since the three points scheme came in for you're better winning two out of three than being unbeaten by drawing two or even three matches. My only concern in his managerial ability was at the time whilst managing Newcastle United, KK foolishly tinkered with his team and bought Aspirilla, the Columbian international. This disrupted a team who were playing brilliantly and David Ginola, my kind of player, was playing out of his skin before the Columbian drug dealer hit the North East. I was in a restaurant one Saturday evening after watching him play at West Ham United that afternoon. I wondered why he stayed down in London until I read the following morning that he was up in Bow Court for a drug's charge. He seemed a nice kind of coffee bean but his style of play was not quite right for the old First Division as it was then and now the Premiership of course. Oh yeah, and the court he was summoned too was opposite where that car hit me nearly seven years ago now. I am looking forward to the Chelsea and Manchester City match more than any other so far this season and especially to see how Chelsea cope with the pace of Anelka, the man who is running Premiership defences ragged this season. Let us not forget the brilliant piece of management when Arsene Wenger brought this unknown front man from his homeland. Then after making him a 'big name' over here he became unhappy, Anelka that is, but the French manager made a massive amount of money by selling him on and replacing him with Henry. I would have found it very interesting to see how both Anelka and Henry would have played together or whether they would have been too alike. Chelsea themselves are having trouble in as much as I don't think the Tinkerman knows his best partnership in his front line. For me, I think in these times he does it wrong for he believes in having two teams, meaning a back-up team, when he can or should play three of them at once. Defenders don't like to face three players with such ability, and also no matter how things are going there are times he should let the team play for ninety minutes if things are going well. I don't mean changing a winning team – just let the players who started finish together. I promise you there is no worse feeling than when you are just starting to play well the manager uses his tiny mind and changes things. If Dave Sexton had had the kind of resources the Talisman has given the club he would have drove not only us, but himself crazy, not that he wasn't anyway. The great saying is, "If things are not broken they don't need fixing", and there were times I am sure he loved us all and then other times he hated a half a dozen of us. I truly believe that and there are several other of our squad would maybe agree!

THE MYSTERY DEEPENS AS TO THE MISSING MILLIONS

So, who REALLY cashed in on the Chelsea sell-out?

This is an exclusive by the *Mail*'s Joe Hare:

For years Chelsea fans have believed that a man being investigated by the US Department of Justice was a serious investor in the Stamford Bridge club.

But now, after 20 years of mystery *Sportsmail* can reveal that Johannesburg Hotelier Stanley Tollman has never been involved in the ownership of Chelsea.

The revelation will lead to speculation about who held the Chelsea Village shares, which were sold to billionaire Roman for £60million. It has been assumed that Tollman, who is facing tax charges in the USA, had made millions from the sale. But it had been disclosed that the first Tollman knew of the dramatic June sale was when chairman Ken Bates rang him the day after to say "the club had been bought by a Russian". If Tollman's version is correct it provokes new questions over the destination of a large chunk of Abramovich's cash.

It was thought that Tollman was the man behind Guernsey-based investment company Swan Management, which has regularly cashed in on Chelsea connections. Members of the vociferous Chelsea Action Group believed that, when BskyB bought 3.9 per cent of Chelsea Village shares from Swan in 1992, it was Tollman who banked a cool £10million. This is now denied by Tollman's friends.

They insisted "Stanley was happy to be on the Chelsea board when Ken invited him but Ken wanted to run the thing himself. He wanted people around him who he could trust but at no stage did he offer Stanley a share."

'Who held the shares?' We don't know but it was someone who could come up with 52 per cent of them very quickly one night to sell them to the Russian investors.

Tollman 73, first became connected with Chelsea in the early eighties but is increasingly annoyed that his name is still linked to the club.

He believes that his American 'troubles' have been exacerbated in this country by the alleged connections.

This week in London, his associates have broken their silence on the deals that have had baffled Chelsea fans for years. One friend said that, "For years Stanley has suffered adverse publicity in London because of his supposed connection with Chelsea. It is simply not true. Because of its problems with the USA Justice Department it had become news here. That would never have been the case if someone had revealed the truth. Stanley hasn't put a penny into Chelsea. He hasn't taken a penny out. The relationship between Tollman and Bates goes back to the early seventies when they met in South Africa. It has been a strange and often distant friendship, which surprisingly led to Tollman joining the Chelsea Board in 1982."

Tollman sources said that, "Stanley was a passive member. He wasn't even a football fan. By 1992-93 Stanley was spending more and more time in the States and was rarely watching matches. At that time Ken asked him to step down from the board and he did so without any question or bitterness".

At that point, his friends claim Tollman thought his Chelsea connections were severed.

But public perception of his involvement didn't change, One of his great grandchildren told Stanley that he was on a website that linked him with Lockerbie, Colonel Gaddafi and Robert Maxwell. He was furious.

"He told Ken Bates that he was thinking of legal action but Bates told him not to go to the lawyers. It is a decision he regretted. It's been something that has caused him great personal damage ever since. And while Bates might claim it did him harm to be connected to Stanley, why didn't someone at Chelsea move to make the position clear?

"Stanley wishes Bates only well. But at the same time many will wonder why Bates failed to move to help clarify Stanley's position with the club".

MORE LINKS

The latest links to Chelsea were quite staggering for they included David Beckham, Carlos Alberto and Rio Ferdinand of all people. That meaning he is still having problems with the FA and they have made it very clear that they are furious over the continuous delaying on the part of Ferdinand for they have asked him for a copy of his mobile phone bill so that they can check to see if he had tried to call them on that very bad day for the England defender. The rumourmongers are out and they are getting bad vibes from Soho Square.

My column in the *Sentinel Sunday* went like this;

'BOBBY HAD BRAINS'

What is the difference between Rio Ferdinand and Bobby Moore? Both came through the ranks at West Ham, but Bobby had brains both on and off the field of play. They call it the Academy and the Hammers still believe that Bobby, Geoff Hurst and Martin Peters won the 1966 World Cup on their own. Bobby was at his brilliant best, Hursty hit that memorable hat-trick, and Martin scored the other goal.

The rest, as they say, is unforgettable.

Looking back, the way Alf Ramsey and his squad went into both the 1966 and 1970 World Cups seems even more fantastic considering what we have seen and heard this week. The England manager today, Sven Goran Eriksson has not only lost the plot but also the respect of all our nation. If what we have heard about the Swede taking over at Chelsea then the Russians will be taking a big step backwards in their bid to build a team of world-beaters. Despite claims to the contrary, the likes of George Best, Frank Worthington, Stan Bowles, Tony Currie and myself were angels, maybe even a manager's dream. Our managers knew where we were and what we were drinking, when I say were, I mean were not at home. These days, some bosses must go to bed in fear of what they may end up reading on the front pages the following morning. Rio Ferdinand has become a second rate superstar, and his two world record moves for a defender seem to have made him believe his own headlines. Certainly, his performances on the pitch are doing little to enhance his position reputation at the moment. I have met Rio a couple of times and thought he was like something out of the 'Simpson's'. On reflection, it is easy to understand how he forgot his drug test. I am a realist, not like those pundits who sit on the fence. I tell it like it is, which is why I have never been employed by club directors, even though I know I could do better than most managers standing on my head. Take my good friend Peter Reid and his decision to buy Jody Morris from Chelsea into a club that has been dragged through the gutter by the night owls over the last three or four years. Now the player is suspected of another sort of attack, this time on a young girl who cried 'rape'.

You of all people Reidy, a man I love and a great football man, what were you drinking at the time, whatever it was I 'm steering away from it!

We cannot possibly take our game any lower at this moment in time in an already very warped world we live in. They say that money is the root of all evil and right now nothing has ever rang truer. When I was a player on top form and free of injury I was a very confident character but most of today's also-rans are truly arrogant both on and off the field. They actually believe that their ability matches the size of their wage packets. My move to Stoke City cost the club a record quarter of a million pounds but all that I did would become more determined to prove my worth for my football club, plus to prove that the manager was right to buy me. I could play with the best, drink with the rest and stand up to any test. Today's players – with the exception of Beckham, Scholes and Owen – are nothing more than a figment of their very own imagination.

Harry Harris in the *Daily Express* states that Chelsea have already have two players for each position but there is talk of a third one in: Buffan, Salgado, Lucio, Ferdinand, Roberto Carlos, Beckham, Emerson, Nedved, Gerrard, Ronaldo and Rooney.

THE BATTLE OF BRITAIN

Dennis Wise, the street urchin bad boy of English football made a handsome profit on leaving Chelsea Football Club. The 36-year-old 'menace' was shrewd enough when leaving the club he captained to be paid out in shares in which he bought 7.5million at 20p and has now made himself £1.5million.

You could say in some ways the introduction of Chelsea's Makelele will play in the role once held by Wise. I have seen this player a couple of times and have doubts about just how good he is, but it may take time, but at this moment in time he and Geremi look to be quite some way off good enough to wrestle in midfield with the likes of Paul Scholes and Roy Keane at Manchester United and of course the top men at Highbury, Vieira and Pires!

It was Tuesday evening, the eve of Chelsea's match against Lazio in the Champions League and the Tinkerman had a very big job on his hands after the defeat at Highbury only three days ago. Both Arsenal and Glasgow Celtic were beaten in the groups, Arsenal in Moscow by Kiev and Celtic by ten men Anderlecht in Belgium. The Gunners huffed and puffed for long spells but did not look up to the job at hand and this result could be the end of another miserable season in Europe. Martin O'Neil will be very frustrated by his team's failure to capitalise on the ten men of Anderlecht and to be truthful the ten men outplayed the eleven in the second half although Celtic could say they had the better chances. John Hartson had one as did Henrik Larsson but the best chance fell to their centre back, who with the ball falling at his feet in the six yard box, somehow failed to convert it into a goal. But when the Belgian side went forward they did so with far more fluency and the goal was a very well worked one. The team over in Moscow are pretty damned good if you remember them having Shevchenko and Rebrov in their side only five years ago but have put a side together who are quite capable of beating anyone on the own soil. Arsenal blew their chances at Highbury when Inter Milan won there by three goals and another shock this evening was that Lokomotive beat the Italians by the same score with an incredible display of free flowing football. This result was just another kick in the teeth for Arsenal for it leaves them as the only team without a win in the group and lag in last place. The

pressure on Chelsea right now will be the main factor after a very disappointing showing at Highbury on Saturday but the Champions League will be a
great test and Lazio will be a great test of their character and once again who
will the Tinkerman select for such a match. All eyes will be on team selection
as there were several doubts in my mind when first looking at the team at
Highbury for in the middle of the week I fancied Chelsea could go there and
give them a real match but after seeing his team sheet I immediately changed
my mind. This was a little late for me for I had written my column saying just
that and fancied Frank Lampard to keep up his good form and maybe have
some say in the result but he looked out of place in a team where it was quite
obvious it had been tinkered with too many times of late. Whilst Chelsea open
fire on Lazio over at Old Trafford comes possibly the tie of the competition
when they take on Scottish Champions Glasgow Rangers. These two teams
bring together two good friends in Sir Alex Ferguson and Alex McLeish, a
player who played for Ferguson at Aberdeen many moons ago. McLeish did a
wonderful job in his first full season as Ranger boss by stealing the championship from the old firm across Glasgow. I was not very pleased by this for I
had quite a substantial bet on Henrik Larsson being leading goal-scorer, in
Scotland, doubled with Celtic retaining the Championship they won in a
canter the season before. That was my last ever bet although I leave for the
Breeders Cup tomorrow in Santa Anita which is about an hour's drive from
LAX Airport. I will be calling on my good friend Jimmy Duggan and look
forward to a nice relaxing week in the Santa Anita Inn. Chelsea's match will
have been finished by the time the wheels of my aeroplane touches down. But
I am hoping to get to the nearest television for Chelsea's match against
Manchester City on Saturday.

'FALLON LOVES ISLINGTON'
ARCADIA, CALIFORNIA;
The headlines of the *Daily Racing Form* read that
'SOME LIKE IT HOT BUT NOT ISLINGTON.'

Somewhere along the way you have to take a break and recharge your
batteries and there was no better place than the United States of America and
the day of the Breeders Cup. I had visited Santa Anita before through my great
friend Jimmy Duggan – the ex-Fred Winter horseman – and this was my kind
of place. But I never imagined for one minute – although I know the Yanks
do everything better than us – that this particular day was better than Derby
Day, Ladies Day at the Royal meeting, Gold Cup and Grand National Day all
rolled into one little basket. This was my treat for working hard in the
gymnasium each and every day and I was very determined to make it one hell
of a trip. I succeeded!

Considering some doctors – specialists – said I would never walk again it
made times like this double the usual fun and enjoyment and what better place

to be than in Santa Anita for one of the biggest races on the calendar. I was ably assisted by my son who looked after my every need as not being in the gymnasium for a week brings me problems, but what I lacked in working-out I made up for in the sun and doing my leg exercises in the hotel pool. The weather was perfect and so was my mood. Last time I visited the Santa Anita Inn I found myself a lovely watering hole where I could relax amongst the locals and in no time I – as always – cracked it off with our friends the Yanks. This trip was going to be fantastic and when I make my mind up that is the way it has to turn out!

Each morning I relaxed at Clockers Corner, and on the eve of the big race had the pleasure to sit chatting with the great Kieran Fallon who told me that if his mount was as good as he was on that morning's gallop – he loved her chances. In other words she would take all the beating. His concern, as always, if the filly knocks herself in her box or if someone tried to knobble Europe's most fancied runner. My words, not Kieran's, I must stress. I promise I do not gamble anymore and have never been in the company all these years where I actually asked, 'give me a winner'. I once I had a bet on our Stoke team winning an FA Cup match and done my money, so I know how jockeys can get it wrong! Sitting with Fallon was quite delightful and I can only imagine that he would have loved sitting with me before the biggest game of my life. Yeah, you get it again, the Germans. I could not have told this brilliant jockey that we could beat Beckenbauer and his team mates but, shoe on the other foot, he would have known by the look on my face that I was very confident that this was my stage, the same as his, it's all the same when the big one comes along. It is called the best!

I must tell you that before the two big races at the track I was looking for a taxi or a metro to get me back to my hotel when a rental car pulled up and asked me where the track was and having all these bags of shirts, trousers and shoes with me, said that "If you drive me to the hotel, which was at the foot at the entrance of this most famous race track, I would thankfully tell you that Fallon loves Islington" and they explained to me that the last time they went to the Breeders they picked an Englishman up and he gave them a winner. But the boys from Boston were not happy with that, they wanted another. I could only say in hope, and I was not gambling, that Falbrav, trained by the dashing and brilliant Luca Cumani, could win for Holland and my buddy Don Shanks who accompanied Darrel there. So is that a coincidence or what?

STOUTE COMMENT

Back to Michael Stoute and his concern was that in the Champion Stakes six weeks ago, "She got further back than I'd have liked and I don't know quite why. It wasn't intentional, but she finished well and I think the effort shows she's every bit as good now as when she came to the Breeders Cup last year". On his final session the *Racing Form* said that, "Islington spent quite a bit of time on the racetrack. Walked the wrong way from the quarter mile chute to the six-furlong pole on the main course. Positioned about three lengths behind a stable-mate, she eagerly travelled a mile on the grass. Got so aggressive around the clubhouse turn that she actually broke into an impromptu breeze, covering consecutive furlongs from the seven-eighths pole to the five-eighths pole in thirteen seconds and change before coming back to hand in the run down the backstretch. Seems to be a bit of a highly strung filly, although she did not get quite as hot as she did the previous morning".

I departed Heathrow Airport with many European, Premiership and Carling Cup matches being played. But my trip was critical for I had been leaving for Mallorca some weeks ago but the death of my mother was heartbreaking and the family George and Julie, the main reasons I could not leave. So I was Breeders Cup bound and one of the worst flights I have ever been on, it was a ten-hour nightmare. Virgin have dropped their standards and I'm sure I'll never fly them again. Anyhow I reached there unscathed and was looking forward to continue my friendship with the as ever impressive Jimmy Duggan, the ex-Fred Winter rider who, if he had knocked the booze on the head a few years earlier could and would have won many more accolades and had several big races under his belt. That is wrong for me to say – knock the booze on the head altogether, just got his priorities right working and winning first, then once making your name in the game like Dunwoody, Bradley, McCourt, Smith-Eccles, Scudamore and of course John Francome probably the 'daddy' of them all. I say probably as John McCririck has pinned 'Greatest jockey' on his lapel. But Jimmy is Jimmy and a wonderful young man who has a beautiful wife, a wedding I attended just four months ago. He picked me up from the airport and was waiting with my son Anthony as I came through the International Customs. I suppose that James, as I always call him, walks a very thin line, but the reason we care about each other, sounds quite silly, is that we know now just where the ice is less thinner!

The journey started here and I never knew I would be bumping into another great pal of mine, Don Shanks the legendary ex-Fulham, Luton Town and Queens Park Rangers full-back and a good one at that. Don and I have worked together many times, coaching the youngsters of Stoke-on-Trent light years ago. So my Breeders Cup began alongside Donald and Anthony, my 22 year-old son, who had only been to the races once before, a Windsor meeting where we had a race ran for Ian Hutchinson who died so sadly about a year ago. I mention this more in my book SPECTACULAR which will be out by the time I reach the end of this book which will be on the day of the FA Cup Final unless the Blues reach the Champions League Final that is!

Once we left the Seabiscuit Marquee after a couple of Smirnoff Ice's, Anthony and I headed for the Grandstand where we sat about thirty yards from the dirt track and not much more away from the winning post. I cannot explain just how I felt, the excitement and expectations so great, especially after speaking to Fallon and Gary Stevens just two days prior. This is the World Cup of Thoroughbred Racing and the atmosphere simply electric with the tension holding. Back to the races and a couple of morning workouts where we watched from the famous CLOCKERS CORNER which was named for obvious reasons. It was here I met the great Gary Stevens, a star in the new blockbuster SEABISCUIT. Gary has been a champion many times and a man of wonderful disposition in a world back in England where so many stars believe their own headlines and carry a chip around with them. Santa Anita racecourse was my destination and I was far from disappointed although I had been there before but not for an event like this one here and now. Sitting with the legendary Kieran Fallon was a complete pleasure and my son was in awe 'star-struck' which is allowed as the Irishman is a genius in the saddle and was going to be on a winner in a couple of days time, we could tell in his eyes when talking about her!

Fallon was cool as cool can be, a character who carries such self confidence it was almost impossible to back against him on Islington, the Michael Stoute trained filly who had about twenty lengths to make up as she ran the back straight which was completely opposite to what he spoke about before the race. Shanks, Anthony and I were on our feet as Fallon sat with five horses in front of him, but he sat as still as a summer's night. When the Shanks – binoculars focused – called "Fallon's sitting pretty, don't anyone panic, hold on to your tickets, he's running". The commentator yelled that Islington was sitting sixth but moving nicely and then Kieran pushed the button into second gear to move closer to the leading pack, this was the moment, turning for home, I was to begin losing my voice and when he hit the front my scream was quite like I would call for the ball at Highbury, White Hart Lane or even that memorable evening against the West Germans before a hundred thousand people on my International debut back in 1975. There were only an estimated 65,000 here but it seemed as if the entire world were there awaiting the two big races on the race card. But back to this race at this wonderful course, "Fallon loves Islington" I screamed as he hit the front on her with the line about fifty yards away, there being no way past Fallon once he presses the button into top gear and as hard as the jockey on the second tried he could not peg the English Champion back. Islington had won and the roar from the Brits was music to my ears!

This victory was a massive one for Stoute and Fallon and I was on cloud nine as I screamed to Sir Michael Stoute, "Sir Michael, I love Islington too". All we needed now was for Falbrav to win the big race for Shanks, who I mentioned was over there to aide Darryl Holland, another of our top horsemen. This was a race for the connoisseur, a one and a half mile on the Santa Anita dirt in the $4million clash. We were still on a real high from Islington and thought this was the day for the Brits to sweep away the rest of the world and, oh boy, Falbraz led everywhere but the finishing line, ridden almost to perfection by Holland, but I could not help thinking, without being critical of Darryl, that Fallon would have got Falbraz home as he just ran out of steam in this mile and a half contest. Our screams from the grandstand seemed to be working about fifty yards from the wire but High Chaparral, the Tabor champion, swooped and dead heated with Sohail with the very brave Falbrav a whisker back in third. We jumped and screamed but could not get Luca Cumani's brilliant colt home in front. Our celebrations were short lived but the day still buzzed and I know that neither one of us three would have rather have been anywhere else in the world. We were unlucky once again by shouting Congaree home, an American trained horse who looked like he would win but ran out of gas also. His trainer Bob Baffert calls Congaree the best horse in the country, but the big question is whether that title comes with an asterisk. Congaree is no doubt the best horse from seven furlongs to a mile and sixteenth. He whipped Aldebaran, the likely favourite for the Breeders Cup Sprint, over seven furlongs in April and in February he won going nine furlongs in the San Antonio Handicap at Santa Anita. All in all this was the best day I have ever experienced on a racetrack and made some new friends also. They say it is better to have love and lost than to never love at all and although I was not gambling I agree with that terminology on this most wonderful of race meetings. I moved on to my local bar, the First Cabin, to finish our day off and drank with Wayne Harris early the next morning. An ex-jockey born in Vancouver, British Columbia, Canada on the 10th of July 1947. He was an apprentice under trainer AG Smithers. He rode his first winner at Fort Erie Racetrack. He moved on to Woodbine and the Ontario Racing Circuit in the May of 1964. He rode all over the USA including Tropical Park, Hialeah and Gulfstream. He moved home to Vancouver in the January of 1967 and rode at Hastings Park till the fall took him to San Francisco. That same year he rode at Bay Meadows and had a very good beginning.

Eventually he moved to Santa Anita in the December and rode his first winner on his first mount for actor/singer/dancer, the wonderful Fred Astaire. "A nice horse Sharp Curve for trainer Lester Holt and it all snowballed from there on in," Wayne told me in modest style. He began riding winners thick and fast on 'very good horses'. He rode a nice filly called Pink Pigeon who was a champion 'turf' runner for three years and won many stakes races, including a world record over a mile and an eighth on the 'turf' of Santa Anita. He also got aquainted with trainer Jim Maloney who was training some of the most powerful stables in the United States at Claiborne Farms with William Hagen Perry and partners. "I rode a mare called Gamely a champion mare in 1969/70 and 71. Horses that included Baffle who set a track record over six and a half furlongs on the Hillside Course at Santa Anita a record that stood for many years" Wayne added. Bahia Key, a champion Californian bred miler. Ancient Title, another California bred sort who won at any distance. He also rode many stakes races back in Canada, such as Merger, who won the Queens Plate in 1968 in the biggest three-year-old race. Then there was Essence who won in the British Columbian Derby in 1970, the year I was a part of that great Chelsea team that won the FA Cup after a replay against Leeds United. This horse was owned by Frank McMahon who he rode a lot of good winners for in California. Wayne added that, "I rode 1300 winners or so and rode for the legendary Johnny Longdon stable." I thank Wayne for contributing to my story and send him my best wishes and hope that we will meet again sooner rather than later. My aim on my travels is to find people and places where I can find pleasure and the FIRST CABIN, about three hundred yards from the entrance of Santa Anita racetrack gave me that pleasure. But I am never amazed with the United States of America for this particular pleasure, or past time, if you like!

Where were we, yeah, back at Heathrow Airport on the 29th of October.

My flight was a little better coming back but I found myself not wanting to leave, however, not to overstay my welcome.

My first Breeders Cup had left me in a kind of daze, probably getting a little past being a youngster, yet on the right side of one of the senior squad.

But it's football once again and Chelsea, who once again kept the heat turned up as they win once again at Everton, a game they usually come away from without a squeak. This really is championship stuff. As regards the Tinker and Talisman I need to catch up on the week just gone, and it is just not trying to remember, sobering up and getting over the excitement of what Santa Anita and all that surrounds it has left with me.

There have been rumblings over another man from the same part of the world as to regards where his money has come from. What I would like to know is; how can the people who try to establish where the Russians get their money cannot justify where and how they got theirs?

My first weekend back was long and my resistance the same, but I found I was finding it difficult to keep up. That is what living or visiting the States does to me, what a country, I just love the United States of America.

At a glance at the newspapers, my face changes from tired to a smile as the bad become good, hiding behind the people who keep them both in and out of work and basically overpaid. Leeds United caught my eye immediately as this club, in the news so much lately for all the wrong reasons, are supposedly pinning their future on an Arab. Now if I am not too far out of the picture they know of only three things, one is oil, then women walking a couple of yards behind them and of course horses. In a nutshell football today sells its soul, if it ever had such a thing!

I can still recall being a young schoolboy who wanted to play the game I loved to play. Oh, how I feel so cheated by all of the work I put in surrounded by such fools. The memories of Johnny Haynes and Jimmy Greaves seem like it never happened and to make it even worse Robbie Williams sings Sinatra, Rod Stewart is recording the likes of Frank, Tony Bennett and all those wonderful voices from the days when I smiled so happily in our prefab just an Ian Hutchinson throw from Chelsea Football Club's front gates. But I have three sons and they think I have been in Vietnam, when I was in the Royal London Hospital for all that time, a time I do not want to dwell on. If you need to know read SPECTACULAR!

I need to catch up on the Kan Bates affair, as to why he has set up certain individuals, but I heard this in the First Cabin where there are serious football-lovers asking in their ignorance. That is not their fault for they have left the country just like I will eventually; the only difference is I have been in abreast of such people. What still harasses me is there is so much money without passion in their hearts for the game that is universal and brings more people together than anything else in life.

The Rio Ferdinand saga hits my face as I return home to leftover newspapers with headlines by the *Sun*: YOU'RE OUT TO RUIN RIO, in smaller print 'United hit back'...On this day Tuesday the 28th of October 2003, the following was reported by Neil Curtis: Manchester United will hit the FA with both barrels when they charge Rio Ferdinand. United have kept quiet since the England star's missed drugs test became public. But they are poised with a powerful statement over what they believe is an orchestrated campaign to ruin Ferdinand. An Old Trafford insider said "There has been a lot of surprise at the leaks coming out of the FA over this case. It is almost as if they have been deliberately preparing the ground to hit Rio with a tough charge". Details of Rio's mobile phone bill have been published alongside allegations of the club's lack of co-operation with the FA Investigation. Old Trafford chiefs are happy that they have done everything by the book.

But *Sunsport* has learned that United believe the FA have been quietly muddying the club's reputation before throwing the book at their player.

Ferdinand attended a preliminary hearing at Soho Square more than two weeks ago and is expected to be finally charged tomorrow (29th of October 2003).

But the alleged offence will be wilfully neglecting to take the drugs test at United's training ground on the 23rd of September, rather than just forgetting to take it.

The more serious charge carries a maximum ban of two years.

United are prepared to fight and have a legal team ready to battle with the FA all the way. And the FA are also sure to face another broadside from the PFA boss Gordon Taylor. He has accused the drug-testers of 'breaching players' confidentiality' by revealing that they have failed tests before disciplinarily hearings are held. But Fulham boss Chris Coleman is urging the FA to carry out MORE tests to in a bid to clean up football's bad boy image.

The former Wales defender said "There has been a lot of bad publicity around the game recently – and maybe if more players were cleared then it will be good for the game".

What I suggest is that the new Fulham manager keep his thoughts to himself at this moment in time for he is very new to the job ahead and in about six months time the same paper will be calling for his head. He was not seen to be saying too much when he had his own personal nightmare, which cost him his career. What I suggest is keep his mind on his own job. I am sure somewhere along the way he has driven over the limit or even taken one more pain killing tablet than prescribed. Only a year ago Coleman was fighting to get fit after a very bad car smash, never dreaming he would become the next Fulham manager. Or did he, I wonder? Anyhow a big part of management, and life in general, is to always keep your own glasshouse in order before voicing your unnecessary views on others.

Chelsea were delighted with their performance against Lazio – but I was not in the country to witness this fine 2–1 win – but had been told that the visitors were nothing to be feared and with them being my brother – John's – local team in Rome, know from him that they were or are on the decline, but they still need to be put in their place by this very expensive Chelsea football team.

There is one thing outstanding at this moment in time and that is the backbone of Chelsea's season rest on Frank Lampard and John Terry, two players improving rapidly, especially young Frank who was not impressing the Chelsea fans at the beginning of his new career here at the Bridge, but I told many, many fans to give him time and give him his right position and you will see the real Frank Lampard. I have watched him several times at West Ham and know he – if played properly – will be a match winner for the Blues on many occasions in this most important of seasons.

Chelsea 2 Lampard and Mutu Lazio 1: 41,140

I returned to London knowing the Chelsea had two good results in beating Kevin Keegan's Manchester City, very luckily in the end, by another Jimmy Floyd loan goal. It was interesting reading Mark Irwin of the *Sun* talking like this "It would certainly be interesting to compare Mutu's mileage with Jimmy Floyd who appears these days to be breaking into a jog now and again." He carried on, "Yet it was the Dutch striker who claimed the only goal of the game, stabbing a loose ball off his shin after David Seaman had pushed Mutu's fierce low cross in the 34th minute." One Sunday headline went THEY THINK IT'S ALL OVER /IT IS NOW FOR CREAKY OLD SEAMAN

Steve Curry has taken a liking to the new Chelsea hero Adrian Mutu as he begins his match report with 'Law Student Adrian Mutu is a mummy's boy, but try convincing the Premiership's best defenders of the fact and they might show you a few bruises and call for a debate on the issue. Of all the galacticos assembled in west London, courtesy of Roman's rouble chest, the Romanian stands out as the most exciting and an antidote to those so-called professionals who have done little to enhance the image of the game. The Premiership is fortunate in its collection of striking talent. There are Thierry Henry, Ruud van Nistelrooy and from Eastern Europe, via Italy, comes this compact, tough little tank full of sophisticated machinery. All three are world-class players, different in their style and physique, but all are capable of scoring goals and offering different perspectives on the art of striking. To upstage two strikers of the quality of Nicholas Anelka and Robbie Fowler is no mean feat, but Mutu eclipsed both, even if Manchester City did demonstrate that their top seven place in the table is not false. Mutu is an all-action participant, a tireless runner and chaser, yet single minded and focused in the penalty area and destined to contribute richly to the continuing success of the English top flight. Claudio Ranieri admits he was wary of a Champions League reaction of the kind Manchester United appeared to suffer against Fulham and that he sensed there was not the required intensity in the dressing room before the game. The Chelsea coach said "United and Arsenal are used to playing in the Champions League in midweek and then playing in the league on a Saturday but for us it's the first time. At least I have a lot of players and I can change. After a good result like we had against Lazio, it's not easy to recharge your batteries. I changed some players and put fresh people in". Mutu was warned by Dan Petrescu about the physical side of the game here, but he says that, "I don't worry because I don't scare easily". Mutu is studying for a law degree with the encouragement of his mother Rodica, who is living in London to look after her boy. Yeah, Steve Curry likes Mutu alright, but I wonder what the winter months bring as the chill is setting in as we ease out of October and even though I have just arrived back from the United States of America I could tell as soon as the wheels touched down.

Chelsea 1 Jimmy Floyd Manchester City 0: 41,040

Back in Manchester there was an even better result for Chelsea as neighbours Fulham put the skids under Sir Alex's team with a very impressive display of all out attacking football. This performance led to headlines a week later in the *Sunday People* that read: FERGIE IN £7.7million SAHA SWOOP. Sir Alex Ferguson is close to tying up a shock £7.7million deal for Fulham striker Louis Saha, says Steve Bates; who goes on to say that he can reveal that Manchester United have identified the 25-year-old Frenchman as their main target for the January transfer window and negotiations are about to begin with Fulham for Saha's release after Christmas. United have done their homework on Saha and are ready to pounce for a player who played a key role in Fulham's shock 3-2 win at Old Trafford. The United boss has been a long time admirer and has instructed the club to make sure he becomes a United player in the New Year.

Chris Coleman, as I wrote earlier, is quickly learning his new trade but the ball is going to bounce a few more times before he will be counted. Arsenal drew at Charlton, which made this a very good weekend for the Blues and next up was a 4-2 win, over minnows Notts County in the Carling Cup and now they travel to Merseyside, where they have already won this season, to face the Toffee Men. This will give the Tinkerman something to chew on, as his team seem to have recovered from that disappointing defeat on their last trip to Highbury. David Moyes' team are struggling a little but they will not be giving Chelsea an inch in this one. As we approach this match the Tinker and Talisman will both be delighted over the three results in eight days while others around them drop points. This was always going to be a close one and

Chelsea are stringing results together without looking like a Premiership winning team of late, but it is points on the board that count around a time English conditions change dramatically, which is always a test for overseas players. After a 1-0 defeat Everton's David Moyes said that, "You cannot miss the chances we got. It is frustrating that we had as many chances against Chelsea as we do against lesser sides". This was also a day when Wayne Rooney said that, "I am not interested in anything Chelsea have to say". This was after rumours of a bid to ease him from Merseyside to London. Moyes' view on the matter was that "Wayne Rooney is playing and that is that. You can see how he is performing and make your own judgement". Back to Rooney and "I am happy at Everton and when I hear stories about Chelsea I just start laughing". As for the match itself it was won by an Adrian Mutu header – which on the TV monitor later showed more than just a glimpse of handball just before taking his chance – this goal keeping Chelsea in the three way mix-up with United and Arsenal who had an emphatic 4-1 win at Elland Road – a win that pushed Leeds closer to the Premiership dungeon. Back at Goodison Park and Mutu the impressive Rumanian. The goal was no classic as Jimmy Floyd fluffed a great opportunity to get his eighth League goal – but Mutu threw himself to head home four minutes after halftime. Moyes was not a happy man saying "I have seen it and he got an arm on the ball before his head". The goalkeeper more than made up for a couple of blunders of late by making a couple of superb saves and that was the difference between the two teams. Off the field of play Jimmy Floyd was once again linked with a swap with Barcelona's Patrick Kluivert. It seems that this crops up every time the Dutch Destroyer fails to score – maybe just a coincidence?

The Wednesday before saw the new players being introduced to the Carling Cup and tasting football against the 'Ragass Rovers' of the English game but Notts County visited the Bridge with nothing to lose – only a football match – and they gave as good as they got before being overpowered by that extra dimension of class once they threatened to spoil Chelsea's party. They really did play well but Chelsea had their minds on bigger fish and were more than just happy to move on from this potential banana skin, and get on with their push to dethrone Manchester United of their Premiership crown!

The Carling Cup match was in between these two big wins for the Blues and the kind of a match that sometimes proves to be that big bad banana skin where players and managers alike cannot work out just how a performance can drop so low. I know the easy answer is the lull after the storm or the just a mere anti-climax but today that should not be the case for, with the kind of squads Chelsea have, they should be able to pick three teams to beat a lowly Notts County. And when you think that apart from having all these players in one's yard they also have a player at Birmingham, Mikael Forssell, who I happen to think is as good as any front player at Stamford Bridge and if I were gambling I will say he'll go pretty close to outscoring all of their big money target men. So be told, keep an eye our for this very talented marksman, who not only scores goals at the highest level – including internationally – but holds the line up well and has the ability to turn defenders and leave them for dead. The mystery continues as to why he is not wearing the Blue of Chelsea instead of the blue of Birmingham!

Anyhow, after a scare from the smaller club in Nottingham, Chelsea finally put the tie to bed after the black and white striped shirted strugglers played a big part in making this match watch-able!

Chelsea 4 Jimmy Floyd, Gudjohnsen 2 and Cole Notts County 2: 35,997

Everton 0 Chelsea 1 Mutu 40,189

My pal Harry Redknapp was not too despondent after watching his side go down 3-0 at Old Trafford for they were still very much in the match until ten minutes from time when Ronaldo and Keane scored inside two minutes. Roy Keane's strike was as sweet as they come and as Ferguson said "It was a terrific strike and probably his first goal for the club with his left foot." It was in fact his 49th goal for the club by the United skipper. Portsmouth though, had just played at Newcastle United and Manchester United after beating Liverpool at Fratton Park. Had you asked Harry if he would have accepted three draws from these three matches I believe he might have taken it. However, they were beaten twice but still got their three points and learned important lessons along the way. With this in mind, losing can sometimes be a far better lesson, although it hurts at the time. Portsmouth have now played all the top clubs away from home except Chelsea so my mate will not be quietly displeased with both his and his team's efforts as the season enters the last final third and that's the time Manchester United usually come good, rather like Islington.

THE BOOK THEY TRIED TO BAN

It was now Manchester United's turn to hit the newspapers for all the wrong reasons, but try as they might the I went ahead and printed four pages of ex-club security chief Michael 'Ned' Kelly in his sensational new book – the book United tried to ban. There are pornographic details, the most horrifying being the one when Sir Alex Ferguson raged that "It's unbelievable, the press would have a field day with this". It all began when Martin Edwards went to award some prizes at an SAS barracks and was seen following a soldier's wife into the ladies' toilets. In 1996 United press secretary Ken Ramsden warned Sir Alex that his Chairman's visits to the ladies' toilet were becoming more and more frequent. Kelly says that, "I know boss, I must be the only security chief in football who has to try and stop the chairman going into the ladies' room." Other revelations included Roy Keane, Ryan Giggs, Eric Cantona and Dion Dublin. Whilst all of this was going on the first signs of trouble in the Beckham household loomed as it was revealed that David Beckham is furious that his wife Victoria had gone back on her word as to moving out to Spain with him. Her refusal follows a few pictures of both parties out on the town with somebody else. The *News of the World's* Rav Singh reports that after repeatedly promising the Real Madrid multi-millionaire and footballer that she and their two sons, Brooklyn, four years old, and his younger brother Romeo, would be joining him very soon. But she has spent just five days in Madrid since his move from Manchester United in the close season. She now says that her singing career comes first. He also says that the Real star told a pal that "Victoria is staying in the UK because of her career. I am really hurt – it's all a nightmare."

"YOU MAY BE DISAPPOINTED IF YOU FAIL
BUT YOU ARE DOOMED IF YOU DON'T TRY"

Beverly Sills

I find this may apply to Mrs Beckham, but if she hasn't
cracked it by now, with all of her powers and high finance
then I think there's something more here than meets the eye.

Alan Hudson

"It is hard for me to take in that my wife and boys are going to stay at our home in Hertfordshire. I love her so much". The Chelsea owner Abramovich will be watching this situation with great interest for he has made noises about if ever it all went belly-up in Madrid he would welcome David to Chelsea with open arms. David continued that, "I am playing the best football of my career but my marriage means everything to me. Chelsea would be an option but in about two years time". His wife, an ex-Spice Girl, told an aide that "This is the last chance to save my solo career and I will do anything to make it work. I am working flat out to make it possible and to do this I have to stay in the UK where my record label and my manager are. If it means we are apart so be it." David is worried about his wife's relationship with rap producer Damon Dash. Real will take this news like a bolt out of the blue skies of Madrid and will be preparing for what could become a real blockbuster, but we ask ourselves can they lose out here?

The quick assessment is no they cannot for I believe the new Chelsea are doing some preparing of their own. This seems a little too spooky to me with photographs of both of them out on the town so many miles apart, can it be a set-up is my question!

I LIVED

So the *News of the World* have been a real mixed bag for the Manchester United manager this Sunday, the second day of November, for it was his wife that Sir Alex transferred more than David. Is this a surprise?

Knowing the media the way I do, they have been banging the drum for the Beckhams in their war against Manchester United, even after the roasting they gave him for getting himself sent-off against Argentina in the World Cup. Since then he was made captain of his country by caretaker manager Peter Taylor and has been a national hero ever since he hit that magnificent last ditch free-kick against the Greeks, that took us through to the Finals of the last World Cup. To say David is an icon is an understatement, getting even more publicity than the great George Best, but they have lived opposite sides of this weird and wonderful football fencing. David is dedicated in every aspect of the game with just one minor flaw, Victoria, and her singing voice that comes with her. The Beckhams have enough money to start up their very own music company, something that would be more logical than all of this palaver. There are plenty of people out there without work who have knowledge enough to be put to the test by the Beckhams, for what is a £1million or two to the biggest earner in the history of the game. That is if you take his earnings both on and off the field!

This storm will give Sir Alex a feeling of warmth, not to be nasty but to let the world know just what he had to deal with whilst David's wife waltzed through Old Trafford as if it were Harrods. The British Press will be sharpening up their knives and rubbing their hands while the blade is on the stove. I have experienced the might of the press more than once, even when I was washed up as a player and trying to find my way through life after my biggest assets were withering away in the Intensive Trauma Unit. They had me on the front pages of the *News of the World* knowing full well I was set-up, yet took great joy in calling me the day before to give me the news that I was now a pimp.

I ask you!

But that sells their precious fish and chip wrappings and we are nothing but a spare potato that they can cut into little pieces before serving the shark. I took it on the chin and laughed it off which some members of my family found a little strange. But as time went by I had the last laugh, for my fight against the bigger demons was tackled in exactly the same way. I worked hard to clear my name but failed, but what I lost in that newspaper I gained tenfold, by finding out once again, who's who!

I used these types of embarrassing situations, the experience of a wandering wife and just plain old sweat and toil to get me through this all. I mentioned in the first few pages that I lived the dream, but I have also lived the many nightmares that life brings with them and fought my way back and it tastes so much sweeter when your enemies – demons – are out of your life and life becomes far more precious.

I lived!

I am not and do not like being the kind of person to say I told you so, but I have said from day one that this marriage will be the biggest story in the history of the world outside the kind of wars that come around every now and then, but I told you so!

My friends will tell you that it was merely a matter of time in my book and this is my book. We are living in the same world as when growing up, only we change the rules. Without the newspapers where would the world be today, much like the aeroplane, the fax machine, the mobile phone, the E-mail and so on and so on, cha, cha, cha!

The next few weeks in football will be gigantic as Chelsea's powers-to-be seem to have everything falling into place with getting points on the board, going steadily into the Champions League without setting the world alight, but as soon as the transfer window opens there will be some serious spending at Stamford Bridge, dwarfing what has been sensational stuff already. Having said that if they are so hell bent on getting rid of the Tinkerman it would be a double jeopardy to spend more money like in the summer, and whoever was responsible for such transfers needs kicking out of the club immediately. But nobody will tell us just who it was, the fly on the wall again!

THE FIRST WEEK OF NOVEMBER WAS TO BE ANOTHER MASSIVE ONE WITH THE FIRST MATCH AWAY TO LAZIO!

On the first Sunday of November, Fulham had a great opportunity to get closer to the big three if they could overcome Liverpool at Loftus Road, the ground they are making more of a fortress than their very own Craven Cottage. They had enough of the ball and at times looked the far better side, but Liverpool hung in there and won with a Danny Murphy penalty two minutes from normal time. The headlines in the *Mail* on Monday read **LIVERPOOL BACK IN THE TITLE RACE**.

Personally I cannot believe that this team can win the championship – or even make fourth place – for they do not have the all-round ability as Manchester United, Arsenal, Chelsea or Newcastle United, although the Magpies have had a very sticky start to their campaign. Charlton are also a very decent team now and give as good as they get whether at the Valley or on their travels up the M1 or M6. The way Liverpool play since Gerrard Houllier took over leaves a lot to be desired and in my mind I can see Mr Bill Shankly walking the steps above shaking his head in disappointment. Okay, the season before last they won three cups: the FA Cup, Worthington, now the Carling, and the UEFA Cup, which goes to show winning is not the be all and end all, for the fans – especially the 'Mickey Mousers' – want entertainment after a week trying to put bread on the table. Manchester United and Arsenal win in style and soon Chelsea will be along those lines set by Sir Alex Ferguson. On the last day of last season when they came to Stamford Bridge and played the Blues for that fourth place in the Champions League, their performance was far too predictable and in a nutshell they went out like a November the 5th banger without the bang, Liverpool are not for me and I would pull the curtains if they were playing in my back garden!

In the same Monday paper the headlines were all about Chelsea's Joe Cole who had his best game in the new away colours of all white with a blue sash right down the middle. Cole also played more minutes in this game than any other in his new Chelsea colours. Peter Johnson wrote about how far Wayne Rooney has to go to catch Joe Cole up, but I find that ridiculous as Cole, in comparison, is an old hand at the game right now and let's be fair. playing at Everton is a little different from playing for Chelsea at this moment in time.

However young Rooney, just eighteen on Saturday, is being expected to win games on his own at Goodison Park – far too much pressure to put on the shoulders of one so young and in his infancy at the top level.

I would use Rooney in spells, but not in a way where you need something extra to get them out of the mire, simply use him to expose the weaknesses you see in the opposition, for that is what great players are all about. I saw no reason to show you any more of this match report!

THE WHIPPING BOY

There was sad news in the *Daily Express* where two men I know, one very well indeed and one who I met just the once when having lunch with Tony Banks MP at the House of Commons. The heading looked like this; **IS REID SET TO BECOME BIRCH WHIPPING BOY**; Now when I met Trevor Birch at the Commons he was brimming with new found confidence that had lifted the gloom of the receivers taking over at Stamford Bridge and I believe Birch was in some way responsible and within a few short weeks he was given a choice to stand down to a lower position under their latest signing which had shipped Peter Kenyon from Manchester United. He chose to take the money, estimated in excess of £2million, and took the first offer thereafter and one of incredible choice of the new chief executive officer of Leeds United. Matthew Dunn wrote after Arsenal had just wiped the floor with Leeds at Elland Road that 'Peter Reid will start handing out the punishment this week, though it his he who must face the Birch after Leeds' worst start to a season in 54 years.' It does not help to read that Australian Mark Viduka is having his very own personal run-in with Reid. The Aussie turned up late twice in two days in some kind of 'stand' against both manager and club. Reid is expected to fine him £130,000 for starters, the sum of two weeks' wages, which is the maximum fine a player can be hit by. Knowing Peter the way I do, he would like to have just shown him the door and gave him a one-way ticket to his homeland and I could not agree with that more. The Leeds manager came into this football club with good intentions, although he knew that there had just been a war there between Peter Ridsdale, David O'Leary, Terry Venables and Professor John McKenzie and there were no signs of the debris being cleared when he agreed to take the job. You might say in a position like that the only way is up, but I am afraid this was a job for the invisible being of Houdini. Peter Reid will get paid a substantial amount when the inevitable happens but I can promise this man is one of great passion and is not at home around 'losers'. I can only feel sorry for Peter and say if he does not want money for getting a team relegated he can put it my way or we can just enjoy it together. Peter is one of the game's great social creatures and our first meeting was at Chester Races when I think we were the last two punters out of the place. On this Monday the top and bottom of the Premiership looked like this:

	P	W	D	L	F	A	PTS
Arsenal	11	8	3	0	23	9	27
Chelsea	11	8	2	1	21	9	26
Manchester United	11	8	1	2	21	6	25
Birmingham City	10	5	4	1	9	5	19
Wolves	11	2	3	6	7	23	9
Leicester City	11	2	2	7	16	21	8
Blackburn	11	2	2	7	15	21	8
Leeds United	11	2	2	7	10	25	8

That is the top and bottom of it in the first week of November and though there is a live Premiership match on this evening it will not effect either of the above.

This is how the goal-scoring list looks at the moment:
- 10   Premiership goals: Henry
- 9   Shearer (Newcastle)
- 8   van Nistelrooy and Owen
- 7   Beattie and Saha
- 6   Jimmy Floyd and Angel

Off the field it was no surprise to find that the *News of the World* story about the Beckhams was nonsense as they were seen lovey-dovey in Madrid yesterday holding hands. How these newspapers make fools of people, never considering people's families at such times. But what's new?

SEABISCUIT

On the eve of Chelsea's massive match travelling to play Lazio, my eldest son Allen and I had to go see the blockbusting motion picture Seabiscuit. From the first time Jeff Bridges set foot onto the Santa Anita dirt track I was back sitting at Clockers Corner as horses glided by, some cantering, others running to the clock and some walking the course backwards. All in a day's work for people who love thoroughbreds and don't want them to be a loser. Seabiscuit is your son, your daughter and everything you want within your family. I had read the book and could not wait to see the motion picture with Gary Stevens – a friend through Jimmy Duggan – who plays his first part in a movie and had been approached by Stephen Spielberg to play a part in an upcoming movie of his. Gary Stevens is a tremendous fella, and I repeat myself once again by saying it never ceases to astound me that the bigger the personality the better the person. Back to this wonderful little mare, who jumps out from the screen like King Kong on top of the Empire State Building and, like that gigantic ape, he is crying out for understanding and by doing so caught Tom, his handler's, attention.

Seabiscuit is a great example of someone being treated wrongly and the old saying of 'If only horses could talk'" springs to mind as I sat watching this marvellous motion picture.

The Biscuit fights for everyone one who wants to fight for some kind of respect and achievement along a path through life, which had him very much understood by many well known horse handlers. Could this be some kind of parallel to the Tinkerman as he seems to not have much time to get immediate success and – as in the States – they don't suffer fools for too long, especially the big cigar blowing boys in sport!

I just wish I could be intelligent enough to write about this incredible part of the history of a mere horse. I was fortunate enough to have spoken to the fantastic Red Rum and he educated me by the way he conducted himself in front of people and took all his successes like a real 'superstar'. It was my pleasure indeed to be alongside a champion of champions one evening at Uttoxeter Racecourse and I have a photograph of this wonderful Grand National treble winner trained by Ginger McCain, along the outback of all places, Southport Beach. Not very USA or Dubai but a quite phenomenal achievement by the trainer who has lived off this one horse forever. This is only one of the reasons I feel as I do about this pony-sized throwback because he beat all the odds and along the way carried everyone's dreams past every furlong pole he ran. The heart is the strongest part of your body but in comparison to War Admiral he was a horse, human being, so much smaller, but a bigger part of the family than anyone who thinks big is the name of the game. I have been fortunate to have had a two-year-old little baby girl as a part of my life, but in reality have three sons without saddles, as I flew the clouds without a passport or visa, those days when my life was in the hands of those fantastic surgeons and consultants over the last six years.

But in time you find out that you have lost all the things that made you happy, you know all of a sudden, through hard work and heartache, these hopes and dreams can really come true. Once finding your mentor, for the want of a better word, you actually see life through different eyes and understand everyone who surrounds you. I truly believe that can happen and Seabiscuit is my example to all men women and children. These are dreams come true, call me a dreamer, but don't bet on it!

You don't walk down the aisle with a young chestnut, you walk down the path of life, she looking after you and you looking after her, but, oh boy, you would die for her not just running herself into a place but coming back home looking you in the eye to tell you that she is okay, so much more than I got from all of my ex-wives and girlfriends for most of the time. I simply loved the 'lady' and if only I could turn the clock back and make the big decision again about all the females I have either lived with, loved or just simply spent a night with 'My Lifetime Lady' would always be in my bed, but not like the one in Mr Wolfe's bed in the movie 'The Godfather' when the Hollywood mogul would not see common sense. The movie Seabiscuit just brought me back into Reg Hollinshead's yard which is a mixture of delight and despair because I was at home with her there, yet never being able to take care of her for the rest of her life. I was nervous when she came out of the box, and proud, and when she was being cushioned into the starting stalls at Ripon, Catterick Park or Chepstow. I was completely out of touch with the real world, as it gripped me and held me from that moment onwards as I sat watching never wanting it to end. I watched Jeff Bridges in this movie and am very sure he will be leaving Hollywood when the time comes with the Oscar for 'best actor'!

His performance was awesome as they say in the USA and loving this country so much, I stick my badge on him, calling the tune in that wonderful situation about great lead actors and screen actresses. This was a simply superb Bridges performance and I will be the first man throwing my hat in the air when he gets his just rewards for his super display.

'A STORY OF HOW THREE MEN AND A GREAT HORSE CAPTIVATED THE WORLD'

An unlikely champion, he was as a rough-hewn, undersized horse with a sad little tail, and knees that wouldn't straighten all the way. At a gallop, he jabbed one foreleg sideways, as if he were swatting flies. For two years, he fought his trainers and floundered at the lowest level of racing, misunderstood and mishandled, before his dormant talent was discovered by these three men.

One was Red Pollard, a failed prizefighter and failing jockey who had been living in a horse stall since being abandoned as a boy at a makeshift racetrack. Another was Tom Smith, 'The Lone Plainsman', an enigmatic mustang breaker who had come from a vanishing frontier, bearing generations of lost wisdom about the secrets of horses. The third was a cavalry veteran Charlie Howard, a former bicycle repairman who had made a fortune by introducing the automobile to the American West.

In the sultry summer of 1936, Howard bought Seabiscuit for a bargain-basement price and entrusted him to Smith and Pollard. Using frontier methods that raised eyebrows on the backstretch, they discovered that beneath the hostility and fear was a gentlemanly horse with keen intelligence, awe-inspiring speed, and a ferocious competitive will. It was the beginning of four years of extraordinary drama, in which Seabiscuit overcame a phenomenal run of bad fortune to become one of the most spectacular performers in sports history.

Competing in the cruellest years of the Depression, the rags to riches horse emerged as an American cultural icon, drawing an immense and fanatical following, inspiring an avalanche of merchandising, and establishing himself as the single biggest newsmaker of 1939 – receiving more coverage than FDR or Hitler.

Laura Hillenbrand beautifully renders this breathtaking saga of one horse's journey from also-ran to national luminary. Seabiscuit; An American Legend is an inspiring tale of unlikely heroes, a classic story of three embattled individual overcoming the odds in the Great Depression.

It was whilst watching this movie, having read the book and experienced Santa Anita, that it all came flooding back. Then I remembered on the eve of the race, my son went for a run and left me at a Metro bus stop on Huntingdon Drive. I had four bagfuls of new clothing and shoes. I had been waiting for the bus to come along for about fifteen minutes when a rental automobile pulled up and opened its electric window on the passenger side. A New York voice asked if I knew where the track was!

I said that if they dropped me over to the furthest side of the car park that would see them into the racetrack itself. "Jump in" said the driver, who by now had learned.

They had travelled down from Boston for the big race. Once in the car the driver said, "The last time we picked someone up looking for the racetrack he was a Londoner and he tipped us a winner. What do you know", in which I replied by saying that believe it or not I was talking with Kieran Fallon and he loves the chances of Islington in the $2million race on the turf. They did not seem too impressed, so I followed up with saying that we were hopeful that Falbrav would also win the other big race worth $4million. The two men from Boston thanked me, I thanked them and they sped away and I just wondered what they thought when Fallon began his beautifully timed run to win on his only ride of the day. You must buy the book, after you've bought mine that is, and go and treat yourself to the movie. If you manage to do so, take plenty of Kleenex!

Today is the big week of Champions League Football once again and it meant that Chelsea flew to Rome to face Lazio whilst Manchester United hosted Glasgow Rangers and the Daily Mail headline read;

'MONTH OF DESTINY'
NOVEMBER HOLDS NO FEARS AS RANIERI
RELISHES HIS BIG CHANCE

It is all Chelsea on the inside of the back page with the first picture of Roman Abramovich watching a training session. On the other side of the page the headline was that **Chelsea to agree £8million Ayala deal in January.**

Neil Moxley reports from Rome that, "Roman Abramovich will use financial muscle to sign Valencia defender Roberto Ayala for Chelsea when the transfer window opens in January.

The Russian will ask the Spanish club to name their price in a bid to beat off interest from several leading European clubs.

Chelsea may fork out around £8million to land Ayala, 31, rated as one of the world's best defenders. He is back in favour at Valencia after being left out for psychological reasons earlier this season'.

Chelsea are preparing to pounce after a proposed move by the player to Real Madrid broke down because of the size of the fee. Valencia's chief executive Manuel Llorente said that "There is interest from Chelsea, but they are not the only team who want to sign him. There are some other important interested teams as well".

This is where my mate comes into the picture, Tony Banks, the former Sports Minister has challenged Abramovich to come clean about his long-term plans for Chelsea.

The lifelong Chelsea fan wants the Russian billionaire to talk to fans still unsure of his motives for investing so heavily in the west London club!

Banks, who flew out yesterday with the official party ahead of tonight's Champions League match against Lazio, has already upset the Russian's entourage by calling for an investigation into Abramovich's affairs. Whilst he has admitted that the 36-year-old's commitment cannot be questioned to date – a £110million spree in the transfer market has proved reassurance until now – he believes it is time for more assurances.

My good friend Banks said that "I am not being critical – just quizzical. It has been some months now since Mr Abramovich assumed control and we still haven't heard anything at all about his long-term plans. The silence has been deafening. I am a Chelsea supporter first and foremost and I am grateful of what he has done so far. However, will he still be around in five, ten or fifteen years like the rest of us?"

Sadly it appears that only time will tell and after I voiced my initial concerns I have met some of his people and they have told me he isn't using Chelsea Football Club as a toy. But it is a fact that this club is now heavily committed to some hefty players' contracts. What happens if he were to walk away?

TONY AND ME

I have known Tony Banks for quite some time now and can assure everyone who is following this case that he speaks for the fans. I must say though, I cannot see what business it is of others about where he got his money and how long he is going to stay, for if he walked away, although the club would be in serious trouble, the players have got enough money out of their individual deals with Chelsea Football Club, after all take someone like Winston Bogarde who was purchased from Barcelona about three or four years ago and has played merely a handful of matches in that time. As Peter Osgood says in his After Dinner speeches, "Winston Bogarde has the best job in the world, he gets £30,000 a week and has Saturdays off". There have always been people in the game who are not as passionate as the next man and I go back to Marcel Desailly, the Frenchman who was leaving the club only days before the Talisman came along. Money still is the very root of all things evil. But for the moment Chelsea have that in abundance, at least whilst Roman is around and I hope that is forever because since Matthew Harding died Chelsea has lost a lot of love and plenty of charm which the ex-Chelsea Football Club fanatic brought to the club and that is apart from the many millions of pounds he put into the club.

As I write these words my mobile rings and it none other than Tony Banks calling from Parliament. It is really my turn to buy lunch but Tony is the most splendid host at the House of Commons, he has absolutely no problem twisting my arm. We talk football over lunch mainly and although Tony is far more intelligent than I am, we are pretty much on the same wavelength when it comes to our passion for the game we both adore. I am very happy indeed to be able to call him 'my friend', and friends to me don't come easily. I suggest that he calls me Monday after his always-busy weekend, especially with the Blues at home, so we can fix up our lunch appointment. He will no doubt want to tell me all about Rome and the drubbing his Chelsea gave Lazio. Before he does though I will give you a couple of headlines and my thoughts on this performance. But just before I do, I would just like to show you how the 'Tinkerman' looked forward to this match. Here's how Steve Curry put it, along with quotes from Ranieri beginning with this: "It doesn't matter what the Italians think of me. I always look forward. The Italian papers believe that the English journalists hate me but I don't believe this. I don't understand this because we have a good relationship.

"We have an important month ahead of us, but it seems to me now that every match is important. To Mr Abramovich every result is important, but he does not put us under pressure. He always seems to enjoy the matches and he is very supportive all of the time."

Curry says that: Frank Lampard has been a revelation, responding to the arrival of Juan Sebastian Veron and Joe Cole by raising his own game. The 'Tinkerman' comes in again with "This is the kind of fixture I came to Chelsea hoping to be involved in.

"We have a winning mentality now and this is one we really want to win.

"We have a lot of internationals with experience of these games and a lot of hungry younger players, and we will all be up to it. It is one of the biggest games I have been involved in. There has been a lot of interest in Italy and Spain in the money we spent in the summer and it makes teams want to beat us".

'The Tinkerman, you sense, is structuring a team in which five or six players are now regarded as automatic choices. Carlo Cudicini, John Terry, Wayne Bridge, Lampard and Mutu are more or less permanent fixtures.

The match in Rome began with Lazio desperately needing a win to keep their Champions League hopes alive, but Chelsea bossed the early exchanges and did not have to wait too long before taking the lead. Once Chelsea were in front Lazio never looked worthy of getting back into a match that became very one sided and once the Italian outfit realised they were going to get nothing they showed the other side of their game by aiming nasty tackles at any given opportunity and when Mutu was spat at by Sinisa Mihajlovic he did brilliantly to hold his cool and simply get on with the match. This was the worst Italian club side I have ever seen in European Cups both here and abroad. They lacked any kind of thought, control or imagination to their game and it was plain to see that Chelsea were cruising into a different world than Lazio were in. Headlines were not better than the *Daily Star* and David Wood's summing up of an emphatic victory, which was very well organised apart from the sending-off of young Glen Johnson. *The Star* said that **CLAUDIOS ALL FOUR IT: A Roman holiday as Chelsea go on rampage**: It was Rome sweet Rome for Claudio Ranieri last night as his Chelsea braves kept their cool in a clash that was something out of Gladiator.

The Blues were subjected to a real battering led by the cynical Serb Sinisa Mihajlovic, but survived to surely guarantee their qualification from Group G with this stunning victory. In truth, Chelsea could and should have won by a bigger margin, had striker Hernan Crespo been sharper in front of goal. The £10million Argentine hit-man, a former Lazio favourite, did score the first but should have been getting his new Chelsea team-mates to sign the match ball as a hat-trick was his for the taking. Having spurned three great chances after his strike in the 15th minute, he was substituted in the 67th minute. And his replacement Eidur Gudjohnsen took just three minutes to claim the second to set up a famous victory for Ranieri on his return to his native Rome. A great individual goal from Damien Duff in the 75th minute ensured it was even sweeter and Ranieri could hardly believe his eyes when Frank Lampard made it four five minutes later. Lazio and manic Mihajlovic found their mauling by the blues hard to take.

The 34-year-old, who was banned by UEFA for two matches in 2000 for racially abusing Patrick Viera, was at it again last night. In the 34th minute he spat in the face of Mutu after the Romanian had caught him in the face with an elbow.

Russian referee Valentin Ivanov missed it but thankfully the TV cameras did not. And the official did spot two horrible tackles on Duff in the 50th and 52nd minutes, which saw him sent-off. At half-time Ivanov had to break up a scrap between Claude Makalele and Fernando Couto in the tunnel. All the Lazio nonsense, though, should not detract from a sensational performance by Chelsea, which inspired their fans to chant, "Are you watching Arsenal". Aside from Ranieri another Roman was left thrilled by the performance. Russian billionaire Roman Abramovich, who has invested £111million on players, must have left thinking it was money well spent.

For Chelsea, with three wins out of four Champions League matches this season looks like they are ready to become real challengers at home and in Europe.

Need time to gel?

They looked as if they had been together for years. But their first goal owed plenty of to poor handling by ex-Ipswich keeper Matteo Sereni. Another former favourite Juan Veron whipped in a curling 30-yard free kick, which evaded the onrushing blue shirts. Rather than push the ball to his left for a corner, Sereni palmed it straight at Crespo. He knew nothing about it as the ball struck him high on the chest and rebounded in.

Just before the break Crespo had two superb chances to claim his and Chelsea's second. Veron, another great performer last night, found him with a reverse pass and although he looked offside the flag stayed down.

But from the left hand side of the box he failed to get enough bend on his shot. Less than a minute later he had an even better chance with Chelsea's sixth attempt on goal in the half, a figure they doubled after the break.

Great work by Duff saw Mutu scurry clear and tee up Crespo. Rather than blast it, he tried a flick and Sereni gathered the ball. In the 64th minute Crespo was guilty again, missing the ball completely as Duff set him up with a great pull back. But the Blues were not to be denied. Lampard, who was excellent all night, set up Gudjohnsen's 70th minute goal with a left footed drive, which the helpful Sereni palmed straight to the Icelander. Duff's strike five minutes later was the pick of the night as he jinked in from the left, beating three men before driving in low at the far corner with his right foot. Gudjohnsen then repaid Lampard by sending in a rasping half volley from 25 yards. The hapless Sereni saved, but of course sent the ball straight to Lampard who bundled it in for number four after eighty minutes.

Celebrations were muted in the last minute when right back Glen Johnson was sent-off. He was booked for a push then earned a second caution and a red card, for kicking the ball away in disgust.

Ranieri was furious with his foolishness, as a one-match ban will follow. At the end Ranieri pushed on Franco Zola, who travelled from Cagliari for the match, to share the acclaim from the 4,000 blues fans. How Zola must be wishing he had stayed one more year at Stamford Bridge because this team is now starting to look like him – something special.

Lazio 0 Chelsea 4 Crespo 15, Gudjohnsen 70, Duff 75 Lampard 80
The attendance in the Olympic Stadium in Rome was 48,000.

In the other Group G match Besiktas beat Sparta Prague by a goal to nil in front of 18,000 people.

Headlines on the Thursday were more interesting as it takes a little time to take it all in and even that great cricket captain Alec Stewart was there to see it. The headlines in the Standard went like this:

'BOWLED OVER BY AN UNFORGETTABLE NIGHT OF BLUES IN ROME': Claudio Ranieri will want me to catch his plane more often. Tuesday's magnificent win over Lazio was the first time I've seen Chelsea in Europe and they couldn't have written the script any better. There are still lots of fans milling around the Vatican and they feel like they've been blessed. I had a word with a guy upstairs and it obviously worked. I honestly feel that I am a lucky charm. I went to see England play Italy in the same stadium when we needed a draw to qualify for the World Cup in 1997; so two visits have brought two great results. Tuesday was an absolutely fantastic night. Any kind of win there would have been a great result but 4-0 was absolutely outstanding. The performance was as good as I've seen Chelsea play in the thirty years I have been following them. Frank Lampard stood out for me but all the players were fantastic. Carlo Cudicini made some incredible saves, John Terry oozes fighting spirit and Adrian Mutu seems to be a unique footballer. It was my best night as a Chelsea fan. I've supported the Blues for more than 30 years so I've got used to taking the rough with the smooth. I picked them before the 1970 FA Cup Final replay against Leeds, not after the game like some people, and it's been that way ever since. My brother is a big Chelsea fan so it's partly a family thing, but dad supports Arsenal. I grew up with the strolling 1970's side of Peter Osgood and Alan Hudson, but John Hollins was my childhood hero. I used to wear the number four shirt for England in one day Internationals because of him. It's obviously a great time to be a Chelsea fan and I have seemed to have timed my retirement perfectly. Everyone keeps going on about the fact that we're buying some great individuals but we're playing as a team.

If we perform like we did against Lazio every week, no one will want to play Chelsea. We'll have frightened a fair few teams. It's been an amazing day all round and there's no way I'd rather be in Bangladesh with the England team. I seem to be busier than when I was playing, with PR and corporate work, dinners and golf days, so it's been good to have some time to myself. Rome is an incredible city and I've been a right Tommy Tourist. We've been there, done it and got the T-Shirt. The Vatican, Coliseum, Forum and Trevi Fountain. One of the reasons I retired from cricket was to devote more time to other aspects of my life; watching Chelsea is one of my main hobbies.

THE GREAT JIMMY GREAVES

I have admired Jimmy Greaves for many years once as a player, then a TV pundit and now *Sun* guest writer. Apart from all of that he is one of the nicest people you could ever come across. On the 8th day of November his Saturday column went like this; 'Manchester United and Arsenal are undoubtedly the two stallions of the Premiership.

'Big, strong, powerful and leading the chasing pack towards the finishing line. Yet I fear both trusty steeds are wearing blinkers right now and cannot see what is beside them. And given the exchange of the Premiership Trophy between Old Trafford and Highbury over recent years, it is hardly surprising. They talk about Scotland being a two-horse race – well it has been no different down here of late. But while this personal duel goes on, Chelsea have well and truly come up on the rails. And if the big two are not careful, they could start to stride ahead. Despite all the big spending and headline grabbing they have done this in a quiet and dignified way. Something you cannot describe of either Arsenal or Manchester United of late. The battles between the two and with the FA seem to be a never-ending saga. Now I am all for a good verbal just now and then. In fact, I think it helps to add more colour to what is already a great product in the Premiership. All I am saying is, these two clubs could become so obsessed with each other that it could be the Blue flag that ends up flying high – and as one of my former clubs I would love to see them do it as well.

'In my travels around the country promoting my book, I can sense an affinity with Chelsea. Like Keegan's brilliant Newcastle of the early eighties to mid nineties, they are starting to become everyone's second team. If they do pick up the silverware this season – and right now I would not bet against it being either the Premiership or the Champions League – people will claim it was bought. But do not for a minute underestimate the job the manager Claudio Ranieri has had on his hands.

'Often when you have a limited squad to work with and no cash, the job can be easier. There are no decisions to make on team selection, the best players are always picked and stay happy.

'Ranieri has two dressing rooms full of stars, which he has had to mould into one team each week – while keeping the rest happy and sharp. He has so far been able to do this without a word of dissension from within the ranks.

'Indeed only yesterday in *Sunsport*, Eidur Gudjohnsen was talking about his determination to stay at the club and fight for his place. Looking from the outside all the players seem to be behind the cause at Stamford Bridge. And to think that Ranieri's job was on the line when Abramovich took over with Sven once again the man in the frame. Yet with quiet dignity and an infectious laugh, the Italian has ignored the pressures and got on with his job superbly. Elsewhere about the club it is amazing how things have turned around. I was doing a dinner at Stamford recently and old Ken Bates was there. Suddenly, he is a hero at that place. Everyone wants to shake his hand and everyone will remember him with fondness.

'Yet Chelsea were apparently only two days from going into administration at the start of the season. Uncle Ken had just one stack of chips left, he gambled; put it all on zero and hit the jackpot. Good on him for that. The game's history is studded with the deeds of gamblers and chancers who helped make football what it is today. To think Tottenham were wary of Roman Abramovich when he first approached them. Ken could not get him signed up quick enough. What a transformation.

'Good for the game?

'That is the question now with a lot of the £120million spent having gone abroad. But it has to be good if Red Rom's readies are going to create a viable opposition to the big two and right now they are.

'That 4-0 win in Rome must have sent shudders through Europe. The most enjoyable thing for me about all of this is that despite all of the millions spent on foreign stars, the shining light right now is Frank Lampard. I have known Frank since he was a toddler and he has become one of the country's top midfielders. The thing I like about his football now is he is not afraid to have a go at goal as well. I remember playing with Billy Bonds at West Ham – one of the best midfielders I ever saw. I told him then he had everything in his game but should get forward and score more. It would be the same advice I'd have given to young Frank if I'd bumped into him – except he already seems to be doing it, and doing it well.

'People argue that the influx of foreigners is stopping good young English players from flourishing. But if you are good enough, you will get there.

'The difference now is once you are there you will get better because of the talent around you. So good luck Frank and good luck to my old club Chelsea.

'You have been a breath of fresh air while Arsenal and Manchester United try to ring each other's necks'.

So there you have it from the one and only Jimmy Greaves, the player who as a player was as good as ever been in the entire football world. A genius with the ball at his feet and the scourge of defenders all over Europe. Like me Jimmy, so tragically, missed out on England's finest hour on that historic day back in 1966 when beating West Germany by four goals to two. Whilst at West Ham United, Jimmy struck up a great friendship with the late great Bobby Moore and a TV company filmed about this wonderful story tale partnership. Two of the world's greatest players united just after I had reached those heights playing against both Bobby at Upton Park and Jimmy at White Hart Lane in only my second match for Chelsea in 1969 when we won the FA Cup which I missed through my own injury and, as I said, like Jimmy missed out on the 1970 World Cup Finals in Mexico. That is not the only thing I had in common with the great man as I wore his Chelsea blue number eight shirt with much pride. I very much hope that that TV company run that show again, for I am sure millions missed it and would love to see such a wonderful show, I for one was engrossed and enjoyed it enormously. I think the show was called when Bobby met Jimmy, wonderful stuff!

Back to the present, the day Newcastle United are in town to face the team that is so very full of confidence after the drubbing of Lazio. Two hours ago Manchester United kicked off at Liverpool and came through that one with all the points but Liverpool missed some great opportunities to 'nick' a point but it seems United are having a little luck at the moment. But you need this luck along the Premiership path and I recall talking to Sir Alex about it in Harry Redknapp's office after one game and he had no hesitation answering my question with a positive answer, tending to agree with me. So now both Arsenal and United kept up the pace by winning their weekend matches so now it was Chelsea's time to keep this three horse race going. Bobby Robson came into town with both Alan Shearer and Craig Bellamy so it was no surprise that I could not see where they would get a goal from.

On the eve of the Newcastle match the Tinkerman was headline news once again as he says that **I'M MAKING A MAN OUT OF LAMPARD.**

"There are few constants in Claudio Ranieri's Chelsea team, but Frank Lampard provides a golden thread of continuity. Ranieri has made the England mid-fielder the exception to his usual rotation rule and declared yesterday that he has done so to 'make a man of him'. Lampard, 25, who scored one of the goals in the 4-0 win over Lazio on Tuesday, is likely to be allowed to pick up where he left off by playing against Newcastle United at Stamford Bridge tomorrow. Ranieri said that, "It is unusual he plays most matches because everyone thinks I am the Tinkerman. Other players are very important, but Frank is someone I count on a lot. I believe in him and for me that is very important".

Lampard's eagerness to learn appears to have been his passport to a regular place in the team. He is Chelsea's only outfield player to have started every Premiership match this season and Ranieri added that, "I am not trying to be his father but I look for the man in the player before I try to improve them. You can be a good player but if you are not a man, you will not learn. Frank wants to improve".

Ranieri is expected to change the side, which battered Lazio in midweek, despite hailing the performances as their best of the season. He went on saying "You can't play every three days at the highest level. It will be different against Newcastle. They showed in the UEFA Cup how good they are. They were losing 2-1 and won 3-2. They may have not started the season very well but they are now in a great position."

'COULD BE THEIR DAY'

Player power at Chelsea has persuaded new owner Roman Abramovich to abandon plans to make any new signings in January.

The Blues were close to clinching an £8 million deal to land Argentine defender Roberto Ayala from Primera Liga title-chasers Valencia. But the current squad made it clear that they felt the squad didn't need further strengthening with the team flying so high at the moment. Claudio Ranieri's men lie second in the Premiership and need just a point from two matches to qualify for the knock out stage of the Champions League. A source close to Abramovich said that, "The players felt there was no need for any more signings with the team playing so well". Wrote exclusively by David Woods of the *Star*.

My view: Is that the last week has got a lot of people caught up in the euphoria of such amazing results, but don't get lost in this state of mind because nobody knows better than Sir Alex Ferguson as to the ins and outs of football teams, good or bad fortunes having lived in this fast football lane for so very long. He will be sipping his whisky with a wry smile on his face as he sees that there are two-thirds of the Premiership to go and a hell of a lot of football to be played in the Champions League. United will be quietly be watching Chelsea knowing that they can overhaul them at any given time. They play the Blues in three Saturdays' time and that is when the real football begins, the one on ones with the top three teams involved. United have cruised through their group and sit there nicely placed with their best players coming into their best form and that spells trouble to those who think they are going to give up their Premiership title without asking a lot of questions from others around them. I remember when Alex was winding Kevin Keegan up at Newcastle and KK lost his rag in front of millions of football lovers and it was quite embarrassing to watch a grown man grovel in tears. I have experienced a KK tantrum at Stamford Bridge when he attacked me outside the players' tunnel at Stamford Bridge, but like Mutu I took it with a smile. So there you have last week's summation and keep what I wrote in mind as the nights draw in and the cold gets into your bones, something United know all about and keep winning. They have said nothing about winning anything, in fact it was good to see Ryan Giggs this morning talk of the importance in Saturday's play-off match against Russia, a game I would not miss and in the other match Scotland take on Holland who have given a comeback to Ruud van Nistelrooy, all of this going on as Chelsea hog the headlines on a daily basis, which I am sure is fine by Sir Alex Ferguson. I will be hoping and wanting the Welsh team to win for Mark Hughes alone, as he has done brilliantly in his first season as the manager of his country. Hughes was a magnificent player for both United and Chelsea and has carried that into his managerial career. Good luck my son!

THE THRASHING OF THE TOON ARMY

Chelsea were 'hot' after scoring four in Rome in midweek but they are aware that they have not been putting teams away at Stamford Bridge, in fact in the majority of their home matches they have found themselves hanging on for dear life in the last quarter. The Chelsea faithful are quite aware of this and were looking forward to a match where their team go for the 'jugular' once going in front, and I had a feeling this could be the day once hearing Shearer was out with the flu, leaving their attacking force pretty desperate. The best result so far this weekend was at Fratton Park where Portsmouth absolutely crucified Peter Reid's Leeds United. Harry has done brilliantly this season and it could be worth having a wager for one of the two domestic cups. Harry has built Portsmouth into a real football team and his shrewd transfer moves have been quite brilliant. He brought in Paul Merson last season knowing that the former Arsenal star could swing a game with one touch of class, and then Harry must have thought that it was dangerous to have any luxuries aboard in the big time. He replaced Merson with Teddy Sherringham and also introduced Patric Berger to the south coast. Portsmouth were leading 2-1 at half time thanks to goals from Stefanov and O'Neill whose goals were interrupted by Alan Smith for the visitors but then, after the half-time whistle, Foxe, O'Neill again, before Berger and Ayegbini made it five then six-one. Berger was a real handful and is enjoying his football under the very shrewd management of both Harry Redknapp and the Bald Eagle, Jim Smith. 6-1 is as good as it gets and more than made up for a slight lapse by Harry's team but as I said earlier they have just had the toughest fixtures and will be delighted that after playing the top teams they stand in the middle of the

Premiership table, only three points off Birmingham City who sit fifth. But it was all eyes on Chelsea this second Sunday of November and the headlines told the story with the *Sun* going **HIGH FIVE RANIERI** Claudio's cover blown as Chelsea turn it on – Rob Shepherd with the *Express* began with: **BRILLIANT BLUES SERVE UP A TREAT** with Frank Lampard shouting that: **THE TITLE IS ON.** The *Mail* went **TURBO CHARGED Grand Prix boss Bernie sees Chelsea roar home** – The *Mirror* reported that **NOW CLAUDIO'S GOTTA BELIEVE IT – HE JUST MIGHT WIN THE LOT – Roman Empire on the march.**

I watched the match on television and it looked from early on that Newcastle might just give Chelsea a game before Glen Johnson opened the floodgates with Chelsea beginning to turn the screw after the break. Johnson's brilliantly taken goal showed that this young player really has a big future. There are not many goals scored by defenders that are taken like an accomplished goal getter but this was one of the best-taken you'll get to see. Let us say that, 'If it were van Nistelrooy or Shearer it would have been hailed as "classic"'. Chelsea then hit two goals in three minutes as Crespo kept his splendid goal scoring run up, then Frank Lampard hit a penalty after Mutu led O'Brien a merry dance, picking the ball up deep, spinning and then headed for goal. O'Brien had a grab at the Rumanian's shirt before finally Mutu went down and Paul Durkin had no other option but to give a penalty and send the Newcastle centre-back the red card. Chelsea did not really look like they had the extra man until Damien Duff, who is quickly becoming the fans' favourite hit the fourth after another 'jinky' run of his. Gudjohnsen – who replaced Crespo – struck the fifth and final goal six minutes from the final whistle. Joe Cole replaced Adrian Mutu. After Gudjohnsen headed the fifth goal Bobby Robson said, "I don't know where my centre-halves were, they must have been sitting next to me". Damien Duff said afterwards that "The boss says he is not expecting us to win the league but we are confident and all the lads believe we can do it. It was a big boost just before the start with no Alan Shearer on their team sheet. The lads have been working hard and were amazed to find out it was the same eleven".

CHELSEA 5 Lampard, Duff, Crespo, Gudjohnsen, Johnson NEWCASTLE UNITED 0 (41,332)

In the *News of the World* the morning of the match Ranieri was headline news once again this time saying that;

'I DON'T WANT ANY MORE PLAYERS'
He is happy with this lot

Chelsea boss Claudio Ranieri last night insisted that he will not spend a penny of Roman Abramovich's millions in the transfer window. The man, who masterminded the midweek 4-0 triumph at Lazio, insisted he wants to work with the megastars he already has to build a super-team.

Ranieri said that, "I have twenty-five players already. What do you want me to do?

There will be no more players in January." Chelsea have been linked with swoops for the likes of Wayne Rooney, Michael Salgado and even Ronaldo. There is no doubt the Blues have long-term 'targets' and owner Abramovich has made it clear he will buy any player he wants. But in the short term starting with today's game against Newcastle he believes he needs to work with the players he already has. He admitted that, "I said before that we had good players but we didn't have a team. But now slowly, slowly I look at them and see they are more of a team. But we still have a lot of work to do. Everybody is talking about Chelsea after the match in Lazio and I was pleased. But I am curious to see the next match against Newcastle. I want to see my team now and how they respond." Abramovich will be at Stamford Bridge this afternoon to see if his new club can match their Champions League perform-ance. He went on "Mr Abramovich is a good man because he always comes into the dressing room after the match and is always smiling and saying 'Well Done'. I said to him that it is important to stick with us even when we lose. And when we lost against Besiktas and Arsenal he was one of the first in the dressing room to shake our hands. It was fantastic. He showed his support. Having him at the club has changed everything. Roman wants to put Chelsea at a high level like Milan, Real Madrid, Manchester United and Arsenal." The Tinkerman is a great fan of Claude Makelele who he thinks is the 'cream of the crop' and told Roman about him telling that Real Madrid are one of the best teams in the world but they have a great player in midfield and everything goes around him – and that player was Makelele. I told him I wanted him to buy him. So Roman got him. Ranieri had a word to say about todays visiting manager Bobby Robson by saying "I would like to be like him when I am seventy. He is full of enthusiasm". If Ranieri, who is 52, does survive at Stamford Bridge until he is seventy he will go down as the most famous pensioner of all time.

In the same paper there was the follow up to last weeks Ned Kelly book 'They tried to ban' and it tells of how Sir Alex Ferguson phoned Maurice Watkins and told him that if he wasn't paid his bonus and pay rise he would not lead the team out at Wembley the year of 1998 against Liverpool. Ned Kelly says that he went to the then Chairman Martin Edwards in the players' tunnel at Wembley and saw that Martin looked very upset and he pulled him aside and asked him what was the trouble and Edwards pointed to the toilets. Kelly said that "Mercifully it was the gents' toilet. Edwards said that "Ned, you won't believe this but he phoned Maurice this morning and told him that if he was not paid he'd better lead the team out". Adding that "The Manchester United faithful would have gone into orbit if they saw the club lawyer leading the team out". Kelly said just how much Ferguson disliked the Board of Directors and told him that if any of them ever tried to stick their noses into the running of the team he would 'be off'. This book is going to stir some trouble and the lawyers must be rubbing their hands together once it hits the streets. On the other side of the coin, Chelsea's new regime keep on coming up smelling of roses and are enjoying a superb start to this campaign. I am not too sure about how highly Ranieri rates Makalele and it is times and quotes such as that find you out. I don't believe that Ranieri is tinkering with anyone with such quotes, for one moment he says just how highly he rates Frank Lampard and how important he is to the team. Then he says Veron is the best midfield player in Europe and now this about Makelele being the cream of the crop. I also think that he is playing a very dangerous game going public about having enough players and will not spend any more of his boss's millions. Firstly he should not say anything about Abramovich's money and where and when will spend it because if Chelsea lost three straight Premiership matches and were knocked out all of the cups he might just wish he had never have mentioned it. One has to walk close to the line here and respect the man pulling the purse strings. At the end of the day if Abramovich clicks his fingers it would be wrong to choose to be deaf. At this moment in time the Tinkerman is going along merrily but football is a game where you can be left talking to the man above about where it all has gone wrong. We have seen it enough, and he has, on the continent where the moneymen give you your work permit even though you might have won the Champions League. England has never seen the likes of Abramovich with the exception of the two Jacks – Walker and Hayward – but even they are not in the same ballpark as the Russian billionaire. Plus in comparison he is years and years younger and has more going on than the two Jacks. Walker bought the Premiership for Blackburn on a shoestring compared to Mr Abramovich and if you were to add it all up the new Chelsea owner should sweep the board if you went by money spent. Kenny Dalglish bought Shearer, Sutton, and the two wide men Jason Wilcox and Stuart Ripley who, like Shearer, came from Southampton and that particular season the big centre-half Colin Henry and goalkeeper Tim Flowers were absolutely magnificent as they kept the goals out whilst big 'Al' knocked them in consistently at the other end.

A TOUCH OF DÉJÀ VU?

This was a great result following the big match in Rome and what it will do is put them in pole position if it did actually come down to goal difference, they are now leading scorers after this emphatic victory. They have the best goal difference of the top three teams whose gap is now seven points above the fourth team, which is Charlton Athletic, managed by the excellent Alan Curbishley. I backed Charlton several times last season because they have proved time and time again that they can play with the best, and beat the rest, and it would not surprise me if Curbishley will be on the short list of candidates for the Manchester United job when Ferguson eventually goes upstairs. To the Board Room that is!

The big news this weekend is that Peter Reid has been fired by the Board of Directors at Elland Road. Peter must be delighted for he will walk away with a cheque for nearly a £1million and have no more sleepless nights. Once again, Directors of Football Clubs cease to amaze me, for they were the ones who gave him the job in the first place and now they are in even worse condition than when giving him the job.

I had lunch with the ex-Chelsea Chairman Brian Mears and told him that it was his fault that they sold Peter Osgood and myself in which he was rather surprised. I explained that if the manager is going to sell a player, in our case the two best players, then the players should have their say. At the end of the day this sent Chelsea sliding down the First Division like Eddie the Eagle and finally relegation. So within a year or eighteen months the Board of Directors sacked the manager, Dave Sexton, and had to dig their way out of quite a mess, in which Eddie McCreadie did a magnificent job in getting back up to the top Division with mostly players who were straight out of their diapers.

Finally Brian, a very nice man, accepted that I might have a valid case to argue. What all the trouble was about was 'petty' off the field stuff, which was crazy because we were the same players that had got to three Cup Finals and finished third in the table the year of that epic battle with Leeds United. Everton won the title that season with the brilliant Alan Ball pulling the strings in the centre-circle, along with co-stars Colin Harvey and Howard Kendall who eventually both managed the blue side of the Mersey. There were some big results at the weekend for Portsmouth, who I have already mentioned, a tremendous win for Leicester City at Manchester City by three goals to nil. Charlton beat Fulham to go fourth in the table.

KEMBER BITES THE BULLET

Only a few days ago Steve Kember, an old Chelsea team mate, got his P45 from Crystal Palace, the team he left to join us in the early seventies. Chairman Simon Jordan has put Kit Symons in the vacant manager's seat for the time being. Steve was the 16th managerial casualty this season and we have only just reached the first third of it. Steve, it says in the Sun, has worked at every level at the Palace and that includes driving the team bus. This was very funny because I believe sometimes managers get it seriously wrong and here are two such cases, the first being the Chelsea signing of Alan Birchenall from Sheffield United. I say this because only the season before I watched this player at Craven Cottage and who caught my eye was his front partner Mick Jones, a player like Ian Hutchinson but a little more class, meaning that in a way he was a better player technically. I believe to this day, because they looked so alike with blonde 'barnet' and both were the same type of player but Jones was superior, once again technically. Chelsea, whoever was to blame, purchased the wrong player, whilst the other player who nearly won the FA Cup for Leeds United, having at first hit Peter Bonetti, who limped through the rest of the match, and not long after scored the first goal in that match in 1970 at Old Trafford. I have mentioned this match before and it still hurts that I missed out through that ankle injury. Well, that is one sorted out and now the case here is why did Dave Sexton buy another midfield player?

I was playing in snatches and had quite few personal problems and ongoing injuries around that time. The day before we played Crystal Palace in a First Division match at Stamford Bridge I went down to Brighton with my friend Danny Gillen, my uncle George and Tony Frewin, my pal around that time. He played at Chelsea as an apprentice professional and could have made it but I think Dave Sexton did not like my relationship with him. For he stayed over in Chelsea some times and we would paint the town pretty nice colours. He lived in Stevenage and to stay over sometimes was good for him, but he ended up being one of the 'boys' here in Chelsea!

On the way back we stopped for refreshments, which led to a real 'session'. The following day I turned up for our pre-match meal at the Montana Hotel just close to the Gloucester Hotel, as it is now, still very drunk, not the kind of nice drunk or playing football drunk, more intoxicated if you like!

I got to Stamford Bridge and felt as bad as you'll ever get, only I was supposed to be playing in a couple of hours in front of fifty thousand people. I had one last opportunity and that was maybe if I had a 'livener', things would look better from behind these eyes, but oh boy, it worked quite the opposite and I felt as if I was going to collapse. I walked past fans coming into the game and made my way to my local, then the Adelaide on the next corner to Matthew Harding's local the Imperial. People were asking me why I wasn't playing and I replied that I was going to have a late fitness test, where a breathalyser would be more appropriate. Whilst on the playing field I was totally oblivious of all around me, and you'll never guess who was playing in the midfield for them, none other than Steve Kember. I promise you that I made him look like a Maradona – while I was more like Maddona – in the middle of a field that I hoped would open up so I could be buried alive. Well, a couple of weeks later our manager approached me at the Training Ground, in Mitcham, and explained that he was bringing in another midfield player and that it didn't effect me or my standing in the team. Of course I knew it would because he played me out wide on several occasions and there was only one place Steve could play and that was mine. Although that is true I recall us playing in midfield together against the closest thing you'll get to the Kray twins; Messiahs Bremner and Giles at Elland Road. I think we did pretty well and the score-line seemed to say that as we drew 1-1 with Peter Osgood scoring against the team he really loved scoring against more than any other. But Leeds United then were the team everyone loved to hate and they were a pretty useful side when getting on top of you, but I am delighted to say I have had my better matches against them. Once when Brian Clough took over and we beat them 3-0 at Stoke City in his first match in charge and also when they were after breaking the record of matches without defeat, thirty-two I think it was, and after leading us by a couple of goals, me and my Stoke City team mates put in a superhuman effort to come back and stop them from such an achievement. Then there were a couple of matches at the

Bridge, where I played in a match we beat them 4–0, although they did lose their goalkeeper David Harvey and I think Peter Lorimer took over the green jersey. There was no better feeling than getting a result against Leeds United!

VICTORIA HAS FOUND A NEW FRIEND IN MADRID
Daily Express Monday 10th of November 2003

After failing to be welcomed with open arms by the wives of her husband's Real Madrid team mates, Victoria Beckham has we can reveal, been taken under the wing of the mother of Latin pop star Enrique Iglesis.

Isabel Preysler, the first wife of ageing Spanish crooner Julio Iglesias, invited Posh, who moved into a sprawling, suburban £4.5million ranch-styled rented villa with David at the weekend, to have dinner at her home last weekend. The outing was the first time that Posh and Becks have socialised together since moving to Spain in July. "Isabel met Victoria in London before she moved to Madrid and they got on like a house on fire" says our man in the Spanish capital. Enrique, the wardling boyfriend of tennis star, turned model, Anna Kournikova, was also at the soiree, along with Ana Aznar, the daughter of Spanish prime minister Jose Maria Aznar and her husband, as well as assorted Spanish aristocrats, bullfighters and models. "The crème de la crème was there," adds our man nibbling the tapas. "Isabel is Madrid's premier hostess and a friend of the Prince of Wales and Camilla Parker Bowles".

The other sensational news on this day was all about Prince Charles and his sexuality told by his senior Royal aide. A royal spokeswoman said the talks came amid 'all sorts of rumour and innuendo'. Yesterday Charles flew back from Oman to face new revelations and renewed storm of an 'incident' between a servant and a senior royal.

The Prince denies this ever took place.

So it's all going on at the moment at both Palaces and it seems that the Buckingham one has more skeletons than the Crystal one.

PARKER

I have not had the opportunity to watch this young Charlton star but several good judges have. He has certainly taken all the headlines today where the headlines in the *Mail* was that **PARKER TO THRIVE IN ENGLAND COMPANY** whilst in the *Mirror* the headlines read **GREAT SCOTT** time Sven gave him a chance? Saturday just gone was a big day for ex-Arsenal and England captain Tony Adams.

Harry Harris in the *Express* reported that, 'Claudio Ranieri resumes his quest for the Premiership against Newcastle convinced he has finally shaken off the shadow of Sven Goran Eriksson'. Ranieri has agreed a book deal with Collins Willow, the next major project for them after their best-selling David Beckham book 'My Side', and it has cemented the Italian's belief that he will still be around when it is published next season.

Collins Willow's publishing director Michael Doggart told me, "He's the man at Chelsea and we don't see anything that Sven is doing to change that".

Ranieri took a jovial swipe at Eriksson during the talks to seal the deal on the book. Doggart added that "It was a good meeting", and Claudio joked, "When I win the title. I will set it up nicely for Sven".

Ranieri has been tormented by the constant speculation but another book is being slated for release next autumn, a diary of the season, with Collins and Willows keen for Ranieri to be around to promote it.

But Ranieri will not profit from the historic account of this season, donating all proceeds to the Great Ormond Children's charity.

Doggart has been impressed with Ranieri, particularly after a mishap with their meeting to tie up the book deal prior to the Carling Cup tie with Notts County.

Doggart said that, "We agreed to meet at Starbucks at around 3pm before this match but Starbucks were being refurbished, so we all went across the road to the White Hart in Parsons Green where, by chance, there were some County fans. They recognised him, naturally, and he signed their tickets".

TV'S ODD COUPLE

Chelsea look set to back Manchester United, though it will clearly not be for the Premiership title. United have been a lone voice in wanting to sell their overseas TV rights independently, but the Premiership have insisted on collective rights.

Now, however, Chelsea are keen to tap into the new market emerging for their games overseas and particularly in China, and the Far East, which can reap in billions for the big clubs.

Italian sources say Roman Abramovich hinted he was looking at the possibility of investing heavily in TV projects. Chelsea chairman Ken Bates told me that, "We are aiming to expose our own channel Chelsea TV world wide".

Bookmakers William Hill had changed the title odds making Manchester United the 13/8 favourite; 7/4, Arsenal and Chelsea; 50/1, Liverpoo; 100/1, Newcastle; 500/1, Charlton and Manchester City.

In the First Division there was an incredible result at Upton Park where at one stage West Ham led by thee goals to nil. Their brilliant young striker Jermain Defoe, two red cards and eleven goals so far this season, scored in the very first minute and Brian Deane hit two. This was with only 18 minutes on the clock. Then Rob Hulse pulled two goals back, one a stunning 25-yarder, before Brian Deane scored yet again, only it was into his own net to square the match before Lee Hughes fired them ahead with thirteen minutes still remaining. The headline in the *Sun* said it all;

SHAME ACADEMY
Hammers are the cock-up kings

This is aimed at the West Ham United Academy of football and apart from Alex Ferguson at United, West Ham have introduced Rio Ferdinand, Frank Lampard, Michael Carrick, Joe Cole and Glen Johnson through the ranks that has five Internationals and apart from them Trevor Sinclair made it to the last World Cup which makes their relegation last season quite incredible, although Ferdinand had gone and young Johnson played in around a dozen matches, not all from the start. This week once again has been all about Chelsea who could have done with the games coming up quickly, but this Saturday brings us a day of Internationals, which the in-form teams could do without, especially being a friendly against Denmark on the Sunday. I was cheered this weekend to see Ray Parlour of Arsenal get the credit for their North London Derby win over Spurs. He is an unsung hero over at Highbury and he grabbed the headlines in nearly every paper, he is a player I have always liked and the best in the game at what he does. England have played inferior players to Parlour for so long and the only man who will be happy with that is Arsene Wenger for he can rely on the fresh-legged Arsenal midfielder to carry on giving him his 110% whilst so many players are on duty for their countries. Saturday saw the 1st Round of the FA Cup and first casualties were 2nd Division Huddersfield who were beaten 1-0 at Accrington Stanley. There may not be any matches this week, apart from Blackburn and Everton tonight, but there will be plenty of news to bring you first hand so don't go away.

Graeme Souness was delighted after their cliff hanger of a match when beating Everton 2-1 and changing places with them in the table, which meant now Everton were just one place above Leeds who were bottom. Blackburn began brightly and found that every time they got into crossing positions they had acres of space and once the ball was in the air it found a blue and white shirt, Blackburn, every single time. Everton missed a couple of great opportunities at the death but overall Souness just about deserved the points.

JOHNSON GETS THUMBS UP

Rob Shepherd, *Daily Express*, 11th November

Sven Goran Eriksson really made his mark as a coach of repute in two spells as manager of Benfica. Yesterday he returned to Lisbon, where he still has a coastal villa, to survey England's training camp for next summer's European Championship finals and announce his squad for Saturday's friendly against Denmark.

The game is one of five friendlies before Eriksson finalises his 23-man-squad for the Euro 2004 campaign. He admitted that, providing he has a full complement of fit players in nine months' time, there is little room for manoeuvre in that he has already made up his mind what the party should be.

Nevertheless, the England coach is not one to close doors – as he showed yesterday by recalling Gareth Southgate – nor is he foolish enough not to realise it is likely that some of his regulars will be injured come the finals.

Indeed, with a long list of autumnal injured and the awkward absence of

Rio Ferdinand under the Football Association directives, Eriksson took the opportunity as expected to give two burgeoning young talents their chance to muscle in and take part in next summer's finals.

If the inclusion of 19-year-old Chelsea right back Glen Johnson and 23-year-old Charlton midfielder Scott Parker were hardly surprises, their selection confirms Eriksson has no qualms about introducing young, untried talent to put pressure on more established England squad members.

Certainly, if Johnson maintained his progress then he could not only force his way into the party for next summer's finals, but also even challenge stalwart right back Gary Neville for a starting place.

Eriksson did not hide his enthusiasm for the way Johnson has performed since his £6million summer move from West Ham to Chelsea.

"He is a very big talent and, what's more, when he plays he has a style about him," said Eriksson.

Eriksson was not even perturbed that Johnson was sent-off playing for the Under 21 side in their last match against Turkey and would thus be suspended for England's opening match of next summer's tournament should he be selected.

"I am aware of that because it's England's next competitive match – but I could live with selecting a player who would just be banned for one game" added Eriksson. "Of course, it's important he learns from a red card because discipline and character is always a big consideration when you pick a squad. Let's just see how he progresses but, like Scott Parker, he is one of the few young players on the edge of the squad who could have a chance. It's too early to say that either Johnson or Parker could improve the team because when everyone is fit we have a very good team. But maybe there could be one or two places in the squad, I will have to look at".

For Johnson it is a meteoric rise. This time last year he had not even made his Premiership debut with West Ham and was on loan at first division club Millwall.

From the Lions Den to one of England's Lions of Lisbon next summer?

That is his challenge.

It is one his club captain Marcel Desailly believes he will rise to. The French World Cup winner said that, "Glen has a great future. Hs is still making small mistakes, but you can feel that he is going to be one of the best right-backs in the world".

Parker has come on leaps and bounds this season since adding an acerbic edge to his undoubted style and has been a major factor in Charlton moving up to fourth place in the Premiership. He said that "There has been a lot of talk about me making this quad and it's wonderful to be included. But I recognise in terms of next summer's finals there are a lot of very good players ahead of me".

Rob Shepherd also reported that Joe Cole has been offered the chance to revive his England career – as a striker. Sven Goran Eriksson yesterday announced the 23-man squad for Saturday's friendly against Denmark but named only three forwards, after axing James Beattie.

The Southampton striker's exclusion is controversial, particularly in the absence of talisman Michael Owen. Beattie – with seven Premiership goals – has struck more than the other three in the party, Wayne Rooney, Emile Heskey and Darius Vassell, put together.

Eriksson conceded that there are few alternatives to bolster the England forward line, but suggested Chelsea's Cole could solve the problem. Eriksson said, "Cole has the ability to play as a second striker. It's a position I have seen him play a few times for Chelsea this season and maybe we should see it for England, too.

"Are we short of strikers?

"I would agree we are more than covered when it comes to defenders and midfield players but not necessarily up front.

"People may be surprised that Beattie is out – but that does not mean his career with England is over. I want to look at things at the moment".

Alan Smith's run of three goals in three games for Leeds has not been enough to command a recall while West Ham's Jermain Defoe and Shola Ameobi of Newcastle are not ready. It leaves Cole with a chance to cement a place in the England squad as either an attacking midfield player to challenge Paul Scholes – who is injured for the Denmark game – or become a Continental split striker. Eriksson has criticised Cole's lack of discipline in midfield but clearly thinks his unique attacking talent still has something to offer England if properly utilised.

Rio Ferdinand was again overlooked because of the ongoing situation with his missed dope test. Eriksson said; "Of course I would like Rio to be available but, at the moment, the matter is over my head".

CHELSEA STARS LINED TO SHAKE MY HAND

Rewind to the 9th of November 2002, and Glen Johnson walked off the pitch at the Dell following a 2-1 win over Preston. On loan at Millwall, this was only his fourth game as a wide-eyed professional footballer. Now, fast forward, to the early evening of the 9th of November 2003, and the youngest player in Chelsea's Roman revolution milked the applause from 40,000 fans.

After scoring the opening goal, he was one of Claudio Ranieri's stars in a 5-0 demolition of Newcastle United – and it was only his 35th start as a pro.

Five minutes later, though, and life got just a little bit better for this likeable lad from Dartford.

Johnson, 19, said that, "Mr Ranieri told me straight after the game about England. He said, 'Congratulations, Sven has picked you. Enjoy it'. It was just minutes after the final whistle went. Everyone was there waiting to shake my hand – all the players.

"They said congratulations and hopefully you'll be there for years. Obviously, I have achieved something being chosen in the squad for Sunday's friendly with Denmark, but I have a lot of work to do. I have certainly not made it. Hopefully, I can get picked for the next one, and on and on, and hopefully start playing for my country.

"But Gary Neville has played at right back for years and deservedly so. There is nobody better than him.

"I am still learning, so I have to be patient. After all I have only played five times for the Under 21 team or rather four and a half as I got sent-off against Turkey".

The fact all the megastars lined up to shake the young defender's hand two days ago is significant. Because during that fabulous win over Newcastle, Johnson was the only outfield player in a blue shirt NOT to be capped at full International level.

So while some youngsters are often overawed when being called up for their country, Johnson's knees are unlikely to be going all wobbly when meeting up with his International team-mates for the first time on Thursday.

THIRTY-THREE YEARS AGO

Whilst reading and writing the last few columns it all came flooding back as a nineteen year-old player in my first full season in the Chelsea team. It was after an FA Cup Tie at Loftus Road, the home of Queens Park Rangers, that Alf Ramsey was quoted as saying "There is no limit to what this player can achieve." This was leading up to the World Cup of 1970 in Mexico where England were to try and retain the Jules Rimet Trophy, the World Cup, and I was a serious contender after such words from the England boss. It was great opening the paper on a Monday morning to read such headlines and I knew if I kept up my good form not only could we win the FA Cup, I would be in with a shout for the most exciting World Cup of my time here on earth. The boys congratulated me, when the World Cup squad was announced and my selection meant that I had a race on to overcome the ankle trouble, which kept me out of both the FA Cup Final and the Replay. There are no words to explain the gut-wrenching feeling I experienced not being able to play in that epic battle against the team everyone loved to hate, Leeds United. I had a fitness test at our Mitcham Training Ground on a surface that was ankle deep in mud but even the soft ground had me saying that it was hopeless, and I remember Dave Sexton walking back to the changing rooms with me looking like it were he who was missing such a match. I went to see doctors galore, acupunctures, and mediums, palm readers and faith healers but we in our home even went to the bottle in the middle of the table trick. I must have upset the man upstairs but could not understand what I had done along the way. What made this situation worse was that it was that I had come through a gruelling season, and a fantastic one, against some of the toughest players ever to play the game. On this particular Easter Bank Holiday at West Bromwich Albion it was me who had to find the biggest hole in the Midlands and a simple ball came to me and as I went to control it, my foot went down it and

I thought the world had come to an end. In seconds it was like I had elephantiasis /elifan'taiasis/ noun (a disease causing gross enlargement of limbs etc.)

The following day I was put in plaster, the worst thing that could happen, and that was the end of a dream season for me. I see these pitches of today and think back to the Hawthorns (WBA) and think just what might have been!

The second blow was missing out on possibly having a chance to play against Pele and the rest of his champions. I had played against the great man in a friendly – although there is no such thing as a friendly with the likes of Ron Harris around – in Jamaica, when he played for Santos, that great Brazilian club side.

What made it even worse was that quite some years later I bumped into Ken Jones, one of Fleet Street's finest, at Wembley after Manchester United had just mugged Chelsea 4-0 in the FA Cup Final. He pulled me to one side and said that he did not know if I ever knew that I was very much a part of the plans made up by Ramsey, in fact in a nutshell I was definitely going to get some time playing in that most wonderful of tournaments. I did not know whether to laugh or cry or if I wanted to know or not!

Anyhow two dreams turning into nightmares for me, after a scintillating rise to the ocean surface. So I am delighted to see this young man get called up and from where I sit he looks quite a remarkable talent. I wrote about his goal against Newcastle and it typified his all round performance, cool as a summer's night in Vermont, Johnson answered several questions on the day he clinched his selection to the full England squad. I look back and in my time there was the ultra-cool and brilliant Bobby Moore, the unflappable Colin Todd, the incredible Kevin Beattie and the stylish Peter Simpson, who like Hinton, could have done more, that this young man can follow. There is nobody who springs to mind after those, and in our Chelsea squad there was the smooth Marvin 'Suave Marv' Hinton, who if he believed in himself would have pushed Mooro all the way. I played with another lad at Stoke City who like 'Lou' found the game a little too easy, for if he had the desire to become the next Bobby Moore could so easily have done so. His name is Alan Dodd!

Another outstanding player – who I played with – like these were Peter Simpson at Arsenal!

Back to Saturday's international that is covering all the nationals at this moment as we run up to the friendly against Denmark. I see this as a great opportunity for the Swede to blood these youngsters but at the same time give them 90 minutes to show what they can do, for there is nothing worse than a man 'tinkering' with the team at half-time and you just might not have had a good first forty-five minutes. As a player I prided my self on my ability and hard work off the pitch to get stronger as the game went on. My training sessions alone would be long distance whilst my main object when training with the lads was the short stuff, no not vodka, short sprints over ten or fifteen yards which are so important when balls are bouncing around and the difference between keeping possession once getting to that ball before your opponent. This is the hardest part of the game for players like myself, it is great when in possession but if you don't get there first you are on the back-foot rather than pushing balls through to your front players. I was not an natural athlete so I had to work twice as hard in all types of running exercises but not only did it improve me and add something else important to my game, for at the end of the day it paid of big time by saving my life whilst in the Intensive Trauma Unit in the Royal London Hospital!

FIVE CHELSEA CALL-UPS MEANS BLUE IS THE COLOUR FOR ENGLAND

THE SQUAD

Goalkeepers; David James (WHU) – Paul Robinson (Leeds United) – and Ian Walker (Leicester City).

Defenders; Philip and Gary Neville (Manchester United) – Ashley Cole (Arsenal) – John Terry, Wayne Bridge and Glen Johnson (Chelsea) – Danny Mills and Gareth Southgate (Middlesbro') – and Matthew Upson (Birmingham)

Midfielders; David Beckham captain (Real Madrid) – Frank Lampard and Joe Cole (Chelsea) – Nicky Butt (Manchester United) – Danny Murphy and Steven Gerrard (Liverpool) – Scott Parker (Charlton Athletic) and Jenas (Newcastle United)

Forwards; Emile Heskey (Liverpool) – Wayne Rooney (Everton) and Darius Vassell (Aston Villa)

In the Tuesday edition of the *Evening Standard* Ken Dyer wrote that, 'There has never been a better time to be a Chelsea supporter than this week.

'After comprehensive victories over Lazio and Newcastle, now Sven Goran Eriksson has picked five Blues players in his squad for Sunday's friendly against Denmark.

'It is even conceivable that the quintet will all be on the pitch at the same time, thereby providing all but one of the back four.

'For defenders John Terry, Wayne Bridge, and young Glen Johnson plus midfield players Frank Lampard and Joe Cole, Sunday's Old Trafford match represents a golden opportunity.

'Provided Eriksson gives them a chance to show what they can do, the increasingly famous five can give their prospects of a place in Portugal next June.

'It was debatable whether Terry was proving more solid than Rio Ferdinand even before his forgetfulness meant that the Manchester United star had to embark on his current protracted disciplinary process.

'Almost on par with Terry is Frank Lampard, who has already been promised that he will start Sunday's match.

'If the England midfielder did not contain an abundance of quality in David Beckham, Paul Scholes and Steven Gerrard, Lampard would already be a fixture in Eriksson's teams.

'Wayne Bridge is second choice behind Ashley Cole at left back, but the former Southampton man is improving with every match.

'Joe Cole hasn't been a regular for England or Chelsea, but Eriksson is keen to have a look at him in a withdrawn striking role, a position Cole himself believes could be best.

'Now Eriksson has added a fifth Chelsea player in Johnson and it is clear the England coach has been really impressed with the teenage full back so far this season. "I love to watch him play", said Eriksson "He plays with a lot of style out there on the pitch". You sense that, as in the Premiership, there is a shift in the balance of power.

'Meanwhile Wayne Rooney is a major doubt with flu, which would leave England with only two strikers, Darius Vassell and Emile Heskey while David Beckham has been told by Real Madrid to rest a back problem for seventy-two hours.'

ANOTHER TINKERMAN METHOD
23 A-SIDE

Chelsea's squad is now so swollen with International talent that Claudio Ranieri sometimes has to conduct 23 a-side training sessions.

Ranieri's latest rotation poser has been revealed by Euder Gudjohnsen and Damian Duff, who paint a graphic picture of Chelsea players jostling for position in the Premiership's most keenly contested starting line-up.

Interviewed in the new *Champions Magazine,* out tomorrow, Gudjohnsen said that, "There are a lot of great players here now. One day we had about twenty-six in training so we had to play twenty-three-a-side. There was no one you could ask to sit out".

His views were echoed by Republic of Ireland international Duff, who said the club's Harlington training ground is now so crowded that even training bibs have become prized possessions.

Duff said that, "We have a squad of twenty-four or twenty-five players, so we could field two different teams every Saturday. Even with the Republic of Ireland team, when bibs are handed out in training you know what the starting line-up will be by the colour. Here if they hand out eleven bibs, there really is no clue as to what the team will be because both teams are so strong. What this means is you can't just go training and mess about. You have to keep on your toes at all times.

"Other places you might get away with a dip in form, but not here. You could score a hat-trick one week and not get in the side the next".

And, with more signings possible once the transfer window opens in January, the Irish winger is candid about the pressure to deliver on Roman Abramovich's squad.

Hw admitted that, "Everyone knows we have to win the Premiership this year after all the money we have spent. I really don't think we can afford to wait two or three years to win the Championship after the quality that has been brought in. There's no point lying, we're all looking to win the League this year".

That is certainly the aim of Abramovich, who has left Gudjohnsen and the players in no doubt about what he expects this season. "He spoke about his vision for Chelsea and made it clear he wanted to take the club to the top" said the Iceland striker. "He said, 'I want to make your life as easy as possible. I want you to concentrate on performing. I'll make sure everything is provided for you'. And I have to say, the man was very impressive".

Abramovich has been true to his word. He realised very quickly that the players were critical of their current training facilities, which are amongst the worst in the Premiership. So the Russian is ready to spend £15million to buy the land for the latest state-of-the-art training complex and has been to London Colney to see Arsenal's new facility. His presence was one of the major reasons Hernan Crespo signed from Internationale. And the striker denied that his Italian team-mates were surprised by his decision to join Chelsea.

"On the contrary, many wanted to come and join me as well" he said "In a way, it surprised me that I swapped Inter for Chelsea, but I can help them become great. At other clubs the history is already written, but at Chelsea a lot more remains to be written and we, the players, can do that now. I need to make myself understood. I'm certainly going to try. It's scary learning a new language, but I'm confident I can do it because when I went to Italy at twenty-one I didn't even know how to say 'hello' in Italian and now I am married to an Italian lady".

Crespo was also asked whether it was true he wanted to become a bin-man?

"Where did they get that from? Oh no, no, no," he said.

My view; I have not been in the Chelsea dressing room for some time now and wonder how the players move around before the game because they are not the biggest changing rooms by a long chalk. As for Damien Duff saying they have to win it this year I think he meant this season because a championship has never been won on New Year's Eve, and as regarding Crespo, I am glad he said he married an Italian woman and not just an Italian. Because Chelsea cannot afford to reach the depths of the likes of Leeds and Manchester United and all that has been brought up in the last couple of months since the 'roasting' situation and the negativity of Rio Ferdinand's case about the drug test. As for the training of so many players in one session it must be a very tough ordeal for the coach because the art of coaching is getting the best out of each individual. Even when we were at Chelsea it was tough enough working on set-plays etc. with fourteen players, where the three not playing could not wait to knock on the manager's door, either that or go change and get to the nearest boozer.

There are so many new beginnings in our game now that are difficult to grasp, even with a team like Real Madrid, probably the best attacking side in the world with the kind of players they have. But I am certain the curtain will fall on the Spaniards as the Russian revolution begins to pick up even more momentum. These successful businessmen could never surely have imagined that this move in the summer would go so smoothly as if they are the masters of the game we invented. But you cannot argue with results in any business and their results up until now are even more frightening, knowing that if the baby cries you can adopt another one. I have said on earlier pages that they have been very fortunate in several of their matches but all of this is a sign that whilst you are getting used to playing with one another and you are taking maximum points through that spell, it augurs well for the future. Before you read any further, I apologise, I was joking about the amount of players that were on each side in training. I was floating away looking how the game would be if it keeps expanding like it is at this moment in time. So let's get back to today and only three days away from the five Chelsea players representing their country. In the *Daily Express* the headlines are JOHNSON UP FOR THE ACADEMY AWARD with Niall Hickman telling the story; West Ham's 'kingmakers' have worked their alchemy again with Glen Johnson's elevation to the full England side as the teenage full-back looks set for a golden future.

Johnson may now ply his trade with Chelsea, but he first made his name in the claret and blue of the Hammers and has become one of the famous five.

In the past few years Rio Ferdinand, Frank Lampard, Joe Cole and Michael Carrick have all won recognition at full England level and the conveyor belt from east London continues to roll out high class players, with Johnson due to make his International debut against Denmark at Old Trafford on Sunday.

Trying to pinpoint where the Hammers get it right while others fail is a tough task for Upton Park's director of coaching Jimmy Hampson, but he does not mind having a stab at it. "We have a great philosophy at this club and it has worked well over the years. We get great backing from the Board and the various managers we have had and the youngsters get treated exactly the same way as the oldest professional". He said that "There is no segregation here between the 13-year-old kid and the 33 -year-old pro and I hope that stays the same".

The Hammers youth set-up is governed by Hampson, who joined from Charlton in 1992. Then there is Tony Carr, Academy Director, who is part of the furniture at the Boleyn Ground, having been in situ for over 30 years. They have a track record, which puts other clubs to shame and continues to serve West Ham well. Indeed, had it not been for their coaching and scouting systems there is every likelihood the club would have suffered financial meltdown as so many have recently.

It is not a point lost on Hampson, who insists he is realistic about the regular departures of outstanding young talent to the Premiership big guns. He said that, "the fact is we got relegated. It is a wrench seeing young lads go who you have worked with from the age of 10 and 11, but it is the law of the game.

"A better way of looking at it is this; we are immensely proud of Glen and all the other players who have represented their country because they have deserved it. Nothing ever comes easy in life and five lads who have made the England team have done so by absolute dedication and determination to be the best they can.

"The youngsters here also know they have a chance and that makes a difference. Frank Lampard was in the first team at seventeen as was Joe Cole and Rio. This week against West Brom the manager put a sixteen year-old called Chris Cohen on the bench. Glenn Roeder gave Glen his chance. We have Mark Noble in the England Under 17's and knocking on the door as well.

"There are stacks of other players coming through like Anton Ferdinand, who is just eighteen, and Richard Garcia. Lower down we have Hogan Ephraim and Ishmail Walsh in the England youth teams and a fourteen year-old called James Tomkins is in our Under seventeen side. We are not afraid to give these lads a chance and they can either sink or swim. Maybe other clubs don't do that as much but we do".

Hampson added that, "rest assured it is not all doom and gloom here. The lifeblood of this club has always been its youth system. There isn't anything magical. We just do the basics right. And what is the old saying, if it isn't broken then don't fix it".

My view: is that I know Tony Carr and have watched him work with the youngsters and as Hampson says they do nothing out of the ordinary, the sign of a good coach. For example Don Howe is the very best I have ever been in contact with. Don did nothing out of the ordinary, he just made a case for everything he brought into a training session and there was never a time when I doubted his ability to get the best out of the players he had to work with. I am sure the players who won the 'double' at Highbury, when Don worked under Bertie Mee, would tell you the same. Players are simple to handle only if you don't try to complicate things. The coaches that try to bring something new, like years ago at Lilleshall, only baffle good players. It is much like a marriage where two people fall in love, get married and then try to change the person they fell in love with, total nonsensical!

Jimmy Hampson is doing a truly magnificent job and whilst reading his comments it hit me that the brilliant Ron Greenwood responsible for Moore, Peters and Hurst, always said that, 'simplicity is genius'. Now the two of those comments add up to common sense. I often wonder what my path through the game would have been like had I joined the West Ham Academy for my father was often pestered by head scout Wilf Chitty to have his son play for the Hammers. Instead of growing up with the likes of Bonetti, McCreadie, Harris, Osgood, Charlie Cooke and of course, yours truly!

I would have been the junior in their set-up of Moore, Peters, Hurst, Boyce, Sissons, Lampard and Brooking which would have been very interesting. The way I always answer a question about certain players is by thinking had I played alongside them, would I have fit in with Brooking say, the answer is 'easily' and would have I got the ball off Bobby Moore early enough for Bobby used to fire pin point balls into Hurst running across the last line of defence. Then I would have had to ignore coming short for the ball and get it knocked into my path closer to the opposition goal. That would not really have been a problem because Bobby was one of the shrewdest judges of the game who ever played it. You simply mix it up so the opposition would have one more problem, because I think a lot of the time West Ham were as easy to read as the *Sporting Life*. Then I ask myself to join the two teams and what would you have?

Here goes: Bonetti, Lampard, Moore, Dempsey and McCreadie at the back with Cooke, Hudson, Peters and Brooking in the heart of the team and up front Hurst and Osgood would have been awesome together. They would have had nearly everything a front two needed and more. Okay 'pace' I hear you scream?

But that would not have been a problem because the way one drops in short and the other goes long it would leave ample space for us four across the middle to exploit.

This is great stuff for you in your local pubs mixing and matching such players and I am sure if you had ten people picking teams from these two clubs at such a time you would get ten different teams. Ron Harris I hear you ask and my answer would be that if 'chopper' played alongside the one and only Robert Chelsea Moore we would lack height, which would have been exploited by opposition coaches. So John Dempsey, a vastly underrated player, would be the perfect foil for Bobby, just as big Jack Charlton was under Alf Ramsey. In midfield there would be me and Charlie, apart from Tony Currie, Glenn Hoddle and Alan Ball would have been the last of the 'real' inside forwards. Players who loved picking it up in deep positions and try to make things happen for those ahead of them. Picking out Osgood and Hurst we could do all day with one or even both eyes closed. Then you had Brooking hugging the left touchline and roaming across the line with his great strength and deft touch on the ball, purely magic. Have you seen the movie 'Ghost', if not have you seen Martin Peters play, for he was the ultimate of figures that crop up where nobody expected, especially his so-called marker.

WELL, THANKS A MILLION

It is Glen Johnson in the headlines once again and West Ham have picked up an extra million pounds after he was called up into the England squad. Johnson was the first player to join the Russian revolution in the summer when he moved in a surprise £6million deal after just fifteen first team appearances. He looks as if he will be given the go-ahead by the Swede, on Sunday for, being a friendly, the manager already knows what Gary Neville can do at this level but he'll be looking for new blood leading into the Euro 2004 finals and Johnson looks like he only needs the opportunity and he'll replace the United player. Whilst all this was going on the club that sold Johnson, West Ham, learned that a group of prominent shareholders are attempting a boardroom coup. They want to remove the chairman, finance director and managing director. This takes me back to about three years ago when Harry Redknapp was in talks with the racehorse 'guru' Michael Tabor about the Bethnal Green owner backing his local club. Harry had it all lined up but the board at that time were frightened off by the size of Tabor's investment and ambition. When

Tabor does something he does not cut corners and this is why West Ham United are in such a mess both on and off the field. In the meantime Harry has enjoyed an incredible journey down at lowly Portsmouth and he is a very underestimated manager, known for his wheeling and dealing, but his great strength is his man management and there will be times this season where that will be the crucial side of his job at hand!

THE SENTINEL

**I write for a terrific Editor Sean Dooley who
visited me in my hospital bed and kept my job
open for me, some others never bothered!**

I mention about Sean because he and several others, Peter Fox, Brendan O'Callaghan, Alan Dodd, Jackie Marsh, Terry Conroy of my ex-Stoke City team mates along with my great pal Brian Shenton were down the M6 to see their mate while some others in London never bothered. Even Terry Neil – my manager at Arsenal, who owned the Sports Bar literally two hundred yards from my hospital bed never came. As for Chelsea Football Club I never received a card from anyone in the place. I was and have always been lucky to have a very close family and you just would not believe what my hospital room was like once I was outside of death's door and into a side room in St Bartholomews. My uncle Charlie would be the Mr Pastry of the family bringing in pies, pies and more pies, all freshly baked that morning. As time went by I was in and out the shower dressed by my uncle George and in my wheelchair heading for the physiotherapist's room by the time he had arrived with his goodies. And then in mid-afternoon my mum would carry the dinner through the streets of London up to my bedside every single day. Yeah, I would say we have quite a family in our time of need and they did not leave a stone unturned right up until Tommy Mason would arrive for my mum around lights out and time to drive her home to Chelsea. But he would and could not leave before we ran through my day of tests once Tom had looked at my now legs which looked more like a roadmap than two organs that would carry me around the world playing the game I love so much. Then there was Bobby Eyre, my first footballing friend in those wonderful days in our Wembley, the 'Cage'. Bobby would be there every Sunday evening bringing my mother and George up with Spaghetti Bolognaise or some other recipe that went down with the finest wine from Sainsburys around the corner. Johnny Westwood, David and Lorraine Rodwell, Malcolm Molineux, my new friends from the east side, would bring me cheer and always watching my progress. My great friend Mel Tame came along with Danny Caine, two men I met at a luncheon and began a rather special relationship with. I still have lunch with Mel as I write, in fact Thursday just gone which holds many lovely memories for they are all scoundrels in one way or another, so we are basically all one of the same breed although we all walked down different pathways through life. Martin Knight, a friend for maybe a year before this happened, become prominent in my life and it was he and Bobby who bought me the crucifix when it came up on my sister Julie's wall. Martin also brought me the thing that kept me sane, a laptop!

It's mid-November and I have been asked by my Sports Editor to concentrate on the England match for my Sunday piece, of which I have for you, whilst on the Friday I thought it a good idea to bring some time into the path of ex-Manchester United, Barcelona and Chelsea legend the terrific Mark Hughes. He was a player of immense power and great control, holding things up while others make ground. There was none better than this player at holding the ball up in any situation and that is why he was not such a prolific goal-scorer for he did so much more than just get on the end of things. He will always be remembered by the quality rather than the quantity when it came to scoring goals. He was also one of those forwards who believed that you had to get your retaliation in before they made their mark on you. This was something Peter Osgood brought into his game after some years of being pushed around, and then the broken leg he received from one of football's 'Mr Nasty', Emlyn Hughes. If we go by that great old Liverpool hard nut Tommy Smith, you will find this to be true, but every dressing room has one as in any walk of life!

OLE GUNNAR, BINGO

Another who ranks aside Hughes is TV pundit Rodney Marsh, a man who loves himself in a kind of way it would embarrass me to be like him, even though he'd laugh at me for having more financial clout, but anyone can be rich when they never put their hand in their long pockets!

I would rather be absolutely 'potless' than taking vanity and greed onto a new level, in fact he would have made a great partner for my second wife, although she wasn't mean until it came to crunch time. It would make Beckham and his missus freak out!

Here is the *Sentinel* column for Friday: Tomorrow's Internationals are vital for both Scotland and Wales and how I would like the Welsh and Mark Hughes to pull it off. Hughes has done magnificently since his taking over the national job and deserves success for the way he turned things around. Hughes was a player I have always thought a great deal of whilst playing for both United and Chelsea. He was honest on the field and this has no doubt followed into his new position of a miracle worker for the country that has not qualified for a major tournament since 1958. He will be relying on a little bit of help from both Ryan Giggs and John Hartson, two players who have the dragon fire in their every breath and hearts, who would do almost anything to get their country over this very difficult hurdle, but they have the kind of players who will run until they drop to stop this terrible run of disappointments. I just hope I do not give them the Hudson Kiss of Death by cheering them on and tipping them to go through, more heart than head stuff though, but we do know they will fight to the very end on a freezing cold night in Moscow. John Hartson can be the player to see them through this very tricky two-legged affair. Hartson has been a revelation since joining Martin O'Neil and his green and white Glasgow Celtic. He is as strong as any forward in Britain and I watched him a lot when having an awesome spell at West Ham under my pal Harry Redknapp, until the wheels fell off and he began putting on weight and losing the sharpness that cost him a place at Arsenal. For the first half of the season he was absolutely brilliant then afterwards looked everything you did not want in a player, but Martin O'Neil has told him in no uncertain terms that if his form dips for going through all the things he did off the field he would show him the door immediately. It has worked for Celtic and he has been a big part of Mark Hughes's transitioning this country to the edge of success. Two-legged affairs are great and they can get the result tomorrow if Giggs and Hartson get on top of their individual games. They are the kind of team who could beat the Russians on their own soil and a draw would put them into a great position for the return in the very impressive Millenium Stadium in Cardiff. Scotland on the other hand could take the backlash of Dick Advocaat's decision to let bygones be bygones and select the very dangerous Ruud van Nistelrooy to get them through this one. Holland are the mystery team who possess some of the greatest talent in the world and this stage tomorrow will suit them right down to the ground where they pass the ball so well. Van Nistelrooy will be hungry for success here as he would feel left out in the Manchester United camp if his team-mates went to the Finals and he had the summer off. This will be his motivation, as if he needs it, for he is a monster of a player when getting the right service and I am sure he will be very much up for this tough tie which should see them go through. Both Wales and Holland are looking for the biggest and toughest players on the field to pick them up and carry them into the second leg with a real chance of qualifying. I cannot say I want the Scots to win for being a 'purist' Holland going through would make for a better competition, but Wales would be fantastic. And of course when you look at Ryan Giggs reminds us of George Best never playing in both the European and World Championships, something that I feel was one of the reasons George would go AWOL every two years when the summer came. If Giggs can perform as he did against Liverpool last weekend who knows, as for George I can see why he went berserk with the 'birds and booze' why these Championships were being played without the greatest player of his time!

I found it very funny this week reading about Chelsea's Tinkerman Claudio Ranieri and his having to play thirteen-a-sides at the training ground for not knowing whom to leave on the side. It read that he sometimes has twenty-six players and wants to play a full-scale match but cannot without upsetting one of his stars. If you were a player and had to sit out a match between the first and second team it would not do your confidence much good. Chelsea's success in Italy has been the talk of the town and I can tell you the new owner Roman Abramovich has a constant smile on his face enjoying every minute of his new business venture. The players say he comes in after matches and congratulates them and shows real enthusiasm even when they lost their only Premiership match this season at Highbury. The Tinkerman is on a runaway train, without a train line to anywhere in particular, but he will definitely be in Manchester to face United in the next three weeks and that will be the real acid test for the Tinkerman and all of his little tinkers!

Sent the same day my Sunday piece, which is a low-down on the International with Denmark:

Here we go again only this time I have the feeling that the Swede will not be following in the same footsteps as the Tinkerman as he tries to get a closer look at Scott Parker and Glen Johnson in their first full International. The thought of him playing his two teams again takes the edge off this match for I would like to see a player judged over the ninety minutes we have always been brought up to play. His constant messing with the team I am certain does nobody any good at all, for surely if you are trying to put the jigsaw puzzle together you only look to change things when there is something going wrong, in other words if a part of the puzzle fits just plonk it in there and look for the next piece!

The other thing is as a player I prided myself on not only getting through the ninety minutes but the extra-time of cup-ties also. I was a player who got stronger as the game went on so I would have never have got a game under the Swede, not that I did under anyone else, but that is not the point here. Players such as Scott Parker will run all day for you and when you have a player like that, that's what you allow him to do. Some players are good at certain times in a match, maybe a little like Ole Gunnar Solksjaer at United who comes off the bench fresh and ruins the opposition in an instant, another is Teddy Sherringham who scores almost immediately when coming onto the field as another example of how certain players respond in certain situations. Alex Ferguson says of Ole Gunnar that he sits and studies the match so well it is almost that he is on the field without being out there, so as soon as he brings him on, he's fresh and clued up, bingo!

JACK CHARLTON

I think the Swede must be pretty sure who are his best players and there are maybe four places up for grabs. I would start the match with Chelsea's Johnson and Bridge as my full backs with another club team mate John Terry the man in charge at the heart of the back four and Gareth Southgate, a player of great consistency alongside him using his vast experience amongst these still 'trialists' in International football. The left full back position can be alternated by Ashley Cole and Bridge, both players are very good going forward so they can take turns at joining in the play down the left hand side. I would maybe give preference to Cole at left back and play Bridge in the role of an attacking midfielder giving us width and a 'getting out ball' down on the left touchline, something we hardly ever have in this country. The most important thing is that whoever it is on the left they must be very positive when in possession and once the other team have it defend in the other team's half. There are so many times we are wide open down that side because it is unnatural for players to go there automatically. Sometimes having a defensive midfield player can be quite a healthy situation for when the opposition have the ball we usually drop off and let them have it in their half but I feel that with four strung across the middle the two wide players push on instead of dropping off. This will try to intimidate the opposition into hitting long balls, which will suit the likes of Terry and Southgate. This is something Jack Charlton did for Ireland as their manager, putting the pressure on as soon as you lose the ball, for Jack it paid great dividends. We don't know if Beckham will play yet because of a back injury but if he does he is good at closing the full back down when the other team has it. Frank Lampard is quickly becoming the man for all seasons in both the blue and the white shirt, a player who looked like a fish out of water when first brought into the Chelsea team but he has worked tirelessly to make his mark and he deserves much credit for the season so far. I used to go to some training sessions when Harry Redknapp was the manager and it wasn't difficult to see that through Frank's father he was doing all the right things, the main thing though was that Frank senior, who was Assistant Coach at the time, gave him his spikes and had him doing ten and fifteen yard 'sprints' when all the lads were sitting down for lunch, this is something really important for that first five yards are crucial in the middle of the field when being first to the 'knock downs' is the difference between going forward or going backwards. And once Frank latches on to those loose balls he has an eagle eye and two great feet to go with it. I am totally baffled by the three strikers in the squad with so much young talent about and I would have brought another young diamond in and gave him his head by playing him in the next five Internationals before the real game gets under way. Jermain Defoe is his name and scoring goals is his game!

This tiny striker is a real handful and shows the kind of education on the field that goes nicely with his terrific first touch and his lightening pace. I have said before but if the £111million spent on players last summer this player should now have been in a royal blue shirt. The Swede cannot keep overlooking this raw talent who has showed me enough to suggest International football is not another world to him. I say if Wayne Rooney is ready then so is Jermain and the better players he plays with the better player he will become and once Owen is fit they could, with the right service, lead defenders a right merry old song and dance. This would have been the ideal time to introduce young Defoe on a ground he scored for West Ham the season before last. A header at that!

He is easy to read when making his run and players such as Gerrard and Scholes would have absolutely no problem picking him out. His pace on the shoulder of a centre back gives him the advantage of anything that is knocked through. The one player I look forward to see in this match is Scott Parker a player of immense talent, a kind of throwback to a young Alan Ball, a 'rare' commodity in our game and Alan Curbishley has brought him through nicely and now he has gained that all important strength his true ability is beginning to shine through. He is a credit to the Charlton manager and has helped him get his club into the dizzy heights of a Champions League place if only they stopped the Premiership right at this minute. What the Charlton manager has achieved over the past five or six years is nothing short of miraculous, a very similar job to that which Dario Gradi has done at Crewe and you can't be paid a bigger compliment than that. And need I say again Harry at Portsmouth. Our old Chelsea coach – Dario – has turned out as many England Internationals as anyone else outside the Premiership and many of them in it. I remember when Kenny Dalglish was the Liverpool manager hearing that Liverpool had first 'option' on their players for quite a substantial amount of money well back then, a hundred grand a season was big money for the likes of Crewe.

So basically Gradi was as good as the Liverpool youth team coach and he did turn some out. The latest being Danny Murphy who is now quite an important part of the Liverpool and England squad.

THREAT TO KENYON PEACE TALKS

This was something printed in the *Evening Standard* on the Wednesday before the Internationals, written by Matt Hughes: The bitter row between Chelsea and Manchester United over Peter Kenyon could move closer towards resolution at a Premier League board meeting. United reported Chelsea to the League last month for making an illegal approach to their chief executive and the matter will be discussed for the first time.

The League must decide whether Chelsea have a case to answer; if so they will set up an Independent Commission to investigate.

Both clubs are hopeful of reaching an agreement that would enable Kenyon to start work at Chelsea this season, but senior figures at Old Trafford are furious over alleged breaches of their former chief executive's gardening leave.

United were willing to release Kenyon after the January transfer window but they are now threatening to make him serve the twelve-month notice period in his contract. The club's attitude hardened after Real Madrid sporting director Jorge Valdano claimed Kenyon called him to register Chelsea's interest in Michael Salgado.

FRANK MUST PROVE HIMSELF TO SVEN

Frank Lampard will be given a chance to cement his place in the centre of England's midfield for Euro 2004 on Sunday.

The Chelsea midfielder has emerged as one of the key players in Roman Abramovich's Stamford Bridge revolution, where he has not only kept his place in Claudio Ranieri's team as a multitude of expensive foreign imports have arrived, but become part of the English backbone of the side.

In the absence of Paul Scholes, Owen Hargreaves and Kieron Dyer at Old Trafford this weekend, Lampard will be given the chance to prove himself from the start against Denmark, where a good performance could be critical to his International future.

Lampard's ability to work prodigiously in midfield for his club, as well as break forward and score vital goals – as he did in the recent Champions League games against Lazio which saw the new Chelsea begin to come of age – have made him indispensable to Ranieri and increasingly hard to ignore for Eriksson. "Frank is playing very good football at this moment" said Eriksson. "He will probably have the chance to start this game, he deserves that, Exactly how we are going to play in midfield I'm not sure yet, but he will be one of them at least. Frank is more mature now, a better passer, and stronger and quicker. That's very important for England. He has a lot of experience but is still young, so it is normal he should become better and better".

Lampard is one of five Chelsea players in the squad. Tony Banks of the *Express* went on to say that: At the moment Lampard has yet to break up Eriksson's first choice midfield of Scholes, Beckham, Gerrard and Nicky Butt – although they have played together just four times since the Swede took over. Butt looks the most vulnerable, having not been a regular at Manchester United this season, but he remains a favourite of Eriksson's in the crucial role of holding midfield role.

The coach said that, "Every time Nicky has played for us, he has done very well. If you talk about Turkey, he was a very important player. He is very clever and always takes up good positions. I'm sure he'll play for United, as the season is long. But he will be fresh for the Euro 2004 finals if he doesn't play too much".

On the same day the *Sun* and Charlie Wyett ran with **GLEN – I WON'T SEE RED – Johnson's pledge over sending-offs**: Glen Johnson insists he will remain super-cool if given his first cap for England against Denmark. The Chelsea defender is determined to avoid a reputation as a loose cannon after two red cards in the last month. Johnson was red-carded for the Under-21's against Turkey last month and then, only eight days ago, the teenager was dismissed again, the sending off being the only disappointing note of Chelsea's 4-0 Champions League win over Lazio in Rome.

Yet Johnson who meets up with his new International teammates tomorrow said that, "I am not a fiery person – I am so laid back and chilled out. I have surprised myself when being sent-off against Turkey and now two red cards in a month. Until now, I have never been sent off in my life at any level. Hopefully, I will put a stop to that and go back to my old ways. Both sendings-off were for two yellow cards, but the second one at Lazio was for kicking the ball away. The manager was unhappy with me and he said a few words. In any case, I knew I had let myself down". Yet Johnson goes into the Denmark match on the back of a very impressive display against Newcastle, which the £6million summer signing from West Ham chipped in with his first goal for the Blues.

Mark McGhee, now in charge at Brighton, following his departure from Millwall last month, insists he always saw signs of Johnson's quality. Arriving from West Ham's reserves, his first game as a professional was against Norwich in October last year – with Millwall crashing 3-1. After seven starts and one as sub, Johnson returned to Upton Park and promptly broke into the first team. McGhee said that "When Glen joined us, he displayed great energy and had irresistible quality on the ball. We stuck him in for his first professional game and he did well. After only a week training with us Denis Wise told me that 'I have just seen the future England right-back'."

Similar words too from Trevor Brooking, who managed Johnson in his first spell as caretaker manager at the end of last season during Glenn Roeder's health problems. Brooking said that "back then, after Glen had broken into the team, I took him to one side and said I felt that he had a chance of getting into the England squad for Euro 2004. I could see that after three or four weeks working with him. Glen is a talented youngster and he did an excellent job at West Ham despite coming into the team at a difficult time. Maybe that is why he has made the transition to Chelsea's team quite easily, as he is used to playing under pressure. He can handle these things superbly and Glen is a terrific, genuine lad who is willing to learn. Sven's attitude with England has always been that age doesn't come into it – it is the attitude that has to be right. Glen has a great chance of doing well".

'DO TRY TO KEEP UP TREVOR'

My view is that: I know Trevor Brooking is very laid back and not one to get excited even in his role as BBC analyser where he is perfect fodder for the two former Liverpool defenders Hansen and Lawrenson, as they see him as an easy target. But Trevor saying Johnson has a great chance of doing well is a little bit of an underrated statement, don't you think? Here is a kid of eighteen having leapt from the West Ham youth team to the reserves and over to the Den with Millwall where he made his League debut and then back to West Ham into the first team, onto Chelsea with all of these so-called world class players and goes straight into the first team. A great chance of doing well, come on Trevor do try to keep up!

INSPIRATIONS

The kid has done miraculously well already. Come on Trevor don't get too excited about this kid's fantastic future now. This is a wonderful story and it was half way through that it dawned on me that although I was in the Chelsea first team at the same age and was elevated into the 1970 World Cup Squad for Mexico in around the same time as young Johnson and understand just what it is like going from the youth team to the International squad inside a year. You grow up very quickly and find that it is by playing against so many players that a year before you were dreaming 'if only'. Then all of a sudden for me it was fantastic playing with McCreadie, Osgood and Cooke and against Best, Law, Charlton at United, Greaves at Spurs, Dave Mackay at Derby, Moore, Peters and Hurst at West Ham, Venables and Marsh at QPR, Graham, Radford, McLintock and Armstrong at Arsenal, Ball, Harvey and Kendall at

Everton, Summerbee, Lee, Young and Doyle at Manchester City. And then after only a very short time into my career it was in Jamaica where I faced the one and only Pele who was playing for Santos of Brazil. Now that is what I call having to grow up quickly!

I remember being in the hotel bar with Tommy Baldwin and Johnny Boyle after this match and the great man came through with a right "tasty" blond on one arm and a drink in his hand and we stopped him to have a drink with us. We asked him if it was alright if we called him 'god' in which he was very flattered and was the complete gentleman, and as I always say that the higher you go up and the greater the talent ninety nine times out of a hundred they are the best kind of people. I had the great fortune to meet him once again in the United States of America before our Seattle Sounders team played New York Cosmos in San Diego. This was for the equivalent of the Super Bowl, the North American League Soccer Bowl. He was once again a little worse for wear but that didn't matter for he wasn't playing the following day and that didn't bother us either. On our return to England, after a very late evening out after the match, we arrived home Thursday and went straight into the Imperial Arms, Matthew Harding's local pub, trained the following morning before flying up to Newcastle for another League match where I scored the only goal from the acutest of angles. There was a loose ball on the left side of the Newcastle penalty area dropping in between Bobby Moncur and myself. I got there first, Bobby was getting on then though, flicked it over his head and caught it right on the touchline where I steadied myself, pulling the ball onto my right foot from an almost impossible angle, and pretending to square the ball to Hutch, on the six yard line, squeezed it between keeper Iam McFaul and his near post. As the ball crept into the net St James's Park fell silent, as nobody knew what had happened, only the sight of me turning away with my arm up thinking about how Pele would have been proud of such a goal. I am a great one for inspirations and this was one fantastic example!

Running after me was Ian Hutchinson who shouted in my ear what he would have done to me if it had not gone in. I looked back at him shouting, "You should know better than that mate". It is moments like that, especially in away matches where the trip home is marvellous, and rounds off a rather wonderful week!

Only a few months later was the time I was selected by Alf Ramsey to fly with the squad to Mexico to defend the title of World Champions, and hopefully, for me, playing against Pele once again, only this time for the best international team of my time on earth, the quite brilliant Brazil. Missing both the FA Cup Final and the Replay against Leeds in that 1970 epic and then missing that World Cup made the saying that it happens in threes quite true and I thought that nothing could be so painful ever again. Little did I know the one upstairs can always go one further and went one further on that most horrific of nights, the 15th of December 1997, in the Mile End Road.

'YOU GOT A DUFF DEAL, CHELSEA'

United chief executive taunts Blues over £17million singing

By Peter Edwards of the *Express*: Manchester United chief executive David Gill last night taunted title rivals Chelsea by claiming Roman Abramovich has paid too much money for Damien Duff.

Gill said Duff, scorer of three goals in 18 League and cup games since moving to London from Blackburn, was not worth the £17million they paid for the Republic of Ireland star. His comments at his first annual shareholders meeting since taking over from Chelsea bound Peter Kenyon are unlikely to go down well in Stamford Bridge's corridors of power. This added further spice to an already intriguing showdown between the two biggest hitters in the capital in two weeks. "We were interested in signing Duff in the summer and we assessed his value" said Gill responding to shareholders' question about why Duff had failed to turn up at Old Trafford. "The assessment of both the manager and the executives was that Damien Duff was not worth that kind of money. Also we felt we had sufficient cover in that area."

And Gill used yesterday's Old Trafford AGM – not attended by Alex Ferguson – to warn off wealthy individuals who may be plotting takeover talks.

"We don't want a sugar daddy", he said. United have been at the centre of feverish speculation following stake building by the American tycoon Malcolm Glazer, Irish racehorse owners John Magnier and JP McManus, and Dutch media mogul John de Mol. It has been further fuelled by Abramovich's takeover of Chelsea, leading to suggestions that other Russian billionaires are circling Old Trafford. "We've received no approaches from any parties regarding a planned takeover bid". Gill added. United plc chairman Roy Gardner, however, warned the 500 shareholders present it was the board's duty to consider bids. "If the board were to receive a valid bid, we would have a duty to consider it, but we are not in that position", said Gardner.

Shareholders also heard that Fabien Bartez's career at Old Trafford will end next summer if a suitable buyer can be found. They were told that the £70,000 a week goalkeeper has been allowed to return to his native France to link up with Marseille on loan till the end of the season following Tim Howard's successful start to his United career. Shareholders were told talks on extending Sir Alex Ferguson's contract are 'on-going'. "We are in discussion with Sir Alex over a new contract. But we're not there yet" said Gardner.

United reported a pre-tax annual profit of £39.3million, helped by the sale of £2.6mllion replica shirts in 58 countries in the past year. "We are expanding our operations around the world all the time" said Gill. "We are close to opening a soccer school at Disneyland Paris so that we can teach children how to play the Manchester United way".

My view is that: it seems that United are now targeting Chelsea instead of the usual war of words with Arsenal around this time of the season and that carries on right through until one side or the other cracks. This tells me that they now believe that Chelsea have become their main rival in the Premiership race. Arsene Wenger will be delighted that he is not targeted about the way his team behave. So it's Chelsea and Manchester United who will fight out the rest of the season both in and out of the ring. Ferguson sees one off after the other as Kevin Keegan got into a verbal match with the United boss and cracked up in doing so, even with him running rivals City Keegan is no longer a personal threat to the United manager. So it is the thinker against the tinker from here on in and I cannot wait to see how Tinkerman handles this as they both prepare to flex their muscles in two weeks' time at Stamford Bridge. This will be a very new experience for Abramovich and his Chelsea sidekicks and I very much look forward to being inside their minds as the match begins on the Monday beforehand and will last right up to the final whistle. The acid test is just around the corner and I for one, cannot wait!

KRAY TWINS
Bobby Moore and the Blind Beggar

I am a great admirer of Sir Alex Ferguson and have met him on a couple of occasions, once in the chairman Martin Edward"s office with Paul McCormack at a time we were putting a pre-season tournament on in Florida. The meeting was good but we did not have the financial muscle that came anywhere near what United carry. I then, again with Paul, Jimmy Duggan and my son Allen, had the displeasure of his being quite rude to us as we passed through the United corridors before a league match against West Ham at Old Trafford. We had a meeting with Bryan Robson and arranged to see him before the match just for about ten or fifteen minutes, in fact Paul and I were not staying for the match because we had two tickets and Jimmy and Allen were a lot keener than we were. We were in the reception and Bryan phoned down to tell the girl on the front desk to send us through. She pressed the door open and we did what Bryan had said, only on the way out we bumped into the United manager who told us in no uncertain manner to get out of his stadium. Now it was only because of Bryan that I did not tell him to go 'fuck himself' which in the end I don't know if that would have mattered or not. Being barred from Old Trafford is no big deal to me and I thought immediately that he was obviously more than just the manager but everything else at HIS Football club. I was very disappointed as I say. I admire the man. The last time I was in his company was at West Ham in Harry Redknapp's tiny wee lounge next to the dressing rooms. I was going to watch West Ham on every given time I could, especially as I was in and out of hospital even to the extent of going there one Saturday after quite serious surgery. I left the Royal London Hospital at midday and was back in the ward at around nine-thirty via the Blind Beggar public house on the corner of Whitechapel Road. This was the one famous for the Kray Twins and also I had been, quite some years before, to an evening with

Bobby Moore, when having his opening night there. Bobby was then involved with Jimmy Quill. This particular day though Alex was as different as chalk and cheese to our meeting at HIS ground. On the football side of it I think he has done absolutely fantastic, but have questioned his choice of goalkeepers and often wonder who really did find Peter Schmeichel!

JORDI WHO

The big Dane was inspirational and quite simply unbelievable in his first couple of seasons there and can say that he was the main reason for United winning their first championship under Sir Alex. If Ferguson thought that Jim Leighton was worthy of being the United goalkeeper it would be time that either him or I go back to see my specialist/shrink in Harley Street. I often wonder what would have happened if Leighton had not have messed up in that FA Cup Final against Crystal Palace, Would he have kept him and ignored the Schmeichel call or would he even have looked for a goalkeeper in the first place?

Instead he put reserve goalkeeper Les Sealey, the ex-Luton number one, and Harry's goalkeeping coach at West Ham until sadly dying all of a sudden just a couple of years ago.

I was also critical of his signing Fabien Bartez as I could not see him having the right credentials to play between the sticks in the Premiership. There was a little bit of Déjà Vu here, for Ferguson made the same mistake when signing Proborsky and Cruyff, the son of the great Johan, after the European Championships in 1996. This surprises me more than anything else, as he knows exactly what kind of players are his type and the right type for Manchester United. Proborsky did one thing in those matches when cheekily chipping the goalkeeper scoring for the Czech Republic, whilst Jordi, which Cruyff prefers to be called, has been seen enough for us to know he is getting a living hanging on, very shakily, to his father's shirt tails!

After all said and done though Ferguson always seems to get out of a mess and his handling of Ruud van Nistelrooy was quite brilliant, once the big Dutch striker got that terrible injury whilst on the verge of signing for Ferguson, but Sir Alex went along with the flow and kept in touch with Ruud throughout his rehabilitation and made sure he eventually became a United player. The rest is history, for Ruud is now possibly or probably the best in the business!

Anyhow that is Sir Alex Ferguson, and it would not have bothered me, or him, had I have lost it in his corridor and afterwards I was pleased I did not. I have had a little run-in with Brian Clough along the way, which I am pleased about the way I handled it. I did give him a piece of my mind and then there is Ken Bates who still thinks to this day that the two scraps we had in the Chelsea tunnel were down to me but he could not be further from the truth. That is what I don't like about people like Bates as he makes decisions without looking at both sides of his particular coin, but once again it's not my loss for if we lived ten lifetimes and came back as different animals we could never have thought any different about one another and that suits me just dandy!

Believe it or not, I did not dislike Bates, the man who signed me the second time around but what he does is make it very difficult to be liked. I think he is one of those people who love being hated!

SICK BASTARD

The news today was shocking as the police had found the body of eighteen year-old Alicia Eborne in a quarry five miles from her home. A local bus driver was charged with her abduction and murder, and I will not give his name for I don't want it on these pages, oh my god with all the evil going on in other parts of the world we have people like this continually bringing heart ache to these poor families. I am sorry for mentioning such a thing but looking around in this club, people were enjoying the company of friends and families alike. I mention this because the murderer is a father of two girls and drinks in the local pub where people were stunned that they had been drinking with him for all these years, never knowing what a sick bastard he was!

INTERNATIONAL WEEKEND

And their headlines **ROONEY AND N'LOONY Boy wonder is star of the show – but madcap defence throw it away** was in the *Sun* while in the *Mail* it was **ROONEY'S MAGIC IS FRITTERED AWAY Robinson slip exposes flaws in rearguard;** The *Daily Mirror* went **SVENDAY BLOODY SVENDAY Danes ruin Rooney show as defenders blow it**. The *Express* said that **SWEDE CHARIOT GOES OFF THE RAILS If we defend like that we have no chance in Portugal next summer says the England coach. DANES WRECK THE JOE SHOW.**

ROONEY IS AN AMAZING TALENT – HIS POWER IS JUST FRIGHTENING Everton team-mate Gravesen, is a big fan of Wayne.

'MAESTRO, YOU'RE FUCKED'

Alan Ball, The Candy Box, March 1975

It was Saturday morning and Australia had just eased into the rugby World Cup Final and waited on France and England's match the following morning to see which team they faced next weekend. But football was on my mind and for a change I was hoping Wales could get some kind of result in Moscow, as I said a few pages back. Also there was a very funny scenario as Bertie Vogts, that great old West German fullback, led Scotland into a Euro 2004 play-off against Holland. I played against Bertie on my England debut and then afterwards had a good time drinking with him and his goalkeeper Sepp Maiuer. It was quite funny because with it being my debut against the World Champions it seemed strange being out with two of there most famous players, firstly in the Val Bonne and after that in the club opposite the Candy Box. It was around about five in the morning when I turned to Alan Ball and said "Don't these German bastards ever buy a drink." To which Ballie said "Maestro, they're alright, they look after us when we go over there." I put my arm around my captain that night and said, "what happens if I never get to go over to Germany." Ballie said "Then Maestro, you are fucked."

I was with my uncle George, Son Allen and George's son, my cousin Anthony and the venue was the Grosvenor Club in Bourne Street just before, if coming through Chelsea, you reach Belgravia where Roman Abramovich has purchased another home for him and his family. Two very intense matches with so much at stake and both the Scottish and the Welsh did themselves proud and gave themselves a real chance to make Portugal next summer. Scotland by beating the Dutch by one goal to nil, and Wales by holding the Russians on a freezing afternoon in Moscow. They play the return matches on Wednesday evening and I will be plotted up for the Welsh match, trying to give them some support against a talented team but one who might just not relish the Millenium Stadium in Cardiff where 75,000 screaming 'taffs' will be right behind their heroes right till the final whistle, and if the Welsh can draw first blood I think that there will be no stopping Mark Hughes players.

Then Sunday was upon us and the friendly against Denmark had arrived with me still in the same venue, but I had been home in between. The talking had to stop and the real business of playing for your place begins. The squad was without Southgate, out with an injury and Wayne Rooney had passed a fitness test as he had been suffering from a flu virus but made the match. And was it a good job he did for he hit a great fifth minute strike to put us in front before the Danes levelled three minutes later through Jorgenson. Then Rooney laid a pass into the path of Joe Cole and the Chelsea midfielder sided footed us into the lead once more with only nine minutes on the electrical Old Trafford scoreboard. In the thirtieth minute Upson clumsily sent substitute Daniel Jensen sprawling and Jorgensen blasted his shot past James from the penalty spot. This was given away by Joe Cole who has a tendency to overdo it in parts of the field where he just needs to put the ball into his front men and join in the play. He has the luxury role whereas he can go where he likes behind the front two yet wants to ignore them when it is his job to get the ball into their feet. You don't win matches beating players on the halfway line and if the Chelsea player does not understand that by now I am afraid he never will. I blame the coaching staff of whoever is supposed to be teaching him such simple things. There are some things certain players don't understand and it might be that Joe will fall by the wayside if he does not put his great ability into the areas it should be used. Players want opposition players to dribble on the half way line. I used to pick the ball up off our goalkeeper and become the last man in defence where I would run into space with it looking for an angle which allowed me to play the ball into the feet of my front man, it is that simple. Cole is doing himself no favours whatsoever and the Danes were delighted by him doing so, for it only makes life for your opponents so much easier, which is the opposite of what it should be. I was very disappointed reading Mark Irwin in the *Sun* who analysed Paul Robinson by the following: marks four out of ten. **Made a couple of top stops after replacing James at halftime before all his work came undone. International ring rust showed as he was caught out for the killer blow**. Now a shot is a shot no matter whether it is for the Sunday pub team or at Old Trafford in this match. Robinson had just pulled off another wonderful save, this time from Peter Lovenkrand's thunderbolt, but Jon Dahl Tomasson's shot, after picking up the rebound proved to be the winner. He hit the first shot with venom and although Robinson was right behind it he spilled it and it bounced kindly for the ex-Newcastle player who made no mistake. Yes, Robinson will be disappointed knowing he should have held the first shot, and it seems sometimes now that most continental keepers have the right idea when punching shots out. With the balls being so light in the modern game I would suggest if a shot stopper is not confident about holding onto these shots punching is definitely the best option. There are no excuses for Robinson, but to say it was International ring rust is truly laughable. Rooney was no doubt England's best performer and his effort early in the second half left the right hand post of the Danish goal shaking, if possible a sweeter struck shot than his goal earlier, although thinking about it they were both struck to perfection. He glided past a defender just inside the box but was at a difficult shooting angle but his awareness allowed him without looking up to hammer what would have a been a goal good enough to win any game anywhere and if he keeps them coming then football lovers in Portugal will be in for a treat. He was supposedly laid up with the flu and these viruses are supposed to make you weak but whatever he has taken to keep his strength up I wish he could give some to me. He is a very special talent, the kind that simply has no respect for defenders anywhere and takes them on, unlike Cole, in all the right areas of the field and given an extra yard he will hit in shots with such venom that I am sure keepers cannot see them. This one particular effort I am sure was coming off the post as the keeper was diving. The keeper was unsighted because Rooney had beaten his marker and hit it without any back-lift so I would not have been surprised if the goalkeeper did not see it on its way to the post or coming back. Yeah, Wayne Rooney is a very special talent and once he begins to relax a little more, meaning concentrating on doing all of the good things instead of some silly little tangles he gets into with defenders, for defenders will love him getting hot under the collar for it detracts from his game.

My view overall: was that it seemed as if I had gone back into a time warp as the Danes looked superior than us all over the field and created much more than we did. It seems if there is an open game we get outplayed by such a nation. People still don't understand that technically these countries have overtaken us whereas when I was playing they were mere amateurs. The main point I am trying to put across is that they are improving as a nation where as I believe at times we have stood still, even gone backwards. Only time will tell and I put my neck on the line by predicting the Danes will go further than us in next summer's finals in Portugal!

I still believe that Teddy Sherringham is good enough for the national team because, with no disrespect, if Emile Heskey is an International footballer I know nothing about our game whatsoever!

JONNY WILKINSON

The one game I do know nothing about, for sure, is rugby, but must say how magnificent the England playmaker is and his one-man show on Sunday was quite extraordinary. The match was all about bottle and this bloke has got that in abundance as he scored every one of our twenty-four points against the seven scored against us by the French. It is not difficult to pinpoint a superstar and this fella is most certainly one after this performance, he must have been something special for this was the first time I have watched a rugby match all through. It is incredible at this moment in time that England has three such individuals as Andy Flintoff, Jonny Wilkinson and Wayne Rooney, three individuals who have excelled over the last couple of weeks and given us something to be proud about. Okay Rooney played in a friendly but Wayne Rooney will never play in a friendly for he is a born winner in every sense of the word and in Flintoff it is the best I have seen a white man since Ian Botham tore the Aussies apart in that wonderful test where it is believed that a couple of Aussies wagered on England on the last day of that test. Nevertheless you have to have the ability to do such a thing and like these three Botham was a real 'superstar' in every sense of the word. The only difference at this moment in time, I hesitate about Flintoff but only because I would like to see him do it against the very best and toughest opposition. Right now we have the two play-off matches on Wednesday before Chelsea travel to St Mary's, the home of Southampton to keep up their part of the new Premiership, which Manchester United have told us that it is the Blues in west London rather the reds on the north side who pose the biggest threat as they go all out to keep a hold of their Premiership title. This week though belonged to the England rugby team as they hogged the headlines in the lead up to their World Cup final at the weekend. There were two ex-Chelsea old boys in the news though, the first being Glenn Hoddle, who since leaving Spurs has tried to say that he was 'Stabbed in the back' at White Hart Lane and the headline in the *Daily Star* said that **A CLEANER COULD DO A BETTER JOB THAN HODDLE SAYS David Pleat, who is caretaker at this moment in time and doing a very good job of it as well**: Tottenham caretaker-boss has relit the fuse on his bitter feud with Glenn Hoddle by insisting a cleaner could do a better job as Spurs manager, wrote Lee West. Pleat has been entangled in a war of words with the former England boss since Hoddle's departure from the White Hart Lane hot seat two months ago. Pleat began the row four weeks ago by questioning Hoddle's management style during his spell in north London. But Hoddle has since hit back by claiming

Pleat should be given the manager's job full time as he is impossible to work alongside. It had appeared that the two had finally ended their bickering following a short spell of silence from both sides. But Pleat, who has taken over the role as Spurs' manager since Hoddle's departure, has now said to have taken another swipe at his former colleague in Sydney's *Sun Herald*. The Spurs supremo is currently searching for a successor to Hoddle and has a large number of applicants battling for the post.

And as Pleat scours through the piles of application forms he insists that none could do any worse than the former Spurs boss. Pleat said that, "We've had everyone, managers, agents, mothers, fathers, dustmen, cleaners applying. To be fair, none of the above could probably do much worse than Glenn Hoddle." The latest remarks will infuriate Hoddle who has made it clear that leaving Tottenham was one of the hardest things he has ever had to do, as he stills loves the club. Hoddle has managed to keep a reasonably low profile since leaving the north London club in September. But he is still hoping for another job in the near future and has been linked with Nottingham Forest, where boss Paul Hart is being tipped for the vacant post at Leeds United. Hoddle said that, "I've got a passion for the game. I've been in this game since I was a kid. It's in my blood. I'm interested in going back into management and I'm interested in doing well." Another ex-Blue was in the news on this day as Jody Morris, now of Leeds United, was charged, along with a friend, of rape. This is not the first time Morris has been in trouble but it seems with him the charge is a lot more serious than 'stepping out of line'. Also on this day 'superstar' status seems not to worry Michael Jackson as he was 'nicked' for sex with an under-age youth. Jackson has already told the world that the young boys who visit him and 'stay over' sleep in his bed with him. Whacko Jacko is one sick 'puppy'!

My view on Hoddle is that: He's quoted saying that he is interested in coming back into the game and also interested in doing well – sounds like a school kid in the headmaster's office. I thought that goes without saying if you have anything about you. I have known Glenn Hoddle, not very well, since he made his debut against me at Stoke City in the mid-seventies and his debut was quite remarkable, also scoring a trademark Hoddle goal from around twenty-five yards out. I said to him coming off the field that if he kept playing like that he was going to be one of the greats. I went to see him when he came to Stoke-on-Trent with his Swindon team, who were playing at Port Vale on this particular Saturday afternoon. He was very cool and very confident about the situation and played this day, as sweeper, and Vale had no answer to the way he set his team out to play. He once again was majestic and his team completely outclassed a Vale team who weren't any pushovers at Vale Park. I thought then that his managerial career was taking off and was not surprised when Chelsea took him on and the reason for that was that Matthew Harding was a massive Hoddle fan. But I began to see things going wrong which were blatant and one in particular was at Wembley in the FA Cup Final against

Manchester United. Chelsea had United on the ropes in the first half and a couple of chances fell their way and they were unlucky not to go in for the break in front. I think Spencer hit a great shot onto the bar, which was the closest either team come to scoring in the first forty-five minutes. On this particular day I was working the BBC radio with the great Denis Law and I said at half-time that Chelsea were giving much more than they were getting, although I should have known Ferguson's half-time team talk was not going to be 'well done lads, same again', very much the opposite.

GASCOIGNE

If my memory serves me well I think it was Mark Stein who had been out injured for quite a while leading up to this match, and looked very tired nearing the half-time whistle and my first reaction was that Glenn should bring him off and replace him with himself who was substitute that day. I was quite surprised to see Mark come out for the second half and thought Glenn must be watching a different game from where I was sitting. United took control and Glenn finally came on with the score two or three nil and made it too little too late as United just grinded them into submission finally winning by four goals. That was the day I first questioned his managerial qualities and from that day on he has continued to baffle me, none more so than in the World Cup with the handling of the Gascoigne incident, when bringing him back from the dead then leaving him out. Gascoigne supposedly burst into his hotel room and began ranting and raving only to be stopped by a couple of other England players who were passing by. And then Eileen Drury and his comments about kids who were born sick were that way because how they were in their previous life. Meaning they were guilty before they were actually born, pretty tasteless stuff I thought and happening just after my accident I wondered if he meant me as well, for I was beaten up pretty badly by that car and the big old oak tree. So to say I am not surprised by what Pleat has to say is pretty much an understatement. What disappointed me most about his returning to Spurs was his handling of Rebrov, a player who could play this game and it was obvious it was personal, something I don't like in any walk of life. Rebrov was a tremendous player alongside Andrei Shevchenko and scored goals for fun alongside the AC Milan 'superstar'. It seems to me that Glenn has made a rod for his own back, and the very last straw to break the camels back is my judgement of him.

CHELSKIING
Now the Russian wants to buy a mountain

By Cameron Robertson of the *Daily Star.* **MEGA-RICH Chelsea owner Roman Abramovich wants to buy an entire Royal ski resort as his latest toy**.

The Russian billionaire yesterday revealed plans to open his very own 'Chelski Land' theme park in Britain. Now he wants to go on the piste by snapping up the exclusive ski-crazy town of Courchevel 1850 in the French Alps.

Abramovich shocked holidaymakers when he flew into the snow-covered resort in his nine-seater helicopter.

Accompanied by his wife Irina and three bodyguards, the Russian – who is worth a staggering £3.5billion – demanded to see all the best chalets in the area. The plush resort gets its name from being 1,850 meters up in the mountains – and it is a favourite getaway spot for Prince Michael of Kent and Juan Carlos of Spain.

Super rich Abramovich – who recently bought a 378 foot mega yacht for £72million – spent hours looking at pads, including those owned by Formula 1 McLaren co-owner Mansour Ojjeh and Irish packaging family the Smurfits. The disappointed oil tycoon appeared to be on his first loser when he was met by stiff resistance from contented owners. But he made their jaws drop by offering to snap up all the plush chalets at three times their current valuations. Resort manager Rene Montgrandi revealed, "I drove Mr Abramovich around for two days as he approached 20 chalet owners trying to buy their properties. He said he would pay double or triple as each owner declined the offer to sell".

One resort restaurant owner said "It would be an ideal location if he wants to bring his Chelsea players away for a short break from football".

My view on this latest coup: is that all I can think of is that because Chelsea did not play this weekend Roman was bored and didn't know what to do with the first weekend break of the season. What with Manchester United looking to open a Disneyland Football Playground it seems like a case of keeping up with the Jones's, and I wonder just what Peter Kenyon has to do with such a thing whilst he is not allowed to come to work at the Bridge yet. At a guess I would say that he is looking around for just what that gentleman said, a lovely place to take the players to, not only for a break but pre-season training in the best possible climate one can buy. What is the point in taking your club to a place that you do not own and twenty chalets seems about perfect for a team with twenty-six players, each chalet probably bedding three players would leave it quite nicely for both management and directors alike. This man from Russia does not seem to miss a trick – or his advisers – and has everyone working for the future of his football club, as for a toy I am not too sure about that, it seems like seriously good business to me!

It was whilst watching the Russians host Wales last weekend I thought the Chelsea owner missed out on a very good PR job for both Chelsea and himself. There have been rumblings from his native homeland that he has earned his money there and is now helping the economy elsewhere without putting anything back. Well, if I were him I would have splashed a few hundred grand – or a long trip on his yacht – for the players beating Wales in Moscow. It would have been a wonderful gesture and one which would have silenced his 'knockers' and won a few admirers both here and back home. Unless there is reason for not doing so I think someone in his set-up missed a wonderful opportunity to settle things down. Meanwhile back in Chelsea the team prepare for a rough ride at Southampton.

MAGNIER AND JP McMANUS

We all know that there are no easy matches in football, let alone the Premiership, but ten days from the crunch match with Manchester United the Tinkerman is having an easier time than the 'thinker' as the United boss declares his case against the Coolmore Farm of John Magnier over that wonderful horse the Rock of Gibraltar. The 'Rock' was a part of a genuine gesture where Magnier invited Ferguson into a partnership, more a sporting gesture than a business one, although Sir Alex will say they have to pay for inviting me into this situation as they looked to get 'snug' as shareholders at Manchester United. Meaning that they, being Magnier and JP McManus, two of the most powerful men in the racing world. The scene is set for a long drawn out investigation and one Ferguson will relish for he has nothing to lose. He has not put a penny in the 'kitty' whether it was for the purchase of the horse, the upkeep of the horse, to even buying a glass of Dom Perignon after this talented animal had broken several records. How Magnier and McManus must wish they never came up with such an idea!

I know from other quarters that two of the most clever and meticulous race horse owners and breeders are deeply upset with the Manchester United manager, but Ferguson being Ferguson, backs down to nobody, and they should have done their homework on the man in the first place. All of this is great for the Tinkerman as he is less involved with things outside of his most important job in life, a game of football and plotting the downfall of United in just two Saturdays' time. As for the Magnier headquarters, they are facing a man who is a bad loser, especially when things look like going against him. Ask Bayern Munich!

I really am shocked that these racing people did not tie up loose ends knowing that the 'Rock' was obviously the best in O'Brien's yard and thinking that this man would take just what they offered. I wrote earlier about Ferguson and his power once behind the closed doors of Old Trafford and nobody, be it, King Kong, Saddam Hussein or Bin Laden will get an inch from him if wanting to use him to get their feet under his table. There is no party with the United boss unless he is wearing the 'hat' and blowing the 'whistle' around his football ground. In a nutshell, you have to pay to enter his empire!

FSA DROPS INTO INSIDER TRADING AT CHELSEA

Having told you about the trouble at United there was trouble at Chelsea on the same day, only this time the Tinkerman is not involved. Wayne Versey of the *Express* reports that: The City watchdog has dropped an investigation into insider trading at the company that owned Chelsea before the takeover by Roman Abramovich.

But there will still be a second inquiry into the 'nature and status of certain shareholdings' in Chelsea Village plc in the days leading up to the billionaire's £140million bid.

Suspicions were raised in the City about the volume of trading following a hike in the company's share price from a year-low of 13p in April 2003 to 28p before the 1st of July when Abramovich tendered his bid document.

He later offered 35p per share in his takeover, leading the Financial Services Authority to investigate suggestions of insider trading.

Having concluded that this was not the case, the FAS turned its attentions to the mysterious ownership of 20.5 per cent of the club before the sale to Abramovich.

In July the FAS announced: "A number of sources (suggest) that the publicly disclosed shareholdings of certain parties may have been inaccurate. The FSA is concerned that the market may have been misled as in the true ownership of Chelsea Village plc".

This led to investigation of eight companies, which agreed to sell shares to Abramovich. At the time the probe was announced, Chelsea chairman Ken Bates threatened the FSA with legal action. He said, "The question of Chelsea shareholders was looked into in 1996 and was accepted by the Stock Exchange. Then the FSA held an inquiry a year ago and found nothing wrong.

"I am fed up with this innuendo. I want to know what evidence they are supposed to have received. I challenge the little worms at the FAS to come out of from behind their stone and justify action".

The FSA can impose heavy fines if it finds that any shareholder has intentionally caused such a financial mystery!

BOSS IS COOL ON COLE

Sven Goran Eriksson is still wrestling with the pros and cons of playing Joe Cole. Chelsea midfield-star Cole, 22, scored for England at Old Trafford on Sunday.

But two minutes earlier he gave away the ball, allowing Denmark to break and score on their way to a 3-2 win. England coach Eriksson said that "Maybe you have to expect he will lose the ball and it's the price you have to pay for having him in. But today if you want to be a complete international player you have to learn a lot.

"That comes with experience. I can talk to him and his manager Claudio Ranieri does the same. Cole can change a game offensively, but unfortunately in football you are not only going that way. You have to take positions and not give your opponents the opportunity to counter-attack easily. I'm sure in February and March he will be in the squad for Portugal and Sweden games, although I don't know if he will start".

Eriksson has also appealed to Newcastle striker Shola Ameobi not to turn his back on England.

My view is that: what I find quite amazing is that players, using Cole as an example, get into the England set-up and still have to learn when and where to pass the football.

When I was a small kid playing in the streets I learned that, and by watching the likes of Johnny Haynes of course. Then after that you sign Apprentice Professional for a couple of years before, if you are fortunate, signing full Professional terms, you should in that time have been taught all the basics of our game. Going back to Ron Greenwood and his favourite saying of 'Simplicity is genius' and nothing is more simple than knowing that you should not be trying to beat players whilst in your own half for the simple reason of it being unproductive even if you do beat him. You may beat him nine times out of ten but the tenth time could cost you an unnecessary goal. Joe Cole at this moment in time has not shown enough intelligence and responsibility, the kind you need when playing in the 'heartbeat' of your team. You should be a leader of men in that role where other players should be able to trust you with the ball and make space for themselves to receive the ball from you, but far too many times Cole plays with his head down, which is not the sign of a great player.

DUFF LEADS THE WAY WITH SOLO SHOW

Damien Duff lit up this low-key friendly with a superb solo goal and Robbie Keane scored twice as the Republic of Ireland swept aside Canada. The game was a low-key friendly and manager Brian Kerr said in the *Daily Mail* written by Colin Young that, "there were only 25,000 here to see Damien amazes me. If I was a parent or a child, I'd want to see him any opportunity he is in Dublin".

My view is that: I am awfully glad that I did not write that for such a newspaper, whether it was Colin Young or a printing error it is not good enough in a newspaper of such standing. That apart, Damien Duff is making quite a habit of scoring this type of goal as he jinks in and out of the full-back, either coming in and shooting with his right foot or going outside, on his favoured left foot, to get his telling crosses in. He has become a great favourite at Stamford Bridge and a player who you can see growing in stature with every touch of the ball, or so it seems to me. I, like David Gill's comments, do not think Duff is worth that kind of money, but that is not his fault. Players today are mostly judged, not on how they perform, but by thy size of their transfer fee, which is not the way it should be.

Quote of the week comes from England fly-half Johnny Wilkinson as he and his team mates warm up to the big match against Australia **"I KNOW EXACTLY WHERE IT'S GOING AND I PUT IT THERE. END OF STORY"** That just might sound a little bit like a quote from a player who has a big ego, but newspapers, and headlines in particular, can make a "mug" of you when you pick them up next morning. This was the *Sun* headline. On the same day Rob Shepherd of the *Express* wrote: **TIME FOR FINE TUNING NOT TINKERING** making a point that 'as we have seen in the cases of

Wayne Rooney and Glen Johnson, players do emerge on the international stage from 'nowhere', one suspects that apart from a couple of either/ors, Eriksson has decided on his 23-man squad and his preferred starting line-up.'

The Swede said that, "Wayne Rooney has been the highlight of the year for us. He has come from more or less nowhere to score three times for England. He played very well against Denmark. What is amazing to see is that when we pass the ball to him, even if it is a difficult ball, he will control with the first touch so he is ready to do something with his second touch. I must say in the eighteen months since I first saw him he has matured a lot. He has made a big leap forward. Even if he has not done as well for his club as he did last season, he has always done very well for England. He has more than exceeded my expectations so far."

My view is that: Chelsea will definitely be keeping tabs on his career at Everton knowing that his club are cash strapped and might just need the money enough to sell their 'boy wonder'. His latest performance was one of great power for one so young and his two strikes on goal were something in the same mould as Geoff Hurst, an example being the fourth goal in the '66 World Cup Final, when you consider that it was a match of great pressure and this goal was struck well into injury time, in fact one hundred and twenty minutes. I played in the same team as Geoff Hurst at Stoke City and can confirm that he had immense power in his shooting, and he never hit any harder than one of his 'rockets' from the penalty spot at Upton Park which was saved incredibly by Gordon Banks in the League Cup semi-final. This save eventually took Stoke City through to meet our Chelsea team in the final, in 1972, at Wembley, which they ran out 2-1 winners, thanks to a goal from veteran George Eastham.

NEW RAPE SHAME

As the game lurches from one crisis to another, from drugs to rape, it is not only the Premiership superstars in the Grosvenor House scandal who are tarnishing the image of the national sport.

Arsenal and England Under-18 star Marcus Artry has been jailed for nine years for his part in a string of sex attacks on women and girls ranging from the age of fourteen. Needless to say Arsenal have cancelled his contract and his career is over.

Judge Colin Smith described the attacks as 'horrific and terrifying' when he sentenced Artry and his three accomplices at an inner London Crown Court. The judge added: "Women must be protected from you".

LIFE BAN

It has been very difficult writing this book in the sense that I began by writing about the incredible take-over of Abramovich at my home club, Chelsea Football Club, but along the way I felt I must go deeper and let you know that whilst the game became even more exciting and that players all over Europe, and at home here, would clean their act up in hope of being signed by the Russian billionaire. Then you read about the likes of Jody Morris and Marcus Artry and think that the world really has gone crazy. What more of a motivation does one need to earn this kind of money for playing the game one loves for a football club like Chelsea. I find it very difficult trying to understand what these youngsters are doing not only to themselves but to innocent people around them. Raping and 'roasting' as it is called now, has sunk the game to the lower depths of our society and I am afraid that the likes of these players should be fined heavily and banned for life from playing the game at any and every level. Not that they would have to be banned because it seems that they would rather rape a young girl than play in front of fifty, sixty and seventy thousand people every Saturday afternoon. I apologise for having to mention this, but again, these are the people who make the love, fun and joy of our game taste a little putrid and I would not mind if half of them were even good players. The players today believe their own headlines and wage packets and with all the backhanders that have controlled outside the game for so long, now I blame the Clubs from the Directorship right down to the manager's office, where I have met many a fool, who themselves believe that they know about the game. Thank god for the likes of Arsene Wenger who had brought complete class into a league that was – apart from Manchester United – quickly becoming the pits. Ranieri has his way, but the Italian looks at the game in a vastly different way from this very unique manager of one of my old clubs, if only I could turn the clock back to sign there under his control and be free of all the injuries I had whilst there, it would have been a dream to have played for him, even though if it was following my mentor and great friend, the late great Tony Waddington!

'PULSATING PLAYBOYS'

This is the end of a Roy Bentley piece that I pulled out of a drawer and could not find the beginning, but there is enough here to allow you to realise what a player he was?

He is talking about the only season Chelsea won the championship and in particular Ted Drake and the team they called 'Drake's Ducklings' just as Tommy Doc called his players 'Docherty's Diamonds' and Sexton his 'Pulsating Playboys', if there were something to call us?

Many of our performances in my first season running through our FA Cup ties were in many ways more pulsating than this team of the moment, and we'll see if any of the big three can become just that. Manchester United have had their best days when their young FA Youth Cup winning lions joined the ranks of the big boys taking over from the likes of Ince, Hughes, Kanchelskis, Whiteside and the fantastic Paul McGrath, leaving only the brilliant Bryan Robson to use his vast experience to coax these boys onto another plateau. Along came Cantona and it was no surprise to me that they could not win in Europe with the Frenchman and was also not surprised that Teddy Sherringham came along to not only fill the void but do it majestically and more successfully, as I predicted way back then. Yeah, they were the greatest days in the club's history although Best and the rest of the boys began the ball rolling but the majority of that side came to the age of no return at the same time, and the 'Belfast Boy' was left alone to go through the kind of changes that happen these days at the likes of Gillingham, Reading and Leyton Orient, sorry to use those as examples, but it would only be the same if I had picked ninety-nine per cent of football clubs out of my trilby hat. George had to go it alone and realised that it was far easier chasing Miss Worlds than getting a pass from his new team mates!

What a waste of talent and in today's market wouldn't it have been just fantastic to have seen George go the same way as David Beckham and wear that number seven shirt of the most magnificent club team ever. Maybe Pele – who also wore the all white – might argue that his Santos were?

What a game this is when you can write about players like these and have experienced being on the same field as them. I had played against Best, Charlton, Law, Greaves, Mackay, Mullery, Crerand, Bremner, Giles, St John, Ball, Harvey and Kendall, Bell, Summerbee and Lee, Worthinton, Currie, George, Bowles, Venables, Dougan, McLintock, Robert Chelsea Moore, Peters and Hurst. Then overseas Cryuff and his up and coming Dutch master craftsmen that brought us 'Total football' and the man himself, Pele, all before reaching my nineteenth birthday. I have obviously missed at least one other great player of those early days for every team seemed to have at least one. Not forgetting a wonderful Real Madrid player named Pirri who nearly beat us on his own in that first European Cup Winners Cup Final in Athens only a year after that epic thriller at Old Trafford when the lads won without me in 1970. This was all happening so quickly!

Anyhow, back to that great Chelsea captain Roy Bentley: "Ted bought seven or eight players, at the same time as Ranieri has done. Ranieri's brought in eight world-class players, but with all respect to our boys they wouldn't consider themselves world class. We were written off as Third Division players, but that was a load of nonsense".

Chelsea was a standing joke long before Drake was mocked for scouring the lower leagues for potential ugly ducklings. In the late nineteen thirties, a comedian wrote a satirical song entitled "The Day That Chelsea Won The Cup" so fanciful was the notion, but Drake changed all of that.

The former Arsenal striker transformed the entire club, bringing in new players, changing the badge and becoming the first manager to take charge of training sessions. Bentley said that, "Everyone was used to Chelsea being a variety, vaudeville team, a complete joke. We were known as a joke club, but if they'd seen Ted speak to us in training no one would've doubted us. Ted changed everything you could think of and was way ahead of the game. No one else did any coaching about how to play the game and he was also the first to get reports on the opposition.

The only thing he slipped up on was the Chelsea Pensioners. He moved them trackside to the top of the stand because there were the last seats to be sold, but a lot of them were very old and couldn't climb up the steps. There was no demand at all for tickets as they'd rather be at the front.

Fired on by Drake's work ethic and Bentley's goals, Chelsea duly won the Championship, clinching the title with a 3-0 win over Sheffield Wednesday at Stamford Bridge in their penultimate game of the season. Although the achievement was grand, the celebrations were remarkably modest.

The ex-Chelsea Championship winning captain went on to say that "I remember the day we won the Championship as if was yesterday. We didn't really celebrate and just had some nuts in the boardroom with the wives. Ted said a few words, I had a few words and then we all went home. Stan (Willemsie) went down for an evening at Brighton races, so he tells me.

Everyone asks what we got for winning the league, but Stanley nearly had the police after him. We were invited to the tailors and could either have a suit or an overcoat as reward. Stan got a suit and an overcoat and when Ted got the bill he wasn't very impressed as Stan got more than everybody else".

An afternoon in the company of Bentley would make even the hardest of hearts pine for the simplicity of a bygone age.

The seventy-nine-year-old was a champion schoolboy boxer, played cricket with the great Wally Hammond at Gloucestershire and is still the proud owner of a congratulatory telegram from his good friend Sir Lawrence Olivier, signed rather theatrically 'goodbye for now darling.'

Among the ups and downs of Ray's remarkable career include becoming the first substitute used by an England team – at B level – reaching the FA Cup semi-finals without getting to Wembley and playing in England's infamous 1-0 defeat to America in the 1950 World Cup.

He came a long way from his first job in football, feeding and grooming the club horse at Bristol City.

Bentley only signed for Chelsea because of the cold weather in Newcastle, an inconvenience, which even a drop of the black stuff couldn't remedy.

He said that, "I couldn't cope with the climate up there and was ill all the time. I was sent to Scarborough one weekend to recuperate and told to drink a pint of Guinness with every meal, as it would build up my strength. It was hard for me to drink as I found it very bitter. It was too strong and I never developed a taste for it."

Chelsea fans have been drinking to Bentley's success for far too long and the man himself hopes they will have more silverware and players celebrate this season.

The Bristolian will be at Sunday's match against Manchester United and, despite his allegiance, is hoping for a repeat of the 1954/55 encounter, which finished 6-5 to the visitors. His last words were that "I'd like Chelsea to win the Premiership, but it would be good to see some goals on Sunday. Ranieri is doing a very good job and if he pulled it off this season, it will be a great achievement".

My interest and view is: becoming a columnist for a very well respected and successful newspaper I am always looking for help outside of my real trade. In this 'big' review of the *Evening Standard*, whoever sends it to print are either totally blind or blind drunk, because I am now and I spotted it. How can you call someone of such stature, 'Ray Bentley'?

I work on a freelance basis, part time really, yet these people on full 'wages' who have never played the game of football cannot even get the name correct. I find that quite extraordinary, disrespectful and damned ignorant!

Let me put it this way, if this bloke writing this piece came and watched me play and I kicked the corner flag whilst taking a corner it would be headlines, and that is what always catches my eye, especially when doing your homework!

It's all right for journalists to make errors such as this but if you are playing they cannot wait to write something negative about you. So maybe, although Fleet Street no longer remains, writers are less educated football wise and less than Premier League as far as being professional.

On the Roy Bentley piece, I am delighted to introduce him into the Tinker and Talisman book, for he was once one of the greats on the field in a royal blue shirt and is now being seen as a player who really were there before Ken Bates said did not exist.

Roy Bentley was a giant in the blue shirt, just like Bobby Moore in a white one, holding the Jules Rimet Trophy. It has happened only once in the history of both England and Chelsea and you could not have asked for better captains.

You read the headline a few pages back about Chelsea going for the

Woodward effect, a piece written by Ken Dyer in the *Standard*.

This is what it was all about: Clive Woodward as a guest of honour at Chelsea's monumental match against Manchester United on Sunday and the triumphant England rugby coach is living proof that the end justifies the means.

Woodward and one of his England heroes, Lawrence Dallaglio and his team mates, have just demonstrated in the World Cup, it doesn't matter an awful lot how you qualify, just as long as you do.

Chelsea, in their penultimate Group G match against Sparta, achieved the point they needed to ensure they reached the next stage of the competition, but in an uninspiring way.

With Lazio and Besiktas also sharing the points in the other game, Claudio Ranieri's team remain firm favourites to win the group, even more so now their final match against Besiktas will be played at a neutral venue in less than two weeks' time.

Sparta made life difficult for Chelsea. They invariably built a wall of maroon shirts in front of their goal and had limited attacking ambitions themselves. Their reaction at the end of a goalless draw spoke volumes. There were high fives all over the place as they kept their Champions League hopes alive.

Ranieri said before the game that Sparta was a tougher side away from home and he was right. While Carlo Cudicini was virtually unemployed his opposite number, Jaromir Blakez, wasn't exactly rushed off his feet either. Chelsea did have their opportunities, however, the best of which came in the 26th minute when Hernan Crespo headed Damien Duff's cross against the bar. Adrian Mutu reacted quickly to toe-end the rebound back to the Argentine who duly netted but the goal was ruled out for offside. That chance apart, most of the entertainment was centred on Ranieri and the Sparta coach Jiri Kotrba, who cussed and cursed and waved their arms around with equal animation.

Ranieri had certainly not taken this match lightly and, with the possible exception of Mario Melchiot, in for the suspended Glen Johnson and Joe Cole replacing the injured Juan Sebastian Veron, this was his first-choice line-up in Champions League encounters.

There was minimal improvement in the second half, although Ranieri was in a more introspective mood and with the crowd subdued, it seemed everyone had an eye on Sunday's clash with Manchester United. Ranieri, the Tinkerman, made a double substitution in the second half, replacing Cole and Crespo with Geremi and Eidur Gudjohnsen. It almost worked a treat when, in the final minute, the Icelandic striker fed Mutu who, with a clear run at goal, put his shot wide.

At least it was another clean sheet, the fifth in a row, for John Terry and his defence. "We have achieved qualification but now it important to get a point against Besiktas and win the group, so our philosophy must be to try and win against Besiktas as we tried against Sparta.

"It is important to win the group and be seeded because then it means you will play a team who finished second in another group – although I can't tell you if that will ultimately prove to be a good thing until I see the draw." Ranieri also believed his team had a perfectly good goal ruled out. "I cannot understand why the linesman put up his flag" he said. "I thought it was a good goal, I didn't think it was offside."

I was invited to this match by Chas Wheeler and had trouble at half-time, only this time not with the officials in the ground, just a combination of a repetition of where I had my colostomy operation and sheer boredom, so I said my farewells to Chas and headed home to watch the second half there. I need not have bothered though, for this was not really a great European evening in a way that it will not be remembered like quite a few before, in fact better forgotten!

This was all about a result but to play well in Europe is a great feeling, especially for those fans that have not witnessed such nights!

All in all it had become a good week for the Blues after winning at St Mary's the Saturday before in another match that was never really one of great excitement, but these were the kind of matches that Chelsea usually come away with a sore head, only this time they came through with all three points thanks to a rare Melchiot goal and that made the visit of Manchester United even the more interesting. A couple of things in particular I was looking forward to in this match for, was the contest between the rapidly improving Frank Lampard and Roy Keane in the engine room where I always say that games are won and lost and my other eye would be down the right hand side of the Red Devils where the loss of David Beckham will figure to be the downfall this season for the reigning champions!

EVE OF THE BIG MATCH

Mark Fleming of the *Express* looks at it this way: John Terry has revealed how Sir Alex Ferguson tried to lure him to Manchester United with a lunch of beans on toast, sitting him next to his idol Eric Cantona.

It was 1995, and Ferguson knew Terry was a keen Manchester United fan – and after inviting him to join the team's pre-match meal, he sat Terry next to the players he most admired – Paul Ince and Eric Cantona.

But for Terry, hoping to inspire the Blues to victory over Manchester United at Stamford Bridge tomorrow, the VIP treatment was all too much. He said that," United made an effort to sign me. They were playing at West Ham one day and invited me to have the pre-match meal at the Swallow Hotel. I was sitting at the same table as Paul Ince and Eric Cantona and had beans on toast, but I was too scared to eat it. It's one of those things that will always live with me, but I just loved it here so much and ended up signing for Chelsea. And I made the right decision. Chelsea is a family club, always made me feel welcome and it felt right as soon as I came here."

My view on the Terry situation is that: you have it from a young lad who was in the deep end without ever going into the shallow one. What a choice to have to make, and reading his words it is not a coincidence that he plays for his club as if it is for life or death. This is a player who speaks how he plays leaving nothing in a grey area. He is a no nonsense player who keeps cooler than an icebox in an igloo. He lacks the finesse at times but that is not a criticism, purely the way he plays the game, leaving nobody around him wondering what he is about to do. He reads things well from a long way away, the sign of a real great defender. Has anyone not heard of Bobby Moore?

SECOND BEST SIGNING?

Yeah, Alex Ferguson must sit back at times and wonder why he did not get this kid which would have saved him a cool £20million from the Rio Ferdinand deal, for he is better than Rio, Japp Stam, Wes Brown and all others that Manchester United has had over the years. Yeah, better than both Bruce and Pallister put together and that is not a knock at these two, simply just how accomplished John Terry has become after making the middle of the defence a safer place for him being there, and the goals against column will have some say in that, and alongside Billy Gallas is becoming quite a formidable partnership. Never leaving out the brilliance of Carlo Cudicini since the Tinkerman has revitalised this goalkeeper, and that must be the best goalkeeping signing since Peter Schmeichel!

Tomorrow afternoon at around 1600 hours the most important man-to-man contest of the season will take place in both penalty areas at Stamford Bridge. This is the battle of two heavyweights and there will be no punches pulled and all that van Nistelrooy will be looking for is that extra half a stride to use his mighty physique and hit one on target. I know in general matches are won and lost in the 'engine room' where Keane and Lampard will be doing battle but tomorrow it will be so tight that it will take a piece of genius or a defensive error to get the break psychologically for them to come out of this match cock-a-hoop. You always know when you are up against teams so strong in the middle of the pitch, for example Johnny Giles and Billy Bremner against Charlie Cooke and myself would fight tooth and nail to create an opening but sometimes you need a bit of genius from Peter Osgood or Allan Clarke to 'nick' it for you. That is why John Terry has the biggest job on the pitch tomorrow and if he can stop the Dutchman from hitting the net then Chelsea are halfway there. As far as the result goes I would not like to call this one, I will just be sitting back in the Grosvenor Club taking in all the atmosphere by closing my eyes and imagining being out there in that royal blue shirt, only that would be strange because there would be no Peter Osgood, Charlie Cooke, Peter Bonetti, Eddie McCreadie or Tommy Baldwin!

The Tinkerman is playing this match down by staying low profile and a lot of that is this match coincides with that wonderful World Cup win in Sydney last weekend. The newspapers have been exploiting every single thing about the best International performance ever by an English team. That is if you take in mind they won it in the backyard of our greatest rivals, Australia. But Ranieri has kept low profile, which says a lot for his common sense, by not getting into the war of words I spoke about some pages back. On the other hand in the same *Express* the headline says that FERGUSON CAN'T RESIST A DIG by Richard Tanner: Sir Alex Ferguson could not resist a couple of thinly-veiled digs at Chelsea despite taking a diplomatic stance before a match that could go a long way to shaping the destiny of the title race.

The Manchester United manager has dismissed the view that Roman Abramovich's spending spree is bad for football and reversed his old belief that money cannot buy success.

But he still made it clear his comparatively low-key summer signings and latest batch of home grown youngsters will prove better long term investments than the ready-made Chelsea superstars they have invested £111million in.

Ferguson, who has shelled out £126million in the last four years, said that, "People keep asking if Chelsea's spending is good for the game. But they have every right to try to change and improve their fortunes.

"I would normally say no to questions about whether money can buy the title, but looking at the start they have made, they will certainly be there at the end of the season".

The competitive juices then got the better of Ferguson when he was asked if he would be comfortable handling a squad of Chelsea's size and quality. He said, "Well, I have that sort of situation. We're very happy with the youngsters we have". But while he believes his squad is as good as Chelsea's, he claims Claudio Ranieri may have more problems keeping his happy in the long run. Ferguson added that, "Claudio Ranieri will be experiencing the things I have experienced in the last few years; which team to pick? Who to leave out?

WHO LIVES, WHO DIES, WHO'S PREMIER

When you have so many players it is not easy keeping them all happy. It is easy to say, "He has all that money, it must be an easy job", it doesn't work like that.

"At the moment he is doing the hard part well – picking the right teams. But they haven't had a blimp yet. That is when the pressure will be on," said the United boss.

Even though there are two-thirds of the season still to go, Ferguson believes that the title race is already between the top three teams. "The way Arsenal, Chelsea – and ourselves – are performing – not making any mistakes – you have to think that the results of the games between the top three could be decisive," he said.

"I can't see anybody else breaking into the top three now. We'll have to play well on Sunday but we've got a good record at Stamford Bridge. The good thing is we will be playing a team who will be thinking they will have to beat us. It could be an open game."

The game is a significant one for Ryan Giggs, who turns thirty today, with

Ferguson revealing his longevity, is in no small part down to yoga. "He has found the answer to all the back and hamstring problems he has had for years" said Giggs' manager. "The preparation and stretching he does has made a hell of a difference." It will be Giggs' 564th match.

Rob Shepherd picks out the comparisons of the two 'destroyers' Roy Keane and Claude Makelele, calling it the midfield battleground. Chelsea is nothing like when our seventies team played, being without the greyhound track keeping us from the spectators which was quite a big disadvantage to us. I know they say you have to give the crowd something to shout about and there are two different ways of looking at that point of view, as Keane said a couple of years ago that the crowd, all 67,000 at Old Trafford, were the 'prawn sandwich brigade' meaning they are now, in the main, corporate guests out for a nice lunch and a few drinks in the pleasant surroundings that comes with Manchester United Football Club. He is right, but they pay his wages, well them and the ones who frequent the club shop looking for a shirt with his name on the back of it. Worse than that, behind our dressing rooms was, and still is the West Brompton Cemetery. Then on that side of the field they began building a new East Stand and I could swear there was more noise in the cemetery some Saturday afternoons. If we had played at the new Stamford Bridge Stadium I am convinced, if Dave Sexton had kept to coaching and not managing, we would have won that elusive second championship for a club that has underachieved for a so very long. Back to tomorrow and Keane and Makelele the two bullfighters who will scrap it out tomorrow, making this match one of such great expectation. Will it be Duff or Giggs?

Van Nistelrooy, Solskaer or Gudjohnsen or Crespo?

Will Jimmy Floyd start, will Forlan?

Then there will be Frank Lampard and who will Sir Alex select to put a stop to his inspirational form?

I believe Nicky Butt, but the United boss might think Neville?

The questions are vast in a match that beforehand could easily become a game of football chess!

The Tinkerman will have the simplest of selections as his players have had two off days against Southampton and Sparta where United are breezing in cruise control at the moment. Team selection will be awaited, as usual, and the atmosphere will be like when the big iron gates crash open and Caesar smiles in anticipation for his gladiators to enter the arena, looking for blood and the scent of agony spills out onto the earth below him. The roar goes up as another gate goes crashing after one tiger, two tiger, three!

This match is more than just a football match, it is the Russian revolution – The Talisman – against the Magnier and McManus – the Coolmore Mafia – Terry against van Nistelrooy, Keane against Lampard, the Tinkerman against the man whose mind games have won many an important football match, and of course the old Manchester United versus the new Chelsea who will discount their very impressive record at Stamford Bridge!

It is almost game on (10.40am Sunday 30th November 2003) and it could go so many different ways as the man upstairs, who gives out the medals, bubbles with excitement and the thrill of having his say as to who lives, who dies and who is going to get their hands on the Premiership this coming May!

Will Manchester United please enter the arena!

ANOTHER BIG TALKING POINT

It was after the Manchester United match against Blackburn that Gary Neville showed a little concern to this visit to the Bridge by saying that, "This coming Sunday is going to be an immense occasion bearing in mind that everything Chelsea have done this season." He told the *Express* "The way it is looking at the top, neither of the clubs we are up there with look like they are going to drop points. That means we are going to take them off ourselves.

"I thought both Chelsea and Arsenal might drop points on Saturday (22nd November) but they didn't, so it is vital we won our game against Blackburn. Now everybody will be looking to Sunday, because these sort of games do determine where the Championship goes at the end of the season".

Sir Alex Ferguson is astonished at the pace being set by the two London Clubs and believes the title could be won with a record number of Premiership points. He said that, "Every game is vital because the top three are giving little away. We have one of our best starts to the Premiership but are still two points behind the leaders. Chelsea have not done much wrong and neither have Arsenal. We must make sure we don't either". Skipper Roy Keane said that, "we are a long way off our best form". And Ferguson carried on by saying that "We will get better as the season develops – we always do".

A plus point for United was the encouraging performance of Kleberson, in his first game back since dislocating a shoulder in August, and Ferguson was clearly relieved that the Brazilian finally started to justify his £7million price tag.

He said about Kleberson "He has been injured for over two months but has worked very hard. He has been great in training. This was an ideal chance to play him and he showed what a wonderful footballer he is. His goal was a superb finish to an exceptional move".

TENSE

On this beautifully fresh morning the streets in Chelsea filled slowly much like there was a big funeral going on. But my guess the men, women and children dressed in blue shirts were a wee bit 'tense' as when United are in town, much like as young kids going to the circus or funfair. And this looked like being some ninety-minute circus and the ringmaster knew he would have a very tough time taming these un-caged animals from all over the world. They are playing like they have been let off the leash for a couple of hours just recently and that is exactly what confidence can do for a player, but when that confidence runs through the entire team, you don't really need a team talk at

2.45pm. I remember saying to my uncle George, as we walked the Kings Road, that this particular morning was my "perfect" playing conditions, with plenty of "give" underfoot and a clear fresh air with not a cloud amongst the blue skies above. Was this afternoon going to belong to that blue or the champions in red?

If this seemed strange for the second last day in November then so it should, the Premiership holders were in town and there was no more time for talk, the performance must do their talking for the Tinkerman and his much improving "tinkers". I picked up the *Mail on Sunday* to get the last of the hype coming from both corners, going straight to the back page, and splashed all across it was that CHELSEA OFFER SVEN AN £18MILLION DEAL and that 'Angry Eriksson to quit England and replace Ranieri in 2004' an exclusive written by Joe Melling follows: Sven Goran Eriksson will quit as England coach after this summer's finals in Portugal.

And the Swede is still expected to take over at Chelsea next season on a four-year contract worth £18million after tax.

Speculation that Eriksson was being lined up to take over from Claudio Ranieri at Stamford Bridge was rife two months ago but subsided in the wake of Chelsea's impressive recent record in both the Premiership and Europe.

But the situation has not changed and Chelsea owner Roman Abramovich's desire to secure Eriksson's services now dovetails with the Swede's determination to step down as coach of the national team after Euro 2004.

Eriksson is furious with FA chief executive Mark Palios after he revealed last week that the England coach has been offered a new deal to keep him in charge until 2008.

The stunt has been exacerbated the deep-seated rift between the coach and the chief executive.

In spite of Palios's glowing appraisal of the man who has guided England to the finals of the World Cup and the European Championships, Eriksson was astounded and angry that the contract offer was made public without his knowledge or approval. His anger has now developed into something close to contempt.

The first cracks in the relationship between the men had appeared even before they disagreed over Rio Ferdinand's International ban for failing to attend a drugs test.

The subsequent clumsy handling of Alan Smith's expulsion from the England squad, because he had been arrested by the police for throwing a bottle into the Leeds crowd, widened the gap between Palios and Eriksson. Smith was released without charge by the police but still faces an FA charge. The shock departure last week of the FA's head of communications and marketing, Paul Barber, has worsened the situation. Barber was popular with both Eriksson and the England players.

Chelsea owner Abramovich has been determined to recruit Eriksson ever since the pair met in London earlier this year. Photos of the supposedly secret meeting appeared in newspapers a week later. Abramovich will not be swayed from replacing Ranieri with Eriksson even if Chelsea won the championship for the first time since 1955.

However, Chelsea are by no means Eriksson's only option. There are two other high profile jobs likely to become available next summer – Arsenal and Real Madrid. Current Real coach Carlos Queiroz was seen as a stopgap by the Spanish club, who have had Arsene Wenger in their sights for some time. If the Gunners' boss makes the switch, Eriksson would be an obvious choice to step into his shoes at Highbury.

If Wenger does not move, Eriksson would be targeted to be move to the Bernabeu.

Ranieri has reacted to the constant speculation with a mixture of dignity and indifference, and today's visit of Manchester United presents him with an opportunity to claim another major scalp.

BLATTER FURY AS RIO PLAYS ON

FIFA are calling into question the validity of Manchester United's results since Ferdinand's failure to take a drugs test. Sepp Bladder, FIFA's president, is furious that a date has yet to be set for the England defender's hearing and that the £30million centre-half has played on for more than two months since the accident. Bladder said that, "He cannot play until the case is settled."

How can you not settle this case when he has played and could be declared guilty by a commission?

And what do you do with the results after?

Ferdinand 24, who is expected to face Chelsea today, denies charge of misconduct. He was dropped by England for the Euro 2004 decider in Turkey but has played for United eight times in domestic competition and five times in Europe since he was charged on October 29th.

This was my column in the *Sentinel* on Friday;

RANIERI MUST IGNORE MIND GAMES

Has the psychological warfare between Manchester United and Chelsea began. I wonder!

Ferguson has already seen off the likes of Kevin Keegan and Arsene Wenger when the title race has turned to mind games.

And now the Old Trafford hierarchy seem to be regarding Chelsea, not Arsenal, as the main threat to their championship.

This week, for instance, we saw United's new chief executive attempt to fire a psychological shot across Chelsea bows.

David Gill, the man appointed to replace Peter Kenyon, told the club's AGM that Chelsea had paid well over the odds for Damien Duff. United had also wanted the Blackburn winger, but the price sent them running scared. Is this the beginning of a war of words between Old Trafford and Stamford Bridge as the Premiership title race hots-up between Manchester and London?

The fact that Gill's predecessor jumped ship to pocket the roubles at

Chelsea merely thickens the plot.

And Ferguson will hardly be tongue-tied if he joins in to try and wind up the Tinkerman at Chelsea. I just hope that Claudio turns the other Trevor Peake and lets his players do all the talking, where it matters most.

That is what they are paid for. Correction, that's what they are paid colossal amounts for. I can't believe the number of stories, arrests, prosecutions and the like flying about the game right now.

I'm beginning to think myself, Bestie and co. were model professionals – certainly compared to some of today's players who think they are far better than what they really are.

Today's stars shouldn't even have enough time to go round getting themselves into bother.

They should be spending their spare time on their knees and thanking god for giving them such a phenomenal standard of living – without either having the ability or the brains to go with it, in the majority of cases. Don't get me wrong, we all knew how to have a good time in our day, but we also knew where to draw the line 99 times out of a hundred. Some of the allegations flying around at the moment leave you sick in the stomach and are terrible for the game's image. And what an insult to those ordinary folk who spend their hard-earned cash to watch these fellas perform on a Saturday afternoon – not to read about how good they are on a Saturday morning.

Maybe today's overpaid should take a leaf out of their rugby counterparts when it comes to professionalism, on and off the field, let alone standards of common decency. Watching the English rugby team the other day was a new experience for me – my God, if you think football's offside law is confusing – but you don't need to be an expert to recognise and appreciate how proud these lads are to represent their country and risk life and limb in the middle of all that violence. It merely confirmed the brief impression I learned many years ago when coaching football to a bunch of rugby lads at Denstone College. Marvellous people!

Just a quick piece of history, as one day I was walking to the bar to meet all the other members of staff, I looked along the corridor walls to find a plaque of Quentin Crisp.

Anyway, good luck to the boys down under tomorrow morning. It takes a lot to drag me in front of the TV screen at that hour of the morning, but the thought of our boys beating the Aussies in their own backyard is good enough reason for me!

This bunch of England players are more like a military outfit going into war, and I did not see one white shirted player that I would have a problem with in the trenches whether in Dunkirk, Vietnam or Old Trafford

---

IT'S A RED LETTER DAY FOR MR CHELSKI'S RUSSIAN FRIENDS
Moscow pals eat, drink and get merry for their away match in London.

The newspapers on this Monday were Chelsea, Chelsea, Chelsea and the first massive test had been passed with flying colours. Blue!

I liked the *Standard* coverage for the picture showed Roman Abramovich with arms stretched out wide and his son looking at him in wonderment. Matheus Sanchez writes the following – When the final whistle went and Chelsea had secured their 1-0 victory over Manchester United, no one was more relieved than Roman Abramovich. Yes, his team had won a crucial match against one of their most important rivals, the champions of England.

Yes, the victory sent them to the top of the Premiership.

But more importantly than that, the Russian billionaire had flown 500 friends from Moscow to watch the game and it would have been embarrassing to see Chelsea lose. At an estimated cost of £600,000, he provided club class seats, paid for hotels and entertained his friends for the weekend. The group went shopping, exploring restaurants and, being Russians, enjoyed a drink. Now, of course, they are all Chelsea fans. "I always dreamed about watching matches in the Premier League," said Evgeny Pezeverzev, 29, who was sporting a Chelsea hat. "We are the champions!" The Russians watched from the £1million-a-season boxes alongside Mini Driver, Boris Becker and David Baddiel – not to mention two – England rugby heroes, Lawrence Dallaglio and coach Clive Woodward. For the visitors, it was the climax to a weekend of the hospitality one comes to expect when one friend is one of the richest men in Russia, worth some £3.5billion. The group, mostly Moscow businessmen and their families were staying at various hotels, including the Millenium Hotel in Knightsbridge, and Chelsea's own Chelsea Village Hotel.

JURGEN KLINSMAN AGAIN

On Saturday night they painted the town red, even Russian capitalists paint the town red. "They are very Russian", said a member of security at the Village Hotel. "They like their drink." "We love London, and have had a great weekend" said Moscow businessman Melku Myanthe, 36, "We have been to clubs and all other things. We had a good time". After sampling the bars and clubs around Soho, for some the night continued to 3am at the Village Hotel where the £4.95 Chelsea rum cocktail was tasted. A British businessman at the hotel said that, "I went for breakfast and there were more Russians than I have ever seen in my life. They did look a bit bleary-eyed". Yesterday the weekenders were joined by another 250 on a day trip. After lunch, either at the hotel's Galleria or in the West End, they arrived at Stamford Bridge. "It's great to be here," said Vadim Semenov, 27, "Chelsea are very popular in Russia right now. This game will be watched over there. We will make a special plan to come to more games". Lifelong Chelsea fan and season ticket holder Bob Taylor, 50, said that, "If you owned a club, wouldn't you want to bring some friends?

"It's his money. This is all good for the club, but only time will tell". As he left the stadium Oleg Lobanov said that, "I think the game was great. I am very happy that Chelsea are number one with Roman Abramovich. We like to see the Russian footprint in England." And the Russian footprint, it seems, is very welcome.

This simply told us that the Russians have joined the Premiership bandwagon. We have had the one-off superstars, my favourite being Jurgen Klinsman in his first season at Tottenham Hotspurs. How many questions were there then and the biggest one being a German playing for the 'Jewish' London supporters' club. He came with a reputation for diving, cheating, so all eyes were focused on the ex-German captain. The athleticism of the centre-forward answered his critics and entertained a pretty gloomy White Hart Lane. Apart from that first point he displayed the finer arts of the game outside of his uncanny knack of being where the ball was once he decided to make his run. I watched him for Germany in the European Championships at Wembley in 1996. Having a seat behind the goal is not the best way to watch a football match but this night I could watch Klinsman from a far better viewpoint as I experienced, by using my imagination as a defender watching him, as he weaved pretty patterns as a lone striker never standing still for a second, only when the whistle stopped he took a well earned short break. He was always in a position for a midfield player to get him off the hook by coming short, then spinning for the one 'over the top', the move defenders loathe. He was the best player from overseas I had the pleasure to watch, scoring overhead kicks, brave flying headers and other superlative efforts. Jurgen Klinsman had come, conquered and shut up his critics once and for all. Long live Jurgen!

£36 MILLION MANCHESTER UNITED DEAL

Whilst Chelsea were celebrating their win over the champions the Manchester club reported that they have agreed a new sponsorship deal worth £36million over four years with Vodaphone. Meanwhile Malcolm Frazer, owner of the Tampa Bay Buccaneers, has stepped up his holding in the club to 14.31%.

VAN THE MAN

My views on both the football and the comments made are that firstly, I would like to know just how David Baddiel's name is linked with such stars. I sat behind him one day watching a match from the Directors' Box with Don Howe, my favourite coach, and George Graham who I chatted with every now and then, as they were sitting directly behind me. But this bloke in front of me kept jumping up and down like a child who was at the back of the class with his hand up. I tapped him on the shoulder and asked if he could sit still whilst the match was going on because he was blocking my view. He turned and said, "You have to show some passion" to which I replied, "show some fucking passion sitting down."

Some people really do get above their station and after watching him on television, if I were him I would be incognito in such places!

The headlines smothered all the last three pages with the match that was a real cat and mouse affair, where certain players were the 'key' to a victory, which would gave the victors a great psychological gain over their rivals. Fulham had done Chelsea a great favour earlier in the day by holding Arsenal to a goalless draw at Highbury, a result that allowed Chelsea to jump over the north Londoners and into pole position. This was made possible by the performance of Dutch goalkeeper Edwin Van Der Sar, who made save after save as Arsenal threw everything into a match that was all the more precious, for they needed the other big match to be a draw. Two points dropped at home is not good for the championship-chasing Gunners and although they, at times, went through Fulham's brittle defence like a knife through butter, they just could not put any of their many chances away. Unfortunately for Manchester United it was the wrong Van Driver on a day when they needed their very own van to break the deadlock and once behind needed him more than ever before.

SELLING QUEEN VICTORIA

I said before the match that the game was on a knife-edge as to who got the better than who in the most dangerous areas. I thought that whoever got the better of the Terry and Nistelrooy duel would win the match. I am not a 'stats' man but there are not many matches a season United fail to score and the Dutchman is the main man where that is concerned, but this encounter would not faze Terry, for it seems to me the better the opposition the better he'll play. Terry did himself proud and showed the kind of qualities that Sir Alex Ferguson is lacking at this moment in time. The outcome was that John Terry was awesome once again and how Ferguson must 'rue' the day he let this rapidly-improving centre-half slip through his fingers, as he watched him make his fantastic Dutch finisher look almost average. Don't get excited you United fans, I know his service was non-existent and that is why I say they miss one David Beckham. The other area on the field that needed winning was the space where Roy Keane usually 'rules' in big matches but amongst Makelele and the equally rapidly improving Frank Lampard, Chelsea stopped the supply to the Dutchman. I can't help feeling that today was the day when, seeming inevitably, the visitors would miss David Beckham so very much. Ferguson has had it his way by playing Giggs on the right hand side but against a very well organised Chelsea he was ineffective. David Beckham was doing nicely, thank you, by setting up the equaliser for Ronaldo in their one-all draw at Ososuna in La Liga, but then left the field after taking a knock. With no Beckham and Scholes, United lacked the imagination of the 'pocket sized genius' and sadly lacked the width and service that Beckham provided so wonderfully for Ferguson's front players and is still doing so now for the Spanish giants Real Madrid. I said it the day they sold Beckham, that he would be sorely missed although all the 'hype' at Old Trafford about this player and that player does not wash with me. The truth of the matter is that the United manager sold Victoria Beckham to Real Madrid and her David was a part of the package deal

I mentioned about players making comments and this time the 'gong' belonged to Sol Campbell who is shouting in the *Sun* to his team mates SEE

YOU IN THE FINAL: was Campbell's message to his French pals. Here we go again, I have warned you that teams that are going to tear Europe apart don't have to shout about it. Have you ever heard Zidane screaming from the rooftops and he has masterminded both the World Cup and the European Championships with France whilst leading Juventus and Real Madrid to many famous victories in the player's unusual number five shirt, and it seems that there is no limit to what this fantastic footballer can do?

Campbell says that, "The banter has already started. It's good we play each other early; we can get it over and done with and won't see them again until the final. We all feel that way. It's better this way, better than being shocked and meeting them in either the quarter or semi finals. It has worked out well, we're happy – but know it will be difficult. You have to go out there and win games no matter who you play and everyone will be playing their hearts out because of the situation. We will need everyone fit, that is for sure. It is just good to get them out of the way. People will want to know what I think because some of their players are here, but it's like the World Cup. We had Kanu and Freddie Lundberg in our group. There was banter until the draw and it will get better as time goes on. We heard it in the hotel before we left for the game. It's no good worrying about Henry because there's Pires – and when you get over him, there's a little matter of Zidane to deal with. Arsenal's Henry said that is "important we are confident of making progress. But we know it will be very difficult for us and we will not make the mistake of being over confident. When you look back at when we won Euro 2000 all the games were tight. We only won the final in extra-time and other matches needed penalties to decide them It will be very difficult to predict which team is going to win it this time."

My view is that: The banter goes without saying and I can only remind those players who think that they will be meeting each other in the final, of the year Denmark won the competition, a nation who did not qualify and only got in on a technicality over a nation that got thrown out. They were the bookies' biggest-ever priced winners, even with Peter Schmeichel in between the sticks. Nations such as the Czech Republic are top class sides who we beat before we play them, if you read the papers that is, but once it comes to the game itself we show we are far better talkers than players. I remember being at all the matches in Euro 96 and we were lucky in all matches except the Holland match, where we had a magnificent night, but the Dutch that evening were in disarray having their best player Edgar Davids sent home and the whole camp might well have left with him. They are an arrogant race we know, but they are like it amongst themselves. At least nowadays the French have that "chip" but at least they stick together when pulling on either the red Gunners' shirt or the blue French shirt over their heads. The first match at Wembley was against the Swiss and they gave us a chasing and these nations tend to improve when we seem to deteriorate. Let's face it, Terry Venables had Shearer and Sherringham at their best with the occasional glimpse of Gascoigne's brilliance, the goal against the Scots probably one of the greatest ever seen in an 'Old Firm' match. Then there seemed to be the real emergence of Jamie Redknapp until his cruel run of injuries halted his progress, and as I have said elsewhere within these pages, he looked every inch the next captain of his country. So how many of today's present team would get in front of those. Owen would get in alongside Shearer leaving 'Teddy''' in the hole or as El Tel says, at the top of the Christmas tree, and that's about it in the attacking half. If I had to pick a back four out of both teams I would pick John Terry alongside Tony Adams, Stuart Pearce and Ashley Cole, with in the middle of the team I would go Beckham, Gerrard, Redknapp and Scholes who would link up to play nicely with Teddy and there is nobody better than the ever impressive and evergreen Sherringham. With both Cole and Pearce we could push one into the midfield area whilst the play is on that side which would move both Adams and Terry moving into the middle with Beckham filling in on the right, something he does so well. So this all began about players winning matches in their dreams, and I have been listening to it for some thirty-odd years, players and managers alike.

Charles Sale is still turning out some good stuff for the *Mail* although I knew the very likeable Charles in his *Express* days, and I no doubt will be seen on his *Sports Agenda* page when this book is ready to go to print. On this Monday though, Charles wrote that, 'Manchester United director Sir Bobby Charlton said on national radio yesterday that chief executive Peter Kenyon's defection to Chelsea in September was "no hardship". This is unlikely to please the United lawyers who are claiming huge compensation for the club or an extension of Kenyon's gardening leave!'

Well, what it tells us is that chief executive or no chief executive, they cannot win you a game of football yet demand such astronomical salaries. Anyhow, Kenyon seems to be in the right camp even though he is doing his work across the Atlantic in the United States of America. He will be delighted that Chelsea had gone to the pinnacle of the Premiership for he is surely on bonuses whilst taking in the sunshine many miles from Stamford Bridge.

The rest of the headlines went like this RANIERI PLAYS IT PERFECTLY YET AGAIN in the *Standard* TOP OF THE PREMIERSHIP Ranieri wants yacht from Roman after sinking United and FRANK AND FEARLESS LAMP LIGHTS THE WAY FOR CHELSEA'S REVOLUTION in the *Daily Mirror.* Back to the *Mail* with BLUE HEAVEN AND CHELSEA TOP AFTER PENALTY STORM and LAMPARD THRILLS ROMAN'S FAN CLUB also that UNITED ROCK AS CHELSEA ROLL TO THE TOP IN STYLE whilst in the *Sun* it said that United were simply RATTLED, as FURIOUS FERGIE LETS FLY AT REF AS BLUES STORM TO THE TOP. Then on the inside page with A BRAVE BLUE WORLD and that FERGUSON SEES A ROMAN LEGION MARCH TO THE TOP and lastly the *Express* with VIERI WELL DONE Roman in raptures as he bids to bolster his new title favourites with £8million striker.

The last mentioned was the move to bring in Christian Vieri into his already star studded squad. It was very clear in Arsenal's 5-1 drubbing given out to Inter

Milan over the last few days that the Italian striker is not happy playing for them after scoring the equaliser, a lucky deflection, he walked away looking very disappointed as the ball ended up in the back of the Gunners' net. He did not even manage a smile and it is quite clear he was unsettled by Abramovich enquiry into his position and was actually the first name mentioned on Chelsea's shopping list. It was said then that Inter wanted eighteen million pounds for the Italian International, yet now they have gone back in with an offer of ten million less. Rob Shepherd wrote that, 'Roman Abramovich saw Chelsea jump to the top of the Premiership last night and then prepared to open his chequebook yet again to ram home their advantage. While Blues boss Claudio Ranieri refused to accept that his team were now favourites for the title after an impressive win over Manchester United, his boss entertained a representative from Inter Milan in an attempt to seal an £8million move for Christian Vieri. Billionaire Abramovich, who has already splashed out £110million on new players this season, watched that investment bear fruit as Frank Lampard's first half penalty saw off the champions. My thoughts are that Chelsea desperately need a Thierry Henry or Ruud van Nistelrooy, a player who will certainly get at least twenty goals a season for you. Having said that, in theory is correct but look at Alan Shearer who leads the goal-scorers after a third of the season but Newcastle have had a terrible start but still the ex-England captain is a rarity. Then again with the rampaging Frank Lampard at last really looking a match winner every time Chelsea play, it goes to show that sometimes it helps to share the goals around. Once again this is pure theory and at the end of the day it does not matter as long as you have a winning formula.' When I had my best spell in English football, our Stoke City team hit the front just before Christmas and were playing some wonderful football and although we hit the top spot we did not have a real out-and-out goal-getter. I always believe if you are playing well and creating openings you will win more than you would lose and with confidence sky high anyone could pop up with a precious goal. I believe that possession is nine-tenths of the law in our game as it is said in life. But when I was playing well at Stoke along with the marvellous Jimmy Greenhoff, I would gauge our performance by the amount of possession we had. As Jimmy said on the video 'Magic Moments', "When me and Alan Hudson were playing well we used to keep the ball away from the opposition, for he knew where I was going and by the time I got there the ball was there waiting for me. It is quite incredible, almost as if we were telepathic". Thanks for that Jim, I love you too me old china, a truly class act was Jimmy, and believe it or not the records show that we took the blows and Jimmy never got an England cap and with the two I got adds up to the miserable state our game was going through. I suppose one should not be surprised that Don Revie did not like me and also he sold Greenhoff from Leeds United at such an early age that he would look foolish if he selected him for his country having not entered Revie's plans for Leeds United's future?

They wondered why in the seventies that we failed to reach the World Cup Finals after the one I missed in Mexico through injury. Jimmy had some memorable times at Old Trafford after he and I left the club, he winning an FA Cup winner's medal against Liverpool whilst I played in a disastrous Arsenal performance when losing to Ipswich Town in 1978.

Back to the Bridge and the match that gave everyone at Chelsea real belief that they can actually mix it with anyone – from Notts County in the Carling Cup, Lazio in the Champions League and Manchester United in the Premiership – all in a space of three weeks. I like reading John Dillon, but only when I have not watched the match myself, in fact I never read a match report if I have watched that particular match, because on far too many occasions I feel I have been watching an entirely different one, but John is as good as it gets after the headlines of: CLAUDIO OVERSEES THE COMING OF AGE plus LAMPARD PENALTY CLINCHER PUTS CHELSEA FIRMLY ON TITLE TRAIL – An hour into the enjoyable rain-lashed afternoon at Stamford Bridge, Roy Keane slid along the sodden turf straight through the legs of Adrian Mutu. When the ball squirted clear, Claudio Makelele immediately did more or less the same thing to Ryan Giggs.

Unless you dared briefly to take respite from the intensity of the contest between Chelsea and Manchester United, the quiet significance of the reactions of the two-tackled players might have passed unnoticed. Neither Giggs or Mutu complained. Or collapsed. Or rolled around in agony.

Instead, there were a couple of minor triumphs for the competitive instinct and the code of proper behaviour. Mutu hopped up with a slight wince and Giggs got straight back to his feet and resumed his chase for the ball. And then, in that fleeting phase of play, came a moment, which confirmed how much the contest at the top of the Premiership has been invigorated by the Russian revolution in London SW6.

The Champions against the new Chelsea was a match reminiscent of one of those epic tussles that United used to have with Liverpool and Leeds. Not forgetting our matches with Leeds United when they were as good a club side as anywhere in the world of football. And given United's supremacy in this fixture – Chelsea had won only two of the previous meetings (not including the Charity Shield) and lost three of the last four – the victory and the elevation to the Premiership summit it brought, was the most powerful psychological triumph of the revolution so far. Even more so than the thrilling, but still freakish victory at Lazio.

This was different because it happened against serious and energised opposition. And because it was secured against a team trying to find fresh ways to attack after Frank Lampard had scored from the spot. Substitutes Damien Duff and Jesper Gronkjaer shored things up for Chelsea along the flanks when United might have surged up them to get back into the game.

But many of the questions posed by Blues boss Claudio Ranieri's incessant alteration of his tactics had been answered in recent weeks anyway. So, too, had those doubts about Chelsea's spirit and their understanding of commitment.

However, this successful confrontation between the two most tigerish, combative spirits in the game, affirmed the new attitude in the most freneti-cally testing circumstances. In a league such as this, you can never remind yourself enough that character and application matter as much as talent.

It is a hard lesson to learn for many foreign players, as the occasional bemused look on the faces of Mutu and Hernen Crespo confirm.

They nearly all get it in the end, though. That is why the essentially physical character of the English game remains unchanged no matter how many foreign players arrive here to embellish it with refined technique.

At Stamford Bridge that notion gave rise to an intriguing question about the prospects for the Euro 2004 as there were several players all over the pitch that would be involved.

That was an excellent piece by Dillon but it seems nowadays that although newspapers give marks out of ten for players in the summation, I feel that there is not enough said about the teams and individuals for the football lover who could not get to the match or even watch it on what today is a crying shame, if you have not got SKY Sports.

Chelsea 1 (Lampard 30th minute penalty) Manchester United 0
The attendance, another full house!

Here is the latest state of play for the three teams who are pulling away with each coming match:

	P	W	L	D	F	A	Points
Chelsea	14	11	1	2	28	9	35
Arsenal	14	10	0	4	28	10	34
Man United	14	10	3	1	25	9	31

Yeah, it is that close and if it stays that way it could go right down to the last match of the season and Arsenal are looking difficult to beat, the closest they came was when Portsmouth went to Highbury, were a goal up and Pires was awarded a penalty which was as harsh a decision given by any 'Mug in the Middle'.

EURO 2004 DRAW

WilsonSports and Racing now go 5/4 Chelsea to win their first title since way back in 1955 and it was quite strange the day as I looked back to our team in the 1969/70 season, the year of the most exciting FA Cup success of all time, scoring goals to take us to that final.

Looking like this: 3-0/ 2-2 Replay 3-1/4-2/ and 5-1 in the semi-final against Watford at White Hart Lane. That was seventeen goals in five FA Cup ties leading to Wembley and of course a 2-2 draw there followed by that incredible Old Trafford victory totalled twenty-one, which was not pretty bad going. This new Chelsea, though, are sitting on a time bomb with Christmas only three and a half weeks away. The first week in January will bring the 3rd Round of the FA Cup and if Chelsea jump that hurdle without fuss they will, just like United and Arsenal, have their taste buds in all four pies. There is always the question asked of which order do you put these competitions, as we look back to only three seasons ago when Manchester United pulled out of the FA Cup. This, the most famous domestic cup in the world and United had put it in the hands of the devil. With the talk of Super Leagues and all that, it makes you wonder just what will happen to this fantastic cup competition with the greatest emphasis being that the entire country take place and if they did take it away that would be the end of so many dreams that this game gives us and those from the lower grades who just want to play against David Beckham. Harry Kewell, Wayne Rooney, Paul Scholes and Frank Lampard, just for sixty seconds – even just walking through the tunnel – let alone ninety minutes?

But this is space age football now and the team buses are replaced by the Chariots of Fire and the players have taken over from management and Directorship whereas in my day you did not have a leg to stand on, if any legs at all. How glad I am to have kept mine, thank the lord and those great surgeons!

The latest talk of the England team going on strike before a big International tells us that 'players and their agents rule'. I say: Good luck to them and all that sail with them. The one thing that I do not enjoy is some of the rubbish we serve up which is not worthy of the spectator. Yet players are judged today, not for their ability, just simply by the size of their wage packet or transfer fee!

Anyhow, right across the Bridge from where I live, Chelsea Football Cub sits in silence like never before, you walk past the place and it wreaks with expectation, if only tomorrow would come quicker so we could find out if Chelsea really cam emulate those greats of 1954/55. And as I walk past once again the excitement rushes my blood pressure and my heart skips a little as I remind myself of, if only!

As you must now be aware that the draw for the Euro 2004 has been made and this is where your country are heading in and around the middle of next June:

Group A: Portugal, Greece, Spain and Russia
Group B: France, England, Switzerland and Croatia
Group C: Sweden, Bulgaria, Denmark and Italy
Group D: Czech Republic, Latvia, Germany and Holland

The Swede's comments are as follows: "The most important thing is that we have fit players, ones who aren't completely dead at the end of May. The players could have played sixty or seventy matches. It could be two tired teams we see. To me the players' fitness is more important than the draw because I know if we have fit players we will have a very good tournament. Of course I will have my fingers crossed. It is the most frustrating thing in this job because you cannot do anything about it".

My view is that: It seems no matter who the manager is, it seems, when the draw is made for a big competition, they look for excuses before the balls are back into the bag. The Swede is talking about fitness and everything else that is inconceivable at this moment in time. Do they go to bed at night and think that only English players suffer injuries and miss big internationals and that would be the best way to go about the job. Tell the punters, who they think are mugs, this that and the other and they'll understand what a job I have got on my hands!

The England players who lifted the World Cup in 1966 I am sure played more matches than any other country in world football with all the domestic league, FA Cup and League Cup and all the replays, European and International matches leading up to the greatest hour our nation has seen on the green, green grass of home. If my memory serves me well, I think that one FA Cup tie went to five matches, and if it still serves me well, I think it was Arsenal and Leicester City, if I am wrong please forgive me, but I am certain one tie did go into a fifth match and given playing each other in two league matches as well, they were sick of the sight of each other!

Ramsey said to his players at the end of the ninety minutes of that pulsating World Cup Final against archenemies number one, West Germany, "You have won it once so you're going to have to go out and win it again". And this was after the hardest slog of a season one can have, but at that moment in time these players would have played on for five six seven hours to win that trophy and not a word would have been said afterwards. And of course you must once again take into account the state of the pitches – some were called that – and did not have the light balls to clip over the top of the human wall.

WERE THE RUSSIANS RELATED?

Well, only that the Russian linesman couldn't keep up with the game, on this particular day, and I'm sorry I can't say that in German. This is the kind of talk footballers respond to, especially all those players he put his faith into along that long path to Wembley, and I don't mean Wembley Way. Being the host nation we had an automatic entry. But there were still many, many friendly matches where Ramsey had to finalise his team selection. At the final whistle I remembered looking at Alan Ball, the baby of this bunch, and the way he looked over at the Germans and Karl Heinz Schnellinger, the big blonde full back who had already chased the brilliant Ball for miles – he was not in the Candy Box with us on that most famous of evenings, for me anyway – and saying to himself "Here we go again my German friend. I hope you have got another half an hour in you, lad", Ball would say in that northern tongue and with the squeak that you couldn't imitate. But his heart is big as a lion, as the Germans knew by the time Bobby Moore had walked the famous steps to collect the Jules Rimet trophy. It was the tiny ginger-haired touch player who changed the whole complexion of this most memorable of all English International matches. He was a constant menace and just kept running at a player at that time rated one of the, if not the, best left back in world football. He got the ball on the right touchline and ran it as far to the touchline as humanly possible and taking a wee glimpse, put the ball into the space for the oncoming Geoff Hurst. The West Ham target man took it superbly, although a fraction behind his big frame and on the half-turn smashed the ball that thundered against the underside of the German crossbar, bouncing back down as quickly and deadly as a silent doodle-bug. The camera switched to Roger Hunt with his arms raised and Hurst, in his usual pose, of hands on his hips as the Russian linesman whispered into the 'Mug in the Middles' ear that the ball had crossed the line. I wonder if this man was related to the Abramovich for he is only the second man to get an English football team out of the mire as time was running out. This was the one point of the match I could not tell you about because it seemed for those few seconds with the silence deafening, the entire world seemed to have stopped. Then it was the hour of Bobby Moore, captain marvel, supreme, messiah and so many other superlatives he has been called before. The crowd were in 'bits' as the ball bounced around the England penalty area and Jack Charlton confessed that he was screaming to his England skipper to get the ball anywhere amongst the 100,000 screaming lunatics who had never ever seen a match like this in the lives, with emotions running high both on and off the field. The West Germans had equalised in the dying seconds of normal time just when Moore and his team mates were thinking, 'that if we can hold on to this we'll have a frosty in our hand in no time', never dreaming that the Germans could beat the world's greatest goalkeeper once again. The screams and whistling of panic got to everyone except Robert Chelsea Moore, who nonchalantly disguised the play by going to kick the ball out, but all of a sudden, once composing himself completely, walked it outside of his box on the left hand side looking up to the tunnel end and with the coolness of the Cincinnati Kid, 'dinked' a lovely ball into the space for his hard-running West Ham team mate. Do you think Hurst knew Bobby wouldn't panic? I do, for he had seen him under this kind of pressure too many times before. But in the last few seconds of a World Cup Final?

The Germans were in tatters, ragged and downright done for as the moment came that made Kenneth Wolstenholme a household name throughout his country. I once asked Geoff, over a few drinks in one of our Newcastle-under-Lyme watering holes, what went through his mind at that precise moment. His reply was quick and incisive as he said coolly that "I aimed for the crowd, the furthest point, knowing if it did not go in, at least it would take them more time to get it back than there was on the clock". The rest, as Paul McCartney would say, was 'Yesterday'. I was just leaving school around this time to sign Apprenticeship forms at Stamford Bridge and this was something that all of us kids wanted to do, first play for their favourite team, then their country, but a World Cup Final, forget it!

TWO OUT OF THREE AIN'T BAD

Well I got past the first two, but the nearest I got was my debut, which I have already told you about, but this was a real special match for me, my own little

World Cup, if you like, on that murky March night, a time I remember for watching the Cheltenham Festival in hotel room bed after my lunch and falling asleep, something so very rare for me. I think someone was telling me this was going to be my evening as the rain lashed down outside my window and those beautiful thoroughbreds slogged up that famous Cheltenham hill to the finishing line. These were my conditions. Maybe my prayers were answered on that rain-sodden afternoon which gave me the confidence knowing that my ankle was not going to let me down in a match I had so long dreamed of. I remember being woken by the telephone and once realising that this really was the day of my reckoning, each raindrop that belted against my hotel window sounded more like Sinatra's drummer – Buddy Rich – than ever before!

I think that was the last time England actually beat West Germany, for not so long afterwards they amalgamated with the Eastern side of the country. This was the first time we had actually seen a German wall knocked down and I took great pleasure in being one of the brickies!

THE RANIERI RIDDLE
Why can't victories silence the rumours?

This is by Matt Lawton of the *Mail*: In time we should know the truth, but reports emanating from Chelsea yesterday – Tuesday 2nd of December – sent out vastly conflicting signals. First came an extraordinary statement from acting chief executive Paul Smith, who claimed to be speaking for all concerned when he said the Premiership leaders had no interest in Sven Goran Eriksson. Then, however, came talk of a possible appointment that points straight back to the England coach!

Paul Newman – not the great actor – Eriksson's close friend and a former FA colleague, has already been interviewed for the post of communications at Stamford Bridge. Newman is currently doing PR work for Eriksson's partner, Nancy Dell'Olio. The problem is, of course, Claudio Ranieri, Chelsea's Italian manager has been under immense pressure this season, and not just because of the £111,000 Roman Abramovich has allowed him to invest in new talent.

That photograph of Eriksson outside the home of Chelsea's Russian owner during the summer triggered off speculation and, contrary to what Smith insisted was the case yesterday, conversations have definitely taken place.

Ranieri has coped remarkably well, maintaining his focus and guiding his side not just to victory over Manchester United on Sunday but to the summit of the Premiership table. Add to that a place in the last sixteen of the Champions League and just two defeats in twenty-two matches and the season seems to be going well.

It is why Chelsea fans want the Italian to stay, and why they are forever being given air-time on phone-ins to convey the message 'Stick with England Sven' they say 'We want Ranieri'.

Smith echoed that sentiment yesterday. "How can you criticise Claudio?"

he asked. "We want him in charge at the start of next season".

The players agree. Frank Lampard, the scorer of the first half penalty that conquered United said that, "He makes us feel that he trusts us and believes in us. It's six games since we conceded a goal, and that's a testament to the work he does with us." Lampard, though, urged caution to those convinced that Chelsea are favourites for the title. He said that, "There's a long way to go. Beating United was one of the highlights of my career, but the manager tells us to look ahead to the next game. We will now be focusing on the Carling Cup-tie with Reading". Winning the Carling Cup is unlikely to provide Roman Abramovich with much pleasure if his team then fall away in the more important competitions, but for now everything appears to be going to plan.

At the moment there is no need to appoint Eriksson, no need to make further changes to a side that have proved themselves serious contenders for the top prizes. It might be different come the summer of course. By then, though, Peter Kenyon will be Chelsea's chief executive and Smith can say the decision was taken out of his hands.

After all, Kenyon was said to have attempted to recruit Eriksson for Old Trafford before Sir Alex Ferguson decided to postpone his retirement.

Not that Kenyon would ever admit to that!

What do I think? I'll tell you straight, that what Claudio 'Tinkerman' Ranieri has done since Roman has appeared has been nothing short of unbelievable and the question that keeps popping up has absolutely no justification. Then again, did the sacking of Gianluca Vialli? Did the sacking of Eddie McCreadie? Did the transfers of Peter Osgood and Alan Hudson?

It has been quite a unique situation watching, waiting, listening, reading and feeling quite stunned by such a fiasco. The latest situation of Roman Abramovich bringing four hundred friends over is quite incredible because I was brought up on the saying, which is quite true, that you can count your friends on one hand!

But looking back to the 'Godfather', the great Don Corleone told his sons and Tom Hagen – his adopted son – that you must always "Keep your friends close, but keep your enemies even closer", this spun around in my head as I researched for this book knowing or more like probing such a situation. It does not matter if you have three and a half billion or three and a half quid, surely you cannot have that many friends and associates. This is fantastic media stuff because I knew in my water the day I got that call from SKY that something big was going down and I don't understand what money laundering is exactly, but there is something going down outside of football. Only tonight I watched the match between Southampton and Portsmouth in the Carling Cup and who was sitting there on a cold evening in an open neck shirt?

None other than the Chelsea billionaire owner!

I am not one for drama but this is the best thing I have witnessed since JR Ewing took Dallas and put it right in the middle of the city of London. It captured the imagination of the people here, mainly because the majority of the elder English folk have never set foot in the United States of America and once getting addicted to that show they thought that was what every blue-blooded American was like. I am fortunate, no, unfortunate to have come across someone like JR and he fired me with one of the most unjustifiable and underhanded dirty tricks anyone has ever played on another. But as that great old song goes 'It Had To Be You'. I did not really know until then that the River Thames was that clean!

But back to this latest fairy tale and how the Tinkerman has kept his cool with so much dignity is beyond anything I have ever witnessed in our game, and don't get me wrong, I know the filth in our game and our country and that is one of the reasons why I am probably happy that I was unemployable. But these people here who have sucked the blood out of our game, before Roman arrived, are no different than the vagabonds and thieves in any other walk of life. As I say, Life takes you where it wants to take you, not always where you want it to go, for I have been dealt some pretty duff cards in my time and if the highs and lows are anything to go with, I have had to take some cards off the top and put them on the bottom, by doing that I do not get too disappointed when I have to throw in my hand!

Getting run over by an out of control driver was by far my lowest ebb, although missing an FA Cup Final and the Mexico World Cup would never be surpassed as a more realistic heartache, in a perfect and most normal lifetime. And then being kicked in the teeth whilst in hospital by a cheating wife was close to breaking me. They say time is a healer but it all depends on how long you are talking about, please believe me!

Apart from that, as in my autobiography, the 'Working Man's Ballet', the story of the evening in a London Hotel was quite exceptional when you are talking about, why me?

'CHAIRMAN FRANK EDWARDS DIES'

I was having a great time in the Royal Lancaster Hotel with my great friend Tony Waddington, who you have read about, and was approached by the Stoke City Chairman, at that time, a lovely old chap named Frank Edwards. I had been told by several people that this man was the right stuff, quality and a man of great stature. I had put in for the vacant job of the manager of Stoke City and Mr Edwards had obviously seen my application just before he left the Potteries for this gathering. He approached me as I was sitting enjoying, as always, the company of Tony, and he asked if he could have a quick word with me. We walked to the corner of this vast dining room where we were out of earshot when he asked if I was serious about running the club. My answer was that I was very, very interested in the manager's position and that I knew what the supporters of Stoke City and the town itself wanted and that I could give them that better than anyone else and far quicker. I say that because they took me in as a second son, if you like!

I also said that I would bring Tony back into the club to guide me through my initial period as first time manager. He gleamed as if I was wasting my time telling him, because he already knew my feelings about the situation. I can still hear his voice as I shook his hand and saw that this man was a very sincere one. His last words to me were that "When are you coming back to the Potteries?" to which, I told him if I had to I would be back first thing on Monday. He then said that "When your train pulls into the station call me from the station" – no mobiles in those days – "and I'll be ready to see you immediately", in other words I had the job. I thanked this charming old chap and returned to our table and ordered a bottle of champagne as Tony and I were back in work together. I could not have been any happier, not even if Liverpool or Real Madrid wanted me!

I wanted to work with Tony and for the people that made me the player I became whilst in my first period playing for them. The 10am train from Euston pulled into Stoke-on-Trent. I checked my watch and it was 'bang on' midday as I headed for the old phones on the wall as you get to the top of the stairs there. I dialled the number and a young girl answered asking me what could she do for me, to which I replied I had a meeting with Mr Frank Edwards and he was expecting me. It seemed like an eternity as I waited for her to tell me to come right on over. Her next words were the words that changed the rest of my life: Frank Edwards had died in his sleep in the middle of the night!

That was the closest I ever got to get on the other side of the fence and I have been asked a million times why I didn't go into management, but there are only certain times you can tell that unbelievable story. That was as close to a Matthew Harding story you'll ever hear, and they were two of the nicest men you'll ever meet. The worst thing is with all the 'filth' in the game the one man, in a position like that, I knew I could have worked for, had died just when I needed him most. Which applies to the wife that left me to fend for myself whilst still in a wheelchair. Isn't it funny how come the worst experiences you have in life seem to have great parallels!

So management never came my way and that is why I feel so very strongly about a man like Claudio Ranieri, the real Tinkerman and a man you know you can trust which is a rarity at any era in our game and by the end of this book I hope they are calling him the best manager that Chelsea have ever had. I have a feeling that will be what happens and we are only a third of the way through the league fixtures, Chelsea play Reading tomorrow in the last sixteen of the Carling Cup, then go into the FA Cup early January and that will be followed by a return to the last sixteen of the Champions League, so don't go away!

MY HARD PAL RAN

Claudio Ranieri may be proving himself a great manager, but he was never a star performer on the pitch. "As a footballer he was a hard bastard", said his agent Vicenzo Morabito. "He was a crude defender. He wasn't top class, but he was a decent defender who played in Serie A. He always had leadership qualities and at half-time in the dressing-room he would be the one the players listened to. He was with Roma from 1972 to1974. He only played fifteen games for them and they were not as big a team back then as now.

"The rest of his career was spent with Catanzaro, the first two seasons in Serie A, then four in Serie B – and he ended his career at Catania in 1981.

"He only scored five goals when he was at Catanzaro, three of them in Serie A, so at least he can say he scored in Italy's top league."

Frank Lampard yesterday warned Manchester United that Chelsea have what it takes to be champions. The England midfielder's penalty gave the Blues a deserved victory over United on Sunday, which took them back to the top of the table.

A reminder that the bookmakers immediately made Claudio's team 5/4 favourites – the first time they have headed the market – with current champs United at 15/8 and Arsenal 2/1.

Lampard insisted that "People wanted to know how far we have come this season, and we have shown that we are here to stay" also saying that, "Beating the champions is special and a great feeling. It gives us a bit of confidence, and people will start to realise we are here to challenge.

"We came fourth last season and now we want to come first. There are a lot of winners in this squad who want to achieve more. All week people had built this up as a massive game, and we performed. We showed a great attitude, imposed ourselves and deserved to win. We have brought in some big names who have worked hard and fitted straight in".

LUIS FIGO

Luis Figo yesterday dismissed Chelsea's chances of winning this season's Champions League. The Real Madrid star is convinced Claudio Ranieri's multi-million pound outfit is too inexperienced to conquer Europe.

Figo, who will be hoping to lift the European Cup for a second time with the Spanish champions, is convinced that Arsenal and NOT Manchester United pose the greatest threat from the three English teams still left in the competition.

Figo also said that: I think Chelsea have great players and have started an exciting project. HOSTILE: I think they will do well in the future because they have quality. But they don't have the experience for the Champions League. That is the only weak thing that can stop them from getting to the semi-finals or final". Real travel to fierce rivals Barcelona on Saturday and Figo is backing David Beckham to cope with what is guaranteed to be a hostile crowd inside the Nou Camp. Figo adding that, "He has the experience of playing in difficult atmospheres so I don't think this will give him any problems at all."

I'M GLAD I NEVER JOINED UNITED

By John Terry 29th of November 2003

Before the crunch match with Manchester United, Andrew Dillon reported that – John Terry announced that he was glad that he never joined the might of Manchester United. He said that; "I definitely made the right decision to come to Chelsea. I was a United fan at the time and had the chance to go up there. United made an effort to sign me and that was a great experience. They were playing West Ham one day and invited me and my family to have a pre-match meal with them at the Swallow Hotel in Waltham Abbey. I was sitting with Eric Cantona and Paul Ince and had my photograph taken with them. It's one of those things that will always live with me.

"They wanted to sign me but I just loved it here so much and ended up signing for Chelsea".

He added that, "Chelsea looked after me and my family, giving me boots and training kit to train in. They might seem silly things but they made all the difference to me.

"This is a family club, and made me feel so welcome. United's interest was a dream come true but when I came back here I loved it so much I decided to sign for the club. When the champions come, everyone is up for it. As soon as the Sparta Prague match was over on Wednesday the manager was telling us to focus. We have to be switched on all game. Playing United is like an International. People will be looking to see if we can match United – they did that before the Arsenal match.

"We lost that game and there were some people who wrote us off and said that "That's it, they're out of it".

"This is the chance to prove we are can compete with the best, as we have shown in the Champions League. But we have got to do it against the big sides at home and they don't come much bigger then United.

"They have done well here in recent years, but hopefully the fans can lift us so we can change that. If we can win tomorrow it will give us the opportunity to try to slowly pull away from them. If you make one mistake they will punish you. That's why they've been the best in the business because they do that. Maybe Ruud van Nistelrooy's all round game makes him the hardest opponent I have to face in the Premiership, although Thierry Henry and Michael Owen are the other two who stand out. I had to start thinking about the game from Thursday and about what van Nistelrooy likes to do in a game. Throughout the season I try to watch him on television. Hopefully, when it comes to playing against him, I know his game a bit better".

What is my reaction to John Terry's remarks: I think that the Chelsea centre-back talks as he plays the game, as I have already said. He is a straight talker, nothing fancy, just purely and simply a young man focused on what he has to do to stop the likes of the Dutch and Frenchman. I like the way he shrugs aside Alex Ferguson's team without saying anything detrimental about them, showing them the complete respect he has for them. But it is that inner strength that makes John Terry the player he is and this season, along with Frank Lampard, they have blossomed beyond all recognition. I have loved the way Terry plays from the first time I saw him, and as a judge I do my analysing in a kind of backward way. Selecting the player whoever it is and make them a bad player rather than the other way around. That gives me the perfect foothold to watch and study the weaknesses more than the strengths. That is how I played the game, playing to my strengths and trying to cover up any weaknesses I had and making sure I gave my very best to the team around me. With Terry, I have had a problem finding weaknesses although he looks to be one-paced, he is deceiving and has a long stride which he uses if an opponent looks like going by him, whether it is on either touchline when a striker tries to pull him out of the middle. Usually big number fives are not too happy being pulled out of the territory in front of the keeper but Terry is at home there as any other defensive part of the field. He has good clean control and passing game – which I mentioned earlier – but as the season goes on the game becomes a little different as fatigue sets in, the nights grow colder and there is always a certain degree of uncertainty with others around him coming into the side and changing the way the back four of late have been perform-ing. Without a doubt the defensive play of Chelsea recently has been their strength. Some people put it down to the sweeping-up job being done by Makelele, albeit in front of the back four. And of course the form of Frank Lampard is so very important because by making those runs of his he is going beyond his markers and taking them into positions they don't like going. Therefore they are more on the back foot rather than the other way around. When I played I prided myself on being able to get beyond our strikers when the opportunity arose. Not just running through the middle but playing one-twos in between the centre-half and fullback. My marker would hate it and I was, when uninjured, fit enough to run from one by-line to the other. This I put down to my personal training where I would stride out three-quarter pace down the side of the field and slow down to a very slow jog behind the goal then reach the other corner flag and just lift the pace up slightly. I would do this kind of run about a dozen times.

What it also does for you is nothing more than mental, knowing that if the worst came to the worst, that is what I would have to do, and I would be confident I had it in the locker. Plus I was always looking for it with both Osgood and Greenhoff, where I would look to play the ball somewhere else and disguise the pass I was making. Once the ball left my right foot I would take off as if in a world of my own, meaning my marker was wrong footed and I had stole a march on him.

The disguise pass I think I inherited from the 'master' of the passing game, the brilliant Johnny Haynes. My overall thinking is that John Terry, like a brilliant young player named Alan Dodd at Stoke City, has this uncanny ability to make the difficult things look easy and that is a sure sign of a truly great player in any position and any part of the field.

'D-DAY FOR VERON OVER PASSPORT ROW'

Juan Sebastian Veron will find out today if he is to be summoned to appear before a criminal court accused of conspiring to forge a passport.

The false document enabled Veron to play for Lazio when they were coached by Sven Goran Eriksson, and he was a key player in the team that won the Italian title three years ago. The midfielder now at Chelsea, was one of twenty players caught up in a scandal two years ago in which bogus passports helped clubs to register stars as European, thereby beating a ban on the number of non-EU players they could field.

Today's case in Rome will hear how a birth certificate in the name of Giuseppe Porcela was used to obtain Veron's Italian passport. The certificate was later proved to be fake and the man named on it never existed.

It is the day of the Carling Cup match at Reading but I am still searching through the many headlines and different reviews and came across CLOWNIO WILL HAVE THE LAST LAUGH The real man behind Chelsea's amazing rise to the top of the Premiership table; Claudio Ranieri has been Chelsea coach for over three years and 161 games, but little is really known of the Roman. With his limited English and sometimes wacky interviews, Ranieri found himself Clownio, but the 52-year-old boss has taken the Blues into the knock-out stages of the Champions League and top of the Premiership. David Woods – who exclusively broke the news that Ranieri would be Chelsea manager – reveals here what makes this fascinating character tick.

GREAVESIE

The timing of Jimmy Greaves's book is perfect. Jimmy is, alongside Bobby Moore and Johnny Haynes, the most modest of men you would ever meet. Their contribution to our game is immense, and as a kid there was Denis Law, the 'Belfast Boy', you know who that is, and Bobby Charlton who took Manchester United to the top of Europe's tree. Some achievement when you have to remember and understand the circumstances of the Munich Air crash that shattered the city of Manchester. Sir Matt Busby was very poorly for quite a long time lying in a Munich Hospital. Then he came back to build another team that could take him to his dream. I will be looking at the great Greaves' book and picking out some nice stories for you.

It was Tuesday the morning before Chelsea travelled a very short trip to Reading down the M4.

ROMAN ROAD LEADS INTER THE G14 ELITE

My friend Harry Harris of the *Mirror* had this to report; Among Roman

Abramovich's hundreds of guests at the Manchester United match was Boris Becker. More interestingly, so was Inter Milan managing director Massimo Moratti.

It set the chattering classes alight, speculation mounting, yet another imminent multi-million transfer.

In fact, on the agenda was Chelsea's entry to the top table, G14, as well as the loose ends of the payments on the Hernan Crespo transfer.

Set up two years ago, G14 has swelled to eighteen and Chelsea are sure to be put forward as candidate number nineteen after Arsenal became the latest addition this season. Four months ago Chelsea were not on G14's invitation list but now, with Abramovich as the owner, it seems inconceivable to exclude the west London club.

Inter have become strong allies of Chelsea since the lavish summit dinner not long after the Russian multi-millionaire took over, when talks hinged on buying one of the Italians club's top three players. At that heady time Inter wanted £25million for Christian Vieri, the worlds highest paid player at £8million a year after tax. Crespo's financial package was far less reasonable and the player was two years younger. In addition, Vieri would not contemplate leaving the warmth of Milan.

But suddenly it is beginning to rain on Vieri's parade and he cannot wait to get away. He does not even celebrate his goals; such is his depth of his loathing for the club and their fans.

Inter might be keen to offload the centre-forward and he might yet regret that he was priced too high for a player over the age of thirty.

FRANKS HUNGER GIVES UNITED FOOD FOR THOUGHT

By John Dillon, *Express* chief writer once again; According to Claudio Ranieri, Frank Lampard was not supposed to take the penalty which beat Manchester United and put Chelsea back on top of the Premiership. It is the job of Adrian Mutu and if he is not there, Jimmy Floyd. "But you know Frank, he takes the ball and takes the kick" said the Tinkerman.

The Italian is an engaging character, but he is still not the kind of coach who takes kindly to deviations from team discipline. He is, though, sharp enough to recognise that there was more good than harm in the excess of hunger and desire which prompted Lampard's impromptu alteration of standing orders, Mutu was one of the first to congratulate Lampard after his successful penalty. This was a moment, which confirmed Ranieri's notion that for all the nig-egos within his expensively assembled squad, the common purpose is the most powerful motivating force, whoever puts the ball in the net.

"People wanted to know how far we have come this season and we have shown we are here to stay", said Frank, the son of ex-West Ham and England fullback of the same name.

Unlike John Terry, Lampard is not a homegrown Chelsea product. Yet, amid the great wave of expensive signings who have arrived this season, he has come to represent the unification of the old and the new within the team.

Claude Makelele was muscularly impressive against United, but Lampard's performance was just as striking. Roy Keane was as fiercely determined, but he was unable to impose his design upon the game in the way the young Englishman and his French cohort did. Here was the triumph, which signalled Chelsea's overturning of the balance of power. United, past experience shows, have perfected the art of running on cruise control before Christmas. It is in the spring when they bolt for home. But they have now been beaten three times in the Premiership. Arsenal remain undefeated and Chelsea have lost only once. It already leaves the champions significantly closer to the widely accepted dividing line of six defeats that separate winners from also-rans. Yet a simple recollection of last season's late surge for glory proves that Sir Alex Ferguson and his team have the one thing Chelsea lack and cannot buy.

They have ridden the full course at the top many times. They have the nous and the knack for repeating title wins, which has so far eluded Arsenal's glittering array of stars on two occasions when they failed to defend the championship.

So, for Chelsea, there is still a journey of exploration in which they must learn whether they can stay the course.

DUFF'S MY NUMBER ONE PICK OF CHELSEA STAR CAST

Says Steve Coppell, ex-Manchester United and England winger: Steve Coppell went to see his old club play Chelsea on Sunday and did not learn too much that he didn't already know. Steve is now manager of first division Reading, the team Chelsea travel to for their Carling Cup this evening at the Medjeski Stadium, just a few miles down the M4 from Chelsea's Harlington training ground. When asked by the *Standard's* Ken Dyer about the team that Chelsea would field, he was just as in the dark as anyone else. Plus at this time I doubt if even the Timkerman knows himself!

Coppell says that, "I don't think it really matters, for Claudio probably has twenty players who are busting a gut to play. On Sunday against United, Chelsea looked so solid yet so adventurous. It must be marvellous to play in that midfield, to be able to play off the cuff knowing that someone like Makelele is floating around behind you, clearing up everything.

"What a joy it must be for Joe Cole, playing in that kind of set-up. Dyer asked Coppell if he had the funds to buy one Chelsea player would it be, Lampard, Makelele or John Terry?

He said that, "I was a winger so I have a soft spot for that type of player because they can unlock defences. I would go for Damien Duff and if I had the choice of one player from the Premiership it would be Ryan Giggs. I think Duff will play against us tonight but I am hoping he doesn't unlock our back four. I am hoping, though, that we will enjoy the game. It's our opportunity for our team to play against top quality players. Whatever the result, we know we won't be judged on tonight's match but on whether we reach the play-offs or not." That is interesting from the Reading manager and it does not surprise me because you find over the years involved with wingers that they have their very own sortt of 'union' or Admiration Society Club, if you like. As a youngster, Peter Houseman was an out-and-out left-sided winger who did tremendously well for the good of that team of the late sixties and early seventies. Then, moving to Stoke City he enjoyed playing with Jimmy Robertson – who I as a kid, watched play for Arsenal and Spurs – and found him a member of such a society. He was in the same mould, a real 'union' man. Moving onto Arsenal the great George Armstrong, who ran miles for Arsenal over the years, must have been a groundsman's nightmare with the wear and tear of the green down that left side. Geordie was a real winger also, and a bloody good one at that, in fact very under-rated, but not inside the Marble Halls and the Arsenal training ground. Then Chippy Brady came in and played a deeper left-sided winger role but drifted about the place when he did not see enough of the ball, but Liam was comfortable all over the field once on his magical left peg. Then onto the USA.

THE BOGEYMAN

In the *Express* on the morning of the team's Carling Cup tie at Reading they ran a story about the mystery man of Stamford Bridge. There are some players who I have come across in my time playing who just turned up for the money, some would spill blood for the cause and then there those in between who took everything for granted, they are the ones like the Bogey Man who turn my stomach, for there are so many players better than them who will kill to pull a blue and white shirt on, but I suppose Chelsea have no luck with Dutchmen and the chips they carry around with them. Having said that, if you are stupid enough to give them such lucrative contracts without reading the small print so be it.

This was an article on the worst signings, which ran along the top of the page as: The Premiership misfits who are laughing all the way to the bank while their club are left counting the cost.

The five players mentioned were Marcelino, a player bought by Ruud Gullit for £5million from Real Majorca and played 19 matches before leaving four years later with his contract – worth £4million over that period – for Spanish first division side Polide Portivo, a team I have never heard of. Well done Ruud!

Then there was Southampton's signing of Agustin Delgado who the Saints knew had a knee problem yet still went ahead with the deal. The 28-year-old played just four matches for the club after a fee of £3.5million plus £300,000 agent's fees then, after picking up wages of £1.5million, £300,000 a start, left to play for Ecuador in the World Cup in the Far East.

Aston Villa have bought some trash over the years but this took the biscuit as Bosko Balaban warned the club he will not quit until they paid an acceptable pay-off package. Balaban was bought for £6million from Dinamo Zagreb and still hadn't played a match for them. This was another one of Deadly Doug Ellis's masterstrokes and it cost Villa in all £8million. Before we get onto Chelsea's mother of all nightmares, look at Duncan Ferguson of Everton. Since his signing from Newcastle in the year 2000 he has started 28 matches but with eighteen months to go on his contract they cannot afford to pay him up, a contract worth £34,000 a week. He costs the club £328,214.29 for each game he played and £656,428,57 for each of his fourteen league goals scored in that time.

I'll let Mark Fleming take you through this classic: The growing excitement that Chelsea could finally win their first title since 1955, does not extend to everyone at Stamford Bridge. Sunday's 1-0 victory over Manchester United has added more weight to the belief at the club that the perennial underachievers are finally about to win something meaningful.

But while the superstars shoot for the Premiership crown, one player is losing the struggle to keep his head above water. At the start of the season Winston Bogarde, an outcast at Chelsea almost from day one, wasn't given a first team squad number and was ordered to train with the youth and reserve players. But the decline and fall of the former Holland international has not ended there. To add embarrassment to a player who once won the European Cup with Ajax, Bogarde has been barred from playing with the reserves for not trying hard enough. The Dutchman, who still pockets £40,000 a week in one of football's craziest ever contracts, was given a rare outing in a Chelsea shirt for the trip to Wimbledon in October. In front of almost 3,500 fans at Milton Keynes, Bogarde was the only big name among a side of young hopefuls selected by reserve team coach Mick McGovern. At Chelsea, not even the reserves play for the reserves. Instead, the team is full of teenagers desperate for a call-up to the first team squad – plus on this night, the ill-fated Bogarde.

McGiven however, was prepared to give him another chance, hoping the 33-year-old former Ajax, AC Milan and Barcelona star would provide a touch of class and leadership to his youthful team of multinationals. But like every single coach before him, he was to be sorely disappointed. On a cold night, McGiven watched in dismay as his side tumbled to a 2-1 defeat. And Bogarde put in such a spineless show in the middle of defence that the coach has vowed never to pick him in the side again.

McGiven later described the team's display as 'careless', a word that sums up Bogarde's remarkable spell at Chelsea, which is now entering its fourth and final year. Throughout his time at Stamford Bridge, the Dutchman has acted without a single care for his career. Long ago, Bogarde decided he would never come close to matching his £2.1million a year deal with Chelsea, so he determined to stay at the club, come what may, and pocket the cash. So far he has banked £6.6million from the club, despite starting just four games. Last season this was a real problem, as Chelsea were feeling the financial squeeze and desperately wanted to cut their disproportionate wage bill. When goalkeeper Mark Bosnich, who was also paid £40,000 a week, failed a drug test, the club were only too happy to wipe him off the payroll. However they have never quite managed to get rid of Bogarde.

Now, with the financial situation at the club better than ever after the takeover by Roman Abramovich in the summer, Chelsea no longer cares about resolving the Bogarde situation. So the player is allowed to live out his strange existence in the twilight zone. He doesn't even live in England any more. Four days a week, Bogarde is required to attend training with the youth team. So, four days a week he boards a plane from Amsterdam, where he now lives, and flies to Heathrow, close to Chelsea's training ground in Harlington. Then, as soon as training is over, he nips back to the airport to catch the 40 minute return flight and is at home for dinner. A club insider said that, "He says it costs him £200 return flight, so that's £800 a week. The season is about 40 weeks long, so that's £32,000 a year on flights".

I was not a good student at school but I can even tell you that is less than he works in a week. Oops, work!

All communications with the powers that be have disappeared. Every now and again the total lack of first team opportunities does hit home, and Bogarde asks to see the manager Claudio Ranieri.

But whereas a few years ago Ranieri would have been prepared to discuss the situation, now he simply refers him to McGiven or youth team coach Steve Clarke. Not that Bogarde is really all that bothered. He just shrugs his giant shoulders and thinks of the money that keeps rolling in and those frequent-flier points.

Rumours from Holland claim that Dutch side Willem ll and Austrian outfit Rapid Vienna might be ready to offer him an escape route in the January transfer window, but both seem long shots.

Chelsea and Bogarde accept the farce will run its due course until June, when he will just walk away from the club £8.4million richer.

During his time at Chelsea, he has started in the first team four times, and come on as sub eight times.

His last Premiership appearance was on Boxing Day 2000 at Ipswich and the last sighting was over a year ago, when he played 21 minutes of a Worthington Cup tie against Gillingham.

He has played twice for the reserves this season, but even that door has been slammed. Bogarde has slipped so far down the pecking order at Chelsea there is no further for him to go – except quietly out of the door for the final time in May!

'LOADSAMONEY'

I don't think you need my view on this one but I must make comment: that this must be the reason for Gianluca Vialli's departure, although that does not add up after giving him such a contract then sacking the manager. I do know that around this time Chelsea were looking for certain players and one of those confided in a friend of mine by telling him that he had been offered a contract in which he agreed terms but when he asked if he should meet the manager before he signed, Colin Hutchison the then holder of the purse strings told the player that he need not worry about that because Vialli would be gone by the time the ink on his contract had dried. The player refused to sign on that kind of deal and quite rightly so. I have told you that story, but thought I would tie it in with the Bogarde story because it gives you two sides to that double-headed coin, one English – or Turkish – and one Dutch. So all I have to say is that who can you trust, in my second spell at the Bridge I was signed by chairman Ken Bates, not John Neal the manager, but I had no problem with that because I have always believed that you sign with a Football Club and deal with the money man about the finer details and then sit down, or vice versa really, with the manager/coach to discuss the role he wants you to play in his team. That sounds simple enough to me and by the way it turned out at the Bridge I was happy to leave when Stoke City cried SOS at the foot of the old first division so again Ken Bates was as good as his word and all went very smoothly, I never had one single problem with Bates whilst a player at the Bridge, but it was crystal clear that I did not figure in the plans of the management team of John Neal, Ian McNeil and my old team mate John Hollins, the coach. There was a funny story about the day we had a practice match at Harlington, which was the usual first team against reserves in which there were the likes of Micky Droy, Clive Walker, Peter Rhodes Brown, Chris Hutchings, Dale Jasper and myself. After about twenty minutes, Neal blew the whistle and asked us for the ball back, because the team that they were playing on the Saturday would not have it for that long. Well, big Micky and I laughed for hours afterwards and on the pitch that day we could not concentrate for being so pathetic. I asked John Hollins – who was refereeing – if winning the ball back was not a part of the game anymore in which he looked into the blue skies above wishing I had never have returned to his beloved Chelsea Football Club.

One of the funniest moments in a reserve team match was playing at Oxford one evening. We finished the match and decided that we would all go for a drink with Rocky Taylor who then had a Night Club in Putney High Street. Rocky and I had played together several times for the All-Stars, a team which included the great Jess Conrad in our goal. Jess took up goalkeeping because he saw a clip of Lev Yashin – that great Russian shot-stopper – not because of his ability but his dressing in all black and Jess thought not only did he want a different coloured jersey than us ordinary mortals but he thought he looked wonderful in black. Anyhow, this particular early morning stint took us into one, two, three o'clock when Peter Rhodes-Brown – a terrific lad – turned to me and said "Al, I cannot believe that we could not beat that team tonight. We had all the ball. They weren't in it, at all." Nobody took much notice at first then we realised he was not having a laugh. He was deadly serious. He thought we had drawn the match, 2-2, when we had won the match 3–2. Peter played on the left wing that evening and for the life of me I don't believe how a footballer at any level could come off a football field not knowing the score. Some time after that match, Oxford bought Peter from Chelsea!

Back to Bogarde – not Humphrey although a better actor – I loved playing and training so much it is very difficult to comment about such a situation because had we played for Chelsea until we were sixty-four we still would not have been paid what Bogarde paid in income tax. It is a truly remarkable story and one that the new owners will take on board, I am sure. This could not possibly happen under the guidance of Peter Kenyon, but it just goes to show, and it must question the business acumen of Ken Bates!

I bet Bogarde has a real laugh back home in Amsterdam along Canal waving his 'dosh' about like Harry Enfield walking in a bar, 'Ah loadsamoney'. You have to make light of this for the damage was done and he obviously had absolutely no interest in playing, sussed the joint out and thought 'hang on here, here we go' and that is about all you can say about the matter, only I wish it were me for the last couple of seasons of my career when I did have a legitimate injury, that really would have been just the job for my life style, after having a great time playing before that. Some people have all the luck and of all the people a Dutchman with a 'chip'.

RUN GOES ON

Wednesday evening saw Chelsea going seven matches without conceding a goal. Reading, some saw, as a banana skin but the Tinkerman has his team at full tilt at the moment and it is really hard seeing who is going to score against them let alone beat them. They simply breezed through Reading and with all of their strike power, though; are not scoring enough goals since the nine goals in one week against Lazio and Newcastle United. Headlines in the *Daily Express* were all about Jimmy Floyd as Mark Fleming followed this headline:

JIMMY HOLDS HIS CORNER IN ROMAN ROAD PAVED WITH PURE GOLD: Jimmy Floyd Hasselbaink proved to be a soldier in the Roman army. He has been left out of big games recently, reviving talk of a move to Barcelona but Hasselbaink showed his worth to Chelsea's owner Roman Abramovch with a worthy winner. The Blues peppered the Reading goal but an inspired display from keeper Marcus Hahnemann stopped them from running away with it in the first half. In the end, however, only Hasselbaink's 57th minute strike separated the sides.

Chelsea manager Claudio Ranieri was so impressed he said American Hahnemann was now top of his shopping list. "He did a fantastic job and I asked Roman if he wanted to buy him", said the Italian. "When we create a lot of chances like this, I am satisfied. It's OK to win just 1-0. It's a good Italian result". Ranieri made six changes from the team who beat Manchester United on Sunday to top the Premiership, with Neil Sullivan coming in to make his debut. But it was no means a weakened side, with eleven full internationals in the starting line-up including French skipper Marcel Desailly, back after two months with a back injury. Chelsea, who won the competition in 1998, played with confidence that befits the team at the top of the Premiership. They hammered Reading, but Hahnemann was masterly as he put up a one-man resistance. Chelsea's £16.8million Hernan Crespo, in particular, was frustrated by a string of outstanding saves. When the Argentinian finally beat the keeper, his luck deserted him. Crespo made space with a piece of sublime skill but his curling shot struck the post and spun all the way along the goal-line before rolling out of play. Reading emerged after the break much more like a team who have won seven of their last eleven matches since Steve Coppell took over. They were sharper, brighter, and almost took the lead when Nicky Forster's direct run and shot was parried by the Chelsea keeper. However, Chelsea scored with their seventeenth attempt of the match when Frank Lampard's sixty-yard ball picked out Crespo.

He held the ball before squaring to Hasselbaink, who found the bottom corner of the net for his ninth goal of the season. But Reading almost snatched an equaliser with ten minutes left when Kevin Watson's corner was met by Ivar Ingimarsson, England star Lampard came to the rescue by clearing off the line.

The *Sun* looked like this; IT HAS TO BE JIMMY while the *Daily Mail* headlines were that JIMMY IS TOO MUCH HASSLE FOR READING; The match report was much the same and the TV highlights showed enough to know that it could have been a cricket score and questions have to be asked about the near seventeen million pounds spent on Hernan Crespo. In an age where there are sheer quality strikers around it seems ludicrous that this amount of money seems to be wasted at this moment in time, it really is an exceptional amount of money for a player who looks like 'he could not hit a cows fanny with a bag of rice'.

Ranieri sympathised with Crespo joking, that "I told Hernan he could shoot at a goal without a goalkeeper tomorrow so he can score again". Sometimes the Tinkerman is quite amusing but for the paying customer they expect a lot more from expensive imports of unknown quality. Chelsea had now just two defeats in twenty-three matches this season and face there old enemies Leeds United on Saturday who had turned over the in-form Charlton Athletic on their trip to south London last weekend. This was a poor display for Alan Curbishley's team who had been producing some great stuff of late. I know that Alan will not be very pleased with this outcome for they would have just strengthened their grip onto the fourth place had they done what every other team has done to Leeds this season.

MENDIETTA

Chelsea, I feel, will have real tough match on their hands this coming Saturday, although having said that if players like David Batty are turning out to be your best performers you are in dire straights. In the next round of the Carling Cup,

Chelsea make their way to Villa Park to face Aston Villa, Bolton who saw off Liverpool at Anfield play hosts to Southampton who beat neighbours Portsmouth the night before. My mate Harry will not be too happy with a poor performance but without my making excuses he was really down to nearly having to pick the bus driver if one more player had gone down with any other kind of ailment. Arsenal after their 5-1 thrashing of Wolves, with some super youngsters playing, travel to West Brom, 2-0 winners over Manchester United, where it will not be half so easy.

The fourth round tie will be between Tottenham – 3-1 winners over Keegan's Manchester City – who'll host Middlesbrough who were inspired by Gaizka Mendietta, a player who never fails to impress me, the kind of player I would love on my outside when playing in the centre of midfield, he works so hard for his team and possesses great skill and composure once around the opposition's goalmouth. One of Europe's great players, he is one of great movement working tirelessly down the right hand side of the field as if making it his own. His displays for Valencia in recent seasons is half the reason I tuned into La Lira, and another player Chelsea could have purchased, for if they keep thinking that Jasper Gronkjaer is up to Premiership standard I am going straight down to see my opticians. I don't like having a go at players but if we were looking at a movie or a racehorse we would judge such an actor or horse or jockey at the highest level so this has to be done. He was abad signing and by keeping on playing him Chelsea are wasting far too many opportunities that fly high and wide behind the Matthew Harding Stand, reminiscent of Graham La Sax, another crosser of the ball, where supporters needed to keep their eye on it just in case they were brought into play. They are short of a right-sided player with such quality and seem to be stocking up with central midfield players, which we all know lopsides your team and give you no balance whatsoever. If Ferguson were to be credited for only one thing it would be that he plays with great width and in Beckham and Giggs had the perfect blend for the counter attack which left the middle open for players such as Frank Lampard – theoretically – to make runs into. Beckham was by far the more superior crosser of the ball but Giggs – when on blob – makes great ground up and takes pressure of his team once winning possession and gets forward so very quickly, however he runs at such pace at times he cannot control his cross as well as the best of the lot, David Beckham!

Back to La Liga and as always one cannot mention such a football league without the mention of the best player in the world once again, the incomparable one and only Zinidene Zidane. Bolton's winner at Liverpool was hit by another super Frenchman Youri Djorkaeff, a player who must surely be taking part in the Euro 2004 finals in Portugal. It was at White Hart Lane that summer signing Helder Postiga scored his first goal in English football against a sorry looking Manchester City. Postiga is another player I like and would like to see him more and more on the evidence of his early season form, but Spurs have been in turmoil for so long now it is understandable that players' form

seems to take a dip here and a dip there, rather like going for a dip which looks like Kevin Keegan's next move by the way he was shaking his head on the touchline. What continues to amaze me is how managers sit there shaking their heads as if the spectators brought these players to the club. Then they get the golden handshake for messing the whole thing up, can't be bad can it, Kev?
Reading 0 Chelsea 1 Jimmy Floyd: 24,107.

The front-page news of the *Sun* on Friday was that; FERGIE HEART SCARE while the back page said; CAN HE CARRY ON?

Followed by FERGIE MAY SNUB NEW DEAL AFTER HOSPITAL SHOCK.

After all the fuss over the United boss he took it in his stride and defied medics by turning up for the usual routine for the match with Aston Villa. This was a must-win match after last Sunday's loss at the Bridge and in my way of thinking they looked a hell of a bet with WilsonSports and Racing at two-to-one on to beat a very average Villa outfit and along with Tottenham at even money the double looked very good value. The big fight for the fourth spot is between Newcastle and Liverpool who were playing at an early kick-off tomorrow.

John Terry was headlines once again in the *Sun* as the headlines read FIREBALL with also IT'S TIME TO TURN SOME HEAT ON MY OLD MATE DUBES, an exclusive by Andrew Dillon: John Terry faces a reunion with football's unlikeliest guardian angel, Leeds defender Michael Duberry who hardly fits the traditional image of a Good Samaritan.

But Terry admits he will be forever in debt to Duberry for sparing him a life of hell as a youngster at Chelsea and helping perfect the skills that have made him an England star. Duberry left Stamford Bridge for Leeds in a £4.5million deal four years ago. But as Terry prepared to lead table toppers Chelsea at Elland Road today, he revealed that, "Michael has had a massive influence on my career. When I was an apprentice at Chelsea, Michael was there alongside Frank Leboeuf and Marcel Desailly. They spoke little English then, so Dubes would help me out all of the time. He taught me little things and tricks that have stood me in good stead over the years. But, most of all, I am grateful he seemed to like me. At the time, there was a little group of senior pros who could make your day hell. There was Michael, Dennis Wise, Jody Morris and Andy Myers. Every so often they would call one of the youngsters into the dressing room. You were given three minutes to make them laugh or they would dish out the punishment. Usually, it was a bit of a slap, even worse they would rub Deep Heat on your balls. It would make you red raw all day. So many times I would peer through the window and see one of the kids desperately trying to make them laugh. They would do a sexy dance, put a bin on their head or just run headfirst into a wall to try to get them to laugh and escape without punishment. Often – you'd spy through the door and see one of the YTS kids with his pants round his ankles getting the Deep Heat rubbed in. It was agony.

"Luckily, for me, Wisey and Michael seemed to like me. So they made sure I never once got called in. It was such a relief!

"I also had to clean Wisey's boots and, at Christmas, he really looked after me. Michael and him would come and give you £100, though some of the other players were not quite as generous. When the draw was made at the start of the season for whose boots you cleaned, you always hoped for Wisey or Dubes".

Yet while there are rivers of cash flowing into the Bridge from owner Roman Abramovich's pocket, Leeds have escaped administration by the skin of their teeth as they battle £80million debts. Terry added that, "That will count for nothing on the pitch. Leeds still have some real quality players, like Dubes, being ex-Chelsea, he'll have a point to prove against us. As players, you tend just to get on with it, whatever the problems of the club. But I'm sure some of the Leeds boys are worried about their families and their futures. Only recently they were chasing the Champions League and Premiership titles. It is incredible how times have changed so quickly there. Things have changed quickly at Chelsea too. We are very lucky to have Mr Abramovich, who seems very committed. On Wednesday, he flew in from Russia just to see us play at Reading in the Carling Cup. After we won, he was in the dressing room practising his English, saying 'Well done and congratulations to everyone'. His actions tell me he is not a five minute wonder".

In the corner of the paper it read that on the way to Reading Terry read about ninety-seven year old Evelyn Jackson, who was in the Manchester Royal Infirmary after a teenage thug beat her up and stole all of her savings. After reading about this in the *Sun* the Chelsea leader organised a whip-round to see that she had enough money to enjoy Christmas. Her daughter-in-law, 34, said that, "It is wonderful. I can't thank the team enough".

THE GREAT NORTH WEST

The World Cup draw was taking place this Friday evening and I was tuned in to Talk Radio to hear that we were very fortunate in being in the same group as Wales and Northern Ireland plus Poland who will always be remembered for knocking us out of the same competition some thirty years ago. That was when English football was at its lowest ebb as Bobby Moore, Geoff Hurst, Martin Peters, Bobby and Jack Charlton, George Cohen, Ray Wilson, Nobby Stiles and Roger Hunt had all passed their international sell-by date. Leaving only Alan Ball who was still in his prime and playing as well as ever. This was around the time that I joined Arsenal from Stoke City to team up with one of my favourite all-time players only to find out when I arrived there that I was bought to replace a player who had done brilliant for the Gunners, but like I was to find out he was out of favour with Terry Neil just like I was to become. To say I was 'gutted' was putting it mildly for a couple of years playing in the middle of Ball and Brady would have been something of a dream midfield. However, I was injured on my arrival and was hampered throughout my entire stay at the club, although playing in a miserable FA Cup Final against Ipswich Town, which we lost 1-0, did not make me feel that I had shown the Arsenal players and fans the real Alan Hudson, who had left his best form and his heart in Stoke-on-Trent. Although I had a nightmare – playing wise – I loved my time there, a great set of lads and the fans magnificent considering they were watching a shadow of Alan Hudson. But as Inspector Clouseau once said "I will return", which I did some five years after leaving them, between that I was falling in love with somewhere else, in the Great North West of the United States of America. I was to become the captain of the Seattle Sounders and started on a journey that I am so happy to say that I had reached the place where I was meant to be, but for another tragic ending just like the Frank Edwards experience in Stoke-on-Trent, I was to be 'done up' once again, this time not by a death as such, but in the life-form of an American who wrecked my career in the States which led to the split-up of my wife and kids. It was a typical Alan Hudson story, just as your life seems to be on the 'up' out of nowhere comes a giant obstacle, this time the giant was an ego-maniac named Bruce Anderson. And when you get an egotistical Yank you get a close relation of King Kong. I love their country and in the main their people, I really do, but as I say, when you get an ego-maniac Yank you get the whole nine yards that goes with it, meaning you cannot win, because they go on a trip where there is no destination. My career was finished right there and then and after a call to Fort Lauderdale, the only team other than the New York Cosmos and Tampa Bay Rowdies I would have left Seattle for. The call fell on deaf ears, I suppose because of the size of my contract, plus Fort Lauderdale had another Hudson as their captain, his name being Ray the player they called Rocky. He was a pretty fine player who I had played against some years ago at James' Park when he was making his mark for Newcastle United. So I pulled the plug on the North American League and headed for a return to the old first division, and oh boy, was I in for a shock. The standard had dropped like throwing an old penny down a bottomless wishing well, and my style of play seemed to be going extinct!

But it was back to Chelsea then as it is right now, and with Christmas 2004 coming up in three weeks' time it seems that this is becoming like a storybook with the loveliest of endings, but this afternoon Leeds United will, for sure, not be looking at it that way. Going to Leeds with seven straight wins without conceding a goal, is just the stuff that dreams are made of!

Maybe so, but don't be telling Sir Alex Ferguson about such things as he faces possibly the most important six months of his entire life, what with this latest heart scare, a court case with the Irish Horse Racing outfit of Manchester United shareholder John Magnier, part of the 'Coolmore Mafia' the FA and FIFA concerning the Rio Ferdinand drugs charge, not being found guilty of the charge but the failure of giving the test by deliberately missing the random test!

I say about the importance of having a very good memory, for although we know he has done some quite incredible things in his management and deserve all his wishes to be good ones. But the man upstairs in the Boardroom does not work in that particular part of our lives, he simply takes each day at a time and reminds us that you only really get out what you put in, and this is where he treads less greener pastures to the 'Coolmore Mafia' because for all what he has done in football they have done maybe that and more in racing terms. This certain 'Rock' might have been a 'gift horse' but the gift should not be abused!

But if there is one man in the world of football, here in England, that can take these people on toe to toe it is definitely Sir Alex!

RANIERI ON TRIP TO ELL

This heading was in the *Sun*, and David Kidd wrote the words: Claudio Ranieri has sworn revenge on Leeds after the defeat that cost Chelsea a title challenge last season. The Blues boss admits he is still wounded from a 2-0 loss, which ended an eleven match unbeaten run and sent Chelsea plummeting down the table. Now the Blues are top and revelling in Roman Abramovich's roubles while Leeds are bottom and £79million in debt. But Ranieri will be delighted to kick Chelsea's old foes while they are down at Elland Road tomorrow.

He said that, "I remember very well last season. We went to Leeds and lost 2-0.

"Now I have unfinished business to attend to. Every defeat is difficult to digest, but this was very hard. We did not play well and we did not recover from it, we then lost to Arsenal and we did not continue our challenge for the title". Chelsea were second going into the Leeds match on December the 28th but their trip to Yorkshire started a run of three defeats in four matches. This time the Blues go into this match with seven straight clean sheets. But reserve keeper Neil Sullivan is still hoping to dislodge Carlo Cudicini after making his debut in the 1-0 win at Reading on Wednesday.

The Scotland man says the Chelsea set-up is far more impressive than his former club Tottenham. He said that, "Being number one is what it is all about but I know it will be difficult to knock Carlo out of the team. It has been a completely new experience for me since I first arrived here. Everything here is geared up to winning the championship. There is a totally different mentality".

Chelsea's next opponents in the Champions League have been plunged into turmoil by a knife-throwing incident. Trouble erupted at Turkish club Besiktas when striker Ahmet Dursun was clattered in a training-ground tackle by Italian Ferderico Giunti.

Dursun reacted by throwing a knife used for cleaning boots at his teammate, cutting Giunti on the lip. Boss Sinan Engin said, "It was a small incident that could happen at any club".

What do I think of the Tinkerman's words?

As I have stated about certain players saying certain things before big matches, now the man who must stop them from singing the Blues is doing it himself. By saying he has some unfinished business in Yorkshire is the smartest way to get the Leeds players wound up and at this moment in time they need all the ammunition possible to start clawing their way back into the place, which is the only place to be. The Leeds players, who were there in the Champions League, will tell you that it is a totally different world. When you are fighting for your lives you become a different player, nerves jangle, confidence slips away and you wish, at times, that you never took up this crazy game.

***

GEORGE, ANT MICK AND AUGUST

Alright – Neil Diamond was right, money talks – but money is no comfort when you are getting legged over each and every Saturday afternoon. Football is there to be enjoyed, loved, passion-filled and at the final whistle a pleasure to come through ninety minutes having played to the best of your ability. That is the reason for being a professional footballer!

But down with the dregs facing the possibility of losing all you have ever wanted is unthinkable and not far around the corner once the upper echelons start tinkering with the purse strings and your manager 'loses it' your future can change in one foul swoop, it may be a pass out of place or a missed chance then everything becomes scrutinised as if a POW camp. Chelsea were so very close this summer that the Russian brought his revolution to these shores otherwise Chelsea would, and I mean would, be in a position very much the same as their foes Leeds United.

Zola would have left and others would have followed to pay the bills, instead Johnson, Mutu, Duff, Makelele, Crespo and Joe Cole cometh!

Me and my gang of uncle George, his son Anthony, Michael, and Stephen August my Eton Place clipper ,were watching the racing after Newcastle had drawn with Liverpool, sharing two goals, theirs scored by, you got it, Alan Shearer!

The half-time scores came through and Chelsea had conceded their first goal in eight matches at Leeds. The Yorkshire club led them at the interval by a superbly taken goal by an on-loan talent from Arsenal – Jermaine Pennant – a player who had caught my eye for the first time this season, through no fault of his own. In fact as a young inexperienced player like this against a team who were beginning to steamroller their way through Europe, he showed no sign of being overawed both by Chelsea's new reputation and the hard facts of them being tough to score against. He did something that many other big names and very costly players could not do over the last couple of months and that is simply score a goal against a defence that were becoming more and more 'stingy'. The ball was down on the Leeds right hand side deep into Chelsea's left-back position. Makelele had the ball but hesitated as if in two minds, and as the ball left him he overstretched and Pennant saw this is as good an opening as his teammates would give him. This started with Alan Smith hustling Joe Cole out of a header and the ball ended up with Makelele who was about to lose control, Pennant saw his opportunity, leaving the Chelsea hard man in a heap then, after jigging past Terry's sliding tackle, cut inside Billy Gallas before beating Sullivan easily at his near post. This was the young man's first goal for Leeds in thirteen outings and now hopes a move could be permanent but sometimes turning in a display like that makes it more difficult for him to move especially in the crisis the northerners are in. The talk of a Sheikh becoming their financial saviour, just like Abramovich, is still rife and if there was a performance to show the oilman that they are ready to battle this was it.

But Chelsea drew level fifty minutes later through Damien Duff, a scruffy affair that Leeds United will not be happy with, but when you are riding high you get the breaks and Chelsea will be happy to come away sharing the points which is one more than they came away with last season. Arsenal will be kicking themselves for conceding a last minute goal at Leicester, one that allowed Chelsea to stay at the top of the tree.

The headline in *Sportsmail* read that; DUFF BAILED OUT THE BLUE CHIP BRIGADE and that PAUPERS LEEDS SCARE SUPER-RICH CHELSEA AS PENNANT STRIKES GOLD.

In the *Express* was that GRAYS POINT JUST PRICELESS – High flying Chelsea stay top but steady Eddie's Leeds so close to hitting jackpot. The *Sun* was middle page spread in Supergoals claiming that LORD OF THE STINGS – Duff shows grit but Pennant injects new life into Leeds. The *Mail's* headlines looked like this: CHELSEA STARS SHOW THEY'RE STREETWISE NOW.

The Tinkerman paid tribute to Leeds after his team conceded their first goal in the Premiership for seven matches. "I'm an Italian manager and I don't like goals scored against us. But Leeds deserved it for their performance. They worked harder than it was possible to do, and Paul Robinson made some fantastic saves. It was a wonderful atmosphere, too, and I really enjoyed this game. Of course, we enjoy seeing that we are still top of the table too. But Sir Alex Ferguson is right when he says that it's not important at the moment who is top". Leeds boss Eddie Gray was in a happy mood as well, saying that, "I hope it gives us a psychological lift to come off the bottom of the table. I have belief that we can climb away from this position. The players worked so hard, and it's all about having confidence to play, especially at home. It's home form that will keep a club away from relegation. The players worked hard, and they'll have to carry on doing so." What do I think of those remarks?

Quite simply, it amazes me when coaches or managers say that their players worked hard. Working hard in any job is a necessity if you are going to get anywhere in life, but when you get between twenty-five and seventy-five thousand pounds a week to play three hours football a week and a couple of hours training each day, staying at the best hotels, eating the best food, buying the best clothes, never having a worry about a bailiff – like in our days – knocking on your door, I should bloody well think they would work their toenails to the bone, nothing less than everything you have should go into each and every match, because today not one professional footballer in the big league has any excuse for anything less. As for the Tinkerman it seems as if he is beginning a goalkeepers' society – after the Reading keeper's performance on Wednesday – or is he just saying in a roundabout way that Chelsea were so far superior that only the goalkeeper changed the course of the final result. I have news for the Tinkerman, Cudicini has saved Chelsea's bacon more times than he seems to remember, In other words that is what they are there for!

GREAT MAN MANAGEMENT

I did not watch this match but I saw some highlights the following day and although you cannot tell from just goalmouth incidents the general consensus is that a draw was a fair result. I thought before the match that Chelsea would struggle to win this match, purely because of Leeds' result the previous weekend at Charlton. Charlton are a very good side and in a great vein of form but Leeds were like the Leeds United of old, tough, resilient, competitive and everything else that goes with a good all round team performance. What strikes me as being funny is why they did not work hard for Peter Reid, maybe it is personal on some players' part, but I find that a real strange thing if players love the club who have looked after them for so long. Like you – I obviously don't know the real story – but surely players have not gone this far down the road of thinking they don't need the club because they have had all of their money and can't expect them to sweat too much whilst picking it up. I remember an incident at West Ham once whilst I was visiting Harry and watching my son Anthony train at the same time. They did not have a match on the Saturday, so a player's spokesman approached Harry and asked if they could have a long weekend because they wanted to go to the Belfry Golf Club in Birmingham, to which Harry said "of course". That was fine by my old mate for there was no match and probably a good opportunity for Aitch to catch up with his horse racing fraternity. So everyone's happy!

On the way out Harry mentioned to his secretary that the players would be having this time off but to make sure they paid for their golf, rooms and all other incidentals. That was fair play from Harry for it was in their own personal time and there was a lot of managers that would not hear of such a gesture. Harry probably had a nice weekend driving Sandra mad because there was no game or even have taken a race meeting in somewhere across Esher way. When he arrived at the training ground on the Monday he asked the young girl if the lads enjoyed their golf and she replied that when she told them about paying for it, they decided not to go!

Now here are players, some not that great by the way, who are getting an absolute fortune, are given a long weekend off and because they had to pay for a round of golf they called it off. Now if you are a manager you better watch out for your back around these kind of players for if it gets a little too much on a Saturday they might just not want to put a little extra in. Harry's strength is his man management and I am afraid if you cannot do your best for a man like this you have a massive problem. I bet at that moment Harry must have quickly thought that he should have had them all in over the weekend running for the sake of it. The reason I slipped that in is because that is what the likes of Peter Reid had to put up with at Leeds United. So let's get back to the story at hand and the Tinker and Talisman as they lead the rest into the Christmas period and next stop is that wonderful character Sam Allardyce, a man I think I know because I played with his good pal Roy Greaves in Seattle, and we were very close.

I don't like the negatives in the game today but after all the hype surrounding Arsenal and their behaviour, Ashley Cole was sent-off with a crazy two-footed tackle on Leicester City's Ben Thatcher which led to Steve Howey, the ex-Newcastle and England centre-half crying 'coward'. I don't like such tackles and agree that players that try to cripple others are unacceptable. The FA are supposed to be stamping down on such incidents but we are getting nowhere very quickly. The bans should be severe in these cases and when a player is out for a long time, after being diagnosed, the situation should be looked at and the guilty party should sit that time out also, and without pay. There is simply no excuse for over the ball tackles!

I remember some years ago watching ITV sport on a Sunday morning and saw Vinnie Jones put in a tackle that half-finished Spurs' Gary Stevens with one of the latest tackles ever seen. Sideways on while the player was on the floor, this is lunacy allowing people like Jones to get away with such a thing. He should have been in the dock and as a punishment sent to pick the Spurs player up each and every day he was in the treatment room, done his shopping for his wife and dropped him home without pay. But in the way of the world he gets a film role instead, terrific stuff!

This particular morning I was put through to presenter Mike Morris and asked him why he was not doing the decent thing and asking for a much sterner approach by the FA. As far as I was concerned, I told Mike that it was almost as if you are condoning such a violent act. Stevens played on but had lost his mobility because of this tackle, and I suppose the Wimbledon lads had a right laugh in the local that evening?

Leeds United 1 Chelsea 1 Duff: 36,305

THE REAL THING

Whilst his old team were strolling past Aston Villa, David Beckham was having the time of his life, and a week after getting through two of Madrid's toughest encounters in Spain. Firstly he was involved in the Madrid battle between Atletico and Real, which went to plan, and then helped his new club to their first win in the Nou Camp in twenty years. The headlines in the Mail were that NOW IT'S NOT JUST MADRID WHO ADORE BECKHAM. THE WHOLE OF SPAIN IS IN LOVE WITH HIM:

The entire Spanish network are now trying to jump on the David Beckham bandwagon now that the world's most famous footballer has won over everything that stood in his way. Even those who are trying to sabotage his marriage are wondering what can they do to dismantle everything that David Beckham stands for. From the moment he walked out of Old Trafford his manner has got stronger and stronger and how Sir Alex Ferguson wishes that he had him back in this frame of mind. His old boss tried constantly to get him to put his wife second and now he has left for Spain, Beckham is coping very well, although the world has turned full circle for him. He is now a megastar in China, Japan, Spain and of course he continues to dampen the spirits of those who cannot wait for him to fall from his tower way above those in the mountainside of Madrid. Beckham is becoming the James Dean of his day. There a very few stars who have had to go to Hollywood, or USA in general, to become the 'real thing'. The Beatles were the greatest pop group of their time but they did not crack it until they won over the Americans, Beckham has far exceeded anything they have ever done, and to do it alone is even more incredible. His football has improved in Spain for playing with the very best players around the globe. Zidane and Ronaldo in particular have benefited from his move there and there is still so much more to come as the Champions League finish this week until the March of next year. This will give him even more time to settle down in his fantastic new life. Where is that immature kid we saw against the Argentines some five years ago?

I am sure that Roman Abramovich will be thinking very deeply about how he can lure the new David Beckham back to his homeland. Money is no problem for both parties, for if Beckham stopped earning from this moment on, he would be more than comfortable for the rest of his life and those of his children and theirs, the only thing though is that his money-making persona is still on the rise. Will he go into films?

I think David Beckham will end up being as big as Marlon Brando if he decides to make movies. He will not even have to speak, rather like Steve McQueen who was the only one person who cut his lines to become more famous. He believed in the movement and the look, Beckham has both and he acts terrifically already and he controls himself superbly under the stress and strain of having to be 'god-like'. Most celebrities have thrown the most amazing wobbles under things far less trivial. What the media did to Beckham after that infamous sending-off was nothing short of barbaric, and how he let them into his afterlife of such an act is beyond belief!

Before we switch our minds onto Chelsea's match against Besiktas tomorrow evening, I must just let you in on a report from the Camp Nou in Barcelona. "Not even when the England captain went to the same corner where Luis Figo was attacked with a choice bit of pork last year did the Boixos Nois, Barcelona's 'crazy boys' take vengeance for his decision to join Real

Madrid instead of their team. Choosing Madrid over Barca, as Beckham did, is one thing; leaving the embodiment of Catalan pride for the team once loved by Franco and still favoured by referees, as Figo did three years ago, is quite another. So it was that the Portugal winger received the bulk of what abuse was going in a match, which was far less intimidating than Beckham might have expected. If bloodthirsty neutrals were disappointed by the lack of incident, England's captain could be well pleased with his contribution to Real's third difficult match in a week.

Having created goals against Osasuna and Atletico Madrid for Raul and Ronaldo respectively, he also had a hand in the opening goal after thirty-seven minutes. His magnificent crossfield pass fell into the stride of Zinedine Zidane, who laid the ball into the path of Roberto Santos. The Brazilian's shot then went in off Barcelona's Xavi. Beckham did not have his most influential of matches as one of two defensive midfielders but he was far from out of place in the exalted company of Real's famous five and the similarly impressive ranks of the home team. There, was, however a notable absentee from the Barcelona team. Ronaldinho was injured and so missed the chance to show that Barca, not Real, had got better value for their twenty-five million or so euros.

Sir Alex Ferguson, of course, had hoped to sign Ronaldinho for Manchester United with the proceeds from the sale of Beckham but he and United missed out at the last minute. Anyhow, Beckham could say he had quite a fantastic week of Spanish football. The statue of Christopher Columbus close to Barcelona's harbour commemorates the fact that it was here that he reported to his Spanish sponsors what he had found on his voyage of discovery.

The news from Spain is that Beckham continues to thrive in his own new world.

What do I think?

My weakness is that I am a sentimentalist semi-old fool so I love following the Beckham progress and it being so satisfactory, for here is a young man who has worked hard on his strength of being about to do what no other person can do with a dead ball. I don't mean in the street or on a beach where the joggers are all that stand between you and the sea. They go by taking absolutely no notice at all, but there were 92,524 in the Camp Nou last Saturday evening where this man has travelled to find as much as Columbus in his own world. He stands up to the task ahead and is resolute despite all of those who see him as something like a 'tart' when he has new earrings and the latest in sarongs. I am not one of those and apart from Zidane on the football field in today's climate as a player, I would possibly have gone the way of a Beckham only I would not have married, although that is a foolish thing for me to say. However, he is a class act both on and off the playing field, and that is what really matters. What will happen to him or how he will react to a marriage breakdown will be just another chapter in the life of David Beckham. I believe it is a foregone conclusion that his wife will walk out on him and if I were still a gambling man I would bet my last bottom dollar. That is just my feeling about the whole situation and don't get me wrong, I hope he remains happy in everything he does because he has put the time in to get where he has got and that is the only way he got where he has got. If that is a prediction then so is it that David Beckham will wear the blue of Chelsea before he forgets the secret of taking the perfect free kick.

Chelsea are flying high and it is quite a way from Reading to Germany where their next Champions League has been moved to because of crowd trouble at Besiktas in Turkey. Nothing changes though and the back-page headlines told the story with the *Express* saying BROLLY GOOD SHOW – RANIERI SALUTE AS CHELSEA HIT BY RAIN OF TERROR – whilst inside went – PASSING TEST OF NERVE IS NO HASSLE FOR CHELSEA – MISSILES RAIN DOWN ON RANIERI'S MEN BUT BRAVE BLUES SHOW STEEL AS BRIDGE FIRES IN HIS FIRST GOAL FOR CLUB. The *London Evening Standard* raved about the Tinkerman saying that FORGET THE TINKER TAG, RANIERI IS THE THINKER:

Blues finish on top of Champions League Group G and the *Star* newspaper comes up with TURK THAT – Jimmy guns down hate mob with inside saying that IT'S HAIL KING JIMMY Ranieri heroes defy Turkish louts to top group. The *Sun* went BROLLY BRAVE and also – Battling Blues see off hate mob with the back-page going MADNESS LAMPS FURY AT TURK MISSILE HELL:

As you can tell by such headlines, Chelsea had more than just a football match on their hands, but it is funny because in most circumstances like this if the home team are inferior the so-called supporters make the match harder for them to win. They simply fire opposition players up, especially Chelsea at the moment, who don't really need any help to stimulate them for everything at this moment is going pretty nicely for them, thank you!

They are playing with great determination and that showed in Germany at the magnificent Aufschalke Arena. It was the first meeting between English and Turkish sides since the crunch international in October and the match was given further spice by the switching of the match to Gelsenkirchen because of security reasons. This move did not amuse the Turks and their fans – many who live locally – were determined to give the Blues an atmosphere to intimidate them, but as I said it rebounded on them. Chelsea played it cool knowing only a catastrophe, like the one at Stamford Bridge against the same opponents, could stop them from progressing further and eventually win their group. One of the most significant things was Carlo Cudicini – who had a nightmare on that evening – played out his ninth match without conceding a goal, Sullivan having played in the 1-1 draw at Elland Road. Cudicini has quickly become a big favourite with the Chelsea faithful even to the extent of talking in the same breath as our Peter Bonetti. Well, he is a very good goalkeeper, but we had the very best, I have no hesitation in saying!

David Hytner of the *Express* wrote: But in a more sinister vein, there were lighters, bottles and coins aimed at the Chelsea players. Glen Johnson appeared to be struck by something and at full-time, the players were forced to leave the field under large umbrellas as yet more missiles came down. This then, was a triumph of temperament as much as talent. On the eve of the tie, Ranieri was asked by the Turkish reporters to describe the term 'to tinker' with great delight and last night he gave them a more practical demonstration. The last time he started with three at the back, his side were unhinged by Besiktas at Stamford Bridge, but he went for the same formation again, clearly believing it was the way to outmanoeuvre the Turks, who played with three narrow forwards. So it proved.

Back to me, and my assessment of this matter: Being that Chelsea were far superior without really demolishing the Turks. They did a very good job under such circumstances and showed that they can come out in front of such morons and perform without 'losing their rag' which is exactly what the opposition wanted. On the stroke of half-time the Turks got through on goal, only their second attempt all night – only to see Daniel Gabriel Pancu escape the off-side trap and with only Cudicini between him and the goal ran the ball a little wide, making it harder for himself before finally thrashing the ball skywards. A minor let-off for Chelsea because at that time the Turks needed a little help from above, but it never came before Jimmy Floyd in the 77th minute and young Wayne Bridge – on the pitch for only three minutes – combined and the young defender hit a sweet left-footer into the far corner of the net after very unselfish play by the Dutch ace, who lined up a shot for the Chelsea newcomer. So all in all it was a great night for the Tinkerman and his boys and no matter what the *Express* people say, that is what he was and still is!

In the same paper there was talk of Jermain Defoe being the next in line as the clear-out at Upton Park continues, with chairman Terry Brown putting his foot in it – rather like Sir Bobby Charlton did – at an AGM meeting – by saying that Defoe, in as many words, has nothing between his ears. There is one thing for sure, Defoe has more between his ears than Brown, that is for sure, as the irate shareholders screamed out that Brown by saying such a thing devalues the player if he is going to get rid of him. If the Tinker and Talisman have their heads screwed on they should be over to the east end of London in his limousine to bring this very talented player to a squad that needs such a player. I know it is difficult to score twenty-five goals a season when you have a system such as this, but Defoe – mark my words – would be a revelation at Stamford Bridge, making West Ham's contribution to the Premiership more than they ever knew. Chelsea already have Frank Lampard, Joe Cole and Glen Johnson from the Hammers and Defoe would make it the 'Four Tops' as they sit proudly on top of the table, thanks to a very late goal conceded by Arsenal at Leicester last weekend.

Besiktas 0 Chelsea 2 goalscorers were Jimmy Floyd and Wayne Bridge 55,350

The Group G finished like this:

		won	drawn	lost	for	against	points
Chelsea	P 6	4	1	1	9	3	13
Sparta Prague	6	2	2	2	5	5	8
Besiktas	6	2	1	3	5	7	7
Lazio	6	1	2	3	6	10	5

LAST SIXTEEN

It was all systems go as the three runaways of the Premiership won their groups to go into the hat for Friday's draw of the last sixteen of the Champions League. This is when the real stuff starts, no losing yet still be allowed to fight another day, although they are two-legged affairs.

The Spanish have four representatives, the Italian just two and with us having three, confirms that these three nations dominate European football, but who will get to a final which is being played, funnily enough, where Chelsea just came from in Germany on Wednesday evening, could that be an omen or what?

Chelsea came back home chirpy but being reminded that the Champions League was yesterday and we have a 'big match' on Saturday at home to Bolton Wanderers. Sam Allardyce has his team in good shape although they outplayed Fulham last weekend and after leading 1-0 missed several easy chances and paid the price as the Cottagers hit them twice in two minutes to secure victory and remain fourth in the table behind Manchester United. His team will be a tough nut to crack and they have big-match players who love the big stage. What 'Big Sam' has done at Bolton has been nothing short of miraculous and his team cannot ever be overlooked as an also ran, so this Saturday's match should be a cracker.

On the Saturday prior to the Champions League match Harry Harris wrote that:

RANIERI STAYS IF HE KEEPS UP WINNING WAYS

Any thoughts that a taxi driver was on permanent stand-by to whisk Sven Goran Eriksson through the London traffic to Chelsea for him to accept the Russian seat of office disappeared in a puff of exhaust smoke this week.

The cloud of carbon dioxide came from Claudio Ranieri's Ferrari of a team as he put his foot down to steer Chelsea to the top of the Premiership.

England boss Eriksson has been, and will always be, a potential candidate for Stamford Bridge, but if Ranieri carries on the same route, then the Italian will stay as boss of the Russian-bought aristocrats.

The Chelsea fans are against the arrival of Eriksson, as Ranieri has grown on them. And, I know for a fact, that Eriksson has not been formally offered the job at Chelsea, so forget any talk about agreement of terms.

Obviously, the man who counts is Roman Abramovich, and the Russian too has warmed to the Italian coach. If Ranieri succeeds, he stays, if he fails, he goes – and knows it.

In fact, Chelsea's interim chief executive Paul Smith has gone to the trouble of refuting the notion that a deal has been laid out before Eriksson by billionaire Amramovich.

Smith this week gave a ringing endorsement to the leadership skills of current boss Ranieri saying "At the moment, Claudio is focusing on the team. He doesn't bother with the rumours concerning Eriksson. I'm not aware of anything, and if it was to materialise then I would be aware of it".

When asked if the club were 100% happy with Ranieri, he replied that "Absolutely. It's clear he's been very successful so far this season. The attitude within the club is that there is complete communication to Claudio and we are very responsible to anything he requires. I've not had to give him any reassurances. His view is that his performances with the team during this season will demonstrate he is the best coach for Chelsea. He is the type of individual who will want to be judged on how he shapes the team and how successful we are". Ranieri's tinkering with the Chelsea squad has often raised eyebrows but Smith again staunchly defends the boss. "Despite having a big squad, everyone knows the players that have been introduced are world-class" he added.

"So they are going to assist in everyone achieving the right result.

"They are also an intelligent group of players, so they understand Claudio's style. Claudio sets out to win every game – the intention is to win and the confidence is there. So what he will do is select a team that adjusts to how the opposition might play".

Ranieri will carry on tinkering with this team, but Abramovich will not tinker with the coach – provided he continues to be a winner.

WE WANT ROMAN TO LEAP WITH JOY

England midfield stars Frank Lampard and Joe Cole insist they want to win the first available silverware to thank the Russian owner for his £260million investment in buying the club and funding the purchase of a host of top internationals. That chance will come in the Carling Cup Final in Cardiff on February the 29th.

As we go into the middle of December, Chelsea now have a clear head as to where they are going in the New Year and the lead up to then will be a Carling Cup quarter-final match at Aston Villa before going to neighbours Fulham at Queens Park Rangers' home ground Loftus Road. This will be a giant test for both teams with Fulham, if they can get something at Leeds this coming Saturday, will remain in fourth place and will be up to the task on a tight pitch that will suit the hosts as they put pressure on Chelsea from the word 'go'. Chelsea will not find many matches this season so intimidating, even more so than the match in Germany, for the crowd at this ground are right on top of the players which fires up both teams and their sets of fans. Fulham have been the surprise packet of the Premiership after sacking Jean

Tigana and replacing him with Welsh international Chris Coleman, a young man who has done quite brilliantly, taking to management like a duck to water. He has passed a couple of rather stern tests already this season none more so than a blinding win at Old Trafford, inflicting one of United's three Premiership defeats this season. So that will have set him up for the season telling his players that if you can win at Old Trafford you have no excuses for not doing so elsewhere. The acid test will come once they suffer two or three bad defeats in a row, something that has got to happen to teams outside of the top three. Look at Charlton, they got into that fourth spot only two matches ago and have since lost the last two rather incredibly, the first being at home to Leeds when the Yorkshire club could not win an argument, whether it was in High Court or on a high pitch. Alan Curbishley was my bet to take over from Ferguson, and that still stands even though Sir Alex is just about ready to sign a new deal, even though he has a couple of problems, one with his health and the other with the Coolmore Mafia and Sir John Magnier, their leader.

'GREAT SCOT'

Magnier and McManus now own more shares than anyone else at Old Trafford and if the court case goes their way, Ferguson will be out of his day job as well. As time goes on the pressure becomes more and more intense and even though Sir Alex is a tough nut from the back-streets of Scotland, he really has his work cut out against these powerful horse brokers who had wished they never got such an idea to offer the Manchester United manager such a fantastic deal. Ferguson is nobody's fool and he is not a good loser, which makes me think he has more up his sleeve than the two Irishman give him credit for. Maybe it might only be cufflinks but something tells me that the Scot has something on the Irish and vice-versa. Chelsea have not got that kind of trouble, for Roman Abramovich would use their money as confetti at one of their four hundred friends' weddings and not bat an eyelid. However, the writing is on the wall for all parties and the amount of money this court case will cost will make quite a dent in one's sky rocket. Bolton have no such troubles either for they are coming into the Lion's Den on Saturday knowing they have nothing at all in the world to lose and lots to gain, and Sam will be reminding them that a similar game to the second half at Fulham will not be acceptable.

I for one will be watching the game with the greatest of interest, apart from the book, I just love the underdog, especially if his team play the game properly which Sam insists upon. Another manager picking his team off the floor is that 'Great Scot' Graeme Souness, a player I mentioned earlier and goes up in my estimation the more I see and hear from him, for he manages his team the way he led his team as a player. No nonsense, get on with it style that I like, and it was on SKY at the Arsenal and Lokomotiv match he brought something so many others have not got. He is straight to the point, no big words – like Ray Wilkins and Ron Atkinson – just tells it the way he sees it.

I am delighted he has brought his team out of quite a disturbing slump for it can get to a point where the game becomes like a snowball rolling over and becoming uncontrollable when things are out of hand, but they rode the storm and the turning point for Graeme was on a televised match about three Mondays ago where they looked like running away with a match, but when at the bottom and so much at stake hung in there, in horse-racing terms 'just hung on', only this time it was a very valuable three points. As the world sleeps tonight three managers will be trying to conjure up something for the weekend and trying to make the dream come true, while many others will be having nightmares before they end in the land of nod. Saturday is no different than any other, although as I said a few pages back this race is now a three-way battle for the first time in the Premiership. Only Blackburn, under the great Kenny Dalglish with the aid of great performers that year and the brilliance of goalkeeper Tim Flowers, the most reliable of centre backs Colin Hendry – oh I am so glad I never played up front – and the man for all seasons, the incomparable Alan Shearer, who is still going so strongly, making the decision he made to retire from international football the correct one. Players know just how much their bodies can take because your body speaks for you and Shearer is a perfectionist who defies his height and weight up front with this wonderful ability to time his every move, whether it be a near post header, a far post one or purely and simply outsmarting his marker which is his real trademark. That is without his wonderful strikes with that oh so reliable right foot of his!

GREAT NEWS FOR FRANK AND RUUD

Alan Shearer is the leading goal-scorer in the all-time Premiership list and he has been a real player – in terms of what you expect out of your centre-forward – the answer being a constant flow of goals at a consistent rate, and that is what Alan Shearer gives you!

Shearer was missing from the Newcastle United line-up that was blitzed – 5-0 – at Stamford Bridge about half a dozen league matches ago, but he'll be ready for Chelsea's trip to Tyneside in the New Year and will be as hungry as ever before and would love to put a large dent in Chelsea's championship push. It is strange – or as 'Greavesie' would say – a funny old game, for had Roman Abramovich had bought Chelsea ten years earlier, the Newcastle centre-forward may never had made it to them and would be just the player in Chelsea's squad who could be the final piece in the Tinkerman's jigsaw puzzle. It is now Friday the 12th and Chelsea are hoping that tomorrow, the 13th, will hold no scares for them, but having said that Bolton will be hoping that Chelsea don't get the opportunity to run riot as they did against the Geordies.

The news from Old Trafford has been quite the same as at the Bridge for United are offering Ruud Van Nistelrooy a doubling in wages making him a £90,000 a week player whilst Chelsea have been reported to have called Frank

Lampard into the office and offered him an almost identical deal. This tells us just how these two players have played right up until Christmas but next year will be the biggest test for both players so far as the three horse race goes into a second period of the Premiership. The weather of change will be a factor, although these players do not get to play on the kind of pitches we had to play on. But slowly the freeze is appearing as the gloves come on and the deep heat vital for some of the continental players who have not played in the North East on a tornado-like wind and rain-swept skies. But as the Tinkerman insists to his players that they don't dwell on the last game and don't look past the next one. His philosophy is simple and that is the best way for players to understand and keeps all the squad on their toes for what is going to be one hell of a year for the Talisman and all that sail with him. The Champions League draw has been called out as I write this and Chelsea have drawn Stuttgart, the German outfit that Manchester United saw off on Tuesday evening at Old Trafford. This is going to be one hell of a difficult match for the Blues, and although some will say they have dodged the 'big guns' there are no water pistols left in the competition, although Arsenal – who have drawn Celta Vigo – would not have minded playing Lokomotiv again after the Russians got through because both Inter and Dynamo Kiev could not beat one another on Wednesday, a win that would have taken either one of them into the Champions League knock-out stages. Manchester United will play Porto in what will be a cracker but this will all take place in March, three months after the transfer window opens which will be interesting to see which managers out the three spends most money for the run-in of all competitions.

DRAW HOLDS LITTLE INTEREST FOR RANIERI

When Claudio Ranieri feigns lack of interest in today's draw of the Champions League second round draw, he is being true to his word. The Italian will not witness the ball-juggling, nor even follow his side's fortunes on television, for he will be doing what he does best – putting his team through their paces in training.

No sooner had his players returned to the changing rooms after Tuesday evening's 2-0 win over Besiktas, Ranieri was beginning to prepare them for tomorrow's match against Bolton.

The battle for the Premiership will occupy all his thoughts as the European Cup is placed on ice over the next ten weeks and he is not concerned who Chelsea draw in the last sixteen, having already avoided AC Milan and Real Madrid by winning their group. Ranieri said that, "I am curious to know the name, but after that I will forget. I told my players yesterday to focus on the Premiership. I'm not thinking about the draw. All the sixteen teams are very good and it's not important who we play.

"We have avoided some of the big guns but all sixteen teams are very strong. The most important thing is to be ready in February, not the name of the team".

Despite this curious ambivalence to the competition, Ranieri is insistent on one subject – Chelsea lack the experience to win the Champions League this season. His team, which he refers to as his baby, have matured remarkably quickly but he maintains they need more time. He said that, "Real Madrid and Manchester United can say they will win it, but not Chelsea. They are used to playing at that level but for us everything is new. Every match is a good step forward but we're not there yet. My baby has started to walk but not yet able to run. She is a baby girl of one-and-a-half. I hope we'll be running quickly but I don't know".

Chelsea players have adapted well to Ranieri's constantly changing tactics and the tinkering will continue. He added, "I am the Tinkerman and will never change my mind. If you prepare your team in different ways your opponents will never get to know you very well. I like to surprise the opposition but don't only look at them, I examine how my players are at each moment. I know when they are tired and what system suits them. We work hard on changing the systems and they are used to it, even during a match. I've always changed my systems as a manager and don't understand why people are so curious".

'FUNNY OLD GAME'

In the 1956/57 season when I was playing for Chelsea Youth team, the first team players rarely saw the manager in the course of a week. Let alone the Youth team.

So I was surprised to see Ted Drake show his face at the training ground one wet and windy morning. More so when I realised he was coming in my direction. I was with the rest of the Chelsea Youth team, training as usual behind one of the goals at Stamford Bridge. "I hear you scored seven goals on Saturday son", Ted said, referring to the previous weekend's game against Crystal Palace.

"Yes Mr Drake" I replied.

I was a bit surprised. I'd been with Chelsea for something like six months and this was the first time the manager had ever spoken to me. I didn't think he knew I existed.

"Do you know that I once scored seven goals in a game, son?" he asked.

"Yeah, Mr Drake, everyone knows about the seven you scored at Aston Villa" I replied.

Every young lad did. In December of 1935, Ted Drake achieved legendary status in football when he scored all seven goals in a 7-1 victory against Aston Villa at Villa Park. What's more, he also had a couple of efforts that hit the woodwork and his feat was all the more remarkable as he had played the entire match with an injury to his knee.

"Scoring seven goals in a game happens for a very, very select few" he told me "and it happens just once in a lifetime. Can you remember your goals?"

I told him I could.

"Then keep running them through your mind. Like a film" he said.

"That way when your playing days are over, you'll always have the memory of your greatest day in football to look back on".

He placed his hand on my shoulder. "Cherish the memory, son" he told me. "Cherish it forever. That day will never come again."

In our next match, against Fulham, I scored eight. After Fulham, we played West Ham and I didn't score at all.

Funny old game!

'It's a funny old game' is a phrase everyone associates with me. Like old-time comedians always had a catchphrase, that has become mine over the years. In the eighties, when I was working on a football programme for Central TV, the producer thought it a good idea if I was interviewed by my 'Spitting Image' puppet. It seemed like a bit of fun, so I went along with the idea. On the day of the recording, I found myself sitting opposite a grotesque but witty carica-ture of myself, the voice, which was provided by a young chain-smoking impressionist. Before the recording we had sat down together and devised a workable script. In the end we had about ten minutes of material, far more than the three minutes allotted for broadcast. The recording went well. I sat there answering questions from my alter ego, but when the scripted interview had run its course there was an awkward silence. The tape was still running and the director hadn't called 'Cut'. I didn't know what to say next and neither did the impressionist. The last word had been mine, so I simply waited for him to close the sketch. After a moment's silence, he turned the puppet to face the camera.

"It's a funny old game", he said.

Although that was the first time I had ever heard the phrase, and it wasn't me who actually said it, it has been associated with me ever since. It was a piece of momentary inspiration on the part of the young impressionist. Harry Enfield has a lot to answer for. But he could not have come up with a more appropriate or poignant phrase to describe football. I have been in the game as a player, commentator and columnist for some fifty years and if there is one thing I have learned it's that football is indeed a funny old game.

That was just one of many wonderful stories from the book of the great Jimmy Greaves whose number eight Chelsea shirt I had the pleasure to have worn some dozen years later, and young Frank Lampard seems to be enjoying carrying on such a privilege!

His autobiography carries so much ammunition against the defenders he used to make fools of, it almost falls out of your hands, whilst you cannot wait to get onto the next page without forgetting so many funny stories before-hand.

Back to the Blues and their first Premiership match since turning over the Russians, sorry Roman, who would have very mixed feelings I am sure, although never wanting his new Football Club to do anything else than win this match and top Group G!

Below are the statistics telling you how Chelsea faired after each of the six group matches;

Aug 13th	Champions League-Zilina-won 2-0
Aug 17th	Premiership-Liverpool-won 2-1
Aug 26th	Champions League-Zilina-won 3-0
Aug 30th	Premiership-Blackburn-drew 2-2
Sept 16th	Champions League-Sparta Prague-won 1-0
Sept 20th	Premiership-Wolves-won 5-0
Oct 1st	Champions League-Besiktas-lost 2-0
Oct 5th	Premiership-Boro-won 2-1
Oct 22nd	Champions League-Lazio-lost 2-1
Oct 25th	Premiership-Man City-won 1-0
Nov 4th	Champions League-Lazio-won 4-0
Nov 9th	Premiership-Newcastle-won 5-0
Nov 26th	Champions League-Sparta Prague-drew 0-0
Nov 30th	Premiership-Man Utd-won 1-0
Dec 9th	Champions League-Besiktas-won 2-0
Dec 13th	Premiership-Bolton ?

LAZIO, PRAGUE, BESIKTAS – NOW FOR BOLTON
Chelsea put Champions League behind them
Ranieri keeps heat on superstars

John Terry revealed last night how Claudio Ranieri's policy of bringing his Chelsea superstars down to earth could pay off with glory in May.

The outstanding win in Besiktas in the face of a disgraceful night of intimidation from the 51,000 fans in the Aufschalke Arena might have been an excuse for an orgy of triumphant backslapping. But instead Ranieri gave his players all of five minutes to enjoy the feat of winning Group G to gain a top seed berth in the 2nd round, the knock-out stages of the competition – before ordering them back onto the pitch for an intensive 30 minute training drill.

Terry said, "Straight after the game the lads were all happy at what we'd done, but the boss came in and told us that we had to forget about Besiktas. He said that Bolton were a good side and told us to start thinking about them. The boss said there was no point in going back to the Bridge after having won 2-0 and then throwing it all away by not beating Bolton.

"That sums him up. We knew we were going to go out training straight after the game.

"It was worthwhile doing it. We needed to shake it out of our legs and get it out of our system ahead of Saturday."

It summed up the renewed sense of purpose about this Chelsea side, as demonstrated by the clinical nature of their display in northern Germany. Ranieri was without Argentine duo Hernan Crespo and Juan Sebastian Veron, and opted to leave Adrian Mutu and Joe Cole on the bench, while giving Damien Duff just a fifteen-minute cameo.

That meant more than £70million worth of talent not involved. Yet with Jimmy Floyd making his first Champions League start with his debut competition goal and then setting up the second for Wayne Bridge's clincher, it was hard to tell.

Claude Makelele's magnificent tempo-setting display was the key, with Frank Lampard and Terry adding to their increasingly mature repertoire as the Blues recorded their eighth clean sheet in nine games.

Jimmy Floyd agreed that 'Tinkerman' Ranieri is setting new targets for his men all the time – and that Chelsea are living up to them. All five Premiership games after Champions League outings have been won, with Chelsea scoring fourteen goals and conceding just one. Jimmy Floyd added "The boss forgets about the game once it's over and just wants to look forward. He knew we had played well, but doesn't want us to be dreamers. Straightaway he said to think about Bolton on Saturday. The Premiership is just as important".

Maybe so, yet after crushing Lazio and superbly dousing the boiling passions of Besiktas, the European elite will be as happy to avoid Chelsea in the next round as Ranieri's players were to guarantee missing the likes of Real Madrid, Juventus and AC Milan.

UEFA's inquiry into the latest shameful episode will doubtless bottle out of imposing a proper punishment and Jimmy Floyd said that "You can't fight 50,000 people, but you can fight them with your football.

"We didn't give anything away, looked very strong and kept the ball well. In the second half we just turned them over and created a lot of chances.

"But against Lazio we played really well for ninety minutes. The best thing is we won the group and we can now grow and take confidence. Now it gets difficult but it's a great challenge."

INSPIRATION

Safely into the last sixteen, Chelsea were now six matches away from a return visit to the Aufschalke Arena for the final on the 26th of May. Ranieri will not encourage his players to dream of that yet. But with every passing game there is more chance of it becoming reality.

That was the interviews and other words from *Daily Mirror* chief Football Writer Martin Lipton, and this is mine: Although it's only a statistic, but if the figures given before this piece are correct, they have not won the six matches following a Champions League match, for after the Zilina match they came back to London and drew with Blackburn Rovers two goals each. There is absolutely no doubt in my mind about the seriousness of Chelsea's intentions this season and they are growing into serious contenders for each and every trophy left in front of them. But as Martin Lipton pointed out that there only six matches between them and a return to the German arena next May, with only Arsenal being in the exact same position and they are both my former teams who are very serious contenders. I cannot say just where my heart lies but Chelsea have not really been too good to me since leaving, whilst I can pick up the telephone anytime I wish to Ken Fryer at Arsenal and he is never any different – a complete gentleman – and that is why Arsenal have that extra class to Chelsea, but who knows what the new regime will come up with, for although there is a fantastic amount of stuff going on at the Bridge these days, barely being out of the morning papers two days in a row and the season is only really now getting into full swing!

Chelsea's ambitions are obvious and the Tinkerman has tinkered brilliantly throughout their run already but there is another fairy tale in Madrid where one David Beckham and his new pals will have a lot to say about where the Champions League trophy is going next May. If Chelsea can take hope from anything, it will be that the Tinkerman will, after watching both tapes and matches, be more than happy that Chelsea have the fire power to show up obvious frailties in the Real defensive department. Their strength, however, far outweighs their weaknesses, but having said that Chelsea are becoming a very difficult team to score against. John Terry, here I go again, has just been so impressive and he is the key to all that goes on around him at the back. Just as Bobby Moore was with the England team from 1964 through to 1972 and Tony Adams for many seasons at Arsenal. These two outstanding players were winners, and the thought of losing the upcoming match, once pulling their shirt over their heads, would never enter their mind. Remember Mexico in 1970, here I go once again repeating such a performance, when the man labelled 'god' took on the might of Brazil, and Pele, almost single-handedly. Adams also put in some quite massive performances for both club and country and, incredibly, once Arsene Wenger arrived, he became a more accomplished individual on the ball. His defensive qualities were there for all to see but at times he lacked the kind of confidence that John Terry has in the modern game. I m not saying the Terry is Franz Beckenbauer by a long chalk but he is never under pressure when the ball is there to be passed. But 'The Keizer' never had the defensive qualities of both Terry and Adams, being pulled from his midfield role by Helmet Schoen, the West German manager, because opposition players were trying to "rough him up" for the want of a better phrase. By pulling him into the back four it gave him the freedom and through his brilliant vision gave him time and space to pick the very best attacking option. I played against the great man three times, the first being in my England debut and although my club form was better than I had played since leaving the school playground, I was confident of carrying that onto the Wembley pitch against the World Champions. If you have that kind of confidence all you need to go with it is inspiration and, once setting my eyes on the German captain as both teams entered the tunnel, he became mine, and I cannot thank him enough, although he'll never know it!

The Keizer has to be the most stylish footballer I have ever seen and this night when I came out of the home dressing room and set my eyes on him entering the tunnel I was thrilled immediately as the studs rattle the tunnel flooring like people were jostling for places as the officials came through to lead the two teams out into a nightmare of a March evening, with the rain lashing down as we hit the entrance to a stadium that had not been a good one for me.

CAPTAIN OF OUR COUNTRY

Missing the 1970 FA Cup Final and then losing to Stoke City in the League Cup Final two years later. Right here and now though I knew alongside Alan Ball I had no trouble as, with his great experience in these matches, I could just go and repeat my club performances. On the previous Saturday we, Stoke City, had just smashed Manchester City 4-0 at the Victoria Ground where I scored a 'super' solo effort running through bodies before Mike Doyle tried to block my shot but I curled a right footer down low into the City net from the edge of their box. After a great debut I, without having any sleep at all, left Ballie from the Candy Box about 6am and went to my mother's prefab, via a lovely young lady I was seeing at the Val Bonne. That lunch time – Thursday – my uncle George and Tommy Mason celebrated the evening before with champagne and Guinness in the Kings Arms, the pub that Bryan Adams bought and turned it into a recording studio. It was a funny carry-on as Adams – who resided next door – complained about the noise in the early hours but it fell on deaf ears so the Canadian 'superstar' after two warnings, bought it and closed it down. That evening back in Stoke, where I lived in Barlaston, I took my father down to the Red Lion just along the way from the main Wedgwood Building. So that is how I happened to be getting ready for our game at Derby County. Then I remember going to the Station Hotel in Derby for our pre-match meal then watching all the 'hype' of an England debut that would surely have my future England career on the up and up but one more match – 5-0 against Cyprus – and I was out, with not even a nod from Don Revie. It was funny how Revie went to the desert afterwards and I am sure – as the saying goes – I would not have got a nod off of him there either?

Along the way, I was told that if I turned up for an England gathering I would become the next England captain. This was when I had booked a family holiday in Marbella because my ankle was knackered and I could no way keep on after such a long season with only the rainmaker making it possible to show my true form. The holiday was actually going away with Geoff and Judith Hurst. Geoff was in the Stoke City team at this time and I could see why he was such a great player at his peak. My form on the Saturday against Derby was extraordinary considering my preparation. I had a hand in both goals scored by the fabulous Jimmy Greenhoff one a great header followed by a Greenhoff 'Special', a typical right-footed volley, the kind that if you were showing young players how to perform such an art, this would be the perfect example. If Rio Ferdinand is guilty today of supposedly missing the drug test, if they had caught up with me on this Saturday I would have been ten out of ten on the scale they count those tornadoes or volcano eruptions like the one I remember in Seattle when Mount St Helens blew its ashes all over the state of Washington and my brand new Camaro. Good job I had the top on!

TOUGH AT THE TOP

Chelsea were ready for Bolton Wanderers, a team one should never underestimate, similar to Charlton Athletic, for they are teams who can win anywhere on any particular day. I looked through the WilsonSports and Racing fixed odds coupon and saw Chelsea as 2/7 whilst Bolton were 8/1 shots to win this very important Premiership match. Manchester United had kicked off at twelve-thirty and got their backers off to a good start – at 4/11 – by beating neighbours City by three goals to one. It was the return of Paul Scholes and he showed all of his great skills by scoring two headers, yeah, the smallest person over fifteen years of age in the stadium holding 67,000 scored with two majestic and trademark headers. That is why it is called the 'Theatre of Dreams'. I would like to have heard Kevin Keegan's post match talk to his two centre-backs!

Arsenal will be delighted with the Chelsea result as United gained post position which was a big surprise for many people, but I told the chaps in the Grosvenor Club that they should not look at this match as an 'easy ride' because Bolton can be dangerous opponents.

And as I explained earlier 'Big Sam' will not put up for another forty-five minutes like the one at Loftus Road last week against high-flying Fulham. There were plenty of headlines before this match with the *Mail* saying that RANIERI ADMITS HE'S A BOLTON WONDERER and the *Sun* heading EASY MEET with both managers face to face – not in same picture – screaming on the touchline with David Facey telling us that: Sam Allardyce says that the pressure the Tinkerman is under makes his job seem like a walk in the park. Since Roman Abramovich's Stamford Bridge takeover, Ranieri has had to live with the constant expectation that he is going to be replaced.

But Allardyce has kept Bolton – who travel to top of the table Chelsea today, in the Premiership for three seasons on a shoestring budget. And he had no doubts to who has the toughest task. The Reebok chief said that, "My job is much more difficult than his. He has the lovely feeling of being able to choose from 25 international players who play in the Champions League and the top three in the Premiership. Most Sundays, he wakes up with a smile on his face because he wins a lot more than he loses. Having said that, he has had to live with the pressure of people saying that he would not last two minutes in the job. But he has kept quiet. And whether you are dealing with someone who has no money to spend – like me – or £140milliom, like him, it is still an extremely difficult job to bring in nine or ten players. The quality of those players has shone through at the right time and, even when they have not been playing well, they are still winning matches. I think I am under a lot more pressure than he is because keeping a team in the Premiership when we are skint is much harder than trying to win it with a bottomless pit of money.

"How much has Claudio spent?

"Around £140 – £150million!

"If I couldn't win you the Premiership with that you could sack me tomorrow. But I don't think anyone is going to get the sack because Chelsea has every chance of winning the league this year."

Allardyce insists he will not give up asking for money to spend on new players until the very moment the transfer window closes on the last day January 2004.

Trotters' chairman Phil Gartside has already said that there is no money to spend but that will not stop the manager trying every trick in the book to squeeze some dosh out of the club. Allardyce went on to say that "I don't go about doing my job by taking no for an answer. I am persuasive and persistent. When you knock me down I'll keep getting up. We need the money to strengthen the side. If the money has not come by the end of the transfer window I will accept it then but not before. We need to enhance what we already have to push on and show we are an established Premiership team this year." Bolton are £38million in debt and there was even talk of the club having to sell some of their stars. But Allardyce insisted that there will be no sales – "we cannot afford to sell anybody at this moment in time, for we are light on numbers as it is. And if you want to progress, then selling a player just cannot be done".

Allardyce says his club have "next to no chance of denying Chelsea of three points today." But he said the same before his team did the 'double' over Manchester United last season. He went on to say that, "It seems to suit us when all we can do is go out there and give it a go and hope that they have an off-day. We seem to relax and play some very good football. But I'm not trying to kid anyone. I've told my lads I don't expect them to win, no-one else expects them to win – so just go out and enjoy it".

What do I think is a very good question: For someone is sure to ask about this match, their manager and his team. My recollection of the last time I played against Bolton Wanderers I have to cast my mind back to the Football League Cup on the way to Wembley with the first match being a one–all draw – I scored this late and vital goal with a strike from about 25/30 yards, something my critics say I did not do enough but there was two reasons for this, the first being I found it difficult hitting balls with my instep because of my ankle injury, and the other was that I was too busy trying to set up Peter

Osgood – mainly – and Ian Hutchinson our two main strikers. Whenever I was accused, and one particular time from Dave Sexton, as he said "why do you want to go through the middle most of the time," I replied with an answer he did not seem to like, telling him that I thought the name of the game, as I see it, still do and always will, that is get the ball to the best player who is more likely to get you a goal rather than a lesser one. So at Chelsea it was Peter Osgood, at Stoke City Jimmy Greenhoff and Arsenal Malcolm McDonald and on my England debut you could pick one from Supermac, Kevin Keegan and Mick Channon, the man who has done so fantastically well as a racehorse trainer. These were three men who played so very differently up front with Keegan being a busy little front runner who was always alert and making himself available for a through pass, having lots of pace and knowing exactly where the goal was. If Keegan had an eye for goal then Supermac had two as he admits to being 'greedy' when it came to him being in possession of the football, the two games I played in the England team – both alongside him – he scored six goals. Mike Channon was like a 'Man for all seasons' with his style of play, nothing fazing him as he was a happy-go- lucky character and I am sure it has worked around his horseboxes. The former Southampton and England striker could run like the wind with a stride that made him very deceiving, being over six feet was a part of that, and also made him very good in the air, although his main asset was his ability to stretch defenders, a defender's nightmare if you like!

Put these three together and you had a potent attack as long as they received good service. The service on the night of the West German game was to be expected from Alan Ball, Colin Bell and myself and it worked out delightfully, especially for me along with Ian Gillard and Steve Whitworth, who were making our international debuts. They both had tremendous matches against the World Champions and inside of them were Colin Todd and Dave Watson of Sunderland fame. I say that as you always envisage him on that Mayday at Wembley with his team pulling off one of the greatest shocks in FA Cup Final memory. The country was in shock when the final whistle came and Leeds United had run out of ideas and time to pull that Ian Porterfield goal back. This was possibly on par some years later when Wimbledon, incredibly, beat Liverpool with a goal from Laurie Sanchez. This was not Liverpool's day for it was the day of the first ever miss from the penalty spot by John Aldridge in such a match. I'm sorry about that John. I am a big fan!

I will put it in perspective for non-football lovers, and that this was not just an ordinary player, he was a player who had the awesome task of following the brilliant goal grabber Ian Rush, and I don't know if there was anyone around who could have filled the boots of 'Rushie' so well. He had the same eye and knack of putting the ball in the back of the net as Ian but Rush has a fright-ening turn of foot, which was his main asset alongside Kenny Dalglish. John Aldridge never looked out of place in Rush's shirt and his goal for game for ratio was something pretty fantastic, considering the task ahead of him. I can only give you one more example of that and it would be when Eric Cantona left Manchester United for movie stardom, a dream that never brought the house down as in his days at the 'Theatre of Dreams'. But Teddy Sherringham was thrown into the 'Lion's Den', funnily enough he started his career at Millwall – and took United one step further by scoring a goal in the second successful European Cup journey by beating the tremendously difficult to beat Bayern Munich.

The first one, obviously, at Wembley against Portugal's champions Benfica, when George Best scored another special, rounding the goalkeeper before sliding the ball into an empty net. I know they all have memories about 'King Eric' but I am more of a Terry Sherringham man, a player of great class and acknowledgeable football brain. He has graced Old Trafford, White Hart Lane and the City Ground – under the great Brian Clough – and who is now under the terrific management of my great friend Harry Redknapp at Portsmouth. If I had one last wish in a football shirt it would be that I would like to play in the greatest side wearing an England Shirt managed by Tony Waddington: The goal would be kept by Gordon Banks, although I am very tempted with my old mate Peter Fox, the back four would be David Nish, Colin Todd, Bobby Moore and Kevin Beattie, whilst in midfield along with yours truly would be Alan Ball and Tony Currie and up front Peter Osgood, Jimmy Greenhoff and Frank Worthington. I can only apologise to the great Stan Bowles but if I had chosen Stan we would have needed three balls with him and Frank up front. But Stanley knows he would always be in my team, but not with Frank. We all have a dream left unfinished!

RANIERI CHARM HAS WORKED A MIRACLE
It has stopped us all hating Chelsea

Until recently Chelsea were probably the second most-hated team in the land.

Whenever Ken Bates opened his megamouth it was to usually to air an offensive or moronic view (ask Matthew Harding's widow). In Frank Leboeuf they had the game's most arrogant foreigner, with Dennis Wise and Graham Le Saux competing for the most slappable Englishman.

In celebrity fans David Mellor and David Badiel they had two of the worst examples of rich kids hijacking the game for street cred, and five minutes spent with their away supporters showed they attracted more racist muppets than Burnley Council.

Not even the beauty of Gianfranc Zola could rescue the damage that lot did to Chelsea's late sixties reputation as the game's most magnificent mavericks. Especially when Ayatollah Bates banned the likes of Ron Harris and Peter Osgood from what was once Stamford Bridge but now is an elitist hotel complex called Chelsea Village.

And when Roman Abramovich decided he was about to buy everyone's best players to land the Premiership, they seemed odds-on to not only become more despised than Manchester United, but two of that city's most favourite – Myra Hindley and Harold Shipman.

So why has Chelsea's approval rating soared?

How come most neutrals want them to put Arsenal's and United's noses out of joint by winning the Premiership and the Champions League?

This wasn't the script.

By now we were either supposed to be burning effigies of the mercenaries who make up the Fulham Road Globetrotters or revelling in the anarchy created by trying to force twenty-two egos into eleven shirts. So what's gone wrong?

Two words. Claudio Ranieri.

The tastiest advert for Italian culture outside of Dolmio sauce has pulled off the impossible. He's made Chelsea loveable again at a time they should have been completely unbearable. We always liked his politeness, dignity, humour and passion for English football. We loved how he how he rose above the petty politicking endemic in modern management and the sneers from bozos less articulate than a lorry load as he struggled to master our language.

TACTICS

But we never realised what a great coach he was until now. Money may be able to buy success, but having a team of internationals costing £110million welded onto a team already packed with them, are ordered to win silverware, seemed mission impossible. Chaos and tears looked inevitable.

Initially he was labelled The Tinkerman for needlessly changing players and tactics, but time and again he has proved doubters wrong.

Nowhere more than against Besiktas this week when he played and won with the same formation he was hammered for after the Turks beat them 2-0 at the Bridge.

Ranieri has mastered the most elusive of tricks. Keeping multi-millionaires happy when you leave them on the bench, motivating them when they are down, and convincing them to put the team before their own vanity. Ask his predecessors Gianluca Vialli and Ruud Gullit how hard that is!

Chelsea have won nineteen of this season's twenty-five matches, are top of the league.

Winners of their Champions League group and are in the last eight of the Carling Cup. But it has been the manner Ranieri has succeeded in – gutsy one goal wins at tricky destinations – which suggests he is building on champions, not show-boaters.

Look at his attitude on Tuesday night. Fifteen minutes after one of the biggest wins in the club's history he had the players back on the pitch training and focusing on today's match with Bolton.

Rather than alienating his superstars, they applauded this action, with Jimmy Floyd Hasselbaink registering his glee at a training session that went on past midnight. They may have millions in the bank but it's medals they truly covet. That is why you haven't heard a peep of dissent from this squad. They trust their boss implicitly, even when he casts them aside. Because they know he will bring them glory.

There is of course a bigger reason why they, and we, want Ranieri to succeed – to destroy the assumption that he is merely keeping the throne warm for Sven Goran Eriksson's coronation next summer.

It emerged again twenty-four hours after the Besiktas victory. Paven Nedved's agent claimed his client was on his way to the Bridge at Sven's request!

Here the nation is united behind the Italian. Not out of a desire to keep Eriksson as the national coach, but out of the respect for the grit and Professionalism Ranieri is showing in the face of such critical pressure.

We want the Roman David to slay the Russian Goliath, and prove there are a couple of things left in our game that speak louder than money.

Talent, dignity and loyalty.

But, if Eriksson does get his job, all is not lost for the neutral. We could all start hating Chelsea again. And in Ranieri England would have a successor as tailormade as one of his suits.

I enjoyed that piece by Brian Reade: although he seems a bluenose, which is not a problem, but between the lines there is blue blood rushing through, if he were the son of the Tinkerman it would still be pretty spot on. About the two most hated teams he must have not been born when Leeds United were at the height of fear, and Elland Road a fortress, not a very nice place to go and play. Bolton are capable of pulling off a shock at 8/1 with WILSONS whilst there is no reason to look at Chelsea as they are long odds on. Maybe correct score as they have not been scored against at the Bridge in the Premiership in four matches, and Cudicini has gone nine matches without conceding. All the questions the day before had me thinking that Chelsea had got away with quite a few things at the Bridge so far this season and it might be a 'law of averages' or merely the time to 'run out of luck'. But if they were going to be real strong contenders this season they have to tear teams apart once getting in front in home matches. They failed to do so once again and all the opposition needs is to smell half a chance of edginess in the home team and they would throw caution to the wind, and Bolton have one or two players who can turn such a match. I felt confident that Bolton would take something back up north with them, and it wasn't a 'good hiding'.

SENTINEL

This was my column on the eve of the Bolton match at Stamford Bridge:

What I would give to don the tracksuit, take a couple of coaching sessions and put several of my theories into practice.

This week's Champions League ties left me screaming at the TV screen as a couple of old chestnuts reared their ugly heads yet again.

How often have we seen great free-kick specialists like David Beckham – and Junhino against Celtic the other night – take advantage of the defensive wall?

That's why I have long advocated scrapping the human wall, placing a defender on each post and the keeper on the six yard box. I guarantee it would cut down the number of goals scored direct from free-kicks – and I also guarantee I would prove my point after just one training session.

My other bugbear reared its ugly head when Arsenal were faced with Lokomotiv's ten men following a dismissal in their tie at Highbury on Wednesday evening.

Arsenal were left with the dilemma of sitting on their two goal lead, or to push forward to exploit the one-man advantage to kill off the Russians once and for all.

I can assure you that a team with an extra player can become their own worst enemy if they are not positive and use that extra player to good effect.

If you took a training session with two defenders versus two attackers, or three versus three, the defenders would always come out on top. But if you played two strikers against three defenders the attackers would get more joy.

He's nuts, I hear you say?

Perhaps, but think about it. If the defenders have the extra man they almost inevitably get confused about who is picking who up, granting their opponents that extra split second advantage in mind and body.

And nine times out of ten the extra player would also think the game was easy, as he stood spare, losing a bit of edge and concentration in the process.

With this in mind I remember Dave Sexton bringing in the system of 'zone' marking, meaning does a defender follow an attacker across the line of defence or does he stay in his 'zone' which is mainly called 'Marking space', which our defenders did not like when it was introduced to our team. Basically defenders prefer to be instructed to 'man-mark' and play one on one with their offensive duties. Centre halves do not like being dragged out of the middle of the team for several reasons, the main one being dragged out to the touchline, which was quite a daunting task. Big defenders like to have people around them and being one on one on the touchline they are far more likely to be exposed. The one great example of this was when Chelsea played Leeds United in that 1970 FA Cup Final.

MY MATE GEORDIE

The first match, obviously, being played at Wembley, saw a one to one duel between right-back – on this day – David Webb facing Eddie Gray the 'wizard of the dribble' and now in charge at the club. Gray had time, space to rip Webby to shreds and it was plain to see that Wembley can be a dream but for our full-back it was a total nightmare. David was a player of great tenacity and one who flies into tackles, but in the middle of the back four that is not so bad because there should be someone there to pick up the pieces if things go wrong, plus cover. This happened more than once during that season and I think it was my good mate at Highbury, Geordie Armstrong, Arsenal's long distance runner who tormented David one evening not long before the Final.

The match was drawn 2-2 and Gray was voted 'Man of the Match' afterwards. The replay was at Old Trafford and Sexton changed the back four by putting Ron Harris out on the right and had no need to tell him why he was making this change!

As if Ronnie needed telling!

Gray was hit as close to the first whistle as humanly possible, and was not seen again. David turned his nightmare into a dream as he strode forward and into the melee straight ahead. Ian Hutchinson threw a 'special' into the heart of the Leeds defence and as several bodies fought to either get it away or get it in back of the net, there was Webby higher than everyone else and the rest is history. A year later we won the European Cup Winners Cup and it was our other centre-half – John Dempsey – who hit a goal, this time though, it was a rather spectacular volley by our unsung hero.

LIGHTNING STRIKES AGAIN

What I found odd, though much later, was that we went back to Wembley, a year after for The Football League Cup Final to face – my next club – Stoke City and Dave Sexton selected to play Webby right full-back again only this time it was Terry Conroy who had the job to get the ball at him and it was that move that paid off for the Potters.

TC – as known by all of his friends, of which I am one – picked up the ball and legged it straight at our right-back and as he took it close to him the inevitable happened. David threw himself two-footed at the Stoke City outside-left and was left on the seat of his navy blue shorts as TC hit a deep cross to the far post for John Ritchie which was enough for him to cushion a header into the path of the lethal Jimmy Greenhoff. Although Jimmy struck his volley well – Peter Bonetti would have saved it ninety-nine times out of a hundred – and as he parried it there was the oldest man in the football league to simply prod the ball past Peter for what turned out to be the winner. But why on god's earth did Dave Sexton not stick to Ron Harris filling the right-back position that day?

That evening we had a post match party in a West End Hotel and the cabaret was a chap called Lou Christie whose record had been number one for quite a while. The name of it was 'Lightning Strikes Again' which was very appropriate, for we had just been knocked out of the European Cup Winners Cup and the FA Cup by Leyton Orient. Lou Christie was the last person we needed on such a dismal evening such as this, one that finished our week off like it was the longest nightmare one could have, only this was without using any sleeping tablets or in my case being hit by a speeding car!

Chelsea 1 Peter Osgood Stoke City 2 Conroy and Eastham Wembley 100,000

JUNINHO

At Highbury the other night we saw the ten men Russians cause a few problems on the rare occasions they got out of their half, and they got some joy by confusing the Gunners' rearguard. Arsenal did brilliantly to recover from a dreadful start to qualify alongside Chelsea and Manchester United for the knockout stages. Spain and Italy are well represented – surprise surprise – but it remains a competition up for grabs. That is unless Real Madrid really did land van Nistelrooy from United!

Then we might as well start engraving the trophy with their name right now.

The heavyweight contenders like Real Madrid are bound to strengthen during January's transfer window and so we may see teams looking a lot different when they return for the knock-out stages after the winter break sale. And the Spaniards would love van Nistelrooy, not that I can imagine Fergie letting him go, especially not to them for any amount of money. They have already taken one of Manchester's prized possessions and if the Dutch ace was to go there it would be a little sickening seeing both Beckham and 'Van The Man' walking out for the final in Aufschalke Arena next May.

My player of the week just gone is Juninho – namesake of the one we know so well – and it would have been a travesty if he'd finished up on the losing side in Lyons clash with Celtic. His ability to strike balls from all angles is comparable to David Beckham or 'Golden Balls', the name he has inherited from his wife and her English public.

He stuck the woodwork from a free kick, where the full back would have been standing if I had my way – then he hit the net with a long range cracker that dipped a little and also could have got a slight deflection.

But Celtic would still have claimed the draw they needed to qualify if only Bobo Balde hadn't handled so foolishly inside his own box as he was late to challenge legally. Yeah, you read it; Juninho finished the tie off with a beautifully struck penalty.

Back home, meanwhile, I'm keeping a close eye on Kevin Keegan just in case United rip his City team apart and he throws all his toys out of his pram outside of Old Trafford. Chelsea will be looking for a slip up. Although the Tinkerman says that he is uninterested in what is going on anywhere else he must know that the Premiership cannot be won without a few hiccups along the way. Ranieri and Wenger would be delighted and enjoy the days leading up to their Carling quarter-final matches in midweek, if City could upset United once again. But it was Bolton who the Tinkerman said that had his 100% concentration and he hopes his players have focused on this match the way he told them to just five minutes after the final whistle in Germany. My uncle George, cousin Anthony and I had our seats ready in the Grosvenor Club for the first match at Highbury where Arsenal hosted Blackburn. Blackburn have turned the corner after having a spell that saw them rock bottom and Souness knew the kind of match his team would be facing after the Gunners successfully overcame the last hurdle in the Champions League in midweek. After the Arsenal match, the headlines were like this: GUNNERS DIG IN TO DENY

ROVERS and SOUNESS FOOT SOLDIERS SHARE SAME FATE AS RUSSIANS – was in the *Mail*. WHAT A GRIND in the *Star*, as Supergoals in the *Sun* reported that Dennis Bergkamp shouted that Thierry Henry is the BEST IN A HUNDRED YEARS – Bergy hails king Henry – all over the back page whilst on the inside it said that IT'S STROP SUEY as Rovers chief hits out at Pires as Gunners hang on. The match at Old Trafford was all about the brilliant return of Paul Scholes as he popped up twice in the middle of two-foot centre backs to bury two headers in David Seaman's net.

Whilst Roman Abramovich is the key to the Premiership with a bankroll just sitting earning interest and biggest interest is the concern of Chelsea all of a sudden putting in a flat performance after all the rage after a win over Bekitas. It was a different story for Bolton though as the *Express* reported that BIG SAM FACING PAY CUT, By Mike Carey. Sam Allardyce could be asked to take a pay cut if football's cash crisis continues. The Bolton boss is halfway through his ten-year contract, which has transformed Wanderers' fortunes. He has won promotion to the Premiership and kept them in the top flight. But Chairman Phil Garside insists he will ask Allardyce to reduce his wages if Bolton continues losing money.

I say that: Nothing changes does it, there are the rich and the poor, and poor old Sam Allardyce looks a pay-cut straight in the eye, although I cannot see a whole lot of truth in such a headline. The big man has done an incredible job and by beating the Tinkerman proved that there is time and space for the underdog in the Premiership as four days after screaming from the rooftops after a very good performance in Germany also-rans Bolton Wanderers really did come to town and give it a go. There was no sign of Christmas cheer at the Bridge and they have a massive match next weekend against west London neighbours Fulham.

Chelsea had been knocked down to third place following Arsenal's victory against Blackburn. The *Mail* said that CHELSEA DEPOSED Misery for Roman as blunder by Terry gives shock win to Bolton: The *Sun*'s headlines read SKILL OR BE KILLED Ranieri needs a hit-man: The *Star* headlines read like this WE SHOT OUR BOLT Chelsea shocker as Ranieri admits he may have too many stars. The *Sunday Express* said that Chelsea BLUE IT with – Terry own-goal sinks Chelsea.

The inside page of the same paper said that Bolton's 'Carpenter' turns architect as his skill designs the late downfall of toppers Chelsea TERRYS OWN GOAL HORROR.

Chelsea 1 Crespo Bolton 2: 40,000

Roman's in need of a £50million fix.

That headline sparked by Thierry Henry's great honour of being runner-up in the 'World Footballer of the Year' to French team mate Zinidene Zidane with his Real Madrid teammate in third spot, the Brazilian superstar Ronaldo. Plus there was a little propaganda going on in Spain as both Ronaldo and Beckham were quoted as saying that they would both be delighted if Henry could cross the channel and wear probably the most famous colours in the history of the game. Henry is playing brilliantly at this moment in time and has made it crystal clear that he wants to play out his football as long as his mentor Arsene Wenger is the manager at Highbury. Loyalty is a rare asset these days and I applaud the Frenchman for such a thing in times where the dollar speaks louder than the motion of our game.

Chelsea's performance is best left alone and I can only think that is the way they would want it!

I started my writing this book by saying if Chelsea were going to be a 'force' and compete with United and Arsenal at the head of affairs they must make Stamford Bridge the football ground that the opposition hate coming to, a 'fortress' if you like!

This is something that will have the Tinkerman thinking more seriously about the way his team performed rather than the result they got. This was just not good enough and if the Tinkerman is to remain with that name he'd better start doing the business right now while the fire is hot and the flames high. First thing he must do is stop his team telling the nation just what they are going to do and get on and do it!

CHAMPIONS LEAGUE DRAW

Chelsea have drawn Stuttgart in the first stage of knock-out football of the Champions League, a team who beat Manchester United in Germany but were not the same team who played at Old Trafford on the same night as Chelsea were overcoming Besiktas in Germany. Stuttgart will be a tough nut to crack over two legs as all German sides tend to be very resilient in away matches and don't give much away at home. Chelsea, and Tinkerman in general, will be looking at the Germans when the time comes closer to the dates of the 24th and 25th of February for the first-leg.

Manchester United have drawn Porto and Arsenal Celta Vigo in what should all be great matches now that the group stages are no more. Real Madrid drew Bayern Munich, the team they beat in their only ever Champions League Final some four years ago. But all three English teams can now concentrate on the Premiership as Christmas approaches and a hell of a lot of points to play for.

Stamford Bridge was not the only place where managers, their team and fans had a real bad day – against all the odds – for whilst Chelsea were getting licked by Bolton, Liverpool were making a hash of trying to beat Southampton and in fact got off lightly being beaten by the odd goal of three at Anfield. The writing was on the wall for Keegan at Old Trafford but he was badly let down by three of his biggest signings, Nicholas Anelka, Steve McManaman and 'buddy' Robbie Fowler, who were not performing and made life so much easier for the champions elect in a match that they never made look like a Manchester derby. There was not enough fire, urgency and the one thing that makes a football match a great one, passion!

I was delighted with the start at Fratton Park as Portsmouth took the lead in a quarter of an hour – against Everton – through on loan Roberts, but ending up losing a match that will be very important between these two sides bound to get involved in the relegation melee come April and May. The heading in the *Sun* will be a big worry for both David Moyes and Sven Goran Eriksson – BAD ROON RISING – Wayne's lucky to escape with a yellow card said Moyes – but still insists that he is calming down. Newcastle found some kind of good form beating Spurs 4-0, with, you got it – Shearer netting another pair keeping him top of the Premiership goal getters' list. How Chelsea could do with a striker like Alan Shearer, a player of such tremendous consistency when it comes to finishing off moves, something Chelsea are very short of at this moment in time. Leeds United had another very good day under Eddie Gray as they beat inform Fulham who still keep their fourth place as they go into the battle with Chelsea next Saturday. That one should be a real cracker!

Over the east side of London Jermain Defoe was pulling his West Ham teammates out of the mire after going two goals behind to Sunderland at Upton Park. The tiny striker had just come back from a five match suspension and his team really missed him over that period where they have had a nightmare. This will make three top managers sit up, especially Chelsea and Arsenal who are finding goals hard to come by recently and the transfer window will see just where this pocket sized goal-machine will be scoring his goals in the New Year.

Tuesday's papers were sparse with their football news, one choosing Sam Allardyce for a two page exclusive joking about his petty run-in with Arsene Wenger over a match played last season where the Arsenal manager chose to pick that performance, the one that stopped the Gunners in their tracks and knocked them out of their stride. Allardyce however simply says is it a coincidence that Arsenal have the worst disciplinary record in the Premiership and yet calls his Bolton team physical. This leads up to Arsenal heading up the M1 and M6 for the weekend fixture.

The only mention in the *Daily Mail* about Chelsea is that along with Arsenal and Manchester United, they'll have to slug it out as to who will buy Jermain Defoe in January, and it is quite obvious that if Chelsea want this player Chelsea will have him, it is as simple as that. In the *Express* there is a story about Hernan Crespo promising Chelsea fans that he will get better saying that "It has not been easy to settle, there is the problem of the language which I have to overcome and I have also a little injury – and don't forget I have been back to Argentina twice already for internationals. All those things have not helped. I am now back for a long time and believe I can settle down more in the team and also living in England. The way the side is playing has helped me, and also the team spirit. There are many changes going on both professionally and personally and things are slowly gelling. It will take time to understand my colleagues. At the moment I am reasonably pleased with my form and my goal-scoring but I know they can improve. I have always felt that I can score goals. Even last season when I missed three months of the season I still became Inter's highest ever scorer in a Champions League season. I want to bring them to this team. How successful Chelsea will become will be decided by everyone being together – it is a squad game. If we stay calm then anything is possible. I say that we can make history and I want to be a part of that".

PRICELESS!
(HOW MUCH IS THAT IN ROUBLES)

On a long haul flight, a man takes a shine to a nun in the next seat, and as the plane comes into land he makes his move saying "sleep with me" he tells her, "and I will give you a fiver".

"Don't be ridiculous" she replies, "I am married to Christ".

"Alright, what would you say to a million?"

"How dare you," snaps the nun. "Do you think I am some kind of whore"?

"Not at all, but what would you say if I promise you that I will give my billions to eradicate poverty throughout the developing world?"

"Untold lives would be saved, now you couldn't honestly say no to that, could you?"

The nun thinks for a while, and reluctantly decides that it would be her clear Christian duty to lie back and think of Rome.

"OK, we have agreed in principle" says the man smugly. "Now let us talk about the price".

It is a very old joke, and even older truth that everyone has their price. So when Arsenal vice-chairman David Dein insists that Thierry Henry is not for sale at any price, Roman must lick his lips at the prospect of stuffing that proud claim down the Dein's throat.

Clearly Henry's price is far above the £40million/fifty million Chelsea offered last week, and a small wonder. As Dennis Bergkamp points out, in the last century there have been few in Henry's league, and – as global football's top coaches ought to have decided yesterday – he is clearly the best in the world.

Without him, Arsenal would be a fine, cultured domestic force with hopes of making the Champions League last eight. With him they have a real prospect of winning it. His ungodly ability to control a football at extreme pace is unparalleled, and as Inter Milan will confirm no defence on earth can handle him on top form. Naturally uniqueness makes him very hard to value. But Thatcherite values control modern football, and in the unchecked free market any commodity's true worth is what someone is prepared to pay.

To Roman Amramovich, sitting on cash reserves of billions, the difference between £50million and a £100million, is meaningless. To Arsenal, on the other hand it is everything. Coffers at the Bank of England long ago dwindled to nothing and the trouble financing behind a move to the larger stadium is paralysing their transfer ambitions. Already their squad is shallower than their two title rivals, and without cashing in on their major asset there is no clear prospect of this changing. The danger of Henry's departure causing a domino effect that will drive away Patrick Vieira, Robert Pires and possibly Arsene Wenger is obvious.

Then again, the terror of Henry rupturing cruciate ligaments and becoming worthless will grow if and when the Chelsea bid edges towards the £100million mark.

Judging by his waspish remarks at Sunday's Sports Personality Awards about Chelsea having two or three teams, the player has no desire to make a move across London.

But it isn't up to him. Thierry Henry is simply a commodity to be bought and sold and the cold realities of football financing place his future in the hands of the person with the deepest pockets.

Whether Roman Abramovich chooses to smash the world record to smithereens to get his man, we must wait and see.

But since there can be no argument about the principle here, it should be fun watching the Russian haggle over the price.

That was a nice piece well-written by Matthew Norman of the *Mirror* and I am sure that all that was said is bang on the button. The most incredible thing in the game – and not only now – is how people put a price on the head of such a player – and will there ever be some normality come back into the life of our game? When I lived in Seattle I would watch the big named basketball, baseball and USA football players and hearing of such a wage structure never believing this would catch us up but that is television for you and now if you are not involved with your promotional and marketing packaging you get left behind.

THE GREAT GREAVES AGAIN

I remember when Jimmy Greaves came back from Milan and went to Tottenham Hotspurs, their manager the great Bill Nicholson would not be the first man who paid six figures for a player and so Milan agreed a price of £99,999. That was when money was money and principles were principles. But this episode has only come about because of Roman Abramovich for – and let's not forget – Ken Bates and all the others who were going to become left out in the rain once the Administrators had come in, are now smoking the biggest and finest rolled cigars. Funny how some people have all the bloody luck, no matter how it comes their way, they take it as if they deserve it, and that is what gets my goat. It is strange as well; because the time had come where everybody were saying this would come to an end and against all of that this happens. I feel the same way now as that first day of the telephone call from SKY about the proceedings that were going on inside the doors of Chelsea Village but I fear for the Blues because they have too many insiders telling the rest of the country just what they intend to do!

You will have learned by now that talk is cheap and in a game where people don't really have a week in the life of a modern day footballer, they don't want to hear about what you are and not going to do to so and so on Saturday afternoon, and unlike a professional gambler you don't get any more points for when you get it right. This would be something I would address to the players if I were the Tinkerman and tell his little tinkers they will be left with an egg on the cheeks if things don't turn out the way they promised those fans once beating Manchester United and went top. So is it that I am so shrewd after that match to say keep it in the dressing room because they have now gone and leapfrogged over you and those papers you shouted in are not even good enough for fish and chips anymore, get my drift!

The biggest worry for the Tinkerman would be that goals have dried up and a couple of players, if I am not fooled, don't particularly look as comfortable on the ball as they do when talking to the media. Sam Allardyce had it right on Saturday and told his players they were on a hiding so go out and give it their all and enjoy the experience.

They certainly did do that, indeed, and I don't think that it was because of playing a smaller club, which is always a copout for a football supporter – not just Chelsea – but almost anywhere you go a fan says "we just can't score goals", well, van Nistelrooy and Alan Shearer don't seem to have that problem. Do you think it is just your team that can't score goals and if you don't know by now that they are not good enough then I pity the rest of your time watching football here on earth.

Chelsea have just lost their very first league game at Stamford Bridge under Roman and after Fulham at the weekend they host Harry Redknapp's Portsmouth in a match I will be attending with my two sons. There never is an easy match in the league nowadays only if you get three in front, but don't tell that to a West Ham supporter after that seven-goal thriller with West Brom earlier in the year and some time later there was a repeat of that at White Hart Lane, but more of that later!

We are a couple of matches away from Christmas and I cannot wait for the new year to begin with the added spice of David Beckham who, through going to Real Madrid, has lifted their profile up even further and SKY showing more and more Real Madrid matches is just fine by me, with Zidane, Ronaldo, Figo, Carlos Alberto, Raul and of course the young man who has won the entire of Spain over and he feels he is playing his best football ever. There is no doubt in my mind that Real got the better of the deal by signing the England captain and the acid test is when the knock-out stages of the Champions League comes around again. How many times does Beckham have to prove he is a great asset to everyone, but he will do once again as he continues to lead his country out onto the playing field and that is all to come after what looks like being the most sensational football season since my being born in Chelsea some fifty-two years ago and that is all down to Roman Abramovich, who is still silent over the future of the Tinkerman, but I feel once Peter Kenyon takes his seat and Ken Bates is slowly moved aside the fireworks will really begin, just you wait and see!

'WHITE HOT LANE' "AND THE BEST CHELSEA PERFORMANCE I HAVE EVER SEEN"

said ex-Chelsea and Spurs Terry Venables, March 1972

It is Tuesday the 16th of December, six years and one day since my automobile accident in the Mile End Road and last night as I sat there watching TV, looking up it hit me, as it was the exact time they were wheeling me into the Resuscitation Room, 9.15am. That is just another year gone for me as I work out day by day and do my best to write as much as I can for I am hoping my other book SPECTACULAR will have been in the shops by the time I finish writing this one for all of you bluenoses and any other football lover who is interested about this ongoing series of accounts that keep the ex-Fleet Street writers in their element. Roman Abramovich's arrival at Stamford Bridge and the day he 'slices' Bates and slides him under the door will have been the most sensational of happenings since Bates himself bought the club for a pound note, something he always boasted. Well, under the circumstances that Chelsea were going to face – administration in the next twenty-four to thirty-six hours – makes this story 'midget' Bates and his crusade to upset as many people in the area as humanly possible. He succeeded!

Tonight Arsenal won through to the Carling Cup semi-finals by beating West Brom at the Hawthorns by two goals to nil and Bolton got past Southampton in the other semi with Chelsea playing Villa tomorrow at Villa Park and Spurs taking on Middlesbrough at White Hart Lane. I still see the match at Spurs after we had won the first leg 3-2 at the Bridge and travelled over to north London for the second most pulsating affair you'll ever have in a cup-tie. I find it so strange that nowadays certain clubs take this as a Mickey Mouse competition, for me no cup-ties are from Disney, but I am a knockout competition lover. This particular evening our Chelsea team gave a huge performance in the kind of atmosphere that was simply electric, and I can still feel the sparks flying now and the memory as great as any of our 'big' match successes in any competition at any time whilst I was first at the club. By that I mean the chips were down after a memorable first leg tie at the Bridge where we let them off the hook by failing to turn our total domination into goals. The match at White Hart Lane was such a magnificent performance that even Terry Venables told me the following day that it was the best Chelsea performance he had ever seen – quite something coming from El Tel. With the scores level on the night at 1-1 – after Chris Garland smashed a blinder past Pat Jennings after picking a ball up on our right side, he then cut inside of Cyril Knowles to fire a stunning left footer past the great Northern Ireland – who was one of the top five goalkeepers in World football – number one, shot stopper – and then with the minutes ticking away I gave away a penalty when a Martin Chivers throw-in bounced awkwardly in the White 'Hot' Lane mud and skimmed through to me and as I chested the ball and volleyed it away, it seemed the entire of north London screamed 'handball'. The referee had no hesitation and pointed to the spot despite all our players trying to get him around the neck to strangle him. The sight of Ron 'Chopper' Harris making for the 'Mug in the Middle' was quite awesome. I was dumbstruck as Martin Peters 'coolly' put them in front on the night but level on aggregate at four goals apiece. But we picked ourselves up and went back on the attack in a match that was – as I said – electrifying, and when these two teams play each other there is no love lost on the playing field and all of the terraces surround-ing it. We attacked them and put their goal under siege with a vengeance when suddenly we won a free-kick on the left wing – about a yard from the corner spot – kicking away from the players' tunnel and I flew over to pick the ball up and waited for the heavy artillery coming slowly up field entering the box like the magnificent seven, only there were just four of our boys. It was reminiscent to the scene at Old Trafford on that wonderful night of FA Cup football with Leeds. The big four of Dempsey, Webb, Osgood and Garland were just fighting for space as I placed the ball down and hit it right footed about four feet and dropping quickly to the surface I thought on a pitch such as this it was the right ball in, a ball which only needed the slightest of touches to wrongfoot my good pal Pat Jennings. With all the jostling between what seemed like the entire crowd coming onto the pitch and most of them trying to get the ball into 'Big Pat's' net. Our Blue Boys from the Shed were worth a goal on nights such as this and like at Anfield where they said many times in the last minute that the 'Kop' seemed to suck the ball into their opponent's goal. It was one of those situations when, whenever the home side won the toss, they chose to kick away from the Kop for the first forty-five minutes and kick into the Kop until they scored which was sometimes ten minutes after the rest of the country had showered, changed and had a pint of lager in their hands in the Players Bar. The ball skidded past the Spurs keeper and through Cyril Knowles, legs and nestled wonderfully in the back of the Tottenham Hotspurs net. I ran the length of the field knowing there would just about enough time for Spurs to kick-off and as they did the whistle went and we were at Wembley once again. Tomorrow though, will be finished on the night, if not won in ninety minutes they'll be extra time and again if no result, penalties deciding who goes into the hat with Arsenal, Bolton and the winners of the Tottenham and Middlesbrough clash at White Hart Lane. Aston Villa really do need to improve their performance if they are to do anything in this match, although they will go into it knowing that they should have won their match at Stamford Bridge earlier in the season. Incredibly enough the man who was responsible for handing the points to the Blues – that particular day – was the destroyer in this tie. Juan Pablo Angel is a nightmare most of the times I have seen him play, but he scored a goal that Roman Abramovich would have loved to have been scored in a Chelsea blue shirt. With the morning headlines all about Chelsea's omission from the competition:

TREZEGUET THE TARGET Chelsea exit Carling Cup, now they'll spend again was back-page of the *Mail* whilst inside went that RANIERI HAS NO EXCUSES AFTER ANGEL MAGIC SHOW Trezeguet next?

GAVIT McCann stabs in to rout Roman soldiers was how the *Sun* printed it out. All along the top of the inside page covered the two ties well saying that Queudrue penalty secures McClaren Arsenal as Chelsea all-stars are humbled for the second time in five days. ANGELS DELIGHT Villa striker shoots down the Chelsea millionaire mob JUAN HELL OF A GUY HITS RAN Were the three main headlines across the two back pages of the *Daily Star* plus a side piece saying simply £100million Rom raid followed by: Chelsea owner Roman Abramovich is ready to break the bank again in the January sales. Ruud van Nistelrooy and Thierry Henry are both in his sights, he wants another midfielder and he won't hesitate to smash the world record.

That is the message coming out of Stamford Bridge – and one that will send shockwaves through Old Trafford, Highbury and across Europe.

Mega-rich Abramovich – who spent £110million on players in the summer – is about to hand boss Claudio Ranieri more funds to improve his dream-team.

He's shopping for top quality but Chelsea's acting chief executive Paul Smith insists they won't be ripped off. Smith said "If Pele was on the market today for £100million then we would maybe go for him, but we won't pay £50million for Joe Nobody.

"But if Ruud van Nistelrooy was priced at £60million and we considered it a good investment, then we would probably pay that. We want the right quality at the right value. Roman is a businessman and is determined not top get ripped off. We won't pay tourist prices".

Abramovich's big spending approach to football has barely made an impression on his personal fortune, thought to be around £4billion. But Chelsea's good start to the season has convinced him that this venture was worth the money, but only on results, not performances and having said that Arsenal were making a terrific start look quite ordinary as they continued their unbeaten run in the Premiership, FA Cup, Carling Cup and their dramatic comeback in the Champions League after looking doomed yet again in a competition, since firstly losing their first home match 3-0 to crack Italians Inter Milan their progress looked almost impossible.

Last week, Arsenal were hopping mad at the rumours that the Russian had made a formal offer for Henry.

The Gunners insisted their star was not for sale but now Chelsea are unsettling van Nistelrooy as the Dutchman ponders a £25million, five-year United contract offer.

A sensational swoop for either Henry or van Nistelrooy would force Abramovich to break the world record £46.5million Real Madrid paid Juventus for Zinedine Zidane in 2001.

But that vast sum would buy something Chelsea don't have; a Premiership goal machine worth 25 strikes a season. Argie forward Hernan Crespo – a £16.8million buy from Inter Milan – has scored six goals in nine games but cannot match Henry or van Nistelrooy. Ten-goal Jimmy Floyd Hasselbaink doesn't look the striker he was two years ago, through no fault of his own. Eidur Gudjohnsen has never been a prolific and consistent goal getter and new boy Adrian Mutu's goals have dried up after an early blitz. Smith claims the Blues are also out to boost their midfield power when the transfer window opens on the 1st of January.

Frank Lampard and Claude Makelele have done the lion's share of the midfield work in the first half of the season.

But Ranieri is afraid of burning them out. Valencia's Roberto Ayala is another long-standing Ranieri target. But he has played in the UEFA Cup and would not be available for the Champions League.

That was from the pen of Matt Barlow of the *Star*, and this is I: must stress that this is nowhere near the halfway point and Chelsea were very fortunate that the flaws in their side happened sooner rather than later. It was quite obvious Frank Lampard could not keep the kind of performances up that have taken him right in there along with Nicky Butt and Philip Neville who play sometimes around the likes of Scholes and Beckham doing that 'anchor role' but that is not Frank's natural game. Frank Lampard had a shocking introduction to his Chelsea career when crossing over from east London. However, that – again – was through no fault of Frank himself, for he was played in a role quite foreign to him, and if the Chelsea fans had seen as much of Frank as I had over the past couple of seasons before he left the Hammers they would know Frank is a box to box player who works tirelessly for the team and, giving him his head, will get you more than the average midfield player's contribution in the goals department. We all know that the blend will always be the main factor whether playing for your pub team or in the World Cup Finals. Both Henry and van Nistelrooy have their very own fan clubs and I am in both of them, however would either one of them fit in with the Chelsea system. I for one, and Wenger, know that Thierry Henry would not be a happy player if tinkered with because he is one of those players, if fit in body and mind, wants to play in each and every game. That is not to say that the Dutchman would like it any other way, but he is a player who needs a day off once in a while because, apart from our Ian Hutchinson and Liverpool's Ian Rush I have never seen a front-man – and prolific goal-scorer – get through so much legwork. Apart from that these two players will get you goals galore and you have to take on board that these two 'superstars' are not only top of the pops in the domestic game, especially van Nistelrooy who will go on breaking records both at home and in the Champions League, having already equalled Denis Law's record in far less games and has four or five years at the very top of his game, god willing, he does not get anything like the injury that put him a year behind signing at United. This is something Sir Alex Ferguson must be applauded, for he actually told the world and their dogs and Ruud then got that terrible cruciate ligament injury. With being a big brute of a player he has to be strong for he really does go through brick walls to get his goals. On the other hand Henry jumps out of one of the pages of my autobiography – The Working Man's Ballet – as he glides through matches like something out of the Russian Ballet, maybe that is why Roman likes him so much?

After all the money Chelsea have spent over the past six months they have still not come up with a player in the same class as both the Arsenal and United goal-fiends?

RANIERI HAUNTED BY THE GHOSTS

The *Evening Standard* and Matt Hughes reported that: Roman Abramovich is enduring his first football crisis. The Russian billionaire has made two fruitless trips in his private plane – from Moscow – in the space of five days, returning with nothing but disappointment. And he doesn't even get to collect Air miles, but does he really need them?

As a well-respected coach with two decades of experience in three different countries, Claudio Ranieri is better equipped to deal with the fickle nature of footballing fortune, but there are aspects of recent performances that will be troubling him. In losing two successive matches for the first time since March, Chelsea have created fewer goal-scoring opportunities against a very ordinary teams in Bolton and Aston Villa, part of a long-term trend that has seen them score only eight goals in the last eight matches. A superb defensive record has helped mask that weakness, but the fact remains that when Chelsea actually concede, they have trouble winning football matches!

Ranieri will also be aware of the ghosts of the Christmas past. This time last year his unfancied side were involved in a three-pronged title race with Arsenal and Manchester United, but a disappointing haul of one point from nine games beginning in the festive period saw them lose ground that they could not recover. History could yet repeat itself, and Saturday's little local difficulty against Fulham is a big game indeed.

Chelsea struggled to penetrate a dogged Villa rearguard all evening, but not for the first time Ranieri did not help himself. His players seemed ill at ease with yet another new formation, a 3-4-2-1, with Jimmy Floyd Hasselbaink as a lost and lonely striker.

Against Bekitas last week Ranieri's tactical tinkering worked a treat as he matched the Turks like-for-like, but last night's changes were a tweak too far that enabled the home side's more rugged 4-2-4 to control the midfield.

The visitors' midfield, by contrast appeared disjointed and disorientated, with Claude Makelele and Geremi getting in each other's way. Joe Cole was the only one to make any impression before Lampard's introduction, and the England midfielder twice went close from the edge of the penalty area before scoring the equaliser created by substitute Hernan Crespo.

The former Internationale striker did little else all evening and would do well to follow the example of another long haired South American, Juan Pablo Angel, who was magnificent throughout, crashing the first one spectacularly from 25yards after dancing around John Terry and William Gallas, and then creating Gavin McCann's 78th minute winner with another searing drive that was spilled by Neil Sullivan.

Crespo has frustrated Chelsea fans since his arrival in the summer, but with just one goal in his last six matches he is not the only striker who is misfiring. Hasselbaink has scored one in his last four matches while Adrian Mutu, the darling of the autumn, has gone nine games without a goal.

Aston Villa 2 Angel and McCann Chelsea 1 Joe Cole: 30,414

Perhaps Abramovich needs to write that £100million cheque after all, because the Tinkerman was not shouting now about the players he has at his mercy being good enough!

After reading and digesting that it makes a complete mockery of a Sunday column as told by Terry Venables giving the punters 'four good reasons' why Chelsea can rule Europe. Terry is in no doubt the tops in his field of coaching but sometimes the headmaster has lost his way. He says in his *News of the World* column that; Chelsea are joint favourites with Real Madrid to win the European Cup – and you have to say that they have a fantastic chance of going all the way. The Blues have amazed everyone with their performances this season.

Nobody doubted that they would, in time, become a genuine force at home and abroad.

Given the money available to them and the players they have bought that much was obvious. But it is the speed with which they have gelled that has sent shock waves round the world. Most fans were concerned that the size of their squad would prove disrupted. How does Claudio Ranieri keep everyone happy and how will they gel as a team?

I would not be surprised to see Venables' lights come up in the frame once Bates has departed for he is a 'master' tactician and the sound of the kind of money in the Russian's Bank Account must make him sweat each and every evening whilst putting his 'busy' head on his silk and gold pillows.

So far the results have been remarkable and it is credit to the players and their quality that they have made the transition seem so smooth. Ranieri has good balance. Defensively Chelsea have looked sound whereas previously, particularly away, you felt they were vulnerable. Claude Makelele has played a massive part in that factor.

He has anchored the midfield and allowed the more attack-minded players to express themselves – and that is an area of the pitch where Chelsea will maybe just edge it over Arsenal and Manchester United. In Adrian Mutu, Hernan Crespo, Jimmy Floyd Hasselbaink and Eidur Gudjohnsen, the Chelsea manager has four genuine goal threats. You feel he could play any combination – and that is without mentioning Damien Duff and Jesper Gronkjaer –

and still be rewarded with goals. He can rest any of those players safe in the knowledge that he has adequate options, although adequate will not be good enough this season to win any of the big pots of gold, either domestically or overseas!

Can the same be said of Arsenal and United?

I fear not and that could be the key.

Could you imagine Arsene Wenger resting Thierry Henry or Sir Alex leaving out Ruud van Nistelrooy?

Even extend that to Alan Shearer at Newcastle or Michael Owen at Liverpool. Not a chance. If they are fit they have to play because those clubs do not possess another out-and-out goalscorer. Of course both Manchester United and Arsenal will score goals from other areas and I expect all three teams to make it through in the next round of the Champions League. England and the Premier League should be proud of our three representatives. Arsenal's dramatic fight-back to qualify as group winners was nothing short of sensational.

Yet I have concerns about their strength in depth to go all the way – particularly in the striking department. United have that experience. They still haven't kicked into top gear, but they have improved defensively and you always fancy them at home.

How they must have wished they had gone for Harry Kewell or a player of his type to give van Nistelrooy back-up.

Diego Forlan has done well but I bet Sir Alex would have liked one more option, a top-drawer striker.

He will look to address that next month, I am sure. Chelsea have the toughest task of the three English teams. Stuttgart are unbeaten at home this year and are pulling up trees in the German league, but I believe Ranieri's side will do it. It could shape to be an exciting climax to this competition and the draw will have given our three representatives hope, especially as Real Madrid or Bayern Munich will go out and Juventus are vulnerable.

United have the edge. They have been there and done it. If I were a gambling man they would get my vote but Chelsea are creeping up on the rails. Will it be domestic or European success?

We will have to wait, but surely their season will depend on Roman Abramovich's spending come May.

Well Terry: I have followed your career very closely – oh and thanks again for your foreword in my autobiography The Working Man's Ballet – and have always admired the way your teams have played wherever you have gone. But this time I believe you have got it wrong!

I see that you have bought season tickets – for once – mate, a long way from Stan Flashman days my friend. And I also know just how much you would love to get your hands on the Russian's chequebook?

'DECEIVING STRIDE'

It is almost as if you have been caught up in the media frenzy the Russian has brought with his buying our club. This time I think the players are getting too carried away far too early and if you see the signs at both Arsenal and United you will see two teams relaxed, apart from Arsenal losing their way in the final group match in the Champions League. I still find it strange when men with so much knowledge and experience get up in front of viewing millions and say that, "my players did not know what to do in the second half, whether to attack or hold onto what we already had". After all they have a full team of internationals on show including the likes of Campbell, Viera, Henry and Bergkamp in the side, just four world-class individuals and they didn't know what to do, I ask you!

There is no striker in the Chelsea camp who is better than Ole Gunnar Solskaer let alone the best striker in Europe 'Van the Man'. And when it comes to Real and Zidane we are talking about night and day here. Real Madrid are in cruise control at the moment and they will overcome Bayern in the next stage before going on to win the competition the same way Manchester United will take the championship over here.

Arsenal will win the Carling Cup, United will take the Premiership and Newcastle United will, if they can get Bellamy back, win the FA Cup. Ruud van Nistelrooy will win the Golden Boot over here and that is about all there is to it. Roman Abramovich, I am afraid, will find the cupboard bare this time around and until he can find a new van Nistelrooy, Henry or a young Alan Shearer they will have to wait in line. I think he should go across town and buy Jermain Defoe before somebody else does and then there will be one more 'quality' striker to answer the Bluenoses plea. The Tinkerman had the right idea by buying strikers but like Ferguson you have to buy the best available, for he does nothing wrong in this department. Well, apart from Cruyff and Proborsky, two who were involved in Euro '96' where El Tel did so brilliantly and should have been given a five or six-year contract no matter what court case was going on, much like the weakness in never giving Brian Clough the top job, a job he would have been magnificent at! Man management! Knowing a player when he saw one, and a true motivator of men. I had a run-in with 'Old Big Head' whilst playing in Seattle after my boss Alan Hinton made a trip back to England looking for players to strengthen our already very useful Sounders team – and he returned to his old boss who was not too busy for him whilst winning European Cups. My name must have cropped up – I was Alan's captain – and Clough told him a story about coming back from Amsterdam and told him I fell off a bar stool at the airport. Our Stoke City team had just been knocked out by Ajax on the away goals rule, but should have won. I was half responsible we didn't, for having a car crash thirty-six hours before the first leg at the Victoria Ground, driving my wife's Mini across a T-Junction, missing a brick wall by literally inches. I am not very lucky when it comes to driving cars or crossing roads, you have been finding out along the way. Not long after buying her new Mini I put that on top of a roundabout next to the Newcastle-under-Lyme Golf Course, which they named aptly after me. By breaking my hand and playing with it strapped and several cuts across my face I underachieved against Rudi Krol and his Ajax side and we drew at home one apiece, had I been fit we would have won this match, for the night of the accident I put in one of my best ever performances in a Stoke City shirt at Carlisle United who were then in the First Division of old. Anyhow, on his return to Seattle he came into training and I asked him how it went. At that particular moment I was on my back doing my routine abdominal exercises when he told me that Clough had asked about me being his captain and mentioned the deal about the bar stool, incident. I was livid, and told Alan so. All the way home I thought about this so when I eventually made home I sat and wrote him a letter saying that 'If you can't say anything good about somebody you don't know say nothing'. Then I moved my pen along to asking him about the time I made two of three goals that helped get him the sack by Leeds United in his first League match in charge at the Victoria Ground. I felt better!

GEREMI? MAKELELE?
'The jury is still definitely out'

The following year, after Alan gave me the title of assistant manager, he told me to pack my bags, as I was going over with him this time. Yeah, you have it, first stop old Big Head himself. We watched a reserve team match at the City Ground, Nottingham, and after the match entered the manager's office and sat around his desk, which was full of champagne and brandy. There must have been about a dozen bodies sitting around when Clough started pouring a drink we badly needed after a long flight and a good old English freezing cold evening. As he poured he turned to me saying "Hello, young man, I received your letter". No sooner had he said that I was on my feet saying "Excuse me, before you go any further, I am telling you this because I don't want you thinking that he" – pointing at Alan – "was talking out of school, he simply said it to make conversation and he and I not only work together but are very close friends" and sat back down. He finished pouring, lifted the first full glass and handed it to me. "There you go young man, you can have the first drink for you have balls", and carried on with the evenings procedures. I liked Clough and forgive him for two things, one by not telling anyone else this story of untruth and the other for not buying me. I would have learned – like under Waddington – something else about the way our game should be played!

Back to the Bridge and in Geremi and Makelele, I believe the jury is still out and the United chief executive was correct in stating that the fee for Damien Duff was far too much.

However Duff has done terrifically well since putting a blue shirt over his head and at the end of the day it is how they play for you rather than how much they cost. Everyone wondered what Ferguson was doing going back for van Nistelrooy after that bad injury and paying such a price but he knew he was getting a player who would get goals in the Premiership. When players turn out like the Dutchman nobody ever mentions the price, but once you buy a 'Wally' the whole world questions how much you forked out for him, for example, Bogarde!

Ferguson has a wonderful record finding front players beginning with Mark Hughes, the managers' dream, then Cantona, there's only one Eric, Cole who'll always get you goals, Yorke until he found better things to do with his spare time, females and other substances, Sherringham a masterstroke, who proved the old Trafford faithful wrong, and lastly, the million dollar question as to who found this wonderful, this red hot, ice cold, baby face, murderer of defences. What these players had, apart from Ole Gunnar, was the look of a goalscorer and a reputation already but don't be deceived by his looks, they all had a good pedigree – instead of Ole Gunner – when Sir Alex took them into the Theatre of Dreams, made all of their dreams come true but that did include the baby faced assassin!

'ACTION WILL ALWAYS SPEAK LOUDER THAN WORDS'

This was John Terry's worst week at the heart of the Chelsea back-line but something he has to get used to, especially if he is going to keep on about what Chelsea will and won't do!

Going into the Fulham match, the one thing Chelsea did not want was to go there having lost the leadership of the Premiership and being knocked out of the Carling Cup – the one that earlier Frank Lampard and Joe Cole said that we will win the first trophy for Abramovich – a promise they could not keep to the new owner who never got where he is today on promises. As I keep saying action will always speak louder than words. The match was live – on SKY TV – as was Arsenal's match the evening before. Arsenal took a very different approach into the match at West Brom – a far tougher hurdle – and came out of it as the only club who can win all the domestic trophies and of course the Champions League. The Tinkerman is now being asked the big question and very quickly because Fulham will be delighted that this could be just the right time to catch them!

What a feather in the cap of Fulham's new manager this would be, but first let's just have a look at the match facts from a game that the Tinkerman said live on air "that Aston Villa deserved their victory, they seemed to have wanted it more than us". When he was asked about his tinkering with the team he looked aggressive for one of the first times amongst the media. He also said that, "I am disappointed. It is not like some managers who might not want to win this cup. I wanted Chelsea to win the Carling Cup. This hurts me. I don't like it. In the first half I thought we were too soft. In the second half it was better but Aston Villa were the better team. They deserved their victory. Nothing much happened for us, but Lampard cannot play all the games.

Others must do it sometimes. Now, after two defeats, we will see how the players react. We must stay together and make this right. It doesn't matter how much has been spent, all teams go through a bad spell. This is ours. All the time I learn things about my players. Everything is new. Now I will see how they deal with this". But in different surroundings he seemed not so disappointed saying, "I thought that we played pretty well but Villa played better. Until two weeks ago we were finding the space to score. But now we do not have the openings. All teams have a bad period and now is the time for me to see how my players react to disappointment".

I spent the entire day in writing so I don't know just how the mood was around the place particularly in the Grosvenor where there are more blue noses than any other. But I must say the folk around these parts have not gone overboard about what has been going on since Roman bought the place, maybe they have waited so long to win a Championship, last won when I was four, so I don't know how they celebrated then and it is strange that I never hear any of the elder statesman talk of such times. All I do know is ,had Chelsea sacked Dave Sexton instead of Peter Osgood and myself, things just might have been different, but as the *Sun* journalist wrote in 'The Working Mans Ballet'. "Had Alan been born on a different day things could have been a far lot better for him".

I wonder what day he was talking about!

CHELSEA'S FLAGGING SPIRITS LIFTED BY TIMELY ROMAN ARRIVAL.

Chelsea's fragile morale in the wake of back-to-back defeats was lifted yesterday by Chairman Roman Abramovich's appearance at the club's West London training ground. The Russian billionaire's visit was ideally timed as a show of support, providing a welcome lift for manager Claudio Ranieri and his star-studded squad in the wake of their Premiership loss to Bolton and Carling Cup exit at the hands of Aston Villa.

He turned up at Harlington for training and a Christmas lunch, which left the Tinkerman saying that, "The chairman is always a nice person and shows his support. He understands that the team cannot always win. There are good moments and bad moments, he is close to the team and we appreciate that."

Ranieri is refusing to be panicked by his team's surprise setbacks and told anxious fans that his multi-million pound outfit are exceeding expectations.

The Italian coach has been hampered by a host of new injury concerns ahead of today's derby match against Fulham. But he insisted he was unaware of the trigger-happy sentiments of a section of his clubs supporters. He said that, "In a bad moment, I want to see my team take a step forward. This is a new examination. We haven't been in good condition but now I want to see our reaction. We have exceeded expectations in terms of results and our position in the table. I expected us to take longer to gel. It is not easy putting in new players who link well together. We cannot have consistency like Manchester United and Arsenal".

For perhaps the first time this season, Ranieri's options are being reduced by injuries and suspensions. Ranieri's favourite 'battery', Claude Makelele, is struggling to shake off a fever and back-up is limited with Juan Sebastian Veron and Emmanuel Petit both ruled out through injury.

But Ranieri is reluctant to make excuses, saying, "I would like to change the team but now I can make very few changes. That should not be an excuse. We have twenty-two champions, if we can't play, some other champions come in".

Chelsea, however will have to spice up the attack to overcome Fulham's obstinate defence. "Fulham are sparkling right now", said Ranieri. "It will be a real difficult game."

So there you have it from the Tinkerman, always confident of the job ahead but I do wish he would stop calling his players 'his champions'. But he goes into today's match knowing his team will have too much for their neighbours and ninety minutes later he was correct. But please Claudio don't keep calling these football players 'champions', it is driving me mad. I will accept it in May if they do become what you are always intent on calling them, quite crazily and shallow!

But as for now I fancy Manchester United to be too strong for both their London rivals. Let's not forget how difficult this season will be as nearly halfway through the season Arsenal are the only unbeaten team in the country yet are second in the table to Manchester United.

THE COUNTRY IS WAITING TO SEE CHELSEA CRASH

"But we won't", says Joe Cole, who wants to prove doubters wrong by getting Chelsea's Championship charge back on track tomorrow. Claudio Ranieri's men need a win at Loftus Road against local rivals Fulham following two defeats on the spin.

Last week's shock 2-1 Premiership defeat at home to Bolton was followed by a Carling Cup exit at Aston Villa on Wednesday night. The dip in form has once again raised questions about Chelsea's chances of glory this term.

But Cole, 22, has called on the Blues to come out fighting and show the country they mean business. He said, "It is important for the club to bounce back against Fulham.

"This will be a big test of character for us because the whole country will be looking for us after the two results and we need to come out fighting. We always knew this was going to be a massive game against Fulham because local derbies are always special occasions. We know you cannot underestimate Fulham because they have had a great start to the season. I have played in big derbies before when I was at West Ham. And I know they all bring their own personalities. But the only way for us to get the last two results out of our system is to get straight back on the winning trail against Fulham. It is a major disappointment going out of the Carling Cup at Villa and losing our second game on the spin. But we hope this run will not last long. I am gutted with the result because I would love to have played in my first major cup final.

"But if the club keeps progressing like I know we can. I am sure we will get more opportunities in the near future". So much as I said earlier about John Terry, Joe Cole and Frank Lampard shouting that they will win the first domestic trophy for Ranieri, talk is cheap chaps, I don't know how many times I have to remind you and your manager is guilty of not doing so himself!

It's me again: I did not go to the match so listened to it on *Talk Sport* and it seemed Chelsea had far more possession than their neighbours but it also gave me the impression that Fulham had some very good opportunities. But unlike my cousin Anthony, I cannot watch the match on the radio!

That is a family joke, but one he swears he could do such a thing!

He really is a lad!

The Chelsea keeper goes from strength to strength and is definitely one of the reasons Chelsea continually go forward knowing they are very confident around their own goal area. That does not take anything away from the team as a whole, because we all know that although Manchester United were a great side winning all trophies in the nineties they owed so much to Peter Schmeichel. The 'Great Dane' was a giant between the sticks for Ferguson and proved that you do need a great keeper if you are going to be successful. The reason for that is for when the team do hit a sticky patch, and that is inevitable – they rely on their keeper to get some shooting practice. I remember one match when Manchester United were chasing Newcastle – under Kevin Keegan – up at St James' Park when Schmeichel made some fantastic saves to keep his team in the match, then Eric Cantona stole the match – which was a real six pointer – and United used that for their springboard to overhaul Keegan's team. Chelsea got the result they needed badly yesterday and sit and hope that Tottenham will steal something of Ferguson's men this afternoon. My prediction is that Spurs will do well if they keep the score down to a reasonable number, remembering that United are at their most dangerous at this time of the year. In a nutshell, they usually begin their run from this time of the year. Chelsea join Arsenal at the head of the table with the Gunners sitting on top only because the A is before the C, as – incredibly – both of their records show up identical, with games played, goals for, goals against and total points all the same. Arsenal were a shade lucky at Bolton not to come away empty-handed at the Reebok Stadium as Bolton kept their great run of form up and came very close to beating both the top two in the Premiership in a seven-day period. Their performance was first class and had the Gunners on the ropes for much of the match, proving if you have good players who play the game properly – passing, moving, and closing the opposition down – you will reap your just rewards. What a magnificent job Sam is doing up there, and of course let's not forget Jay Jay Okocha!

I fancied this match could be a draw and Wilsonsports Betting and Racing went 12/5 while Chelsea were 4/5 to win at Fulham and this afternoon's match at White Hart Lane have United as 8/13 shots with Spurs going 7/2. The Spurs match would be better backing correct score maybe 3-0, 4-0 or even five, then Ruud van Nistelrooy scoring the first goal is nicely priced at 7/2. Then you could have a correct score and the United striker in a win double.

There were a couple of good pieces in yesterday's newspapers and one was with Brian Woolnough, that brilliant journalist who headed with: THREE WISE MEN FACE SANTA'S SACK.

When you have spent £110million on some of Europe's top stars and then lose successive matches that is a crisis.

It is cruel, yet a fact of life in the Premiership. You buy, you play, you win. If not, someone else can have a go. The pressure to be a success has never been greater. Claudio Ranieri at Chelsea has hit his first mini crisis. But it won't take long to develop into a major one for him. A draw at Leeds, defeat at home to Bolton and then knocked out of the Carling Cup at Aston Villa. He simply must pick his best team, playing in the right formation, to win at Fulham this afternoon.

No other result will do to prevent the likeable Ranieri having that infectious smile wiped off his face. No-one else can help him as the rumours continue about Sven Goran Eriksson and owner Roman Abramovich looks down from the directors' box.

The most worrying things for Ranieri are that at Villa Park on Wednesday, his team were not as passionate as the Villa. Clearly, David O'Leary's side wanted it more and that is unacceptable. Chelsea have been outstanding in Europe so far and stayed in the top three of the Premiership all season. It will not be enough for Ranieri, certainly not for Roman Abramovich. Chelsea must be the best and a poor result at Fulham and over the busy Christmas period would have Abramovich playing the role of Tinkerman instead.

Is all this pressure fair?

Yes, it is. Managers are handsomely paid and they survive, or are sacked, on results.

Time has never been shorter for them such is the thirst for success from PLC boards, directors and supporters.

Liverpool's Gerard Houllier, like Ranieri, must win today. He takes his side to Wolves – which was abandoned – with most fans believing the Frenchman has run out of ideas and time. Floundering around in the middle of the Premiership is no good for both Liverpool and Houllier knows his job is on the line, despite recent claims and denials behind the scenes.

Kevin Keegan also needs good results over the busy holiday programme to end rumours of dressing room unrest at Manchester City. Surely Keegan would not walk away from football again?

Ranieri, Houllier and Keegan should be football's three wise men going into Christmas. Yet they need to bear some gifts, otherwise the New Year looks very bleak for them.

They know management is a rat race – but they still love it. Only one thing matters for them now, results.

Time is not on their side with patience never shorter from the men upstairs. Football is demanding like never before, with the pressure on from all sides.

It will be a surprise if all three of them have managed to fight off football's win-at-all-costs attitude before the end of the season.

Back over to me: I would not be too disappointed if Houllier was given the old tintack for I did not like the situation when Roy Evans was joint manager with him and all of a sudden Houllier was given the job on his own. What did Roy Evans do wrong, which did not include the Frenchman?

I have heard stories about Houllier being linked with someone high up at Anfield?

Keegan, on the other hand, has shown incredible naivety in the purchasing both Robbie Fowler and Steve McManaman, two players who we know are great buddies but one has thrown his career away. For Fowler, whatever the reason is just something that is one of the great losses in my time, playing, coaching and writing about the special performers in the game we love to play!

Robbie Fowler looked the greatest striker since Jimmy Greaves and that is not exaggerated, he did not have the same 'gift' for taking the ball like Greaves but he had that special talent of always having time on the ball and his timing of hitting balls from any angle a sheer joy to watch. Sometimes you will get great strikers but they are not great players, this doesn't apply with Fowler, he had it both. For example, Gary Lineker was a brilliant goal-getter for both club and country but he was not someone you would cross the road to see play. Years ago, Roger Hunt – a World Cup winner – was a prolific goal-man but not an exceptional player. Alan Shearer was a little different and would get himself goals at any level, if teams play to his strength, and that is simply get the ball to him anywhere from the thirty-five yard line – an invisible one – and he would make things happen. He really has improved over the years and is more a complete player now than ever before, although he has lost a little pace, but don't let that fool you defenders. But like Teddy Sherringham he uses his head more than his legs and that saves you using up your energy, therefore being brighter when the ball gets to you in the last third of the field which gives you more time to do what you're best at, hitting the back of the net.

So there you have it, and it is with great disappointment I write about Fowler because there are not many talents coming through like him over the years. When we have to play Emile Heskey in front of players such as Fowler it proves my point of being a wasted talent. I think when it all comes down to the 'nitty gritty' it must be down to the money being earned and that money is more important than personal pride in your performances. If a man stepped off a flying saucer and saw both Fowler – when he first started and Heskey – he would not accept that Heskey would go on to get more England caps than the ex-Liverpool player. On the other side of the coin Michael Owen is a manager's dream – if Fowler's the nightmare – and a player with immense talent to go with his immense attitude playing up front all on his own, showing such courage surrounded by defenders who would have a breakfast far bigger than the local Merseysider. Another one, Michael Owen!

SAVAGE OLAMA BIN BLADDER

The news had just broken that Rio Ferdinand has received an eight-month ban and a hefty fine – although the money does not matter these days – and the country was up in arms about how the entire thing was dealt with. If these same lawyers are the ones representing Sir Alex Ferguson in his fight against the Coolmore Mafia he will not be too encouraged about this outcome. The Ferdinand affair has been shabbily handled and there were far too many ifs and buts from day one. FIFA were looking for someone to put up and make an example of and Rio – although not having the drug test done – was the fall guy and the headline above is right on the button. Osama Bin Bladder, the head of FIFA, has never impressed me since the day he first took over the reigns in Switzerland and Rio has my deepest sympathy and should, and is appealing against this barbaric ban. I have said from day one that football clubs should not have random drug tests, they should in these days of high profile superstars make it a rule – right across the universe – that players contracted by their particular club should be tested twice a week, one after a Saturday or Sunday match and then again on the following Friday, the day or two before their weekend match. This would be looked at as a routine arrangement where they would also see the blood levels of certain players and then the club doctor would be right on top of the situation. After all the reason this random testing was introduced was to get rid of the drug taking in our game or, for that matter, make it a rule throughout professional sport all over the world!

Manchester United solicitor Maurice Watkins read out a statement from the club like this "We are extremely disappointed by the result of this case, in particular by the savage and unprecedented sentence which makes an appeal inevitable. I can confirm he has the full support of Manchester United and the PFA. There will be no further comment at this stage".

The *Sunday People* Sport section had this case all over the first five pages and one more on page 22.

All of us who know Manchester United and Sir Alex Ferguson – in particular – will know that they will be tougher than ever to overcome. The resilient manager has never been one to duck any situation involving his beloved Manchester United and it is with this in mind I feel that this latest injustice will spur them on to regaining the Premiership title. As for Rio he will be out of the limelight for a very long time, in terms of a footballers career, and if he gets any joy it will be – at the most, halved. Then the FIFA body would have, although backed down, shown their intent for all to see.

There are too many grey areas in this case against the ex-West Ham and Leeds United centre-half and that is why this could have been prevented. They could have said because of these areas we are giving him a sentence of which he will serve if there are any traces of drugs in his blood stream in the future. In fact the ban for anyone from here on is found with anything like this in the future will get an automatic two year ban and this will not go in front of a committee that have already made their minds up before the Manchester United and England player had walked into their room.

MORNING PAPERS

It was Saturday the 20th of December and the inside page of the *Daily Express* was a headline that said, 'I WOULD NOT SWAP WITH RANIERI' by Fulham boss Chris Coleman. The Fulham manager Chris Coleman says that Chelsea may have a budget of £110million but his team are true Premiership leaders. Coleman could be forgiven for feeling green with envy as Chelsea head for Loftus Road with a team full of international superstars. But he says he is relieved he does not have the pressure Claudio Ranieri is under in today's west London derby. The Blues may have spent £110million in the transfer market since Roman Abramovich arrived, but they are only one step ahead of fourth placed Fulham in the Premiership table and have lost their last two matches. Coleman said that, "As far as I am concerned, in fourth place we are top of the table – because the other three are in a different league. Nobody is going to catch them now and although Chelsea now have had a couple of wobbles you know they'll finish in the top two or three at the end of the season. We are just a little club in comparison and we can't go comparing ourselves. People keep asking me if I'm jealous of Claudio Ranieri having so much money just up the road, but I'm not.

"I wouldn't want £100million to spend because that would be too much pressure for a manager in his first year. The pressure is on them every game because they have spent so much money on high-quality players. Every match is under scrutiny and every defeat you are looking at the reaction of the fans. Of course every manager in the country would love money to spend and to be able to bring in quality players, but it does bring that extra pressure and I don't envy Claudio, that's for sure. We spent a lot of money in the past, I know, but compared to what Chelsea have got it has just blown us out of the water. Maybe if you gave me £50million at the start of next season I would be ready for it, but not yet."

Fulham go into the derby with Jerome Bonnissel fit again after an ankle injury, but with Mark Pembridge still out injured.

On the bottom of the same page Claudio Ranieri admits that his Chelsea team are currently feeling flat but says there is no crisis at the club and the players have exceeded his expectations. Despite making their best start to a Premiership season, Chelsea have once again been going through their customary Christmas wobble, with only one win in four matches. But Ranieri, preparing for a derby against Fulham, said, "Now is not a good time but we have gone beyond my expectations. We have added ten players to the side since last season and they have gelled far quicker than I would have imagined". Questions have been asked about some of the foreign players failing to learn English, but Ranieri insists there is no communication problem. He said that, "The most important thing is that they understand each other on the field".

Chelsea have been linked with a host of players ahead of the transfer window but Ranieri was giving no clues, saying, "We are only thinking about the Fulham match, which is another important step for the club".

Once again the Tinkerman handled the media well and it is his sense of humour that keeps him sane in a world where you have so many friends whilst you are winning but one of isolation if going the opposite direction. I have not met Chelsea's Tinkerman but like him a lot for he has one of the greatest qualities a person can have and that is his honesty. As for the Talisman, he has brought great power to a Football Club which has always been a sleeping giant although playing poker with success through the sixties and seventies but never had a card player that could pull the aces out when needed. The who's who of Stamford Bridge from Hughie Gallagher to Roy Bentley, Jimmy Greaves, Bobby Tambling, Terry Venables, Peter Bonetti, Peter Osgood, Charlie Cooke and Eddie McCeadie, were players of immense talent with very special qualities. Five of those I had the great pleasure to play with in my first full season, one of complete and utter sensational experiences. For me – it was like taking a train ride through the country stopping off in big towns and leaving the like the James Gang with their satchels full and fans all over the place never forgetting such a band of players. OK, the James Gang left with the cash where we left with the points and another pass to the next round of cup matches that we thrived on. The disappointment was something so difficult to put down on paper but so easily to talk about. Being the youngest player it was my job to show that my legs were strong enough to do that bit extra for my elderly team-mates and that was my pleasure and anything else that came my way, I absorbed it like the greatest love you have ever experienced. And years later that I found that my heart was truly strong to handle such an incredible automobile accident when the men in green garb thought that my heart could give way at any given time, such was the trauma of so many individual and life-threatening injuries. I was the 'Kings Road Kid' alongside Peter Osgood the 'King' and Charlie Cooke the 'Prince' of Stamford Bridge and we were so close to having a team that could wrestle the championship from the likes of Arsenal, Liverpool, Everton, Manchester City and United, although by the time I broke into this Palace of a team the two teams from Manchester were broken, up with Law, Charlton, Crerand and the 'Wayward Genius' of George Best names of the past. George walked away at a crazy age of somewhere around twenty-six years of age as the others' legs were truly spent through their very own voyages around Great Britain and Europe.

NEIGHBOURS

Also at the bottom of the page of the *Express* this day was the first blip of the season, call it a negative or whatever you like but the bookmakers are rarely wrong. With the headlines CHELSEA ODDS-ON TO WIN NOTHING led into some useful information by Graham Sharpe, the man who works for one of the biggest betting organisations around.

He says that for the first time this season some Chelsea punters have the blues. The Premiership's biggest spenders were backed at 1000/1 to clean up by winning all four major tournaments – Premiership, FA Cup, Carling Cup and Champions League – this season, but now they are out of the Carling Cup they are as short as 2/5 with Bet365 to end the season with nothing. This might encourage people to take Hills' 4/1 that Sven Goran Eriksson will be in charge at the Bridge at the start of next season. Chelsea are still serious title contenders at 9/4, while Manchester United are 6/4 and Arsenal (250/1 with Skybet to win all four and 8/1 to remain undefeated in the league) are 15/8.

Fulham will be keen to administer Chelsea's third consecutive defeat and at 4/1, the side, which already boasts a win at Old Trafford must be a sporting wager. The Gunners are now 5/4 favourites to win the Carling Cup while Aston Villa are at 4/1, Bolton 9/2 and Middlesbrough 11/2. Liverpool are 13/8 in 'betting without the top three' Premiership odds – Newcastle are 7/4 second favourites – but manager Gerard Houllier is now odds-on at 5/6 to depart Anfield before the end of the season and 6/4 favourite to be the next manager for the chop, ahead of Kevin Keegan at 4/1 and David O'Leary at 10/1.

Thierry Henry just missed out on the FIFA World Player of the Year Award this week but has been installed as 7/2 favourite to win it next season. Henry is a 9/2 shot for the Golden Boot, with Ruud van Nistelrooy 15/8 and current leader Alan Shearer backable at 9/4.

Harry Harris reports that Roman Abramovich has transformed Fantasy Football into Chelsea's reality show. So when the name of Ronaldo pops up as a potential target, no one will laugh it out of the Russian oil billionaire's west London court. Both Peter Ridsdale and David O'Leary wanted Ronaldo for a year's loan as a part of the Leeds United's dream team. At that time, though, Ronaldo was seeking match fitness after a serious knee injury. But nothing is beyond the biggest chequebook in world football at the Bridge. The chance, any chance, of bringing Ronaldo to these shores must be encouraged. And the inclusion of Ronaldo on Chelsea's next wish list will not lead to further confusion about who recommended him, Claudio Ranieri or Sven Goran Eriksson.

Even the tea lady at the Bridge could tell you the 27-year-old with the goofy teeth is still the best striker in the world!

But who else is on the list?

I can reveal the players Abramovich and his advisers have lined up. In each department, Ranieri and his aides have a contingency plan if they cannot get their preferred choice.

In attack, apart from Ronaldo, Wayne Rooney is a long way from being considered on the list of strikers, while Roma captain Francesco Totti falls into the same category as Thierry Henry – they are part of the very fabric of their clubs and it would take more than money to take them away.

Michael Owen might have come under consideration with 18 months left of his contract, but his preference is to go abroad, with Real Madrid and Barcelona chasing him. David Trezeguet is a reasonable addition to the list of goal-scorers admired by Chelsea. A proven striker, clever on the ground, potent in the air, he has been coveted by Arsene Wenger but he is way out of the Gunners' price range. He could come in with Ronaldo. Chelsea will need one, or possibly two strikers next summer, Ranieri has acknowledged they are struggling to break teams down. Jimmy Floyd will be allowed to go to Barcelona on a free transfer. Eidur Gudjohnsen is still out with ankle injury, but has the rest of the season to prove he is up for the job. Although short-sighted critics felt that Ranieri had acquired too many midfield players and that Frank Lampard would not get a game, the reality is that with both Juan Sebastian Veron and Manu Petit injured, they have been short in this depart-ment. Emerson was close to a move to the Bridge, last summer, and there is bound to be another big attempt to sign the Brazilian. He is the preferred midfield target.

Pavel Nedved has always been high on the list, and there will be a renewed effort to sign the Czech midfield playmaker from Juventus. After Zidane, Nedved is the best, my kind of midfield player, one who covers acres of ground but whilst doing so, keeps superb control and balance and gets more than his fair share of vital goals in the very biggest of matches in European ties.

David Beckham will not be a target unless his wife gets fed up with Madrid. If he did go to the Bridge it might be a familiar one – for his dad once used to mend the boilers there.

A fullback or two may be on the agenda, and definitely a world-class centre-half, with Marcel Desailly coming to the end of an industrious career possibly as early as this coming summer!

Roma's Walter Samuel has all the credentials, but Lucio, of Bayer Leverkusen, and Valencia's Ayala are more likely alternatives.

Alessandro Nesta would be first choice, but he is highly valued by AC Milan.

A selection of the above would certainly cost another £100million, but who cares when you are having so much fun?

Yet one of the untouchables on Chelsea's list, Henry, believes Ranieri already has a squad capable of wining the title this season. Ranieri has regularly ruled out his side's chances of beating both Manchester United and Arsenal, despite the clubs newfound wealth, but the Blues are two points behind the leaders and Henry laughs off such talk. He said that, "You can say five teams are in the running for the title this season, because Chelsea have three of their own. Sometimes I hear the Chelsea players joking or saying they have no chance of winning the league title this season. I always said Chelsea were a threat for the title even before all the big signings".

So there you have it from Thierry Henry, a player who seems to become a better player with each season – like a good vintage wine – and to think he was a wide player when Wenger brought him over from their native country and turned him into a locomotive train that is always on time, never breaks down and you will never spill your drinks whilst he is in possession of the steering of the train. This was a little of Wenger's magic shown as Nicolas Anelka did a 'runner' from Highbury leaving Arsenal with a massive wad of bank notes but no-one to partner Dennis Bergkamp up front. Then the Arsenal ringmaster gargled with the idea of moving Henry away from the touchline and get him more involved down the middle where games are won and lost. So it is no surprise these days when he drifts out wide and uses his electric pace to torment those poor full-backs by going both inside and outside, causing havoc with the ball almost glued to his feet, taking off like Linford Christie leaving defenders in his wake. If I have one criticism it would be that he does not score as many goals as he should. I know Wenger will say he is more than just a goal getter for he provides many goals for his fellow team mates and I cannot argue with Mr Arsenal after all he keeps bringing such great quality into the Highbury home dressing room. And I will be delighted to be shown around the new one in Ashburton Avenue!

The great comparison now is between the superhuman efforts of Ruud van Nistelrooy and one of the two players who I should have had on the front of my first book 'The Working Man's Ballet' – Henry or Zidane – instead of me and another one of my all-time favourites, Franz Beckenbauer. Of all the players Harry touched on, the one special player our of the pack is Czech international Pavel Nedved, a player who is the perfect midfielder in a climate where to be the very best you have to be mobile, especially on the biggest stages in the world, the Champions League and the European and World Cups. Nedved is my player of players in that area and only Zidane could be judged as better, but that is not a problem if you are second best to one of the greatest talents of all time. So now you realise that I chipped into Harry Harris's summation of Chelsea's wills and will nots this coming season by wondering how he did not rate Nedved so highly. But, oh yeah, Harry never played the game or as I said earlier 'Lived the dream'.

DERBY DAY

So the stage was set for a terrific showdown between the third and fourth placed teams in the Premiership at Loftus Road. Chelsea had won by far the lions' share of these matches with their neighbours and this was a great opportunity to get back to winning ways. And that was the way it turned out to be with Carlo Cudicini and John Terry – once again – being the outstanding performers when Chelsea – if a boxing match – would have won by quite a distance on points. Hernan Crespo scored with a magnificent header in the first half and from there on in, although Fulham huffed and puffed could not blow Chelsea's defence down. There was one problem coming out of this match and that was the injury to Damien Duff and they would not know until the following Monday, if it is a simple dislocation of his shoulder or there is muscle damage which would keep him out for six weeks. But Chelsea leapfrogged back over Manchester United and tied for the top spot with Arsenal with both teams having the exact same goals for and against column, which is incredible as we enter the New Year and half the season almost over. Ferguson took his in-form team to White Hart Lane and a good hiding looked on the cards for David Pleat's team. United began strongly and were overrunning the home team from the first whistle. It took John O'Shea to head the first goal with van Nistelrooy hitting the second but with a big score looking good for the visitors for – looking at Chelsea and Arsenal – it might just go down to goal difference come May. Back with the Blues and some headlines, with the *Sun* writing that BLUES ON THE CRESP OF A WAVE: But mums the word as Ranieri finds he faces a Duff dilemma. The *Sunday Express* read THE AGONY AND THE ECSTACY: and Crespo puts Chelsea back on track but Duff's injury is a worry for Ranieri: In the *Daily Mail* it said that CRESPO SUPPLIES A CRISP FINISH: and that: Roman is smiling again as Chelsea get back on course.

Peter Higgs of the *Sports Mail* saw it this way: Hernan Crespo scored a stunning goal to ensure that Roman Abamovich's £120million toy was mended in time for Christmas. But on the day Chelsea put their recent setbacks behind them to reclaim a share of the Premiership leadership with Arsenal, a worrying injury to Damien Duff marred a highly successful afternoon for Claiudio Ranieri – and the coach's 84-year-old mother Renata.

He was at least entitled to be happy that his expensively assembled team showed the character he had demanded to put their Premiership title challenge back on course. Victory was secured by Crespo's towering 62nd minute header, a typical old-fashioned centre-forward's goal from a player who at last appears to be coming to terms with English football.

Chelsea's manager was delighted by the way his players responded to the surprise defeat by Bolton Wanderers and the midweek Carling Cup exit at Aston Villa.

But the prospect of losing Duff for up to three weeks after the Irishman was carried off in the seventh minute and taken to hospital with a dislocated shoulder, brought dismay to the Ranieri family. Signed for £16.8million from Inter-Milan to deliver 20-plus goals and take his new employers to their first championship for forty-eight years, the longhaired Argentine has taken some time to adapt. But his eighth goal of the season suggested he is getting there. And he could prove to be a key-figure in the second half of the season.

"Crespo is improving", insisted Ranieri. "He's only at sixty or seventy per cent of his quality. This not the true Crespo, but he is getting better. It takes time to understand English football, the atmosphere and everything. But he is a goal scorer, and when he gets in good condition he will score more goals". Chelsea will need him to do so if they are going to keep up with the pace of the other big two. Yet, this was another example of how Ranieri's team can grind out a single-goal victory if necessary. Anything less than full commitment would have been costly against a Fulham side that have already embarrassed Arsenal and Manchester United, the only other realistic championship contenders. But the early loss of Duff could not disrupt Chelsea's fluent passing game in difficult windy conditions, with Joe Cole coming on as a replacement to show the watching Sven Goran Eriksson how well he can play in England's problem position on the left of midfield. Once Carlo Cudicini had rebuffed Fulham's bright opening by turning away Saha's header at full-stretch, it became a question of whether his opposite number Edwin van der Sar could repeat his match-saving heroics which forced a goalless draw at Highbury earlier this month.

Chris Coleman was honest enough to admit his team had not been good enough.

"We huffed and puffed but our general play was poor", said the new Fulham boss.

"We looked a bit panicky and needed to show more composure." But he believed that his team had not reached fourth spot without deserving to do so, and claimed that they would bounce back in the Christmas matches against Aston Villa and Southampton.

As for Chelsea, they go in to the holiday period in good heart. After fading in the closing stages last season, Ranieri believes he has the players to sustain a challenge. So does his mum, especially when Damien Duff is fit again.

His mother calls her son and grills him about not playing Damien Duff!

Drug testers from UK sport were in action at Loftus Road, where Fulham players Sylvain Legwinski and Facunda Sava were randomly selected to provide samples. Chris Coleman said that, "It is part of football now to have testers turn up at any time."

But as I have already pointed out these tests should not be done at random. Here is a situation where they want players tested so why doesn't the club have the authority to do such a test on players on the morning before and after the match, because if they took it the day before it would not stop them from taking some substance either the evening before or the morning of a match and if it is performance enhancing drugs then that is the correct time to be tested. It still needs to be done, ok, the authorities might think if a player is found positive the club could hide it, but there must be a way to employ people with medical background to do such a job all around the country, after all we are not short of a few quid in this country now judging by the sizes of players' and managers' pay packets, the money at the Football Association and the PFA!

Fulham 0 Chelsea 1 Crespo: 18,244

STILL DIGGING

Outside of Chelsea the great Ferguson and Beckham saga continued as the Scot said that Real Madrid are the team to beat this time around in the Champions League stating that "I can't look beyond Real Madrid this year because they have four great players who – on an individual basis – can win a game: Ronaldo, Zidane, Figo and Raul".

That says it all does it not? On the same day Beckham was headlines in a competing paper saying that, "I want to win the real treble" and goes on to say that he is a far better player than he was at Old Trafford and he aims to beat United trophy haul. His coach who knows him from their days at Old Trafford – Carlos Queirez being Ferguson's number two – said that, "David is doing very well, and I think with each match, he takes a step forward. He has shown a lot of maturity in the last two or three months playing in central midfield. It is not his natural position because he was not 'born' there. But he is getting more and more comfortable. David is learning when to move, when to stay, when to pass and how to reach a balance between short passing and long passing. A lot of things are new for him so it is natural that we expect more and more from him".

Back with Chelsea's rivals United, where there was bad news for the Blues as Paul Scholes was back with a bang in the Manchester derby scoring two headers that have become his trademark in and around the opponent's penalty box. Scholes, the smallest man on the field, got between two City defenders to dispatch two Denis Law-like jack-knife headers that the great man would have been proud to have put away. This is a big move forward for Ferguson because it comes at a time when his team will be expected to be moving into top gear in the early part of New Year and overdrive by Easter, their usual road to the championship.

MUTU PLANS TO RUN OUT ON ROM Strike ace sets up secret deal.

This was an exclusive written by Jim Keat of the *News of the World*; Adrian Mutu will walkout on Chelsea to join his dream club, his father has revealed. The £15.8million striker has a 'verbal agreement' with Steaua Bucharest president Gigi Becall to return to Romania in two years – despite signing a five-year, £40,000 a week, deal at Stamford Bridge.

BIZARRE

The latest piece of news coming out from the Bridge is that Adrian Mutu's father told the media that his son will only play two of his five-year contract for Chelsea and stated that his son has already shaken hands on a deal with Steaua head coach as to his future plans, his father continues. "But I don't think he will stay. You will see that in the next two years somebody else will have him in their side".

Steaua chief Becali confirmed a secret deal had been hammered out in principal, when the pair met last month. He said that, "I talked to Mutu when we played Liverpool in the UEFA Cup. He said that he was a big fan of our club and it is his dream to play for Steaua. Mutu insisted that, despite enjoying his time in Chelsea, playing for Steaua is his dream. He knows we do not have the kind of money to spend like Chelsea – but said that by then he would be rich enough to not think about money".

Well I can only say that that is a slap in the face for the advisers of the Russian and I would not like it to be me who was being misled. It just goes to show that certain players from these countries are very difficult to figure out and I know through my friendship with Harry Redknapp that these chaps are quite incredible with their approach to the game. Next it was Geremi to hit the headlines with IT WONT BE A TRAGEDY IF WE LOSE THE TITLE. Another *News of the World* exclusive by Rob Beasley. I know Rob from his days working in Stoke-on-Trent for the local radio and newspaper; Chelsea star Geremi knows the true meaning of the word tragedy. So the thought of Roman Abramovich's Blues ending up empty-handed at the end of a money-spinning season doesn't even come close. Not when you have seen a close friend collapse and die in front of you on a football pitch. And not when you have suffered the agonising loss of your beloved mother just weeks after you've left home in pursuit of fame. That sort of heartache puts it the soccer hype all into perspective.

And Geremi sums up his philosophy in a far different way than most other footballers in this country. And says this just as their impressive Premiership form is beginning to falter as well. Last weekend Bolton became the first league team to win at Stamford Bridge this season and that slip-up came hot on the heels of a scrappy draw at crisis club Leeds. So if Chelsea's season comes to nothing – despite the roubles of their free-spending Russian benefactor – their season will inevitably be labelled as a disaster. But not for Geremi for he was just twenty when newly arrived at Spanish giants Real Madrid when his mother died.

And just this summer, Chelsea's £7million man watched in horror as fellow Cameroon international Marc-Vivian Foe died during a Confederations Cup match in France. No wonder he has a dramatically different outlook to your average Premiership footballer.

And the African ace remembers how he was on an all-time high when tragedy struck for the first time.

He said that, "Going to Spain to sign for Real Madrid was one of the greatest moments of my life. But then my mum died soon afterwards and that was truly the worst moment of my life".

Geremi goes in to talk about his football boots, which he says he loves as much as his girlfriend and the advantage Chelsea have on all the rest of the league because of the ambitious spending of Abramovich. He said he was unhappy at Real Madrid because he was not playing on a regular basis and that is why he spent a season with Middlesbrough.

This story came a little too much for me and I can't help thinking that Rob was chuckling a little himself. It had now become Christmas Eve and I thought I might just add a couple of funnies used by the *Sun* chief writer Steven Howard. This was a column beginning with Ron Atkinson, who since stopping managing football teams has become a little bit of a bore on his commentaries of late, at a match with West Ham United at Anfield. The Hammers were getting stuffed three goals to nil when Ron Greenwood – one of the games deep thinkers – moved to the touchline and told his troops to 'apply the principles'. Paisley heard this and turned to the great Shanks saying, "We've had it now boss they, are going to apply the principles". This is an old Tommy Docherty gag that always goes down well at an After Dinner Function; "Doug Ellis called me into his office one morning and told me that the board had given me the vote of confidence". So I replied with "Thanks Chairman I'll pack my bags now". My favourite one which was not in Howard's list was again as manager of Queens Park Rangers for only a very short spell of something like forty odd days, he was called into the office of the then Chairman Jim Gregory to be told that "We are parting company Tommy, this does not seem to be working out" to which Tommy replied "Mr Chairman, I'll be sorry to see you go. I thought you were doing a very good job".

They were the best that Steven could do and I can't get a bloody job writing anywhere. But I must include a funny by Tommy Steele – a man I remember playing for the Chelsea Old Boys some years ago with my father Bill and uncle George – with his flashy blonde hair and huge vibrant grin. Anyhow, the story goes that many of his contemporaries would take drugs or become alcoholics but Tommy was never ever tempted. He's a Londoner from a loving southeast London family and now lives not far from where he grew up. He's sold the mansion he had in Petersham, near Richmond Park, Surrey, and bought a riverside penthouse in the famous block where Jeffrey Archer lives. "It's called Peninsula Heights and I've wanted to live there since 1968, when I was doing a film with Stanley Baker. Looking down the river seeing Bermondsey, where he lived as a child he said to Annie – his wife – that "it's taken me fifty years to move fifty yards, my mum would have been absolutely thrilled".

As Chelsea were to go into their Boxing Day fixture against Charlton Athletic Gary Neville was screaming that 'CHELSEA HAVE NOT GOT A SQUEAK' which was like taking a leaf out of his boss's mind games encyclopaedia. Bill Thornton of the *Star* said that; Title pretenders Chelsea have been warned about the pressures they must conquer if they are going to lift the big prize. Last season Alex Ferguson wound up rivals Arsenal by referring to the run-in as 'squeaky bum time'. A few weeks after he made such a remark the Gunners had cracked and United pulled off one of the great comebacks to claim the title. Now United's Gary Neville, who has played his part in all eight of the Reds' championship successes, has drawn cash soaked Chelsea's attention to the 'twitchy' days that lie ahead in the months to come!

And the vastly experienced defender said he cannot look any further than Arsenal as United's main challenger – because they have been there and done it so often. With more than a hint of the cunning of his manager, Neville said that "I'm not trying to threaten Chelsea or say they won't win it, but when March or April comes around the pressure starts to get you a little bit. I've won a few championships. I've been involved in United teams that have blown up, and ones that have held their nerve. You get to April and every match is televised. It gets twitchy believe me!

"We still get twitchy after eight titles. Everything you have been fighting for over the last ten or eleven months is coming to a head in three or four matches and you are watching other teams and praying they'll do you a favour and if they do it gives you a great buzz but if they don't it makes the next match as tough as ever."

If only we could get into the mind of the mind of the manager who is primed for every last intricate detail needed to pull the big one off. There is only one Alex Ferguson and his record cannot be knocked in any way whatso-ever, that is why he is so brash in his movements along that touchline in front of their adoring 67,000 fans at every home match. Old Trafford was my coming of age, although my second ever first team match was at a very packed White Hart Lane against none other than the great one himself, Jimmy Greaves!

I had been there many times on my father Bill's shoulders never dreaming that one Wednesday evening in August I would be sweating the sweat with Jimmy and then as the year turned and I was enjoying my stay in the first team, the time had come to travel to Old Trafford and Best, Law, Charlton and that great old war horse of a right half Paddy Crerand. The Stretford End was fully packed as this seemed like a storybook affair on the field with such illustrious names. That summer Ian Hutchinson and I were warming up for a season in the 'stiffs' then all of a sudden Hutch got into the first team and formed a quite remarkable partnership with Peter Osgood and I was assigned to play alongside Charlie Cooke and Johnny Hollins not long afterwards. It was at Old Trafford which was the most exciting as the sound of the buzzer in the home Dressing Room can be heard in the hall leading to the tunnel and you hear the Home Team dressing room swing open and the aroma of their very own liniment fills the air and the studs are heard as they enter the tunnel like a team that were just going to show us around the building beginning with the trophy cabinet. Their look was one of 'welcome to our playground, this won't take long'!

This match was on BBC Match of the Day and it saw us put in yet another cracking performance where once again both Ian Hutchinson and myself were pretty sure we were here to stay, for if you can take on and beat a team like this on their own 'toby' there is not much more you need to be 'primed'. It was at Old Trafford that I scored another disallowed goal when hitting a sweet half-volley past Alex Stepney from the edge of his bow, shooting inside the post leaving the Manchester United keeper flatfooted and pinned to his line. The referee gave an off-side position against Peter Houseman our left winger. In today's game it would have counted for he was so far away from where I shot he might as well have been in the Players' Bar. So in many ways the officials have not changed that much, and it is only the television that changes them as they believe the cameras are there to film them, such are their egos, acting more like policemen and parking wardens with each game.

Back then I was privileged to have been on the field with the great Jim Finney the most respected official, possibly, in the history of the English game. One of the outstanding things that I remember from this match was in the early stages Bobby Charlton picked up a loose ball and taking it a few strides let fly, hitting a right footed special which was in all the way. I was standing behind him as the ball seemed to be in and as the Stretford End were up in arms screaming 'goal'; the Cat came from nowhere to tip the ball past the far post, and I can still see Bobby holding his head in his hands with disbelief. You know the way Bobby used to celebrate a pile driver like that as he seemed to take off and once hitting the ball would kind of jump and end up in a crouching position, as was the way the strike had taken him, the ball given everything he had. A truly amazing save from the man nicknamed the Cat for his agility around his goalmouth, and us Chelsea Blues would not have swapped Peter Bonetti with any goalkeeper in the world, that was just how brilliant he was.

My half volley – right at the end – was struck from just outside the United box into Alex Stepney's right hand corner of the net and the funny thing was that we played them at the Bridge where I scored once again only for it to be disallowed. This time I ran along the left touchline – rather like the goal at Newcastle – that I told you earlier Pele. and all – and crept it inside the near post once again. But there will be Ipswich supporters who will say "What is he going on about, after the goal he claimed against us that hit the side netting and the ref signalled a goal". Which brings me onto our match against Ipswich when David Webb kept goal against them at the Bridge, after Peter Bonetti was injured and Tommy Hughes also, so an SOS was called out to a young man named Steve Sherwood – the son of the Olympic pairing of two great English track stars – but Steve did not get to the Bridge until a quarter to three and we were told by Dave Sexton who had seen the referee and had agreed that as long as he was there for the first whistle he could play. When he arrived I believe that Bobby Robson had changed his mind and after Webby had taken off the green jersey and thrown it to the youngster it was all systems go as the bell rang and our centre-half had to change back into the green of Bonetti. That was all we needed to be fired up and Webby was a hero as he kept a clean sheet but the lads did not need a team talk this particular day as Robson gave us a new kind of determination which saw us protect our goal superbly for David to boast a clean sheet. There is an amazing stat here for it was two Christmases before that our centre-half scored a hat-trick against them at Portman Road. There were 43,896 inside the Bridge to see David Webb make history on this day and they enjoyed Steve Kember and Chris Garland banging in the goals for us. On that day in 1971 Manchester United and their fiercest rivals City topped the table on level points of thirty-five from twenty-three matches, with Leeds in third followed by Sheffield United who got off to a flyer as newcomers, then Derby, Liverpool, Spurs, Arsenal, Wolves then us lingering in tenth place, nine points behind the leaders. Derby County won the Championship that season with Leeds United runners-up and Nottingham Forest and Huddersfield were relegated into the old second division. Also on the back pages was the record transfer of Alan Ball becoming the most expensive player in Great Britain joining Arsenal from Everton for £220,000. Also on the quiz page the answer to last week's question was Peter Osgood who became the last player to score in every round of the FA Cup including the Final against Leeds United with a fantastic flying header from a beautifully flighted ball in from Charlie Cooke which levelled the scores and gave us the impetus to go on and come back – after being behind three times – to beat the team everyone loved to hate.

'DEATH VALLEY'

I feel that although Alex Ferguson has done wonders at Old Trafford, Alan Curbishley has been the manager of the decade as to the way he has brought Charlton Athletic from obscurity to now sit amongst the elite in terms of football clubs and the power they have had over the years. Whilst you see the likes of Leeds United floundering, what Alan has done is nothing short of miraculous and the way he goes about his job; and if you look at what Chelsea have spent this last summer Curbishley has spent a mere £16million in eleven years as manager of this incredible football club. This was Chelsea's next stop on Operation Premiership. Chelsea were coming in after a win at Fulham but Charlton – on any given day – could upset the best of the rest and what I like about them is they win football matches by playing the game of football properly. They had Paolo di Canio in the side today, a player I drooled over at West Ham whilst Harry was in charge and a player they should have never have let go. With Manchester United beating Everton 3-2 and Arsenal beating

Wolves 3-0, Chelsea had to make this match one that they dare not lose but Charlton had ideas of their very own and hit the front in the first minute of a match that would become a frantic affair and one of those matches that, when Charlton put their game together, they really can rip the heart out of visitors coming to south London. This was the match before a home one against Portsmouth – who were torn to shreds with injuries – but they had to find a way back into this match as Charlton should have scored again just before Chelsea levelled through John Terry. So the match was set-up at one apiece with under ten minutes played. I'll run through the headlines before telling you about certain aspects of a very entertaining football match, if you were either a Charlton fan or – like me – a neutral.

The *Mirror* DI CANIO HELPS ADDICKS SPAN FOURTH BRIDGE plus WE BLUE IT and Arsenal and Chelsea win and Ranieri admits lose twice more and our title race is over.

The *Mail* said RANIERI FEARS FOR CHELSEA'S TITLE HOPES and DOUBLE TROUBLE as Holland and Parker show their worth as Roman's troops take a real beating whilst on the back page it simply said OH CLAUDIO. The *Sun* went SCOTTCHA Snubbed Parker takes his revenge on Ranieri, and that BUY BUY OR BYE BYE with Failings of old come back to haunt Ranieri and TWO BAD Fuming Ranieri warns his Blues they are close to blowing the title. The headlines in the *Express* told the best stories in that IT'S THUMBS DOWN TO THE ROMAN GLADIATORS as Di Canio and Pareker lead the way as Charlton's unsung heroes pile on the title agony for Chelsea's slack defence whilst Ranieri lays down the law to his faltering stars and finished up with CRISIS AT XMAS as Ranieri title blast for his fall guys.

The match itself told the real story, although some of the things that you are to read are silently deafening. They make a mockery of paying out such large sums of dough and Alan Curbishley's players at times toyed with Chelsea, no one any better than Di Canio at doing such a thing. I mentioned about myself being a neutral and that allows me to enjoy my football more than the wound-up, gut-twisting supporters who are so in love with their underachieving heroes. This is much like watching a big horse race without laying any cash down on the favourite who you could see would not win with still three fences to jump. I am a great admirer of the way Alan Curbishley goes about his work for all his signings are technically good players who work so terribly hard to get anything out of a football match. When I was gambling – stopped nine months ago now – I would never bet against his team. They are likely to make a fool out of even the shrewdest of judges and one match in particular springs to mind a couple of seasons ago – over Christmas again – by going to Highbury and winning 5-2, a result that shocked a lot of people but not me, for I fancy them to score at any given time. They play great stuff and they play it direct, going at the heart of defences and if they don't get any joy there they have players who can pull out wide and go another route. The route in this match made – for once – John Terry look very ordinary as he was pulled all over the place. The magic of the Italian was there for Charlton's biggest ever crowd in the Premiership to see. Once, when getting to the byline he turned and twisted Terry and about four thousand others behind that particular goal. I have witnessed this many times at Upton Park and – although bias – I must give my mate Harry Redknapp all the credit for taking a player who had been brutally treated for pushing over a docile referee against Arsenal whilst playing for Sheffield Wednesday. It was one of those that he should have saved for Christmas because it would have gone down great in either, 'What happens next' or 'The Bloopers of 2001'. I laughed so hard I lost touch with all that was wrong about a situation where the Italian let his feelings known without one trace of good sense. He wears his heart on his sleeve and sometimes his sleeve gets caught up a little in the heat of a real Premiership battle. Punters at Upton Park have seen him score majestic goals against Arsenal and Manchester United over the years and sang his name so loud they could be heard way back in Whitechapel.

The Tinkerman looked lost and lonely on the Valley touchline and if I had some of the Chelsea billionaire's fortunes I would have paid any asking price for what was tinkering about in that extremely imaginative mind of his. As for Chelsea let's read what Matt Lawton wrote; Blame Roman Abramovich. He was the one who paid off Chelsea's debts, gave Claudio Ranieri £111million to spend on new players and so persuaded the Italian to change his plans. At one stage last summer Chelsea's manager had an option on Scott Parker. He bought Juan Sebastian Veron instead.

In front of Charlton's largest crowd in the eleven years back at The Valley – 26, 768 – that decision proved costly. But so did Ranieri's failure to identify a bargain when Ipswich let Matt Holland leave for next to nothing. Ranieri signed Claude Makelele.

Charlton partnered Holland with Parker and, during this enthralling encounter Chelsea paid the price.

The Charlton pair were magnificent, driving their team forward from midfileld with the kind of industry and invention one would normally associate with the Premiership's leading trio. Paolo Di Canio, who followed Holland here on a free transfer, added the finishing touches. Wonderful!

Alan Curbishley said that most Chairmen would choke on their cornflakes if he told them how much he has spent on his team in thirteen years as manager – a net £18million – and while Abramovich is more likely to breakfast on Russian caviar, yesterday's experience must have been unpleasant. A club who splashed out just £750,000 last summer made fools of his highly paid superstars, scoring after 44 seconds before beating Carlo Cudicini on a further three occasions. It may be two years since Chelsea last conceded four goals in the Premiership, but defeats are becoming a touch more frequent. This was their second in the Premiership in three games after losing at home to Bolton, their third in four competitions. Ranieri attempted to dismiss a run that puts a chink of daylight between Chelsea and their two main rivals in the championship race as nothing more than a blip, but both his body language and his actions suggested otherwise. Replacing Joe Cole with William Gallas with eight minutes left and Charlton still sitting on a two-goal advantage was extraordinary, even when his back four appeared capable of conceding another four before the final whistle. Defensively Chelsea were awful, Marcel Desailly looking every second of his 35 years along with a strangely hesitant John Terry. For a player who has impressed for much of this season, this was not a good day for Sven Goran Eriksson's assistant Tord Grip to be watching.

Chelsea had no answers to the free flowing play that Charlton play and when things go their way, at home or away they are a very entertaining side, and that is why I am a big fan of their brilliant manager!

All in all if the Blues are going to win any silverware they must stand up to performances, such as these?

On the eve of Arsenal's match against Boro – Chelsea and United play tomorrow – the *Evening Standard* and Ken Dyer wrote that it has been:

A BLUE CHRISTMAS
The excuses are difficult to find for Ranieri's Chelsea form
comes down with the festive lights yet again

What is it with Chelsea and Christmas time?

We've just emerged from what Andy Williams assures us with perfect pitch is 'the most wonderful time of the year', but try telling that to Chelsea fans.

While everyone else is wondering where all their money went, anxious Blues fans are asking similar questions about lost points. Something seems to happen to Chelsea at the turn of the year and Claudio Ranieri will be wanting to know why!

Since the 13th of December, when they lost 2-1 at home to Bolton, Chelsea have now played six matches and won just two, 1-0 at Fulham through that smashing Crespo header and a 3-0 win against Portsmouth with goals from Bridge – just to annoy the South Coast supporters with his first goal for the club, then one each from Frank Lampard, hitting a beauty after a blind side run through Pompey's wide open defence, then a goal from Geremi that I doubt he will ever score one like again. The game was in the bag as the ball swung into the path of Geremi who brought it down on his chest and hit a blinding volley from a full thirty yards and that glossed over all of the uncertainty of their earlier rather raggedy play. I was in the West Stand to keep an eye on my mate Harry's team and to tell you the truth, until Bridge scored Portsmouth should have been in front when Yakubu went through like taking a walk in the park and incredibly rolled the ball into the most welcome hands of Neil Sullivan. If Harry can get this Nigerian to finish as easy as he turns defenders and creates his own chances, my mate will have no trouble staying amongst the Premiership runners next season, but that is a 'big' if. Last season, it was uncannily similar and in seven matches Chelsea played before, during and directly after the festive season, they again only managed just two triumphs, a 2-0 win against Aston Villa in the Premiership and a 1-0 home win against Boro in the third round of the FA Cup.

Chelsea 3 Bridge, Lampard and Geremi Portsmouth 0: 41,552

Whilst on the FA Cup, Chelsea had a tricky tie first at Watford who are managed by former Chelsea midfielder, the very popular Ray Lewington, who came into the team when my great friend and team mate Eddie McCreadie took over once Sexton was booted out just as he did to Osgood and myself. And Chelsea supporters wonder why they haven't won the championship for so very long!

I certainly don't have that problem with that kind of running of this Football Club.

Anyhow Watford gave Chelsea a mighty scare having them on the ropes more than once and their aerial threat was one that nearly pulled off the shock of the round. But Chelsea hung in there and clawed a draw with goals from Frank Lampard once again and an Eidur Gudjohnsen penalty. This was a good result for the Blues for the pitch was one you Londoners would know about if ever playing at Wormwood Scrubs or Hackney Marshes back in the old days. But it was a Frank Lampard led revival – once again – and young Frank was becoming more and more important as the season goes on with his all-action approach, his newly found passing ability and his wonderful percentage of shots on opponents' goal, and believe me this ex-West Ham youngster really does carry a powerful punch with both feet, something else he has worked on. For whilst watching him at the Hammers he was very much a right-sided striker, as Paolo di Canio would build the play up on the left Frank would arrive late on the scene and get more than many of his contempories in that position.

FA Cup 3rd Round Watford 2 Chelsea 2 Lampard and Gudjohnsen penalty: 4,584

Chelsea failed to fully recover from their mid-season malaise 12 months ago and it is the Tinkerman's task to make sure the same thing doesn't happen again this season.

The rumours of the Italian's imminent demise however are certainly premature. For a seemingly condemned man, the Chelsea coach has devoured many a hearty breakfast over the last few months and he will surely be given the rest of the season before being judged. Chelsea's frailty may seem temporary but Ranieri is enough of a realist to know that, if his side should lose at Leicester, the pressure on him will inevitably increase. Ranieri says he is not worried and there are a few billion reasons why he is still smiling.

Money doesn't always bring happiness and the man who has £50million isn't necessary happier than the one who has £48million.

The resources with Roman Abramovich as put at the Tinkerman's disposal so far, however, bring with it a much more acceptable kind of misery and Wednesday's 1-0 home defeat by Liverpool is likely to have Chelsea's Russian owner reaching for the roubles again.

Whether they go out now and spend another £10million or £100million on new players will not solve the conundrum of Chelsea's Christmas crack-up and until Ranieri finds an adequate answer, he will be looking forward to this fun-filled time of the year as much as the turkeys.

Some significant factors have contributed to Chelsea's difficulties at the mid-point in the season. The opposition, for example, seem to have worked out a system, which the London club seem to find great difficulty in combating. They came, as Liverpool did on Wednesday night, strung five across midfield and played one striker up front on his own. In addition, Liverpool's wide midfield players El-Hadji Diouf and Harry Kewell, operated high up the field and worked hard at preventing Chelsea left-back Wayne Bridge, and to a lesser extent right-back Glen Johnson from foraging forward to support their attack.

The Chelsea players have taken part in a lot of games recently but to put forward tiredness as a reason for their anaemic displays is an inadequate excuse.

Ranieri loves to rotate his squad at every opportunity and fit, young athletes should not be tired just halfway through the season.

The Chelsea coach is more concerned, I believe, about his players' mental approach.

The last couple of weeks, it seems, has eroded the teams' confidence, particularly players such as the otherwise excellent Adrian Mutu, who it appears just can't buy a goal at the moment. Ranieri needs to get the former darling of Stamford Bridge, Jimmy Floyd, involved in the action again.

The Dutchman remains the club's top scorer with ten goals but has, somewhat strangely, not figured in the last three matches, and was left out of the squad altogether against Liverpool.

At the back, Ranieri has also had several problems. Goalkeeper Neil Sullivan failed to impress when he deputised for Carlo Cudicini against Watford in the FA Cup while the once outstanding central defender Marcel Desailly is beginning to look as though he might need WD40 for his three-match rub.

The one absolute necessity is that midfielder Damien Duff is back in the team as soon as his mended shoulder will allow him to return.

Raneri has tended to use Duff a little more sparingly than the Irishman himself was happy with earlier in the season but on evidence of the last few matches Chelsea have badly missed the impish inventiveness that he brings to the team. It would also be a boon for the Chelsea coach if he had the option of playing Juan Sebastian Veron.

The Argentine midfield player has had his detractors since he first arrived at Manchester United but he was beginning to pull the strings for Chelsea before his back gave out at the beginning of November.

Abramovich is said not to be over-chuffed by his team's recent results and that is no surprise considering the size of his investment.

Chelsea 0 Liverpool 1 Cheyrou: 41,420

With Chelsea's next five Premiership matches against Leicester City – today live on SKY-pay per-view-at 2pm – Birmingham, Blackburn, Charlton and Portsmouth, however, the urban Russian could be considering that modern day prayer 'Dear God. I pray for patience, and I want it now!'

Leicester City have skipper Matt Elliott back after suspension and Frank Sinclair has finally recovered from an Achilles injury.

RESULT OF THE WEEK

I said earlier that I am a neutral football lover. I am not one to see a team – your own – win at all costs, although in today's climate its pretty much just that. The result I followed with most interest was going on at Fratton Park whilst sitting in our club – The Grosvenor – I had one eye fixed firmly on the Premiership update.

This was a six-pointer – if ever there was one – Portsmouth and Manchester City were playing it, although there will be plenty more of these matches from now until May

I thought when first seeing Robbie Fowler that he would become the best English goal getter since Jimmy Greaves but time and again his troubles seemed to pile up. I don't want to go into his personal life so I will just leave it as one of the great escapes. There are so many kids who would have dreamed to have such ability but Robbie has abused it and rarely used it. What he does not understand is it is players with his talent that pull the fans through the turnstiles. Anyhow, yesterday – I am so happy to say – was not his day as he struck the woodwork twice with marvellous efforts and had another one miss the net by one of Ken Bates' whiskers, and as it turned out this day finished grey also, for all connected with Manchester City.

I said earlier that Harry must save his big guns for home matches and try to strangle sides away from Fratton Park, just as they did beating Leeds United 6-1 and Tottenham 2-0 in recent home games. He said afterwards that, "outside of the top three there is nothing between the rest of us". Harry knows that – whilst bringing in Eyal Berkovich from Manchester City – that he has the proven talent to steer clear of basement trap door.

He now has the quality in Teddy, Patric Berger and the little Israel playmaker Berkovic. I have no doubt that these three players can do enough damage on their home ground to ensure their safety. What with Leeds losing at home to Spurs yesterday you can see how important winning home matches is. My 'fling' with Charlton remains – I just love watching them – although this win against the unlucky Dave Jones and his Wolverhampton Wanderers. Everton slipped into the battle zone once again by losing at Fulham whilst Southampton – who will lose manager Gordon Strachan – at the end of the season – seem to be falling apart. Bolton had a great win at Blackburn after trailing 3-1 with the 'Dynamic Duo' of Dwight Yorke and Andy Cole scoring goals only to see there defence run ragged by Bolton's 'Do or die' battlers. So the heat is on Chelsea after Arsenal thrashed Boro by four goals at Highbury, the first time they have 'buried' a team in front of their home fans. Thierry Henry was once again the 'jewel' amongst Arsene Wenger's crown!

My seat in Sloane Square – along with George and his son Anthony Mason – is reserved and I am looking forward to a match that not many of these Chelsea players have played in before, and if they think the Champions League is tough they have another 'thought' coming. Micky Adams' sides know only one way to play and that is to 'go for the opposition from the first whistle, don't let them settle, close them down from the very minute and when attacking get it wide and lets just see how the two lads at the back like it'. Adams will no doubt have looked at the tapes of Chelsea's failings at both Charlton and Watford in the last fortnight and he would have been stressing that they can capitalise in dead ball situations, and their provider of those dead ball situations will be ex-Chelsea midfielder Muzzy Izzet. I spoke to the Turkish international in the week and – he loves playing against Chelsea – told me that his team are revved up and ready to give as good as they get today.

Before we go into the match, I would like you to read a very good article by Karren Brady – the 'first lady' in our game – who runs Birmingham City for ex-porn king David Sullivan and whoses husband Paul Peschisolido scored a hat-trick yesterday for Sheffield United in a terrific 3-0 win over Gillingham in the first division. Pesch is a Canadian lad who – it seems – has had more clubs than Tiger Woods – is a very decent player who has not quite reached the heights I once thought he would. Let's not forget this was the Gillingham side that knocked Charlton out of the FA Cup, one of my fancied teams in this year's competition. What do I know?

I have met her once when visiting St Andrews; at the time my son worked there and found her a lovely young lady and 'yeah' she is actually more attractive and sexier than any photographs you have seen of her in the media. In fact very, very tasty!

Anyhow her story is worth adding to the Tinker and Talisman, here goes with the headline THE BRADY PUNCH: There is a strong case for saying that January last year was the most crucial in the past fifty years of Birmingham City's existence.

All right, so that claim won't echo too loudly around the football world. My club haven't in cricket terms troubled the scorers too often.

But even if they had, January 2003 was such a pivotal time for us that I will stand by my assessment of its impact for the future.

The transfer window opened and we grabbed goodies with all the eagerness of Iraqi looters. Except we had to pay for our spoils!

I take off my hat to Steve Bruce for his guile in buying four players who, in my view, were essential to the club's survival. With clinicalness, he extracted each at keen prices and all four of them – Jamie Clapham, Stephen Clemence, Christophe Dugarry and Matthew Upson—remain first team regulars this season. And they are a fair part of the reason why we feel we may not have to be so busy in the transfer market this month. Other clubs will be mulling over major moves. Now Sir Alex Ferguson would like to snare a strike partner for Ruud Van Nistelrooy.

And with the probable absence of Rio Ferdinand until next season a centre-back of Upson's calibre may also be on the Old Trafford shopping list. And, no, they can't have him.

Manchester United may well be the club to take the title of big spenders we won last January. But while the current window is ajar, no one would be surprised to see Roman Abramovich throw it wide open with another money-no-object signing or two for Chelsea.

Red Rom is not the only person looking for bargains in January.

It is exciting that the oil-baron has used his experience from governing Chukotka (total spending £112million). Let's hope he is more successful in West London since the province went bankrupt.

Chelsea are in a position to trump any club financially but no one will underestimate the attraction of United to the world's best players.

West Ham's Jermain Defoe could eventually figure in that bracket—if only he would make up his mind not to be among the world's silliest.

DIAMONDS

Both Chelsea and Arsenal are said to want Defoe, although unearthing the truth in such matters is harder than solving the Big Bang mystery!?

If Chelsea are a rich, rogue element, it must also be said that they go for the obvious targets. When you buy diamonds, you know what you are getting. Buy an unsigned painting and it could be the inferior artist's work or a masterpiece!

No one doubted the ability of Hernan Crespo, Claude Makelele, Adrian Mutu and Damien Duff. And you don't need an FA coaching badge to make a judgement on the quality of Thierry Henry. Chelsea have offered £50million for Henry and Arsenal laughed it off. Abramovich would have to part with the price of Gunners' planned Ashburton Grove Stadium plus a bit more to get Henry.

While there are big buyers, there will always be a big seller.

Leeds must be leading candidates, although they would perhaps see the departure of Mark Viduka to Old Trafford as less of a blunder than letting Eric Cantona go.

Viduka is reported to be earning £65,000 a week at Elland Road. Henry gets less than £50,000 at Highbury. It's a crazy business!

Henry and van Nistelrooy will stay where they are. And we would surely say the same of Michael Owen at Liverpool. No questions – the club want to keep the England striker.

QUEST

But, with eighteen months of his contract still left and a new contract unsigned, Owen has few strings attached to a move bar loyalty. It is no coincidence most interest centres on the strikers.

Boro and Newcastle are not alone in their quest for more firepower. Indeed, you could add my club's name on that list. I know how successful my proposal for loan deals to be permitted among Premiership clubs has been. We borrowed Mikael Forssell from Chelsea and his fourteen goals account for half of our total this season. And, no, you can't have Forssell either!

Halfway through this season only a handful of points separate a dozen clubs in the Premiership. Many fans are dreaming of flights to Europe next season – and many more are having nightmares of late-night coach trips, to places such as Crewe and Rotherham.

Wolves, I am afraid, need more of a miracle than money to save them. But no doubt they will be scouring the most unlikely places for a saviour from Burundi or Lesotho. Don't knock it, we would all take a risk – but Wolves may have to take more than one.

Portsmouth and Leeds also have problems up front. But Leicester, Spurs and Blackburn can take comfort from their goals-for column. Defenders cost less.

It is a stark warning to those First Division clubs chasing promotion that the three who came up at the start of this season could all be going straight back down in May.

I still believe that the newcomers are unfairly penalised by the transfer window, a system that otherwise has benefited longer-planning in football and to some extent curbed the excesses of agents.

Among the lower teams, there is a great shuffling of schemes to acquire new blood by a mixture of Bosman, ingenious loans, slick deals and even the occasional purchase.

Previous homework is essential. Otherwise it is more sensible to stick to West Bromwich Albion's game plan of last season – live to fight another day rather than risk financial ruin. That is why every chairman should hang a sign above his shaving mirror warning 'beware of panic buying'.

A chairman who is persuaded in January a certain player is essential to his side's chances of success can easily learn by March that he was another club's unwanted cast-off.

Out of work actors claim to be resting between engagements. The cynical among us have re-written that to suit transfer-seeking players as those who have 'fallen out with the manager'.

And, yes, anyone can have him. At a price!

Signed Karren Brady.

I think that the world now is a woman's one. They are commentating on the game of football in numbers and I cannot say that is good or bad because there are so many 'berks' making a good living on television these days. If I see

Ray Wilkins on the television I turn it over and that goes for Andy Gray, Ron Atkinson, Rodney Marsh and several others. The best on television is – without any doubt – Martin Tyler, for he is sensible and knows about the game and does not go over the top like so many ex-pro's who think they are in Hollywood. I played in a testimonial against Tyler once at Wimbledon and you can tell if one has any idea or not!

He has and he delivers better than anyone on television, though, doing a different job Des Lynam is also the business.

Karren Brady has earned the right to be on the front pages of football magazines and newspapers. She is bright and intelligent otherwise she would not have been in her job for so long.

She represents Birmingham Football Club with style and grace and does not allow her position to stand out in public, something I like in a woman. But I made two blunders marrying quite the opposite, and that does not work if you are looking for a happy ending.

Back to the game and the big match at the Walkers Stadium where Chelsea must hang in there, if they are to be taken seriously. It will be interesting to see just how Chelsea go into this match after a dreadful Christmas and also how Leicester will approach such a match knowing that they are desperately in need of points.

The headlines on Monday were more favourable than the last week's with the *Mail* saying that CHELSEA ARE RIGHT BACK IN TITLE TRACE on the back page and inside simply said PERFECT REPLY and CHELSEA END DOUBTS WITH TIP-TOP SHOW FOR RANIERI. The *Express* back page read that JIMMY'S HOT AGAIN whilst inside CHELSEA STRUT AGAIN. The *Mirror* splashed out that EVERY CLAUDIO HAS A SILVER LINING and that CHELSEA'S BLUES ARE OVER AS HASSEL-BAINK BOUNCES BACK. The *Sun* had a double page splash with my favourite POSITIVE TINKING and CLAUDIO CONJURES UP A WINNER FOR BLUES WITH OLD GUARD RECALL.

What a turn around as Manchester United drop two valuable points against the rapidly improving Newcastle United who took the game to the champions from the first whistle and went on to show that that fourth spot is not out of reach. One thing has not changed and that is the pathetic refereeing of Paul Durkin, the man who was involved in the Paolo Di Canio trouble at Hillsborough, when the Italian was playing for Sheffield Wednesday against Arsenal. He pushed the Premiership's worst referee to the ground in an incident that involved Patrick Vieira and Nigel Winterburn. In the first minute of this match Alan Shearer was brought down by American goalkeeper Tim Howard but the man in green waved play on – which saw the ex-England captain chase him half the field in disgust. Just as well Shearer never put a hand on him because we all know what terrible balance the man has!

In the second half he disallowed a perfect goal scored by Silvestre, the Manchester United centre-back. The scores remained scoreless and the

Magpies got a well deserved point, leaving United just five points ahead of the Blues and just one in front of the Gunners. Both Chelsea and Arsenal did their cause one hell of a good one by both blasting four-goal warnings to Ferguson's team. Leicester City sadly missed Muzzy Izzet and failed to come out of the traps quickly enough, making every word I wrote earlier seem a load of trash. Leicester boss Micky Adams must have been absolutely sick watching his team go all afternoon a poor second best all over the Walkers Stadium pitch. Steve Curry of the *Express* began his piece with CRISIS WHAT CRISIS?

If Leicester had not been so pathetic this would have been a five-star performance from the Blues. It seemed at times that Chelsea had fifteen players against the blue-shirted Foxes. I can make just one prediction after this performance and that is the Leicester will be relegated come next May and that Chelsea had better forget their performance otherwise they'll be giving themselves false hope of catching Manchester United and Arsenal, who had Thierry Henry in spectacular form at Highbury the previous day. The Tinkerman showed the Talisman that he could rejuvenate his tinkers as Jimmy Floyd and Adrian Mutu took a lot of pressure off the Italian by notching the first two goals before the interval. Gudjohnsen looked a class act and his partner Jimmy Floyd the 'bull at the gate' performer and the man who broke the deadlock with a simple flick of his heel into Ian Walker's near post. As Curry said the first goal was inevitable as Melchiot put the ball through to Cole, whose cross was slightly deflected and Jimmy Floyd finished quite nonchalantly.

The second came a minute before the break when Jimmy Floyd hit a free kick that deflected wickedly off Nikos Dabizas leaving Ian Walker wrong-footed for goal number two. Jimmy Floyd – who was given the second goal – should have made it three when he found himself in the clear with only Walker to beat – and Gudjohnsen in a better position – but failed to go past the keeper. That should have been his hat-trick and opened up the match to be the avalanche Chelsea needed as they were falling behind with their failure to put goal chances away recently. Mutu came on as sub and delivered Chelsea's third goal with a sweet strike after a neat one-two with Babayaro, who himself hit the fourth with little fuss from the home team.

This was Mutu's first goal in fourteen matches and the full-back's first of the season. Chelsea will find Watford a different proposition – that is if Lewington's players did not read too much into this footballing massacre, for had this been a boxing match it would have been stopped before the interval.

I am not really giving Chelsea's performance enough credit because of the utter gutless and spineless performance their opponents put in, but I will change that by saying that their passing game and movement was as good as anything seen by their two Premiership rivals this season. And let's not forget that Arsenal dropped a very valuable point at the Walker Stadium earlier in the season, although Leicester did have a much stronger team on the field that evening, and of course their commander-in-chief Muzzy Izzet was there to put some fire into their play, And at the back no Matt Elliott, a player I rate as one of the best in Europe over the last five years or so? The Tinkerman remained unmoved by this display saying that, "When things are going wrong I prefer to take the responsibility. I don't want pressure on my new squad. It is like with children, put them under pressure and they won't grow up with confidence" said the Italian. Adding "I prefer it when people are against me because I'm older and have seen all of this before. It was important today to check out how my players reacted to a bad period – and they answered very well. They gave me the maximum", carrying on that, "We are like a family. When everything is right we all enjoy it. It is good to see how the family react when things are going wrong. The right family link up with each other well. I wanted to check this and I was very pleased with the outcome".

Leicester City 0 Chelsea 4 Jimmy Floyd, Mutu and Babayaro

The Tinkerman has his very own way of putting himself across and it is quite refreshing from the sometimes, devious minds of the two head bosses in the Premiership.

Claudio is somewhat crackers and gives out the vibes that he is so very sincere.

So that cannot be wrong in a game where there are so few laughs in this generation of high finance businessman running their football clubs. The next step looks like more trouble for the Manchester United boss as the authorities are looking into the move of Tim Howard from the United States of America. A statement from *Sportsmail* read like this: Manchester United will demand an explanation from Alex Ferguson after it was alleged that the signing of Tim Howard last summer ended with a six-figure sum being paid to a business partner of the Old Trafford's manager's son, Jason.

Sportsmail said they can reveal the following: That chairman of the plc Roy Gardner was urgently seeking a meeting with Ferguson after yesterday's goalless draw with Newcastle United at Old Trafford. He wants to discuss reports Mike Morris received £139,000 for 'commission concerning signing of player Tim Howard with Manchester United'.

This comes at a time that Ferguson is still awaiting the court hearing regarding his ownership rights of that brilliant Aiden O'Brien horse Rock of Gibraltar, with John Magnier. As far as United officials are concerned they paid FIFA registered Swiss agent Gaetano Marotta for brokering Tim Howard's £2.3million transfer from New York Metrostars to the English champions.

But it now appears that Marotta was then involved with Morris, who owns the Monaco-based World Football Agency but also had close links with Jason Ferguson and Elite sports Group Limited, the Manchester United-based agency of which Sir Alex's son Jason is a director.

A United insider said that, "If this story is true, then it is even more serious than it was before. It means they have gone to extraordinary lengths to disguise the fact that that either Jason or his business associates are involved".

David Davies, the FA's executive director, said "That various documents are now in our possession. They will be studied very carefully and any breach of the rules and regulations that they show will then be discussed as a matter of urgency."

Another source said that: the agents involved may have been paid by both the buying and selling club, while the methods that were used to gain Howard a work permit are also now raising questions.

Apparently, Howard's lack of international appearances for the United States meant that he had to call on the nationality of a relative, thought to be Hungarian.

A Manchester United issued statement said that, All our transfer deals are approved by the board of Manchester United plc and are conducted in accordance with the FIFA and FA rules. Details of all payments involved in those deals are sent to the football authorities as required under the regulations.

Well I say, with all the fuss about Roman Abramovich and his background being checked it looks like we are in for some real interesting issues on our own doorstep.

The Manchester United boss is becoming rather a little like JR Ewing from Dallas for his financial situation is always being banded about and he has to sign a new contract yet and that may now be put on ice.

TERRIFYING

The *Evening Standard* on Monday had two pieces about Chelsea players with one on the front page about Juan Sebastian Veron with the headline CHELSEA STAR IN RAID TERROR with Veron and family attacked at home by machete intruder; Chelsea star Juan Sebastian Veron and his girlfriend were threatened by a man with a machete who burst into their bedroom.

The couple woke to find the man standing over them at their home in Barnes, it was revealed this afternoon.

As the intruder stood there one of the couple's two young children wandered into the room.

The man demanded jewellery and cash and is believed to have threatened to harm the children if the 28-year-old player and his girlfriend Maria Vinaccia did not co-operate.

They handed over £360,000 worth of gems before the couple and two other women in the house were pushed at knifepoint into a bathroom and ordered to stay there. The family waited until they heard a vehicle driving away before raising the alarm yesterday morning.

Scotland Yard said that the man got into the house through a bedroom window at about 7.30am. Eight people were staying in the house at the time.

One police source said; "This was clearly a frightening experience. Threats were made against the children".

When Veron signed for Chelsea from Manchester United for £15million last August he was hailed by manager Claudio Ranieri as the best midfielder in the world.

The £80,000-a-week player was one of the owner Roman Abramovich's first purchases.

The raid comes only days after a court heard details of how Chelsea millionaire vice-president Joe Hemani and his teenage daughter were attacked during a terrifying raid on their home.

Mr Hemani was beaten with crowbars and 13-year-old Francesca was thrown to the ground when a gang burst into the family's £3million home in Wargrave, Berkshire.

A 35-year-old man appeared in court this morning charged with aggravated burglary.

Veron, while playing for Lazio in Rome, was one of twenty players caught up in a scandal in which bogus passports helped Italian clubs to register footballers from South America as Europeans to beat a ban on non-EU players.

LAMPARD 'WE CAN STILL BE CHAMPIONS'

At the other end of the newspaper it was Frank Lampard again shouting of Chelsea still being good enough to peg both Manchester United and Arsenal back in the hotly disputed championship race after the champions dropped two points at home to Newcastle United yesterday. He said that, "The title race is far from over. There is a long way to go and we've had our slip-up over the past few weeks. United and Arsenal have been picking up maximum points so it was important for us to get back on track and get our confidence back.

"We haven't been as good as we could be in the last month but yesterday we were back to our best. We felt under pressure buts it's mainly brought on by ourselves. It was a test of character because a lot of people were giving us stick, but we have bounced back. There was a lot of determination before the game to put our performances right and we showed what we are all about from the first minute. Everyone's been working hard and we were always going to win the game".

Jimmy Floyd took over saying that, "I was fired up to score but we were all up for it. We had a point to prove and had to show what Chelsea are all about. I'm pleased to be scoring again and had enough chances to have had a hat-trick but it wasn't to be.

"We need to build on this win and have to believe in ourselves. We have to believe we can win every game and that is all we can do. We still have to play all the other teams so we have a chance".

I thought by now that the Tinkerman would have his players say nothing after this terrible spell, especially as it is over now and they should learn from all that was said after beating the champions at home some weeks ago. There was one thing for certain this morning and that was that Chelsea would not be bringing Edgar Davids to Stamford Bridge as he signed for Barcelona yesterday and will make his debut next weekend

COX OUT TO HAND CHELSEA BLUES

Neil Cox bounced back from suspension to help Watford claim a vital point – then promised FA Cup misery for Chelsea. The hornets take on Claudio Ranieri's millionaires at Stamford Bridge on Wednesday in the crucial third-round replay.

Cox – who missed the first clash – warned "All the pressure is on Chelsea, not us. Pressure for us is making sure we avoid relegation. But we still go to the Bridge believing we can win. We were unlucky in the original tie".

Ray Lewington said about Wednesday's match that, "I gave my lot a bit of a rollicking, because they seemed to have their minds on Wednesday's replay during the opening forty-five minutes. I suppose that's understandable to some degree, but our fixtures against Coventry and then at home to Crystal Palace next Saturday are far more important than the FA Cup. We will bank around £700.000 from the televised games and that is a great bonus for the club. But we must not confuse it with the damage that losing First Division status would inflict".

It was interesting listening to Leicester boss Micky Adams on the television after Sunday's match, for he said although he had players missing the ones who came in had Premiership experience but so many of them played poorly'.

I cannot remember the last time I saw a Premiership match won so easily, although Arsenal are the masters of playing away from home and their recent four goal demolition job at Leeds was a good example. Within the next month we will see quite a few changes and with the Carling Cup semi-finals and Champions League due in about five weeks it will be all systems go for the top three as they test their players' ability to stand the pace by playing three matches a week from there on in.

As for important matches, the next one is always the most important whatever it may be. Winning is a great habit although Arsenal have the habit of not being beaten yet are still in second spot.

CHELSEA SWOOP FOR SAHA

Ken Dyer of the *Standard* reports on the day of the Watford match that Chelsea have made a late swoop for Fulham striker Louis Saha. The star of Loftus Road at the moment is linked with Manchester United – who offered £8million – but Fulham have turned that offer down. However Chelsea yesterday put a late bid in to halt that deal.

They threw the whole thing wide open. Saha has made it clear he wants the stage of the Theatre of Dreams and to team-up with van Nistelrooy. United identified – Dyer's words – Saha as their number one window target but balked at Fulham's asking price of £12million. Saha has scored thirteen Premiership goals this season, but has been unsettled since United's interest was made public. Fulham manager is reluctant to sell his star front man and the only consolation would be him getting a chunk of that fee to strengthen his squad. Having said that if you sell your main source of goal power how can you be strengthening your squad?

Chelsea are also looking for a goalkeeper and a central defender before the window closes, but the Tinkerman's side has struggled to score goals at times this season and the Italian sees Saha as a prize capture.

What amazes me is that how Chelsea have waited until Ferguson made it public that he admires Saha and would see him as a great back-up and partner for his Dutch superstar. If Chelsea pulled off the coup, it would take their spending on just four forwards – since the summer – to £60million. It would also be a blow to United, not just because Saha was their main transfer-window target but, following the defection of their former chief executive Peter Kenyon to Chelsea, it would prove again the Blues' purchasing power under Roman Abramovich.

Over the other side of London lies the biggest mystery in football at the moment with David James leaving West Ham to replace David Seaman at Manchester City, proving once again that Kevin Keegan is not the full ticket. If 'Calamity' is the best goalkeeper in our country we are in dire straights. It was revealed that West Ham were offered Seaman in a swap deal for James before the big Yorkshireman damaged his shoulder against Portsmouth last weekend. Terry Brown – the West Ham United chairman – and his directors believe that the deal made sound financial sense.

But then again, he thought that letting Harry Redknapp leave was also a sound business deal – and they got relegated the very next season, whilst Harry passed them on the way up with his Portsmouth team. Keegan is thought to have paid a million and a half pounds for James who is thirty-four next birthday. In most cases goalkeepers get better with age but that is not the case with both Seaman and James. As I just pointed out, James was in the West Ham United goal in their relegation season so I can't see how he is any help to the ex-England manager. For instance if Gordon Banks had not have had that terrible car accident – where he lost an eye – I would have had a championship medal in 1975 – with Stoke City – and he would have gone on playing for another decade perhaps.

I say this because Banks was a great athlete and was – unlike Shilton, James and Seaman – not musclebound. He was a great reader of situations and it was not a coincidence that he made that incredible save from Pele in that famous 1970 World Cup match in Mexico. It was also no coincidence that was possibly Bobby Moore's best ever performance in both an England and West Ham shirt.

Along with Alan Ball they were the real last world-class internationals.

CHELSKI HUNT FOR TREZ

Was the headline in the *Star* with David Woods writing that; Chelsea are lining up a £25million bid for Juventus ace David Trezeguet.

Stamford Bridge representatives were in Turin last night for talks with the Italian giants over a deal for the French hit-man.

Trezeguet, 26, has scored twenty-two goals in forty-three appearances for France and this season boasts ten in nine Champions League matches.

Despite a £111million spending spree, Chelsea boss Claudio Ranieri is desperate to land a proven goalscorer.

He has already been knocked back in a £50million bid for Arsenal's Thierry Henry and is now turning to his international team-mate.

Juventus might want to hang on to the player whilst still in the Champions League. In any event, he wouldn't be eligible for Chelsea in the later stages of the competition.

Owner Roman Abramovich is determined to put the Blues back on track for glory and that means splashing out even more cash.

The Stamford Bridge outfit are already on collision course with Charlton over midfielder Scott Parker.

Chelsea have offered just £6million for the England midfield player, who is valued at £18million by Charlton boss Alan Curbishley.

Parker has already learned his wages would rise three times to around £45,000 a week. And Charlton fear agents will continue to target Parker, and the bid could blow up into a Saha-style saga.

French striker Saha is the main target for Manchester United and has attacked his club Fulham for not selling him.

A Charlton source admitted that, 'There's plenty that Chelsea can say to Scott to tempt him. But we see Scott as being as important and influential to us as Damien Duff was to Blackburn. They sold him to Chelsea and looks what has happened since'.

Chelsea expect to wrap up a £5million deal toady for Czech international goalkeeper Petr Cech.

In the Sun it was said that, 'The FA have blocked non-league Scarborough from moving a potential clash against Chelsea to Stamford Bridge.'

The Conference club host Southend in an FA Cup third round replay tonight, with a lucrative home tie against the winners of the Chelsea and Watford tie up for grabs.

Scarborough are already assured a £500,000 payday after SKY agreed to screen the fourth round game live. But they were hoping to double that with extra gate receipts from playing at Stamford Bridge.

The Yorkshire club's McCain Stadium holds only six thousand fans – and last season Farnborough switched their tie against Arsenal to Highbury.

But the FA have blocked Scarborough's scheme – insisting clubs can only move games for safety reasons. Third Division Southend have pledged to keep the match at their Roots Hall home if they win tonight's replay.

MINNOWS BRIDGE KO

Michael Morgan reported that Chelsea could face double trouble in the fourth round of the FA Cup. Claudio Ranieri's millionaire Blues may meet non-league Scarborough – and a player who earned £400 a day as Henry's lookalike.

Ashley Sestanovich was chosen as the Arsenal and France superstar's body double in that famous Nike advert for the 2002 World Cup finals.

Sea Dogs midfield man Sestanovich 22, said that, "It was fantastic. I went to Rome, got paid £400 a day plus £35 a day spending money – and stayed in a five star hotel into the bargain".

Clapham born Sestanovich is on loan at Scarborough from Sheffield United until the end of the month.

His side play Southend tonight and the winners will host either Chelsea or Watford.

He revealed that, "My mate answered an advert when Nike were looking for stand-ins for all the football superstars in that World Cup ad. I just went along with him to the audition for a laugh. While he was doing his bit, I messed around in the background practicing my skills. Then one of the guys shouted at me, 'Hey, you look good – how do you fancy standing in for Thierry Henry because you look like him?'

"The next thing I was being flown over to Rome for twelve days' filming. All I had to do was stand in for Thierry when they were shooting rear view shots and high angle camerawork.

"You wouldn't expect footballers as important as Thierry Henry to stand around all day long for a few mug shots. Roberto Carlos, David Beckham, Ruud Van Nistelrooy, Ronaldo, Ronaldinho, Louis Enrique and the great Eric Cantona were also there. It was a thrill".

Well that was a nice little story and one he will one day tell his grandchildren no doubt, but in the meantime he was helping Scarborough knock out Southend and the next step would not be a stand-in part for the young midfield player but a real life experience amongst the Premiership elite. What a dream match for the non-league outfit and it once again shows the magic of the FA Cup. You could be a nobody in the eighty-ninth minute of a third round match then 'bingo' a late winner puts you right in front of millions of viewers with the opportunity of further glory if producing a performance of a lifetime. I find that the FA are completely out of order by not allowing this club to switch this match and if it only holds six thousand I can see that as dangerous ground. Plus it is the chance of a lifetime for all the folk in Scarborough to see their famous old club in a match with the players they only read about every day, never dreaming at the beginning of the competition that the magic and mystery of the most famous club competition in the world would bring them together. Come on you lot at the FA, don't keep living up to your initials.

On the morning of this evening's match there were some interesting rumours that Joe Cole was going to be used as bait for the signing of Scott Parker at Stamford Bridge.

I cannot see Curbishley allowing Parker to leave and because of the interest in his young player he has left him out of the squad for the weekend's match at Everton.

*The most talented player in the country, Matt Le Tissier and I discussing our caps
– or lack of them – before a match at the Bridge in '95*

*A picture to treasure, in the tunnel with Matthew Harding
at that same Southampton game of 1995.*

In a match at Stoke where Bill Shankly came into the dressing room afterwards with that wonderful compliment, 1974.

(Coloursport)

Peter Osgood's Testimonial in 1975, George Best's only time in a Chelsea shirt.
What a shame that was!

Tony 'Working Man's Ballet' Waddington proudly leads his team onto the
Wembley pitch before beating us in L.C. Final.

(Sentinel)

*John Terry and Thierry Henry trying to psyche
each other out in the Champions League.*

Jimmy Floyd celebrates his 100th Premiership goal. A great achievement!

The ever-impressive Carlo Cudicini saving that penalty at Old Trafford.
Not bad considering it was Van The Man.

Crespo and Gudjohnsen celebrating taking the lead in Monte Carlo.

Joey Cole showboating at the Bridge. The match where the Blues beat the reigning Champions by Frank Lampard penalty.

New boy, Scott Parker – a great buy – scoring against my mate Harry's Portsmouth.

What a moment! Wayne Bridge knocking my other club out of the Champions League.

Who said the Chelsea boys would not get their hands on the Premiership trophy?

ENGLAND TAKE THE ROCKY ROAD

They begin with two away games and then face Wales as Ryan Giggs' ban is over, writes Matt Lawton of the *Daily Mail*, and he believes that England's route to the World Cup suddenly looks a lot more daunting.

Those with suspicious minds and vivid imaginations would have taken one look at the fixtures England agreed at yesterday's World Cup meeting in Cardiff and questioned the motives of Sven Goran Eriksson. Was it his intention, they might have made life as difficult as possible for his successor?

The Swede has never lost a qualifying match, but whoever leads England into September's encounter with Austria will do well to emerge from the 10-game campaign unscathed. This after all is an England side that so nearly slipped up at home to Macedonia, away to Slovakia and almost missed out on an automatic place in the last World Cup in a game against Greece at Old Trafford.

The optimism that followed last week's draw in Frankfurt had subsided a little yesterday.

The teams England face should present David Beckham and his international colleagues with few problems, but the path to Germany now appears more daunting.

Two away games top start with the prospect of facing a Welsh team that includes Ryan Giggs and a concluding fixture that will evoke painful memories for those old enough to remember one of the most desperate nights in the history of the national team – England 1 Poland 1, Wembley 1973, and the saves from Jan Tomaszewski which blocked their passage to the last World Cup to be staged in Germany.

Assistant coach Tord Grip and FA executive director David Davies were keen to focus on the positives yesterday, not least the fact that England will not have to play in June 2005.

"You have to make compromises," said Davies "We didn't expect to play our first two games away but we didn't expect to play our last two games at home either".

The main thing Sven wanted to avoid was playing in June, when the players are tired at the end of a long domestic season. Wales were also keen to avoid that, and we have done so. "We were on the phone with Sven for the last thirty minutes of the meeting, and it was his decision to go ahead with these fixtures. Nobody was keen to come to England for their first game, and although it would have been very good to have met Wales without Ryan Giggs, the chances of the Welsh agreeing to that was nil".

Before I give you the fixtures I would just like to say that, how come all of a sudden we want Wales main threat out of this match when all I keep hearing is about how many world class players we have in our team. England should be able to pick three teams from our nation that should beat Wales, and I make no apologies to Mark Hughes and his players, it is just that is the way it should be. Hughes is doing a blinding job for his initial job in management and I am sure he will become a great manager wherever he chooses to go. There is a distinct lack of good English managers in fact; I cannot remember the last time an Englishman took his club to the summit of the Premiership at the middle of May. Matt Lawton carried this article out for much longer than I thought necessary because we have heard it all before:

September 4th 2004	Northern Ireland v Poland
„	Azerbabaijan v Wales
„	Austria v England
September 8th 2004	Poland v England
„	Austria v Azerbaijan
„	Wales v Northern Ireland
October 9th 2004	England v Wales
„	Azerbaijan v Northern Ireland
„	Austria v Poland
October 13th 2004	Wales v Poland
„	Northern Ireland v Austria
„	Azerbaijan v England
March 26th 2005	England v Northern Ireland
„	Poland v Azerbaijan
„	Wales v Austria
March 30th 2005	Poland v Northern Ireland
„	Austria v Wales
„	England v Azerbaijan
June 4th 2005	Azerbaijan v Poland
September 3rd 2005	Wales v England
„	Poland v Austria
„	Northern Ireland v Azerbaijan
September 7th 2005	Northern Ireland v England
„	Poland v Austria
„	Azerbaijan v Austria
October 8th 2005	Northern Ireland v Wales
„	England v Austria
October 12th 2005	Austria v Northern Ireland
„	England v Poland
„	Wales v Azerbaijan

THE SENTINEL

The transfer window is open again, and peering through it is Manchester United manager Sir Alex Ferguson. Fulham boss Chris Coleman is not impressed by the way the United boss has been slowly upping his bid for Louis Saha while at the same time, giving young Dutch star Arjen Robben a tour of his the state-of-the-art training ground facilities, something which has had his PSV Eindhoven club up in arms.

Next it was Ronaldo, who travelled to London to see his old teammates play against Liverpool on Wednesday. The Brazilian, though, was contacted before reaching the stadium and told in no uncertain terms to do an immediate U-turn. Did these shenanigans go on in my day?

Of course!

One of the funniest signings I witnessed was while on tour with Stoke in Cyprus. Manager Tony Waddington came to me by the swimming pool and asked if I would join him that evening to watch Sheffield United play the locals. My first reaction was "not really guv'nor. We are all sorted out to go to Nick's club tonight and football is the last thing on my mind". Waddo then said that if I came for the first-half he would return with me to this great little watering hole, so I agreed. When we arrived at the match he asked me if I thought I could play him. I said the way he is playing he might be replacing me. Sammy was a left-footed wide player who would add to the balance in our team. He was impressive, admittedly against ropey opposition, however all the fun was still to come. On leaving Nick's place at around 3am we headed for the hotel where Salmons was holding up the bar with a couple of other lads. Sammy, who was soon to become my roommate, was in good form and Waddo soon had him pinned against the wall to talk business. In no time, the player had agreed terms, but told Tony that there was one problem – namely that he went out on a Friday night for five or six pints of bitter. "It is the only way I can relax before a game", he said.

By the following morning's boat trip, Sammy was a Stoke City player. That trip was the beginning of a very good friendship with my old sparring partner. It was if we were out to break all drinking records from Stoke-on-Trent and London on the night before a match.

The next evening we were in the hotel bar once again, when Waddington had Francis Lee in exactly the same position, but this time he failed to lure Franny to our club. This reminded me of my signing for Stoke City, because I received a telephone call from our secretary at Chelsea to say that Tony Waddington was in town and wanted to meet me at the Russell Hotel at 7pm. I was halfway through a boozy lunch with Peter Osgood, who like me, was transfer listed. I arrived at the hotel and as I made my way up the steps, the porter told me a gentleman was waiting for me in the park opposite, Russell Square itself. I walked across the road to find Tony in one of the telephone boxes with nobody on the other end of the line. He soon had me seated on the park bench talking about a move to the Potteries. He impressed me greatly and I agreed to sign as Stoke were the only club who had shown any interest in me at that particular time. Waddo asked if I would like to travel with the team to the following day's match at Ipswich. I said I had a lot to do before leaving for the Potteries on Monday, so he said he would meet me at Stamford Bridge at 10.30 the next morning to put the transfer to bed.

I told my local publican-landlord to make sure he threw me out at 11pm, and that in no way should he ask me to have 'afters'.

When I arrived at the Bridge the next morning I need not have bothered. Tony had been at his favourite nightclub into the wee small hours. The rest is history and we began our great love affair with the game and its social side.

There was one funny instance when I was tapped up when I was having a great day out with one of my closest friends Michael Carter, at Chester races. We were drinking with the chairman of Blackpool Football Club. He was a really nice chap and we enjoyed each other's company for the entire afternoon.

Out of the blue he asked me if I would like to become player-manager of his beloved Blackpool. It was a great offer and, if I had not been so ambitious and in a great situation at Stoke City, I would have been tempted.

But once again it shows it doesn't matter where you are, a move can be lurking in the most unexpected of places.

WATFORD AT LAST

Well it was good news all round for the Tinkerman as his very pricey striker Adrian Mutu hit the 'onion bag' at last, after fourteen matches in fact. The headlines were ringing the praises for the little Romanian and Jimmy Floyd who is beginning to find his touch and remains top of the striker's league at Stamford Bridge. The *Daily Mirror* went MU-TWO Chelsea strikers hit form as Blues join race for Saha, all over the back page with the inner saying that JIMMY'S THE TRUE BLUE Old maestro Hasselbaink still has the killer touch and MU-TWO LIGHTS UP BRIDGE.

My favourite headline was that RANIERI TO TINKER WITH HIS FORWARD THINKING. The *Mail* said CHELSEA STAGE SHOW FOR NEW CHIEF and that Ranieri's ready to sign £10million Parker. The *Sun* came up with YOU SILLY OLD MU. But ref Al redeems himself as he rules Adrian goal is okay. The *Express* said that; Chelsea front men suggest they don't need any more help. They also said that Dream tie for high-flyer Quayle, and Chelsea in Saha swoop. Mark Quayle scored the goal that booked Scarborough a dream fourth round tie with Chelsea and then admitted they don't stand a hope in hell of beating them.

His simple tap-in seven minutes from time from Jimmy Kelly's cross was enough to sink third division Southend 1-0 and see the Yorkshire town into the fourth round for the first time in their 125-year history.

The match will be played in the cramped McCain Stadium a week on Sunday and the financial reward will be huge for a club who were in administration last year. But the match winner has no doubts about the effect facing the world's richest team will have on their footballing prospects. "Do you think we will win? No – I am a realist," said Quayle. "But I am looking forward to enjoying the day. I have never played in the fourth round of the FA Cup before so to score the goal in the third round must be my most important. It is a delightful feeling. People are looking now to Chelsea coming here and that is the magic of the FA Cup – to be on the pitch with players like that".

Despite Quayle's reality check, Chelsea boss Claudio Ranieri is predicting a 'big battle' when Chelsea travel north. The Conference side pulled off a remarkable 3-2 victory over the Londoners in 1989, and Ranieri joked he knows little about his next opponents. "I have never been there but I know it has a nice beach" he said. "I am looking forward to it because the FA Cup is wonderful for this reason. It will be a big party up there, but on the pitch it will be a big battle, that's for sure".

Ranieri praised his strikers for the way they saw off the challenge of Watford, particularly two-goal Adrian Mutu, who had recently gone thirteen matches without scoring a goal. "Goals are like oxygen for strikers" he said. "All my strikers scored very, very good goals, and I am happy".

Matt Lawton reported that: The need to impress the new boss has become a recurring theme during Claudio Ranieri's tenure at Stamford Bridge.

But last night another man with power and influence to push him through the exit door was reminded of Ranieri's qualities as a coach. Peter Kenyon, appointed in October as Chelsea's new chief executive, but still on garden leave at the behest of his former Manchester United employers, attended his first match here since Roman Abramovich's roubles lured him away from Old Trafford.

Presumably he was encouraged by what he saw, given that a spirited Watford side who had frightened the life out of them at Vicarage Road earlier this month, were no match for their illustrious opponents on this occasion.

A trip to Scarborough for the next round was secured with ease during an entertaining replay, goals from Mutu, who scored twice, Jimmy Floyd Hasselbaink and Eidur Gudjohnsen confirming their supremacy. If Chelsea thought they needed a new striker, it seems Abramovich can put his bulging wallet away again.

Ex-Watford and England boss Graham Taylor reported on the radio that, "They have smacked Chelsea's bottoms once. But it will be very hard to smack it again".

As we well know a giantkiller has only one attempt and when you are giving them a grilling you must capitalise on it otherwise the return trip becomes a formality for the giant. That first match when they had them on the ropes was a marvellous attempt but you felt any time Watford scored Chelsea would just go up the other end and scrap their lead. This replay has been a great opportunity for Chelsea strikers to get out of firing blanks at Stamford Bridge and their response was emphatic. I have never doubted the ability of Jimmy Floyd to score goals and if I have one criticism of him it is that he should be pushing his weight around from dead ball situations instead of taking them himself. I don't mean from the David Beckham situations but from corners and free kicks around the corner flag area. It is pretty amazing that he scores so many goals yet never scores from a corner kick. When I look at this situation, I think back to Brian Clough, when in practice match once, a striker, Roger Davies possibly, ran over to take the kick and 'Old Big Head' screamed at him to get where he belongs. So the Blues have hit seven goals in their last two matches – although against weak opposition – but they will have regained a lot of their lost confidence in front of goal, and Jimmy Floyd is as lethal as ever. His link-up play with the Icelandic international is good but I believe they should be kept together, as the 'dynamic duo' and just play the rest around them. I am not really sure of Hernan Crespo, for me the jury is still out. Mutu needs a helping hand from players from deep for he is sharp but it no good possessing lightning pace if you are not getting balls threaded through the right channels. The great plus for Chelsea is that Frank Lampard has kept his good form well but he must understand, although he wants to be in the team every match, he needs to have his batteries charged through a very long season, especially with big matches here and then going to places like Stuttgart where you need to be on your mettle from the first whistle.

I was kindly invited to Stamford Bridge by Mervyn Wilson of Wilsonsports and racing betting shops, a very nice man who has been ultra-successful in his business life. With him was a stranger to me, another man of great wealth, Kenny 'Up on the Roof' Lynch, a man I have had the pleasure to have known for many years. It all came about because of an old friend of mine, Doggan Ariff, arriving in London from Cyprus and Mervyn thought it would be nice to sit over lunch – before the match – and then afterwards chew the fat about all the space between us whilst Doggan has been away from his many south London businesses. So this would have been me and three blokes with business in Cyprus. Hotels, casinos, travel agencies and a lot more. But Doggan had not arrived in time for the match so it was just the four of us. It was a match Chelsea needed to win for Manchester United had slipped up at Wolves the day before – losing 1-0 at Wolves – and Arsenal had beaten Aston Villa whilst we were having lunch. There were televisions in the Wise Suite so we were able to see Thierry Henry continue his unstoppable form. Twisting, turning, dummying and always in command of his opponents. The first goal reminded me of a goal scored against our Stoke City team when Leeds United came to the Victoria Ground in one of the greatest matches I have ever had the pleasure to have been involved. Leeds had just been knocked out of the FA Cup on the Wednesday – a match our entire squad were taken to see – and had arrived in the Potteries needing to avoid defeat to break the first division record of 31 matches without defeat, with us obviously making it thirty-two. This was a massive match for me, also having missed both the FA Cup Final and replay against them in 1970. There was an incredible beginning to the match as – like Henry and Arsenal – Leeds were given free kick about twenty-five yards from our goal and as the wall – more about the wall later – was being lined up, our keeper John Farmer came rushing out leaving the goal unattended. The great Billy Bremner cheekily chipped the ball over the wall into an empty net, 0-1 and the Boothen End silenced. Before we could regain any rhythm we were hit by a second goal from another 'Jock', Peter Lorimer the man with the hardest shot in football, 0-2. Slowly we somehow clawed back into some kind of form but not before Bremner and Giles had completed their show to make us look inferior beings!

The two-goal cushion gave them the opportunity to stroll nonchalantly across our Victoria Ground pitch as if the match was already over. Then about ten minutes from the break we got a lucky break as the ball dropped to me right on the edge of their penalty area and on the half turn I hit it to the left of David Harvey's right hand post, 1-2 and 'game on'. They were not so nonchalant now as we were laying siege on their goal knowing if we could nick an equaliser, the second-half kicking into the Boothen End would favour us as we would be going for the 'kill' and they would be happy coming away by having avoided defeat. In a nutshell they had the opportunity to hit us a third time – whilst we were regrouping – but they chose to just play the game of 'keep ball'. Then it happened, we were given a free-kick in much the same spot as their first goal and I grabbed the ball – whilst they put up their wall – when, all of a sudden, our left-back Micky Pejic came storming forward, screaming at me to roll the ball in his path. I did just as he asked and he hit a 'blinding' left-foot shot in the same spot that I had beaten the Leeds keeper, 2-2, and moments later the half-time whistle was heard, although I don't know how for the crowd were going crazy as we mounted attack after attack. Our dressing room was like a furnace with emotions running sky high as we all knew that this would turn out to be our day and that they would be thinking that about thirty-five-yards along the corridor they would be as sick as pigs knowing they might just have thrown the match away. In a way we did not want to hear the half-time whistle because it broke the momentum we had built up, but it did, and we knew we needed to get straight back into that groove, and as quickly as possible. The buzzer went for the second half and we entered the arena to the most electrifying welcome I have ever witnessed on a football field in my twenty years playing the game. We turned the screw and with Greenhoff and myself 'keeping the ball away from the opposition' – as Jimmy puts it on the tape 'Magic Moments' – and sensed that a winner must surely come our way as we banged at their door time and time again. Then all of a sudden we gained a corner on the right-hand side under the Players' Lounge Seating and as usual Geoff Salmons struck a sweet left-footer onto the head of Denis Smith, who in turn flashed a header in the direction of Geoff Hurst and as you all know about Hursty he does not miss them from eight yards out. And this time he didn't need the aid of a Russian linesman, 3-2, and the ground erupted. The second-half was an absolutely brilliant performance from the boys in the red and white stripes, although the trouble was still not over as the final whistle went there was fighting in the players' tunnel and Jack Charlton we heard had smashed the away-team dressing room window, which was sweet music to our ears. We had pulled off a sensational win and I am sure that everyone at that match – except those in all white – would put that match down as the best ever seen at the Victoria Ground. I thank Henry for scoring such a goal for it gave me the perfect opportunity to tell you about one of the greatest matches I have ever played in, if not the greatest!

Anyhow it was Sunday the 18th of January and Stamford Bridge was sold out once again for the visit of Steve Bruce's Birmingham City. The headlines on the 19th read in the *Independent* that BRUCE EXITS STAMFORD BRIDGE A PROUD MAN, Whilst the *Mail* simply said RIGHT CROSS WOULD BE A CHELSEA KNOCK-OUT. The *Sun* was more controversial saying that SCOTT'S MISSED and RANIERI REALLY NEEDS PARKER BOOST. On the back page of the *Sun* it read that FERGIE GETS SAHA £12million seals move.

On the morning of the match there was not much in the *Mail* on the game except that CHELSEA V BIRMINGHAM 4.05pm live on SKY Premier Plus, followed by; Like Rocky Balbao, 'Italian Stallion' Claudio Ranieri turned to someone called Adrian in a time of crisis and Mr Mutu came up with the goods. Including two goals in the all-important FA Cup rematch against Watford. Having bounced off the ropes, Chelsea's pretty boys must show they are true contenders against Robbie 'Aptly named' Savage and the rest of Steve Bruce's bruisers.

So, after a very average lunch we took our seats in the new West Stand seating area outside of the Directors' Suite and the one we were in. Birmingham had come to town missing five first team regulars while, as I said, Chelsea had hit eight in their last two matches. The first half dwindled away and my conversation with Kenny was far superior. Chelsea huffed and puffed but as they huffed the 'Boys from Brum' got numbers back and I left my seat to make some notes over a nice glass of red wine, with the TV on in the suite just in case anyone would begin to take the match by the scruff of the neck and make Chelsea look like real dangers to the two teams above them. If Manchester United's defeat at Molineux the day prior was not enough to 'spark' Chelsea into life then nothing could!

The thing is that you do not need to be a rocket scientist to know just how Steve Bruce would have his team play, especially as he was missing his best two strikers, one of who is Mikael Forssell, on loan to the visitors for the season from Chelsea, and has scored more goals than any player the season so far. Forssell is a player I like and it is just another incredible mystery as to why he is not scoring goals for Chelsea and is doing so regularly for the opposition. It was lucky for the Blues of Chelsea that this talented striker was not allowed to play for the Blues of Birmingham because it was all a part of the loan deal that he must sit the two Premier matches out when the two teams meet.

Whilst drinking my wine I made several notes about the first-half, the first being that there was 'too much average-ness' within the Chelsea team. Another point was that at times it was like watching a circus act with 'flick' here a 'flick' there, a 'drag back' here and a 'rollover' there, etc, etc, etc!

There were a couple of close-ups on Bruce as he paced the touchline and sat back on the wall looking like he had no pre-match meal as he nibbled at his nails throughout but at the same time he must have been thinking 'if only'. You got it, Forssell, maybe?

Chelsea had a couple of great chances late on, one in particular to Jimmy Floyd who would put this chance away ninety-nine times out of a hundred, but with Maik Tailor to beat he drove the ball low into the keeper's feet, as he ran out of his goal expecting him to thunder the ball waist high. The Brummie keeper got lucky but he deserved his luck for his handling all afternoon had been excellent, and with a makeshift defence he definitely deserved all the luck needed to keep Chelsea goalless. They were all the notes I made apart from the one other thing I said at our table afterwards, which was that "I never thought I would ever say this but Robbie Savage was outstanding" and my new friend from Cyprus agreed as I had heard him say that a few seconds prior. But I was impressed with his handling the match in the middle of the field, winning tackles, coming away with the ball almost every time he went into a tackle and setting up the play for a very brittle forward line. Two pints dropped against a makeshift Birmingham City team is just not good enough if you want to challenge for the crown and I must disagree with the Tinkerman who plays down such performances. The main point I made afterwards was that if I had the kind of money Roman Abramovich had and I was serious about being the best team in the world, instead of buying a new set of players for approximately £111million I would have paid the exact amount of money to steal Zinedine Zidane off of Real Madrid!

There is not much more I can say about this performance so I will leave you with the Tinkerman's gems after the match. Monday's *Evening Standard* headline was stolen by Adrian Mutu, looking like this Ranieri keeps his cool as others lose their head MUTU IN TUINNEL BUST-UP. But the FA are likely to act over the striker's row with Purse by Matt Hughes. Here is what Ranieri had to say after it was written that his expression of pleasure after yesterdays goalless draw was deadly serious. "I prefer to see the glass half-full rather than half-empty and I'm always positive. I'm happy with out league position and will see how we finish the season. When we played Bolton we tried everything and got nothing, but yesterday at least we got a point. My team is in good health and I said well done to my players afterwards because they gave everything they had. We have six points more than we did this stage last season. I'm happy because it's not easy to buy eleven new players and link them straight away. We have a very good group and everybody is fighting for each other". Chelsea did create several chances but not enough to worry about the final score-line. Joe Cole – who continues to flatter and frustrate in equal measure – hit the post in the first-half and Hasselbaink put a firm header wide, but the best opportunity fell to Billy Gallas, whose 49th minute shot was cleared off the line by Olivier Tebily. Mutu created two openings for Hasselbaink and Gudjohnsen in the closing minutes but by then a sense of resignation filled the winter air. Not the manager's of course.

Ranieri continued by saying that, "We're not frustrated that Arsenal and Manchester United are so far ahead. We're still building and will hopefully be closer by the end of the season. We're trying to stay close to them, but it's not our target. I've said from the beginning that we are building a foundation and do not have to win anything this season. Chelsea do not have to win this season." Perhaps next season, maybe with a different manager?

Those words could well come back to haunt the Tinkerman and it concerns me that he feels Chelsea don't need to win anything this time around. Some Chelsea supporters have been waiting fifty years to win the championship again and I am sure, after paying out serious money for season tickets over the years and now seeing a billionaire taking the seat at the top of the table, I think they would be concerned also!

The Tinkerman is definitely not the full ticket at times to the extent that he sounds like an actor who is waiting for his last line and the final curtain will fall so he can get to his drawer in his dressing room for the whisky bottle?

The Mutu situation was 'handbags at five' so we'll leave that one there and go on to the pitch being dug up straight after the match with a new one hopefully being ready for the next home match on February the 8th, ironically against Charlton. There was a point in the match that Lynchie turned to me and said about the pitch being a shade 'iffy' to which I replied by asking him if he could still remember the pitches we played on at White Hart Lane in the FA Cup Semi-final in 1970 and a lot more like it from Christmas right through to the end of May. Kenny smiled!

Chelsea 0 Birmingham City 0: another full house

NATASHA DEMKINA

I must share this with you, about a young lady from Russia by the name of Natasha Demkina, who has stunned the medical world with what appears to be her incredible gift to spot illnesses with X-Ray vision.

I would suggest that Roman Abramovich contact this young woman and get her in to see the Tinkerman straight away. This report came from Igor Monichev in Moscow. It mentioned several cases, one in which a woman went to her about an injury to her wrist some years ago and told her only that she had fractured a limb and wanted to know if she could tell her where it was. Natasha said, "Oh, this is just another test, very well". She stared in silence then smiled saying, "It has healed very well but I see it". With two fingers she gripped her left wrist to show her where the fracture was. The woman was stunned. Natasha said that she sees everything that happens inside the human body – so Roman, I suggest you bring her into the manager's office before it is too late.

I have just watched the live Monday Night match between Newcastle United and Fulham and for the first forty-five minutes it looked as if the Geordies were the ones who have just spent all those roubles, but Fulham fought right down to the wire and left St James's Park 3-1 losers. Laurent Robert was tantalising the Fulham defence and fired in one or two screamers with that wonderful left peg of his, then scored the third goal with an overhead kick to make it 3-0. He was man-of-the-match deservedly so, and Newcastle to continue their progress up the Premiership table sitting poised behind Alan Curbishley's Charlton Athletic. Tomorrow night is the first leg of the Carling Cup semi-final between Arsenal and Boro and the evening after Sam Allardyce's Bolton face Aston Villa at the Reebok Stadium. Arsenal beat Boro by four goals at Highbury only in the last week or two, but I feel the visitors will not be so charitable this time as they defended quite appallingly. I'm hoping for an Arsenal and Bolton day out in Cardiff for 'Big Sam' deserves some recognition for the way he has pulled this club around. Next Saturday Chelsea will travel to Scarborough in a match I hope will be a draw so the non-league outfit can have a major payday from a Stamford Bridge replay. There was a double page feature in the *Daily Mail* with headlines;

MAGIC OF THE CUP
Malcolm's minions versus Roman's millions

Chelsea's FA Cup fourth round tie at Scarborough on January the 24th will see two footballing worlds collide. John Edwards talks to the non-league club's chairman Malcolm Reynolds about life after administration and how he signed cup hero Mark Quayle for only £2,000.

QUAYLE

Roman Abramovich was ripping another page out of his chequebook at the time, after quickly agreeing to Parma's £15.8million asking price for Adrian Mutu.

Three hundreds miles north, Malcolm Reynolds and Russell Slade were deep in negotiations on the telephone for a proven goalscorer of their own, but were finding the going a little tougher.

Finally, Slade took another call from his Nuneaton Borough counterpart and flashed a knowing smile across the table "we've cracked it, chairman" he beamed. "They'll let us have him for £2,000".

The details of Mark Quayle's arrival at Scarborough via such outposts as Grantham Town, Morecambe and Telford, took on storybook proportions when he stepped out against Southend in the FA Cup third round replay the Wednesday before last. An 83rd minute winner sent the Conference side marching through to the fourth round for the first time in their 124 year history and guaranteed a half a million payday against Chelsea, exactly twelve months after administration and the threat of extinction hung over them like one of the mists that roll in off the North Sea. While Abramovich laid out £111million on new players in the summer, Scarborough limited their spending to £2,000 on a 25-year-old who was sent packing by his home club

Everton. Even that modest outlay was sanctioned only after hours of haggling.

Anyone who thought the FA Cup might be losing its magic should have tried contacting Reynolds yesterday as he attempted to cope with the public, as well as the media, response to a tie that illustrates the competition's enduring appeal better than most. *Sportsmail* finally succeeded at around 1.30pm and, after catching his breath, Reynolds recounted the background to the first transfer fee paid by Scarborough in ten years. "I have never known a day like this in my life" he said. "I have fielded at least fifty calls already from all sections from the media and from well-wishers who just wanted to say 'well done". To go from obscurity to the national spotlight so quickly is too much for a simple chap like me. It's funny to think that while Chelsea were paying all that money for Mutu, we were worrying about how Nuneaton wanted £2,000 for Mark and trying to chip a grand off the asking price. It might not sound much, but to us it was the difference between signing him or looking somewhere else. Russell had built a good littler squad but we needed a finisher. He knew about Mark's record and that Nuneaton were anxious to remove him from the wage bill (this is me, and Chelsea have Winston Bogarde) after being relegated.

"He was the one we were going for and I sat round a table with Russell in one of our sponsor's lounges, while he a call into the Nuneaton manager. They were pals, apparently, but it didn't seem to make much difference. They wanted three grand. We did a few calculations on the overall package and had to accept that it was too much. Several calls later, we asked if they would consider knocking a grand off. Their manager took it to their directors and a while later the phone went again. I looked anxiously across the table for the nod of the head and saw Russell break into a beaming smile".

Reynolds, who knows about high finance after running a merchant bank in Vienna, insists he is no Abramovich, despite taking on the debts of £1.5million two years ago before steering Scarborough towards the promise of prosperity.

An unpaid tax bill of £350,000 proved the cue for administration 12 months ago, but Scarborough survived it and are now looking ahead with renewed optimism after surrendering the McCain Stadium for developing 200 houses and building a new £6million ground, complete with tennis and athletics facilities nearby. Reynolds once confessed to donating 'several thousands of pounds' of his own money to the Scarborough cause but was coy on the subject as he assessed their comeback from the brink. "The only thing Mr Abramovich and I have in common is that I visited Moscow several times during my days at the bank" he said. "Don't make me out to be a wealthy benefactor, because I am not. I have contributed occasionally – we all put our hands in our pockets when we can. It's incredible that we should land a tie with Chelsea on January the 14th because that is precisely the date that we went into administration twelve months ago. They were dark days, but what bailed us out was owning the freehold for the site where we played. Selling that enabled us to start work on a site down the road. Under the current set-up, we stand to lose a quarter of a million pounds every year on average. At the new ground, where we hope to be playing by next Christmas, there will be facilities that will generate enough income to put us on sound footing".

'TAKING MY OWN LIFE'

Quayle reflected on the shattered dreams he left behind at Goodison Park, saying "It left a massive hole in me, being released by Everton, I felt lucky just being there in the first place and the memories have spurred me on to try and get back to a higher level. A lot has been made of the fee, but it doesn't exactly stand comparison with some of the ones Chelsea have laid out. In fact, let's be fair, you could just about get a decent secondhand car for what Scarborough paid for me".

Well that is a dream draw for the non-league side, and a great example of not giving up when things are going haywire all around you. My dark days in the Intensive Trauma Unit – for my family – seem light years away but when I came round fifty-nine days after leaving Jamie's Bar on December the 15th 1997, was something quite extraordinary even though I did not know what was going on for being on so much morphine. But as time went by I slowly put my life in order – after my wife walking out on me – but it was not until about a year ago I could come to terms with the future. Had they amputated my legs – as they were moments away from doing – I would have had to re-evaluate my future with so much more seriousness. In my book 'Spectacular' I explain what my plan would have been, for after leaving my body in the ITU I went above and saw my father and best friend Leslie May and after just losing my mother I would have no problem of taking my own life and joining them above.

My writing has filled a great gap in my life and helps me explain all that went on before me, and now I find that swapping my life for a PC was not a bad deal at all.

I am still passionate about the game I love so much although it has never really done me many favours but like a marriage you sign the contract!

Having said that the million-dollar question is say I was playing in today's financial climate?

My answer was and still is that time moves on and use the example of Frank Sinatra taking all that time to reach the top being eclipsed by the Spice Girls. That is the one and only way I can put it!

Going back to Scarborough's big day this coming Saturday and a reminder that the last time the two teams met was in 1989 in a 3-2 League Cup win for the underdogs after drawing one each at Stamford Bridge. The Chelsea team at that time were lying second in the top flight and were leading by two goals but three goals in seven second-half minutes devastated a Chelsea team with players like Kerry Dixon, David Speedie and Micky Hazard, a player I admired so much. Simply, my kind of footballer!

There was another twist in the tail last night as Arsenal lost the first leg tie of the Carling Cup against a Boro team they had annihilated ten days earlier. The little Brazilian Juninho struck the winner after going close with a couple of other good efforts as the team from the North-East searched for a winner. The big question now is who will Wenger choose to play in the second leg with a trip to Cardiff only an hour and a half away.

Tonight is the first leg of the Bolton and Aston Villa match, one I mentioned earlier that I am hoping for a Bolton win.

GREAVSIE

I always enjoy reading the Jimmy Greaves page in the *Sun* and last week's was no different as he said that: As Abramovich himself will know, Roman wasn't built in a day.

Therefore I cannot quite believe all this pressure being put on Claudio Ranieri at present. Is it us in the media at fault, the new super-wealthy owner himself or dark forces working for Sven Goran Eriksson?

Whatever, it seems absurd to me that this man's job should be under threat because of a few dodgy results.

'THE RUSSIAN HIT LIST MISSED JAY JAY'

I don't apologise for butting in on Jimmy's piece but I have to explain this before I go to bed having watched the best performance of the season by Jay Jay Okotcha. It was his signing-off match for Bolton having his bags packed to go off to the African Cup. I had just come in from a nice afternoon and thought I would go home to see Bolton beat Villa in that other semi-final and as luck would have it we all witnessed one of the all time great performances by an individual. This player will be wanted by every club on the planet – big Sam's worry now is to keep him – and it just goes to show that Sam gave him the opportunity to make it here could very well rebound on him. But is that is sods law!

On Monday we saw Lauren Robert strike a wonderful free-kick, but Jay Jay made a mockery of the art of taking free-kicks, by hitting a ball which arrowed into the only place he should not have aimed at. Quite stunning!

His overall performance – especially later on – was breathtaking and has confirmed about these black countries that they will take over the game. Although I will write this in my column and this book is about finding value for your money, why on earth has this player's name been mentioned on the Russian hit list. The good, the bad and the ugly was also on view tonight as that 'Man in Green' again Durkin, and his side kicks somehow were the only three people on the planet that did not see that Angel was offside on three occasions before hauling Villa off from a three goal deficit, quite astonishing how these people are not cautioned – just as players are – for such diabolical a decision – for such errors. The officials have much more time to make a decision than players do making a rash tackle, and after all it is a man's game and a contact sport. So, I cannot believe that between the FA, UEFA and FIFA they do not put three and three together and for a change make it six. But that aside, I am looking forward to the rest of the season and in hope that I see a better performance than this, and I for one know it will not come from a Chelsea player. I say that with respect and also would like to be a fly on the wall of the Russian's quarters as they sit, watch and wonder why the Tinkerman has not mentioned Jay Jay?

The great one, Jimmy Greaves says that: "Who in their right mind truly believes that because £110million has been spent in the summer, Chelsea were automatically entitled to win the Premiership?

"At very best I believed it was going to take two or three seasons. Both Manchester and Arsenal are way ahead of Chelsea in their plotting and planning to land another Premiership crown. Let no one at Stamford Bridge forget that it took Sir Alex six years to get everything in order before he started dominating the game.

"Arsene Wenger too, needed time and money to mould together one of the most entertaining teams this country has seen.

"I believe the Tinkerman – Ranieri – deserves the utmost praise for having already been able to get all these stars into a side that can not only entertain but win games as well."

PANIC

"Yes, they have slipped up, but that was inevitable for a squad constructed in such a short space of time.

"What Chelsea have done is to lay a foundation to establish themselves as one of the big three clubs for years to come.

"That for now should be enough. Panic never won any team anything. If Ranieri were to be dispensed with, who on earth would be able to walk into Chelsea and win them the title this season?

"It simply would not be possible.

"It seems clear Ranieri has a good relationship with his players he has brought into the club. What he now needs is time to forge them into a team that can consistently produce results.

"If he is given that, and I don't mean just one or two seasons, I mean time like Ferguson was given, there is no reason why Chelsea cannot do a United. However, if Abramovich were to bow to pressure coming from all sides, Chelsea would only go in reverse. Chopping and changing a boss never achieved anything. Name me a club that has won the title in recent memory who have not had consistency in the managerial and backroom department prior to that success. I can't think of one!

"Ranieri's position, however, is in stark contrast to that of Gerard Houllier at Liverpool.

"It is no secret my old mate, Ian St John, has been laying into him recently.

Houllier has had money to spend and time to forge a team. They probably peaked in their own trophy treble season. But now things are in reverse and the reds are as far away from winning the title as they have been in the last decade. But at least chairman David Moores gave Houllier a good run at it and could not be criticised for releasing the Frenchman now.

"There is no doubt Houllier has done a decent job. But there comes a time when a man has to realise he has taken things as far as he can.

"That time is now for Houllier.

"For Ranieri it remains a long time off."

Thanks Jimmy, always one for the underdog is our Jimmy and I get the feeling while reading his piece that the elite group in the Roman Empire will be throwing that straight into the basket under the Tinkerman's desk. I believe if he does not win a pot this season the curtain could very well fall down around his heels, for these people did not get where they are today through being patient, a 34-year-old billionaire, come on James my boy!

The main story on this Thursday was that goalkeeper Carlo Cudicini could very well be leaving come the summer although he says different as Chelsea line up Czech international Petr Cech to replace him. Mark Fleming of the *Express* explains that; The ties that bind Carlo Cudicini to Chelsea are stronger than ever. The popular Italian has enjoyed a five-year love affair with the Stamford Bridge club, rising from the Third Division keeper in Italy to become one of the best stoppers in the Premiership. And Cudicini has confirmed he is here to stay, despite a turbulent time recently which has seen his marriage end after just fifteen months. "It was just one of those things" said Cudicini yesterday. "We had been together for years but being married and living together was another thing completely. It just didn't work out".

The Italian keeper had wanted to keep his heartache private but has been forced to go public to deny he is eyeing up a return to his homeland in the summer because his wife, Carola, has been unable to settle in London. "People say that my children are unhappy in London but I don't have any children" he said. "They say I will return to Italy because my wife is homesick, but how can that be when we separated four months ago?

"I want to stay at Chelsea for as long as possible. I have a contract until 2008 and I intend to see it through. Of course if Chelsea wanted me out of the door, there is nothing I can do about that. But if it is up to me, I will stay here for the rest of my career. I love the club. I love the fans. I love everything about it. I don't want to leave Chelsea.

"I don't want Chelsea fans to think that I am trying to move on and make money now that I have made a name for myself at Chelsea. That could not be further from the truth. Chelsea have been good to me the whole time I have been here and I want to pay them back for the faith they have shown in me".

Cudicini was a virtual unknown when he was brought to Chelsea by former boss Gianluca Vialli in July 1999. During his early career his fame as the son of legendary AC keeper Fabio Cudicini had marked him out as someone special, and he played for both AC and Lazio.

But a succession of injuries hit him hard and he ended up in the Italian Third Division playing for Castel di Sagro before Vialli took him to London.

During his time at Chelsea he has rediscovered his old confidence and has established himself as one of the top goalkeepers in the country.

He had a slip dip in form at the start of the season, which coincided with the breakdown of his marriage.

An uncharacteristic mistake against Besiktas in the Champions League was followed by him dropping the ball at the feet of Thierry Henry in a tense match with Arsenal, a gaffe that cost Chelsea the match.

However, the reaction of the Chelsea fans in the following game, a Champions League tie with Lazio, was enormous comfort for Cudicini. "They gave me a wonderful reception and it was very emotional for me", he said. "It is always a difficult time when you make mistakes but the fans were fantastic. Everyone makes mistakes. We are human beings not robots. Fortunately the fans, the manager, my teammates, everyone at Chelsea understands that. It made me stronger and it helped me so much because I recovered well. Soon after we went eleven games without conceding a goal".

Cudicini insists his future at the club will not be affected by the imminent arrival of Petr Cech from Rennes, who will make his £9million move in the summer. The 6ft 5inch Czech international believes he will be first choice next season, but Cudicini said, "He will find a tough opponent in me".

"We will both challenge for the place and the manager will decide. It is perfectly normal that Chelsea want to buy another goalkeeper. We need to have competition for places and greater strength in depth. It is perfectly understandable. I am not scared of competition. I have had to fight my way into the team before and I will always have to fight for my place. All I can do is play my best and hope the manager picks me.

"I don't have any problem with Chelsea signing another keeper. Whatever happens, I don't intend going anywhere. My life is in London. I want to win trophies with Chelsea".

Eidur Gudjohnsen has also pledged his future to the London club.

The Iceland striker has been linked with a move to French side Bordeaux before the transfer window shuts.

But Arnor Gudjohnsen, his father and agent, said that, "If Eidur is playing and scoring he is more than happy to stay".

Thanks dad, I wish I had been in a position where I could have had my father as my agent, what a way to keep it in the family. I am a massive fan of the Icelandic but I think he has the ability to score more goals, for when he gets into good positions in the box he is as cool as his nationality. He has great control and composure when in key areas in the box and his wonderful overhead kick against Leeds United – when Terry Venables was managing them – was as good as it gets, and Chelsea should be showing that goal on their screens every match day. It was surely the goal of the season in my book and in that same book, this player should be amongst the goals far more often. That is not a criticism – or maybe it is – just that he has all the ability in the world to be more adventurous up front and be a little more like his sidekick Jimmy Floyd who eats sleeps and drinks goals.

On this same day there was more transfer fury – following the sale of Saha from Fulham to Manchester United – it was the Charlton chairman who said that 'GET LOST. We don't want your money Mr Abramovich, someone has to make a stand' which was on the back page of the *Express* but the *Sun* had a bigger splash with a big photograph showing Scott Parker on the move with the ball at his feet. The headline read 'I DON'T WANT ROMS READIES says Charlton chief Martin Simons'.

Charlton chairman Martin Simons last night blasted Chelsea over Scott Parker and said "Get lost Roman, we don't want your money".

Billionaire Chelsea owner Roman Abramovich has sanctioned two bids for midfield star Parker – the latest being for £7.5million with bonuses based on appearances.

Charlton have told them to keep it and the angry chairman Simons insists there will be no caving-in like Fulham did over Louis Saha's move to Old Trafford, even if the Blues double their offer.

He said, "We are fourth in the table, they are third. In the last few weeks we have been catching them up. So it hurts when, with their buying power they have the ability to see the club beneath and say, 'Oh, lets spend a few million and have their best player.'

"Well I say 'Get lost Abramovich' and I think I speak for the rest of football. Somebody has to make a stand. We don't want Chelsea's money. We are not the Charlton of old, where if someone offered us a million pounds for a player we would ask for £1.25million. Chelsea must be shown they can't take our best players without us putting up a fight. We don't want the gap between us and the top three to get wider, if that happens they might as well go off and play in a league of their own".

Abramovich has rampaged across England in his search for players. He had no problem swatting aside the likes of West Ham when he wanted Joe Cole and Glen Johnson – paying £12million for the pair. And there was precious little resistance from Southampton as he snapped up Wayne Bridge for £7million. Hernan Crespo arrived from Italian side Inter Milan for almost £17million without too much fuss and French club Rennes have just agreed to sell keeper Petr Cech in a £39million deal which was too good to resist. But Charlton refuse to budge over the 23-year-old Parker. Simons added that, "We want to send out a message that our best players are not for sale. Our feeling is that we want to build for the future. Scott Parker is a pillar of our building. He is unhappy because he can see more money down the road but we want him to stay. We are not denying Scott the chance of a lifetime at all. He signed a new contract in June for five years. He has still got four and a half years left on that contract. All we are saying is that 'Scott you have signed that contract. We don't want to let you go. You are a part of Charlton Athletic. We want you to play for us and honour your contract.' Obviously, he is being tempted by huge financial incentive and it's very, very difficult for the guy and I understand that. But please Scott, I am saying appreciate what you signed six months ago because we want to keep you".

Simons insisted, contrary to the claims by Parker, there was never an agreement that we would sell him to a bigger club. "We have not made any deals to let him go and we will not be doing that. The rest of the team want him to stay and we want to build a team around him. If he went to Chelsea how many games would he play?

"Maybe twenty-five a season?"

Simons believes that Parker's England ambitions will be just as well served by staying at the Valley.

And, at yesterday's 'Kick Racism Out of Football Campaign' 10th anniversary dinner the Charlton supremo found himself beside England boss Sven Goran Eriksson.

Simons revealed that "I was sat next to Sven and he was saying that he sees Scott as one of his main guys for the future. He wants him to play. Scott might say he can get Champions League football with Chelsea.

"But we may be only a season away from it ourselves and I think if he stays with us I think he could be there. Obviously money often talks in football. If they were to offer us say £25million, then that is an offer you can't refuse but we are trying to stand out against that direction. A bid of £10million a few years ago would have been the lifeblood of our club. But we have now built our club by keeping our players".

'I DON'T KNOW'

After listening to the Charlton chairman I am not so sure he did not put his foot in it when saying £25million would be an offer they could not refuse. On one hand he is saying to this young man, money is not the be all and end all and that is why we want you to stay, for you are the pillar of the building of Charlton Athletic, then on the other hand he is saying everyone has a price. If I were this terrific young player, I would have serious doubts about a man who would be foolish to make it known that if Mr Abramovich was to come back with a quarter of a century then, young Scott, we'll help you pack your suitcases for you. No this stinks to me and it is almost as if he is enticing the Chelsea owner, saying between the lines that if you came back with that quarter of a century the player is yours, signed, sealed and delivered personally by Charlton Athletic Football Club. I remember after my first season in the game which was rather sensational as regards a player of eighteen coming into a side that really were not challenging for honours and ended up winning the FA Cup and finishing third in the First Division with that great Everton team winning it. At the end of that season I went in to renew my contract. The manager – Dave Sexton – asked me how much I was looking for, to which I replied that I did not want to earn any more or any less than any of my teammates. I thought that was the general feeling after such a season. He told me in return that when I came back into his office with a half a dozen England caps I could demand such a wage. The wage offered me was £75 a week, that was £25 less than Johnny Haynes was earning for Fulham some ten years prior. That season also there was talk of AC Milan showing interest in this young lad from Chelsea, but that died a death for some unknown reason. Italy was the place I wanted to play as well, but if given the opportunity I would have gone to Spain in the present football climate, the most exciting football anywhere in the world. .

Anyhow, as my career panned out, if the manager had me over that barrel I would have been earning that paltry £75 a week for the rest of my life because I could have only put two international caps on his table. So there you have a conundrum, which is not far away from young Scott Parker, he is a victim of his own ability. It also worries me if he were the son of the Charlton Chairman would Simons advice his own son to stay put. I have great respect for Alan Curbishley of which you have already read, but come on, let's all be straight here. If the chairman talked a good game he had an off day here and if I was Scott Parker I would play him at his own game by keeping the ace up his sleeve and say you have tried to kid me, so here we go, if Charlton are not in the Champions League next season would you agree – if Chelsea, Arsenal or Manchester United still wanted me – to let me go?

So the Carling Cup first legs have come and gone and could not be better balanced; on one hand Arsenal have to decide if they want the trophy in their cupboard which seems a shame having come all of this way. I felt that Wenger should have had Henry, Viera and Pires on the bench just in case he felt they could go on for the last half an hour and turn the game their way. I cannot see why he has not given his team more of a chance, okay the youngsters have done well, but play them and, if it looks sticky make changes for there is no better way for a young player to learn at this level. He gave Boro the initiative and I cannot say that is good management when a cup final is at stake, and a big gate at Cardiff on a Sunday afternoon. What better way for your players to relax?

Bolton, on the other hand have taken the bull by the horns with Sam Allardyce saying – only last round of the FA Cup – that he was delighted that they were knocked out so he can concentrate Bolton's Premiership status. But he knew he had one foot in the door before last night's first leg and he felt that his squad would be at full stretch if involved in three competitions so he opted – quite wisely – for the Carling Cup. I must agree with Sam's comments this morning that Jay Jay Okocha – his Nigerian captain – is the best player ever to play for his club. This player – who played his last game before flying to Tunisia for the Africans Cup – was sensational against Villa at the Reebok Stadium, scoring twice from free-kicks, the second was as sweet as you'll ever see a football struck. From the angle of the box wide on the left he arrowed his shot into the only position the goalkeeper could not have got it. Absolutely magnificent!

But this player is a total one off for a black player, for he plays just around the spaces left in between the back four and the midfield players. But he – unlike so many of our players – is so comfortable receiving the ball either up front, or in the centre of the field. He makes ground like a gazelle and carries the ball as if tied to his toe, that is unless he wants to rocket one at your goal. He works tirelessly for the team and Bolton will have to be very careful whilst he is away unless Sam was clever enough to get him to sign a contract before he left for the airport last night. Having said that, what does it matter if a contract is signed these days, just ask the chairman of Charlton?

JAY JAY GOTCHA
Villa rocked as Nigerian hotshot bids fond farewell

This was Peter Ferguson of the *Daily Mail* just confirming of my reckoning of the Okocha performance; Jay-Jay Okocha conjured up a flamboyant farewell to savour last night with the bravura performance that all but propelled Bolton into the Carling Cup Final in Cardiff next month.

Maybe has been nudged into it by manager Sam Allardyce, who gently pointed out before this semi-final first-leg that for all Okocha's mighty influence, he was overdue to improve his meagre goals tally.

So Nigeria's gifted captain duly signed off before parading his sublime skills in the African Nations Cup by hammering in not one but two free kicks to open and close Bolton's most impressive game of the season.

The in-form midfielder will be back from Tunisia in time for the Millenium Stadium final, which would be Bolton's first since 1995. No Wanderers fan greeted Okocha's second goal more than Allardyce, who nominated him as the club's best ever player.

While those who recall the Lion of Vienna, Nat Lofthouse in his pomp might beg to differ, Allardyce said that, "I've been associated with this club for seventeen years and not seen anyone better, not even Nat Lofthouse. Jay Jay's talent is unquestionable. If that goal is not the goal of the season I don't know what is".

It was Okocha who dominated and beguiled with another performance that probably makes it that much harder for Bolton to keep a hold of him for next season with Europe's top clubs taking note.

His opening goal after two minutes owed a lot to a blatant dummy run from Giannakopoulos and some poor defending by Villa, as his free kick beat both the poorly constructed defensive wall and the poorly positioned Thomas Sorensen.

But his eightieth minute closer brought the house down, swerving the ball past defenders and Sorensen from a particularly difficult angle with such sheer power that the goalkeeper was beaten all ends up.

By rights he should be already practicing those at Nigeria's training camp in Tunisia and Allardyce said that, "He's done a magnificent job staying as long as he did. He's been strong enough to resist huge pressure. Now we have to make sure we go through so that wonderful display is not wasted." Okocha, still to discuss a new contract said that, "It's been a difficult week for me. I played under massive pressure tonight and I am glad it's over. I hope to stay at the club. I am having a great time here".

He is not the only one playing with a smile on his face at the Reebok. Bolton's football has blossomed and matured this season, and Villa walked straight into an opening blitz that stopped them in their tracks. Okocha's first had barely registered before Nolan held off Peter Whittingham, then beat Mellberg and finally Sorensen for the home side's second after eight minutes.

Then Giannakopoulos came up with his own candidate for goal of the game with a bicycle kick that put Bolton three-nil ahead on seventeen minutes, only for Juan Pablo Angel to trump that with a stunner that dipped over Jaaskelainen from a tight angle three minutes later. Angel's hotly disputed and scrambled second for Villa after fifty-five minutes, when the TV replays appeared to confirm Bolton's protests that he was offside, seemed to set up a storming come back.

Instead Bruno N'Gotty highlighted Villa's woeful defending by stretching Bolton's lead with a free header from Youri Djorkaeff's seventy-third minute corner kick, before Okocha, inevitably, applied the 'coup de grace'. There was also a terrific display from French international Youri Djorkaeff, a player who has impressed me enormously since joining a club that was destined for nationwide football on his arrival. He has brought a thing of the past, the fetch and carrying of the football, the man in there who keeps things going, meaning he is forever keeping the ball moving, putting the opposition forever under pressure, a player that Chelsea have not got. In Lampard they have what I call a box to box player and although his game has improved out of all proportions after the sticky start he had in the royal blue shirt of Chelsea Football Club. With players like Okocha in the team you need that flowing football, for if you knock the ball about, nine times out of ten the Nigerian will be sure to get the service he requires to get at the back four. I am sure Djorkaeff will lead Bolton through to Cardiff because he will influence the pace of Bolton's game in the return at Villa Park.
Bolton 5 Aston Villa 2 Att: 16,302

Before I go onto my next point about defensive walls, I sat wondering just how Roman Abramovich spent £112million on over a half a dozen players and the mention of at least a dozen or more top class players did not include the brilliant Nigerian. I know there may be a question about his age – thirty-years-old – but they cannot use that as an excuse, for Okocha has at least four good years left in a body that is fit, strong and looks like he really takes care of it. There is not a Chelsea player who has put in a performance like that since Abramovich has taken over, or long before actually. He was majestic in all he did and made players like Makelele and Geremi look like selling platers. I just hope that when he returns from Tunisia he will repeat such a performance at Cardiff in late February. The black countries really are producing some wonderful talents these days but, as I said before, this is a black player with half white attitude, for many are moody and do not like the other side of the game. The thing that comes natural in English players – from their schooldays – is that they are prepared to graft, and know that there is a defensive side to a football match. Discipline is something that – even with the Brazilians over the years – sometimes go AWOL.

ANOTHER P**** IN THE WALL

I must go back to the two Jay Jay freekicks for the Villa keeper was finger-wagging his players for the diabolical setting up of the defensive wall. I have been saying for a long time now that if I were a coach or manager of a football team these days I would scrap the idea of the wall. The reason being that it attracts great strikers of the ball to shoot and the number of goals today scored with the keeper unsighted is incredible. I once said to my mate Harry Redknapp that he should try it in training, by putting a player on each goalpost and the keeper standing on his six yard line, and I would lay money that the kicker would think twice about taking on the shot. What you would have is the free-kick taker facing a situation where he could not aim at any given spot and this would deter him and unlike having a wall – make the goalkeeper the one who has the clear picture and could actually stand on his six yard line and invite the shot to be taken. Mark my words, if one team went through a routine by doing this others would follow. The argument against my theory is that the players on the post would be playing the opposing players onside, but that is no big deal because all you would have is a matchlike situation as the ball is played, and the players on the line quickly push out about ten yards leaving any stragglers offside. There are just too many goals scored these days with the ball being lighter and all, and of course what is the worth of having a goalkeeper if he cannot see the ball. I just hope when this book is published someone might just take me up on this crucial situation. If it were not for the defensive wall David Beckham would not be such a household name!

'SCARBOROUGH FAIR'

That, apart from cricket – Yorkshire being my team years ago – the fair is all I know of such a place and I am sure threequarters of the Chelsea team know even less, but at 12.30 Saturday lunchtime they will know a little more. Isn't fate fantastic when two balls are pulled out of the bag like these two, with the richest club drawn against the poorest, almost like something out of 'Roy of the Rovers' which is what the FA Cup is all about. I don't know how many hundreds of teams begin the season in this competition – the greatest domestic cup in the world – and that tells you just how marvellous Scarborough have done and I believe they should have been given the option to play at Stamford Bridge so that they could reap the benefits of such a wonderful cup run. Okay, some will say that it is great for the city to have the 'elite' travel to town, but at the end of the day money pays bills not memories or day trips!

It is also interesting that the bookmakers differ a little with Ladbrokes going Chelsea at 1/10 Scarborough 16/1 with the draw an 11/2 shot. On the other hand William Hill go 1/8 Chelsea with Scarborough 14/1 and 5/1 the draw. My bookmaker WilsonSports and Racing are far more generous than the others, always offering better odds, only slightly, but when you are betting five timers that 'slightly' becomes far greater than you can imagine. Bookmakers are rarely wrong but would it take a very brave man to lay out eight grand to get nine back if Chelsea win this intriguing cup-tie. Surely Chelsea have far too much firepower for Scarborough although some will say that the last time these two teams met Scarborough went through to the next round of the Football League Cup in 1989.

'WE'LL WIN THE LOT'
'I'm gunner help us make history by bagging four trophies'

Gilberto Silva cannot wait to sink his claws into Junhino as the Boys from Brazil warm up for the latest round of football's longest running feud.

Arsenal's World Cup winning midfielder confidently declares that the all-conquering Gunners can create soccer history by four major trophies. He said that, "This season could not have gone much better for Arsenal so far. We are top of the Premiership, through to the next round of the Champions League, in the Carling Cup semi-finals and still involved in the FA Cup. We have a great chance to win many trophies and I think we can pick up all four. Of course, that will not be easy – because there are many other good teams waiting out there to beat us. We need to keep believing in ourselves to work hard and play hard. But if we can continue to perform like we have been over the last month, then we will have a very good chance.

"It is not a problem for me to play so many games – I am used to that. In Brazil it was crazy. We would play Sunday Tuesday, Thursday and then Sunday again – up to eighty games a season. So I don't need a rest. Everything is so different in England. I had to change some parts of my game and become more physical. I wanted to do that as quickly as possible. I could have gone to other countries after the World Cup yet I chose Arsenal because this was the best opportunity to show what I can do".

Arsenal hammered Steve McLaren's team 4-0 at the Riverside and 4-1 at Highbury earlier this month. Boro beat a second string Gunners side at Highbury last Tuesday and the two clubs lock horns for the second leg at the Riverside next Wednesday. Gilberto said that, "I told Junhino I don't want to see you anymore on the pitch this season. Normally we are good friends, we played together when Brazil won the World Cup in 2002 and talked many times of football in England.

"He loves this country and loves the football here. If he didn't he would have not come back to Middlesbrough. He would have stayed in Brazil or joined a club in Spain. After Wednesday's match we will get together and talk about the game, our lives and many other things. But until then, we are not talking – and we are not friends".

Well, I have warned players of shouting from the rooftops because the whole country can hear them and that only spells trouble with a capital T. Confidence is one thing but this kind of talk is sheer lunacy. Did you ever hear Tony Adams saying such things as he led one of my old clubs through match after match marshalling a defence superbly?

Arsenal went on the rampage again against Boro scoring four goals against them in three times this season when fielding their strongest team, which is a feat in itself for McLaren's team are well drilled and have always been a tough nut to crack even if you do come from Brazil – excuse the pun.

This article came out on the eve of the FA Cup fourth round, and it seems that Gilberto is intent on putting more pressure on his team by bragging that Arsenal are going to sweep the board. I have already warned the likes of Norbert Solano at Newcastle and also Frank Lampard and John Terry at the Bridge. Gilberto Silva, the Arsenal and Brazil midfielder has said he has played eighty matches in a season before now and is not fazed by the long hard English season one iota. But once again I remind you of such statements and, as I wrote earlier, the manager Arsene Wenger himself put his foot in it last season by saying they would go through the entire Premiership season unbeaten.

'PUB TEAM'

I will not apologise to anyone for what I am about to put down in front of you, the reader – but this Chelsea performance against non-league Scarborough was nothing short of scandalous. Being their best player on so many occasions this season already, Chelsea owed this victory to John Terry who buried a header for Chelsea's one solitary goal against these gritty and determined no-hopers. We were at our usual table in the Grosvenor Club at twelve noon to settle down for the 12.30 kick-off and the chat was all about the gambling side of this match. The best being betting John Terry to score the first goal then after that – as it turned out – Chelsea were 2/7 to be winning at half-time. That means if you put £7 over the counter you would collect nine back, no matter how the game ended. In the opening half Frank Lampard crashed a sweet thirty yarder onto their crossbar and from there on in it was a calamity of calamities, and 'no' David James was not in goal.

I wrote about Eidur Gudjohnsen not scoring enough goals and this match was a perfect example of what I am talking about. Firstly he went through with the keeper to beat and rolled a pathetic right-footed shot into his hands. Then not long afterwards he missed an even easier one, but he was not alone in what was to become almost like watching a match over Battersea Park between two pub teams who had been to a late night party until the early hours. Passing was hit and miss and at times quite appalling, and I will not stand for excuses about the playing surface because we played on the pitches like that for the most part of our season back in the seventies. This was not a performance good enough from the new Chelsea and even the most ardent of supporters in this 'blinding' little drinking club were not impressed. Okay, they created several great chances and some were harder to miss than to score and once again we had yet another blundering refereeing display. Scarborough should have equalised with about a quarter of an hour to go when a cross found defender Colin Cryan all alone on the edge of the six-yard line. His header – into the hands of Cudicini – equalled all of Chelsea's glaring misses. Cynan said that, "I wish that chance had fallen to Mark Quayle instead of me. You could see the heartache on my face as I ran back".

Mark Quayle himself said that "John Terry was awesome, it was a pleasure to play against him".

This could be the reason Quayle has made it in the big time, finding it a pleasure to play against the best central defender in the country.

But the blunder was still to come, after Cynan missed what was as good a chance as we saw all day and their very last throw of the dice. But then minutes later when Billy Gallas went up for a high ball only to bring his right arm up and somehow knock it away. Penalty!

Absolutely nailed on penalty, which even those same bluenoses scoffed at. The cowboy with the whistle was Barry Knight and him and his two little friends along either touchline were nowhere to be seen either. This was the third big match in a row that the man with the whistle has made terrible decisions, which could be of great importance as we enter the last third of the season. For Scarborough alone it cost them another moneyspinning match at Stamford Bridge on Wednesday week, and of course the players – who battled so bravely – the opportunity to experience a night in the FA Cup at the new Chelsea's stadium!

I felt for Scarborough because they deserved a replay for the way they went into this match. There were no 'bashing' tactics to try to stop their illustrious opponents and once in possession they played some nice football, just as Yeovil had done in the previous round against Liverpool. Chelsea – in the end – could not wait to get off the field and as far away from Scarborough as possible. I did not bother listening to the aftermatch analysis for we had seen enough of what I can only explain as a match to 'forget' and as the Tinkerman had put it after the Birmingham game, that he looks at it as 'a half full, not half empty', meaning the negatives were too embarrassing to talk about so just try to pick out the positives, and on this day of a shambolic cup tie the country saw a new side to the Tinkerman and his new Chelsea. Jesper Gronkjaer continues to disappoint and there was one time when John Terry picked up a ball wide in his own half and ran at the home defence as if to show all of these so-called strikers the way to go about their job. He finally struck the ball just wide but it was one piece of constructive play and I am sure Terry will not be happy with several of his superstar teammates. I will not pour any more petrol onto this already blazing fire and will just say well done to the non-leaguers and if it had not been for yet another refereeing "blunder" they would have earned themselves a well-deserved replay at Stamford Bridge. And for all of these players it would have been an experience of a lifetime but again the third eye was not focusing and one of the most blatant penalties you'll ever see went Chelsea's way. It is little bits of luck like this that win you cup competitions, so who knows?

The *Mail on Sunday* headlined it best by printing MILLIONAIRES FIND IT'S NO BEACH PARTY and CHELSEA SURVIVE AS SEADOGS ARE DENIED SPOT OF GLORY. The actual write up will tell you no more than what I have and as I said a little earlier, it is a match best forgotten.

On the same page the Charlton chairman – who returned from holiday today – seems to have changed his tune according to Rob Draper. The latest offer fro Chelsea for Scott Parker has reached £10million, £15million less than Richard Murray said would be an offer he could just not refuse. It only took a couple of dozen lines at the foot of the page so it really does not carry much weight.

The draw for the fifth round will be drawn at 1.30pm today so let's have a look at how your teams fared at the weekend in the FA Cup:

Arsenal 4 (Bergkamp, Lundberg 2 and Bentley) Middlesbro 1 (Job) 37,256

Birmingham 1 (Hughes) Wimbledon 0 22,159

Burnley 3 (I.Moore and Blake 2) Gillingham 1 Henderson 9,375

Coventry 1 (Joachim) Colchester 1 Adebola own goal) 16,341

Everton 1 (Jeffers) Fulham 1 (Davies) 27,862

Ipswich 1 (Reuser) Sunderland 2 (Smith and Arca) 21,406

Liverpool 2 (Cheyrou 2) Newcastle 1 (Robert) 41,385

Luton 0 Tranmere 1 (Mellon) 8.767

Manchester City 1 (Anelka) Spurs (Doherty) 1 34,000

Notts Forest 0 (Sheffield United 3 (Lester penalty, Morgan and Allison) 17,206

Portsmouth 2 (Taylor both) Scunthorpe 1 (Parton) 17,509

Scarborough 0 Chelsea 1 (Terry) 5,379

Swansea 2 (Robinson and Trundle) Preston 1 (Eluhu) 10,2000

Wolves 1 (Ganea) West Ham United 3 (Deane, Harewood and Connolly) 24,419

'QUOTES OF THE WEEK'

Quotes of the week come from my mate Harry Redknapp, who has been travelling Europe looking for a front partner for Teddy Sherringham. Harry said, "I've travelled so much I am not sure if deep vein thrombosis is an illness or a Greek centre-forward". And followed up with "I have been lying in bed the other night thinking about strikers. Now I know a few years ago I remember when there were always better things to do in bed than that". I suppose Sandra had a little smile when reading that, but she knows by now that Harry has a sense of humour all his very own. He needed a sense of humour once listening to the draw of the fifth round of the FA Cup as his team drew Liverpool away from home. The complete draw is to come, with the biggest match bringing Arsenal and Chelsea together once again – in fact the fourth time in four years – with the Gunners winning the other three. This is a massive opportunity for Chelsea to get one back on the team, who at this moment in time have a sign over them, just as Chelsea has the sign over Arsenal's north London neighbours Spurs. This match will be the perfect stage for Chelsea to hit the heights that they are searching and aiming to become a part of. So one of the 'Big Three' will be missing from the sixth round draw, and I wonder if the Tinkerman will use Gilberto's claim that my other old team can win all four trophies this time around. The perfect 'motivation' ploy if Ranieri can put it across to his players in the right manner. This is the match – psychologically – that can be Chelsea's launching pad into the rest of the season. They were unlucky in the league match there earlier this season – their first Premiership defeat under the new owner – when Carlo Cudicini made a horrendous mistake letting in Thierry Henry for the winning goal. A strange 'assist' for the ultra-reliable Italian goalkeeper and one he will need to get out of his system once making his first save in what will be a real 'humdinger' of a cup tie.

This brings back memories of our Chelsea '70' team who drew Arsenal at home and after two great goals from Johnny Hollins – the goal of the month – and the 'wizard of Os' who sent a sizzling volley into the left side of Bob Wilson's goal, a strike that 'Megs' as we called the Arsenal shot stopper then, never looked like getting to, in fact, the ball was coming back out off the stanchion as Wilson was still in the air. That is not being critical of Bob, just simply reminding those Chelsea fans of the kind of goal that was Osgood's trademark and the bigger the matches the better his goals. We were mugged in this match, although Arsenal came back strong and thoroughly deserved the result, but at Highbury on the Wednesday evening's replay we should have been home and hosed by half-time as Bill Garner gave the Arsenal defence a real chasing, although it was his aerial threat that they could not cope with. When big Bill was on song, as he was this night, there was no player who could jump higher to head balls around his marker. However it seemed that he did not really have the best time at the Bridge but that was because it was a real difficult time for everyone at that time, with the problems between certain players and the manager. But Bill on this evening should have been our match winner and although we led one–nil after another one of his headers found Peter Houseman, all Nobby had to do was simply knock it past Wilson.

The game was heading for extra time when Steve Kember was adjudged to have brought down George Armstrong and the ever reliable Alan Ball kept his cool and stepped up to knock us out of a tie that could have gone either way. I must say, one reason for our getting knocked out was my form taking a dip and I was short on confidence for a reason I cannot remember, but I felt responsible, for had I played anywhere near my best, I am certain we would have won this tie. But that is the thing about cup football, you only have one chance unless the obvious, going into a replay.

Apart from that, Highbury was a good ground for me, until I joined them that is, in my first season we thrashed them in tremendous style winning by three goals and once leaving for Stoke City I returned – although terribly drunk – and scored the only goal in a very good City win. The evening before my roommate Geoff Salmons and I went on the town after a bad two first games of the season and Sammy had to get one of our teammates – Eric Skeels – to lace his boots up for him for he had the dreaded 'shakes'. Not a good way to prepare for such a big match in London!

I must stress that this was not the norm, just one of those times when things were not going right and we thought we might as well try to change our preparation and it worked, but I don't think that this would work over a season, but we got away with it and won the match. The strange thing is though, that I scored there half 'Brahms' and when I joined them, I never scored there once sober in about eighteen months, funny old game!

Things have changed dramatically since and you would have to be some kind of fool to abuse the kind of living players have today. But times change and move on and it was only since SKY TV came onto the scene and brought a whole new ball game with them. And I must say it is great for the spectator with the fantastic coverage, although the commentators leave a lot to be desired, instead of Martin Tyler as I mentioned earlier on. This next match between two of my old clubs will surely be televised in a match that could be sold out five times over but before that Chelsea travel to Blackburn at the weekend for yet another live SKY match. Anyhow, here is the draw for the next round; Manchester United versus Manchester City or Tottenham /Tranmere Rovers will play Swansea/ Telford or Millwall will play Burnley/ Sunderland against Birmingham/ Sheffield United against Coventry or Colchester/Liverpool against Portsmouth and Everton or Fulham against West Ham United.

The bookies make Manchester United the 3/1 favourites with both Chelsea and Arsenal 7/2 shots.

But the biggest news in the papers today is the bitter row that goes on at Old Trafford and as promised the 'Coolmore Mafia' have turned the screw on Sir Alex Ferguson. They dominated the headlines all through the nation such as UNITED CHIEFS WILL FIGHT FOR FERGIE DEAL with beside it Board back boss as Irish duo turn screw covered the *Mail* on Monday IT WON'T WASH as Irish pair keep up pressure as United refuse probe covered the back page the following day. The *Mirror* headline was that MAGNIER POWER BATTLE HOTS UP and FERGIE GOING TO ROCK AND

RUIN also that Boss warned, as fight gets dirty. The *Sun* covered it as UNITED BOSS ON THE BRINK and ROCKED as Fergie faces push as rival plans a crisis summit at Old Trafford. The biggest piece was on the inside page of the *Mail* saying that FERGIE IS FACING A FIGHT TO THE FINISH. The *Evening Standard* says those IRISH TYCOONS' 63 QUESTIONS SPARK UNITED DEAL PROBE. I liked the *Express* on Tuesday with a photograph of Sir Alex chewing with that grin that shows us it's another goal for his beloved Manchester United with all around it VICTORY FOR SIR ALEX IN THE OPENING ROUND OF UNITED POWER GAME and DEAL ME IN plus Ferguson will sign contract to thwart the Magnier threat. Opening up there is a double page saying that FERGIE IS DUE A GOOD KICKING also that SIR ALEX WINS ROUND ONE BUT GLOVES ARE OFF AS RIVALS WANT TO SEE BLOOD. Surrounding Richard Tanner's piece was OLD TRAFFORD POWER GAME; UNITED MANAGER CAUGHT BETWEEN A ROCK AND A HARD CASE AS COOLMORE MAFIA STEP UP THE PRESSURE and then CLUB READY TO INVESTIGATE DEALINGS, BUT IT MAY NOT BE ENOUGH FOR MAGNIER. The *Sun* came up with THIS IS A FIGHT TO THE DEATH and UNITED CHIEF; MAGNIER WILL STOP AT NOTHING.

Sir Alex Ferguson is under the microscope as Manchester United last night pledged to investigate their transfer 'gravy train'.

United responded to allegations of inflated transfer fees and illegal payments to agents by promising a 'thorough internal review' of player moves in and out of the club. Their surprise move came in response to calls from the club's biggest shareholder, John Magnier, for greater transparency in the breakdown of the sums paid in transfer deals. Magnier, along with other leading sharehold-ers, has been alarmed by allegations that associates and friends of Ferguson's agent son, Jason, had received commissions from deals. Under scrutiny will be last summer's purchases of American goalkeeper Tim Howard, Brazilian midfielder Kleberson, Portugese winger Cristiano Ronaldo and French striker David Bellion. Rio Ferdinand's British record £30million move from Leeds two years ago, which caused unrest among some shareholders will also be looked at, as will the £28.1million deal for Juan Sebastian Veron, who was sold to Chelsea at a £13million loss.

Magnier is unlikely to be satisfied at the move because the review will be conducted internally. He is demanding an independent audit and is threaten-ing to call on an extraordinary general meeting of shareholders if it is not forthcoming.

United, however, insist that everything has been above board and that while Ferguson identifies the players he wants, he is not involved in the financial side of the deals.

The champions took the unusual step of issuing a full statement to the Stock Exchange of their policy and procedures on the buying and selling of players and a copy of it is printed below.

The statement repeats that the plc board decides on the buying and selling of players and the handling of monies, and Ferguson's only involvement is in identifying players to be bought or sold.

United have also pledged to provide additional information on transfer deals. It started on Friday – it is Tuesday today – when they unveiled £12.25million buy Louis Saha.

The club revealed that £750,000 would be paid to agents. Club sources say there is little they can do if agents are a part of their cut to associates or friends. But why such a large amount was paid when it was clear the former Fulham striker wanted to join United is not explained. Magnier and other shareholders will also want answers to allegations that United paid £6million more to Sporting Lisbon for Ronaldo than any other club offered. They will want to know what work was done by Swiss agent Gaetano Marotta in the deal to bring Howard to the club from New York/Jersey Metrostars. Marotta was allegedly paid £150,000.

Other questions needing answers relate to why Kleberson's official agent in Brazil was elbowed aside and the deal was brokered by two others stipulated by United and whether Jason Ferguson's Elite Sports Agency had paid for Bellion's car and mobile phone while he was a Sunderland player.

United's decision to spend £7.5million on Uruguay international striker Diego Forlan two years ago has long been queried, while nearly £3million of the £28.1million paid for Veron went on agents' commissions. Also, the Veron deal was agreed with Lazio while the Italian club still owed United money from the purchase of Jaap Stam.

As it said above they gave the following; United's statement that outlines the policies and procedures followed during transfer and contract negotiations.

What makes me laugh is when Roman Abramovich entered the scene by saving Chelsea's hide, he was questioned, yet all this has been going on for so long, and if it had not been for the 'gesture' from Magnier to Ferguson to put his name to this wonderful horse none of this would have come out and they would have all been bosom buddies and the show goes on. Manchester United have become so powerful but they might have been a little more careful as to whom they let into their football club. Magnier and McManus, the two biggest shareholders never go to a match and I don't even think they like football too much, and yeah, I know that is immaterial in this matter but I find it surprising that the Old Trafford boss got involved with people who have no interest in the club, just like he had no interest in horse racing before they made him this more than generous offer. How the world turns in such mysterious ways, as Sir Alex said that he needed to find something outside of football to take the pressure off him and a day at the races suited him right down to the ground. They still show the photographs of him leading the Rock of Gibraltar back to the winners' enclosure with a beam as big as when United hit that late winner in that dramatic finale in the Champions League Final against Bayern Munich. Anyhow, let the battle go on while we get back to the game of football. The last piece of news out of the Bridge today was that PETIT CHASING DEAL FOR LIFE by Matt Hughes of the *Evening Standard*. Emmanuel Petit today urged Chelsea to offer him a new contract so he can end his career at Stamford Bridge.

The midfielder's deal expires at the end of the season and the club have yet to begin talks about a possible extension.

Petit made his first Chelsea appearance for four months in their 1-0 FA Cup win over Scarborough and knows he is playing for his future. It was reported last week that Petit plans to return to France with Paris St-Germain in the summer. But the Frenchman, whose side face a London derby at Arsenal in the fifth round said that, "I want to win the title with Chelsea and after that we'll see what happens. I saw in the newspaper a week ago that I was going back to France but I didn't say those things.

"I would like to stay at Chelsea for the rest of my career".

With manager Claudio Ranieri blaming his side's recent slump on the tiredness of Frank Lampard and Claude Makelele, Petit's recovery from a knee injury is a timely boost. Ranieri hopes to increase his midfield options by signing Scott Parker by the end of the week. One of the longest running disciplinary cases in football will be resolved today when Joe Cole's appeal against a misconduct charge for last season's fracas at Bolton is heard by the Football Association.

Cole, who was then at West Ham, was given a two match and a £15,000 fine last month for his part in the heated exchanges last April.

The 23-year-old admits to using abusive language on the pitch but denies the tirade was directed at the fourth official.

As for the Manu Petit situation, I feel Chelsea will be foolish to offer him an extension on his contract because he has been one of the biggest disappointments I have seen in a player since leaving Arsenal. I watched him several times for Barcelona and he looked out of his depth and through that and his unimpressive form with the Blues I would go elsewhere to find a more exciting and imaginative midfield player. I think looking back Patrick Vieira must have carried his French international teammate in that wonderful double winning season before Petit and Dutch winger Marc Overmars both left for Barcelona in yet another Wenger masterstroke of a deal. Isn't it funny how the Arsenal manager was not interested in him when he came back from Spain and that alone tells me I must not be far off the mark on this one. I think if they do offer him a new contract, it will be just another step in the wrong direction for the Tinkerman and I would fear the worst and Chelsea might begin looking for a new manager before the ink has dried. It would not surprise me if Roman Abramovich has checked out Martin O'Neill at Celtic as the Tinkerman's predecessor. The Northern Irishman has a great CV and I know that Manchester United would love him to take over the reigns from Sir Alex. His teams play without fear and he has obviously learned his trade from the great Brian Clough, if not totally, a little here and there. He gets the best out of averageness, which is a great asset to have and he would leave the Russian in no uncertain terms about how he is or would tackle such a job. He does not stand for players telling just what they are or are not going to do, players are there to perform. There is a lovely story in Brian's Clough book about his former right winger as to a day in the Charity Shield and Martin was having a field day having scored two goals and was looking for his hat-trick, in fact looking far too hard to the point of 'hogging' the ball to such an extent he was disrupting the teams performance. Clough said that they were murdering Ipswich by five goals in this Charity Shield match at Wembley. He takes over, "If he thought I was against him before that day, he must have been absolutely certain when I made my decision to substitute him. Two goals to his name and he wanted to be a bigger hero still. He wanted a bloody hat-trick!

"Gerrim off" I said to Jimmy Gordon alongside me on the Wembley bench. "You can't do that". "Can't I? If you don't get O'Neill off that pitch right now, I'll sack you". It was unusual to talk to Jimmy like that. Given our background at Middlesbrough – him among the senior professionals and me still wearing L-plates – I regarded and treated him like my elder brother. I paid him as much respect as any manger ever paid any coach. Anyway, he did as I asked, or demanded, and O'Neill came off. He didn't say a word until after the match and then I knew it was coming.

"Why did you bring me off?"

"To save money for the FA" I told him. "The way the match was develop-ing they'd have to chuck on an extra ball – one for everybody else as well as the one you were keeping to yourself".

"Well" he protested, "I had got two goals".

"I know – but you weren't going to get a third by playing on your own. That was a certainty and that is why you had to come off".

Of course he didn't like it. Players never do like decisions that go against them, decisions that let them know the truth. But they do remember them and for any contemplating a career in management, those are the decisions worth remembering.

O'Neill just wouldn't give the ball to anybody. He was after his third goal but in looking for it he had stopped playing for the team. We were playing Ipswich off the pitch. I don't know what the biggest score ever was for a Charity Shield match but we were threatening to break all records. Nevertheless, even though victory was assured against a very accomplished side, O'Neill's selfishness still had to be eliminated in the wider interests of the team. It took him weeks and weeks to get over it. There were many times when I clashed with him, usually when I left him out of the side, and I was forever hearing him moan, "I might as well pack my bags and go back to university". I heard it once too often and pulled him in front of all the other players. "Martin" I said, "I've done you a big favour".

"What's that boss?"

It was a growl or a sulk more than a civilised tone I was entitled to from an educated young man.

"I have arranged that flight for you back to Ireland and I've organised a place at university. Get on it".

He never mentioned university again. Eventually, despite our clashes, he did become an integral part of the side, but for somebody so bright it surprised me that I had to teach him the game. He didn't know at first, not properly. He finished up as second highest goalscorer one season and he might have been our top scorer but he didn't know where the goals were coming from. He hadn't twigged, until I pointed out, that most of those goals could be traced back to the feet of his now assistant, John Robertson.

"Your goals are coming from the left. You're standing there on your own when the ball comes to you because the opposition have been drawn to the magnet on our left wing. That's why you are getting so many chances".

I had to explain things like that to him. It took him a couple of years into his managerial career before he asked John Robertson, "What was all that that the gaffer used to shout at me – Get the ball"?

"He used to shout it at me all the time and always after we'd scored".

"If we had the ball, the other side hadn't got it" Robbo replied. "Simple as that." Robbo had known what I meant.

This can be read in Brian Clough's book 'Walking on Water'. A book I highly recommend on the great man's life in the game. I had a run-in with him once but it turned out fine. I think the bloke was absolutely brilliant!

THE SENTINEL

Our newspaper in Stoke-on-Trent, has a new sports page in its Saturday edition where on the back page Richard Adams writes a piece titled BACKDATE. On this Saturday it was dated 18-4-74 with the headline HUDSON MAKES DREAM START plus RECORD SIGNING EARNS PRAISE FROM BOSSES SHANKLY AND WADDINGTON;

Stoke's biggest gate of the season watched new signing Alan Hudson shine on his debut in a 1-1 draw with Liverpool at the Victoria Ground. It was nearly a perfect day for City in front of 33,000 fans as they took the lead against the Reds following a strike from Geoff Hurst.

However, in injury time Tommy Smith turned quickly in the box and fired home to level the scores and deny Hudson a fairytale start to his City career.

"I was pleased with my game" said Hudson. "I did a couple of things right early on and it helped me settle down. The rest of the lads were great and played just as they told me they would. I thought Jimmy Greenhoff in particular was superb because he was always available when I looked up. It is just a pity it is not the start of the season as there are some good players and I fancy we could finish in a high position in the table".

Stoke boss Tony Waddington watched his record transfer pay an instant dividend with an excellent display.

He said that, "It took Gordon Banks a couple of months to prove he was world class, and Jimmy Greenhoff a season to establish himself with the fans. Alan had those fans eating out of his hand. It was a tremendous debut".

Legendary Liverpool manager Bill Shankly was also glowing in his praise for Hudson. "The boy showed his quality" he said. "It is always difficult for a debutant, but he did well and will probably improve his form in time".

Hudson was heavily involved in Stoke's goal. Jimmy Robertson began the move when he crossed for Hudson who let fly with a firsttime shot which ricocheted out of the packed Liverpool defence for Hurst to smash the ball home.

Reds striker Kevin Keegan was a constant menace to the home defence and had a goal disallowed early in the second-half.

Robertson could have wrapped up victory late on, but after being sent clear by Hurst he shot wide. This miss proved costly as, in the dying minutes Smith struck to spoil the Potters' party.

Teams were STOKE; Farmer, Marsh, Pejic, Dodd, Smith, Bloor, Robertson, Greenhoff, Hurst, Hudson and Mahoney.

LIVERPOOL; Clemence, Smith, Lindsay, Thompson, Lloyd, Hughes, Keegan, Cormack, Heighway, Waddle and Callaghan.

Well it always a treat to be mentioned in glowing terms by two managers such as Waddington and Shankly. I can also remember someone saying that another very well respected manager, Stan Cullis of Wolverhampton Wanderers, said on the radio that it was the "finest debut I have seen in all my days in top class football". Thank you for that also Mr Cullis!

It was almost a year later when I gave another super performance against Mr Shankly's team, which I think I mentioned earlier that he entered our dressing room to shake my hand afterwards. This was a match over Easter – when we played three matches in four days – after a 2-2 draw at West Ham on the Friday morning where the impressive Terry Conroy scored both goals; the second one was a treat as I nutmegged my good friend Frank Lampard out on the right before sliding a cross into TC's path to put us back in front.

The following afternoon we drew 1-1 at Highbury with a well struck free-kick from my old roommate Geoff Salmons. The two matches had taken their toll on my still badly injured ankle – from the match at West Bromwich Albion – and my chances of making Monday's clash with the league champions looked highly unlikely. I told my boss in the North Staffordshire Hotel – opposite the station – that my ankle was aching like hell and that it would not stand up to another match on a hard pitch. We had a couple of drinks and before we left he told me to "Go home, put your feet up and prepare as you usually do for a match, just in case it rains". Well, I had a few more drinks knowing that there was no way my ankle would stand up to another ninety minutes against a team like Liverpool – in fact against anybody – so although I went home and put my feet up and kept out of my local pub on the Sunday, I was still a long shot to make the match. I arrived at the ground at my usual time – 1.45pm – and went into our dressing room and to my amazement my kit and boots were laid out. I thought that my boss was up to one his old tricks as to getting me to play just like he told me he talked Sir Stanley Matthews into it some years earlier. Anyhow, I walked towards the tunnel and I was simply shocked to see Liverpool coming off the field asking where we did we get the rain from! There had been no rain from Birmingham to Manchester and Liverpool for days on end and now out pitch took a long stud!

Tony had telephoned the Stoke-on-Trent Fire Department – and I was in seventh heaven able to keep our good run going and also, of course, to play against the team who were the best around.

Anyhow this led to probably my finest display in a Stoke City shirt and Mr Shankly confirmed that it was the best display he had ever seen.

Before I go into the big story of the Chelsea signing of Scott Parker I write to you from a South West train from Portsmouth where I had just been watching their scoreless match against Wolves. This was my first match with Harry of this Premiership season and I thought I might bring him some 'Donald'. I didn't!

They shook the woodwork four times and I jumped into the lap of a good-looking young blonde on the first occasion, thinking that they had taken the lead. But my luck just like Harry's on this day was out!

Teddy Sherringham once again gave a polished and classy display and I could not help thinking of him only two seasons ago doing the same business with Manchester United. What a marvellous player he has been for his every club and country, in very difficult conditions today he was still a player a level ahead. I left Harry at the ground and that great old footballing warrior Jim Smith dropped me at Fratton Station. I know Jim had passed all of his coaching badges but I am not quite as sure has passed his driving test. Thanks Jim!

Portsmouth 0 Wolverhampton Wanderers 0 Att: just over 20,000

The big news was still at Old Trafford and the Ferguson and Magnier affair, one that looks far bleaker for the Scot as the Coolmore Mafia really turn up the heat. This is the first time the nation has seen Sir Alex facing the kind of defeat none of the likes of Sherringham, Beckham, Scholes and now van Nistelrooy can get him out of.

That is the ongoing situation at Old Trafford, whilst elsewhere it was business as usual, buy, selling and buying again. Chelsea once again and Scott Parker!

I wrote earlier about the Charlton Athletic chairman being stuck in between the devil and the deep blue pockets!

The one man so disappointed is the man who has been his tutor for so long at the Valley, manager Alan Curbishley.

Chelsea have, once again, flexed their financial muscle and this time they have bought a player who once again is unproven in the big time. These players that they have bought and bought over this period since the Talisman took over seems to me like as close to a circus as anything in a big production I have ever witnessed?!!

How can you bring nearly a dozen new faces — at over a hundred million pounds — from all around the world, before a ball is kicked, and then six months later need to replace half of them with 'real' players?

I say if you want to go in the right direction — quite simply sell a yacht and or a 747, even both, to get Zinedine Zidane the greatest player in the world. If you cannot get the best player in the world with over £4billion then you have a massive problem!

If you can't steer Zidane away with all of that money the money is not worth the paper it's printed on! The other opportunity is give me the cheque-book and I'll go get him!!

All I'll want out of it is a drink, a large one!

WEEKEND OF WINS FOR THE BIG THREE

It was Manchester United's match first and Gordon Strachan's team made Ferguson's champions fight right to the death. A comeback to form Kevin Phillips fired in the two Saints goals, after heading Saha's free-kick into his own net and then missed a glorious chance almost on the final whistle, as he slid into the six yard box as the ball went straight through his legs out of danger!

This would have made it quite a day for Kevin for there are not many visiting players scoring a hat-trick at Old Trafford, in fact not many teams!

Manchester United could now sit back and hope that their neighbours City could upset Arsenal at Highbury and that Blackburn could do the same against Chelsea. Graeme Souness's team would certainly make it tough going for Chelsea — for like City — they are desperately in the need of the points to get clear of the old trap door!

BIG THREE WIN

After this weekend of wins for the big three it was plainly clear to all of them that even though they are a class apart there are no longer easy matches – even though Aston Villa hit five second-half goals to torture Leicester City, who along with Leeds United – losing 3-0 at home to Middlesbrough – look down and out in their battle to keep Premiership status. As I mentioned earlier, I was not only at the Portsmouth match but also in the manager's office both before and after the match and both sets of coaches were looking anxiously at the day's final results. Life in the basement is absolutely no fun at all!

Harry was struggling so badly to put out a team capable of getting three precious points that he had to wait for his centre-forward to get to the ground from Heathrow Airport, having been sent home from the Nigerian team's manager for being late for a team meeting. This meant that the race was on to get him to Fratton Park to take part in some of the game, and when you have to live like that, you end up living on your nerves. He had a police car get him through the crowds and appeared in the second half, when he missed the best chance of the match, spinning clear in the area and with only Jones to beat hit the goalkeeper with a stunning drive, but should have gone either side of him by placing the ball in to one corner or the other!

Harry must have wished – at that precise moment – that his aeroplane had been delayed?

That cost two Pompey the points which could be very costly come May, but afterwards the blow was a little less severe as Leeds and Leicester City lost – and yesterday Blackburn were dragged closer the drop zone by losing to Chelsea with two minutes on the clock. The headlines read as follows A NICE PAIR FOR FRANK Lamps is simply the best in the *Sun*. RANIERI SALUTES FRANK He's flying in the *Mail*, whilst the *Express* went LAMPARD FINDS ALL THE ANSWERS. The Star put it this way; JOHNSON SAVES THE DAY FOR CHELSEA AS ROVERS SLIP UP Glenn keeps them in title chase. That afternoon's *Standard* said that JOHNSON'S GOAL HAS BLUES IN RAPTURES.

With both Manchester and Arsenal winning their matches it was vital that Chelsea kept in touch with a very late strike from Glen Johnson. Frank Lampard once again was quite brilliant if for only for the way he took his goals and was so close to grabbing a hat trick with a header that Brad Friedel somehow got a hand to.

The astonishing thing about Frank is his ratio of shots on target and as I said earlier in my writing that he works very hard – on the training ground – on his technique. And it was funny just over the last few weeks when – along with Tommy Baldwin – I met up with Charlie Cooke who was visiting from the United States of America. Somebody told me he was interviewed and said of Lampard that "He reminds me so much of Alan Hudson". His header would have made the scoreline 3-1 and Chelsea would then have made life a lot easier for themselves, having lost their lead inside the last five minutes only to hit back with that superb strike into the top corner of Friedel's net. Scott Parker made a satisfactory start after his £10million signing from Charlton. Did I not tell you about the Charlton chairman?

The importance of winning this match was shown at the final whistle as the Chelsea players ran and jumped all over Chelsea's third goal getter. There has been talk about bringing in new fullbacks but maybe this super strike might change certain people's minds.

This was the most important goal of the season so far, for had Chelsea left Ewood Park dropping two points – against a team slipping into the danger zone – they would have lost important ground with the two at the top. That is really just how important this match was?

The Tinkerman said that, "When they scored in the last few minutes, I thought the match was finished. But my players have very strong character. They wanted to win and it was good for us. We started very badly. After this, we played very good football. We must be more cynical – surely he means clinical – When we have the chance, we must kill the game off. We had two or three chances to finish the match. If you don't the other team can still win or draw. We must improve on this. We want to arrive at the top like Arsenal and Manchester United because we aren't like them. They are used to this position. For us, it is the first time and we must continue to build our foundation". Ranieri said of Parker that, "It was a good debut for Parker. I'm very pleased with his performance. He had only one training session with us but played very well. I changed his position three times – there's a shock – and now he knows me very well". But once again it was up to the midfield player and left-sided defender to deliver the goals that won this match, which surely must be a big concern after all the dough they have spent on strikers!

The match began in a frantic fashion when after only two minutes they were caught stone cold and only the brilliance of Carlo Cudicini kept it scoreless with a superb reflex save from a Jon Douglas volley. If that wasn't a wake-up call then the next Rover's attack definitely was, as a minute later Marcus Babbel headed back a cross from new signing Michael Gray into the path of Garry Flitcroft, who nonchalantly volleyed past Cudicini. 1-0.

As the Blackburn captain celebrated his second goal in successive matches, Cudicini must have been wondering what was going on for this was the first goal he had conceded in 420 minutes of football. That was after only three minutes, then following that he panicked with a back pass from John Terry – and hit a ball, which thankfully ricocheted out of the path of the oncoming Dwight Yorke. Chelsea all of a sudden were now living very dangerously. But they eased into the match, and Jimmy Floyd went close before Frank Lampard latched on to a Jimmy Floyd pass and steered it sweetly into Friedel's far post with the inside of his right foot. 1-1 and very much game on!

Chelsea had now taken over and ten minutes later they went ahead when an awful pass from Tugay's misjudged pass found Manu Petit – not half the player he was at Arsenal – who played a square ball into the path of the oncoming Lampard – once again – the bang-in-form midfield player made no mistake. 2-1 and Rovers came back immediately with substitute Paul Gallagher hitting a fine goal which was judged offside and it was the same player who got Blackburn back in the game with only three minutes on the clock, rifling home a first time cross from Tugay. Chelsea looked down and out and just as I turned around to my uncle George and said "Georgie, I fancy them to get another one", as the last word came out of my mouth the Chelsea fullback Glen Johnson – in the middle of a goalmouth melee – fired a sweet shot into the top corner of Blackburn's net. This is always a great time to go ahead and so it proved as Graeme Souness must have wondered just what was happening in a defence that would not give you too much confidence going into the Premiership run-in at the wrong end of the table?

Michael Hart – a West Ham United supporter – was quick to point out that Lampard's form is more than good enough to hold a place down in Sven Goran Eriksson's team which will play in Portugal. Would that be because Frank began his career at the West Ham Academy?

In Ken Dyer and Michael Hart the *Evening Standard* have two very talented and experienced writers. This is why I have chosen the *Standard* for so many quotes and stories, which include the Tinkerman!

His article in the Evening Standard was headlined

FRANK CUT OUT TO BE SVEN'S DIAMOND

When the Tinkerman was asked if Lampard was the best midfielder in the country he was quick to answer "I think so. I'm very pleased with him. In this league, it's amazing. He's strong with good long passing, good vision and strong in the tackle now. I think he has scored ten goals now which is quite unbelievable, very, very good".

CARLING CUP FINALISTS

All heads were now turned to both second legs of the Carling Cup and on this Tuesday evening Bolton took a three-goal advantage to Villa Park and were they lucky to leave there with a place booked for Cardiff at the end of the month. Sending-offs were becoming second nature now – rife in fact – and the home side played with ten men for over an hour. But O'Leary's team threw everything at Allardyce's side but could not get that all-important third goal. Overall Bolton deserved it through their performance in the first leg and that wonderful performance by Jay Jay Okocha, who missed this match through being in Tunisia with Nigeria playing in the Africans Cup. The score-line of Aston Villa 2 Bolton 0 was not good enough on an evening of high passion and dramatic goalmouth incidents. The following night the red card was out again and this time it was the very experienced defender Martin

Keown who was the culprit and, like the night before, the 'Copper in the Middle' had no choice but to send him back to the away team dressing room. Arsenal who were trailing by one goal – through Jonathon at Highbury – were once again under strength – which gave Boro the initiative to take the game to them, something they would have had to be careful about had the likes of Pires and Henry been about. Arsene Wenger got both the first and second legs wrong and was dumped out for his ignoring the fact that any Cup Final is one you cannot turn your nose up at. Chelsea's on-loan midfielder Zenden did the trick after a lovely weighted pass from Menietta. The Dutchman coolly slipping the ball past Arsenal's young goalkeeper which meant the Gunners had to fight an uphill battle with their ten men having to really pull something out of the fire. Arsenal did pull one back, but minutes from time their new £17million player Reyes came back to help in defence and as a loose ball ran across the edge of the penalty area he took a swipe at the ball which ended up in his own team's net and that was what they say was 'History'. It was now a Bolton and Middlesbrough Carling Cup Final. The top three were all now back to the drawing board as they strive for both the Premiership and the Champions League, not forgetting FA Cup glory. But one thing for sure was that only two of them could progress into the sixth round of the FA Cup as Chelsea and Arsenal were due to fight out their fifth round tie at Highbury in ten days' time.

CLOSING THE WINDOW

On that last day of window-shopping, there was a scramble for three top players and Chelsea were the only one of the three who didn't go for the chequebook, for a change!

Manchester United had recruited Louis Saha from Fulham for a cool £12million whilst the Gunners paid £17million for Reyes – as you already know – but it was Spurs who got the best of the bunch by capturing Jermain Defoe for a 'paltry' – in these days – £7million from West Ham with Bobby Zamora – a sensation at Brighton a couple of seasons ago – part of the deal, going over to Upton Park. Defoe is a player I rate highly and a player I felt that Chelsea should have snapped up as their forwards are still not hitting the net enough as Frank Lampard takes over as their leading goal getter!

I am surprised that the Tinkerman did not call Frank in and get his opinion on this very talented 'tiny'' striker. Or maybe he did?

The other big news is still the Ferguson and Magnier battle and I hear from certain quarters that the Coolmore Mafia have the Old Trafford boss just where they want him. In fact if there were a firing squad ready –and waiting – to pull the trigger it would be the Manchester United manager facing them?

I believe that this time Sir Alex has bitten – not only the hand that fed him – but far too much to chew, and we all know how much he chews.

He would have been better taking the £7million 'get-out' offer and made up his money with a chewing gum advertisement!

In the *Express* Harry Harris writes about the MANCHESTER UNITED CRISIS SPECIAL and that EGOS PUT PEACE DEAL ON THE ROCKS.

John Manier intensified the growing pressure on Sir Alex Ferguson when his lawyers yesterday – Monday the 2nd of February – took the row over Rock of Gibraltar back to the Dublin courts.

Leading Manchester United shareholder, Magnier's lawyers applied to the High Court for a 'motion to comply' after club boss Ferguson apparently missed three deadlines to clarify and detail his claim over the horse's stud fees.

After Ferguson issued the writ, Magnier's legal team applied to the High Court for details of the claim for half the horse's stud rights. They could be worth up to £100million over ten years.

The clarification Magnier sought did not materialise on January 12th. A seven-day extension was granted and then another deadline of noon on January the 30th came and went without any response from Ferguson's side.

Yesterday from his Barbados retreat, he instructed his lawyers to go to court and a hearing before the High Court judge is set for ten days time.

So what will it take to broker a peace deal?

Ferguson has been advised by the club to settle the acrimonious dispute.

On the table?

Just £45,000 a year – or stud season – from Magnier. That is just one stud session by the champion horse. Is that enough to bring Ferguson to a deal?

Not likely.

He knows the pressure is on to settle, and quickly. But the smart money will be on him wringing at least a little extra from Magnier. That could be two, possibly three 'stud covers' from the Rock. If he gets it, Ferguson's legal action over the horse will be dropped.

An insider told me yesterday; "One cover a season is worth 64,0000 euros and, who knows, next year if the fillies start winning, then one cover could be worth £200,000.

"The offer of one cover has always been on the table and John Magnier is not sitting down to talk about it".

Effectively, with pressure being applied on Ferguson from the club, Magnier has the manager over a barrel. No wonder he is considering his legal tactic to force Ferguson into a Dublin Court to 'show his hand'.

Lawyer's negotiations could increase the number of covers but Ferguson would have to forget any ideas of a multi-million pound dividend from the horse. The Rock's stud career could be worth a total in excess of £100million but that sort of money now looks out of reach. The message from the Magnier camps in Dublin and Barbados is certainly an uncompromising one – back down or the scrutiny of Ferguson's transfer and other dealings goes on.

The insider warned that, "This issue is still heading for the courts if Sir Alex believes there is a big cash settlement to be negotiated".

Ferguson, although he insisted the legal proceedings, knows he cannot now pursue that path to the bitter end either. That is why an out of court settlement could be reached as early as this week.

The difficulty is finding any face saving compromise – in such a fierce clash of large personalities and egos.

RONALDO

On the SPORTS AGENDA with Charles Sale read that: There have been strong denials from Stamford Bridge but those connected to Real Madrid's want-away striker Ronaldo, insist he will be in London today to discuss personal terms with Chelsea. Even if overweight Ronaldo makes an appearance – he's due to have treatment in Spain for a thigh injury – the 15lb he's said to have put on over the last two months is not a great advert for his services.

It was one day last week in our club that we heard the news of both Ronaldo and Beckham having been seen inside Stamford Bridge. The rumours were twisted like Spaghetti Junction but it came from more than one source, which is to be taken as if they were there. It could have been a promotional trip or a real deal, and let's not forget Beckham and Peter Kenyon know each other from their Manchester United association. However, I cannot see the England captain leaving Madrid, unless of course, his wife is still complaining about living in Spain!

PLEATS NEW AGE BELIEF
Spurs ditch old buying policy and go for young guns

On the afternoon of Tottenham's massive replay against Manchester City – with a trip to Old Trafford for the winners – David Pleat, their caretaker manager, had this to say about a club who were in a transition after the mess Glenn Hoddle made of the club.

This was written by Adrian Curtis of the *Standard*: When Tottenham fans get their first glance of Jermain Defoe at his White Hart Lane unveiling tonight, they will be glimpsing into the future in more ways than one. Aged 21, Defoe fits perfectly into a new strategy pioneered by acting manger Pleat and chairman David Levy, which will remain in place no matter who eventually arrives as first team coach. The days of Teddy Sherringham and Tim Sherwood are officially over; from now on Spurs will buy young players with a residual sell-on value. The dream scenario sees them build a team capable of winning top honours and improving the balance sheet. If all goes to plan, in four years Defoe will be a seasoned England international commanding double the £6.75million that Spurs paid for him.

Of course the best laid plans have a habit of going skew whiff at White Hart Lane, but there is no doubting the prevailing philosophy because it extends beyond Mondays to the players Spurs have failed to bring in during the transfer window.

Their targets all fitted the new Blueprint; Andy Reid at Forest, Diego from

Santos, Paul Robinson and James Milner at Leeds. All are talented young players who almost certainly would have been dismissed as too expensive and too inexperienced by previous managers Glenn Hoddle and George Graham.

It has taken David Pleat and Levy four years to cut the wage bill and install a policy that will, given success on the field, rasp the benefits in future years. Add to that promise of youngsters like Johnnie Jackson, Stephen Kelly, Lee Barnard and Philip Ifil, who have progressed through the club's youth teams, and the scale of the transition is clear.

WHAT DO I THINK? What surprises, or does it, is that it is the year 2004 and they are only just realising that the future of any football club is the young players coming through, just ask Sir Alex Ferguson and Harry Redknapp and his terrific backroom staff led by Tony Carr, whilst my pal was at West Ham United.

That article about the future plans at White Hart Lane was far longer than what I have written for you, but it is quite repetitive and whilst writing it I come over a little light headed about the fact of what age we are living in. The reason I chose to include this is because of the transfer of Jermain Defoe – a player who Chelsea should have bought the very minute the window opened – and I have already told you that I think he is better equipped than all Chelsea's front players to give you the one thing you want for your outlay. Goals!

These were headlines after his signing for Spurs forty-eight hours ago, the reason I did not write this earlier was for the coming to terms with the player personally. And he had to sit and watch a Jekyll and Hyde team performance on the following day.

THE TRANSFER CLOSES, BUT ANOTHER OPENS FOR CONTROVERSIAL STRIKER; There was a big photograph in the Mail but the main headline was all about the Saha and Parker deals with just DEFOE GOES.

The following day in the *Mail* it read THE DEFOE DEBATE – BAD BOY OR BARGAIN BUY; Claire Nash wrote the other headline saying that when Jermain Defoe joined Spurs this week, many West Ham fans were delighted to see him go. Despite his talent, the striker has as many enemies as he has friends.

The *Sun* went SPURS SWOOP AS THE TRANSFER WINDOW SLAMS TIGHT adding STROP IDOLS and Sulking stars have held their clubs to ransom and So Long Jermain; The *Express* simply said DEFOE SNATCHED.

YOU CAN BECOME THE NEW GREAVSIE; Pleat hails 'exceptional' Defoe, was how it read in the *Mirror*, whilst inside the back page read that DEFOE'S FINAL INSULT with Fans' fury over Spurs sale.

The one thing I hope does not happen is the pocket-sized goal-grabber does not hit the target on his debut against Portsmouth tomorrow, and Harry Redknapp echoed my feelings as in the next four days Harry's team face both Spurs at White Hart Lane and a Frank Lampard inspired Chelsea team. These are two players Harry had at West Ham and of course Frank is related to Harry through Harry and Frank Senior marrying the twin sisters Sandra – my ex-hairdresser – and

MISSING COPY

SENSATIONAL STUFF

The last two days are the first that all newspapers have been Chelsea-less. And on this Wednesday it was an FA Cup fifth round replay that became the match of this – and possibly any other season as Spurs hosted Manchester City. The match began well for the 'lily whites' and were cruising 3-0 with goals from Ledley King, a very well taken effort for a big defender, before Robbie Keane made it two with a brilliantly taken goal and then a David Beckham style free-kick from German left back Christian Ziege leaving Kasey Keller stranded to the spot. I keep telling you about these defensive walls, when will coaches and managers learn?

GUTLESS SPINELESS HUMILIATING

Was the headline in the following day's *Evening Standard*.

Anyhow, the whistle went for half time and with the score staying at three it looked very much like the north London outfit would be travelling to the other half of Manchester for a 'plum' fifth round match, which would leave them only a hundred and eighty minutes away from Cardiff and an FA Cup Final. A lot of spectators in the ground – which was buzzing with excitement – would not have seen the 'Copper in the Middle' show young Manchester City's Joey Barton a red card for an earlier incident of dissent and on the whistle he continued to give Rob Styles verbal in such a manner he was sent walking off not to be seen in the second half. I would lay money that the majority of the 30,400 attendance did not realise that City were down to ten men as the whistle blew for start of the second half!

So with Nicholas Anelka having left the field with a groin strain, City looked doomed having lost their best player with injury and young Barton off for abusing the 'Mug in the Middle' all looked doom and gloom as Kevin Keegan took his seat on the bench looking a hundred and ten years old and a chin that could have swept the touchline, it was that low. But minutes into the restart captain Distin 'ghosted'" into a goal scoring position and headed the goal that began this remarkable comeback. On the hour Paul Bosvelt pulled another one back after his shot was heavily deflected off of Anthony Gardner and then the best player on view, Shaun Wright-Phillips, streaked down the right side of Spurs defence and kept his composure – at full speed – to chip in City's equaliser. 3-3 and Keegan was up on his feet going bananas from the City bench. His face had gone from one of a ghost to one of a clown and I don't know which one suited him most!

But whatever, he could now pick his chin off of the track and spur his team with some of the most animated moves I have seen from a touchline. With extra-time lurking Spurs were now the ones vulnerable, and with virtually the last tick on the clock John Macken became the next 'ghost' now as he went on the blind side of Gardner and King to head the winner, 4-3, and the whole place went berserk as poor Kasey Keller just sat there and looked into space, the one between his two defenders and Macken, the hero of this extraordinary FA Cup tie.

This was truly remarkable and to make things worse my great friend Michael Carter had Fulham to knock out Everton – which they did by two goals to one – and three other winning teams – including Middlesrough to beat Arsenal – the evening before, all going onto a Tottenham victory.

At 3-0 up and City with a man short he was counting his winnings!

And as the great Jimmy Greaves would say once again "It's a funny old game".

Thursday was full of Kevin Keegan and his 'miracle' halftime team talk, but I did not see it that way. With ten men you have absolutely nothing to lose, except your pride and it took that pride to get them out of deep trouble, and it also proves again that the team with the eleven players on the field are more vulnerable than the team with ten. Because if the team with ten have a player like Ian Wright's adopted son Shaun, then your ten then becomes at least twelve for this kid was absolutely terrific in everything he did. His work rate was phenomenal, which had me thinking back to what I said about Aston Villa's Darius Vassell when his team had ten men against Bolton, it made Wright-Phillips' performance even the more special, well done my son!

Tottenham 3 Manchester City 4
Fulham 2 Everton 1

Manchester City now travel across Manchester to face neighbours United in round six whilst Fulham host West Ham United and Chelsea go to Arsenal, which makes it three local derbies in the fifth round of the FA Cup.

But it is back to the bread and butter of the Premiership with matches at Wolves for Arsenal as United travel not far to Merseyside and Everton, who were dreadfully unlucky to lose at Loftus Road on Wednesday.

The *Evening Standard* had the scoop of all scoops on this Friday the 6th of February.

The headlines looked awesome as the top of the page said that:

Former Old Trafford chief Peter Kenyon sets out his 'Blueprint' as he starts his reign at Stamford Bridge

Then in big black frightening letters, it read that: "'THIS IS THE MOST EXCITING CHALLENGE IN EUROPE. I'M DELIGHTED TO BE A PART OF IT'.

It may have been 6.15am and still dark but Peter Kenyon came bounding into the hotel lobby.

All that fresh air from his six months 'gardening leave' had put a healthy bloom on the cheeks of the new Chelsea chief executive, or perhaps it was just the prospect of the challenge ahead, which so energised him at such an ungodly hour.

Kenyon, who first cut his teeth as a sportswear company executive and then underpinned his reputation as Manchester United's highly successful chief executive, was about to fly to Holland on club business.

But before departing, he spoke for the first time about what had persuaded him to leave his native North West and the team he had supported avidly from childhood and come to Chelsea.

He is a personable man with an open face and a ready smile but behind the public persona is a shrewd businessman who has been headhunted by Roman Abramovich because the Russian billionaire feels he is the best at what he does.

It must have been a wrench to leave United, the club he had worked for almost seven years, but if the rumoured package of £7.5million over three years is anywhere near close, it should ease the pain of parting.

He says the break with United was amicable on both sides, but there were recriminations. United didn't want to lose him but now, although Kenyon is working for one of their closest rivals, the fans at Old Trafford would readily recognise the scale of his achievements for the club.

Now, though, his brief is to utilise that invaluable experience and help Chelsea emulate United and then even usurp their lofty position as the flagship of English club football.

"Roman Abramovich is a serious businessman" he said. "He is committed to the vision of making Chelsea the number one club in Europe.

"It is my job to run it on his behalf and help achieve those ambitions as a board".

A glance at the Premiership table suggests Chelsea are a little way adrift of United at the moment but, in terms of the club in general, Kenyon is clearly aware there is even more ground to make up. "There are huge differences between the two clubs" he said. "I had the privilege to work for the best club in Europe and I've been fortunate to have been a big part of the United story over the last decade. The reason why I joined Chelsea is because they represent the biggest opportunity and challenge, both professionally and personally in English football. Chelsea as a club are based on history and that history suggests that, for their size and position, they have underachieved on the field. Now they have an owner whose investment of more than £200million so far emphasises his commitment to make it the biggest and best. It can happen, but what we have to do to be realistic about is the time frame. The expectation is there from fans and other people from within the industry but these things don't happen overnight, it's a continual process".

If developing Chelsea into a blue chip European power will take some time, though, neither Kenyon nor his employer will be satisfied with anything less than a trophy of some sort by the middle of May.

"If you leave the investment aside it will be a huge disappointment if we don't win anything and I am sure the fans will agree with that" he said. "If you include the investment, however, it will be a failure if we don't win something. That's the way the manager will see it and the way we see it because we're expected to win things – that's what we do". That statement is unlikely, on the face of it, to decrease the pressure on Chelsea's urban coach Claudio Ranieri, but Kenyon is not about to fuel any more speculation about the Italian's future beyond the end of this season.

"I'm used to speculating about managers," he smiled, as he recalled his years straight-batting the incessant rumours surrounding Sir Alex Ferguson. "But as we sit here today, Claudio has a contract until 2007 and we are involved in all the major competitions. I really want to close down all the speculation, although I am realistic enough to know that is most unlikely. What we really have to do, Claudio and myself, is to focus on winning something and the other stuff doesn't help. What we should not forget, however, is that the team are still third in the Premiership – although there may be some disappointment because of the start we made – and have done better in Europe than many expected. With all that in mind, let's put the shutters up on the speculation and deal with reality".

One of Kenyon's greatest achievements at United was to mastermind the brand marketing, to tap into the lucrative Far East and American markets. Can he do the same with Chelsea?

"That is the aim but first things first" he said, "Manchester United and Liverpool are so far ahead in the marketing sense and why?"

"Because Liverpool dominated English football in the 1980's and they were followed by Manchester United. The Premier League is still the best in the world. More people watch it and more tune into it than any other league in the world. The stage is there and now Chelsea have to perform, we have to start winning trophies, that's the base from which we have to work. The rest will follow".

Kenyon believes a promising start has been made but now is the time for a long-term strategy for the club.

"There was the perception last summer that, if any high profile player was available, then Chelsea were in for him. To continue to progress now, though, doesn't mean wholesale changes every season; it doesn't mean spending £100million every year, because I'm afraid that doesn't guarantee you anything. Not long ago Chelsea did not have one English-born player in their team but now we have a realistic chance of having six in England's squad for Euro 2004.

"We have players like Frank Lampard and John Terry, who we want to be a part of the team for years to come. We need to supplement that base with other world-class players but always within a strategy. It's about finding the right mix, not changing the mix all the time".

Part of Kenyon's 'Blueprint' is to look at ways of improving the infrastructure of the club, to ensure that progress on the field is matched by improvements off it.

"We have to invest in the club's facilities, some of those have been neglected in the past. We can't have the best team in the country based at the worst training ground in the Premiership. That has to be a key objective although planning and construction will take time. Another area of neglect is that we haven't got an academy and that's just not acceptable for a top flight Premiership League club. These are things we have to put right and which need investment to signal longevity and future benefit".

Kenyon also hinted that Stamford Bridge might yet be further expanded to meet the demand of supporters eager to watch a consistently successful team.

"We have a fantastic stadium holding 42,000 fans and it is now selling out regularly. I believe however, that a 50,000 capacity is a good size for a high performing London club and we have to look seriously at that idea. All sorts of issues are involved but I think the success of Chelsea will warrant a stadium of bigger capacity than it is now.

"We won't be moving though, Stamford Bridge is the heartbeat of the club and will remain so".

Kenyon also sees a definite place for feeder clubs, places where young Chelsea talent can be developed in a competitive environment.

"Changes in academy structures have made it more difficult to sign talent outside its immediate area. We've also seen the influx of European players, which has been generally good for the game. Talent today doesn't just come from this area of London. It's important to have the best scouting set-up and have the ability to work with other partner clubs. In that way youngsters coming through the system can play in competitive football. We can also identify talent that we wouldn't otherwise have access to, so that they may grow up in France but in their hearts they are already becoming Chelsea players".

Beyond the hotel's revolving door, London was awakening slowly but, in the empty lounge, Kenyon was bright-eyed and bushy tailed. "This job represents the single most exciting challenge in Europe over the next five years and I am delighted to be part of that, to really contribute and make it happen. The issue is to develop a strategy, both for football and the business. I've only been at the club for a few days but I am delighted with what I have seen. Like any organisation, it's the people who make the difference and there is a great loyalty, a great willingness, a great buzz".

Kenyon has plans to move his wife and young family down from Cheshire when he can find time. The first thing he should do when he is in his new house is to find a gardener. That interview was with Ken Dyer and a terrific one it was. You feel if you know this man Kenyon and for a change his words jump out of the page as you are reading them. He has passion for both sides of the football club and his ideas are something that are brutally honest whoever comes into the line of fire. His CV is quite magnificent and if the players can match his willingness to learn about what a football club is really all about then Chelsea, for a change, have a man who will eat, sleep and drink Chelsea Football Club and I have great admiration.

WE WILL BE RUTHLESS IN GOING AFTER OUR TRANSFER TARGETS.

Chelsea will be 'ruthless' in scouring the world for new players, Peter Kenyon said. Asked if Chelsea would bid for David Beckham however, Kenyon replied that,

"Just so there 's no headline, he's not available. We need to have a strategy, though, and if we are looking to strengthen a position we will be ruthless in scouring the world for the best player in that position. We have to be careful about this, however, because the criteria has to be, are they much better than the players we already have?

"Can they improve the team?

"Do they fit into the next seven or eight years and that is a wonderful position to be in.

"We have the nucleus of the next generation of the national team. Those are the real strengths and that gives us the great flexibility of being more focused on the rest of the team and more focused on what size the squad needs to be. We need to move away from the perception that because a player happens to be the best striker Chelsea have to sign him whether we are strong in that position or not. That was unfortunately how it came across last summer but that is not how it works. There needs to be framework because that is what brings success. Other clubs brought in as many players as we did last summer but it was the value of the players we signed which grabbed the headlines. This is a team game and ultimately we have to mould a team. I firmly believe that you can't just lose your heart to football. I am not trying to take the passion out of it, because that is what the game is based on, but there has to be a strong business case for what you are doing.

"We don't want to win and go bust. A lot of our fans have supported the club, man and boy, and they want to be able to take the next generation to Stamford Bridge."

NO PARADE FOR PARKER

Chelsea have abandoned plans to unveil Scott Parker to fans on Sunday for fear of antagonising Charlton, writes Matt Hughes.

The visitors only agreed to sell the midfielder for £10million on the condition that they would not face him this weekend.

Parker will not be treated to Chelsea's custom of parading new players before the kick-off. He said that, "It will be a very emotional day and it's best that I'm not playing".

Jesper Gronkjaer is set to fill in for Parker, while Joe Cole serves the second match of his two-match suspension. John Terry is suspended for reaching five bookings, so Marcel Desailly will partner Bill Gallas at the centre of defence.

Damien Duff – Achilles – and Celeste Babayaro – hamstring – are out, but Hernan Crespo could return to the bench after recovering from a calf injury.

The *Sentinel* sport page had another BACKDATE: 24-01-74 involving yours truly and it was about my first match against Chelsea in a Stoke City shirt at the Victoria Ground, once again reported by Richard Adams – and I promise you he is no relation of mine!

SPOT ON CITY GIVE CHELSEA THE BLUES

Geoff Hurst fired home a late penalty to give Stoke a crucial home win against Chelsea at the Victoria Ground.

Hurst made no mistake from the spot sixteen minutes from time after Alan Hudson had been brought down in the area by his old team mate Gary Locke.

Stoke's new signing was again hugely influential, but was surrounded by controversy after Chelsea argued long and hard over the awarding of the penalty.

However, City's skipper – for the day – was in no doubt the correct decision had been made. He said that, "I was definitely brought down. I had beaten David Webb and I knew I would have to beat Gary Locke if I was going to get a shooting chance, which is what I did."

Stoke manager Tony Waddington was glowing at the form of his recent capture, agreed with Hudson.

He said that, "It was a definite foul. Hudson's change of pace took him past two defenders and then he went down. Chelsea can hardly complain at the result because we might have had four or five. Chelsea were not threatening to score, and their only danger was in the air, and Denis Smith had a great game against Bill Garner.

"Hudson had another great game. He can take players out of things with his acceleration. He wants responsibility and we give it to him. He is forming a fine partnership with Jimmy Greenhoff."

Hudson almost blotted his copy book when a miss hit back pass was picked up by Bill Garner who hit a shot against the bar, but he more than made up for the error with a dazzling display.

His strike partner Jimmy Greenhoff went close to extending City's lead with a couple of fine efforts and Alan Dodd smashed a shot over the bar, but Stoke were never in danger of losing their advantage and held on to a crucial victory with ease.

This is me: I remember this match well for I think it was the first ever Sunday old first division league match to be played?

However – incredibly – with it being packed out, they never had another one scheduled thereafter!

That was of course until the play-offs began, all through SKY TV and then as we know right now Sunday matches are a big part of our football calendar.

I was full of confidence after my debut against Liverpool and that perform-ance had set me up to become very popular with our Boothen Enders, who would eventually sing, "Alan Hudson walks on water". I didn't really need any inspiring, for when you are playing that well you build on it, especially in big matches like the one against my old club. My performance was near flawless apart from setting up my big friend Bill Garner and I was just delighted that it wasn't Peter Osgood, otherwise it would have turned a few heads and also have cost us a point which we badly needed if we were going to reach the UEFA Cup spot as fifth in the table. My form was as consistent as one can get and with each match I felt more and more like I was born to play for Tony Waddington. He commented that he gave me responsibility which was right and my response to that was one of gratefulness for I was the kind of player who needed to be in a the thick of every one of our attacking moves ,with my ability to link the defence to the attack, especially with the great Jimmy Greenhoff. Also, as I told you earlier it was my boss who was quoted as saying "Alan Hudson will play for the World XI before he does play for his country." That was after another great team performance at White Hart Lane – which was becoming a very lucky ground for me. I scored the second goal after nipping in and nicking a ball off the toes of another good friend Terry Naylor – Terry fancies himself as the last Frank Sinatra – to record Stoke City's first win at this ground in a hundred years, so you can imagine we were setting new records in those days of the mid-seventies.

This match reminds me of the times now when players complain about racial abuse and other situations from silly spectators who shout out crazy things. It is merely a Saturday when they can relax on their day off and they choose to be louts. I mention this because at 1-0 a ball ran out of play and I moved to pick it up when a voice in the crowd said "Come on Hudson you w★★★★★", and just as he got to the last word I turned my head to see him standing in the paddock with a lady on his arm. I had the ball in my arms and said to his companion "Excuse me love, what does that idiot do for a living" and the lady slowly moved her arm from his as much to say, "I am not with him". I then threw the ball in as the crowd were screaming at me – and the Copper in Black blowing his whistle like a train guard – to get the game going once again. So you can imagine my delight when I scored the second goal that clinched our victory, as I waved to that area of the paddock.

But back to my first two matches against my old club Chelsea. Where and when this particular day turned out fantastic for me, and in the second last match of the season at Stamford Bridge I scored the goal that won us the match in another 1-0 win.

I can tell you, that was some feeling after all the rumours that Chelsea put out including one of me being an alcoholic?!

So I reckoned that if I was an alcoholic, where did that put the Chelsea team after I masterminded both of our wins against them?

And by the way, I reckon I was very close to being an alcoholic, but if I were, it did not affect my football, that's for sure, just ask the Chelsea manage-ment after those two matches!

HUNGRY FISH CHASES LURE OF EUROPE

Mark Fish believes Charlton will use Sunday's visit to Stamford Bridge to restate their European credentials. Scott Parker's move to Chelsea and last week's home defeat to Bolton sparked fears that Charlton could collapse as they have done in the past two seasons. But the South African defender insists the current team are made of sterner stuff.

Alan Curbishley's side are fifth, after Newcastle's win yesterday in the Premiership and Fish is confident they will finish the season strongly.

He said that, "Playing in Europe is a dream for all of the players and the belief is there that we can do it this year. Playing against sides from across Europe would be a fantastic experience but we have to keep putting our best foot forward to make it happen.

"There is a positive vibe around the training ground and we feel we can push on and finish the season where we deserve to be. It is in our minds how we have fallen away in the latter stages, over the last couple of years and the fact that so much has been made of it makes us even more anxious to avoid it."

Fish is also hoping a successful end of the season will convince Curbishley to offer him a new contract at The Valley.

He said that, "Being in the final year of my contract has given me an extra incentive to do my best. I feel as if I have to prove my worth to the Charlton management, but also everybody else watching."

Curbishley is waiting on the fitness of Jason Euell before naming his squad. The former Wimbledon striker limped out of the Bolton defeat with a bruised foot and could be replaced by Paul Konchesky.

Carlton Cole is unavailable because of the terms of his loan deal but Shaun Bartlett could return to the bench after four months out with an ankle injury.

WHAT ROMAN DID FOR US

By my old friend Nigel Clarke that avid bluenose: West Ham could have gone to the brink of administration if it hadn't been for Chelsea's Roman Abramovich.

Hammers' manager Alan Pardew says his raid on Wimbledon for their three top players has almost certainly saved the Dons from going out of business, while the Hammers, relegated last season with debts of £44million, were able to sell Joe Cole and Glen Johnson to Chelsea for £12.5million.

Pardew said, "If Abramovich had not gone into Chelsea you would have had to seriously worry about West Ham's future because a lot of those deals kept us from a Leeds situation."

Jermain Defoe has gone to Tottenham but Pardew has brought in eight players, which has helped crisis club Wimbledon.

He has singed Nigel Reo-Coker, Adam Nowland and John McAnuff, and added: "While Chelsea's money kept us going our money has kept Wimbledon going. I have tried to buy players who could turn into Premiership stars. I have gone for a fresh feel."

GOALS, GOALS AND MORE GOALS

It's Sunday the eighth of February and the time of the big match against Charlton Athletic and Chelsea have been very quiet – indeed – in their build-up to a match that must be called 'revenge' for Charlton blew Chelsea away not so long ago at The Valley.

Both Manchester United and Arsenal kept up their relentless gallop by beating Everton and Wolves respectively. But they did not have it all their own way on their way to precious victories away from home. Manchester United were in a right 'ding–dong' affair after leading the Toffees by three goals to nil at half-time with two goals from Louis Saha and one from the 'Flying Dutchman' Ruud van Nistelrooy. These two are quickly becoming the 'Dynamic Duo' as the new boy from Fulham has settled in immediately in his role alongside 'Van the Man'. It looked for a few moments that Everton were going to repeat the feat of Manchester City in Wednesday evening's FA Cup fourth round tie at White Hart Lane. After hauling themselves back from a three goal deficit, David Moyes' team went about the second half like men possessed and had the champions reeling as they pulled back to three apiece. Wayne Rooney entered the match in the second half and was fabulous and so unlucky to not score on a couple of occasions, but when it looked set for a 3-3 draw, Van Nistelrooy popped up at the far post to nick all three points for his team. This was just another reminder of the drama the Premiership holds as the fans were treated to an incredible seven-goal thriller, and my pal Harry Redknapp was cursing his luck as his Portsmouth team were involved in one themselves at White 'Hot' Lane after the Spurs faithful were served up two fantastic matches where there were fourteen goals in the past four days. Harry's nightmare became reality when new signing Jermain Defoe hit a wonderful first goal as the Portsmouth manager had feared beforehand.

Harry was once again left wondering what they have to do to have just a share of the luck, as for two Saturdays on the spin had seen them the better team only to come out of them with only one point. But once again the results in the basement went for them as Leeds crashed once again – 2-0 at Villa Park – Leicester went down 3-1 at Newcastle and of course, Wolves loss against the Gunners was his only consolation. Another team involved is Manchester City who host Birmingham at two o'clock this afternoon.

At Molineux, Arsenal took the lead through Dennis Bergkamp and looked to be cruising until Wolves once again showed the fighting qualities that were so evident when they beat Manchester United only three weeks ago and then drew with Liverpool.

But after Wolves equalised, that man Thierry Henry scored yet another 'pearler' to put them in front and then Toure made the game safe with a third later in the second period, after more superb work from Robert Pires.

Charlton's form at Stamford Bridge has been impressive since arriving in the Premiership and after reading Mark Fish's comments about his side 'high' on confidence, although they were beaten by Bolton last weekend, which was a minor set-back as they chase that fourth spot which Newcastle hold before the live 4pm kick-off at Stamford Bridge. SKY are really dishing up some fantastic matches of late and I have a feeling the one at the Bridge this afternoon will add to this weekend's goal feast. Chelsea will be without John Terry and I think that will give Charlton an added 'gee-up' as Marcel Desailly replaces him alongside Bill Gallas.

Bookmakers LADBROKES will be hoping for a Charlton win or draw as a lot of punters will have backed the 'Big Three' in a win treble and although they would have had quite a scare with Manchester United pulling the game out of the fire in the final minute. They had Arsenal at 2/5 – Manchester United at 4/7 and Chelsea today as 1/3 favourites, which I think is very 'skinny' against a team more than capable of beating the Bluenoses. If you have backed the treble you would have been given a little over 5/1 so if you had a pound on the 'Big Three' you would get back six.

The scene was set on a pitch that had just been relaid which always has me thinking of the pitches we played on.

Big news from the Bridge read like this on Monday's *Daily Mail*: BATES IS PUT OUT IN THE COLD with a story shared by Steve Curry and Claire Nash: Ken Bates is the first casualty of the bloodletting which seems certain to result in Claudio Ranieri's removal as manager, despite their tenacity in the title race. Chelsea's 1-0 win over Charlton yesterday, courtesy of a hotly-contested Jimmy Floyd Hasselbaink penalty, followed last week's win at Blackburn and was their first back to back win since November. But Bates' waning influence at Stamford Bridge was underlined when his notes were unceremoniously axed from the matchday programme. So long a platform for Bates's vitriol, the column was dropped just days after American lawyer Bruce Buck replaced him as chairman of Chelsea Village.

Bates told *Sportsmail* exclusively last night that, "I was told by Bruce Buck that they would not require my notes this weekend because they wanted to keep the programme free for the new chief executive. I didn't see why this should effect my column, which has been a feature of the programme for so many years, so I told them I would not be doing it again."

Bates is also believed to have made his last appearance on Chelsea TV and has been dropped from the club's centenary committee. The symbolism was clear as Chelsea chairman Roman Abramovich flexes his muscle through his new chief executive and enforcer Peter Kenyon.

My thoughts are: that old grey beard has very gently and slowly been given the cold shoulder and I also think he is very fortunate that Roman Abramovich was so generous to him when buying the club. He could easily have allowed the club to go into administration before saving the life of Bates and co.

It was Trevor Birch firstly and Bates second in the rebuilding of the new Stamford Bridge and it is quite well known that new chief executive Kenyon and Bates are far from being friends, never were and never will be, as this latest move is very transparent. Peter Kenyon is a winner and has vast experience in this role of chief executive and his very constructive column in Friday's *Standard* – reading between the guidelines – were there for all to see. It will not be long before 'Captain Birdseye' is out in the cold with only his £27million to keep him warm. He has had a very good run and must be applauded by the way he filled the holes of this very fast sinking ship, although the disturbing 'vibes' I receive from close Chelsea connections tell me that the writing is well and truly on the wall of Ken Bates' office. I have had a couple of run-ins with the man – my first being when he called my home in Seattle and asked if what he had heard about me wanting to return was true. In Seattle our matches finished near to midnight – before we got out of the ground that is – and on this particular morning after the match the night before I was wearing a severe hangover. As the telephone rang at about 6.30am and I answered to the voice of Bates. He asked the question to which I answered that I would love to return but only on a loan deal which meant out of our season in the North American Soccer League. I added also that it would be a great deal if Chelsea took me to the Bridge once again and that Seattle in return could have both Micky Droy and David Speedie when Chelsea finished their season!

He was very receptive to that idea but his next words were like a hot iron put to my forehead to go with a very late night on the booze. "But what about your manager wanting something out of this", which hit the nerve I have always had about my good friends and fellow professionals. I called him a four-letter word and slammed the receiver down as my first wife Maureen stirred and asked me who I was calling such a word, and I replied to her saying that it was the chairman of Chelsea Football Club. She then said "Oh, Al you cannot call people like that such names", to which getting out of bed and heading for the kitchen saying "I just did."

It was quite incredible though, quite some time later when I had left Seattle I approached Chelsea once again about signing me. At first it was Danny Blanchflower, as their manager – who I found delightful and the deal was all but done. And I felt in need of a celebration drink in our afternoon haunt, the Town House just off Gloucester Road – the same one that I took Jimmy Gabriel after we agreed terms for me to go to Seattle Sounders. Whilst I was celebrating my return it came over the news – after I had received a telephone call – that Danny had been fired. This was very similar to the Stoke City chairman – Frank Edwards – dying the day I was to see him about becoming the manager of his club. So you see, I am far from the luckiest man on earth and after reading the second chapter about my injuries in that car accident you just might agree?

What was to follow was quite astonishing, as I heard that Geoff Hurst, who

I both lived and played with – took over the reigns of the Chelsea manager. The picture is still very clear in my mind that I was walking through Earls Court with my father and uncle George and went to telephone box to call Geoff. I asked the position after I had already agreed with Danny and he replied that, "If you turn up on time for the rest of the week's training he would sign me" That nerve of mine was struck once again and foolishly I told him to stick his training sessions and Chelsea Football Club. I was in a terrible state of shock, because Geoff knew that I was a good and dedicated trainer and had played in the same side when I made my fantastic entrance into the Victoria Ground. It was times like these that you wonder if the world had gone totally crazy. It was not long afterwards that, after an appalling record as their manager, Hursty was given the bullet, one I wished at Earls Court that I had fired.

But incredibly, quite some time later it was Ken Bates who finally signed me himself and some six months later – after never making the first team – he allowed me go back to Stoke City – in such a way I thought he could be quite a Jekyll and Hyde. He did me a great turn which had me wondering if deep down he was a little kitten, but going back to work for him in Drakes Bar I saw that this kitten was had grown into a starving rockweiller. This latest news is not the kind that pleases me, just one that tells us that every dog has his day and there is lightning that strikes where you would never have thought it would! The one pleasing thing is that as I approach the last third of this book, I can live in hope that I will have access to Chelsea Football Ground to bring this to the Chelsea fans!

THE RUSSIAN ROMAN

The big news following the Charlton match was that in the *Daily Mail* BATES BEEN PUT OUT IN COLD and BATES WRITTEN OUT OF ROMAN PROGRAMME. The *Express* went with FURIOUS BATES SIGNS OFF IN CHELSEA "GAG" ROW and that ANRGY BATES SIGNS OFF while in the *Sun* it was all about the Tinkerman, who stormed: SHUT IT and also that he: WANT'S TROPHY EVEN MORE THAN KENYON.

So the arrival of Peter Kenyon – as expected – will see the departure of the Chelsea chairman – and the rumblings from Stamford Bridge were very transparent for the simple reason that Ken Bates and his Chelsea Village empire was tumbling under the extreme pressure of this brand new world. Rome was not built in a day and Roman moves in exactly the same direction as he has waited patiently for his new chief executive to finally move into office, following his 'garden leave' and this latest news was simply telling the entire football world that Chelsea were now going to steamroller all that gets in the way of the Russian Roman. This was bigger news than the match itself, where Chelsea won the match with as dubious a penalty as you'll get to see in a catalogue of 'howlers' from the 'Coppers in Black.'

Bates at last looks cooked and it will be interesting to see, after he has finally left the building, just how all of his 'sneaks' and 'spies' are treated by the brand new regime.

Peter Kenyon has made it very clear that Stamford Bridge has no room for the man who claimed to buy the club for a £1 note. It seems that Mr Bates has been bushwhacked by some very clever individuals and bit the cherry at leaving him out of the programme, giving the Russians exactly the response they wanted, playing straight into their hands. So much for the brooch!

JIMMY FLOYD'S LUCKY THIRTEENTH

The match itself was a big disappointment with the only goal of the game coming after 'The Mug in the Middle' gave a very dubious penalty for Fish getting tangled up with Jimmy Floyd, who got to his feet, brushed himself down and coolly sent Dean Kiely the wrong way. This was just another example of having the 'third eye' as this decision could cost Charlton the fourth place in the Champions League if they are two points out of the frame. But in all fairness, their performance deserved nothing and that is even more the reason that Chelsea must begin putting teams away. This Jimmy Floyd effort was Chelsea's first league goal at the Bridge for 215 minutes, and that tells you the story without me saying anything. It is just not good enough and if Charlton had turned up they would have got something out if this match, which is why their boss Alan Curbishley was so incensed with such a poor performance.

The most disappointed player in a blue shirt must surely have been Adrian Mutu who missed four great opportunities in the last ten minutes, one which hit the angle of the bar and post and after a great piece of work from substitute Eidur Gudjohnsen, he hit the goalkeeper with his fine low cross. Robert Huth was a big bonus in for the suspended John Terry. Having said that Charlton offered no threat and Paolo Di Canio even looked an average 'Joe' which I was very disappointed about.

The Tinkerman thought that Huth was outstanding and I was surprised to see him play in front of Desailly, or is this just a nudge to the Frenchman, as to him being on his way back to France, come summertime. The three clubs I played for were all doing well. We know about Chelsea and Arsenal but Stoke City in the Nationwide first division are on a roll and on Saturday they went to another team in fine form, Millwall, under the guidance of ex-Bluenose Denis Wise. Tony Pullis, the Stoke boss, is a man I have been impressed with when meeting him at the Victoria Ground and he seems to have turned things around in a club who have been going nowhere for so very long. I think it is seven wins and two draws out of the last nine league matches and Saturday they shared the points in the Lions Den. Incredibly, though, they sit in the middle of the table, but only five points off a play-off position, but the most important thing for them is they can play out the remainder of the season without any fear of relegation!

Chelsea 1 Jimmy Floyd Charlton 0 40,255
Millwall 1 Dichio Stoke City 1 Clarke 9,024
Wolves 1 Ganea Arsenal 3 Bergkamp, Henry and Toure 29,392

GUS POYET

Whilst Chelsea were struggling to score once again, an ex-favourite of the Stamford Bridge faithful shot Spurs into the lead for the fourth and final time

– with only a minute on the clock – to overcome Portsmouth. Gus Poyet – the player without a position – was booed onto the field at White Hart Lane as substitute for Jermain Defoe, but was in the right place at the right time to break Pompey's hearts after another good performance from Harry's men. The headline in the *Express* read: POYET HAS LAST LAUGH AT SPURS BOO-BOYS while there were two conflicting stories in two different rags about David Beckham and Peter Kenyon, the man who had the job of telling him that he was no longer wanted at Old Trafford. The *Sun* said England skipper's Chelsea hint and BECKHAM: I CAN WORK WITH NEW BLUES BOSS whilst the *Mail* reported that BECKHAM SNUBS KENYON also that DAVID'S LIFT FOR KENYON.

The *Mail* read that: Peter Kenyon's vowed attempt to persuade David Beckham to follow him to Chelsea is doomed. The former Manchester United chief executive, now at Stamford Bridge, said that, "Any club would like to see David Beckham wearing their shirt. He's that type of player."

But after goals from Ronaldo and Roberto Carlos earned Real Madrid a 2-1 victory over Malaga on Saturday, Beckham reiterated his desire to see out his contract with the Spanish champions. Beckham said "There will always be speculation if I am going to move back to England but I have only been here six months. I am enjoying my football and people can see that. I don't want to move anywhere yet."

The twenty-eight-year-old England captain did admit that his relationship with Kenyon had not been sullied by the acrimonious nature of his £25million departure from Old Trafford. "He is there to do a job and obviously it's his job to sign players. He is a really nice man and I worked really well with him when I was at Manchester United. He is one of the ones I spoke to about me and Alex Ferguson. I have always had a good relationship with him. He treated me very fairly and I will always respect him for that. If the speculation carries on, then so be it, but as everyone can see I am happy here."

However, Beckham looked far from happy against Malaga. He was suffering from a stomach upset and struggled to complete the match.

He said that, "The stomach cramps kicked in near the end. Over the last three days I have lost quite a bit of energy."

But the *Sun* put it a very different way saying that: David Beckham has admitted that he would have no problem linking up with Peter Kenyon at Chelsea.

Instead of ruling out a return to the Premiership with the Blues, Beckham has hinted it could happen when he is ready because of the enormous respect he still has for the new Stamford Bridge chief executive.

It was Kenyon who headed Manchester United's secret operation to sell the England skipper behind his back last summer, after the Old Trafford boss Alex Ferguson decided he wanted Beckham out.

Twenty-eight-year-old Becks, holds no grudge against Kenyon for helping to end his love affair with United. The Real Madrid star said, "He is a really nice man. I worked well with him at Manchester United and would have no problem doing so again."

Kenyon has only just begun his new role with the Londoners, has already made it clear he would be keen to team up again with the midfield ace once more by bringing him back to this country.

He revealed his interest in seeing a 'Blue Becks' by telling *Sunsport* exclusively at the weekend that, "Any club would like to see David Beckham wearing their shirt. He is that type of player."

England's captain was away on holiday when he was stunned with the news that United had agreed a £25million deal to offload him to Barcelona.

He will never forget how Kenyon confirmed his worst fears about his irreconcilable feud with Fergie and made it quite clear he had no future at Old Trafford and added that, "He was honest enough with me and I respect him for that. I have always had a good relationship with him. He is one of those people that I spoke to about me and Alex Ferguson."

Once Becks knew he had to go, he made sure he got his own way and joined the Madrid giants instead.

The England hero has proved a major hit in his six months in Spain so far.

He helped Real stay top of La Liga thanks to a 2-1 win against Malaga on Saturday night – although he played with diarrhoea. Becks joked that, "There was no mad dash to the toilet at half-time. But there had been for the last few days."

There was not much wrong with his 'runs' on the pitch either, and his 40 yard pass helped set up Real's 25th minute opener for Ronaldo. Despite Kenyon's interest in him and the talk already mounting of another move, Beckham insists he is in no rush to quit the Bernabeu.

He declared that, "Working with Peter Kenyon for so many years was very good and I enjoyed it. But I have said that I am a Real Madrid player.

"He is there to do a job, obviously. When I signed my contract and things like that, I spoke to him and he treated me very fairly. For that reason he will always have my respect. There will always be speculation about whether I am going back to England or not. But I have only been here in Spain six months.

"I am enjoying my football and people can say see that. I don't want to move anywhere else yet. It his job to sign players, and if the speculation continues, so be it, for everyone knows I am happy here."

BECKHAM AND CHELSEA

I think David Beckham would be off his rocker to join Chelsea at this moment in time, for the simple fact that real Madrid will be knocking on the door for the Champions League this year and how many opportunities does one have to play alongside such players as Zidane, the world's best, Raul, Ronaldo, Figo and Carlos Alberto. He will win the Spanish League – La Liga – whilst his old club will finish runners-up in the Premiership, which will be a great boost for him over the Manchester United manager. Ferguson has hinted, quite nastily, that United are a better team now than they were last season, but I don't buy that. A team without David Beckham is not a better team than having him down the right-hand side of the field. His ammunition to his front players is second to nobody in world football and even his best pal at right-back does not seem the same player now that he has left. Beckham made life so easy for Gary Neville by always being available and his movement is quite outstanding. I remember having a conversation with Eddie McCreadie – I might have already told you about this – about Beckham, and my old Chelsea team mate said that he would whack him early and if he came back he would whack him again, but I said "No mate I don't think so, because he will drag you to places you don't want to go and if you did go the ball would be 'on' for someone else in your position which would make you think twice." If you were to ask any front-man about David Beckham they would tell you that he is a striker's dream. So, he will see it out at Real until something quite incredible happens once more in his – so far – fantastic lifetime. He is a footballing James Dean and if it weren't for his shyness, he would be a brilliant star of the big screen. I must also say that with all of his experience he gives a diabolical interview and these last two pages have been quite boring to write.

BACKDATE: 31/1/74

The *Sentinel* was kind to me for the third week running in their look back into those heady days of the mid-seventies. This time it was my eighth match in a red and white striped shirt and we were unbeaten in all of those, and after the match at Wolves, it read:

Stoke City manager Tony Waddington described new signing Alan Hudson as "A 'racehorse' in a ploughed field" in his team's 1-1 draw.

As well as Waddington, Hudson's teammates were also full of praise for the former Chelsea star.

Centre-half Denis Smith said that, "He makes my job easy. All I have to do now is to nod the ball and Alan takes it on from there.

"We were in quite a good spell before Alan joined us, but we have that extra confidence now and I cannot see any team taking us apart."

Stoke City coach Alan A'Court echoed Smith's thoughts by saying that, "Alan's performance on a sticky pitch was tremendous. We were booed off the field today, but that is eight matches unbeaten for us now."

I don't know how Denis Smith – our hatchet man – could say they were in a good spell because the night I looked as the result come up on the BBC teleprinter my new team were third from bottom after a hard-earned draw at Ipswich.

MIND WE HANG ON TO THE TINKERMAN

I enjoy reading Matthew Norman of the *Evening Standard* and on Monday 9th of February it was no different as he wrote: While next season's Premiership may not be as dull on the pitch as this year's three way boreathon, it is certain to be less amusing off it. One of the two drollest managers in English football is certain to leave his club and the other is odds-on to depart.

It may be possible to soldier on without the postmatch interviews of Gordon Strachan, whose deadpan damning of referees and sublime comic timing have been such a joy. To lose Claudio Ranieri as well would be a catastrophe.

Ranieri may not be as good a coach as Sven Goran Eriksson, but he's an infinitely more hilarious comic turn, whose bemused air of resignation about the Russian madhouse and majestic grasp of Pidgin English are a constant delight.

It's widely believed that he speaks perfect English but simply loves his pantomime Italian shtick and it is essential that he remains in Blighty if Chelsea sack him. It's true that Barry Evans and Joan Sanderson are dead, while Francoise Pascal is getting on a bit. Even so, with Ranieri likely to be available in May, is it beyond the wit of TV to revive a show curiously omitted from the top ten sitcoms (it's PC gone mad!).

And bring back Mind Your Language?

Well done for that Mark, my sentiments entirely. The Tinkerman not only tinkers with his little tinkers in Blue shirts but tinkers also with the English dictionary.

I have not met him and if you'll remember I invited him for dinner in my *Sentinel* column along with Harry Redknapp, Alan Curbishley, Kevin Keegan and Roman.

Which was pure fantasy.

EIDUR: 'WE'RE ALL UNDER THE COSH'

Eidur Gudjohnsen insists it is not only Claudio Ranieri who is feeling the pressure at Chelsea – every player is under the cosh as well.

New Stamford Bridge chief executive Peter Kenyon caused a major storm in his first week by declaring it would be a failure if boss Ranieri did not deliver a trophy this season.

But the players, most of whom have cost millions, know Kenyon will also be casting his eye over their futures should they flop.

The Icelandic striker said that, "This is Chelsea Football Club. Everyone is under pressure. At a club like this, especially the way we are heading, there will always be pressure to win things.

"That is not only on the manager but also on the squad. We are all fighting, all wanting to show we wish to be a part of the changes and part of the team.

"We are still in three competitions. In the Premiership there is everything to play for as we still have to play the top two. If we do our jobs, we will put pressure on them towards the end of the season. I am sure of that!"

But defender Mario Melchot backs Kenyon's claim that Chelsea need to bag some silverware to show the current campaign as being a success.

The Dutchman admitted that, "I can understand why Peter Kenyon has said what he has. The club have invested a lot of money on players and in return that creates pressure to succeed. All the staff and players are aware of that. Last season we got into the Champions League, which was an achievement. But this year they expect more – and we want to give it to them. Peter Kenyon's words don't worry me, as a player I put myself under pressure to win regardless."

Czech Republic goalkeeper Peter Cech, 21, will join Chelsea from French outfit Rennes at the end of the season after completing his £9million signing yesterday.

The Londoner's £17million wing wizard Damien Duff has declared himself fit to face Portsmouth tomorrow, having not played a full game since dislocating his shoulder against Fulham just before Christmas.

HEAVEN HELP THEM IF ANYTHING GOES WRONG FOR £17MILLION IRISHMAN CHELSEA GAMBLE OF DUFF
Damien ignores doctors in a bid to help Ranieri

Mark Fleming of the *Daily Express* writes that: Damien Duff is prepared to put his career on the line to save Claudio Ranieri's skin. The £17million Irishman, who has not started a match since dislocating his shoulder before Christmas, has been told he needs an operation to heal the joint properly.

However, under-fire manager Ranieri is desperate to have the brilliant winger back in his team as soon as possible. The club are going to delay the operation until the summer, hoping that Duff does not do any permanent damage in the meantime.

Duff admitted that, "I am hoping the shoulder will heal itself with a lot of rehabilitation work but doctors say there is an eighty per cent chance the injury I had before Christmas will come back."

The risks are huge. If Duff dislocates his shoulder again it could become a regular occurrence, much like the injury that blighted former England skipper Bryan Robson's career.

Chelsea club doctor Neil Frazer said, "Players often use shoulders when they fall, particularly someone in his position who goes past people with speed. They need to be able to land and, if he dislocates it again, he's very liable to recurrent dislocation.

"A percentage of sportsmen who have such a fall suffer recurrent dislocations. The last big name you remember was Bryan Robson."

It is a measure of Chelsea's desperation to win something that the club are willing to risk waiting until the summer for Duff's operation. Ranieri knows he will be sacked unless he wins at least one trophy this season and believes Duff holds the key to his chances of keeping his job. "We miss him so much because he is the type of player who dribbles, gives you a chance of two-on-one and creates space", the Chelsea manager said. "We will need him for the next month, which will be probably dictate where our season goes."

Duff, who has also been struggling with an Achilles injury, was one of twelve first-team stars that were forced to miss Sunday's 1-0 victory over Charlton.

However he is in line for a return for tomorrow's trip to Portsmouth, and then for a ten-day stretch that will decide Chelsea's season.

Ranieri's side travel to Arsenal in the fifth round of the FA Cup on Sunday, then host the Gunners in the Premiership the following Saturday, before travelling to Stuttgart four days later for a vital Champions League clash.

The former Blackburn star, who has been a sensation since his £17million move to Stamford Bridge in the summer, is dying to be a part of the first team again.

"I expect to be back to face Portsmouth on Wednesday" Duff said. "I had better be because there are some big ones after that and I don't want to miss any of them. I want to be flying for them.

"Being injured gets me down. It's the one thing I really hate. I live for playing football. It's the only thing I am interested in. And when you are injured, you do a nine-to-five job like everybody else."

Duff has spent the past few weeks working on his upper body strength so he is less likely to be shoved to the ground by desperate defenders. "I feel much more confident when I am taking a player on now" he said, "I know he won't knock me off the ball."

The monotony of working in the gym was at least lifted once, when the Irishman fell hook, line and sinker for a typical football wind-up.

"Some days I have to pinch myself when I think about the size of Chelsea and where they are heading," Duff said.

"A couple of weeks ago someone ran into the gym and shouted out that Ronaldo had signed for us. We were all gobsmacked. We bought it completely. But that is how big this club is now, and will be as long as Roman Arbramovich is around."

Chelsea want Duff to have his shoulder operation as soon as the season is over. But the winger wants to delay it further, so he can turn out for Ireland in a friendly tournament in America at the end of May.

Duff said, "I will play international football until I drop. I love it and treasure every Irish cap I have. If I go off with Ireland and then have the operation when I get back, that would mean missing the first two weeks of next season and I don't want to do that either."

It's me again: Firstly I think Chelsea are making a massive mistake about delaying the operation on Duff's shoulder and particularly letting the world know about it. If they were to choose to ignore the doctor's opinion then they should have done so by leaving the problem in-house. I know just what the next right-back will be thinking of when facing the vastly talented ex-Blackburn left-winger, and it will not have sympathy written on it!

Apart from Charlton, teams are closing Chelsea down a lot quicker as the season unfolds and with not only Chelsea's importance in mind. There are ten teams who are not out of the trap door yet and Leeds United's four-goal win over Wolves yesterday – Tuesday 10th of February – was quite a reminder that they have not thrown in the towel yet. It would only take a run of four matches, with, say, three wins and a draw to take a team marching past fellow strugglers reversing places with them!

I think my second spell at Stoke City was quite an escape act, as just into the New Year the team were 'tailed off' and looking no hopers for survival, when I turned up on a month's loan. I was a little washed out as a player but the challenge and the times I spent the first time around lifted my body to new heights, a body that had been well lived in but still had enough for such a fight. That first month we won three matches and drew the other one out of my four games and a new contract was written up which I signed with a great relief knowing I did not have to return to the Chelsea reserve team and, whilst slowly getting to know my new teammates saw something within the dressing room to build a serious fight against the drop. Our team was my great pal in goal Peter Fox, he was revitalised and superb, Steve Bould who would later move onto Arsenal with a 'little help from his friend' yours truly. He became everything I knew he could be, forming a wonderful partnership with Tony Adams. We had three centre halves in George Berry, an old Wolves player who was game for the fight. Paul Dyson from Coventry who used to run into brick walls for the team and Brendan O'Callaghan, possibly the toughest man to get on with I ever knew. But once I did, he was different class both on and off the field, just like Foxy. He represented his native Southern Ireland on a regular basis and was very useful in both penalty areas, whether playing up front or at the back for the cause! At left back there was Peter Hampton an ex-Leeds United player. Hammy was quality and like most players who do not believe in themselves, never fulfilled his talent, with an educated left foot and a good footballing mind. Hammy was my first line of attack when receiving the ball off of Foxy, for I trusted him and built up his confidence to such an extent he even held the 'whip' on our end of season tour of Tampa Bay. Robbie James – who sadly died about a decade ago – was our right-sided midfield player, one who deceived not only the opposition but our players as well. He also carried an awesome shot. I was the quarterback of the team and that suited me greatly for, as I wrote before, it was Waddington who first gave me responsibility and my game went onto a different level thereafter! On my left was young Chris Maskery a local lad who 'died for the cause' a typical young 'Stokie' who apart from Fox became a roommate of mine and boy, was he funny. If I had asked him to do handstands he would oblige and I tried my utmost to make him a better player. Had Frank Edwards – the old chairman – not have died and I had taken over, I am sure I would have succeeded. Mark Chamberlain was the player who could have gone on to great things and once again, had I been manager I would have got more out of him than he gave his teammates. He could cross a ball at a pace Linford Christie would have been happy with. Ian Painter was our centre forward, a player who was crippled with a back problem, a problem which would have been dealt with in the modern game.

'Panner' was a great lad with bundles of pace and had a good coach worked with him, he could have become a far better player, just another one who is neglected by diabolical coaching at that time. I called them 'A Nightmare on Lilleshall Street' where all the badgers set out to ruin this great game, and my god, did they succeed. Sammy McIlroy, the next 'George Best' he was hailed when first coming onto the scene at Old Trafford, a wonderfully gifted ball-player who was my 'First General' in all attacking strategies. I just told Sammy to get into that position where you did not get picked up and through Peter Hampton I would get the ball into his feet, where he could turn and destroy defenders at the wink of an eye. He was exciting and lifted the Boothen End when on a solo. Paul McGuire was Brendan's big pal, a quality player who hit deadly free kicks and corners and was the player who took all the accolades on the final day of that incredible season. We played Wolves at home and needed to win, but goal average was vital. Paul scored all four of our goals to complete this amazing escape!

The funny story was that afterwards I ran into the manager's office, sat in his chair and put my feet up with a bottle of bubbly. The boys were running on and off of the field to a rapturous crowd but I needed to watch the teleprinter for our relegation rivals' results, the champagne was quite apt as we not only won the battle but the war also. The story goes that 'Squire' was behind the goal at the Boothen End with his arms raised when the manager – Bill Asprey – grabbed one hand and stood there with him. Then turning to Paul said that "I scored those goals today" to which Paul replied, "What are you on about?" The manager said. "If I had not picked you, you would not have been able to score then would you?"

Once again as Greavesie would say "Funny old game".

He became the steppingstone of our survival. We had several other fringe players such as Philip Heath who came and wen,t but overall it was these players mentioned who pulled off the 'Great Escape' in the mid-eighties.

As for Ronaldo being seen at Stamford Bridge, I can confirm that both he and David Beckham were seen within the grounds, which had tongues wagging from Putney Bridge to Sloane Square, which is where I was when learning of such a thing. One punter said that they were there discussing a promotional deal with a boot company!

SEVEN MILLION A YEAR

Harry Harris wrote that: Chelsea will pay Claudio Ranieri's successor a massive £7million a year, dwarfing any other deal in football.

Ranieri, who is on £1.4million a year, faces the sack if he does not win a trophy this season and Romam Abramovich will spare no expense in replacing him.

A five-year contract for the new boss would have a value of anything between £35 to £40million depending on the level of Champions League success achieved. That, plus limitless funds to spend on players, would attract any coach.

England coach Sven Goran Eriksson is favourite for the job and Abramovich can afford to buy the Swede out of the last two years of his Football Association deal. But Eriksson is pondering his next move and if he wants to stay with England, there are two leading candidates. His main rival is Fabio Capello, who has privately indicated that he wants the job. He is out of contract at Roma at the end of the season, where he is mounting a Serie A tile challenge on a shoestring budget, in marked contrast to the Chelsea riches.

And the arrival of former Manchester United chief executive Peter Kenyon – who made clear how tenuous Ranieri's hold on the job is when he took charge at Stamford Bridge last week, could see an attempt to bring Sir Alex Ferguson to Chelsea.

Ferguson's future still hinges on the power struggle at Old Trafford. If John Magnier and JP McManus, who own 25 per cent of the clubs shares through their company Cubic Expression, gain any boardroom control, the United manager of 17 years is likely to walk out.

But if there is an out-of-court settlement over the stud fees for Rock of Gibraltar, Ferguson has hinted to close friend Bryan Robson he would want to continue at Manchester United until he is seventy.

Ferguson has just signed a £4million a year contract but can expect, with bonuses, to earn £6million a year if United continue their phenomenal run of success. But the package Chelsea would offer may be hard for Ferguson to resist if his situation at Old Trafford becomes untenable.

Transfer funds of £150million would also tempt the Scot, who has struggled with the restrictions imposed by the United plc.

Kenyon's public demand for trophies has heaped pressure on the players, too, as Eidur Gudjohnsen revealed last night.

MY COLUMN

The following is my *Sentinel* column on the morning of Chelsea's match with Charlton.

Jermain Defoe's move from West Ham is not only great news for Spurs – but potentially significant news for England.

He was the bargain of the transfer window and I can't believe that moneybags Chelsea let him slip through the net. And I'll go as far as to predict Defoe will be a major part of the Swede's plans when he selects his squad for this summer's European Championships. I see Michael Owen and Defoe as the best partnership in the country, partly because the new Spurs striker has the temperament not to be fazed by the presence of the Liverpool man and to rise to new heights alongside him.

I have watched and studied this young player and he has it all. Not only that, he also has the ability to make Owen look an even better hit-man. Owen has been the lone ranger for far too long, for both his club and country, and Defoe's introduction would take so much pressure off our best striker. At last, he would be working more in tandem with a player on the same wavelength

– rather than someone at least two steps behind. Owen has been badly hindered by playing alongside Emile Heskey, a player who just does not cut it at international level.

But there is a genuine partnership in the making for England now that Defoe has jumped on an international pad by joining Spurs.

I just love the way he weaves his way around defenders in the penalty area, while his brain works just as quickly as his feet. He plays on the shoulder of his marker, a great art in itself, but he also has the pace of Owen and possesses a tremendous first touch.

He has suffered a nightmare at West Ham this season after being sent off three times and thinly disguising his desire to leave.

I see that as being totally honest in a world of football where loyalty and ambition become secondary.

This young man, though, is hungry for success and his first ambition will be to win over the Spurs fans before gunning for an England place. His only problem at the Spurs is, perhaps, whether his teammates are be tuned in to such a cute players wavelength.

Owen will read him, though, and that is why they will be tailormade for each other by the summer, if the Swede does his job right!

This could be the first time England have had a good combination leading the line instead of relying on a one man band.

With Manchester United spending £12million for Saha and Arsenal £17million for Reyes, I reckon Spurs have got a 'snip' with Defoe.

He still has a little chip on his shoulder, but that isn't such a bad thing for an out and out goal-getter who needs a mean and selfish side to him. It was true that Fergie wanted Defoe at Old Trafford, but there were too many ifs and buts, while Defoe also had his very own agent. Sorry, I could not resist that one!

The young East Ender lets his football do the talking and is a smarter, better all-round player than Saha. As for Reyes, I couldn't help smiling when he scored his own goal on Tuesday, because I doubt if he had ever been in his life before.

I thought Arsene Wenger got his tactics wrong, I know the Champions League is crucial, but I don't see how 45 minutes from Pires and Henry was going to make that much difference in the months to come.

Boro got through on merit and good on them. It is nice to see two fine sides in Boro and Bolton going to fight it out in Cardiff at the end of the month.

JEFF POWELL

Jeff Powell has just a few lines to put to the public about the current managerial situation: While it is never easy to tell where Sven Goran Eriksson is coming from, could it be that we now have a clearer idea of where he is going?

The England manager has hinted that, if Beckham and the boys go down something like 3-0 in all of their Euro 2004 group matches in Portugal, he will be free to toddle off to Chelsea and help himself to Mr Abramovich's millions.

The word from the England dressing room is that Eriksson doesn't really do team talks. But if the Swede makes an exception this summer, how can he possibly motivate them to win?

SPORTS AGENDA WITH CHARLES SALE
'NEW BOOK PROBES ROMAN'S BILLIONS?'

Chelsea owner Roman Arbramovich, who prefers to keep a veil of secrecy over how he acquired his billions, is unlikely to welcome a major probe into his life and times. Top sportsbook publishers Collins Willow have commissioned an in-depth study of Abramovich, who has spent more than £220million on his Chelsea revolution, as one of the major books on their autumn publishing list.

The sizeable advance given to author Dominic Midgley, a former editor of *Punch* magazine, and Chris Hutchins, an author of books on royalty, includes plenty of funding for trips to Russia to investigate Abramovich in his home land, where they intend to talk to friends and work colleagues – if allowed.

Abramovich is keen to move out of the limelight at Stamford Bridge and let newly arrived chief executive Peter Kenyon build a profile at the club.

That would explain Kenyon's busy media programme over the last weekend, including a chat with Garry Richardson on Radio Five Live in which he changed from being a Manchester United supporter to a Chelsea fan during the course of the programme.

PORTSMOUTH

Chelsea knew that they would get a good test from Harry's team and that is exactly what they got. But it seems the addition of Scott Parker looks as if he will become the best signing since Roman Abramovich invested all of his roubles into the football club.

The following day's papers were all about the new signing from Charlton and from the first whistle he made his presence felt with a couple of crunching tackles and that wore off on Lampard and the rest of his new teammates. The *Daily Mail* put it this way: PARKER LIFTS RANIERI FOR THE BIG PUSH followed by the *Sun* saying that: SCOTTY PARKER and RANIERI'S LAST BUY SHOWS HE COULD BE THE MOST VALUABLE. Running along the top of the *Express* looked like this: Chelsea boss given breathing space while late Boro winner sees Ferguson's men falter in title race and RANIERI ENJOYS HIGH LIFE THANKS TO SCOTT.

So you can figure out that Chelsea got the result needed to keep on the heels of the two top clubs in English football for the last ten years. I personally was gutted for my mate Harry as his team gave everything and more to pull this match out of the fire, and had Yakubu taken that wonderful opportunity when Sullivan hit Hon Terry with an attempted clearance which left the

Nigerian with a near open goal, only for him to blast it into the Fratton Park crowd. Had this fell to Berger or Berkovic, it would have levelled the scores and lifted Portsmouth onto another confidence level. Okay, Chelsea were the better team but that was always going to be the case and Harry and Jim Smith have been about too long not to know that: but their team, if given one break, could have upset Chelsea's rhythm.

I made my notes early on that read: Portsmouth are far too clumsy in possession and it will be fatal if that continues. Chelsea could have had them dead and buried before the half hour mark but I know the way Harry works and if they could just hang in there until half-time things would change and then who knows just what the last forty five minutes would bring. You would not have thought that Portsmouth were down near the basement on yet another fine display – after being robbed at Spurs and at home against Wolves the week before. But this was to become a big night for the Blues, as just about two hundred miles away Manchester United were being given a real hard time by Middlesbrough, which had the headline in the *Sun* saying that:

BORO SINK FERGIE AS MAGNIER WINS WAR WITH UNITED.

The Tinkerman changed things a little by playing Makelele, Lampard and Parker in the middle of the field and that – as I always say – is where most matches are won or lost.

On this evidence one headline in the *Sun* got it right by saying that Scott Parker showed that he was the best signing to date by the Russian and in time, with both he and Lampard, Chelsea will be a real tough nut to crack. They are both long distance runners whilst Makelele sits behind them keeping the opposition away from the back door. After Yakubu's miss Patrick Berger skipped past three defenders before unleashing a wonderful drive that – once again – hit the woodwork and, if Portsmouth were given points for doing such a thing over the past three matches they would be halfway up the Premiership table. But this night belonged to Chelsea with Parker the main man alongside Frank, who for once took a back seat as the new boy went about his business with the kind of desire and passion needed to win football matches. Chelsea had all of the ball in the early stages as Portsmouth found it hard to come to terms with, for they needed to get the ball to Berkovic much more and without Sherringham they were missing their link between defence and attack, So it was no shock that Chelsea took the lead when a lovely, though simplistic, move where Bridge, collecting a throw helped the ball into Parker who played a neat one-two off of Mutu before controlling with his right and blasting with his left, a ferocious volley that ended up high into the top of Shaka Hislop's net.

The ex-Charlton midfield man became the seventeenth Chelsea player to score this season which is possibly one of the reasons the Tinkerman does not want to go back into the market for another much needed striker. In that first forty-five minutes he showed all of his qualities in his ability to win tackles, use the ball sensibly, and of course scoring the opening goal, as Matt Lawton in the *Mail* said: "In a fiercely contested first half, the former Charlton midfielder displayed a remarkable gift of ubiquity – he was everywhere making tackles, completing passes and scoring goals."

With so much said about players taking time to settle in – especially after all the emotional hassle surrounding his move – he made a mockery of such a theory.

The match was never all Chelsea for Portsmouth came out with their sleeves rolled up and gave it a real go. Luck at this moment in time is not on Harry's menu, with Steve Stone suffering a stress fracture during the warm up and Berger coming off late in the game with what could be a serious knee injury. With Teddy out, along with Sherwood, Harry's woes just get more and more hard to take. Although afterwards, he only had praise for his patched up team by saying that, "We couldn't have played any better, but we're just not getting the breaks."

As you know I was at the home match against Wolves and those squandered chances when hitting the woodwork four times could be two very precious points dropped come April and May time. After Chelsea had been pushed back by a spirited home team with Lua Lua getting into the thick of things, Chelsea broke away and put the match beyond their reach as an inspired piece of tinkering by Ranieri replacing Mutu with Crespo and Gudjohnsen with Jimmy Floyd. Lua Lua saw a header flash wide and then straight after forced a great save out of Sullivan before Chelsea broke away with Frank Lampard putting Jimmy Floyd through and the Dutch striker lobbed the out-coming Hislop, only to watch his attempt hit the bar but, unlike at the other end, it fell kindly to Crespo, who chested the ball into an empty net. Claudio Ranieri watched intently with his usual stance and with his right hand on his chin and beneath a very happy Chelsea manager. No matter what they throw at this man he will fight it with his wonderful humour and if he is bombed out he can walk away with his head held high and his pockets bulging, and that is the bottom line!

Chelsea had now inflicted five goals and six points on Portsmouth but the Premiership strugglers more than held their own for two of the three hours played, both at the Bridge and Fratton Park. But at the end of the day, if you have not got someone to put away chances – when they are at their premium – then you are going to suffer!

Harry Redknapp has now got an injury crisis as his team faces two matches at Anfield against a Liverpool side who are battling once again for that fourth Champions League spot.

Portsmouth 0 Chelsea 1 Jimmy Floyd 20,624

As for the Blues, it was a timely confidence booster as they go into two very exciting matches against leaders Arsenal beginning tomorrow at Highbury in the fifth round FA Cup tie.

The *Mail*'s headlines read like this: WENGER AIMS BIG GUNS AT

CHELSEA and that Wenger won't be rested as Arsenal boss picks best XI by Ian McGarry:

Chelsea fans may have hoped that Arsene Wenger would rest some of his key players for tomorrow's Cup game at Highbury. If so, they are going to be disappointed.

In the past the Frenchman has had one eye on the league when selecting sides for Cup games. Middlesbrough, for instance, were spared another caning by Thierry Henry in the last round, while Chelsea themselves did not have to face the French striker in their quarter-final last season – which they lost 3-1.

But Wenger made it clear yesterday that Chelsea will face the big names tomorrow, including Henry. "I will play Thierry" said the Arsenal boss. "In such a big game in front of 38,000 fans we need to play our strongest team and we want to put out a team with the best chance of winning.

"I would have preferred a lesser opponent but Chelsea is such a big game for us, even if we have a very good record against them."

Twenty-five games unbeaten in the Premiership have Arsenal five points ahead of Manchester United and six in front of Chelsea. Perhaps, from that pint of view, they could afford to be a bit more relaxed!

"No, because the championship is ours to lose and win" said Wenger. "A five point difference with thirteen matches left. Ten points maybe. Anyway we will not relax in the FA Cup because we want to win it for a third time consecutively. We remember last season when it helped make up for the disappointment of losing the title."

Arsenal certainly have the psychological advantage going into this game. The clubs have met in the FA Cup in each of the last three seasons – including the Final in 2002 – with Arsenal winning each tie, though they required a replay victory at Stamford Bridge last season after drawing the sixth round tie at Highbury 2-2.

In fact, Arsenal's unbeaten Cup record against Chelsea stretches back more than fifty years, to January 1947 – while Chelsea have not won at Highbury in thirteen years, save for a meaningless League Cup match.

With Claudio Ranieri's side facing Arsenal at Stamford Bridge in a week's time for the league showdown and an international week squeezed in between, Wenger is more worried about tiredness in his players, who also face a Champions League match against Celta Vigo on February the 24th. Chelsea have one day's extra rest before playing Stuttgart.

As Wenger assesses the opposition, he admits the admiration for Frank Lampard, one of the best midfielders in England.

He said that, "Lampard has been outstanding for Chelsea this season. He has always been talented but he has matured since he arrived there and now has improved every aspect of his game. For instance, he was always good at shooting from outside the box but now he times his run into it to score as well.

"Winning this cup game would give us a psychological edge for next week and that could be important, especially with so many matches to play in such a short space of time."

Time is something which, Ranieri seems to be short of to please his employers, but Wenger offered a little consolation, "We are all under pressure it is a part of the job."

He said "His is different because it is a financial pressure due to the money that has been spent on the team, while with other clubs it is to win trophies because you have done so already."

Ranieri remains upbeat as ever. He said that, "Why should I think the season could be over in February?

"I am a positive man. Why would I think I could lose these two matches?

"I think about beating Arsenal twice which means we are still in the cup and the title race is still open.

"We will go to Arsenal with a lot of respect, but we have improved a lot since we lost our first game against them. We beat Lazio twice, we won against Besiktas and we won against Manchester United. They were good for our confidence. Now we have to prove that we have improved".

CHRISTMAS HANGOVER CURED

The Tinkerman and his little tinkers have now recovered from the nightmare run around Christmas and has seen his team win six and draw one of their last seven Premiership matches, and that will give them the much-needed confidence going into face Arsenal twice in the next eight days. The first encounter will be at Highbury in the FA Cup – for the fourth time in the last four seasons – whilst the second will be at the Bridge the following Saturday. Both matches will be televised live. The second encounter Sir Alex Ferguson will be wanting a Chelsea win to close the gap – if they win their next match that is – to three points, but Arsenal have superior goal difference to both Chelsea and United which is like an extra point. Although the Gunners are free scorers they also have the meanest defensive record in the Premiership.

Although I have a feeling – in the FA Cup match – Chelsea might just at least play out a draw and get them back at the Bridge for a fifth round replay. Which again will leave them once again still facing the unbeaten Premiership leaders twice in eight days, the only difference being that both matches will be on Chelsea's home soil. What two fantastic matches that would promise to be?

You have obviously gathered by the Manchester United headline – earlier – that they were beaten by Middlesbrough by three goals to two and you can read my feelings about that in the following column of mine in the *Sentinel*. The first is my Friday piece and will be followed by the mess Manchester United have got themselves in, and Sir Alex in particular!

My *Sentinel* column read like this:

BARBARIC COMMENTS

There were two ex-Spurs players in the news this week for entirely different reasons, with Joe Kinnear taking over Nottingham Forest, whilst Southampton had a brainwave to bring back Glenn Hoddle as their head coach. But at the thirteenth hour two local MP's stepped in and put the brakes on the deal. John Denham, who holds Southampton Itchen, expressed his fear that the fans would go 'ape-shit' if Hoddle were to take over the club he used as a vehicle when the Football Association ousted him for his incredible behaviour whilst managing the national side. The fans have every right to be stunned by such a move, because as Denham points out, when Hoddle left the Saints he never had one nice word to say about them. Hoddle has become a monster in sheep's clothing in his managerial career by upsetting the majority of players who played under his management. He also came back to the Saints and bought Dean Richards for a near £8million, but little did he know he did them a right favour, for under Gordon Strachan they looked better defensively and have played some terrific football along the way. Strachan and Hoddle are opposites, one wears his heart very much on his sleeve whilst the other has no sleeves. I was going to say heart but that would be stooping down to his level. Any club who took Hoddle on after his barbaric comments about the many children who are struck by illness was unforgivable!

He once said as England manager that Michael Owen was not a natural goalscorer, now come on, will somebody tell me where he came up with that theory?

He left England in tatters, then did the same to Southampton and Spurs, a club he said he was born to manage. Some will say that under him, Southampton reached their highest ever Premiership position and I'll hold my hands up on that but it is not always that kind of success that tells the true story. When you have a situation like he had at Spurs by bringing in Teddy Sherringham and then insulting Teddy Boy's intelligence, I think you are definitely playing with fire. I have seen Sherringham several times so far this season in a struggling Portsmouth side and he is still 'top notch'. I have written before – in this space – that it is incredible how such great players such as Alan Ball and Glenn Hoddle make such a 'pigs ear' of management. With Alan Ball, I believe he was frustrated that the players he had could not play the game like him, but he forgot there were not too many players in the world who could do that. But with Hoddle – if what I read is true – he would want to be the best player in five-a-sides almost to the point where he was showing off all of the kind of talent that is such a rare gift. Put those two ingredients into a casserole dish and it would be a definite candidate for food poisoning. The greatest asset a manager can have is his ability to 'man manage' and that means getting the very best out of what you have at your disposal. For example, when I arrived at the Victoria Ground, I did not know what the future would hold for me, all I did know is that I wanted to play the game the way I love playing it, and by doing so other players around me would benefit from it. So to my great fortune Tony Waddington – as he said so often – gave me the responsibility a player like me needs. Add confidence to that and hard work on your fitness and you have the perfect scenario. Being the manager has done his job properly and the rest is up to the player. But far too many mangers want to play the game for the player. I read just lately that Chelsea's Jesper Gronkjaer said in the press that, "When I was at Ajax I thought I was a great player, but here I have gone sideways, and the reason being that the man who bought me played me on the wrong wing, I am a left winger not a right winger". That is just one example of such management. At Chelsea Dave Sexton would sometimes put me out wide on the right and really he would have been better getting Stevie Wonder to play there, and I love Stevie Wonder. Back to St Mary's and the job at hand. The fans will revolt, the players will not respond and the board of directors have put this deal on hold until today and, as I see it, Friday the Thirteenth looks gloomy for the ex-England boss!

MORE COOLMORE MAFIA PRESSURE

My Sunday *Sentinel* piece read like this:

Once upon a time there was a manager who had all the answers to any problem that came his way. But it seems that that has changed and he may be thinking twice about throwing in the towel that was once white, but is now turning a different kind of red. Whilst Arsenal – and Thierry Henry – cruise along like a Rolls Royce in the fast lane, Alex Ferguson's team are waiting for assistance on the hard shoulder. The Scotsman once had a motor like the Frenchman but, through personal vendettas, he has lost his road map and the vehicle that once got him to his destination safely seems to have had the tires let down. It has been a long road for the last decade but one of incredible successes, but it seems now that the Frenchman and his very skilful team are pulling away. The Scot has been called everything in his long and illustrious managerial career but never a 'shirker' so now is the real 'acid' test for both him and his players.

His one man band seems to have bitten off far too much to chew since taking on the Irish and all their 'Mafia' connections and my mole tells me that he would have had more chance climbing the Empire State Building and bringing down King Kong over his shoulder. Greed is a terrible illness and there is absolutely no cure for it, so the players at Manchester United – for the first time – have a bird's eye view of a man slowly slipping down the ladder that for so long took him to the top floor of such a building. Whilst Arsenal keep up their relentless gallop to the winning line and Chelsea keeping in touch on their heels, Manchester United have a definite case of collapsing and how Kevin Keegan will be wishing he was still at Newcastle with the team who once handed the championship to the man who laughed in his face in front of millions of viewers. Keegan, however, has a date with destiny himself this coming weekend and he will never have a better opportunity to pull something back from the man who has toyed with him so many times in the past. Manchester United plc will be sitting down after the weekend and take stock of an experience they have never faced before. The Coolmore Mafia will be smiling to the gods, as their manager seems to have lost the plot for the very first time!

The Premiership champions are on the ropes and waiting for the bell to ring but there is still time for even more humiliation, as their defence – if that is what you call it – leak goals like never before, except if you go back as far as Jim Leighton, a goalkeeper who the United boss thought was the best man for the United cause. The alarm bells have been ringing for quite some time at Old Trafford but the manager – who once could tinker with great results – has to face the music alone. He is the one who buys the players and takes it on those once broad shoulders to take on a fight, which is impossible to win!

At this moment in time, the man from the back streets of his beloved Scotland seems to have reached his destination with fate. If Rock of Gibraltar could talk he would be asking those at the Coolmore stud "just who is this man who feeds me only polo mints"?

You cannot walk into a world that has flourished by the genius of Magnier,

McManus and Tabor – the man who wanted to buy West Ham and keep Harry Redknapp and all of his homegrown talents. Yeah, I know Ferguson is powerful in his own back garden but what we are talking about here is a garden as big as the Santa Anita and Kentucky racetracks. Not forgetting Dubai. Ferguson could never have got it so far wrong in his thinking that he could use his beloved Manchester United for the growth of his family's future business. I have seen a side of Ferguson that turned me off him, although still holding respect for the magnificent job he has done on the football playing fields. I was invited one evening to go and see Bryan Robson before a match against West Ham at Old Trafford and, after the receptionist had spoken to the ex-United and England captain, she showed us through the door which would lead to him. This was bad timing because walking towards us was the 'big boss man' who looked at us as if we were four terrorists and quickly fronted us to say "Go back out from where you came from" with the kind of tongue I can only imagine he saved for David Beckham and his unadorable wife, the Spice girl.

I was quite shocked, as I had seen the other side of him in a meeting with Martin Edwards – the ex-chairman – and he was a pussycat. The million-dollar question right now is where does he go from here. He has always had a problem in finding great defenders – Denis Irwin apart – and that record of his still remains. They have leaked in eight goals in three matches and not against top teams!

Yet, he goes out and buys a striker for £12million and I don't care who you are, you cannot expect your team to keep scoring four goals to get you out of the mire!

As the Champions League comes closer, all of Europe will have been watching the results of Manchester United and thinking that if you are letting in goals like that in your domestic game, what chance have you when you face the likes of Real Madrid and Juventus?

The one person who will be quietly chuckling is Beckham himself, after being insulted by his ex-manager once too often. While Real Madrid stride on majestically, Manchester United splutter like that old beaten-up Skoda.

DRINK CANADA DRY
'An offer they couldn't refuse'

Beckham does and did not deserve the kind of grief his one time boss gave him because it is not as if he was an image of George Best, whose breath once turned heads in the United dressing room and following Best there were Robson, Whiteside and McGrath, who saw that sign at the Airport – just like George did – and boarded the aeroplane to Vancouver and once seated were asked by a passenger what were they doing going to British Columbia and quickly the ex-England captain replied that "We decided to come away but did not know where we were going until we got here. So after having a few drinks in the bar Paul McGrath went to the men's restroom and passed the sign saying: 'Drink Canada Dry', so after returning to his pals and telling them about it they all agreed that this was an offer they could not refuse!

Sometimes that can be forgiven, if you are continually winning league titles like Beckham has done for so long at a club he was born to play for. This latest setback against Steve McClaren's – of all people – team on Wednesday evening was just a reminder of just how his season was heading. Then just as he thought things could not get any worse he heard that Magnier and McManus had increased their shares by buying eight million more shares from Dutch media magnate John De Mol at a cost of £21.2million. Then to add to his already painful story, American billionaire Malcolm Glazer is reported to have made an offer to become the first ever American owner in the Premiership. This could work one of two ways for Ferguson, but I have feeling the Yank and his three sons Joel, Edward and Bryan – all United fans and advisers – will not tolerate the kind of business that has got out of hand in Manchester. Glazer owns the Tampa Bay Buccaneers, a place where I have played and once had a home, and this man with untold 'dosh' said that "Manchester United is the only club to buy." Back on the playing field though, the biggest problem he has is that when a player like Junhino scores two headers against you, it does not take shareholders to tell you that Junhino is a tiny pocket-sized genius with the ball at his feet, so how is it he comes to our ground and scores with two headers?

The problem mounts at Old Trafford and I cannot see how they – all of a sudden – lock their back door, because even if they did it may be too late because the burglars have been, taken and gone long ago!

IMPRESSIVE LAMPARD ON INTER'S WATCH-LIST

This was reported by In McGarry of the *Daily Mail* prior to the Charlton match eight days ago: Inter Milan will monitor Frank Lampard's progress for the rest of the season with a view of bidding for the Chelsea and England midfielder in the summer.

Sources at Inter confirmed they have had the England player watched on several occasions. The club has also received a detailed technical dossier on his style of play and suitability for Serie A. Coach Albert Zaccheroni confirmed his intention to revamp the Inter midfield by recruiting Serbia and Montenegro star Dejan Stankovic from Lazio during the January transfer window. Now he has his eye on Lampard, who cost Chelsea £11million when he signed from West Ham two and a half years ago, and is one of the few Premiership players to have maintained his value in a falling market.

Lampard's contract expires in June of 2006 and Inter hope to pick him up for a lower fee, though Chelsea want to extend the 25-year-old's deal in the summer.

RANIERI WAS AFTER YOUNG STAR HENRY

"Frank's the best midfielder in the country on current form" the Tinkerman said and "I'm not Sven Goran Eriksson, but he deserves to play for England. He can do everything."

In fact Lampard has featured in all five of England's matches this season, scoring an impressive first goal when coming on in the 3-1 win over Croatia in August.

Barring injury, he seems to be certain to be named in Eriksson's Euro 2004 squad. Ranieri yesterday clinched the £7million signing of Czech goalkeeper Peter Cech from French club Rennes – taking his spending to £128million. But the Italian said that, "I am working for now but I am also working for the future – though maybe I will not be the manager in the future."

Ken Dyer wrote a piece about how Claudio Ranieri revealed how close he was to signing Thierry Henry. Chelsea meet Arsenal in the FA Cup fifth round tie at Highbury tomorrow and their Italian coach described him as the "Mohammad Ali of football", and "that I had tried to sign him as a youngster."

I must interrupt here, because when Arsene Wenger brought Henry over to north London he was a winger and it was not until Nicholas Anelka done a runner with the help of his family's organisation, that the Arsenal boss chose Henry to replace him through the middle of every Arsenal attack, and that also explains how and why Henry drifts out wide in so many of his team's attacks. A place he can show his electric pace and is so comfortable, going either outside or inside the poor opposing full-back. This was possibly one of the greatest ever buys before the transfer fees in this country went through the roof?

The money the French manager made on Anelka – although not wanting him to leave was quite a masterstroke!

This is just another art of great management and if you weighed up all of his transfer transactions the scale would fall mighty heavily in his favour!

Ranieri continued and said that, "I watched him a long time ago when I was manager of Florentina and he was playing for the French Under-21 team.

"I said to my chairman 'Please buy him because he is one of the best' but it did not happen for some reason.

"I told him that Henry was like the Mohammad Ali of the football pitch because he has so much style and grace."

So how does Ranieri intend to stop the man who Chelsea's England midfielder, Frank Lampard now rates as the best striker in the world?

"With a gun" said the Chelsea coach. "But seriously, I have my best players and we will do our best to stop him on Sunday.

"All players have a price and that includes Thierry Henry. I wouldn't like to put a price on him, though. Only Arsenal can do that."

Meanwhile, Arsenal fullback Ashley Cole has paid tribute to Ranieri.

He said that, "You keep hearing that he is going to get the sack. I don't think that's fair. I feel sorry for him because he is a great manager and, from what I have seen, a nice man.

"Any manager who has that sort of money would build a great team. But they are under more pressure than us. We'll go into the Cup game as if it were a normal match — but they have spent all that money and I think that they have to get results now."

RANIERI TO PRESENT CONVINCING CASE
Double jeopardy for Chelsea manager but Henry's absence
gives his career prospects a lift

I came across a nice piece in the *Independent* written by Chief Sports Writer Nick Townsend, it went like this: Another day, another blowpipe dart directed between the shoulder blades of Claudio Ranieri. Just as well the Italian possesses a rhinoceros hide, and a humour that protects him like an antidote to the poison. On Friday, it was idle talk from Arsenal's Ashley Cole, and a tabloid's narrow interpretation of his sentiments, which could have unsettled a less resolute man. "If we beat them we could end up getting Ranieri the sack" was Cole's relatively innocuous quote, which produced the headline 'We'll Sink Tin', a reference to Chelsea's self-styled 'Tinkerman'.

Ranieri charitably regards such speculation as 'the spice of our job'. Nevertheless, it would be fair to say that what the Chelsea coach, with the spectre of Sven Goran Eriksson at his shoulder, does not need now is a double-header within a week against the League leaders located only sixteen tube stops away. The first comes at lunchtime today in the knockout competition, which Ranieri and his counterpart Arsene Wenger have regarded with a respect not observed throughout the Premiership.

Under Ranieri, Chelsea have been defeated by Arsenal in the FA Cup every season — including the 2002 final — since he succeeded Gianluca Vialla in September 2002. The portents are equally ominous from a historical perspective. It was just after the war that Chelsea last accounted for Arsenal in the cup and they have never won a tie at Highbury. Typically, Ranieri has a ready response to such statistics. "In Italy we say, 'That isn't two without three'. We lost three FA Cup games against Arsenal. Now is the time for a win. It is a big rock in front of us, but we are ready."

The persistent Eriksson takeover claim is a strange one. Most of the evidence is circumstantial, and as far as this observer is aware, there is no substance to the rumours though, as we are all aware, six months can be an eternity in football politics

Anyway, are the Swede's credentials any superior than Ranieri's?

Still, you assume the latter must yearn for the freedom that Wenger — and, indeed Sir Alex Ferguson back in 1986 — enjoyed to create a team, without the constant pressure and talk that the Stamford Bridge regime are poised to change the manager.

Ranieri maintains that: "At the beginning there was a chairman and a chief executive who chose him (Wenger). I want the new owner — Roman Abramovich — and new chief executive — Peter Kenyon — to believe in me also. That is my job. I try everything to try and convince them. If Abramovich and Peter Kenyon had chosen me in the beginning, it would have been a little easier, but I have the possibility to show what I can do and that is important to me. A lot of managers want to come here. That's understandable, but at the moment I am here. I have the stability and I am strong."

In his corduroy jacket, he looked anything but a squatter. Yet, effectively Ranieri was claiming squatters' rights. The message for would-be interlopers is that you'll have to bundle him out of the place, bound hand and foot.

Certainly the players have vindicated his faith, having emerged from a Christmas period where their grasp on the championship became increasingly tenuous, with renewed vigour. It does not surprise the Italian. "After the Liverpool match, which we lost 1-0, I said that I'm sure my players would come back. Slowly we have recovered, and are in a good condition. We can improve again."

But sufficient to eclipse the Gunners, who have just about every rival locked into their firing line at present?

And not once, at Highbury today, but at Stamford Bridge again on Saturday?

Much will depend on the proficiency of the defending of John Terry and company – even in the absence through injury of arch predator Thierry Henry.

Terry, who will almost certainly feature alongside Sol Campbell for England against Portugal on Wednesday, was a colossus against Portsmouth on Wednesday night. Ranieri almost purrs with enthusiasm for his captain.

"I like Henry's elegance on the pitch, but of course I believe in my player. I brought him in for Frank Leboeuf who was a world-class champion, and I believe in him. He is progressing every year. I said two years ago that in my opinion John could become like Tony Adams not only for Chelsea, but also for England. He's got very close this season. He's strong with a good personality. He's a fantastic player and still very young."

Henry was ruled out last night because of a bruised foot, but Ranieri is conscious that Arsenal possess other treasures, including the record acquisition from Seville, Jose Antonio Reyes, who has already exhibited his vision and trickery. "Arsene always looks forward and Reyes is a fantastic player", says the Chelsea boss. "I'm sure he has bought a player with a long future ahead of him".

Ranieri faces an Arsenal team who remain undefeated in the League this season.

Their manager attributes a principle reason for that to the contribution of his captain, Patrick Vieira. "If you look at the reasons for our consistency since the start of the season, it is of course down to the attitude of my team, but also down to the work Patrick has done with the players," says Wenger. "He brings a mental understanding to the side, which we saw before when Tony Adams was playing. Maybe today it is forgotten that at one time he felt victimised and was on the edge. I was worried he would go."

Vieira has stayed, and provided the cement to bind the brickwork of the Arsenal team together. There is still a feeling that Chelsea remain a construction of individual pieces, which are still prone to falling apart under sustained assault. Yet you cannot argue with what Ranieri has achieved. The only question is, will he become the first coach to secure significant Champions League, Premiership and FA Cup success, only to be dethroned as the culmination of it all?

The next six days will provide us with some fascinating clues.

BERGKAMP

Dennis Bergkamp is set for a recall on Sunday after being injured for the midweek game while £17.5million Spanish striker Jose Antonio Reyes looks like missing out.

My score-line read: "DURK THE JERK"

As I said earlier, I fancied Chelsea to leave Highbury with at least a replay and the Blues had a massive boost when hearing the golden boy of the moment would miss the tie and the 'still adapting' Spaniard would replace him. The Arsenal team sheet looked quite empty without this fantastic bang-in-form Frenchman, but it is the FA Cup and we know one thing, and that is it will always throw up an unexpected hero somewhere along the way and this Sunday morning was no exception. This was to become an enthralling derby match and Chelsea began the game well and closed down the Gunners from the first whistle, led by Scott Parker who crashed into the Arsenal captain Patrick Viera in the very first minute, which set the tone for the rest of the early afternoon, and that would suit Chelsea if the game became a scruffy affair. Arsenal's strength is passing the ball around the pitch quickly, changing the angles from right to left, moving opposing defenders from one side of the field to the other. They don't play with wide men and therefore there are always spaces down the flanks that attack-minded Laurent and Cole thrive on. The match would finally end up with six yellow cards and the Arsenal skipper was the first one to be waved at by Paul 'The Joke' Durkin. Viera was still arguing with 'Durk the Jerk' as the players disappeared up the Arsenal tunnel and should know better for all his team needed was to lost their most influential player in a battle like this. Chelsea had given a little more than they got in the first half and were very unfortunate to have a Gronkjaer header ruled out through offside before Adrian Mutu put them into the lead closing in on half-time. Frank Lampard hit a long drive to the far post which found the Dutch winger standing all alone at the far post and he met it sweetly to bury his header into Lehman's net as the Arsenal number one looked on helplessly.

The Chelsea end erupted and so did the Grosvenor Club with bluenoses dancing and singing in the hope that at last they were going to put Chelsea into the next round at the expense of a team that had not lost a cup tie against

Chelsea since as far back as the forties. But the cheers turned into tears as the 'Copper in Black' signalled it as no goal. Billy Gallas almost scored just after John Terry made a magnificent tackle to halt Gilberto as the Brazilian latched onto another superb pass from Bergkamp – who played delightfully throughout – but the Arsenal midfielder dwelled just a second too long, giving the magnificent Chelsea centre-back just enough time to clear the danger. My first thought at that moment was 'If that were Thierry Henry?'

Moments later that Gallas effort looked in, but to the relief of the Gunners the ball crashed into the side netting. Then Ashley Cole had a tremendous opportunity to put the home team in front but chose to drive the ball, instead of getting his toes under the ball and lifting the ball over Cudicini. It was great stuff as Chelsea poured forward once again then with the Blues holding more than their own at this particular time, it was no surprise when they took the lead. The Arsenal keeper Jens Lehmann's poor clearance was blocked by Scott Parker – who found Adrian Mutu – with only Toure between him and the German shot-stopper. Mutu feinted to go right and switch the ball onto his left foot before letting fly with a beautifully struck left footer into Lehmann's left-hand side of the goal. The tiny Chelsea striker had a little luck as the ball eventually went through Toure's legs, leaving the keeper with no chance of stopping Chelsea from taking the lead. Arsenal 0 Chelsea 1 flashed up on the scoreboard and the Chelsea fans were now delirious as the half-time whistle went and their thinking was at last their time had come. From whre I was sitting Chelsea deserved their one goal advantage and if they could keep Pires quiet then this terrific cup-tie was as good as won. But we know the 'cool' of the Arsenal manager and the way he will approach his half-time team talk, just telling his players to take the game to the Blues because he felt they would try to hang onto that one goal lead – which is the Italian way of thinking – and there were fifteen minutes for the Tinkerman to make his mind up whether to go for a second or hold fort and try to keep this very dangerous team at bay. The big chance was that there was no Thierry Henry, so Chelsea had one less worry and in my mind I would have come out and gone at Wenger's team. Arsenal, though, had other ideas, having not been beaten in the FA Cup since Liverpool had beaten them in the final four seasons ago. Eighteen consecutive matches in fact, so you knew that Arsene Wenger would be calm in the home-eam dressing room and telling his players to move the ball quicker but at all times be patient. The second half began and the match took a different kind of shape as the home team looked like the side in front, Robert Pires came more and more into the match whilst Dennis Bergkamp was still a threat whenever the ball came into him, but overall Patrick Viera took the match by the scruff of the neck and powered his massive frame all over the pitch, and now this had become the 'acid test' for Scott Parker, Frank Lampard and Claude Makelele.

It took you back to being a kid when playing on one of those pinball tables where the ball pinged around the table like a hot potato, the only difference was the Gunners had full control of it. Their passing became slick and quick, not giving their opponents time to block the spaces now being occupied by the brilliant Pires and the inspiring Bergkamp.

The bookmakers made Arsenal odds of between even money and 6/5 against whilst Chelsea were11/5 with the draw the same price. But I did not look into how the odds changed as they went up the tunnel at the end of the first half, for today you can bet at any given time in a match!

SUNDAY BLOODY SUNDAY

It seemed as if the manager of the home team had told his players to go back out there and show the millions of viewers just how they got to be five points in front of the rest of the Premiership and – if that is what he said – then it certainly did the trick. There were spaces there that were not there in the first forty-five minutes, and although we all know as the game goes on it opens up, but you still needed to be able to utilise that space. Arsenal now were turning the screw and Chelsea could not keep up with a team looking to win the FA Cup for the third year running. With Bergkamp playing the lone striker role and the new boy Reyes dropping off a little, Arsenal began using the spaces left by Chelsea's inability to hold firm once that fantastic equaliser was struck. More about that in a minute!

The Gunners' fans sometimes get frustrated with the team because they play such a short passing game once in the final third of the pitch. I can relate to this because Dave Sexton would 'dig' Peter Osgood and myself out for exactly the same thing. On one occasion when being given a roasting – not the kind players talk of today – by our manager, I replied that I thought the name of the game was to give the ball to your best players, which did not go down too well. You could say this was five-a-side football and you would be perfectly correct, because that is how we learned our trade. But at Highbury the pitch is so tight that teams get numbers back closing down passing options, trying to push you out wide, but Wenger's team go into either Henry – when playing – or Bergkamp, and if that is not on they use the spaces down the flanks left by Pires, who drops off deep and uses that wonderful ability to run at speed, making ground whilst the opposition were still getting over another breakdown in attack. Pires is the master of this kind of play and he takes the ball right to the edge of the box before stopping and weighing up the situation around him.

Bergkamp's role was one which many English players cannot perfect apart from the brilliant Teddy Sherringham. There were players years ago that would drop off into the 'hole' but nowadays we lack a player of such class. Paul Scholes is possibly the best at playing this role but it seems that the Manchester United schemer seems to have to play so many different roles for both club and country. For example, I'll look at Brazil in 1970 when the legendary Pele played the role of 'coming off', although Tostao was the man who did it more often, and if they were not 'on', the ball would go out wide to either Jarzinho or Rivelino. This game really is very simple but the problem is when the opposition cannot cope with teams like Arsenal running at top speed at their goal, and the second half on 'Sunday Bloody Sunday' was just like that.

Now, the problem is for all the money they have spent, have Chelsea got a player who can play in the 'hole'?

Gianfranco Zola could, but he – for me – was not consistent enough, especially away from Stamford Bridge!

WHAT'S GONE WRONG WITH SULLIVAN?

Before him, Mark Hughes was brilliant at coming off and holding the ball up but, through doing so, gave up so much as regards his scoring duties. Hughes should have been a player who scored twenty-five goals a season without breaking sweat!

Going back to United and we have Eric Cantona whilst Jurgen Klinsman was superb in his first season at Tottenham. You see the best players in these situations are foreigners and Paolo di Canio springs to mind as such a player, although mostly when doing so more as a wide player. Chelsea were sadly and badly lacking such a player in this match and because they have not got that kind of player – Eidur Gudjohnsen – I hear you say, is the closest at the Bridge to a player such as the ones mentioned. Again the Icelandic front man should score more goals than he does and for the love of god I cannot figure out why!

Arsenal's leveller was a picture book special as Jose Antonio Reyes picked a ball up some thirty yards out and moved effortlessly to his left hand side and, once realising he had a clear path to goal, let fly with as stunning a left foot cross-shot as you'll ever witness and that sounded the warning bells for the Premiership leaders were now not thinking about replays here. Five minutes later another slick move found Reyes clear on the left and as substitute goalkeeper, Neil Sullivan, left his line to front him, did not stand up long enough as the Spaniard squeezed the ball past him, and although the Chelsea number two goalkeeper got a piece of it, it was not enough to keep it from crossing the line. This was now a real uphill struggle for the Blues as Viera – had by now – taken charge of the engine room and the 'acid test' seemed too much for Scott Parker, Frank Lampard and Claude Makelele. This was their big chance to get amongst Veira and co and although they stifled them right up until the break, they could not compete with the massiveness of the French midfield captain. We hear the word 'awesome' used many times but this Patrick Viera performance was nothing short of it. The Tinkerman looked ten years older as you could see his mind working overtime but could come up with no answers to the superiority of the 'Sunday Bloody Sunday' demolition job, and who knows just what might have happened had the fantastic in-form Thierry Henry been on parade. The big question now is can the Tinkerman come up with a suitable solution for this Saturday's match at Stamford Bridge and also will this win give Arsenal a psychological advantage over the team six points behind them. Once again I would love to be that fly on the wall in the office of the Russian's one more time!

My next step with this book is to approach *Loaded* Editor Martin Daubney for some kind of sponsorship, for this is a magazine that has held up whilst so many have fallen apart at the seams, and of course it is very much 'in' with all sorts of readers!

Arsenal 2 Reyes both Chelsea 1 Mutu 38,136

The gory details of Monday's headlines went like this: REYES LANDS OLD ONE-TWO and Wenger loses his heavyweight champ but Jose is just as deadly in the *Mail*. The *Standard* went Arsenal £17million man puts Ranieri under pressure and that JOSE RAISES THE ROOF AS BLUES JUST FADE AWAY while on back pages of the *Express* said: REYES THE ROOF and Jose's double turns up heat on Chelsea boss, and on the inside that Spaniard shows he is settling in as his double deepens Chelsea's gloom and piles the pressure on Ranieri whilst Wenger is able to Reyes a smile. Also that NOW THAT'S THE WAY JOSE.

The *Sun* printed: REYES THE ERASER alongside Wonderkid fires a double as gunners rub out soft blues. As all Ranieri could say was that WE LOST THE PLOT.

Take it as 'Red' that the Bluenoses skipped through their morning papers, some even not bothering to purchase one. The headlines say it all and it's best left as Chelsea did a great job in the first half containing their fierce rivals and with no Henry those ten minutes before the buzzer went for the start of part two of four forty-five minute halves over the next six days. Yeah, half-times can prove the changing point in so many matches, where teams lose momentum, giving the opposition the opportunity to straighten out all the things they were doing wrong whilst the big question asked is can Chelsea maintain a performance that was not great, but one of a fighting nature which was equal to their far superior rivals. It was the second quarter that new signing Reyes turned the match on its head and Chelsea could not answer the questions the fans asked: Do we have both the bottle and ability to get back into this match? I remember – although I was sidelined through injury – when that Chelsea team of the seventies went behind three times against Leeds United in that epic final and each time they came back strong to pull themselves off of a carpet that gave you more than sore knees. This was an epic battle in every meaning of the word and then the answer was asked the same questions of our illustrious and sometime brutal opponents?

The answer was no, for we had knocked the wind out of their tails three times and where we found that little extra courage the 'football gangsters' from Yorkshire had no such answer, for being totally drained, having thought they had us nailed three times but the character of our team was far stronger than they ever knew. That is the acid test and we came through that test of all tests in 'Blue Flying' colours!

But the new Chelsea have a wonderful opportunity to put the record straight as the Gunners come to Stamford Bridge in a live match on this coming Saturday afternoon. Arsenal – not let's forget – are carrying a torch into this match, having gone through the Premiership this season unbeaten and will not be in any mood for that record be taken away from them, knowing Chelsea must win this match to stay in the championship hunt. The Tinkerman will be looking at several different types of combinations to tinker with, like who would partner who up front? And also can he play Parker, Lampard, Geremi and Makelele all in a match that must be won? The first two names are more than capable of getting forward and causing the Gunners problems so it may be he will have Makelele sitting tight in a role that will try stopping the supply to Henry if the 'main man' has overcome the injury to his bruised foot!

It was after the Chelsea match that I settled down in our club to watch Harry's team play Liverpool at Anfield and oh, what a fright they gave the red side of the Mersey.

A goal down after two minutes from a Michael Owen goal, they looked like lambs being led to the slaughterhouse but they settled down, rode their luck once or twice and then Harry brought young Matthew Taylor off of the bench to grab a great late equaliser. Portsmouth deserved the replay if only for the way they were defiant and stood tall as a team who were ravaged by injuries to crucial players such as Sherringham, Berger and Sherwood, and then of all things, Steve Stone fractured a bone in his leg in the pre-match warm up. How's your luck?

But my mate's teams have always got character and no matter what they – at all times – do is keep on playing their way through a match and this time it paid off big time and I found myself – in a very depressed Grosvenor Club – being the only one jumping out of my seat when young Taylor's terrific effort crashed into Dudek's net. So it is back to Fratton Park on Sunday afternoon for this fifth round replay, and my hopes and best wishes go out to my mate!

INTERNATIONAL WEEK

Portugal is a nice place to vacate and the match was played just the same way. In a life where both managers and players complain about too much football, I for one do not see the use of such a match as the Swede changes his team more than the Tinkerman which maybe why the new Chelsea regime are likely to replace one tinker with another. Ledley King made a surprise appearance after injuries to John Terry, Jonathan Woodgate and Sol Campbell. The Spurs youngster played alongside Gar at the heart of the England defence, a position he had not filled this season, for playing a major part in David Pleat's midfield. In midfield Frank Lampard, out of position on the left-hand side with Steve Gerrard and Paul Scholes in between him and David Beckham whilst Michael Owen was partnered by Wayne Rooney.

The pace of the match was pretty sedate and the most important statistic of the evening was that it was Louis Figo's one hundredth international for Portugal.

Ledley King scored a 'messy' goal from a David Beckham free kick and the home side equalised through Pauleta in yet another situation where the ball was whipped over the human wall – when will coaches and managers see the light – giving James no chance. Dead ball situations are now becoming the main threat these days and I cannot help but repeat myself by saying someone has to try defending such kicks without the goalkeeper being blinded at the precise time the player makes contact with the ball. I don't spend too much time on these matches because with changing the team around so often, I feel like it is a little like being at a school trial where a hundred boys turn up and everyone has to play. Totally ridiculous, and wasn't it the Swede that said that we cannot sustain our good first-half performance for ninety minutes after being knocked out by Brazil in the last World Cup?

If he really believes that, then why does he keep changing players when the match is in the balance and players must be examined as to whether they can last the last twenty minutes of an international match?

BATES IS TOO WISE FOR THE OWLS?

The game was drawn and all I can say is that I could not wait to get back to the real thing, beginning at Stamford Bridge on Saturday. But before that the *Express* claimed – through Harry Harris – that Sven Goran Eriksson has been made an offer of a five-year contract by Roman Abramovich to take over from the Tinkerman. This would be worth a staggering £5million-a-year basic wage with a £1million bonus for each trophy he brings to Stamford Bridge and on top of that a £100million to spend on new players in the summer. The Football Association have publicly declared that they could not match such a figure as they try to get the Swede to sign a new two-year extension on his present deal. The *Express* also revealed that the remarkable conflict behind the scenes involving Sheffield Wednesday chairman Dave Allen and Ken Bates over rumours of a Bates bid to buy the Yorkshire club. Bates said that, "I plan to stay as Chelsea chairman, but I had been asked for advice from Sheffield Wednesday. Why should I want to buy a club in such a financial mess?"

Dave Richards, their former chairman, is a mate and I was glad to help as he asked me. I met the chairman and asked for all the facts and figures and Allen told me that his financial director would provide them for me. That was on Sunday and by Wednesday I was told that the financial director couldn't give them to me. Why not?

Are their finances worst than what they say?

They are supposed to be £23million in debt and losing £55,000 a week, but why wouldn't they let me see all the facts, instead of draft accounts which are unsigned and uncertified?

Wednesday, thirteenth in the second division, last week announced debts of £23.6million for the year to May 31st, 2003.

Bates pocketed £17.5million from the sale of Chelsea to Roman Abramovich. Owl's vice-chairman Mick Wright confirmed the talks with

Bates, insisting he had been given the information asked for. Bates added that "I am happy to give advice but I cannot do that from a blank piece of paper."

All I have to say that is for someone who always insisted on his love for Chelsea Football Club it has not taken old 'Grey Beard' too long to search for another club!

In another international, Cardiff striker scored a hat-trick for Wales in a 4-0-demolition job of Scotland whilst Norway beat Northern Ireland 4-1 at home and Southern Ireland held the mighty Brazilians to a goalless draw at Lansdowne Road.

Louis Saha scored one and made the other on his French debut replacing Thierry Henry – out with a bruised foot – scoring from a move set-up by Zidane in the 82nd minute. Chelsea hitman Adrian Mutu was on the score sheet twice as Romania outclassed Georgia at the Cyprus International. In the same tournament Southampton's Marian Pahars scored for Latvia against Kazakhstan, 3-1.

Aston Villa new signing Norberto Solano gave Peru the lead against Spain in Barcelona but the home side fought back to win 2-1.

CZECH BLOW ADDS TO CHELSEA JINX

Chelsea have an anxious wait to see if their new £9million goalkeeper Petr Cech has picked up a longterm injury before joining them.

The 6ft 5in Czech Republic keeper, whose summer move from Rennes was completed during the January transfer window, dislocated his elbow in a French league match against Lens at the weekend.

Cech fell awkwardly making a save after twenty-five minutes and left the pitch in agony. Doctors put him in plaster and told him to rest for at least five weeks. However, there are fears of long-term implications, which Chelsea are to monitor closely. They will not want to complete the deal if there is any suggestion that the injury has caused permanent damage.

Cech, the most expensive goalkeeper in British history, is the latest star struck down by the club's injury jinx.

Many of Chelsea's big name recruits have been affected, giving Stamford Bridge the most expensive sick list in Premiership history.

Juan Sebastian Veron, who cost £11million from Manchester United last summer, has been ruled out until next season with a serious back complaint. Record signing Damien Duff, a £17million buy from Blackburn, is still recovering from a dislocated shoulder and an Achilles tendon injury. Doctors have decided the Republic of Ireland winger needs an operation on his shoulder in the summer and risks further, perhaps permanent damage, if he injures it again in the meantime.

Chelsea have been robbed of £16,6million striker Hernan Crespo for much of the season with a nagging calf injury. Cech, 22, has been signed as cover for Carlo Cudicini, whom was himself forced out after an hour during the Chelsea FA Cup defeat at Arsenal on Sunday after aggravating a groin injury.

The Italian is hopeful of returning for Saturday's rematch with Arsenal, this time in the Premiership at Stamford Bridge, but insists he will not rush back.

"I felt it with the last kick of the first half and during the second half it just got worse" said Cudicini. "It's too early to say if I will be fit or not. I am having treatment and we will have to wait and see. I don't want to take any risks with this kind of injury."

Chelsea and France captain Marcel Desailly realises he is no longer an automatic first choice for the club and country, but believes he is good enough to play a part.

The 35-year-old defender, who has a hundred and eleven International caps, started for France in their friendly against Belgium last night – Wednesday – having missed their previous two games against Germany and Israel.

He has not played for Chelsea since their 0-0 draw against Birmingham, a month ago after suffering a calf injury.

"Claudio Ranieri has asked me to get back into shape," said Desailly, "but if two players are at the same level, he prefers to play the younger one and that is better for the club. It is a new situation, and I have to deal with it. I have forgotten how much effort was needed to come back from injury. With age, I need more time.

"I still think I am up to it. I won't carry on if I'm not, but I still enjoy going to training."

THE DAY ARSENAL WON THE CHAMPIONSHIP?
CHELSEA 1 GUDJOHNSEN ARSENAL 2 VIERA, EDU

The scene was set for Chelsea to take quick revenge for their FA Cup knockout blow at Highbury six days ago, but in their favour this time it will be in front of their own faithful supporters. 41,847 fans were present whilst SKY TV allowed many millions more to witness the day that Arsenal won the Championship. To cancel out their advantage though was the return of the mercurial Thierry Henry who replaced the two-goal hero from last week, Jose Antonio Reyes. Chelsea defended the Shed End and the atmosphere was at boiling point as the Gunners kicked off against a club who had not beaten them in the last seventeen league matches and to rub their bluenoses into it even more have disposed of the Blues for the last four seasons in the FA Cup. Revenge today would be terribly sweet if only Chelsea could win a match that was a serious six pointer. The match could not have begun in a more exciting manner as Arsenal kicked off and the play began by going down the left side midway in their own half when a square ball was played to their captain who so uncharacteristically let the ball slip under his right foot and run loose to the closing Geremi. Vieira could not recover as the Chelsea midfield player made ground swiftly down the left and hit a powerful cross-shot that shot through the Arsenal back line and creeping in at the far post was Eidur Gudjohnsen, who coolly sidefooted firmly past Lehmann in the Arsenal goal. The time in the corner of the screen showed us that it was twenty-seven seconds as the Chelsea faithful jumped from their seats in wonderful delight. Stamford Bridge had erupted and the Blues had the perfect start, or did they?

This can work one of two ways and if you cannot take the game to the visitors after starting a match a goal in front, then you are sitting ducks for the likes of Vieira, Henry and Pires. In other words there is no in between, it is either sink or swim and Arsenal were dab hands in the murkiest of Premiership waters!

Chelsea now had to hang on to this lead but it did not look good as Arsenal had the lion's share of possession, as the home team seemed to be making up the numbers. An Arsenal team a goal down was a rare occasion this season so Chelsea had the opportunity to pursue their ability to fight back under pressure, but that defiance they showed in the first forty-five minutes at Highbury just under a week ago was not coming through. There were many arguments – as usual – as to did the Tinkerman pick the right team for such a match and if you are a tinkerer then the time to change your team is at moments when you need that extra attacking force. For instance, Chelsea had four players in the middle of the field who are not very creative, unless you take the tenacity of both Frank Lampard and Scott Parker's ability to throw themselves into every attacking move. That is okay, but you need that player who calms that early storm and this was just down my street. My forte if you like!

As the Arsenal captain does for his team when in the middle of a battle, he composes himself and strides around the centre circle like a ringmaster in Barnum and Bailey. Or even a lion tamer amidst a jungle of many terrors, that is what a hectic struggle for territory can be like and as I said earlier for Chelsea's 'Four Just Men' the acid test.

Great teams need that player who drifts into spaces unnoticed whilst his midfield partner keeps roaming and probing for openings. An Alan Ball, Billy Bremner, Johnny Giles, Charlie Cooke, Tony Currie, Jim Baxter, Johnny Haynes, Glenn Hoddle or yours truly. These were when positions were still wing halves, not wingbacks, inside forwards and not midfielders! There is one thing about me, and it is not big headedness, please believe me, I just I love putting my name alongside such greats.

ANOTHER FLOWING ARSENAL MOVE

Whether in front or behind early on, you must try to maintain possession especially against the likes of Arsenal who will punish you big time if you cannot maintain possession and at the same time put even more pressure on their back four. Against Arsenal you must try – at all times – not to give the ball away cheaply, by making them work darned hard to get it back, because once you've lost possession you are in for a long ninety minutes. Going a goal in front can work one of two ways just like – so often lately – going down to ten men, where you have to work out as a team how you are going to face such a happening. Anyhow, Chelsea looked lost in front and it was no surprise that the equaliser would come and it came from the man who had miss-controlled the ball for the opening goal, but as the saying goes: 'You can't keep a good man down!'

A flowing Arsenal move ended with Bergkamp – given far too much space – turning quickly and sliding a delicious pass down the left hand side of the Chelsea defence and Vieira was on the end of it. He took one touch and slid the ball past Cudicini with the utmost of ease. 1-1 and game on again!

The Chelsea crowd only fifteen minutes ago, were led to believe that their team could at last end the Arsenal jinx, but in no time Arsenal reminded them that dreaming doesn't win football matches and a nightmare was only six minutes away as the very quiet Henry slung over a right footed corner which whipped across the six-yard line about a yard over the hands of the out-coming Sullivan. With the Chelsea keeper stranded there was chaos amongst the Blues defence as the ball fell to Edu who smashed a sweet left-footer into a Sullivan-less goal. 1-2 and big trouble for the Bluenoses!

The question now was would Arsenal go for the jugular or simply maintain possession for the next hour or so, something that they are wonderful at doing. Chelsea were not playing badly but needed that little bit of imagination of, say, a Zola or a Cooke of our day, who could twist and turn defenders and conjure up that element of surprise with his brilliant ability. It was times like these that the likes of Peter Osgood and Ian Hutchinson were needed, two players up front who would let the Arsenal defence know that if they were going to take the points away from Stamford Bridge, they were going to do so knowing they had earned the right. In the end with Manchester United being held at Old Trafford by bottom of the table Leeds United, I felt that we had just witnessed Arsenal win the Premiership. As I was thinking of this, I came across a headline in the *Daily Mail* on the morning of the match which read: RANIERI MAY MAKE CHANGES AGAIN IN A BID TO SHOCK ARSENAL BUT COULD HIS BEST STRIKER BE PLAYING FOR BIRMINGHAM?

Followed by Chelsea's missing link is Forssell: This is a player I rate very highly and I cannot buy that the strikers Chelsea who have been brought into the club for mega-bucks are better equipped than this fresh-faced flying Fin. Neil Moxley reports that: When Mikael Forssell was thinking over a loan move to Birmingham in the summer, he made one thing abundantly clear. "I wanted to be able to play against Chelsea in the Premiership," he remembers with a grin. "In fact, Birmingham had done the deal and I threatened to pull out unless I played against Chelsea."

Chelsea were his employers, of course, but having become one of their fringe players, the Finland international had a point to prove, "I thought the best thing for me was to show what I could do against them."

The contract on the table specifically denied Forssell that opportunity, but he insisted the issue was considered – and was not afraid to take it right to the top.

"Roman Abramovich was told about it, but put a stop to it and said that I couldn't play," said Forssell, before emphasising: "But I wanted to. I'm a Chelsea player, but if I had to score against them to show them I could play for them. I would have done it."

Forssell's self-assurance will no doubt strike a chord with those Chelsea fans who believe he is playing in the wrong Premiership derby this weekend. While the west London club look for finding a way of beating Arsenal, Forssell will be seeking to add to his nine Premiership goals this season against Aston Villa.

And, eight months on, Forssell has no doubts that he was right to join Birmingham, even if he can't play against Claudio Ranieri's team. He said that, "They can spend money on anyone. You hear talk about Ronaldo and because it's Chelsea, you don't discount it.

"That's why I came to Birmingham. I could have stayed and fought for my place. But I know I will play here in the Premiership. It is good for my development. I know Ranieri likes me as a player but I understand his situation. If you buy someone for £18million, he has to play".

It is a conundrum that might recur this summer when Chelsea will no doubt be linked with plenty more highly priced strikers – and may even buy one or two.

Would Forssell, who will be twenty-three next month want to return?

"What would be ideal would be if Ranieri came out and said I was definitely one of his first four strikers", said Forssell. "Ideally, I would like to be in the first two. But I understand that with the number of competitions Chelsea play in, you are likely to start around thirty games a season. So being one of four strikers is all right. Even though they swap around, everyone gets to play." – except Bogarde – I could not help myself throwing that one in!

"I could go with that, but I would have to know for sure. If Chelsea said I was going to be one of those strikers, I'd go back."

And if not?

"This could be a good place to come, if Chelsea say they don't want me. Birmingham want to go forward. They are ready to put money into the facilities, and better players. But I am not talking about when I'm going to go, or where I am going!"

If he does return to Stamford Bridge, Forssell will be going back to a club he first joined when he was a seventeen-year-old, when he was one of the most admired young players in Europe. "A big reason why I came to Chelsea was Ruud Gullit" he explained. "Bayer Leverkusen wanted me but Chelsea came in late."

His first impressions remain vivid. "I trained with the first team once at the age of seventeen. It was on a Friday before they played Sheffield Wednesday in the League.

"I had the goalscoring session of my life. The goalkeeping coach must have thought, "Who the hell is this?"

"It all felt good. Everything I hit went in, overhead kicks, the lot.

"But it wasn't enough. I wanted to know what their plans were for me. Colin Hutchinson (the former managing director) was there at the time. They told me I would go straight into the first team. At first, they were as good as their word. I was in the team for the first month, and then they went and bought Chris Sutton for £10million. That wasn't what I was expecting."

Forssell reacted with characteristic bloody-mindedness. "I wasn't playing at Chelsea" he recalled, "and if you are not playing, you want to do more."

The problem was that Chelsea restricted the amount they wanted him to train. "They took the balls off me but that wasn't a problem. I just went and trained by myself. There were some pitches in Chiswick I used.

"I have a contract with Nike and I asked then for a bag of ten balls. I would take my stereo, put my rap music on and do my stuff for a couple of hours at a time. I would have defenders in front of me in my mind. I think that's important for you to have defenders in front of you, even if they are only imaginary.

"So the goal last week (his superb slaloming effort against Sunderland) may have looked quick but it wasn't for me. It was normal because I have practiced it so much.

"Sometimes the park keeper would come along and say, "Go home."

"Then they would see who it was, shrug their shoulders and say, "Oh it's you Forssell" and he would let me stay. Well, one of the park keepers would. He was a Chelsea fan. I had to go if the other one was working. He supported Arsenal."

It was not just his football that Forssell worked on in those days. "I'm a Fin and in Scandinavia you are not encouraged to be a sportsman. You are encouraged to do your education. My mother said that I could do anything I wanted with my life – only I had to finish my exams. She moved with me in my first year and after training she would tell me to do my studies. The thinking is that you might be talented, but you have to get yourself an education. I had a Finnish tutor in London and I took Finnish, Swedish and English."

For all of his linguistic skills – he has also picked up a fair bit of Spanish and Italian – Forssell like most footballers in foreign lands, likes to socialise with his fellow countrymen.

One particular friend is goalkeeper Peter Enckelmen, who is now with Blackburn and probably relieved he will not be turning out for previous club Aston Villa against Birmingham after his gaffes in last season's derby clash.

The pair hope to meet up again soon. They might even go to the cinema. What was the last film they saw together?

There can only be one answer from a man who speaks five languages.

"Lost in Translation", he said

That for me was a brilliant piece of journalism and put a lot of things into perspective, especially that the main point being if Forssell had been banging in goals in Europe, Chelsea would probably have bought him, for his record stands up to any other player on Chelsea's new rostrum. There is a sincerity about this young player, a hunger to play at the top level and writing to Nike for ten footballs as enough to tell you that this boy is a thinker and a learner of his trade. I have spoken to quite a few Brummies and they love the way this Finish international plays the game for them. And with all due respect to Steve Bruce, if he can score goals for a team who are mainly defensive minded, what would he be like with a team that loves going forward.

It is an absolute mystery to me just how nobody at Stamford Bridge has not asked the one simple question, being why is he not playing at his own club?

Those loan deals are all well and good but you don't loan out internationals for such a long period, and after all if he is not wanted back by now, why not sell him?

Would it be because someone would end up with egg running down his tie?

I repeat that I am a great admirer of Eidur Gudjohnsen, but he is becoming rather costly in front of the sticks and in a game coming up will tell you the self-same story. But it is Sunday and the replay at Fratton Park where Harry's team take on Gerard Houllier's underachievers. As I said I was at the Wolves match at the home of Portsmouth and left wondering just what they had to do to win a football match, but at least they are creating chances and if they could only get Teddy back, he and Eyal Berkovich could open up defences which would allow those vital goals to come their way. They play good football and in times of desperate trouble they give their all for the manager and Jim Smith his right hand man.

There was a big week ahead as Arsenal travelled to Spain for their first leg tie against Celta Vigo, Manchester faced a tough encounter in Portugal against champions Porto and of course Chelsea travel to Germany to play Stuttgart, a very tough and resilient outfit with that typical German outlook of what we got we keep and then slowly creep into the match once they have sussed out their opponents. They will have watched Chelsea's matches against Arsenal, which is part of doing your homework and will have liked what they saw from Chelsea, in the respect that they know they have a chink here and a chink there, and I don't mean a Chinese or Japanese player. They will have noticed that Chelsea were suspect in aerial threats, although Cudicini would be replacing the out of form Neil Sullivan and that will give the Blues a real boost for such a match. It seems as if the Italian shot-stopper had now recovered and will be needed in a match that will not be for the faint hearted. The Germans have got over their midseason break and are very difficult opponents on their own 'Toby' but that should suit Chelsea right down to the ground, as the pressure will be on the Germans to get a result to take to Stamford Bridge with them in a fortnight's time.

BETTY SHINE

'Another Miracle.'

The scene was set for a surprise replay at Fratton Park and Harry did not have too many options as to who would play, let alone where they would play. As he always says, "We are down to bare bones", a saying that will always stick with him, but he is the type of bloke who says if it makes those people happy then it can't be that bad! But the thing about it is, all the people who question his managerial ability would not know what day of the week it was, if in the kind of mess Harry's club were in. Some time after my accident Miss Betty Shine — that wonderful healer — said to my ex-wife that one day one of the medical staff will tell her that my living was a miracle, well Harry — by getting Portsmouth out of the Nationwide First Division — performed another one!

His big signing of this particular season was Teddy Sherringham and he was playing some great stuff before tearing a hamstring, but he knew that he just had to find someone who could be just as instrumental, although an entirely different player, and that was Eyal Berkovich, the little Israeli who played some magnificent football under Harry's management at Upton Park. I said to my pal David Rodwell and the boys in the Grosvenor Club that this player could be the match winner. Not by scoring the winning goal, simply being around the ball at every given moment, keeping the tempo up and making sure they kept the ball at all times, then once free the type of player — I just mentioned — could thread the ball through the eye of a needle and there was going to be plenty of needle in this crunch match today. The clock struck two and with our table full of drinks the six of us sat back and prayed for Portsmouth, and by halftime they had more than held their own, only allowing one opportunity to Liverpool and as luck would have it, it fell to Emile Heskey who hit Shaka Hislop with a first-time shot. We sighed heavily as we picked up our glasses and sat through the half-time interval quite happily. The manager's half-time team talk should have been a simple affair. By telling his players that they had done enough in the first five sessions against Liverpool already and go out and do it again — Portsmouth had beaten Liverpool earlier in the season and drawn the original tie which, broken down is four sessions. Then in the second period of this replay all the watching millions saw the 'Mug in the Middle' award the away team two penalties — one which the linesman changed his mind — the other one, a brilliantly-timed Taylor tackle saw him give another, which Harry said afterwards was "the most diabolical decision" he had ever seen and those watching millions once again agreed. 'The Mug in the Middle' must have been the only one in the country who saw it as a penalty, but justice was restored when the out of touch Michael Owen placed his spot kick poorly to the left of Shake Hislop who just seemed to fall to his left and wait for the ball to roll into his body. Still scoreless, but this gave Portsmouth the impetus to now go on and search for that incredible winner. And incredibly — as it turned out – it was as a swift passing move which ended up by Yakubu turning quickly to feed Richard Hughes to his left, and the player struck a real sweet left-footed strike into Chris Kirkland's far post. 1-0 and Portsmouth were on their way to one of the great recent FA Cup upsets. I'll let Harry finish off by saying that, "They were entitled to walk all over us given the quality of their squad but we showed such great spirit." He said after Houllier had his say, stating that, "We played some terrific stuff and I thought our two centre-halves were outstanding. I have said many times before that if we had we not been struggling for numbers so much, we wouldn't be fighting relegation, we would be seventh or eighth."

FRIENDSHIP

Harry has made some tremendous signings in his managerial career, which include the brilliant Paolo di Canio and the strong old-fashioned centre-forward John Hartson at West Ham and the players now he is depending on are the still tidy and classy Teddy Sherringham and now Eyal Berkovich signs for him for a second time and is instrumental in all Portsmouth's attacking plans. The small Israeli is a truly wonderful player and along with Teddy, Patric Berger and young Matty Taylor, will be the saviour from the dreaded drop. And of course this coming Saturday a home tie against Arsenal in the sixth round of the FA Cup.

My pre-match prediction of Eyal Berkovich was bang-on as he played that role where he is allowed to go anywhere he wanted, and by doing so his quick thinking and ability in tight spaces saw that the home side had enough of the ball to pull off such a great result. FA Cup Fifth Round Replay: Portsmouth 1 Hughes Liverpool 0 19,529. Portsmouth had earned themselves a shot at Arsenal in the last eight of the biggest domestic cup competition in the world of football and the tie will be played at Fratton Park!

'HOULLIER HAS VERY SHORT MEMORY'

Along with Harry afterwards I was disappointed that Liverpool manager Gerard Houllier did not once mention Portsmouth's outstanding perform-ance, for all he could talk about was his team being 'unlucky' which is total rubbish. I have never been a 'lover"' of Houllier over two things, one being he left the great David Ginola out of the French national side and then I do believe he was behind Roy Evans – that great Liverpool servant – getting the sack when they were a joint managerial team?

All in all the Frenchman has a very short memory and should think of Roy Evans at times like these, for I am certain Evans would not have squandered the kind of money he has on very 'iffy' players.

The reason I have talked of Portsmouth in this particular book is because Harry Redknapp has been a great friend since our days together in Seattle where he was my coach. His wife Sandra and two sons Jamie and Mark grew up for a little while with my son Allen. Football can be a cruel game for you can make great friendships but because of the transfer element those ties can be broken just as quickly as they began. But luckily enough for me, I moved to the East End of London and only a half a dozen stops away from Upton Park. Our friendship was rekindled and I am so happy for more than one reason, because later Upton Park and Harry in particular, became a great therapy for me after my eleven months – 59 days out cold – hospitalised in both St Barts and the Royal London Hospitals. Even a couple of days after visiting the operating theatre, I would creep out through those hospital doors and head to Upton Park from Whitechapel Underground Station. How I looked forward to those home matches after a week of all kinds of tests and of course my physiotherapy, which was a big part of my rehabilitation. The reason I tell you this is because for the eleven months I was hospitalised – as I say eight and half weeks in a comatose state – I never received either a telephone call, or a get well card from Ken Bates and the rest of Chelsea Football Club. So when I am in the company of Chelsea supporters they have to understand my love for my home club is not really what it should be. I was taken to Stamford Bridge by my father – who taught me all I have ever needed to know about the game – and from there on in it looked like I would one day captain the team and go on to win at least one Championship, for we had the basis for one but Dave Sexton sent Osgood and myself packing in such an extraordinary affair. Only this affair had no love lost!

One of the good things about writing this book is that I am completely impartial and enjoying the 'every minute' of the happenings so far without wanting one team or another to win the Premiership, although having said that, another old club of mine – Arsenal – are playing football which the Dutch once called 'TOTAL' and it would be great to see them go through the season unbeaten, because they have thrilled football crowds all over the country. I felt I had to let you know about my keeping Portsmouth a part of this book, as they are the first result I look for each and every Saturday with Chelsea – obviously – second, exactly where they are in the Premiership as I write. Now we can get back to the Tinker and Talisman!

OVERKEANE OR JUST PLAIN STUPID?

We were still on the cup only this time it was Europe with Arsenal going to Spain to beat Celta Vigo, Manchester United to Portugal to face Portuguese champions Porto, who outplayed Ferguson's men and should be going to Old Trafford with more than a one-goal cushion. Then of course there was that man Roy Keane once again grabbing the headlines for being sent off for the eleventh time in a Manchester United shirt, when he foolishly put his studs into the back of Hildebrand as the goalkeeper collected an over-hit through ball, which ran into the keeper's hands. Instead of jumping cleanly over the German keeper, he quite stupidly used him as a paving stone as if playing hopscotch, as a kid. Bennie McCarthy was the Porto hero with two fantastically taken goals, the first a brilliant struck half-volley from a difficult angle whilst the second was a superb headed effort out-jumping both Gary Neville and Wes Brown to plant the ball into Howard's top right-hand corner. This will go down as one of the best goals of the Champions League, of that I am certain!

Once again the Manchester United boss continued to keep the blame away from his 'king' midfielder but he must have been the only one in the stadium that saw it that way. Ferguson of late has slightly lost his way since the Coolmore Mafia have turned up the heat in the Ferguson's family's kitchen, and it is showing both on his face and his judgement of picking the right team to win certain matches. This is the time of the year that his team usually put together a string of wins, putting pressure on all those around them, but since they lost by that single goal at Wolves they have looked second rate, and as I have said on numerous occasions the team would miss the kind of perform-ances Beckham has given them in those runs. I said from day one that allowing David Beckham to go through the exit door at Old Trafford was a glaring and unforgivable mistake which would come back to haunt the manager!

Beckham is sorely missed, no matter what the Manchester United manager says. Ferguson knows exactly what I am talking about and it is only his stubbornness and pride that keeps him from admitting it, for he knows all about the Manchester United way, and should do because he instilled it – for the sake of a better word. And, also the Scottish manager never transferred Beckham, he transferred his wife Victoria, and if she had to go so had he!

When you look back when Sir Alex was like a rampant vampire as he sucked the blood out of big name players – showing the likes of McGrath, Whiteside, Kanchelsis, Ince and Mark Hughes the exit door – and injected new blood into a team that went onto so many incredible successes without them!

Back to Keane and his wrong doings – only the ones seen by the 'Mug in the Middle'. Along with them his bosses comments on his midfield general:

1/ In the April of 1995 – for stamping on Gareth Southgate – then of Crystal Palace – in the FA Cup semi-final. The boss said that, "Roy deserved to be sent off, but he got a bad tackle and needed seven stitches in a gashed ankle."

2/ In the August of 1995 – against Blackburn – a second yellow card for diving, but Ferguson said that, "Roy didn't try to con anyone."

3/ In the October of 1995 – against Middlesbrough – for throwing a punch at Jan Aage Fjortoft. Ferguson's opinion was that, "If you lift your hands in football you pay the price. Nobody could dispute it – but I don't want to talk about it anymore."

4/ In the October of 1996 – for dissent after stamping on Claus Lundakvam. His manager said that, "We didn't get any crucial decisions."

5/ In the April of 1999 – against Arsenal in the FA Cup semi-final – being booked twice for tripping both Marc Overmars and Dennis Bergkamp in that match where Ryan Giggs scored that 'wonder'' goal after Bergkamp missed a penalty in the last minute of normal time. Ferguson was speechless!

6/ In the February of 2000 against Newcastle – for being booked twice once more for late tackles on keeper Steve Harper and then Rob Lee. Again Ferguson was in silence.

7/ In the August of 2000 against Chelsea in the Charity Shield at Wembley – for a lunge on Gus Poyet. Ferguson said that, "Roy will be disappointed."

8/ In the September of 2001 against neighbours City – for one of the worst tackles I have ever seen, which later he said that it was intentional, he had been waiting to get this player. His manager said that, "I've not seen it but our secretary told me he thought it to be a sending off."

9/ In the September of 2001 against Sunderland – for throwing the ball at Alan Shearer, which had Ferguson saying that, "Shearer stopped us from taking a throw-in but Roy left the ref with no option."

10/ In the August of 2002 against Sunderland – for elbowing Jason McAteer, which had Ferguson commenting that, "The player went down quickly which is disappointing. It was a soft dismissal."

11/ In the February just gone against Porto in the Champions League – for treading on goalkeeper Vitor Baia – which had his manager saying that, "It's not the kind of thing that Roy would do. The keeper made a meal of it."

Myself, I think that Keane is very fortunate only to be shown the red card eleven times for I would say at least fifty per cent of his tackles are either late – which is the sign of an assassin – I know that because I played with the biggest and toughest assassin since I began watching and playing the game. Ron Harris' timing of tackles were uncanny as he would 'put the anchors on" when sussing the situation, making his opponent a dead duck, leaving himself no opportunity to pull out, which set himself up for the 'kill'. There was no equal to 'Chopper' in those days and more so now, where players go over after being whacked by a feather duster.

I have seen Ronnie perfect this over my days, months and years playing both with and against him. Ron was the master assassin – there is no argument about that!

As for Sir Alex Ferguson, he has always backed his players to the hilt and what amazes me is that he seems to see what nobody else does when it comes to what his players do. I say that because where he stands – in that odd dug-out at Old Trafford – which must be the worst view in the 72.000 capacity stadium, where how many times have we seen him jump up in the air a couple of seconds after a goal is scored?

He is merely judging the goal by the response of the home fans around him?

That is because more times than not he waits for the crowd reaction around him, because he cannot see from such a position. As for him sticking up for his captain Keane, that is acceptable because that is what he is there for, putting the frighteners up his direct opponent, and as I said, the tackle on the Manchester City player Alf Haaland was as bad as it gets on a football field, as the 'over the top' tackle is the most severe and dangerous of all. Once again, if only he had played against the likes of a Dave Mackay, say, which would be a simple case of 'men and boys'.

GUDJOHNSEN IN PLEA: 'GET OFF RANIERI'S BACK'

And also: VfB Stuttgart in the UEFA Champions League, tonight: FALL GUYS DELIGHTED TO BE BACK IN THE SADDLE;

Ken Dyer reports that: The people say that, when you fall off a horse, the last thing to do is to search for broken bones before climbing back on immediately. That's easy to say but hard to do when you've just been catapulted 10 feet in the air before landing on your head but the theory is sound enough. It's unlikely that John Terry has ever worn a pair of jodhpurs but the Chelsea defender and his teammates are metaphorically desperate to get back in the saddle, as they look to put their season back on track in freezing Stuttgart tonight, following that double whammy against Arsenal. "The best thing about those results is to play again quickly," said Terry – and his coach, Claudio Ranieri, is hoping that the German team suffer a backlash tonight in the Gottieb-Daimler Stadium.

'BINGO'

Hardly a day goes by without Ranieri having to answer a question about his future and the Italian knows that defeat tonight will only heighten the speculation about his likely exit at the end of the season.

"I am confident with Chelsea, Roman Abramovich and Peter Kenyon," he said "People continue to write something different but what can I say."

Take away those two recent results by the best team in England and to be frank, Chelsea are still in reasonable shape as they go head to head with Felix Magath's Stuttgart.

The Chelsea match believed that the Germans would have a distinct advantage following their winter break but that is not exactly the way it has turned out.

Ranieri looked enviously at the Germans as they took a short holiday in the sun, recharged their batteries and regrouped before the final push.

At the same time, his Chelsea team were playing three matches a week and sometimes looking very jaded.

Next year English football will have its first official winter break, but it's as well to look at the experience of Stuttgart since they returned to action. In their first game back they beat Hansa Rostok, but since then they have failed to win, losing to Kaiserslautern last weekend to put them even further behind Werder Bremen than Chelsea are adrift of table-topping Arsenal.

Up to now Chelsea have reserved some of their most impressive performances for the Champions League. The 4-0 victory over Lazio will live long in the memory of every Chelsea supporter who was lucky enough to be in Rome and the 2-0 final Group win over Besiktas watched by 50,000 ex-pat Turks in Germany was a triumph of professionalism.

Now though, Chelsea have arrived at the business end of the competition, two matches instead of six, and what Ranieri describes as "Bingo".

How tough it will be to pick them-selves up after the Arsenal disappointment?

That was what Ranieri must have been thinking as he drove into the club's training ground on Sunday for their post-mortem.

Abramovich was also present as the players drifted in, downcast at first but increasingly bullish as the meeting went on. They looked at the Premiership table and, although they saw Arsenal nine points clear, there was no talk of throwing in the towel. They looked back at the Champions League and saw a realistic chance of pride and glory.

A word of caution though, Stuttgart who finished second in their group, three points behind Manchester United, scored a memorable 2-1 victory over Sir Alex Ferguson's team in Germany despite missing a penalty.

Terry will also have been warned about lone strikers who scored in that match. Brazilian-born Kevin Kuranyl, who has an identity problem – he has three passports from Germany, Brazil and Panama – but there is certainly no confusion where scoring goals are concerned, having netted fifteen in thirty-two matches last season.

Magrath has also recruited defender Boris Zivkovic, signed from Portsmouth during the transfer window, but taking time to settle in.

Behind him is goalkeeper Tino Hildebrand, who some believe to be Germany's best, despite the pressure of Bayern' Munich's Oliver Khan and Arsenal's Jens Lehmann.

For their part, Chelsea hope to have Carlo Cudicini back from injury and Damien Duff is also fit again.

The impish Irishman has been badly missed and might just prove to be the talisman that Chelsea need at this important time.

The evening before Arsenal won a thriller by three goals to two with great goals from Edu and a beautifully worked third from Pires, after he and Henry teased and tempted the Celta defence with a five-a-side-like winner, ending with the brilliant Pires sidefooting a neat return into the Spaniard's net. Now it was the Tinkerman's big evening after those two very damaging displays against the Gunners, but John Terry was defiant in his backing of the Italian and he once again was Chelsea's Man-of the-Match. This was a match where Chelsea never had one shot on goal and their winner an own-goal in the twelfth minute – by Meira who was stretching out to stop a terrific Glen Johnson cross getting to Crespo who would have had only the Tino Hildebrand to beat from twelve yards out. Once again Eidur Gudjohnsen missed the easiest opportunity of the match when, after good work from Geremi, Crespo angled a nice ball into the path of the Icelandic International who unbelievably skied the ball over the target when scoring would have been a lot easier. My theory of Gudjohnsen having some kind of phobia when in front of goal has time again proved right and this tie should have been put to bed, instead the resilient German outfit will make it very difficult for Chelsea in the second-leg in twelve days time at Stamford Bridge. This was a very gritty performance after such a nightmare of a fortnight in both south and north London but they stuck to the task ahead and in Carlo Cudicini had the man who looked unbeatable in the Chelsea goal. A couple of his saves were top drawer and that gave his teammates the kind of confidence that Sullivan had not over the past couple of weeks. The headlines read in the *Sun*: CLAUDIO NINE and RANIERI THE ROMAN SOLDIER MARCHES ON TO EURO GLORY; Which was followed by a match report from Mark Irwin who saw it this way – We came to bury Claudio, not to praise him. But this stubborn citizen of Rome is still one step ahead of all the backstabbers after another victorious night in Europe.

Claudio Ranieri has been aware of whispers surrounding Chelsea for the past few months. But the soothsayers predicting a bloody ending for the leader of football's Roman Empire had better take another look in his crystal ball.

For boss Ranieri will not be giving up his job without a fight. And the players are clearly backing him all the way.

And though Chelsea remain in Arsenal's shadow at home, on the Continental front they could yet be rulers of Europe.

For make no mistake about it, Chelsea are serious Champions League contenders. Any team that can win all five matches away in Europe – as the Blues have done this season – must be major players.

Ranieri confesses even success in Europe's most prestigious club competition might not be enough to save his bacon.

SURVIVAL

He said that, "If Mr Abramovich has decided to change the coach at the end of the season I surely can't change his mind.

"I told him I would leave when he arrived last summer and he said 'No. I believe in you.' But I don't know if he said that out of conviction or necessary because he hadn't been able to find a coach to put in my place."

Yet even if Ranieri is not getting too excited about his survival prospects, this was an emphatic message of intent from his squad.

Fernando Meira's own goal was enough to wreck Stuttgart's impressive home record and leave the Blues with one foot firmly planted in the quarter-finals.

As I said Eidur Gudjohnsen could and should have made the return leg at the Bridge a formality had he buried a glorious first-half opportunity – but Chelsea will still be big favourites to go through after the second leg at the Bridge in twelve days time? What made this result all the more remarkable was that Chelsea had entered this crucial match under a huge cloud following successive defeats by the Gunners.

Stuttgart coach Felix Mageth claimed Ranieri's inability to keep a settled team had created a disunity within Chelsea ranks – which would prove their downfall.

Yet those jibes came back to haunt the former German international as the Blues Brothers put on a daunting display of togetherness.

Marshalled by the magnificent John Terry and bolstered by the return of keeper Carlo Cudicini, Chelsea were always in control of a match they simply could not afford to lose.

Hernan Crespo led the line magnificently, while Glen Johnson showed the adventure and composure, which lit up his early games for the club.

It was the fullback who carved Stuttgart open to set up the killer goal in the twelfth minute. Collecting a ball from Cudicini's throw Johnson then exchanged passes with Geremi and continued his run deep into opposition territory.

His low angled cross was aimed for Crespo but was intercepted by Meira – who misjudged his attempted clearance and belted the ball past Tino Hilderbrand and into his own goal. After Gudjohnsen's miss, Chelsea failed to go any closer as the Germans – later on – seemed to be dejected after those early super saves from Cudicini and Chelsea had done quite a feat in winning their fifth away match in this season's Champions League and if they could only get some consistency in their play, they could be a major threat in this competition. I don't buy that they are better equipped in Europe, I just believe there is not so much pressure on them for these matches because the pressure is not as huge as the Premiership in terms of being the best team in the country, but wouldn't it – in this already crazy season – be something if they drew Arsenal at some stage leading up to the Final or even the final itself?

Other headlines said that: Champions League special: LAMPARD RELISHES A EUROPEAN BREAK in the *Standard*, as the *Mail* popped up with TOUCH OF LUCK AS RANIERI MEN WIN BACK SELF-RESPECT and that Ranieri joy as Chelsea cash in on lucky break: The rest of the headlines were pretty much the same as Chelsea returned home both jubilant and relieved that that great big dark red and white cloud had been lifted from their shoulders. The next stop for the Blues is the brand new stadium in Manchester where City have found it very difficult to win. In fact they have won only twice this season, although I feel for my old sparring partner Kevin Keegan for, although they are miserable defensively, he always encourages his football teams to go forward in search of goals. Having said that he made a proper Charlie of himself whilst in charge of the National team by claiming that with so many world-class players in his dressing room, the job was too big for him!

What I can never understand is why people like Keegan have to make outrageous statements like the one of so many world-class players. World Class players are players that somewhere along the way win a World Cup, and with the exception of George Best and Michel Platini that has always been the case. From Pele to Johan Cruyff, Franz Beckenbauer, Diego Maradona and of course our very own Robert Chelsea Moore.

So the million-dollar question was that: Could City put another nail in Ranieri's Premiership coffin?

I thought this match would suit his team, for Chelsea had a tough match in Germany whilst City had rested after a relieving and much needed win last Saturday against Bolton. Chelsea have been terrific in Europe but not just as a football team, purely as a team who have showed the kind of steel needed to travel to all countries with so many different conditions.

Stuttgart 0 Chelsea 1 Meira own goal 50,000

The weather in Germany was certainly different from the climate in Spain and Portugal where their two main rivals were performing. Other headlines of the week were like this: VAN WILL OVERTAKE ARSENAL shouts Japp Stam all over the inside pages of the *Sun*. Also in the same paper the huge headlines read that BIGGEST HOME WIN EVER FOR GUNNERS as they were given the go-ahead to start building their magnificent-looking sixty thousand seated home ground in Ashburton Grove, not far away from Highbury. And on the strength of that the Arsenal Board announced that they wanted Arsene Wenger to finish his managerial career with them. Arsenal, one of my old clubs, where Ken Friar – who helped me so very much when leaving Arsenal – said that "The major banks all did their own diligence on the plan and they all approved it. That gave myself, and Danny (Fiszman) a great deal of comfort. Ken continued, "we have been told by all the professional lawyers that it is the most complex finance that any of them have ever been involved with. The new stadium will produce a substantial amount of extra cash flow, which allows the debt to be paid quite comfortably." The repayment on loans totalling around £250million will be high, but Fitszman is convinced that the club have no problem making the commitment and that Arsene Wenger's budget will not be damaged. Friar added that, "The business plan we have allows for us to have additional income from banqueting and conferences, things of that nature. We wouldn't be doing this unless we felt confident it would work. We are putting the ranch on this one, as they say."

Ken Friar was the only man who helped me financially in my playing career by coming into a meeting with the Managing Director of Seattle Sounders – Mr Jack Daley – at Heathrow Airport. He asked me if I would like his assistance and I was delighted to have him do the business side of the deal for me, for he knew exactly what my wages were at Highbury – being the Managing Director himself – and got me a contract that for four great years there allowed me to live the life I dreamed of, I have told Ken since that he will always be in my debt. He is a wonderful man in charge of a wonderful Football Club and as always I wish him the very best of health for the rest of his days with us.

Other headlines went like this, "IT'S TOUGH FOR US BUT EVEN TOUGHER FOR ARSENAL and also that FERGIE IS DEFIANT.

Harry Harris wrote that: Chelsea must be regretting their decision to drop their interest in Jose Antonio Ryes after considering him overpriced and not quite as good as billed.

But the Arsenal man's double against the Blues in the FA Cup will have left them thinking their assessment was possibly a little awry. Chelsea were sceptical about the £17million price tag for a player not recognised as one of the best in Europe, albeit one with immense potential.

Christiano Ronaldo at Manchester United was another youngster Chelsea scrutinised before deciding the price was too high.

Chelsea want to buy into talent that will last for a decade, but do not want to be rushed into hasty positions – even though Reyes and Ronaldo show such promise.

That is the reason why a big bid for Wayne Rooney can be discounted, at least from Stamford Bridge. Sir Alex Ferguson may also be having reservations about his value!

Rooney's return to domestic football is poor because of Everton boss David Moyes' refusal to start him every time.

I cannot see, myself, what all the fuss is about with Wayne Rooney fir in these days of big money Everton have a gem and like Beckham, Schloes and the rest of United's youngsters coming in at Old Trafford, Ferguson never had any problem in his bringing them up and playing them at all the right times, and let's not forget these were young players who were taking over from real big name and game players.

FOWLER FLOUNDERS

Chelsea were heading for a very tricky match at Manchester City knowing that they must win because the runners-up position in the Premiership was up for grabs. The entire Grosvenor Club had their eyes locked onto SKY to keep up with Chelsea's match and the biggest 'yell' of the afternoon was when it flashed on the screen that Eidur Gudjohnsen had sneaked the winner – completely against the run of play – with only five or six minutes remaining. And around the same time the same voices were heard again as Luis Boa Morte had equalised against the champions down at Loftus Road. Luis Saha had put the reds in front against his old team and should have had a penalty that would have put the match out of Fulham's reach, but the 'Berk in Black' messed up yet again. The United manager came under fire – three days after a bust up in Portugal with their coach – once more for leaving van Nistelrooy and Giggs out of his starting line-up, in such an important match, but I have no doubts there was a method beyond his madness, once again. Arsenal were two goals up in four minutes against Charlton at Highbury only to finish the match clinging on for dear life as Charlton rallied after such an horrendous beginning. Chelsea were taking a right old pounding at Manchester City and how Robbie Fowler never took the match ball home one will never know?

Fowler, a player I rated so highly when bursting onto the scene, looked like his old self but the only thing missing was him hitting the back of the net on numerous occasions so Chelsea rode their luck for the second time in four days and scraped out two 1-0 wins. The City striker missed a couple of easy chances – by his standards – but was desperately unlucky with a left footed volley that scraped the post, a typical effort with his back to goal, he seemed to hit the ball over his shoulder which gives the keeper no idea of where it would be going and only fresh air kept the ex-England centre forward from putting City in front. There is no doubt in my mind that City deserved something out of this match and even Ranieri and a couple of players interviewed afterwards echoed my thoughts.

The headlines in the *Mail* and *Express* looked like this: EIDUR PUTS CHELSEA SECOND AS CITY BLOW THIETR CHANCES and CLAUDIO'S GOOD LUCK

The rest were mainly on Keegan's plight of being in THE DROP ZONE and that KEEGAN HAS WORDS BUT NO ANSWERS.

This was a big win for the Blues and helped them leapfrog over Manchester United and into second place and in another season that would have been good enough to be realistic about winning the Premiership, but my other old club Arsenal are playing out of their skin, and although Charlton gave them a fright, they carry the kind of confidence that could well see them going through their Premiership programme unbeaten come May.

The statistics speaks volumes about how Chelsea had set out their stall after those two very damaging matches against north London rivals Arsenal. The stats show that in the two matches in both Germany and Manchester City at the brand spanking new stadium which is becoming more like a graveyard for Keegan's team they hit every part of the City of Manchester Stadium except the back of Chelsea's net and were left 'mugged' by the kind of chance that Eidur Gudjohnsen has been missing too regularly lately:

Manchester City 0 Chelsea 1 Gudjohnsen 47,304

Beginning with the *People* the other Sunday headlines said CITY GUD FOR NOTHING plus King Kev is caught cold as the iceman cometh for Chelsea.

Which had the ex-England head-coach saying that, "To lose 1-0 was a body blow but we have got to get over it, because we play Manchester United next."

The *Mail on Sunday* went: RANIERI SPARED BY FOWLER and that Keegan's suffering as Robbie's howlers hand it all to Chelsea: Peter Fitton wrote that: If Robbie Fowler had possessed that piratical touch of old, he would have been celebrating another hat-trick and Chelsea would be championship history. Instead, the redoubtable Claudio Ranieri, scowling and agitated for most of the afternoon, was able to summon salvation through Eidur Gudjohnsen.

It was cruel for Kevin Keegan's buccaneering City and Chelsea must acknowledge that, if fortune had favoured the bravest, they may well have been humiliated.

Somebody suggested at one point that Roman Abramovich, was consulting a map for a gulag in which to detain Ranieri. But it was Keegan, a prisoner of his own fate, who was left to reflect: "If you don't win matches when you play like that you are really in trouble. We need Lady Luck now. She's deserted us. And we're being sucked down.

"It's tough to take because on a good day Robbie would have had a hat-trick. He missed one good one and had a couple of hard luck stories as well. Claudio has just summed up the match better than I could. He said that, "You played fantastic, we played poorly. You lost the game. We won. That's football, it's crazy."

All it needed for disaster to become triumph was a perspiring, prowling and fearsomely committed Fowler, now 28, to roll back the years, sadly, he couldn't oblige.

I did not see the entire match. But I did see the highlights and if they were anything to go by the Tinkerman can thank his lucky stars, because this could have damaged his chances of survival – in the manager's seat – and have some after effects on a team who looked everything but championship contenders, but as it is always said 'When you are down there the luck eludes you' and this day definitely made that look quite true.

Chelsea are in great need of a player who can take the 'fizz' out of the game when your team has its backs to the wall. If not, the firing brigade has an easy target and how Fowler never hit that target will – if he still has that passion – have haunted him that very evening. This is a player who I was once thought would be our greatest striker since Jimmy Greaves, but too many off the field distractions sent him the wrong way, because there is a very thin dividing line in any walk of life and only the most positive and bravest attitude will keep you on the right side of it. At the end of the day Chelsea 'stole' the points, which keep them in touch with Manchester United, although still a little more behind Arsenal.

A few days prior to this match I was interested in reading the thoughts of ex-Newcastle United, Spurs and England star Chris Waddle who had this to say:

'TINKERING DOESN'T MAKE SENSE'

It doesn't matter how much money you offered me, I would never play for Claudio Ranieri's Chelsea.

No player in their right mind would be happy to sit on the bench for half the club's matches and turn out once a fortnight. Chelsea's title bid is over because they have too many players and Ranieri is too keen to keep all the players happy.

But all of this talk about rotation policies is complete nonsense. It is a cop-out.

Arsene Wenger picks his strongest team in virtually every Premiership match and his team are unbeaten. Alex Ferguson rested Roy Keane against Leeds United and paid a major price by dropping two points.

And Ranieri is the worst culprit – chopping and changing his side to keep players sweet rather than doing what is best for the club.

If a player came to me and said he wanted a rest., I would put him straight on the transfer market.

Scott Parker does not suddenly need a rest after an hour just because he has moved to Stamford Bridge.

He played virtually every minute of every game for Charlton. He's fit and it cannot be doing his England chances any good to sit out as much action as he will for the rest of the season.

This is me: I don't agree with Chris on this point because if I were the England manager, I would love for my players to play a little less rather than a little more, for the manager knows exactly what such a player is capable of and, by the time the Euro 2004 and World Cup qualifying matches come along, he will have a very fresh player who has not been playing with any injuries that would hinder his performances for the country. The player would also be hungry to have as much of the ball as possible and there would be no excuses regarding that we play too much football in this country.

When England were not playing in World or European Cup matches in the old days they would be involved in the Home Internationals and Alf Ramsey expected 100% out of each and every one of them and any players involved would get about four to five weeks off before returning to the club for pre-season training. I quite understand Chris Waddle's point but if by playing as much as a player does now his career would last another two or three seasons, even more, if you were lucky!

The greatest example is Teddy Sherringham who is near thirty-eight and looking tremendous although he is out injured with a hamstring injury at this moment in time!

Back to Waddle who says that: Just look at Wayne Bridge, who broke records in playing in every match for more than three seasons when he was at Southampton – so why does he need to be rotated now?

If it is not true that Ranieri is just following some foreign trend either?

I used to play fifty-odd games a season at Marseille – in the league and the European Cup – and I wouldn't have wanted it any other way.

MIDGET

Now players are fitter than ever so why do they need more rests than a midget snooker player?

You do not see Real Madrid resting Ronaldo very often. That is because they want to win football matches.

On the whole, Ranieri has not spent his £120million or so too badly. He has just bought too many similar players. Parker is undoubtedly a quality player, but if Ranieri was going to make any major signing it should not be a box-to-box midfield player.

Chelsea miss a Gianfranco Zola, a creative player who can unlock a defence with a moment of unpredictability.

If Roman Abramovich had bought Chelsea a couple of weeks earlier the little Italian would still be at Stamford Bridge.

But by the time the Russian billionaire arrived, the striker had already agreed to join Cagliari. Zola might, by now, be slightly too long in the tooth to make a difference, but Chelsea need a fantasy player like him – whether it's a playmaker, a winger or a man in Zola's old role just off the main striker

Ryan Giggs can always conjure up something for United and Henry does it more consistently for Arsenal, but who have Chelsea got to provide that element of fantasy?

Joe Cole, on his day, but he does not have the chance to do it week in week out.

The Blues have lacked width since Damien Duff suffered his injury last December. They have missed the Irishman with Jesper Gronkjaer a frustrating replacement who rarely produces the telling final ball. While Chelsea have an enormous squad and are stacked with strikers and central midfielders, they are still lacking the back-up on the wings. There are very few of Ranieri's recruits who could be labelled as failures.

It is just that they have yet to gel and they do not have the same team spirit as Arsenal or United.

But they have far too many midfielders who do the same job, including Frank Lampard, Parker, Makelele, Geremi Manu Petit and Juan Veron.

That is before you even think about the Russian captain, Alexei Smertin who has been loaned out to Portsmouth.

Up front there is Adrian Mutu, Hernan Crespo, Jimmy Floyd Hasselbaink and Eidur Gudjohnsen – then two more proven Premiership scorers out on loan in Mikael Forssell and Carlton Cole.

In Ranieri's favour, he has always insisted this season would be too soon for his team to challenge for the championship.

But that may not be enough for Abramovich!

THE BLUES OVERTAKE UNITED

The top six of the Premiership is all about regarding the Champions League for there is no team below there that can possibly put in the kind of finish that would take then into the elite money-making Champions League:

	P	W	D	L	GD	PTS
Arsenal	27	20	7	O	+35	67
Chelsea	27	18	4	5	+27	58
Manchester United	27	18	4	5	+26	58
Newcastle United	27	10	12	5	+10	42
Charlton	27	11	7	7	+4	40
Liverpool	26	10	9	7	+ 9	39

The match Liverpool have in hand is against their conquerors Portsmouth – in the FA Cup – last weekend, a match that will take Harry's team up to Anfield for the second time this season. Portsmouth have played the red half of the Mersey three times this season, winning twice and drawing the other which led to that fine 5th Round of the FA Cup Replay victory.

Then, whilst all around them, teams were picking up points on Saturday, Harry thanked on-loan striker Lua Lua from Newcastle for equalising for them on Sunday in a match they played so very well once again. But, as we all know by now – Harry has that wonderful ability to get a quality player in who will do the business at a cash-starved club such as Portsmouth.

BACKDATE: 21-02-74

It seems like 1974 was the best time in Stoke City's history, apart from beating my Chelsea team in the 1972 League Cup Final and then of course there was the rejoicing of the return of Sir Stanley Matthews. It is evident that I am still alive and kicking in my old playground in the Potteries, a place where strangers think life is pretty dull, but my early days there were buzzing with terrific night life, almost a pub on every corner, but the best was in my village of Barlaston the closest pub to Wedgwood, the world's most famous pottery centre. The proud owner of the Red Lion was Lenny Bacon, a nice man – in his sixties – who was famous for wearing his unsightly green suit. He became my own personal barman in the days when pubs were pubs and the cost of a pint would not burn a hole in your pocket.

BUCKINGHAM PALACE

In my researching, going through daily papers, magazines and more than anything else keeping my ears and eyes very wide open, I came across an article about Thierry Henry and although it was quite long I am cutting it down to the important points: Arsene Wenger has told Barcelona: "You have as much chance of getting Thierry Henry as I have of buying Buckingham Palace".

The Frenchman is confident his fellow countryman has no intention of seeking pastures new and that the club would refuse to sell their superstar striker – even at the price of £100million. That is despite them having taken on a £285million debt to finance their new ground at Ashburton Grove.

Henry is the most sought-after striker in Europe. But Wenger made him what he is, converting him from a winger in the wilderness to king of the goal-scorers – and Henry knows it.

Wenger is so sure of the player's desire to stay, he has changed his approach, for a couple of weeks ago he snapped at Real Madrid for declaring an interest. Now he has just taken to laugh off all the talk.

Barcelona President Joan Laporta said he believed they could get Henry because he would be moving to the 'best club in the world'.

Wenger responded by declaring: "I want to buy Buckingham Palace. But that does not mean to say I can have it. There are many at our club who are bored by all this because we have no desire to sell Thierry. Why would we build a superb new 60,000-seated stadium and then sell our top players."

After the Manchester City match goal-scorer Eidur Gudjohnsen said that,

"The gap between us and Arsenal remains the same after the weekend but nobody at this club has given up. We have gone above Manchester United and now we are aiming to go one better.

"There are still eleven games to go and, who knows, maybe in four or five matches the gap will be much narrower than it is now.

"But to finish second would be a great achievement as well. All the new players are still getting used to each other, yet we could finish up runners-up or better.

"And believe me we are still hoping Arsenal slip up."

In a different interview, the Icelandic striker followed up by saying that, "Finishing second is what we are aiming for and to end up in front of Manchester United would be an achievement. It would be a measure of our progress under Claudio. He has always said that he wanted an improvement on last season, when we finished fourth.

"I can't tell Chelsea what to do but I think people should get off his back. If we could finish second, hopefully that would end all the speculation about his job. The manager has not been affected by all the talk and neither have the players. We are all 100% committed."

He continued by saying that, "I'd say we are still in it but definitely trailing. But we have got to believe. I refuse to give up even though I won't say I'm very confident of winning the title. I'd still like us to put some more pressure on if we or when Arsenal slip up. At least we will have done our jobs."

Me again: Chelsea are in some kind of time tunnel with the lights switched off or is it just the experience of being in between the top team in the country for almost a decade. As the old adage goes 'It's one thing getting there, but another staying there'.

The Blues – most of the time – look lopsided with no balance on either side of the pitch. Look at Manchester United with David Beckham in the side, they could knock balls into Cantona, Mark Hughes or Sherringham who held up the play, knowing that the ball would finally end up on the flanks with Giggs or the England captain. Stretching defences was and still is Alex Ferguson's theory and a great one at that. All the great teams had great wide players and although Ferguson always bought goal-scorers and centre-backs and dodgy goalkeepers – Scmeichell excluded – it shows just how important Giggs and Beckham were in his jigsaw puzzle but somewhere along the way the manager has lost his way amongst the trials and tribulations with the Coolmore Mafia. He has got personal once too often but more of that coming up. The Red Devils are no longer!

The Devil now is now Dead, and while the sweet sound of my old football club Arsenal are making such wonderful waves. Chelsea must be a little confused as to how to reach that level and stay there because United and Arsenal could not be any more different in the football classes. One team is tough, determined and purely struck by winning whilst – although the other one is of the same idea – is like experiencing a night at the Royal Ballet – The Working Man's Ballet once again – with their most beautiful introduction that has the country – United fans excluded – 'purring' with delight. And this is one of the reasons why our international team are not real live contenders in this upcoming European Championships. Look at the Arsenal side and you will see a German goalkeeper behind a host of fabulously talented Frenchman with a touch of Dutch here and Brazilian there. Sol Campbell and Ashley Cole are exceptions – along with Ray Parlour, but overall their attacking strategy is phenomenal based on the three degrees – Henry, Pires and Bergkamp – who are masters of using the football like it was the most valuable and fragile piece of art in the world. Their football is sublime and sometimes frightening as they break at the kind of speed that Linford Christie would be proud of, but unlike the black sprinter – Arsenal amazingly do it whilst keeping it under complete control. This is the level that Chelsea has got to reach if they are going to make good use of Abramovich's riches. I promise you faithful Bluenoses that this is not something to try at home, and your team cannot expect to be able to perform this way just because they are now the richest football club on the planet.

Chelsea's next match is against the Germans in the second leg in the third round of the Champions League in about ten days. In the meantime will catch up on some of the latest news as Jeff Powell's *Daily Mail* column reads:

'WERE FA TOO QUICK IN DENYING SVEN CLAIMS?'

The denial came so quickly that it beat the story to the punch. Hours before the Sunday morning tabloids hit the streets claiming Sven Goran Eriksson is trying to recruit Pavel Nedved, the best footballer in the word today, for his prospective employer of tomorrow, the Football Association had rushed out a denial from the England manager. How dare anyone suggest such a thing?

This was a journalist first. Not the notion that Eriksson might be recommending players to Chelski FC, but the fact that an institution as august as the FA would react with such alacrity to the glimpse of a headline on late night television.

The timing of their statement was 10pm Saturday night, still well before the hour of which many a Premiership celebrity is taking his fancy at London's Chinawhite nightclub, but most of the game's administrators are already tucked up in bed. Quite apart from how they knew which bed to fine Mr Eriksson – not a question to which Ms dell'Olio has always had the answer – the FA's haste was unseemly.

It smacked of the spin–doctor being called out at the dead of night. The FA were said to be tired of all this. Although, whether they are tired of having to refute all the gossip or weary of their manager's discretions was left unspecified.

It was as indiscreet to take tea with Roman Abramovich, and his Mr Fixit, Pini Zahari, as it was to raid the refrigerator with Ulrika Johnsson.

So it is not too difficult to imagine Erksson being naïve enough to telephone Pavel Nedved and ask him if he would care to join him at Stamford Bridge next season, as newspaper headlines suggested.

Not only that, but there are other indicators which make the revelation by

Nedved's agent, fellow countryman and former Czech international Zdenek Nehoda, unsurprising. For a start, in the eyes of many observers including this columnist, the Juventus midfielder is currently the finest player on earth and should have been voted the World Footballer of the Year in December.

That makes him a natural target for Abramovich's next shopping expedition to football's equivalent of the luxury goods department at Harrods.

More significantly, like so many of Chelsea's extravagant signings since their Russian revolution, Nedved's prospective transfer would appear to have something that looks like Eriksson's fingerprints all over it.

Like Juan Sebastian Veron – remember him? – Nedved played under Eriksson at Lazio. The Italian connection was also detectable with Adrian Mutu and Hernan Crespo.

You do not have to be all that cynical, either, to trace Joe Cole, Glen Johnson, and Wayne Bridge back to England's senior and Under 21 teams.

Is it really any wonder that Claudio Ranieri, who often seems to be in the dark about which players Chelsea are signing, simply shrugs and smiles when asked if he will still be managing them next season?

Not when Eriksson prevaricates about his future beyond Euro 2004 and he raises the question of what will happen if England lose all three group matches in Portugal this summer. But in denying the Nedved speculation, is he really being convincing?

Well, this is the man who promised the FA that their £3million a year would be enough to secure him against outside commercial distractions – only to start appearing soon after in advertisements for anything from classical discs to spaghetti sauce.

Whether all the uncertainty affects the players is unclear, although England and Chelsea appear focused on the job regardless.

It is the FA who gave the impression of being the most agitated about what might be happening. But whilst they were so fast in reacting to the latest story, I doubt we have heard the punch line yet.

As for Jeff Powell's piece: I think that he is so on the ball and showing all his expertise in a job that has seen England managers come and go just like visiting Harrods change of prices. But us players of long ago, we could only afford a look around, although I might have mentioned that my brother – John – and I visited the top floor for their 'way out' clothes for the new breed of the Chelsea 'jet set'. That was the time when the young and free girls in the Kings Road were wearing hot pants on a beautiful summer's day. Which brings me back to George Best and the question of 'where did it all go wrong?'. It was the swinging sixties and as I have always said that your teens are the greatest time of your life, because if you haven't got it 'sussed' by then forget the future.

As some of you may remember it was not long before my accident that the 'News of the Screws' had me on the front page calling me a 'pimp' because I had two coloured young ladies on my knees and a glass of champers in one hand, and I was accused of not seeing my hand without a drink in it. But time passes and although I should not mention the biggest fish and chip paper of all time, I must write to you about their headlines on the last Sunday in February:

SVEN: 'IM NEW CHELSKI BOSS'

This piece is written by Rob Beasley: Sven Goran Eriksson has sensationally confided he will quit England for Chelsea in the summer.

The Swede confessed all in an extraordinary telephone conversation with Juventus star Pavel Nedved.

Amazingly, the England coach called Nedved to find out if the Czech Republic international would join him at Stamford Bridge next season..

Nedved's agent, ex-Czech international Zdenek Nehoda revealed that: "Mr Eriksson phoned Nedved and said that, "I will be taking over Chelsea this summer – would you be interested in signing for me?"

Nedved and Eriksson have worked together before when the pair were at Lazio.

The news will stun both Chelsea boss Claudio Ranieri and the FA chief executive Mark Palios, who only last week revealed in the *News of the World* that he hopes Eriksson will stay until at least 2006.

Only two weeks ago at a press conference, Eriksson was asked "Can you say hand on heart that you will not be Chelsea manager after the European Championships?"

The Swede replied: "Yes, because I don't have any offer to go anywhere, absolutely not, and that's the truth!"

The FA have been in talks with Eriksson on two fronts – over an immediate £1million pay rise on his current contract which runs out in 2006, AND over an extension to keep him until 2008. But Sven has still to put pen to paper.

This is where I came into the equation: If this love affair between the new Russian revolution and the Swede had been planned that long ago – in the newspapers almost every day – why if what we have read and believed did Nedved appear on the list of the first £111million Mr Abramovich spent in the first place. I know that the new Chelsea owner has a money tree in his back garden, but please this seems so 'off the wall' to me. Money, like love of both football and women has tapped me on the shoulder once again, and money can certainly make fools of oneself, and this statement is aimed at all of the so-called magicians. And the way this new Chelsea team are performing at the moment they need both the magician and his roommate!

The feeling and vibes you get from the 'real' Chelsea supporters is that they are baffled more than ever. In fact they do not know if they are coming or going!

Oh, how delighted I am that I don't share their disappointment!

I will return to Stamford Bridge only when I am invited, until then I write from afar.

SENTINEL

It was the first week in March – the time Manchester United are known to put a spectacular run together – and a full page was for a story, headlined: ROMAN'S REVOLUTION IS BEYOND OUR KEN followed by Bates to go after being frozen out by 'new' Chelsea: Ken Bates is preparing to bring his extraordinary 22-year reign to an end after being forced out by the clubs' new regime, writes Steve Curry of the *Daily Mail*: But, typically, Bates intends to have the last word with a broadside at his detractors when he hosts one of his renowned supper club meetings tonight at Stamford Bridge.

Football's best known chairman is determined his departure from the club he helped rebuild on London's fashionable Fulham Road will be every bit as explosive as his entrance twenty-two years ago.

The 72-year-old bruiser was hoping to ride gracefully into the sunset in the summer of 2005 but the axing of his famous programme notes and his increasingly marginalisation at the club may accelerate his departure. The conjecture about his future was heightened last week when, for the first time in memory, Bates was not on the flight carrying the team, VIP guests and the media to a European fixture and just about everyone was asking where he was!

Bates would only say that the decision not to travel was his and his alone. But the presence in Stuttgart of Chelsea's new chief executive Peter Kenyon and Paul Smith, the man who stood in while Kenyon was on gardening leave from Manchester United, only fuelled the rumours.

The dumping of his column has been crucial. Every two weeks Ken would pull up a chair to the oak table in his vast office and, in long hand, write out his chairman's notes for the match programme, a discourse that became required reading for every supporter. Quite often the pen was dripping with vitriol, often rumbling members of his industry. Indeed, it became a badge of honour to get a mention even if the diatribe was insulting, which it usually was. He once accused a football writer on a London newspaper of suffering from Alzheimer's, another of being an alcoholic.

He would act as watchdog for the welfare of the game, not afraid to berate the FA, of which he is councillor, which generally speaking, he championed.

Quite who wanted Bates gagged is not clear, but a chief suspect must be Bruce Buck, an American lawyer and one of the new executives.

There is great warmth felt by the vast majority of Chelsea fans towards the chairman, who turned Stamford Bridge from a decaying old ground into a modern complex of shops, restaurants and hotels.

Famously, Bates bought the club in 1982 for just a £1 so that when he sold to Roman Abramovich, and collected £17.5million, it represented good business. Naturally, it was not as simple as that.

Bates had bought the club but not the ground, which is like buying a

Bentley but not the garage. And the deal came with debts of £1million plus. Chelsea were wallowing in the old Second Division with gates around 13,000.

The club also had a hooligan problem and twelve acres of prime real estate seemed to be going to waste, as property prices in Central London rocketed. Marler Estates gave the club notice to quit when the lease ran out in 1989.

This was Bates' finest hour as he used every device at his disposal – confrontation, litigation and sheer bloody mindedness – to delay the clubs relocation.

The recession of the Nineties meant Marler cooled on the building apartments and the ground was sold to Cabra Estates.

In 1992, the Royal Bank of Scotland acquired the freehold, gave Bates a twenty-year lease and the cubs home was secured. The option to buy was taken and Bates' vision of a complex of shops, hotels and restaurants began to take shape.

When he collected his cheque from Abramovich, Bates accepted he was, in his own words, "selling the toy shop to somebody else."

But is it not Red Rom who is marginalizing the chairman. He has made no obvious effort to gag Bates since the takeover last summer. The fact that the programme notes were axed in Kenyon's first week at the club might be more than coincidence.

Bates' notes have been missed. Laced with good humour – "There is no truth in the rumour I have been seen at our youth matches distracting the opposition's goalie' – they could be deadly serious, too."

Perhaps his pièce de resistance came, however, not in the Chelsea programme, but in his resignation letter as vice-chairman of Wembley Stadium Ltd.

Writing to Adam Crozier, the FA's former chief executive, he complained: "Even Jesus Christ suffered only one Pontius Pilate—I had a whole team of them".

It was perhaps ironic that the further diminishing of Ken's influence at Chelsea came on the day three weeks ago when the FA was crowing about the new Wembley. Almost to the last brick, it is the design given to them by Ken Bates before his resignation two years ago.

The fact Bates was always a loyal friend and a frightening enemy. There will be those, former players amongst them, who will be delighted at his demise but the vast majority will be saddened.

Bates, for all his contradictions and confrontational style and political incorrectness, is a man of honour who loves Chelsea to the core. He will be sorely missed.

On the opposite page the headline went: WHAT CHEEK! AS RIVALS PULL A FLANKER ON FERGIE: I write in more depth about the Robben signing but the first this is what Mark Fleming – of the *Express* – had to say: Chelsea have made a dramatic swoop for Holland superkid Arjen Robben and set up a £14million deal that will infuriate Sir Alex Ferguson. Robben, a target at Christmas for Manchester United,

Had a medical at Stamford Bridge yesterday and the deal will be rubber stamped in the summer.

Robben is rated one of the most exciting wide midfielders to have come out of Holland for years and was courted by Sir Alex, who gave him a personal tour of Old Trafford.

But United's haggling over the fee angered PSV, who decided to sell their prize asset to Chelsea in a calculated snub to Ferguson.

PSV chairman Harry van Raaij said that, "Because Manchester United were first in the queue we kept Chelsea waiting, but when we had our second discussion with United over the fee for Robben we were very surprised and badly disappointed over how low they thought they could push us on a transfer fee.

"They seemed to think that he was worth more than £4million less than Chelsea were willing to pay. That was a big letdown because we expect a reasonable price for such a talented striker and it was only then we opened negotiations with Chelsea."

There was already bad blood between the two clubs, with PSV believing that Ferguson had illegally approached Japp Stam before signing him, had unsettled Ruud van Nisterooy in the run-up to his move and then invited Robben, who has played four matches and scored two goals for Holland, to Manchester in the Dutch winter break without PSV's knowledge.

'COULD BE SHOCKS IN EUROPE COMING UP?'

The Champions League second leg against the German side Stuttgart was now upon us, and oh, how they needed to go through this tie. On the Tuesday, Chelsea hosts the Germans and Manchester United did the same to that smart team from Portugal, the champions Porto. My fancy of all the three English teams left in the knockout stages would have a hard time going through. I thought that Chelsea would come undone against Stuttgart and the champions of the Premiership would feel very lucky if they could overcome the very talented Portuguese football team. And as the match went on, it looked as if Sir Alex Ferguson's luck was down to the minimum, and as Betty Shine told me whilst dining out in one of Knightsbridge's most plushest of restaurants, that no matter what all these 'know-it-alls think, the time comes when the spiral turns and that there will be payback time, in other words what goes around comes around'.

Don't get me wrong, but she was absolutely against the hideous comment and thoughts of both Glenn Hoddle and Eileen Drury about being some kind of crusader in a past life, which is and always will be absolutely nonsense.

I think now that Manchester United have sucked the first lemon in the Champions League and with the Blues having overtaken them in the Premiership that club who have had it all their own way for so long have now become a serious threat no more!

I have always beat the drum for Beckham and if one player could have changed the fate on this evening it would have been the player who is now choking with laughter over his paella. That's if the football Royal Family eat such nutrition, I know David doesn't, but the posh one should at least try to keep up with her husband and all of his incredible successes. He has become a 'One man band' just as Leo Sayer was when we were taking home pittance in the swinging sixties. I am a fan of Leo!

Back to the business at hand as Ian McGarry wrote this — as I said — in the *Mail*:

THE LAST THING THE UNITED MANAGER NEEDED NOW WAS TO MISS OUT ON HIS TOP TARGET

The news that Arjen Robben is signing for Chelsea will be as welcome to Sir Alex Ferguson as a visit from John Magnier. Losing a player you assumed had agreed to sign for Manchester United this season is bad enough. But the timing of the deal, which will see Robben move to Stamford Bridge instead, could not have been worse.

Apart from the fact that Chelsea leapfrogged United into second spot last weekend, Ferguson finds himself facing the most serious crisis of his time as manager.

Magnier and JP McManus continue to demand an investigation into the transfer policy at the club. Robben may be one signing that got away, but the infamous 99 questions from the Coolmore Mafia just became one hundred.

Add to that Champions League defeat by Porto last week, the fact that they now trail Arsenal by nine points in the League and throw in an FA Cup quarter final against Fulham — a team they have yet to beat this season — on Saturday and there is the potential of further trouble.

However, losing Robben not only damages Ferguson's present position, it weakens his vision of the future. He had earmarked the PSV Eindhoven player to take on Giggs' position on the left, releasing the Welshman to play behind Ruud van Nistelrooy. To that end, he used his full array of contacts to ensure that news of his interest in the player reached the correct ears before Christmas, and on the afternoon of January the second Robben was driven out of Manchester United's Carrington training HQ with his father Hans, leaving behind them a very satisfied manager. Ferguson had spent almost two hours showing the Dutchmen around the club's state-of-the-art facilities as well as introducing him to some of his superstar players.

"I was quite realistic about the visit beforehand, because I wasn't really obsessed with United", said Robben Junior afterwards.

"It's clear they want me. I make the final decision together with my girlfriend, as I have top play there, but we have to live there. But the clubs have to sort things out first. I don't play a role in that. I went there without any real expectations. Sir Alex explained that he saw me as a regular player. He expected me to play about forty matches in my first season."

It was Ferguson at his charming best. Warm, courteous and, most important of all, patriarchal. When it comes to wooing an impressionable youngster, Fergie loves to play the father card. Ted Beckham still has the photographs of a younger Ferguson round his house in Essex when David was signed aged fourteen, come to United was the message, where we are all one big family.

Fast forward to June the 19th last year when United's boss broke off a family holiday in France to share coffee and cake with Ronaldinho and his brother Roberto Assis in a Paris hotel – all without contacting the Brazilian's club Paris Saint-Germain first.

It was not Ferguson's first such 'offence'. PSV chairman Harry van Raaij complained bitterly about the way Japp Stam and then Ruud van Nistelrooy were enticed. He will take great satisfaction in turning over his old foe now.

Ferguson will be fuming, but should appreciate the irony of someone else enjoying the last laugh on him for a change. Only time will tell whether the consequences of Robben's flight of fancy will be more harmful for United and their manager.

Splashed all over the back page of the same newspaper was THE GREAT ROBBEN ROBBERY.

No, it has nothing to do with my great pal Tommy Wisbey!

This followed that Chelsea grab £14.3million Dutch winger from under the noses of Manchester United: Chelsea have snatched Arjen Robben from under the noses of Manchester United after the winger last night agreed to move to Stamford Bridge for £14.3million.

The 20-year-old Dutchman has agreed a five-year contract worth around £2million per season that will see him complete his transfer in the summer – despite having pledged his future to Sir Alex Ferguson just eight weeks ago.

Negotiations with United broke down a month ago when PSV Eindhoven were told that the Old Trafford club were refusing to pay more the £8.6million for the player.

Chelsea stepped in and Robben is understood to have met owner Roman Abramovich and manager Claudio Ranieri in London two weeks ago. He was flown to Stanstead Airport by private jet at lunchtime yesterday, with PSV technical director Frank Arnesen and his agent Ton Smit. He was whisked to the Chelsea Village Hotel, arriving at 1.45pm and underwent a medical at a west London hospital in the afternoon. An official announcement by the club is expected today.

Chelsea will pay a percentage of the fee now for what is effectively an option to buy Robben in July.

Robben, who is currently suffering from a hamstring injury, is believed to have passed the preliminary examination, although the results of some of the tests will not be known until today. PSV chairman Harry van Raaij confirmed that all talks with United had ended.

"There's a very good chance that we will finalise the transfer to Chelsea on Tuesday" he said. "The negotiations started three or four weeks ago, just after the deal with Manchester United fell through.

"We tried to keep these things secret as long as we could and I think we succeeded. This is a big transfer for PSV, especially in the harsh economic climate for our clubs."

The fact that Manchester United are unwilling to meet PSV's asking price for Robben will raise further questions about the way in which future transfers will be conducted at the club.

Ferguson met Robben and his father, Hans, on January the second at United's training ground and convinced them that the player's future lay at Old Trafford. Robben Senior was then made aware of Chelsea's interest, but in mid-January he declared that, "Arjen will only play for PSV or Manchester United."

The deal represents victory for Chelsea's new chief executive Peter Kenyon over his former employers at United. It is also another step in Chelsea owner Roman Abramovich's campaign to turn the club into the best team in England and a major player on the European stage.

Robben will be expected to provide keen competition on the left of midfield for Damien Duff, although he is versatile enough to be used on the right as well

This was the big news of the week and it led to other headlines such as the *Express*: Chelsea steal £14million starlet from under United's noses: plus ROBBED OF ROBBEN: and that Fergie loses top target to Blues as PSV take revenge: In the *Sun* it simply said ROBBED and Chelsea nick £14million superkid from under the noses of United: The following day's *Mail* looked like this: ROBBEN FLEW THE NEST AND CAUSED A TRANSFER FEUD: and that the youngster had gone FROM MUMMY'S BOY TO MOST WANTED MAN: Also, in the *Sun* was MY BLUE HEAVEN: and the Transfer that rocked the reds with Robben himself commenting that, "CHELSEA SHOWED THEY WANTED ME SO MUCH MORE THAN UNITED". Ex-Manchester United centre back Japp Stam had this to say about him, "Arjen is only twenty and has had two seasons in the Dutch League with PSV but has made a very big impression. His exceptional performances got him a call-up to the national team and since has been a part of our squad, he's done very well and already scored at full level, too.

"He is an out-and-out left winger who is extremely quick, has a superb left foot, is a great dribbler and has the vision to pick killer passes. For someone of his age, he really is a complete player. The only thing he lacks is experience, otherwise he has it all." Robben has won four caps and scored two goals since his debut for Holland in April last year. I have not seen anything of this player but I am getting to a stage where I don't believe what I am reading about most of Chelsea's new purchases.

On the day of Chelsea's big Champions League match the *Sun* wrote that: I'M OFF which goes on Cole to hand in transfer request: Mark Irwin had to say this: Joe Cole is ready to hit Chelsea this summer with a transfer request.

The fed-up England midfielder has run out of patience over his lack of first team football since a £6.6million move from West Ham in August.

Cole, now 22, has not played a full ninety minutes for Chelsea and fears that could wreck his Euro 2004 dream. He has started just eleven Premiership matches and has been subbed in every one of them including last week's win at Manchester City.

Now he plans showdown talks, and unless his situation improves dramatically over the next two months, Cole will ask for a transfer.

His only consolation has been hanging on to his England place. But that could change as Euro 2004 approaches and that would be the final straw.

Tuesday's headlines were all about Ken Bates the man who – allegedly – bought the club for a pound note – and has turned that pound into a cool £17million, although I have been told by my mole, it was ten million more. The *Standard* went like this: D-DAY FOR BATES and Chairman Ken may quit Chelsea post at last supper. Inside read: Is it goodbye to the Bridge for chairman Bates and ROMAN EMPIRE TO SACRIFICE CHELSEA'S SAVIOUR. The three back pages of the *Daily Express* were covered with Bates beginning with: Last supper for chairman as Blues line up tasty new signing and in big letters were: BATES; I'M OFF and that Culture clash with Abramovich forces Ken to call on his Chelski reign: Inside a page size photograph of Peter Kenyon's face red: It's all coming up roses for Kenyon as he returns from 'gardening leave' to cut Bates and Fergie down to size and that VICTIMS OF THE SMILING ASSASSIN I then picked out a quote that simple read: 'To score direct hits on both men, two of football's most powerful figures in football, is a remarkable coup.'

SO FAR

I must admit that when I began this project I thought that the politics would far outweigh the football and I think I am right on that score, but what has happened on the playing field since the Christmas period has changed things dramatically, with the Tinkerman really mounting immense pressure on himself by over-tinkering, which seems to have blinded him. Let's not forget from one line to the next – you the reader have read – that the pressure has been incredibly dynamic in the shape of a tornado brewing. The Germans were next up and all eyes will be on the team selection, which will tell us if he is confidently cool or throwing wrong cards onto a very dangerous blackjack table.

That is just how high the stakes are right now!

There is something huge brewing in the plush offices of Bates, Kenyon and Abramovich and with only eleven Premiership matches to play, I reckon that my timing of writing from the beginning to the end of this book – for once in my life – will be perfect timing!

That is unless – of course – I had a football at my feet!

The headlines kept coming, as Ken Dyer's were that: We haven't seen the last of Ken – easy life isn't for him!

In the *Daily Express* the headlines read that CHELSEA CAN'T BUY A GOAL and that RANIERI LIVES TO FIGHT ANOTHER DAY and that it was also a CHAPTER OF DISASTERS: With the *Mail* saying that CHELSEA TAKE THE BACK DOOR ROUTE the headlines of the Premiership champions were not so good as they crashed out of the competition after being a goal to the good going into the ninetieth minute at Old Trafford: FERGIE STUNNED BY BOLT FROM THE BLUE and 36 seconds to go, then Howard lets it slip away: The back page showed a mass of red bodies at the final whistle with Gary Neville on his knees, Scholes, Brown Phil Neville and van Nistelrooy with their heads in their hands whilst Giggs looked as if he just seen his future go up in flames as Nicky Butt faces the turf and Solsjkaer in no man's land. The result was that United were BUSHWACKED and that one cruel blow cut and there's no way past Jose. It also stated that this devastating exit will have cost United £10million, but the biggest blow of all will be a great club's pride.

Then there came LINESMAN ROBS SCHOLES, THEN PORTO STRIKE AT THE DEATH TO SEND UNITED TUMBLING OUT OF EUROPE.

The biggest shock of the Champions League week was the home defeat of Juventus inflicted by Spanish side Deportivo La Coruna with a twelfth minute Pandiani goal adding to their slender one goal first leg lead of two weeks ago in Spain. It has now become quite fascinating that Chelsea were not only one step ahead of the champions but also still in with an opportunity of Champions League glory.

I just wonder what chief executive Peter Kenyon has on his mind as his old club looked down in the dumps and adding to that they face this brilliant Arsenal team in the FA Cup Final next month.

This latest performance against Stuttgart was a long way off being vintage, but they got the result they set out to get, although if the Germans had their shooting boots on then Chelsea would have followed United out of the competition.

ZINEDINE ZIDANE

I did not like the team sheet when it flashed across our screens and I am still bewildered by the constant selection of Jesper Gronkjaer, a player who throughout the season has been not only disappointing, but totally out of touch when it comes to delivering crosses into danger zones of his opponent's penalty area. Damien Duff looked rusty and was taken off with eight minutes left on the Tinkerman's wristwatch. Desailly entered the scene after Glen Johnson limped out of the match on the half-hour mark, and Parker was replaced by Geremi, as the clock struck the hour. The Germans looked pretty useful opponents and Chelsea never helped their cause by defending far too deep – the Italian way – allowing the red-shirted Germans to come forward in numbers, which for most of the match had Chelsea chasing shadows. My overall assessment of this Chelsea performance was one of a team holding onto anything that would and could keep their season going. But had the Germans finished off their good approach work, it would merely have been another nail in Ranieri's coffin. So Chelsea, with Lampard and Terry always in the thick of things, once again ground out an all-important victory which takes the team into the last eight of the biggest club tournament in Europe and now the stakes were piling up, Chelsea needed desperately to introduce some more effective attacking plans because apart from Gudjohnsen's goal at Manchester City it seemed that their very expensive strikers were all out of touch around their opponents' penalty area.

For those around Europe who were not tuned into this match the result looked a good one against the German champions and at the end of the day that is really all that matters in this and any other cup competition. It has become tougher and tougher to look outside of Lampard and Terry when praising great performances from individuals and that is a big worry, for over at Highbury there was Henry, Bergkamp, Pires and Campbell all playing superbly in this latest and fantastic run of theirs, being unbeaten in the Premiership and only in the FA Cup over the last four seasons and that was in Cardiff when they were robbed by Liverpool after another diabolical decision by the 'Mug in the Middle'. But back at the Bridge, Ranieri said of their latest victory that, "When you are building, sometimes you play well, sometimes you don't, sometimes you play well and don't win and sometimes you don't play well and do win. That is what happened tonight, we didn't play well but we are in the quarter-finals – and that's important. Stuttgart are a fantastic team on the counter attack and maybe we were nervous. I wanted to play better than that, to keep possession of the ball better but it was not possible." "Tell that to Zinedine Zidane" is what all of these people with all the "nelsons" overlook!

He went on that "I wanted us to close them down and to play three up front to put them under pressure but the important thing was that we did not concede. I hope there is a lot more to come from my team."

Stuttgart came out for the second half looking like a team who meant real business and had Phillipp Lahm not missed a glorious opportunity in the first minute of the restart, life would have been very uncomfortable for the Blues, because what you get in such a situation after defending deep for so long is that you have given the initiative to your opponents and it is very difficult to just switch into an attacking mode. The Stuttgart coach Magath said that, "We are all very disappointed. We played the 180 minutes and I don't think we have been the worst team. There was a balance between the sides. I think it would be very fair to say that Chelsea were lucky.

"They are not a bad team but we were surprised that they played so much on the counter-attack.

"We pressed forward throughout the second half and created good opportunities that could and should have changed the tie."

The headlines were not good but Chelsea had made it to the next stage of the Champions League, and that is all the eyes of Europe are on, the result. The *Sun* went that Chelsea were STUTTERY and SO NERVY FOR RANIERI AS HIS MEN SLIP INTO LAST EIGHT whilst the *Standard* simply said that RANIERI PLAYS IT SAFE and CAUTION SEES BLUES INTO QUARTER FINAL DRAW AS FANS DELIGHT IN UNITED'S EXIT; The *Daily Mail* called them BLUE BORES – But Ranieri's dour tactics are paying off.

Chelsea 0 Stuttgart 0 36,657

The first signs of anguish on the Tinkerman's face was in La Manga some six weeks ago – a place some weeks later three Leicester City players were caught and charged with gang rape whilst on a mid-season break from their battle against relegation – when he told the *Standard*'s Graham Hunter that WE'RE STILL SHORT OF WINNING FORMULA AND WAYS with a photograph of him looking down at a standing ball whilst resting his right foot on it. Hunter said then that: Claudio Ranieri looked tanned and refreshed in the Spanish sunshine of Chelsea's La Manga training camp. But the Italian refused to relax for one second, admitting that his team are still 'lacking something' before they can win the Champions League. Sinking into an armchair in the same lounge bar where scores of footballers, step forward Stan Collymore and Paul Gascoigne, have let themselves down, Ranieri showed the same impish humour and disarming candour to a Spanish audience as he does each week in England. Asked if Chelsea count themselves among the favourites for the Champions League he said that, "The favourites are the perennial names like Real Madrid, Juventus, Manchester United, AC Milan and Arsenal. Chelsea?

"We are there or thereabouts, we are working towards that aim – but are still lacking something. We are not yet at the level of Real Madrid, although everyone who plays against us as if we were.

"Look at Ferguson and his team. He's been there fourteen years, but it took him until the sixth or seventh season to really start winning.

"People may say we have the best squad in the world if they like but it is not even the case that you can have the best eleven players in your side and expect to win top trophies. I do have fine players but I remind everyone that what I am doing is making a team right now. I view myself as someone who is still laying the foundations, which explains why we started the season in England really well and then hit a big slump.

"Right now there is no question that we are fighting our way up again and with the Champions League coming around the corner at us it is vital that Chelsea is once again really strong and ready."

He continues to repeat himself in every interview which I feel is getting a little 'old hat' and fans don't want to keep hearing it. When I played my first match for England against the World Champions West Germany at Wembley, it was the first time I had played with the other ten players in our team and I felt very comfortable and that applied in my first match for Stoke City – when leaving Chelsea for £240,000 – against First Division League Champions Liverpool at the Victoria Ground. It was as if I grew up with my teammates on both occasions, and as I see it football is football no matter what language you speak – and there will always be barriers of some sort – no matter what position you play. I maybe can understand with the language barrier if playing in another country and other players not accepting you straight away but I had to prove myself over and over again at Stoke City and that challenge was enough to motivate me which meant getting the best out of oneself. Ranieri cannot afford to keep playing on foundations and redeveloping tactics because the game is a very simple one made difficult by the kind of tinkering he does at the wrong times. As I said, this is the first time I have seen him so very deep, though maybe thinking is all the hype against him being there, worth it all?

THE KING AND I
'A storm in a teacup, to boot'

I know you can say that his ability to stand on the touchline like a man of stone waiting to be removed to his place amongst other great Romans. He has this incredible control over his emotions, which is something very rare in today's climate with the usual touchline scenes between the two benches or with the fourth official. I have always said – when still searching for a managerial post – that I would not be a dugout manager. I believe the manager should be in the front of the Directors' Box or in his own galley – just like the one Tommy Docherty once watched his 'Docherty's Diamonds' from – almost on top of the roof of the old East Stand. It was a particularly strange walk from the dressing room to such a viewing place, as the manager would have to walk through the long East Stand Bar before climbing a ladder to get to his viewpoint. I remember when I was injured once and watched the match with all the Chelsea fans who were local lads, although much older than I. On this particular afternoon, Dave Sexton walked through the bar stone-faced as usual – and saw Tommy Baldwin and I supping with the chaps. He was not amused to say the very least!

He felt this as being unprofessional and not caring about the boys out on the field.

The one Friday morning we arrived for training at the Bridge – the only day we trained there – to see a letter on the notice board which said that players who were not playing for any home match were banned from drinking alcohol in the East Stand. The next home match it was a real cold day and a drop of brandy would always go down well, so it was what you might call 'A storm in a teacup' – a great song in those days that not only took the teacup by storm but the charts also, flying to number one and staying for quite a time, oh what memories of the sixties and seventies!

And as for the brandy in that cup, Sexton knew – of course – but as usual 'bottled' it up inside to use for another day. One of those days was whilst playing against Stoke City at the Victoria Ground – I think it was on a Monday evening – and at half-time Sexton threw a massive 'wobbly' in the away team dressing room and pointed the finger at our main source of goals – and mainly great ones – and ended in Ossie throwing his shirt across the room, much like the Beckham and Ferguson fiasco, which ended with us going out for the second half without the 'King of Stamford Bridge' and the next to we saw our centre-forward was in a night club which one day would become my local haunt, The Place in Hanley, a very famous place for big stars in the backwaters of this country of ours – oh sorry, is it still ours?

It was also a place where I met the majority of my new teammates for the first time, as I had arrived on a Monday morning to find it was the players' night each and every Monday and the venue The Place. Hursty told me this as I was looking forward to an easy and early night when told that it would be a no-no to miss these evenings.

So the first meeting, I was out until three in the morning and the second time I met them was the following morning still not sobered up, not really the perfect preparation to face the League Champions in your first match in front of your own fans, and this was a match I had to make a good impression, being by far the biggest signing Stoke City have ever paid for a player, £240,000!

This was just the beginning of events that led to the manager telling the pair of us that we were no longer needed or wanted at the club where I was born and the club that Peter Osgood was completely in love with. If Stamford Bridge were a woman, Peter Osgood would have been married for life, never ever contemplating a divorce of any kind at all, not even a short split up, that is how much the 'Big Man' adored Chelsea Football Club. But as we all well know, all great things come to an end, and in this case it was so unnecessary!

'MILLWALL MICK AND DENNIS THE MENACE'

Back to today and over in south London the tiny but legendary figure of Dennis Wise was having his very own party as new manager of Millwall as he guided them into the quarter-finals of the FA Cup and had taken them on a fantastic run of twelve unbeaten matches which puts then in with a big chance of the play-offs, if not keeping them out of an automatic second place with so many teams beating each other week in, week out.

Only last weekend, though, they missed a glorious opportunity to go through and face Sunderland in the semi-final by being held to a goalless draw against lowly Tranmere, missing a penalty ten minutes from the end. This let me down personally, for I doubled them up with Celtic – who beat Rangers in the Scottish Cup – and was rubbing my hands together when the 'Mug in the Middle' gave them a dubious penalty which Wise should have taken himself, for he has become quite an inspiration in the Millwall dressing room, and then of course he's been up the staircase on several times with both Chelsea and Wimbledon, but that was not in Cardiff!

If they could dispose of Tranmere – in the replay – and then Sunderland, they would face Arsenal – who will surely drive one more nail through the heart of Ferguson's worst nightmare – since first winning the FA Cup under his management – in the other semi-final. Though some people said that when Sir Alex went in for his heart surgery, it took longer finding the thing than fixing it! This would possibly make that a third miracle in this book up until now!

Wise has, obviously, brought his very own passion for winning into the club and that is no surprise to me after working under so many top class names of the football world. My pal 'Millwall Mick' will be like a man possessed as his team enter a ground that has seen so many a cup upset over recent years, the last being when John Aldridge was in control and they came back from three goals down against Glenn Hoddle's Southampton side to win a fantastic match 4-3. I know for sure that the ex-Chelsea and Wimbledon player will be successful in management, because apart from his vast experience and background he carries the most important torch, luck!

This is another case of being in the right place at the right time for Wise – unlike my appointment with Stoke City chairman, Mr Frank Edwards – for he will use this as a steppingstone to go on to further managerial posts at a higher level.

I know that Wise is close to Ken Bates and I wondered what he thought about the headlines of the *Evening Standard* only hours after Chelsea qualified for the next round of the Champions League: BATES SUES IN £2MILLION ROW which was followed by Former chairman issues Chelsea writ and wants to call Roman as his witness: The acrimonious departure of Ken Bates from Chelsea has hit new heights after the former chairman issued a writ for £2million against the club. And Bates has threatened to subpoena Chelsea's multi-billionaire owner Roman Abramovich to give evidence against his own club in what would be a sensational case if it ever went to court.

As revealed by *Standard Sport* last week, Bates is seeking a £2million settlement for what he claims is a breach of the contract he signed last summer following the Russian's take over. Bates pocketed £17million for his shares from Abramovich but signed a two-year deal to keep him chairman of Chelsea.

When that ended he would then become life president.

Although there was no salary linked to the contract, it is understood the terms provided for generous travel expenses and other allowances, estimated to be worth around £200,000 a year, as well as the continued honour of representing the club at Football Association and Premier League meetings.

But since the arrival of new chief executive Peter Kenyon at Chelsea, Bates has been marginalized and he believes his treatment, after taking legal advice, constitutes a breach of contract for 'unfair dismissal'.

Although Bates only resigned as chairman officially last week, talks have been going on for several weeks to find a settlement.

It is understood that Chelsea have offered £1million but this was rejected by Bates.

The 72-year-old made it clear during various discussions that he was quite prepared to call Abramovich to give evidence for his action.

If this happened it has the potential to be hugely embarrassing for Chelsea regardless of the result.

After resigning, blaming a clash of East and West cultures, Bates then criticised the new club regime when the club's in-house TV station would not show tributes by ex-players of Bates' chairmanship. He said that, I didn't realise Vladimir Putin (The Russian President) runs Chelsea TV.

Bates is now looking into getting involved with Sheffield Wednesday but was told yesterday by the Yorkshire club's chairman Dave Allen: "Ken Bates is the last person I would turn to for advice. When he jumps in the water the sharks jump out".

Paul Thompson of the *Standard* wrote this!

As for Dave Allen at Sheffield Wednesday, I love the last remark and overall find it such a brilliant piece of news not far off really of the Ferguson and Magnier affair in Manchester and Coolmore.

This is how I reacted to such news in my *Sentinel* column: "I'M NOT BLUE FOR KEN": Regular readers will know I will not be walking around wearing a black armband since hearing that Ken Bates was finally leaving Chelsea, the place I was born!

We go back a long way and he's the reason I was kicked out of the club a few years back.

Captain Birdseye is one of those weird characters that just loves to be detested and for that reason when asked about him, I reply that I liken him to the Leeds United team of the mid sixties for a decade or so. He's made an art form out of rubbing people up the wrong way with his acid tongue. The Russians have been quite clever in levering him peacefully out of the club – then again – it has cost them about £27million to do so.

So the bearded blunder walks away with his pockets full and a big smile on his face and they haven't seen the last of him at Stamford Bridge. He's still got a penthouse suite in the Chelsea hotel the Russians want to demolish in order to extend the ground, so there's every chance he'll sit tight just to be spiteful.

I first spoke to him more than twenty years ago when he called and woke me in the wee small hours when I was out in America. He wanted me back to Chelsea, but his negotiating skills were an insult to my manager in Seattle – the old Wolves and Derby County winger Alan Hinton – and I told him so in no uncertain terms.

My missus heard my end of the conversation and could not believe I called him a certain four-letter word. But he is not one of those to bear grudges, to be fair, and he eventually brought me back to Stamford Bridge some three years later. He was as good as gold when he allowed me to return to Stoke City for a second time and asked no fee.

But I would not go as far to say that there is a good side to him, he just simply lets his guard down now and then. He kicked me out of Chelsea after Kevin Keegan, who then was the Newcastle manager, twice set me upon in the tunnel at Stamford Bridge – the first time by ex-QPR and Birmingham goalkeeper Mick Kelly and then the second time.

Like so many other football chairmen, he couldn't be bothered to hear both sides of the story before jumping to conclusions.

'FUNNY OLD LIFE, EH'

So I haven't been back too often since, although I live only an Ian Hutchinson throw-in from the new stadium. So at this moment in time I do not know the position I am in with the new regime, and hope that this book will mend a few bridges, but in all honesty I have never been one to hold my breath!

It has always stuck with me that I never received a get-well card from Chelsea Football Club whilst being hospitalised for eleven months in the year of 1998.

I got a card from a little old lady in Stoke-on-Trent who I once helped getting onto a bus with her shopping, funny old life, eh!

This made it terribly difficult for me to have much love for Chelsea under Bates' chairmanship and once out of hospital, could be seen walking the opposite way past Chelsea fans going to the Bridge as I visited my old pal Harry Redknapp in a box ran by Mel Tame – a dear friend still – at West Ham United. It would not surprise me to see Captain Birdseye pop up somewhere else in the game – if only to show the world that it can't write off this old duffer as easy as that.

But for now, he's being hounded out of football after meeting his match in the form of Roman Abramovich and his Russian comrades – much like Alex Ferguson will eventually be run out of Old Trafford after biting off too much more than he could chew with the Coolmore Mafia, and he does love his gum!

Leaving van Nistelrooy out only last week against Fulham because of his complete honesty about the team missing Beckham – in the media – is just another example of how he is finally losing the plot. I cannot believe people who have been in the game for so very long fly off the handle over such trashy headlines. What Sir Alex must remember sometimes is that – thank god – everybody he deals with is not like him?

This was a simple case of the Dutch striker being asked if he thought they were missing the wonderful talent of Beckham, to which he answered, "yes I do" and the following morning it is blown up out of all proportion by the dregs of the ex-Fleet Street gang. It seems like that there are only two people can 'mouth it' at Old Trafford and that is he and his captain Roy Keane!

I hear from a grand source that these Irish fellas intend to drag him through the gutter and out of football after he dared to challenge them in the courts over ownership/breeding rights for Rock of Gibraltar. On a lighter note this week, I can't sign off without giving a mention to Leeds United front man Alan Smith for his brilliant performance against Liverpool last weekend which – for me – sheds a whole new light on him as a player. Instead of dogging his natural ability by snarling at everything in his wake, he finally let his football do the talking and showed us a repertoire of great passing in tight situations around the Scousers' penalty area.

If he carries on like this, he could become one of the four young skilful and clever strikers in England's Euro 2004 campaign, alongside Michael Owen, Wayne Rooney and Jermain Defoe and oh, Robbie Fowler had the best credentials at an early age, his loss is also the nations!

I wonder if that prospect would be enough to persuade the Swede to stay put with England and it amazes me that neither the Football Association or Chelsea Football Club can come clean and tell the people in this country what there intentions are. Don't get me wrong, they have every entitlement – as a business these days – but let's never forget that it is still the fans that make the game because without them there would be no game. You can have all the television channels on this planet but without no paying customers there is no game and that is why they have the right to know. I know many old Chelsea supporters who have stopped going – even before they raised their prices through the roof!

'WE'LL MEET AGAIN DON'T KNOW WHERE, DON'T KNOW WHEN?'

With both Chelsea and Arsenal still remaining in the Champions League, the entire of north and west London were asking just one question, could they be drawn once again in a cup competition this season?

The one thing for sure, Arsenal – at this moment in time – fear nobody in Europe as they just keep moving along sweetly in the Premiership and as they do, the English champions just can't keep up with them. Just when the talk of a Chelsea and Arsenal Champions League Final was being talked about their two balls were picked out of the bag one after the other and the *Evening Standard* headlines called it the £10million CLASH – Chelsea versus Arsenal for a place in the Champions League semis: Arsenal and Chelsea are to meet in the quarter-finals in what will be the biggest ever English club confrontation, of that there is absolutely no doubt. The stakes were high and so were everybody who are turned on by such ninety minutes of 'scary' football. This match would not be one for the faint hearted, but I was 'cool' because my heart once passed the biggest test of all.

The Premiership rivals, first and second in the table, were today drawn together to set up a mouthwatering Champions League quarter-final!

The two games – at Stamford Bridge on Wednesday 24th of March and Highbury on Tuesday the 6th of April – together are worth £3million purely in prize money and gate receipts for the winning club. On top of this will come television revenue! Arsenal received £15million of that last year, even though they went out at the second group phase. Qualifying for the last four would be at least another £2million from television. Add that to the potential £4.3million prize for winning the competition and these two matches open the way for a possible windfall of more than £10million.

It is the first time in history of the European Cup that two English clubs have been drawn together at this stage of the competition.

This historic tie will also be the first encounter between English sides in football's elite competition for twenty-six years. Arsenal are third favourites, behind Real Madrid and AC Milan, and will now face a series of massive matches over a 10-day period which will make or break their Treble chances.

'WHAT DOES DAVID BARNARD KNOW ABOUT FOOTBALL?'

Beginning on Sunday the 28th of March, they play Manchester United at Highbury in the League, followed by the first leg of the Champions League quarter-final.

They play the Old Trafford club in the last four of the FA Cup before the second leg of the Chelsea tie at Highbury. Arsene Wenger believes Arsenal have a psychological advantage over Chelsea.

He said that, "We know we can beat them, But we have to play well to do that and they have quality players who will respond in a big game.

"But it doesn't matter what the competition is, the Premiership League or the Champions League, it is Arsenal against Chelsea. And they won't be intimidated against us. It will be an interesting tie."

Whoever progresses from this tie will have to face the winners of the Real Madrid-Monaco quarter-final in the last four. This raises the prospect of David Beckham returning to London to face one of the two clubs favourite to sign him if he returns to England from Spain. Wenger said that, "The problem with Real Madrid is that there is not one problem. They can give you problems everywhere."

Arsenal have already beaten Chelsea three times this season, including twice last month when Arsenal won 2-1 in both the FA Cup and the Premiership. The Stamford Bridge club have not beaten the Gunners in the last eighteen attempts and have not tasted victory against them since Claudio Ranieri became coach.

Chelsea secretary David Barnard said that, "It's an historical event as neither club have got further than the quarter-final stages before.

"We have a great opportunity to put right our previous results against Arsenal this season. It will be like a chess game, both clubs know each other so well."

Arsenal vice-chairman David Dein said he would rather have avoided Chelsea until later in the competition.

He said, "I think one of the joys of playing in Europe is playing against teams from overseas and having played Chelsea three times it is a bit anti-climatic."

The last time two English clubs met in the European Cup was when Liverpool and Nottingham Forest played in the first round in 1978.

As for me, this is a fantastic draw and I look forward to it counting the days. What I must say is how can the secretary of a football club talk about performances like David Barnard did. Any team at this moment in time who think they can take Arsenal apart better think again because they are still going like that runaway train and entertain everyone aboard it!

The Arsenal Express train does not look in any way jaded, in fact they have looked sharper as the season has progressed, but the 'finding out' will be when, or if, they lose their first match but that does not look like happening at this moment in time and the season has not got very long to go and they are hot favourites for both the Premiership and FA Cup and third favourites for the Champions League, what a position to be in with April only two weeks away!

Well, the media boys were at it again – on March the fourth – with the following CUT UP DUFF and Damien 'kicked in the teeth' by £12million Robben deal: from the *Sun* while on the same day Alex Ferguson appointed Walter Smith as his assistant in a desperate attempt to save his club from failure, the *Mail* said that: KICKED IN THE TEETH with Duff shocked by the Robben signing!

Ian Cole wrote it like this: Chelsea's record signing Damien Duff has admitted that the news of Arjen Robben's imminent arrival at Stamford Bridge has been a 'kick in the teeth' for him.

Duff, the £17million winger, is just coming back after missing two months with shoulder and Achilles injuries.

The Republic of Ireland star was stunned to hear of Chelsea's £12million swoop for PSV star Robben, who also plays on the left wing.

I must butt in here: because it has only come to our attention that Jesper Gronkjaer has blamed his poor form – for over three years now – onto him being played on the wrong – not right – wing and it has us thinking again that the Tinkerman is running out of tinkers, especially ones who are playing in positions that are foreign to them. I can only say if Claudio has got it right, then the rest of us are nothing short of being complete fools!

Duff says that, "I must admit it was a bit of a kick in the teeth after two months out to hear about it. But I'll just have to carry on doing what I always do and work hard. I heard that he (Robben) is a left winger, but I don't play there very often so maybe I'll get a game somewhere else in the team!"

Duff also revealed that he expects to be hampered by his Achilles problem for the remainder of the season. The former Blackburn man played a full ninety minutes as Chelsea reserves lost 2-1 to West Ham last night to press his claims for a return to the starting line-up.

Duff, who has managed just three substitute appearances since Christmas said that, "I think I will struggle with the Achilles for the rest of the season but I'll have to grind it out.

"It's been the worst two months of my life. When you come to a new club you are desperate to impress and it's been very disappointing.

æBut it was good to get a full game under my belt. I felt a little ring rusty but it was good to be out there.

æI was gutted not to get on against Manchester City."

On the same day Harry Harris was writing about the speculation of the talk of David Beckham's move to Stamford Bridge. His column named AHEAD OF THE GAME headlined this as BLUE BECKHAM and MADRID LEAVE EXIT DOOR AJAR FOR ENGLAND CAPTAIN: David Beckham has been added to Chelsea's spectacular summer shopping list after his coach Carlos Queiroz confessed he does not know whether the England captain will stay at Real Madrid for next season.

The one thing for certain – or are we to be misled by the media through clever administration – is that the Tinkerman will not be Chelsea's main man next season – this is one of one of the most unjust decisions that I have seen in my days in and out of the game.

There is a massive few weeks ahead of Chelsea Football Club and only the people within the walls of the new regime know that answer!

Myself, it seems the more power – financially – this regime have, the more trouble they seem to find themselves in. Peter Kenyon will not have the time he had at Old Trafford to bring this club to the pinnacle!

He may be the best at what he does – merchandise and all the contacts abroad that made his ex-club the richest Football Club in the world, but you must remember Chelsea do not have a David Beckham or a George Best to fall back on. Chelsea have had wonderful players over the past generations, but who hasn't?

Len Shackleton, Raich Carter, Tom Finney and Matthews are just four examples. Chelsea can go back to Tommy Lawton, Hugh Gallagher, Roy Bentley and Jimmy Greaves. Yeah, Spurs were magnificent with Greaves again, Dave Mackay, Danny Blanchflower and the rest of that great first 'Double Winning' side, not forgetting the forever sight of 'bustling' and dangerous Bobby Smith, the battering ram of all battering rams.

So, all that means nothing to the new Chelsea Brigade which I understand, and that is why all this money spent on the overseas players in the summer makes the local diehard wonder are they believing what they see, or is this just some kind of 'mirage' of a different kind than they have been used to for so very long?

Promises costs both love and lives!

I myself think that Chelsea are heading into a cul-de-sac, for they are buying above-average players – compared to Wenger's signings of Nicholas Anelka, Patrick Vieira, Thierry Henry and Robert Pires – which make them look anything but wonderful. The new regime had the toughest job on their hands once taking over – we all know that – but the question is just how long will it take to catch up the Gunners?

And the goings on with the Tinkerman have been nothing short of awful if you look at the gap between the two teams – playing wise – and the club's position in the general background. Although the majority of my time on the field was like playing in the sitcom 'Mash' I adored the club and the running of it by a gentleman in Ken Friar. If only he had been at Stamford Bridge, some kind of sense and stability would have been brought from the top, which would have sorted out the horrible day-to-day stuff between the players and management.

I, as an ex-Chelsea and Arsenal player, do not sit on any of the fences that make our national sport a crying shame but after quite a long time in my rehabilitation have found time to sit up reading and writing to the wee small hours waiting for the trolley to take me down to the Operating Theatre. Once under a different kind of bright light, I am sure that I have touched something out there, and have returned – sometimes in the most horrific pain – to put certain things in my life in the right order. There is pain and then there is pain and I can assure you that after twenty-four trips to the Operating Theatre – many major and many incredibly awesome – never knowing of such pain. I have played through the barrier on many, many occasions and was thought no better of – like many of my kind – but what I experienced has stood me in good stead for the remaining years of my life. That one thing in life that tears people, lovers and friendships apart, has caused all whatever is going on at Stamford Bridge. Money!

The kind of propaganda that has entered into the once rundown Stamford Bridge football ground is sensational, but I wonder now if this extremely large bubble is looking ready to burst because the new regime can go out again this summer on a spending spree and a year on look no nearer to catching Arsenal up. This is a question that not even a billion English pounds can answer!

I repeat that in the early days in choosing to write this book I thought of calling it 'A Fly on the Wall' and have been tempted to change the title each and every time there is something floating around in the media sewer that more than ever makes this incredible season – so far – more and more like a rerun of Dallas, only with JR Ewing you knew exactly where you stood, much like with Bates. Unless you are hellbent on getting into the clutches of such people for whatever reason – mainly financial – I would rather pack up my PC and head for the nearest airport. Chelsea Football Club is not the place where I was brought up anymore, it is simply like another building along the Las Vegas strip. The only difference is in Vegas there are big hitters in each and every one of such empires. Who would have thought that someone would waltz into Chelsea and Kensington Borough and make the Harrod's boss look like Harold Steptoe?

I think at this moment in time, Mr Abramovich has overrated his agents who select his players and managers and it just goes to show that all the roubles or punts in the world cannot buy you love, fame, or success, unless you have a several oil wells to fall back on, only that can be very sticky. The oil that is!

Chelsea are facing some massive matches from now until the last kick of a ball come mid-May and what will happen after that will give me the opportunity to clear my head and once again look into a different kind of world that has brought these Russians into the country. That meaning they have given me the perfect opportunity to keep on writing, something that helped me keep my sanity whilst hospitalised for so long. And when you think we have the biggest war ever known going on – outside of our front doors – the media are focused more on all of these issues of someone like the Swede who is having the time of his life. I would like to see him on 'Who wants to be a Millionaire' with Chris Tarrant and after getting stuck on the £1million question has three options to take or as Chris says 'lifelines', phone a friend, in we which would see him put his hand on his chin, rubbing it like a great drummer brushes his skin, then say 'no', in which the presenter would reply what is "no" to which the Swede would say "A friend is out". Tarrant would then say, "I can assure you your friend is in". The Swede now looking like he wished he had never said how much running the English National team meant to him would finally say "I have not got any". "That brings you to the audience then", in which he would after taking another layer of skin off his face say "That is also a 'no' for they don't like me". "How about a fifty-fifty then?" Tarrant would say as he waits to go into a break and just as he is going to say "Don't go away we will find out the answer after the break, the Swede would interrupt and say "Don't bother, I'll take the money".

After the ads have finished and Chris has gone into his position that looks like coming out of the tunnel at the old Wembley Stadium he would say "Well it's been a mad and magnificent night for our last contestant who went away with a half a million, and whilst leaving asked if he could come on again at some time having never answered a question wrong, I'll have to talk to my superiors."

"Before I introduce our next contestant I must say he was very lucky that he never got any football questions!"

'BARMY MONEY'

Chelsea's winning through to the next round of the Champions League was a massive boost for the club, but still left a cloud over the future of the manager. This was not a vintage performance by anyone's standards but in cup football – in general – being in the 'hat' – for the next round draw is what it is all about. That is even if you look at it as simply financial in a football world, which has gone totally barmy.

The last piece on Ranieri after the Stuttgart match was put rather childishly by the *Evening Standard* by heading the back page with CLAUDIO PLAYS IT SAFE and that Caution sees Blues into the quarter-finals as fans' delight in United's exit: By far the biggest cheer on yet another successful Chelsea

European night at Stamford Bridge came after the final whistle, when the result at Old Trafford was announced.

The Chelsea fans hadn't just watched anything approaching a Champions League classic against Stuttgart.

But at least their team were through to the Champions League quarter-finals, which is more than could be said for Manchester United.

Claudio Ranieri thought it was sad to see United capitulate to a 90th minute Porto goal, but his team's supporters were generally not that sympathetic.

Arsenal may be in a class of their own but Chelsea are proving, both at home and on the European club front, that they are in second place and are ahead of Sir Alex Ferguson's team so far this season. Whatever happens during the summer, Ranieri, his coaching team and players must take a great deal of credit from that. The Italian has always insisted he is constructing something special and all the signs are that the building is moving along nicely.

This goalless draw against Stuttgart may not live long in the memory, in fact most of us may have forgotten it by the weekend, but this was a night when the ends justifies the means.

Ranieri the Tinkerman often does things to his team which mystify most of us, but against Germans, and mindful of that slender one-goal lead from the first-leg, he reverted to Italian type.

He said afterwards that he played an attacking 4-3-3 system, but it looked far more like a 4-5-1.

The wide players, Damien Duff and Jesper Gronkjaer, seemed to be mainly employed in this formation to keep Stuttgart's adventurous full-backs quiet. It looked for all the world like a sensible solid formation based on the knowledge that Stuttgart would have to go on the offensive if they wanted to pull this tie out of the fire.

In the end, Felix Magarth's side were some way short, although he felt Chelsea rode their luck. It's difficult to agree with him on that.

Although Stuttgart did go close to scoring on a couple of occasions, so did Chelsea, most notably when Gronkjaer hit an upright with just two minutes left.

In truth and although Chelsea were far from fluent all night, this victory will have given Ranieri and his players much pleasure.

It was a classic two-legged performance, do all the donkey work away from home. Nick a goal and then shut up shop in the second leg.

Ranieri conceded that, "we wanted to play a little better" but added: "We play sometimes and don't win. This time we didn't play particularly well but we are in the quarter-finals."

Some of us would certainly have liked Chelsea to play a more expansive game at home, but the bottom line for Chelsea fans is that their heroes are through to the most prestigious club competition and ready to take on all cormers. Another big plus for Ranieri was the return into the European arena, of that fleet-footed Irishman.

"The first twenty minutes were difficult for Damien Duff but after that he got better and did well," said Ranieri.

In fact, Duff was the focal point for most of Chelsea's attacks early on but was then switched into the midfield by Ranieri, before finally being replaced by Adrian Mutu with just nine minutes left.

Scott Parker, making his first Champions League start after his move from Charlton during the transfer window, also began well in his favoured central midfield role, but looked far less happy when he was moved to a wide position as Ranieri changed to a 4-4-2 system.

In the main, though, Ranieri can hardly be faulted. His team stifled the Stuttgart threat from the start and it was only when the Germans became desperate towards the end that they finally looked anything like a team who had beaten Manchester United this season.

The only worrying note for Chelsea came early in the first half, when Glen Johnson pulled up in some pain from an injured left ankle.

The full-back battled on after treatment but looked less happy and was eventually substituted after half an hour after twisting the same ankle again.

The former West Ham defender was undergoing a scan today t assess the extent of the damage, but all indications suggest that he could be struggling to be fit for the quarter-finals in two weeks time.

"The good thing is that, apart from this injury, I am recovering most of my injured players," said Ranieri.

"Duff's return is important to me and I am also hoping Juan Sebastian Veron will be able to help us."

Veron had undergone a back operation but Ranieri said that, "Seba should be back with us at the end of the week and I hope that he could be ready to play in another month."

Elsewhere for Chelsea, goalkeeper Carlo Cudicini had a relatively quiet night, but Frank Lampard worked as tirelessly as ever in midfield and John Terry again hardly put a foot wrong all match.

It was the expression on their faces at the end, which also spoke volumes about last night's achievement.

For them it was job done.

Bring on the quarter-finals!

FROM STUTTGART TO BOLTON

I told you earlier about my eight and a half week stint in the Intensive Trauma Unit where several of my family feared to tread, for being told that it would be the final time that they would see their son, nephew, uncle, father and best friend take his last breath. I know for certain that would have delighted quite a few people, and by knowing this, that alone gave me the kind of determination – once realising what had happened to me quite some weeks later – that I can only say I never really thought I had inside of me. I know your will to win on the football field is undoubted, but this was really a far different ball game, although Professor Williams once told me that I was a tiger while under anaesthetic, but put in another way. But I am resurrected and stronger and a better person than before, but that does not mean that anyone escapes criticism and only a half a mile away from where I write I have a brand new reason not only to live, but write, the second best – great sex is somewhere in between – thing to playing the game I love so much.

In the Chelsea programme against the Germans the fixture list read that they had eleven Premiership matches and the two Champions League semi-finals against the team who had now become something of more than just a hoodoo. Now, if Chelsea fail to knock the Gunners out of the biggest European club championship tournament in the world those eleven matches would bring the most incredible happenings to a club who were still hellbent on dethroning the Tinkerman and bringing in the Swede to replace him. That still concerns me, because once again if you have all that financial clout you must make sure you get the very best of everything available and I do believe Chelsea are dancing in the dark. But the next stop will be up north to try to get revenge on Sam Allardyce's team Bolton Wanderers, for their sloppy 2-1 home defeat at the Bridge!

'OSGOOD REALLY SHOULD HAVE FOLLOWED ME TO STOKE CITY'

The *Sentinel* were still keeping up their BACKDATE and this week looked at the match played at Coventry which was out first defeat in eleven matches since joining them. I remember this match as well as I do some of my great performances there, but believe I wish it had never happened. If anyone was responsible for this defeat it was yours truly, yeah, I did a have 'stinker' here and there. For some reason I had been over hitting my good friend the 'bottle' only this was much too close to kick-off time. Geoff Hurst and I were rooming the night before in the North Staffs Hotel and I was in a bad way and prayed that the next day I would be 'rid' of my demons but my prayer fell on deaf ears. Coventry was a match – that if I were up to scratch we would beat ninety nine times out of a hundred – although they had the great Tommy Hutchinson, later a teammate and good friend of mine in Seattle – but today I was not myself and let the boys down terribly. It is one of those things that happens very rarely and not one that you can stand up afterwards and apologise in the middle of a very disappointed dressing room. The report went this way: WINNING STREAK ENDS FOR STOKE: Hurst disallowed goal completes a miserable day for the Potters: Stoke City's eleven game unbeaten run came to an end following a 2-0 defeat against Coventry City at a freezing Highfield Road.

Manager Tony Waddington named an unchanged side as the Potters looked to better their improving league position, but his team were not able to produce the goods in a disappointing performance.

The Sky Blues had much of the game in the first period, but they were unable to convert their possession into goals.

They also started the second half brighter and took the lead when Tommy Hutchinson found the net following a deep cross from Smith, which was only parried by Mike McDonald. The goal woke up Stoke and they soon began to create chances through Jimmy Robertson and John Ritchie. Midway through the second half Geoff Hurst should have equalised but, following a superb piece of control in the area, his tame shot fell into the keeper's hands.

Despite a valiant fight, Stoke were constantly overrun in midfield and Coventry extended their lead after some poor defending, after a dire back pass by Alan Dodd intended for McDonald, was cut out by the alert David Cross who shot home from a tight angle.

Stoke City's poor day was completed when Hurst finally found the net seven minutes from time, but the referee disallowed the goal for offside.

The game finished 2-0, with Coventry manager Gordon Milne more than satisfied with his side's victory.

He said that, "I could not have asked for any more of the players, yet we could have lost."

Underneath this tiny report was a titbit saying that: Stoke were continuing to pursue Chelsea striker Peter Osgood.

City Chairman, Albert Henshall was hoping a deal could be struck if Chelsea were prepared to accept a straight cash offer for the player.

He said that, "If only Chelsea would change their adamant attitude about wanting players in part exchange, then we would be back in business. The ball is in their court now and any move must come from them."

TERRY: WE ARE OUT TO MAKE BOSS FIREPROOF

John Terry says it would be impossible for Chelsea to sack their manager Claudio Ranieri, were his team to win the Champions League this season.

The Blues are into the last eight after digging deep for the 0-0 draw against Stuttgart on Tuesday which handed them a 1-0 success.

They will have to play a lot more fluently if they are to achieve their dream of going all the way in Europe's elite competition, but their collective desire to keep Ranieri in his job gives them an extra incentive.

The Italian knows he must deliver a trophy this season if he is to have any hope of prolonging his stay in west London, and he knows the Champions League now represents his last shot at salvation.

He has been forced to live with persistent rumours he will replaced by Sven Goran Eriksson in the summer, rumours that the club have done little to deny. Skipper Terry, however, has had enough and has called upon the board to come clean and clarify the situation. And if they cannot do so, he plans to take matters in his own hands, win the Champions League and ensure they simply cannot dismiss him.

"Every player in that dressing room is going to try their hardest to win the competition, and that would make it almost impossible for them to replace Claudio." he said. "The club should come out and say something. Claudio has been great to Chelsea and it wouldn't hurt for the club to come out and support him. Hopefully they can do so soon and everyone can just concentrate on their football. All the players have had enough of it, and Claudio, obviously has had enough of it. Every day there's a link with Chelsea and Eriksson or whoever.

"It's frustrating for Claudio because he works so hard. We see that because in a lot of his own time, he comes in and works hard with us. He has been brilliant, he's the person who has given me a chance, and it's the same for the other players. We are all 100% behind him and getting through to the champions League quarter-finals shows that. Everyone in the dressing room hopes there won't be change this summer, we all want to come back to Claudio in the pre-season.

"We owe him a lot and if we can go all the way in the Champions League, it would be a great repayment."

The spectre of Eriksson is destabilising and with so many of the players full-square behind their boss, there is a distinct possibility of a rift developing with owner Roman Abramovich and his board.

Were a new man to come in, he would have to battle to win over some disappointed players.

Ranieri has certainly drawn the best out of Terry – ironically bringing him to the attention of the England coach Eriksson in the process – and defensively Chelsea do look sound.

They have not conceded a Champions League goal in five matches and Terry said that: "We all know exactly what we are doing. The fans realise it's not going to be a goal feast every time, sometimes we have got to be patient. It's frustrating for them and frustrating for us as well, because we always want to win three-nil.

"But we can't go tearing into teams and opening ourselves up at the back and in midfield. Against Stuttgart we had to stay solid and wait for something to happen and that's what we did."

Terry urged striker Jimmy Floyd Hasselbaink to think again about quitting the club.

The Dutchman was not even on the bench on Tuesday and says he will leave if he continues to be overlooked.

But Terry said: "We don't want to lose players like Jimmy, he has great hunger for the game."

BLUE BECKHAM
Madrid leave exit door ajar for England captain

By Harry Harris in his *Daily Express* 'Ahead of the Game' column: David Beckham has been added to Chelsea's spectacular summer shopping list after his coach Carlos Queiroz confessed he does not know whether the England captain will stay at Real Madrid next season.

Queiroz who coached Beckham at Old Trafford for a season under the management of Sir Alex Ferguson, has never been totally convinced about him, as this column printed out from the time Real Madrid bought him from Manchester United.

And then after a family dispute with wife Victoria, the *Mail* followed up with "Is Becks ready to quit Madrid and come home" which also involved the developments of Chelsea Football Club and their interest in the finest right-sided player in the world. That is my opinion of David Beckham, although I repeat myself sometimes it is only to remind you, the reader!

Chelsea have been monitoring the situation since Roman Abramovich bought the club last year. The Russian has made recruiting the best English talent his priority as he attempts to make Stamford Bridge the number one in Europe. And Peter Kenyon's appointment as chief executive following his move from Old Trafford, has served to strengthen that policy. An approach for Beckham was first made before he officially signed for Real Madrid but Abramovich is prepared to go to extraordinary lengths to make England's leading footballer the figurehead of his revolution.

However, sources close to Beckham are playing down the speculation he is preparing to quit. They said he had only failed to renew the lease on his mansion in the capitol because he would be away with England from late May prior to Euro 2004.

It was said in the *Daily Mail* that, although Real were happy with what he has contributed to the team in his first season, he is still a walking case of unpredictability. Would that be something to do with his wife?

After all, that is the reason Sir Alex finally pulled the plug on his career at the club he adored. This woman is fierce and more dangerous than his crosses and deadly free kicks. You will find out by the end of this book that the loving husband and proud father is not far behind George Best when it comes to seducing beautiful women, and that is through my experience in playing the game. Life does not change that much, the man is multi-talented, good looking and a real athlete, and with these attributes he has high sex level which is something he cannot hide. That is not a criticism, just something that comes with the package – a luxurious luggage if you like!

How many young men of his age would like to be in his very expensive shoes, I for one would!

POLL-AXED

We are in the year of 2004 and times have changed dramatically, marriages don't last like days of old, no matter how much men or women play behind their partner's back and, through my experience, one is no better – or worse – than the other!

Anyhow, back to the future and Chelsea's win at Bolton, which kept them in touch with Arsenal and Manchester United, who were now showing signs of not beginning the run that usually puts the championship in a different light. In other words, they usually make a run for the winning post a winning one. Sam Allardyce – who has done magnificently at Bolton – felt his team were let down by the 'Mug in the Middle'.

This time the mug was Graham Poll!

Sam stated that: "Graham is a smashing bloke, but he shouldn't be making mistakes like that – and as I have stated on many occasions in my *Sentinel* column – that if players are punished for their slightest mistakes in the heat of a battle, then so should the 'Mug' for he has more time to overlook such a situation, but refuses to see commonsense because of his uniform, the uniform of a policeman, parking warden or clamper!

"These people in uniforms really disgust me in times where there are muggers of old women, paedophiles and, of course terrorists, running around killing the innocent."

Bolton were fortunate that they had enough points on the board, for it is decisions like this that could get you the sack and see your team fall into the Nationwide. The most important thing for Chelsea was that they bagged the points and came back to London feeling not only relieved – after a first half battering – but happy with what really was a real decent result. In the *Mail* it was John Terry once again screaming the 'war cry' much the same as you have heard so many times this season and still I repeat that he might just choke on some of his words come May or June. John Terry should stick to being a real good centre-half and sometimes when you shout from the rooftops, it can make his performances – which are far more important – suffer. And he is the backbone of a very efficient Chelsea defence.

The photograph showed him standing like a gladiator after a wonderfully taken first goal, the kind of finish that an Alan Shearer would be proud to add to his wonderful collection of goals he has scored over years so consistently. It was a sweet half-volley at the far post, and what sprang to mind was that after all the money Chelsea have spent on strikers, it is Terry and Frank Lampard who lead the way when it comes to putting the fear into the opposition. I wrote earlier about Jay Jay Okocha, the Bolton show-boater, and in this match he once again looked the part, but still could not find the back of the net which is quite incredible this season for he hits the ball with such sweetness and power, but is always hitting either the post, bar, side netting or the poor goalkeeper's hands. He is still quite some player!

The Nigerian would have the Stamford Bridge faithful crowing if only the powers to be could recognise such a talent!

I give the benefit of the doubt to Chelsea and their Tinkerer as regards Jay Jay not being a youngster, but when you think they tried to keep Zola – once the Russians arrived – Jay Jay is pretty much a spring chicken. Anyhow, that is just another great talent slipping through the Russian fishing net. And talking of age, the evergreen Teddy Sherringham is still showing – along with his vast experience – class and seeing things quickly cannot be bought in a raw youngster from overseas. This once again is full credit to my mate Harry. Is he a shrewdy or what!

Bolton 0 Chelsea 2 Terry and Duff Att: Nothing like Stamford Bridge

---

THE HEAT IS STILL ON

This was a weekend of high drama as England had bowled the West Indies all out for an embarrassing 47, whilst at Manchester City the Champions were being battered 4-1 which kept Arsenal in an even stronger position in their quest to not only take over the championship but become the first team to ever to go through the entire season unbeaten, by winning 2-0 at Blackburn Rovers. The Blues were now second, three points and a six-goal better goal difference than the red side of Manchester. But Arsenal are surely out of reach at this moment in time!

The Tinkerman has woken up to some propaganda relating to his position as the Chelsea Head Master, but what's new?

The two latest names in the news in the *Mail* and the *Mirror*, one stating that Hitz all over for Ranieri, the other saying that Final insult for Claudio as Chelsea move to poach Bayern coach:

The *Mail* said that: The plot is thickening at Stamford Bridge – Hitzfeld link spells doom for Ranieri: Between Matt Lawton and Steve Curry the *Mail* read like this: Claudio Ranieri's position as Chelsea manager was further undermined yesterday when it was claimed that Ottmar Hitzfeld had turned down the opportunity to take charge at the Bridge. Reports in Germany said that the Bayern Munich coach had received 'an offer' from the Premiership big spenders. But Hitzfeld – who now denies making the claim – has expressed a desire to honour his contract and the remaining sixteen months remaining at the Olympic Stadium. Sven Goran Eriksson remains top of the Chelsea shopping list, but he is due to hold informal talks with the Football Association next week, after which the Swede will agree to sign a new deal that will run up until 2008. If Chelsea indeed made a move for Hitzfeld, that would suggest Roman Abramovich and his chief executive Peter Kenyon are not entirely confident of signing Eriksson for themselves, and the FA certainly saw yesterday's developments as an encouraging sign.

Hitzfeld was quoted as saying in a German newspaper that: "I have had an offer from Chelsea, but I will see out my contract with Bayern until 2005."

Within hours of the story appearing in *Sport Bild* – a top sports newspaper over there – both he and Chelsea denied it.

There was no question as this mission goes on that there were not too many people telling the real truth!

Kenyon – who had lined up the German to replace the retiring Sir Alex Ferguson during his time at Manchester United, issued a statement, but only a brief one, saying that: "Chelsea have not made an approach for Ottmar Hitzfeld. The story is totally untrue and without foundation."

Which was pretty much what Hitzfeld was saying also: "I don't know anything about this," he maintained.

This now was becoming a little too much for me as I write from the peaceful waters and tranquillity of Magusa – used to be Famagusta – because the plot that was once so simple has thickened out of all proportion. Surely there is an easier way to run a football club, especially with all of those sheckles in your back 'sky rocket'?

When is somebody going to come clean and tell the Chelsea public – no one else – what the hell is going on, even if they don't tell the manager of their football club.

Back to Tobias Schild and Ramain Hinko, the two journalists who wrote the story, who were astonished when they were informed of the denials: "I talked to Hitzfeld," said Hinko, one of Germany's most respected sportswriters and a man who had reported on Bayern Munich for more than thirty years. "And he didn't just tell me once that he had received an offer from Chelsea. I went back to him on the issue and he told me for a second time."

Hitzfeld had even explained to Hinzo how he received the offer. He had been approached by Pini Zahavi – the agent largely responsible for bringing Abramovich Kenyon and a whole host of top players to Stamford Bridge.

It might be that Zahari has acted without Chelsea's knowledge and there remains a difficult period in an otherwise distinguished career. Out of the Champions League and nine points behind Werder Bremen in the league, Bayern are only two points ahead of Stuttgart in the race for the second Champions League place for next season's elite tournament.

The Bayern board appear to be split on Hitzfeld, with club President Franz Beckenbauer – the man pictured on the front of 'The Working Man's Ballet' – hinting strongly last weekend that a move for Stuttgart's Felix Magarth was on the cards. For Hitzfeld and Ranieri, this is a time of real uncertainty, a time when events might yet prove to be beyond their control. Hitzfeld prides himself on never having broken a contract. On this occasion, it may well be broken for him – Matt Lawton wrote the bones of this: Apart from the words – mostly lies – the outstanding thing for me was the 'glum' face of the main character in this book, the Tinkerman!

STOP BUYING

These were the headlines in a *Sun* exclusive with photographs of both the Tinker and Talisman on the opposite side of the page facing one another. This is supposed to be the time of the talks of the 'showdown' between these two extraordinary characters. Andrew Dillon wrote that: Claudio Ranieri's rift with Roman Abramovich has deepened after it emerged the pair had a bust-up over Chelsea's growing army of stars. Boss Ranieri told Blues' Russian owner during the January transfer window he was satisfied with his team and the spending spree must stop. But the club signed £10million Scott Parker just days later. And now keeper Peter Cech and Dutch winger Arjen Robben have also been lined up for the summer. Newest recruit Robben is the fourteenth signing in nine amazing months since Abramovich began his Chelsea transformation with a £140million buyout.

CLAIMED

The row has caused major confusion in the camp over who is directing transfer policy. Ranieri has also drawn a blank in his bid to clear the air over his future, after Bayern Munich coach Otto Hitzfeld claimed he had been offered the Stamford Bridge manager's job this summer. The Blues' squad now totals forty-one, more than rivals Arsenal and Manchester United, and MR Abramovich has spent more than £122million assembling a huge collection of starts. Ranieri fears that overcrowding would cause problems have proved correct. Fed-up striker Jimmy Floyd Hasselbaink asked to leave last weekend because of his frustrations of lack of first team action.

Midfielder Geremi is also unsettled – and fellow Cameroon ace Joseph Desire Job – sounds like a wind-up name to me – insists that Geremi would be a big hit if he returned after his season's loan at Middlesbrough. Job revealed that: "I'd love to see Geremi back. I think everyone would because when he was here he showed a lot of qualities on the field and was very popular in the dressing room. He had a good season for Boro and all the fans would be happy to see him again. He can see we're a good side now, now we've won the Carling Cup and looking forward to Europe."

That was a *Sun* exclusive and the more I read, the more I feel like throwing up. The season that Geremi played up north, I must have been either out with George Best and Oliver Reed or back in the Intensive Trauma Unit.

Players from overseas come and they go – like everything else in life – but being not only in love with, educated and knowledgeable about our game I continue to be astonished. Klinsma, yes, Ginola, yes, Di Canio, yes, but so many of the others, absolutely no!

These three players I have mentioned had so much to prove to the British public and came through like the unthinkable. I watched the German through the Euro 96 Championships here in England and he was an education to front players of all ages.

LIKING GERMANS AND FRENCH

Once you have crossed that incredible finest dividing line that took the fresh young schoolboy into his Apprenticeship and the door to professionalism, these are the kind of players who are the masters of their trade. I am a massive Klinsman fan and his main asset − was like mine − his unselfishness. And me liking a German, well two if you count Franz, Christ!

So it was quite appropriate that my England debut was against our oldest enemies a relationship of love, hate and everything else thrown into the grapevine, that is not everyone's taste of the wine. That is the only way I can explain my feelings about such things in life. As my great friend Harry Redknapp's dear father − Harry senior − himself, says quite simply "right or wrong."

Then along came Ginola − the man with the strangest walk of an athlete I have ever seen − who would never be fed up with having that 'bag of wind' at his feet, and then came along George Graham, who finally got his nicely painted finger nails running through the Frenchman's lower back. One of the worst days in English football history was when Sir Alf Ramsey killed off wide players and David Ginola is the greatest example I can give you of such a player. Football − like life − needs depth and width and that should be provided by the likes of the Frenchman and the Italian Paolo Di Canio, players who the paying customers loved to watch flying down the touchline with the ball on the end of their toe and in Ginola there was no better in world football. He was unfortunate at Spurs because he was more popular than George Graham and also 'Gorgeous' George as he was known at Chelsea, took the hump because he was also better looking than him, I can say that with very much confidence. Had I played with Ginola, he would have had so much of the ball he would have thought it was his birthday every Saturday afternoon and it would have been my pleasure to run around getting the ball back just to get it back to him, sit was such a pleasure to watch such wonderful skills. Now all of a sudden, I seem to like the French!

As for the Italians, I love their restaurants and hospitality, and it is actually my favourite food. That brings me to Paolo, the artist who paints pretty pictures and has east Londoners singing Bocelli. Now that is quite something!

He will never die because of his passion and his nuisance and I have witnessed that first hand on the training ground at Chadwell Heath. My mate Harry thought he had overcome all of his troubles when purchasing this brilliant individual, but he never really understood that here was a man who was crazier than Harry − and me − himself.

But what happened was the Italian 'genius' could not only drive you potty, but turn the stadium into a place which you only see on special occasions at the Royal Albert or the Royal Festival Hall. The man when not kneeling down, praying to the gods, with his name singing out loud, was not only a genius but something life lacks at that time of need. A comedian, if you have any sense of humour!

He receives the football in tight spaces and it looks – for the normal punter – totally impossible for him to create something, but my word, I have seen him many times make the man in the different coloured shirt look such a fool. Charlie Cooke was – on his finest day – incredible and I can only compare the Italian to the Scot when sober. Charlie that is, not Paolo!

Wonderful control, with balance so different from the rest of us humans, if he could light a cigar as he was making the likes of Emlyn Hughes – who tried to patrol him for Liverpool – look stupid, it would have filled the billboards from here to Dundee United and back to the west End of London. I saw this man destroy Hughes one evening at the Bridge and the man in red did not know what knee to bounce back off the ground on!

The Italian is a genius of a very different kind, talented of course, frustrating, like most geniuses (George Best) and childish when things were not going their way. Throwing tantrums when the simplest of things did not go right, that is the Italian magician.

Unlike the Germans and French, the Italians I have always loved. Be it their food, hospitality in restaurants, or simply their mannerism and passion for all of the things that are important in our lives. Yeah, I think the Italians are great!

My visits to Upton Park when Aitch was in charge were made special by this talent who at times sent my mate into a nervous disposition. His frustration and problems in life became and belonged to everyone in the football ground.

That is why they sang his name in such a way that the people outside of the Boleyn Ground thought that the football had been postponed and was substituted by an Italian Opera.

I know Harry had sleepless nights over this 'crackpot', but the paying customer saw something they had never witnessed before – sheer class with a difference!

I have heard about Trevor Brooking and how the West Ham faithful adored his shimmy but this man charmed the crowd and made them realise why they left home on a cold Saturday morning.

Di Canio will go down in the history books as one of the all time great West Ham players, enough said, apart from being a little too far down the road for the Tinkerman, although I feel he could have brought him to Chelsea, just to educate the uneducated youngsters of today.

Before leaving Paolo – on the lighter side – I cannot ignore the time he pushed over 'Durk the Jerk' when being sent–off in a match between Sheffield Wednesday and Arsenal. Again Harry took a big bold gamble bringing him out of his football hibernation. The name of 'Durk the Jerk' was referee Paul Durkin, who had lost control of this match and fell down like he was in the penalty area and had he been both a player and referee would have given himself a penalty kick. And I have no reason to think that he would not have scored had he taken it himself!

FORSELL AGAIN

On the same page as the Roman and Russian's showdown, a loaned-out player's future at Chelsea was like an oarsman on the Thames with a very tiny hole in the bottom of his boat, because whilst Chelsea were still not hitting the net enough, up in the Midlands Mikael Forssell was still banging them in for Birmingham City and this player is not just a goal-scorer but a fine all-round player who could match up to any one of Chelsea's strikers so far this season, in fact he is Chelsea's leading goal-taker in the Premiership, which makes a mockery of such a loan deal. And this oarsman knew that the hole needed fixing and quickly for he is very ambitious, talented and still only twenty-three. He has been a revelation under the guidance of Steve Bruce – a manager who badly wants to keep him – but the Finland international is hell bent on playing for a top Premiership club and who can blame him?

Steve Bruce should know a real centre-forward when he sees one and this was one of the shrewdest moves in the Premiership this season, for this player is turning in performances of great consistency – yet Chelsea continue to ignore him in a season which has us asking simply, another why?

Leading up to the Chelsea and Fulham match, the *Sun* ran a newspaper article on all the grouches Ken Bates left behind him at Stamford Bridge – oddly enough buying two bracelets were not amongst them – after being slowly removed from all of his positions under the roof of the new regime. Then within literally days, he was seen to be quoted as saying that he would like to join Sheffield Wednesday, only they cost more than the pound he forever boasted about. Here was a man who had Chelsea so very much in his heart, don't make me smile, how many faces can one man have?

Bates was less than thirty-six hours away from taking Chelsea into liquidation so he should say a very big thank you to the Russians, but some people have very short memories, especially Bates, for he has said on several occasions that Chelsea did not exist before he arrived at the helm. What about Jimmy Greaves and Roy Bentley?

The headline before the Fulham home match read that: 1 'Rom taken to the cleaners warns Bates.' 2 'Too many players, too much cash.' 3 'He's keeping quiet over Ranieri.' and 4 'People at the top have no experience.'

I will not print the rest of what he has to say, for the simple reason he is not really a big part of this book and has had nothing to contribute in a season that is now really hotting up. There were quotes also from John Hollins – a flop as a Chelsea coach – David Webb – a manager who wanted to run the place lock stock and barrel – Tommy Docherty – the man who signed me Apprentice and is never short of a word about both Manchester United and the Blues, and is now the top man – along with Jimmy Greaves on the After-Dinner circuit. The manager most hard done by was Eddie McCreadie who led them back into the old first division only to be sacked for asking for an extra car for his wife Anne – which was given out to the media – but that was nothing further from the truth. There is quite a good story about my mate Eddie and it goes like this: It is a 'done thing' at the Bridge and many other clubs, I suspect, that the manager must go up to the Directors' Room after matches – something I know Harry loathed at West Ham – but Eddie refused to do so. One day he was asked why, and he explained that he did not want to go into their room because he did not like any criticism aimed at his players by Directors, telling them that if they had any such criticism it should be aimed at him because he picked the players. The Directors agreed with his wishes and kept 'stum' whenever the manager was present. Then the obvious happened, Juan Mears, the smallest of the Mears family let his tongue run away on one of Chelsea's lesser performances. Eddie lost his 'cool' and grabbed him by the throat and pinned him against the wall, the rest is – as they say – history. The following manager was Ken Shellitto who was given two club cars!

I wish Eddie and Linda well in their new lives in Tennessee where I visited them a couple of years ago and he was in pretty good form.

The back page of the *Sunday Express Sport* on the 21st March read:

ANOTHER FAILURE FOR ENGLAND OPENERS – FERGUSON SENT-OFF – CHELSEA HANG ON

But the biggest headline was: ROARING ROARING ARSENAL: Unbeaten Gunners on brink of history: Arsene Wenger last night saluted his Arsenal players for an 'outstanding achievement' as they equalled the all-time record of twenty-nine unbeaten league matches from the start of the season. 'They deserve a lot of respect.' You may remember me telling you of one of the greatest matches I have played in when scoring the first goal against Leeds – we were 2-0 down at the time – and had the pleasure to end Leeds United's sensational run of the same amount of matches in the 1973/74 season. The only other team to do so were Liverpool in the 1987/88 season!

Wenger added that: "at the start of the season this looked so far away but the players have shown a wonderful attitude. They deserve all the praise for the class of their play, their motivation and mental stamina. The quality of the Premiership is so high and I think it makes it such an outstanding achievement in modern football. The record is very nice, but what I am most sensitive about is that the players can so quickly be criticised – and I think they should be congratulated for what they have done. Now we have a massive match against Chelsea in the Champions League quarter-finals on Wednesday. I promise you that will be a big game of football."

Arsenal romped to a 2-0 lead against Bolton with some sublime football, but then endured a nervous finish as the visitors rallied in the latter stages, something that happens when having a long run of unbeaten matches, when the opponents have absolutely nothing to lose. Unless they are in that fight in the dungeon!

Bolton boss big Sam Allardyce had some ultra-complimentary things to say of the Gunners' football: "In the first forty minutes they were wonderful, and

I cannot see any team stopping them – or even beating them, for they are so strong and deserve great credit for the run they are on."

As for that massive match on Wednesday, there was a small piece saying that:

RANIERI WILL BE AXED WIN OR LOSE

It was reported that Claudio Ranieri will be sacked as Chelsea boss in the summer – even if he leads Chelsea to Champions League success. Owner Roman Abramovich has finalised his list of replacements with Fabio Capello high on it. So in managerial terms, Ranieri is a Dead Man Walking. Abramovich – with chief executive Peter Kenyon – is determined to bring in a man who will combine the Russian's desire for good football and big trophies. Roma boss Capello, one of Italy's most successful managers, especially in that golden spell with Milan in the early nineties, fits the bill – and he wants to manage in the Premiership. Ranieri was not appointed by the new regime, who have made it clear they want their own man and he is on borrowed time. Even winning the Champions League wouldn't be enough to save him, because the process to appoint a new manager is already under way. Ironically, if Capello is secured on a salary of around £5million a year, Ranieri would be in the frame to replace him at Roma.

Ranieri is a native of the Italian capital city, is well respected by the club, who are set to make next season's Champions League. The other names on Abramovich's list are Milan's Carlo Ancelotti and England boss Sven Goran Eriksson. But Capello would be the easiest to attract to Chelsea, as he is frustrated by both cash problems at Roma and the likely loss of some top players in the summer. Capello was contacted by Peter Kenyon – the then Manchester United chief executive – when Sir Alex Ferguson announced his retirement – a process spearheaded by Kenyon at Old Trafford. Capello was disappointed when Ferguson changed his mind and continued as the United boss. His main rival to becoming Ferguson's replacement was Eriksson, who again finds himself part of Chelsea's future planning. Any move for Eriksson is thought to be fraught with problems due to his involvement with England in Euro 2004 in Portugal this summer.

'JONATHAN PEARCE HAS IT ALL WRONG'
'The biggest voice in sport'
'WENGER TO GIVE CHELSEA DOUBLE DOSE OF THE BLUES'

I like Jonathan. We have only worked once together at a match between Everton and Arsenal at Goodison Park and was terribly impressed and have always liked his enthusiasm for a game he would have given his right arm to have played. This was a long trip and one that when you arrive there find it a little tough to get excited, well I do, but I am not paid to scream down the airwaves like a raving maniac, but that is Jonathan, and I am the laid back me!

Here is what he has to say about the upcoming Champions League matches between our remaining two clubs: "Chelsea will come desperately close to the thing they covet most this week. Roman Abramovich and Peter Kenyon will be within touching distance of their main target, the Champions League! Thierry Henry?

They'd be terrific by-products of the Russian Revolution. But it is Arsene Wenger that they really want!

"Chelsea's high rollers can forget it though. They may beat Arsenal this week, and even knock them out of the Champions League, but Wenger will not desert Arsenal now.

"People wondered why I put so much importance on the Gunners being able to raise the £10million to buy Jose Reyes from Seville. It simply meant that Wenger had been freed from financial shackles imposed on him during the search for the backing of the new Stadium project. So the backing had to be in place. Therefore Wenger will be staying. I had no doubt that the French Professor would have left his French Academy this summer if this hadn't happened.

"Henry, Pires and Vieira would not have hung around. Abramovich might have got the lot. He yearns for a manager with Wenger's all round ability. He is a brilliant tactician. He can rejuvenate players who have lost their way and turn them into world-beaters. He is an astute businessman and planner off the field, as his London Colney Training Ground input shows, and there is not a player in the world who wouldn't sign for him given the chance. Chelsea won't get him, but within months they will have found the nearest thing they can get to him. Claudio Ranieri could beat Real Madrid 5-0 in the Champions League and yet still be booted out. We know it. He knows it. His players know it. That's why they won't beat Arsenal over the two matches."

Jonathan, come on now, Cup football – Champions League or a cup of any other nature – is purely and simply a completely different ball game my friend. I promise you, mate, that no matter what the cup is, everything else goes out of the window. Times have changed in the Champions League because it is not a knockout competition anymore, until we get to these stages where the groups are scrapped. So rethink, Chelsea are the underdogs and they like it that way. They cannot win an argument against my other old club, but the bookmakers will tell you that the odds will show that this will be closer than you are predicting. Also, if I back them, then the opposition are certainties!

Back to you mate: There is great sympathy around the country for the Italian who had endeared himself to the nation with his delightful bumbling English. Mind you, we all loved Peter Sellers hilarious fumbling with the English language as Inspector Clouseau, and he was a slapstick comedian!

Don't get me wrong. Chelsea are involved in a tremendous campaign. A top two finish would continue the upward curve in the club's fortunes. I think they'll beat Arsenal on Wednesday and go into the Champions League quarter-finals with a lead. Highly creditable!

But with the players Ranieri has at his disposal, he should be hitting these levels. I believe the Chelsea hierarchy think of him as incapable of taking the club to the next level – and they have a point.

Why joke or titter about his Tinkerman reputation?

For too long he has given the impression he does not know his best team. I have said before in this column that there seems to be too much free spirit about the way Chelsea play and not enough drilled discipline in their method.

I must take over again here Jonathan, for I believe quite the opposite has happened this season, for Chelsea have dug out results through performances from the likes of the fantastic Frank Lampard and John Terry who have this burning desire to take Chelsea wherever they want to go. Young Frank has improved his entire game dramatically, becoming Chelsea's 'Man for all Seasons' if you like. He'll cover every blade of grass and then he'll pop up and hit as spectacular a goal as any other player in the Premiership and that includes front players of the highest order. The only player in the league on par with Frank Lampard is Alan Shearer for sheer power and consistency in hitting the white of the goalkeeper's eyes. And in Terry this player has earned his number five spot in Portugal – along with Frank – with or without the suspension of Rio Ferdinand, these two players have been Chelsea's edge this season when things looked like going pear shaped. Add the odd flash from Dunn and the introduction of Parker and Chelsea have a great base of British talent and that is where they get their discipline from. So I disagree with you, I think they lack that free spirit of Arsenal, quite definitely, and that is where your prediction could come unstuck. I'll let you finish now, as you go back to the Tinkerman: There has been sympathy for the way he has been treated. Is he the man spending the £140million on new players or have some been brought in without his approval?

How can he instil a true Arsenal style togetherness in the dressing room when the players know he won't be around much longer?

But he is the man to challenge and beat Wenger or Sir Alex on a regular basis!

Chelsea can sign a Crespo or a Makelele with Ranieri in charge, but can they get Shevchenko, van Nistelrooy or Beckham?

Those players don't need cash, they just want winners' medals. So the search will be stepped-up for a replacement. Forget Otto Hitzfeld. He has always been angling for one more year at Bayern to tide him over until he decides to take over the German job from Rudi Voller in 2006.

Sven Goran Eriksson won't leap straight into club management if he makes a total mess of Euro 2004. The fans wouldn't want him. The pressure would be too much. But Carlo Ancelloti is a strong candidate. He might be able to persuade Shevchenko – 'My favourite striker' that is me, the author – to come to England too. That would be a huge coup for Abramovich, who won't settle for second best. He and Kenyon are hugely ambitious. They know they need a world class finisher, and there are not too many around. If Real Madrid are denied Henry – as seems possible – they'll go for Shevchenko this summer. It could be a fight between the two clubs for the Ukranian. Ronaldo might then become available, though. Roman would love him too. What is certain is that there's too much uncertainty about Chelsea at the moment to make them a worthy bet against Arsenal. I believe that Cole, Crespo, Geremi and Makelele don't convince the club's top brass. All of them could be going. The players will be aware of the whispers. How can those levels of doubt help going into a game of this magnitude?

The lack of a spirited unity throughout the club is more damaging than an injury to Cudicini or any other poor performance on the night.

I don't think the talent is there to win a one-off game. I don't think that they'll beat Arsenal over the two legs. I did tip them to win the Premiership in August. They won't do it now. I do admire Ranieri's fortitude, humour and love of the game. I don't think he is a kingmaker, and that is what Chelsea need.

The Abramovich/Kenyon partnership won't rest until they have their king, throne, empire, palace, the lot. The Chelsea tale may discover a sad chapter or two in the next fortnight, but the story is just beginning!

TERRIFIC

Well that was the man that screams and hollers down your radio sets and your football channels, and for all of you that thought him to be just a loudmouth, you have just learned that Jonathan Pearce is a very astute follower of our game, and that cannot be said for too many in the media nowadays. He talks sense, he knows his stuff and does his homework in great detail. On our trip to Merseyside, he wrote for quite some time on the journey, leaving me to fiddle with my thumbs. But seriously, that was a terrific piece, well written and great reading. I am glad he mentioned my favourite Shevchenko so we have more than one thing in common, Jonathan my son!

As for his prediction, we will just have to wait and see. Whilst on the Jonathan Pearce story I must take time out to say 'hi' to Bill Kenwright who shared our taxi from the station to the ground that day, he's a real nice man and I can only say that I am sorry that he has to suffer so much in that Everton Directors' Box!

That's a big 'hello' Bill. Bill still cannot believe my story that I told on the Brian Moore show one evening, about turning down England and only wanting to get one England cap – that one against West Germany – he was dumbstruck and tried to get me to say that I was joking. Bill I wasn't my friend!

But those reasons could fill another book, on another day!

Back to Jonathan, and it is times when I write I look for certain answers that aren't there. For instance could he have been the crazy lunatic driver who ran me over?

But no Jonathan, I know it was an out of control Asian driver. Your passion for the game sometimes clouds your vision – just as my love for the odd tipple sometimes clouds mine. For example, I have lost more money gambling through my heart than with my head, in other words I don't count sleep at night. I am enjoying my fourth life, after Maureen – who mothers my two sons Allen and Anthony – then Laurel – who mothers Adam – and a third wife not worth mentioning. Football is my first, second, third and fourth love and can never be replaced like a wife or a car or a house and, as I write, my fifth life will begin in Cyprus. Crazy world considering I really did die at least once!

When I left Jonathan, once reaching the smoke late on that Saturday evening I liked him much more than when I met him at the station. His sincerity was his main asset, but now I must tell him that if he did not think the game so predictable he would be an artist at work with the pen, but, because of that predictability, you therefore should stick to the microphone because you liven up the dullest of football matches, and that is a great compliment to you for there are a zillion players who do not have this ability and are getting paid fortunes for doing so!

On this Monday morning there were more rumblings from Madrid as to the future of David Beckham and Roman Abramovich had obviously advised chief executive Peter Kenyon to keep his eyes firmly on the situation, but that was the furthest thing from Chelsea captain John Terry's mind as he roared, as the headline in the *Sun* put it as: BLUE AINT SEEN NOTHING YET as Terry insists the title race is still alive. Neil Curtis reported that: John Terry has warned Arsenal that Chelsea's best is yet to come. And that means the Gunners are going to have to work for title glory. As for the Champions League clash, centre-half Terry believes the Blues are ready to overcome their Arsenal hoodoo. The England defender, 23, was excellent once again on Saturday as Chelsea kept their 16th clean sheet of the season. He said: "Right now we are winning games without playing well. But that does not worry us – it's a good sign.

"Our boss, Claudio Ranieri, he does not care about performances right now, he just wants results. Well, we are getting them. Sooner or later it is going to click and then we will be winning by three, four or five goals. This season is not over, there is plenty to play for and we are ready for it." The phenomenal force of Arsenal stands between Chelsea and glory this season. Terry added that, "I cannot put my finger on why we have not been able to beat them. I don't think it is a psychological thing. We still believe Arsenal are going to slip up in the league sooner or later – and then we will be waiting. I don't want to talk too much about our meeting in the Champions League yet. We have reached the last eight without playing our best football and that it still to come. There is still so much to play for this season." Terry started and finished a move with a sweeping half-volley that opened the scoring in the 72nd minute. Damien Duff bundled home the second goal from a Jimmy Floyd cross just three minutes later. It had been Joe Cole's introduction as a 65th minute substitute that turned the tide.

Unhappy at being left out, the England midfielder showed Ranieri why he should start the next match as he gave Chelsea energy and life in the closing 25 minutes he was on the field. Terry said: "Joe was a little bit frustrated about not starting the game. But he is going to give the manager food for thought, if he comes on and plays like that. He changed the game for us." But the real Chelsea hero was third choice goalkeeper Marco Ambrosio. Injuries to Carlo Cudicini and Neil Sullivan have given him his big chance on Saturday and he did not let anyone down with a string of fine first-half saves. Ambrosio, who was Chievo's reserve goalkeeper before joining Chelsea in the summer, has hardly had a career to talk about. Yet now he could be the hero in Chelsea's most critical stage of the season.

Ambrosio, 30, said that: "I don't know if I am ready for it. But it is the first big chance in my life and I want to do my best for Chelsea and change my career. I was nervous at the start of this game because I had a lot of pressure on me.

"Everbody will have been looking at me to see if I was ready to play for a big team like Chelsea. Well, I kept a clean sheet. It is another three points and we continue to try to catch Arsenal."

It is a shame Ambrosio's heroics did not rub off on Hernan Crespo. The Tinkerman had to play him with Adrian Mutu and with Eidur Gudjohhnsen suspended – he was totally ineffective.

As for Bolton, they had so many shots on goal in the first half and were denied two penalties, which should have been given. Jay Jay Okocha has had 105 shots in the league this season – and has still not scored. Ambrosio made sure of that on Saturday but it was a sickening defeat for a team whose great start is beginning to stumble.

PUNISHED

Bolton boss Sam Allardyce said that: "We dominated Chelsea in the first half. But what we failed to do was see them off when they were on the rack. When you have a team of Chelsea's quality in a position like that you have got to take full advantage."

CHAMPIONS LEAGUE QUARTER-FINALS

It seems right that I have picked the perfect season
to write such a book with both my old clubs Chelsea and
Arsenal going head to head in the Champions League!

The biggest week in Chelsea's history was here and north London neighbours Arsenal also had theirs as they face the first leg of the first phase of the treble that only Manchester United had done before them. Incredibly, it was Chelsea in the Champions League and Manchester United in the FA Cup semi-finals that stood in their way, as the gap they have opened at the top of the Premiership was far too much to make up for both the aforementioned football clubs, though Chelsea, unlike Manchester United, have galloped on relentlessly as we close in on the last ten matches of the Premiership season.

On the Monday of the first leg, staged at Stamford Bridge on Wednesday evening, the Tinkerman was all over the back page of the *Daily Mirror* with the words 'LET ME STAY' and that Ranieri wants a job in the Premiership when he gets the Chelsea axe.

It goes on to say that: Claudio Ranieri this week goes into the most important match of his career pleading for another chance in the Premiership

The Chelsea boss, whose side takes on Arsenal in the quarter-finals of the Champions League on Wednesday, is resigned to the fact of being sacked in the summer.

And last night Ranieri admitted that the result against the Gunners would make no difference to his long-term prospects at Stamford Bridge.

The Italian's agent Jon Smith said that, "Claudio is on a good contract at Chelsea, and we are not about to jeopardise that, or any other future settlement of it, by making any moves now.

"But if he were to be fired, there are clubs at home and abroad who have indicated their interest in him.

"Should the situation arise, I know he would prefer to stay in this country."

Ranieri admitted: "I don't think this game is important for my future. It is important for Chelsea's. I don't think about Ranieri, I think about Chelsea."

Wenger, who last week laughed off an offer to lure him to Real Madrid, has joined a list of Sven Goran Eriksson, Ottmar Hitzfield of Bayern Munich, and Roma's Fabio Capelo, Martin O'Neill and Milan's Carlo Ancelotti as targets for Chelsea.

The Frenchman said that: "I find it strange Ranieri has put up with it. I have a lot of sympathy for him."

Despite all the speculation as – the Tinkerman – Ranieri has this season managed a multi-million pound squad into a formidable team!

While Arsenal were lapping up the adulation for matching Liverpool and Leeds' record of the best unbeaten start to a season, over the same 29 match period, Chelsea have been no slouches either. Since the Premiership started, only four sides – the present Arsenal team, Manchester United in 2000/1 and 1993/94 and the Blackburn squad of 1994/5 – have a better record at this stage of the season.

Arsenal – who at the moment have the best 29-game statistics since the top flight was overhauled in 1992 – are on course to claim the title, while the other three line-ups did so. Inside this morning's *Mirror* the headlines went like this: Stamford Bridge scandal: Chelsea in turmoil 48 hours before Champions League showdown against Arsenal: NO WAY TO TREAT YOUR MANAGER: No justice for Ranieri as Roman's axe hovers.

On the football side of the business at hand under the headlines of: COUNTDOWN TO THE BIG ONE it says also: DUFFED UP AND READY TO GO after Damien Duff, the Southern Ireland left winger bounced back to score the winner in Chelsea's last match at Fulham before Wednesday's big clash.

Claudio Ranieri hailed Damien Duff as a boxer who has bounced back off the ropes after the winger scored the winner against Fulham.

And the Italian manager identified the £17million man as the player with the big punch to knock out Arsenal in the Champions League quarter-final on Wednesday.

Duff had described Chelsea's signing of PSV wideman Arjen Robben as a 'kick in the teeth' as he fought back from shoulder surgery. But he has scored two goals in two games and Ranieri opted to withdraw him after 45 minutes to save him for Europe. Ranieri said that: "Now everyone understands how important he is. He scores and makes good final passes, is dangerous, very quick and could do something important on Wednesday." Duff had voiced his concern at the Stamford Bridge policy. But his manager added that: "He's a good boxer. Maybe he had a kick in the teeth but he's bounced back off the ropes."

Other headlines were led by the *Express* who printed, ITALIAN DIGS IN AHEAD OF ARSENAL SHOWDOWN and that RANIERI FIGHTING TO THE END and that Sack talk cannot faze Chelsea boss.

While in the *Daily Mail* underneath the CHAMPIONS LEAGUE SHOWDOWN it read exactly like this: CHELSEA IN A SPIN OVER CLAUDIO.

The Tinkerman says that, "The players give me strength", while UNREST PLAYS INTO ARSENAL HANDS AS BIG CLASH LOOMS.

As for the Fulham match, Fulham boss Chris Coleman, whose Fulham side performed well below par, suggested Chelsea were there for the taking and if his side had been a little more attack minded, he might have achieved just that. "Ours was a lacklustre performance, which was surprising given this was a full house in a great stadium. I can't tell you why that happened", said the disconsolate Welshman. "The bottom line was that we had too many underperformers."

One of the problems is that, with the exception of Damien Duff, they have big names not offering big performances. There are far too few players who feel you with a sense that they can make things happen, the feeling you get when Thierry Henry has the ball at his feet.

There is little doubt they are prepared to play with caution, a no-risk philosophy that happens to be the mindset of a coach whose football education was in the Italian school. This game was a perfect example. They were enjoying success out wide with Duff's sorcery and Jesper Gronkjaer's direct running, the two wingers switching flanks to some effect. At half-time Gronkjaer was withdrawn and the diamond formation replaced an orthodox 4-4-2.

"I know we were dangerous on the flanks but we were conceding too much space in front of our defensive line. Geremi and Frank Lampard were always facing four players in midfield", explained Ranieri.

"With two wingers it was very difficult to close the space and this was the reason why I changed the system. Football can be played without wingers."

This Tinkering, it seems, does not impress owner Roman Abramovich, who wants a settled team playing football that has become less second nature.

The plus side once again was the performance of John Terry, the driving energy of Lampard and the penetration of their most exciting player Duff.

It was suggested that Duff is to Chelsea what Robert Pires is to Arsenal. "Pires is more elegant and Damien is more direct. As one of you wrote, Arsenal are the Musketeers and we are the Gladiators," smiled Ranieri.

Unfortunately, he is a Gladiator about to be put to the sword!

This is a typical way of the Tinkerman describing these two teams and going back to Pires and the way he plays and in his photograph he is surely D'Artaignan!

Chelsea 2 Gudjohnsen and Duff Fulham 1 Pembridge: 41,169

Whilst browsing through the *Mail* I came across Duncan Ferguson – in a photograph – literally trying to strangle Leicester City's Steffen Freund, which led to his obvious dismissal. He would no doubt later be fined and suspended and I suggest could be better off with someone like Frank Warren as manager, rather than Micky Adams.

The best news of the weekend for me was that I backed Portsmouth at 6/4 to beat Southampton and Harry's team did so with a late strike by that incredible striker Yakubu – not for all the right reasons, he does so very well getting into scoring positions but once there seems to be like he is facing Freddie Kruger in a dark alley.

On the other hand we have Teddy Sherringham in the same team, who makes the black striker look even more docile. Harry was clearly delighted and relieved as chances came and went until the Nigerian international striker hit a dramatic winner with a quarter of an hour to go on my watch. My pal said that, "It was a massive game. If we had been beaten we would have been in desperate trouble and it would have knocked everyone flat. They all worked extremely hard and the centre-backs were heroes. We missed some gilt-edged chances and it was all hands to the pump at the end."

There were however warning signs for Portsmouth – especially as their run-in includes key away matches at Leicester and Leeds. They dominated the first half as befits a side with an impressive home record, but Yakubu was guilty of missing a handful of chances. Teddy was once again the instrumental and orchestra leader who just gets better with age, although Harry tells me that he is now getting little niggly injuries – latest one a hamstring – where at a much bigger club would have time to rest them, but Portsmouth are in desperate need of his services as he sets up moves, keeping the attacking movement going by brining players into the game through his wonderful speed of thought and superb delivery of the football, and let's not forget, it gets pretty blustery on the coast there, which makes his passing even more spectacular.

My favourite headline of this Monday morning was simply:

YAKUBU STRIKES TO GIVE POMPEY AN ESCAPE ROUTE

And I jumped for joy in the Grosvenor Club whilst my son went to pick up my winnings, so it was – once again – drinks all round and a wonderful result for my mate who I am certain will keep his team up, and the clash at the Walker Stadium against Leicester will be the match that will clinch it, I will be backing them to win that one and hopefully will be there to see it.

The headlines on the inside page of the *Evening Standard* said that:

SPURS MAY OPT FOR RANIERI IF TRAP BID FAILS

Matthew Norman says that: RANIERI RUMOURS COULD BRING FLUSH SUCCESS AT CHELSEA and goes on says that: The most closely guarded secret since George Michael was flushed from the closet by that urinal detective in LA is out. According to reports in just about every Sunday newspaper, Claudio Ranieri will leave Chelsea this summer.

It's difficult to know how this leak will play down Stamford Bridge. On one hand, you needn't be a top psychologist to know that nothing is more liable to damage players' form than sure knowledge that their boss is a lame duck. On the other, Roman Abramovich might console himself with the thought that whatever chance Chelsea have of beating Arsenal over two legs in the Champions League quarter-finals rests on them on no account taking the lead. So maybe players, depressed at Ranieri's harsh treatment, will start sluggishly and go behind; and then, struck by the need to impress the new boss, whoever that might be, storm back to win. But the decent thing to do is leave speculation about the tie for today and quietly observe that, while Mr Abramovich is entitled to hire and fire, Signor Ranieri has been delightful and hilarious blast of fresh air in a fetid managerial pool, and will be greatly missed.

I follow and like the Norman columns for they are close to the bone and never without humour, something that has kept the Tinkerman sane.

In the same *Standard* there is a huge picture of Robert Pires leaning against a lamppost looking like a film star, poet or rock star of the sixties. His French good looks with that tiny moustache and thin line of hair from his chin to his lip are outstanding. If you don't follow our game you would never believe that this man is a genius on the football field, a player I have come to admire more and more as this season goes on, and even now he is maintaining the kind of form that Arsenal will be looking for over these massive matches against both Chelsea – in the Champions League – and Manchester United in the FA Cup.

The heading went like this: THE GAMES OF DESTINY and that PIRES INSISTS THAT THE GUNNERS CAN TAKE THE HEAT AS THEY FACE DAUNTING RUN: Four games, two opponents and thirteen days which could decide Arsenal's season. There is no doubt what is at stake as Arsene Wenger gathered his players around him at London Colney today for the build-up to one of the most pressurised sequences in any of their distinguished careers.

Two clashes with Chelsea in their Champions League quarter-final will dictate whether Arsenal can progress beyond the last eight for the first time. Sandwiched between those capital encounters come two games with Manchester United at Highbury and in the FA Cup semi-final at Villa Park six days later.

If Arsenal come through this match, the Treble dream lives on. And while Robert Pires reflects the determination among players to take nothing for granted after the experiences of a year ago when an eight-point lead was squandered, he is certain of one thing: his teammates can handle the heat.

"We like matches with pressure," said the 30-year-old French midfielder. " It means that you are involved in the chase for trophies, if you are involved in such matches at this stage of the season.

"Everyone wants to beat us. So the higher the pressure, the better Arsenal are."

On Wednesday they face Chelsea at Stamford Bridge in the first-leg of their European quarter-final. On the face of it, statistics suggest Arsenal can already start checking out facilities for the semi-final in either Monaco or Madrid. After all, the teams have met three times this season and the Gunners have won the lot. Three-nil to Arsenal. Pires, though shrugs off that record as irrelevant. Again, the lessons of twelve months ago have clearly been taken on board. "The problem a year ago was we anticipated victories in the league. Everybody else was saying it and we thought the same. It taught us a lot.

"Okay, so we have beaten Chelsea three times this season, but that will not mean anything in the Champions League games.

"We are careful about that record. We don't think those victories, not at all. Chelsea have big players like Adrian Mutu, Hernan Crespo, Marcel Desailly, William Gallas, Claude Makelele…so many of them. They will love the big games. All they need at the moment is time. They have a new President (Roman Abramovich) and new players. They have to find a balance.

"This is the main difference between Arsenal and Chelsea. We have played together, basically, the same players, for three or four years. It has created links between the players. That is important for the atmosphere on and off the pitch. Chelsea do not have that balance just yet, but they will want to win something this season.

"I believe there is a possibility that they can win the Premiership but it will be a big achievement for them if they were able to beat Arsenal in the Champions League. They will be very motivated, we know that."

Planning a strategy against Chelsea is difficult because Claudio Ranieri changes his line-up so much.

"All I know is that it will be a formidable team against us," said Pires, who scored another cracker in Saturday's win over Bolton.

And he has equal respect for Manchester United whose decline has been rapid, as suspensions and injuries have slashed the options for Sir Alex Ferguson at a critical stage of the season.

"They are going through what we went through last season at this time," said Pires.

"Look at the game at Blackburn recently. We won 2-0 where last season we lost 2-0 and we had basically the same players.

"The difference is we are going through a good period and United are not.

"But they will want to protect their Treble. They won three major trophies in 1999 and that was a marvellous achievement, a formidable thing. They still have great players – I especially like Paul Scholes, he is tremendous – and they will be like a wounded animal at the moment. And wounded animals are the most dangerous.

"They will want to beat us to prevent us achieving what they achieved. It will be tough – in the league match and the FA Cup."

Pires, however, is convinced that Arsenal are equipped for the massive challenges ahead. He epitomises the transformation of a year ago and he is now willing to give as good as he gets on the field. Witness the scene when Aston Villa came to Highbury back in August.

Villa's Swedish defender, Olof Mellberg, waved an imaginary card that he felt should have been shown to Pires after what he regarded as an exaggerated response to a challenge.

Rather than forget it, Pires confronted Mellberg and the argument, reinforced by several members of the Villa bench, continued in the players' tunnel at half-time.

"There was a lot shouting," he recalled. "Then it all went quiet. I looked around and Patrick was there."

The 'Patrick' in question was Vieira, always so fiercely protective of his teammates.

"He is now the best in the world in that midfield role," said Pires. "He used to be just defensive but now he does everything. Defending and attacking.

"He is a natural leader. He organises dinners for the rest of the players and that the bond between us strong off the field as well as on it."

And Pires has changed, so have the team. Arsenal will now settle for the pragmatic when necessary. "It is goods for us when we win playing spectacular football," he said. "But we didn't produce that at Blackburn. It was efficient. Sometimes you have to win using your head. It is very important that we win playing super football. We just need to win."

After Chelsea's 2-1 home win over Fulham Ken Dyer's *Evening Standard* piece was headlined that: NOTHING CAN KEEP RANIERI SAFE NOW.

The *Daily Mail* spelt it out this way: IS IT ONLY SVEN WHO FITS THE CHELSEA BILL?

In the Sun under the words CHAMPIONS LEAGUE CRUNCH – TWO DAYS TO GO was that Ranieri: All the backing from the players has given me strength.

On the eve of the biggest European Cup match played in this country, the double page inside the *Daily Mail* portrayed Peter Kenyon as the 'Messiah' holding out his hands in front of the wonderful new West Stand, where the boxes cost £1million a season. The headlines surrounding it was that RANIERI WREAKS HIS REVENGE alongside MANAGERS SWIPE HAS TORMENTORS AT CHELSEA SQUIRMING.

On the back page it was said that Claudio Ranieri finally admitted defeat in a battle to save his job at Chelsea yesterday, when he told his squad he will not be their manager next season. A tearful photograph – I don't know where they get these kind of things from, showed next to headlines of: GOODBYE BOYS as TEARFUL RANIERI STUNS HIS TEAM BY ADMITTING HE IS BEING FORCED OUT.

Claudio Ranieri may have been portrayed as a tactical halfwit in recent weeks, but at Chelsea's training ground yesterday he performed something of a masterstroke.

The Stamford Bridge manager, victim for so long of a whispering campaign, which has made his position untenable, finally responded with a beautifully delivered swipe at his tormentors.

Tired of the employers who have remained silent in the shadows while the speculation continues to rage about his future, Ranieri had them cornered last night. Cornered, squirming and nowhere to hide.

"Now it's Chelsea who must help the Chelsea team," he said, knowing full well that it would be impossible for them to respond with an answer.

It was something Ranieri had been building towards. It did not take a genius to work out that a briefing with a senior club director had fuelled the weekend's headlines that the manager was history. At training yesterday morning he conveyed as much to his players.

In an emotional speech, one tempered with sadness, Ranieri told them that this season would be his last, and that everything happening behind the scenes at Stamford Bridge pointed to his departure. Not quite a final farewell, but an attempt to deal with the uncertainty before focusing on a Champions League quarter-final match against Arsenal.

By the time Ranieri had showered and changed for his TV interview with Sky, his intentions were clear in his mind. The interviewer was almost too embarrassed to raise the subject of another round of newspaper stories, which spoke of Rainer's imminent dismissal, but the Italian seized the moment with a forthright, uncharacteristically candid response.

Rainer has acted with nothing but dignity from the moment a photographer caught Sven Groan Eriksson visiting Roman Abramovich's London home last summer and yesterday was another demonstration of that. If the club's Russian owner wants him out, it will not be on his terms.

He certainly succeeded in scoring points against his employers in the build-up to tomorrow's encounter with Arsenal at Stamford Bridge. After all, it will not be Ranieri and the players that the supporters round on if Arsene Wenger's side inflict yet another defeat to their London rivals.

TOO MUCH MISTRUST AND DISRESPECT

All Kenyon had to say was that, "This wave of media speculation about Claudio's future and false links to other managers is unhelpful to our manager and the players in the build-up to an important match in the Champions League. We will not add to this speculation by responding and reiterate that Claudio Ranieri has over three years left on his contract."

At this moment in time, the Russians seem to be playing their most famous game, no, not lottery, but lottery of another kind, the real roulette. Chelsea are in a position where they could press Arsenal all the way to the death in the Premiership and, considering the Gunners are unbeaten throughout this amazing season, this is a 200% improvement on last season. I don't really put that down to the players coming in because it has been the same players this time around that have performed admirably. Frank Lampard has been outstanding throughout, shoving Chelsea to the brink of their opponents' penalty area at any and every given opportunity, putting them on the back-foot. Then there is a the constant improvement and maturing of John Terry, a player I liked at first sight, just as I did when first setting eyes on Sol Campbell so long ago now at Tottenham. I remember when living in Bow, East London, my great pal Malcolm Molineux was running the closest pub to my new home there and we began our friendship from there. One evening Mal told me that Sol Campbell was in the pub last evening – being a Spurs supporter – he said that I know he is only the Spurs centre-half but he is a really nice fellow. My reply was that Sol Campbell was quickly becoming the best centre-back in the country, which quite shocked my mate, and when he was going to leave I told him that if he joined Arsenal they would take over from Manchester United. That season they won the Double!

Sol Campbell is the first-choice back player and John Terry has made huge strides to make them the best partnership at the middle of defence since Peters and Lee, but one could see and the other could not. What I am trying to say – in jest – is that who could picture that gangly figure of Jack Charlton alongside the one and only Bobby Moore, probably the only player who pulled on the shirt and became a different person. His ambition to lead our country never waned, in fact it got stronger each and every game. Please don't get me wrong, but in today's marketplace – and that includes since 1970 – there has been nobody with the class of such a player. This is not a knock at all the centre-backs since – although there are so many – only I have not got enough pages left to name them all!

Bryan Robson and Tony Adams are the other two most outstanding figures, with Robson being the best, for he carried England for so long through the changing times of our game. Moore once told me that I should concentrate more on playing for England than my club – Chelsea at the time – because that is how you become a world name instead of just a great player on these shores. I begged to differ, because of being the way I am I think the club pays your wages and you owe your 100% to them and that anything else on top is a bonus, however, I am the person who never looks further than the next day and that has applied and proved to be right both in my football and my marriages, two loves that are not that much different. If there is a difference, it is that football is in your own hands where the other is always in the balance!

I have loved and lost on both battlefields, but the success at the top of the tree in football far outweighs any type of happiness with a woman, for you know it is just for the moment.

I found that out after my accident where although – if playing – I would still have been contracted to the club and got the best treatment, my wife broke all the codes that that love brings with it. The love of the women in my life have been more like flings, whereas the love with a football at my feet is something I cherished and worked hard for, knowing that the more you put in the more you get out. On the other side of that matrimonial coin you can work your fingers to the bone to satisfy your partner and in a life – that is far too short as it is – you waste far too much time in bothering. That will be on my headstone anyway!

'MONEY DON'T ALWAYS BUY YOU LOVE'

Back to the great Robert Chelsea Moore, whose ambitions were worn on his sleeve even by just watching him lead his nation out of the tunnel at Wembley. He was right and I was wrong, he had more courage than I did, he could hang in there no matter what the problem was and nothing showed that more than the bracelet situation in Bogotá at the time of the 1970 World Cup in Mexico, the one I should have been a part of. He was let down terribly by Alf Ramsey, but sat his ground and acted like the great Steve McQueen in one of his many roles as the super cool 'dude' with the class of Sean Connery playing Bond and the wonderful 'togetherness' in one of many of his extraordinary Anthony Hopkins screen performances.

I have always said if Bobby had been this great in the United States of America, he would have been taken from the playing field and placed onto the big screen playing the super-cool McQueen with his light grey suit, powder blue shirt, dark red tie and that 'Barnet' which made his appearance so outstanding.

At the end of the day, after the way Chelsea treated me – and Peter Osgood – Bobby could not have been more correct, for Ossie and I fought our corner and the only regret is that there was not the money around that there is today, so instead I settled for meeting the greatest man I have ever met in the game, Mr Tony Waddington, so money doesn't always buy you love, although it would have come in rather handy right at this minute. I could not have played any harder, for better or for worse, and could not have put my football any higher on the agenda than it always was!

Anyhow we were still just thirty-six hours away from the first leg at Stamford Bridge and this time it was Arsenal's Edu who was shooting the fat to the newspapers, something I had already warned John Terry and Frank Lampard about. The *Daily Star* covered their paper with 'We couldn't have got a better draw' with threequarters of the paper saying that CHELSEA HAVEN'T GOT ONE PLAYER WHO'D GET INTO OUR SIDE in an exclusive by Danny Fullbrook, going on to say that: Edu is risking a war of words with Chelsea by claiming that not one of their players as is as good as his Arsenal teammates.

The Brazilan is usually the unsung hero of Highbury, quietly going about his business.

SWAP

But with a Champions League quarter-final showdown against Chelsea to come tomorrow, he has decided to air his views.

And Edu insists he would not swap one player at Stamford Bridge for any of his Gunners' teammates – despite Chelsea having spent £22million on the likes of Damien Duff and Hernan Crespo.

Yet the midfielder's attitude is hardly surprising – after all, Arsenal have not lost to Chelsea since a meaningless League Cup tie in November 1998.

"When I look at the Chelsea team, I do not see a player that is better than anyone we have at Arsenal," said Edu, who scored a league winner at Stamford Bridge last month.

"We know we can beat them from the results in the last few years. This is a good draw for us. It could have been Real Madrid or AC Milan. And we do not really have to travel, so we will have fantastic support from our fans at the Bridge.

"But Arsenal have now proved this season we can go away and play anyone. There is no fear.

"Chelsea will be under much more pressure than us in this game on Wednesday, because they will be playing in their own stadium.

"If we score at Stamford Bridge we will know very clearly what we have to do at Highbury to reach the semi-finals. A match against the Blues for me always brings back good memories and in the Champions League these matches will be even better, because the taste of victory will be even sweeter.

"The team is playing with focus and there is a feeling we can do something great in Europe this season."

No wonder Edu feels like that, especially with Thierry Henry in his side.

The French striker has terrorised both the Premiership and Europe this season and Claudio Ranieri's side know they will have to put in one hell of a show to stop him from scoring.

Edu added: "Thierry Henry is the number one striker in the world in my opinion but we all work for the team.

"At the moment though, it is impossible to stop him.

"The key to the first match will be in our defence and holding the first attacks of the Chelsea team."

HOPELESS

"I am sure they will throw everything at us. They will know that the situation will become more hopeless if the goal does not arrive and that situation will be positive for us. Chelsea have had a lot of publicity this season. But, truly, up until now, what have they done?"

Edu has improved as rapidly as Frank Lampard, as for Chelsea, which makes it even more interesting in the engine room of these two battles, but it was Jimmy Floyd who hit back in this war of words by saying – in the same newspaper – that YOUR'E TOO COCKY with the same writer telling us that: Chelsea hit-man Jimmy Floyd Hasselbaink has accused Arsenal of becoming overconfident and arrogant. And the outspoken Dutchman has insisted that could cost them in their Champions League Battle of England.

The Gunners have not lost to their west London rivals in their last 16 meetings in all competitions. But fired-up Hasselbaink is convinced Chelsea are set to erase the pain of that run by winning the biggest showdown ever between the two sides.

Chelsea's Russian supreme Roman Abramovich has offered a bumper £2million bonus to his side for beating Arsenal and reaching the Champions League semi-finals.

Hasselbaink, however, says he is not interested in the money, preferring to concentrate on the glory of rumbling the Premiership leaders.

Speaking in Spain he said that, "It has been terrible losing to Arsenal so many times since coming to England.

"But as far as I am concerned, the moment has come for revenge and to break that record. I am convinced that we are going to beat them at Stamford Bridge and I would give anything to be the player who scores that goal."

CONFIDENT

"The Champions League is going to be different for us than the League or the Cup. Arsenal will arrive calm and be totally confident that they are superior to us. That is going to be their greatest mistake. As far as I am concerned, Arsenal have seemed to become arrogant by their success. For us these two European matches are going to be like two great finals.

"Roman Abramovich has promised a special bonus for us to eliminate Arsenal, but I do not want it for just reaching the semi-finals. We want to get to the final."

KENYON LIFTS RAN

Chelsea chief executive Peter Kenyon last night attempted to quell speculation about the future of boss Claudio Ranieri.

Ranieri had called on Kenyon and owner Roman Abramovich to break their silence earlier yesterday – and last night Kenyon did just that.

He said that, "This was an unprecedented and continuous media speculation about Claudio's future and false links to other managers is unhelpful to our manager and the players in the build-up to an important match in the Champions League.

"We wish to reiterate that Claudio Ranieri has over three years to run on his contract."

As the game edged nearer it was now the turn of John Terry to have his say with headlines, which read: WE CAN TERRY-FY GUNNERS.

John Terry insists Chelsea should stop worrying because Arsenal are not invincible – and neither is Thierry Henry. Chelsea have not beaten Arsenal for six years, but Terry believes a win this time would see them go on to win the Champions League.

He said, "Arsenal are not invincible – nor is Thierry Henry. So let's stop worrying about them and go out and beat them. I think this could be our year, so let's go out and do it. Yes, Thierry Henry has got everything. He's got pace, a great first touch, good movement and times his runs so well. He also has the ability to finish and overall he's the toughest striker I've played against. But, again, he's not invincible.

"And they're not unbeatable. They have great players throughout their team and have played well all year. But we know, on the night, we are as good as them and we've shown that in the games we have played against them already this season."

SCARE

Chelsea have already lost to Arsenal three times this season, but Terry still believes there is nothing in the tournament to scare them.

Even with Real Madrid likely to be waiting for them in the semi-final – the Spaniards face Monaco tomorrow – Terry thinks Chelsea can go all the way.

He said, "Why not?

"We've come a long way this season and I've watched some of the other teams on television and there is nothing to scare us. If we beat Arsenal, there's no reason why we can't go on to win it. We'd have no problems with Real in the next round. We're not going to get any easy sides at this stage of the competition and we have to take confidence from what we've done so far. It's the first time myself and some of the other players have played in this competition.

"But others like Marcel Desailly, Jimmy Floyd Hasselbaink, Claude Makelele and Hernan Crespo have plenty of Champions League experience. With our youth as well, that is a great blend."

VICTORY VIE: Patrick Vieira insists his Arsenal side are bracing themselves for a Chelsea onslaught tomorrow. Vieira knows Chelsea will be gunning for revenge and looking to end an amazing record, which has seen them go sixteen matches without a win against Arsene Wenger's team.

Vieira said that, "The Chelsea game is going to be a very difficult match. They will be determined to beat us because we have such a good record against them.

"Things can change very quickly in football, including winning streaks, and we will have to be at our best to get through. We will be ready for them."

WENG'S DUTCH COURAGE: Now it is Mario Melchiot who speaks out on the eve of this delicious upcoming match: Dutch international Mario Melchiot has given a revealing insight into how Arsenal have become such a dominant force. Melchiot, who joined Chelsea from Ajax five years ago, said he had noticed the similarities between the Gunners' game and the one made famous by the Dutch masters.

Melchiot believes that, although Arsene Wenger's approach is largely based on lightning quick counter attacks, Arsenal play football, which had been pre-programmed on the training ground.

SIMILARITIES

"At Ajax there was a lot of football, which was automatic, in that players go into certain positions for certain moves.

"It is practiced time and time again on the training ground, so you know exactly what to do in particular situations. With Arsenal you see that a lot.

"For example, you play a ball into the strikers and the midfielders move off it and when they do that, the wingers go deep.

"Arsenal have a lot of similarities to Ajax. The major difference is at Ajax we were not always playing on the counter-attack, whereas Arsenal often play on the break.

"They drop down and you attack them, then they suddenly come at you with pace. When you have such moves already worked out and then you have the sort of quality they have, you can understand why they are doing so well at the moment."

Arsenal and Chelsea face each other in the Champions League quarter-final, first leg tomorrow.

The Gunners have already beaten Chelsea three times this season but

Melchiot commented: "People will go on about the supposed psychological problem. But I believe that after you have gone through a number of games where you have failed to beat a team, eventually you become stronger because of it. This is a Champions League game, so it is different because we have not played them in the competition before.

"We always run like crazy against them but we'll be trying even harder this time. People have been having a go at us but you can't always play your best football. At the moment Arsenal can't do a thing wrong. You need a thick skin in this game because we were hammered after losing to Arsenal twice last month.

"Last year everyone was praising Arsenal, saying how wonderful they were, yet they slipped up."

RANIERI'S PLEA OVER RUMOURS
Chelsea boss speaks out in defence of his players

This was an exclusive by Ken Dyer on the evening of the big showdown: Claudio Ranieri believes raging speculation surrounding his future will eventually affect the performances of his Chelsea players.

As his team go into their biggest match of the season against Arsenal tomorrow night, he said that, "I hope it is not a distraction. The players were okay in training, but every day they see this and that – it must have an effect eventually."

There are unconfirmed reports today that the Chelsea manager made an emotional speech to his squad after training, telling them he will not be in charge next season.

Ranieri, talking to *Standard Sport* after he had seen his players, appealed to Chelsea to give him time to finish the job he had started.

He also insisted that the club should issue a statement over his future after dismissing the latest rumours that he will be replaced as 'rubbish'".

His demand for someone within the club to 'come out and defend us against all of this rubbish', was later answered by chief executive Peter Kenyon, although the statement stopped short of unequivocal backing.

Kenyon said that, "This wave of unprecedented and continuous media speculation about Claudio's future and false links to the managers is unhelpful to our manager and our players in the build up to an important match in the Champions League. We will not add to this speculation by responding and only wish to reiterate that Claudio Ranieri has over three years of his contract left to run.

"We are at an exciting stage of the season where we stand second in the Premiership

"And have the chance to advance to the semi-final of the Champions League.

"It is important that we all work closely together to maintain our momentum and challenge for honours at the highest level."

The Italian, who has a contract until 2007, compared his job with Arsene Wenger's at Arsenal and said that, "He has worked a long time with his players. He is calm and he is able to give his players time to adapt to a new culture. All managers need time. We have a good project at Chelsea and I hope I can conclude the job. I have a contract until 2007 so why not?

"I spoke with Roman Abramovich and Peter Kenyon and they both say that if it is any different they will tell me.

"At this time they are happy with me but I cannot believe this latest rubbish. This is not an attack on Ranieri but on the job we are doing here.

"But of course the club should say something if I'm under pressure. I want the club to say: 'This is all rubbish. Continue to work – not for me but for the players for all their sacrifices.'"

Sven Goran Eriksson, who was initially linked with the Chelsea job, is believed to have had more contract talks with the Football Association.

Meanwhile, Thierry Henry today insisted Chelsea's failure to beat Arsenal in the last sixteen matches is irrelevant to the outcome of their European clash.

"Those games don't matter," the Arsenal striker said. "We have never met in this competition so the record is clear in the Champions League. We're not looking beyond it. We may be only five games from putting our hands on the trophy but there is still a long way to go."

Running alongside: RELAXED CLAUDIO SEES THE FUNNY SIDE, AGAIN were the odds of his successor at Stamford Bridge, with: Sven Goran Eriksson leading the market at 7/4. It says that: The England coach has not yet signed the contract extension offered to him by the Football Association. A friend of Roman Abramovich, he has been closely linked with the Chelsea job since being photographed 'going for tea' at the Russian's London apartment last summer.

Ottmar Hitzfeld is quoted the same odds of 7/4: The Bayern Munich coach claims he did not say that Chelsea had made him an offer despite reports to the contrary in Germany. He is keen to take up the challenge of another big European club although his Bayern contract does not expire until 2005.

Martin O'Neill is next in the betting at 4/1: It appears only a matter of time before the Celtic manager takes on a major Premiership club – or Spurs. With a school of thought at Stamford Bridge tempted by a successful 'British style' manager, the former Leicester City boss would appear to fit the bill.

Arsene Wenger, not surprisingly is quoted at 20/1: Arsenal laughed off speculation that their inspirational manager is top of Chelsea's hit list. But could Wenger really resist the kind of wages Chelsea will be offering?

As usual, he will be linked with Real Madrid job next summer.

Ronald Koeman, the ex-Dutch captain, is an outsider at 33/1: The charismatic Ajax coach has already been touted as the next manager of Barcelona – where he enjoyed a successful playing career. He has impressed many with his assured transition to coaching and looks an interesting outside bet to replace Ranieri.

'TWENTY-FIRST CENTURY ROLLER-COASTER RIDE'

According to reports after the Tinkerman had meetings with Kenyon, Abramovich and his players, he was very jovial as if he had not got a care in the world. And so he should feel that way, for he is in a tremendous position where he cannot lose. He has been given a new bunch of players – that nobody knows who congregated – and sits being idolised by fans and players throughout Stamford Bridge. Some time ago he was looked at as something of a freak as Bates had to hire one of his gatemen to take Italian lessons so that he could not only communicate for him with the media but also report all that was said back to Old Grey Beard. That Ken Bates does not miss a trick and that is why he sacked Peter Osgood – I am told – after one of his spies reported back to him that Osgood had laughed at his expense in one of his question and answer evenings. Now we all know the banter that goes on in these gatherings, and if you cannot have a laugh with the guests then you might as well all stay at home. When I worked in Drakes Bar for Chelsea Football Club, I had a great relationship with one of the 'top men' at the Bridge, Peter Price and believe me I had a bad time standing in front of a couple of hundred irate fans – that was a pound a man for my work – as if I had just played in the match. They would be furious that they had not won anything for so long and wanted the answers off of me!

I really could have answered them if I was the manager but on that 'skinny' £200 a time I was not in any position to put my blood on the line. This was around the time when Hoddle was in charge and Matthew Harding was trying his utmost to bring big names to the Football Club he ate, drank and slept for. However, it was quite a relief when I was asked not to come anymore although my pal, Malcolm Molineux and me did enjoy the matches and meeting faces I had not seen for so very long.

A glass of wine in a box or two did not go amiss either, and if you knew what I had to face come post-match proceedings, you would have needed maybe something a little stronger, but back to the job at hand and this incredible fixture that is causing waves up and down the Kings Road in pubs, bars and restaurants alike.

There are as many Gunners in restaurants here now than ever before because once again it just goes to show Chelsea is the place, whether it be in the 'Swinging Sixties', the 'Sexy Seventies' the 'Orrible Eighties' the 'Naughty Nineties' or this rollercoaster ride with the Russian Revolution at the start of the twenty-first century. Yeah, things really have changed, but all the football world is asking, can Chelsea with all of their new found 'dosh' takeover and dominate like Arsenal, Manchester United, Liverpool and Leeds United before them?

PACE WITH GRACE

The *Evening Standard* showed a photograph of Thierry Henry in 'Working

Man's Ballet' like action. Underneath the quote says that, "Thierry's technical mastery is giving spectators the most enriching experience of their sporting lives."

Michael Henderson writes: Why Arsenal star is finest player in the world. But there was no question mark. He describes through his imagination of players being waterlike characters. He says that water is the one element that flows through our daily lives and what do you see?

For instance Kenny Dalglish is a river, perhaps, a majestic, teeming river, like the Rhine, sweeping past the Lorelei; Eric Cantona as a lake, sparkling like a million diamonds when the sun dances upon the waves but also reflecting the darker moods of the troubled sky. Denis Law was a waterfall, Jimmy Greaves a geyser. Among current players, Paul Scholes may be a secret spring. Emile 'Where's the goal?' Heskey, alas, is no more than a puddle.

Thierry Henry is an ocean. So vast is his repertoire, so convincing is the intimate welding of his head, heart, feet, that he can now do pretty much as he pleases – and it pleases him much. He is not carrying this Arsenal side, because there is one other great player, two others of exceptional quality and a handful of very good ones, but he is the one who provides its unique flavour.

He makes goals, he scores goals – and memorable ones, too. He adorns games and he changes games – as Cantona did, though not always in Europe. Perhaps it is better simply to say that he adorns the game. With the possible exception of Zinedine Zidane – and even that caveat shows how far Henry has progressed – he must now be considered the finest player in the world. Football supporters who fail to respond to Henry's brilliance – and by the extension Arsenal's transformation under Arsene Wenger – are not true supporters at all. They have changed English football irrevocably, but to leave a permanent mark upon the game, they must first win the champions League, which Liverpool made their private property when it was known as the European Cup and entry restricted to genuine champions.

No team deserves to win the world's premier club competition, for such titles have to be won the hard way, but only Chelsea fans are hoping that Arsenal are not England's representatives in the semi-finals.

It has been said before, but it needs to be stated firmly once more. The Gunners are playing football of such refinement, beauty indeed, that one can scarcely forbear to cheer. Watching them spin a golden thread across Highbury last Saturday, in the face of a ferocious wind that made the practice of handsome football a distant prospect, it was hard not to recall with a mirthless chuckle, that this was the club that gave up the world the unlovely Double-winning side of Peter Storey and Peter Simpson, from which the world did not withhold its defiance.

This was the club, even when Liam Brady was at his height, commonly associated with the dour victory and the grim draw, offered as a blood sacrifice to those high priests of anal retentiveness, Don Howe and George Graham. Such were the joys!

So the superb football that the Highbury crowd now takes for granted takes some getting used to.

As a grateful member of that crowd, no doubt as astonished as the rest of the country, said last Saturday: "No opportunity to watch this side must be wasted."

Certainly no opportunity to watch Henry in his coat of many colours should be overlooked. He has reached the stage, like George Best before him, Viv Richards, to use a handy comparison with another sport, when his technical mastery, married to the confidence that comes with knowledge and the sheer thrill of being alive, is giving spectators the most enriching experience of their sporting lives.

It is reflected most clearly in the way he holds himself. Has any footballer ever looked more graceful than Henry?

Not in an attendance-seeking, what-a-dandy-I-am sort of way. He simply looks more at home on the football field than the other 21 players who happen to be sharing it with him, although Patrick Vieira doesn't actually resemble a duffer. The other thing, of course, is his lacerating pace, which may well make some England defenders look old when France begin their defence of the European championship in June.

When a striker combines that poise and pace with the skill that Henry has on the ball, wherever he accepts possession, with the way he keeps the ball moving, with either foot, for the benefit of the side, and when he scores the kind of goals that Henry has made a habit of scoring, then he is entitled to be judged by the highest standards.

So how good is he?

Dalglish, most decent judges agree, was the last truly great player (as opposed to good, or very good) in English football. It is now clear that Henry is his heir, not in style – they could hardly be more different – but in his contribution to the wealth of the team and the discomfort of the opponents.

The breathtaking second goal he scored against Internazionale in that celebrated 5-1 victory in the San Siro, when he turned Javier Zanetti inside out before scoring left-footed, making an utter fool of an experienced international defender, has come to represent all Henry's formidable strengths in a single burst of inspiration. He may never score a finer goal, but he is having a jolly good go.

Arsenal are not perfect. Wenger's memory is selective, Ashley Cole is a petulant young cuss and Robert Pires goes to ground far too easily. But these are minor quibbles. Almost single-handedly, it seems, they are bringing the game into repute by daring to play football of a generosity and grace that puts a spring in the step of every spectator going to watch them.

It takes talent of a high order to do that. It also takes moral courage because it means risking failure. The Leeds United side that Don Revie managed, who did not lack talent, did lack courage and, as a result, failed to transform their potential into glory. Arsenal glory be, have opted to take the high road – and what a giddy adventure it is proving to be.

You don't have to look far to see what is wrong with English football and if you harboured any doubts, these nice chaps from West Ham will have banished them with their decorous behaviour at Millwall, although the crowd disturbance could just as easily have been t'other way round. It's too often a slum sport, with players, managers, chairmen and supporters all intent on claiming a piece of infamy they can call their own.

Yet at Highbury, the air smells of lavender. Thierry Henry has received the ball 40 yards out and all that separates him from the goal is a garden of primroses.

My opinion of Henry:

A man could come off the moon and tell you immediately that this is player is something very special, but when I hear of the complete player, I think people have to stop, think and don't get too excited because that is some statement. For starters, Thierry has no heading ability whatsoever and that for one makes one incomplete and if you were to run his strengths and weaknesses alongside George Best, you might even think again, again and again. George Best could do just about everything but played in a very different way and, whilst he was shaking off defenders he was pulling Miss Worlds the very same day. I am not one for comparisons for I believe players have their very own way of translating the game over to the public, for instance Pele could not be compared to Best, Maradona, Greaves or Cryuff, and then there were the footballers' footballers like Franz Beckenbauer, the most graceful wing-half converted to centre-back one will ever set eyes on. The 'Keizer' even made Glenn Hoddle look like just another inside-forward, but again Franz could not head the ball. Anyhow, Thierry Henry is a wonderful player who has been converted – by his very intelligent coach – from a winger to the spearhead of Arsenal's every attack.

His confidence is his big 'asset' as most players of such wonderful talents, and this springs Peter Osgood to mind for I have never seen a player with the confidence of the 'King of Stamford Bridge', only George Best is comparable when he really was in full flow and proving to the football world in those early days of the sixties that there was a contender to Pele's crown.

Having that kind of confidence is the reason for players like that scoring the most spectacular of goals and these three players all have this amazing quality to do so.

If only Chelsea had Osgood in these two matches coming up, then we could all see for ourselves what the real word 'complete' meant!

And Chelsea's chances of that elusive victory would be so much more in their own grasp!

The 22nd of March 2004 was a big day at Leeds United for all the reasons that would have Don Revie turning in his coffin. A new consortium have saved their skin and ex-Leeds United and Scotland winger – very much a part of the club it seems these days – said "A lot of people have left this club very wealthy. They probably were carried away with a bit of success but it was Leeds who were left to suffer."

And that came from the heart of one of the real good guys of that team of 'gangsters' and boy, could he hit the ball. Just ask Peter Bonetti when he thumped one of the hardest shots I have ever seen at Villa Park in that semi-final when Tony Hateley headed a Charlie Cooke cross past Gary Sprake to take Chelsea through to the 1967 FA Cup Final to face Tottenham Hotspurs at Wembley. I was sitting right in line when the free kick was rolled about fifteen yards into Peter's path and the rest is history. Good for Chelsea and bad for Leeds as the referee said, he had not blown his whistle, it could not have happened to a nicer bunch of lads!

I recall 'Catty' taking off as the ball was coming back out of the net, such was the force behind the Leeds' player's hammer blow, but Chelsea and all their marvellous fans breathed the biggest sigh of relief when the 'Mug in the Middle' pointed for the kick to be retaken!

KENYON BEAMS

Then – on this day before the match – Harry Harris wrote that, 'Sven Goran Eriksson would cause shock waves inside Soho Square, if as I suspect, he informs the FA that he is quitting after the European Championships.'

Damien Duff took most of the headlines as the man who holds the key to unlock the Gunners' defence – in several newspapers – but in one in particular, Duff said that he was scared of the Gunners. A lengthy lay-off after a shoulder injury sustained at Loftus Road some weeks ago Duffs' return is timely, but when asked about the prospect of tackling the rampant Arsenal in tomorrow's Champions League quarter-final at Stamford Bridge, he simply said it was 'frightening.'

Duff will surely need the run-out against a bang in form Gunners but at least it will give Chelsea another option as they have been relying so much on goals through the middle of the field, mainly through the ever impressive and inspirational Frank Lampard.

Beside a photograph of Peter Kenyon 'beaming' with laughter as if he had just won the lottery and now had more money than his employers, Mick Dennis of the *Daily Express* wrote a good piece, very short, but very much to the point: There are several ways to prepare for a big, midweek football match. Some encourage players to have a nap or report for a massage in the afternoon. Others partake in light exercises.

But nobody recommends undermining the manager and demotivating the players. Yet, incredibly, that is how chief executive Peter Kenyon has approached tomorrow's Champions League showdown with Arsenal.

Last week Kenyon spoke to Sunday newspaper journalists. And the papers all had pieces explaining why Claudio Ranieri will be sacked at the end of the season. Reasons given included the suggestion that Chelsea had played dull football under the Italian.

There were no direct quotes from Kenyon, but it was clear that he had briefed against his manager and team. Kenyon gave one other interview, to Sky

Sports News, in which he said that in the quarter-finals of the Champions League 'you can smell brasso'.

But there is another smell coming from Stamford Bridge. The way they are treating Ranieri stinks.

Chelsea have been in the Champions League once before. Four years ago they lost in the quarter-finals against Barcelona, Rivaldo scoring twice in the Nou Camp.

This time Kenyon has done the damage – before kick-off. Thanks to him, Ranieri wears the expression of a boss marking time in his job and the players know, regardless of any facesaving statement yesterday, that whatever they achieve, a new man will be installed this summer.

Ranieri is a dead man walking. He knows it. His players know it.

What a shabby way to treat a decent man and what a crassy, inept way of preparing for a massive match.

TERRY AT THE PALACE

John Terry leads out Chelsea tomorrow for the biggest game of his career – and arguably the most important London derby in the history of the game. The outcome will be worth so much more than the mere millions and billions that the Chelsea owner possesses. The only other time Chelsea staged a Champions League quarter-final, first-leg clash, Terry – then a rookie defender – was turning out for David Platt's stiffs before only fifty people at Crystal Palace Athletics Stadium. For Terry, that rainsoaked evening became a landmark for the best young centre-back in Britain. For many fans it was the greatest night of their lives – April 5th 2000 – as the Blues beat Spanish giants Barcelona 3-1 before travelling to Spain to get turned over 5-1 in one of the craziest matches ever seen, with the great Rivaldo notching two super strikes for the team who have since been overtaken by Real Madrid in both La Liga and Europe, but things can still change!

After all, the new owner of Chelsea looked at the Spaniard's match on his satellite TV and decided that not only was there money to be made, but football really is 'the beautiful game', also it seems at this moment in time he does not understand – for all his financial clout – that every 'Walk in the Park' in our game is a summer's day and all the kids have a Frisbee!

In other words as the boss – Frank Sinatra – would say. In other words!

The Chelsea Captain swore that the next time Chelsea played in such a match he would be at the heart of their defence and, boy, is he the heart of the defence. Terry is ultra-confident in both his and his team's ability this time around and is playing out of his skin, so much so, that he defies logic, such is his super-cool attitude and only Sol Campbell can be talked of in the same breath and surely the Swede must have made him an automatic choice for Portugal this coming summer!

I certainly think he is the best and is improving at such a rate of knots there is no telling just where he will not only lead Chelsea but England as well.

Well, he swore to be there and in twenty-four hours he will be facing the awesome Thierry Henry and Robert Pires, as the Gunners set out to destroy Chelsea for the third time this season, but let's not forget they have pushed them right down to the wire on each occasion and only a couple of bizarre errors – one by Cuisine – have stopped them from taking anything out of their showdowns with England's finest football team.

CHELSEA'S TIME MUST COME SOON!

The Tinkerman at this moment in time is in a situation that looks so much unhealthier than Arsene Wenger, but he keeps coming up trumps against all of those that are against him. I myself thought that the man was a fraud when he first came here, but that is not insulting him, simply stating that Chelsea at that time did not know – after all these years under both Bates and Mears – just who to employ to make this Football Club – one that could have had the kind of decade of success that major clubs have had before them – but who am I to have such knowledge?

Nobody!

SADLER GIVES IT TO YOU STRAIGHT

John Sadler of the *Sun* is a straight talker and a wonderful writer and over the years has been the only journalist the great Brian Cough has confided in. On the eve of this contest he writes: A lesser man than Claudio Ranieri would do something dramatic and very satisfying this week.

He would tell Roman Abramovich where to stick the manager's job at Chelsea.

Not at the end of the season, either, just before the confrontation with Arsenal at Stamford Bridge tomorrow.

With a suitable parting shot to the club's seemingly dissatisfied owner: "You think you can spend £122million and the team beats everybody? You want a new manager? I make it easy for you. I go home and you take my place tonight. Eets OK?"

Wouldn't that be luvverly!

Unfortunately, Ranieri is too much of a gentleman to wash his hands of his contracted managerial responsibility. More's the pity.

VOCAL

For Chelsea in general, and Abramovich in particular, do not deserve a manager of Ranieri's impeccable manners and talent.

They have not appreciated or understood the size and complexities of the task they gave him in expecting unity and total commitment from a bunch of expensive strangers who would not be guaranteed regular places in the team.

I do not include Chelsea's fans in this. Their support for the Italian has been consistent and vocal, declaring their objection to Sven Goran Eriksson, or anybody else replacing him.

But their protests still fall on deaf ears among Chelsea's arrogant hierarchy. The fact that yesterday Ranieri got the players together and told them he was off at the end of the campaign shows he knows the game is up.

He appealed publicly stated support from those who control the club. But Chelsea's attempt at reassurance convinced no one. Ranieri's insecurity was clear when he said: "The club should come out and support me. Not for my sake, but for the players, for all they have sacrificed, all they have fought for."

Still not a word from Abramovich though, instead we heard from chief executive Peter Kenyon of a 'wave of unprecedented and continuous media speculation about the club's future and false links with other managers'. When Chelsea have done much of the card marking themselves.

We know Ranieri has a contract for a further three years or more. What was needed was an unequivocal statement of support from Abramovich himself.

Rather than a warm embrace for their beleaguered manager, Chelsea offered little more than cold comfort.

The leaks have kept flowing. If it is not Eriksson replacing Ranieri after this season, it will be Ottmar Hitzfeld. If not him, Carlo Ancelotti or Fabio Capello, maybe Martin O'Neill. As for Arsene Wenger, somebody is having a laugh.

In normal circumstances we would opt for wishing Arsene Wenger, somebody is having a laugh. In the meantime, long-suffering Ranieri has continued to smile and steer Abramovich's overloaded collection of stars in to second place in the Premiership and to within two matches of the Champions League semi-finals.

Two decidedly difficult matches loom against Wenger's Arsenal.

In normal circumstances, we would opt for wishing Arsenal a place in those semis because of the way they have played throughout this remarkable season, as Wenger has created arguably the finest club side ever produced in England.

***

FIRED

And it is nothing like one-sided an issue as that in this double-header. It is now a clash between integrity and insanity, dignity versus disrepute.

Nobody wants to see a Russian walk into English football with a mountain of money and buy immediate success. Certainly not the Champions League at the first time of asking.

And Chelsea's appalling treatment of Ranieri has divided the nation's allegiance tomorrow night and for the return at Highbury.

There has been a widely-held belief that Ranieri could win the Champions League and still be fired.

That would be so unjust as to warrant an FA disrepute charge – but it seems it would indeed happen.

It is why, at a push, I join those hoping Arsenal represent this little island of ours in the last four of the Champions League.

Especially, if Ranieri walked out on Abramovich prior to the most important match in Chelsea's history, to the certain prospect of fresh employment in the Premiership or abroad.

STOP DUFF
BRAVE SOLDIER KNIFED BY THE ROMAN ARMY

The day had come and the two big headlines in the *Sun* leading up to this evening's Champions League crunch match were about the Tinkerman fighting off, not only the enemy in red shirts but also in blue inside of the offices at Stamford Bridge. Whilst this was going on, the Gunners' manager made it quite clear that the return of Damien Duff caused him the most concern about these two extremely difficult and demanding cup-ties. The Arsenal boss said that, "He is the one we have to keep quiet." Following on with, "I would say Duff adds something to them – he is a major danger. He has had a great season and can run at you, provides crosses and goals."

Arsenal face what Wenger calls the biggest fortnight in the football club's history. Ashley Cole repeated his boss's words by saying that, "Chelsea are a great team and when we played them he was their best player. He has been hit by injuries this season but now he is fit again it will make it tough. The likes of Duff, Hernan Crespo and Adrian Mutu can turn a game just like that. There is a lot of pressure on us. Everyone is thinking the run has to end because they haven't beaten us for so many years." The call of 'arrogance' by Jimmy Floyd had the Arsenal boss saying "I don't feel that we have become arrogant. But you have to accept what people say. I feel that to repeat performances for 29 matches like we have in the Premiership you need humility. If you think you can walk on water, you will sink very quickly. Before, we did not know how to win in Europe. But our confidence has never been as high as it is now. Our basis is quite strong but football is not predictable. Chelsea are a good side and we need a top class performance.

"We are favourites because we have beaten Chelsea before, but you could say there was no pressure on us because we were 99 per cent out of the competition. It is the biggest fortnight in the club's history. There are not many times when you are playing for the league, you are in the Champions League quarter-finals and the semi-final of the FA Cup."

He carried on by saying that, "United seem so far away, I don't even realise we are playing then on Sunday, that's just how big this match is.

"We want to take this chance because we feel that last time against Valencia it was very tight. You don't get these chances often. I've not had to tell the players that because they know. For them it's been long enough."

The story that Claudio has been knifed by the Roman army runs next to a picture of the Tinkerman looking as if he really needs a friend. Steve Howard wrote that, "Claudio Ranieri wore a navy blue suit and a shirt open to the neck. All the more easy, you thought, for the Chelsea hierarchy to apply the noose, but the Italian was fighting to the end as he prepared for his club's Champions League quarter-final showdown at Stamford Bridge tonight.

The Chelsea boss said that, "I will not be resigning. I am not stupid. I am not crazy.

"I am a gladiator – like my boys in this team. I have some of that English spirit too. And when I fight, I do it face to face." Touché.

In the old days of the Imperial Rome, gladiators would enter the Colloseum, turn towards the Emperor, and repeat the fabled fighting motto: "Those about to die salute Caesar."

It is not, as it sounds, a death sentence. A heroic performance and they were spared. Ranieri, though, never stood a chance. For the thumbs down were delivered the moment Roman Abramovich walked into Stamford Bridge.

Now as he stands on the brink of Chelsea's finest hour, success or failure is of little consequence to him personally.

What an extraordinary situation to arrive at.

Tonight we should be celebrating one of the greatest milestones in domestic football – an all-English meeting in Europe's premier club competition. The only time we went down this road before was in 1978/79 when Brian Clough's Nottingham Forest stunned defending champions Liverpool with a 2-0 aggregate victory.

Clough would go down in folklore by winning the cup that very same season and retaining it the next. Bob Paisley would return to win the competition for a third time – and another four league championships. No such luck for Ranieri, though.

Even if he steers his side past an Arsenal team – unbeaten in 16 matches against Chelsea – and into the semi-finals, it will not be enough.

Even if he wins the trophy, it will not save him.

At the moment when Ranieri's name should be shouted from the rooftops of West London, he is already dangling from one of the Stamford Bridge rafters.

For Abramovich's insatiable demands and Kenyon's limitless ambition dictate that the Italian is not good enough for them. Perhaps the new chief executive should be renamed Grand Kenyon.

Yet Ranieri took it all in good spirit and with his customary humour as he faced the media in the bar of the Imperial College training ground at Harlington yesterday.

Though I did notice he was in no hurry to fork out £2 for the Red Russian that was on sale.

SHARKS

Addressing the Press pack he affectionately refers to as 'my sharks', he said: "I see I am known as Dead Man Walking.

"And that is how I will continue. Step by step, day by day. That has always been my philosophy. I am an Italian manager and have been brought up in a world where you win one game, draw the next, lose the third…and then you are sent home.

"I was asked when I first came here if it worried me that Chelsea had so many managers. I said that in Italy we sometimes have six a season. That is the culture. For me, I look only at tomorrow, tomorrow and tomorrow. The pressure on me is not important. But I am an emotional man and it's important for me to feel the support of my players and the fans.

"It is not important to have support of other people within the club...."

He had talked earlier about having time to build solid foundations – the four years or so Alex Ferguson had been granted when he needed it most. He laughed his hyena laugh

And said that, "You must build very quickly now – everything, the foundations, the first floor and the roof garden!

"All in twenty-four hours.

"But it takes time. I know that because I am a man who works with his feet on the ground."

Except he has had his legs cut from under him. He also joked that, until this season, he had watched the Champions League only on TV.

"Well, apart from at Highbury," he said. "I had a good time with the Arsenal fans but this is so much better."

PACK

He finished by admitting that, whatever he may have achieved this season, it would never have been good enough. He even told his wife Rosanna on the day Abramovich arrived, that she should be prepared to pack at any time, and that his own personal destiny had already been decided. But not that of Chelsea's.

He said that, "AC Milan and Arsenal are the best teams in Europe. But if we can prevent Arsenal scoring we will go to Highbury with a good chance. I am looking forward to seeing what destiny has in store for this club."

Should it be masterminding the downfall of Arsene Wenger's 'superteam' then Ranieri might respond with some sign language of his own.

No, not the thumbs up. Two fingers!

DEAD ON THE FIRST OF JULY

Claudio Ranieri admits he knew he was finished at Chelsea the minute Roman Abramovich took over.

Ranieri, who takes on Arsene Wenger's Arsenal tonight, revealed that: "Right from the very beginning, from the first of July, I have known that even if I had won everything this season I could still be going home in the summer. That will not be a surprise for me."

Russian billionaire Roman Abramovich completed his sensational takeover on the first of July. Two days later, Sven Goran Eriksson was pictured visiting the oil tycoon's home along with top agent Pini Zahavi. Now the Blues have made it clear Ranieri will be axed even if Chelsea overcome Arsenal and go on to win the Champions League.

Ranieri insisted that: "None of this is new for me. I first heard rumours on the third of July. There is nothing I can do about them but continue in my job. A manager in my position must continue to work and not listen to anything else."

Players have been quietly advised to keep quiet. But skipper John Terry said that: "Every player is 100% behind Claudio. He has done a fantastic job here."

I DREAM OF BEING LIKE PATRICK VIEIRA

Under a photograph of Frank Lampard, with his head back on the sofa in a trance, were the headlines of above. About halfway through lunch on Monday, Frank Lampard is disturbed by the shrill of his mobile phone. "Frank, I just rang to tell you" the voice on the line says. "In the players' player of the year awards we voted for you. The whole dressing room."

The caller was Patrick Vieira and Lampard is chuffed.

"It's a great honour and nice of Patrick to tell me," he smiles. " It just goes to show the bond of respect between the players."

That Vieira should be speaking to Lampard at all, let alone two days before their sides meet in tonight's mouth-watering Champions League quarter-final, might surprise fans of both Chelsea and Arsenal.

Their burgeoning friendship is largely down to Steve Kutner, the agent they share. "We have met up recently a couple of times and get on well. I think we are going to go out for dinner with our girlfriends soon."

Such friendship seems unlikely after their first few encounters – when Lampard was a young colt at West Ham, and Vieira just beginning to make a name for himself at Highbury. "We had a few problems, me and him. I pushed him over when I was nineteen and he kicked me in the groin."

The memory is a painful one. "The stud marks were there for ages, it looked terrible. That carried on for a couple of years."

Now their relationship is very different. "I respect him and he respects me."

Lampard has been seeing a lot of Vieira lately. On the pitch. Off the pitch. On the TV. And sometimes even in his dreams. The image of the Arsenal midfielder racing towards the Chelsea goal to score at Stamford Bridge last month is one which still causes some discomfort. His admiration for him is almost unqualified. "If you are not at your best then he will eat you alive," says Lampard. "He not only has the quality, but has the experience now as well. He's got those long legs that tackle you and drag the ball round you. He always comes through in the big games, and he has the ability to surprise you as well. He was the last person you expected to see running onto a (Dennis) Bergkamp pass at the Bridge to score."

So how good is he?

"He's the best all-round midfielder. Steven Gerrard has been fantastic recently and Roy Keane is still brilliant in the big games. But Patrick is the man."

So did Lampard vote for Vieira?

"Thierry Henry," he answers without apology, and it is immediately clear that Lampard has as much time for the brilliant French striker as for his midfield compatriot.

"A lot of people look at Henry and think he's an arrogant man, the way he plays sometimes with that style of his. But always in the tunnel he shakes your hand, as if he knows you, and asks how you are. It's a measure of the man. For me, he is probably the best player in the world at the moment."

Lampard's admiration for Arsenal as a team is unequivocal. "When you are on the pitch playing against them, you don't see a weakness.

"They've got talent, team spirit and fight – everything really. I look at their team and I see strength. You get the feeling they know what the others are doing. There's a telepathy to them."

So how good are they?

"They are the best club team since I have been involved in football, the Manchester United team of a few years ago with Cantona, a young David Beckham and the rest. But overall this team is a bit special and it's the best."

That Chelsea should be playing in a game of tonight's stature hardly looked likely last May, when the club were days, minutes, away from financial meltdown. Then their world was turned upside down by the arrival of Roman Abramovich.

"I was in Vegas on holiday, lying by the pool last summer, " remembers Lampard, "and Rio (Ferdinand) rang and said that there was a billionaire taking over Chelsea. He told me this geezer was really rich and was going to buy everyone and I was a goner, but I took no notice. A week later I came back and it was all true."

At that time Lampard was 24, had established himself as a reliable Premiership midfielder and won 11 England caps. But he knew the arrival of Abramovich and his money meant his place would come under threat.

"I said to myself you can either go look for another club, or become a better footballer and play every game. I decided to become a better player."

The extraordinary thing is, he has. The Arsenal dressing room are not the only ones to regard Lampard as one of the players of the season in which he has missed just one game, in the Carling Cup.

How has he done it?

Lampard insists he has not changed anything in particular, but is adamant that one man deserves as much credit as himself, his manager, (at least for the moment) Claudio Ranieri.

The Italian has always placed great emphasis on "intelligent players" and in Lampard he knew he had signed one of great natural, ability and intellect, but over this season Lampard has become more mature and more able to handle different situations.

"It's not just been this season, but over the past three years Claudio's helped me." He reveals. "He's made me much more aware tactically. I was too naïve for Champions League football when I came here but now I know I can compete at that level. I have matured a lot mentally. A significant part of the game is in the mind – confidence and awareness. I knew I had the ability but I knew I had to learn.

"The most important thing Claudio did was take me aside when I first came to the club. I loved to run forward at any opportunity and scored forty goals in four seasons at West Ham, but he explained to me that I shouldn't run all of the time. The difference is making the right decisions and he has taught me how to do that.

"He's a good man. He's strong but fair. He talks a lot about the team being his family and he protects us."

Family indeed. The joke around Stamford Bridge is that the two are so close, Ranieri could be Lampard's surrogate father ("Yes he is" says Frank without embarrassment).

Whether Ranieri will be around to pick the team next season is a daily debate, and while the players' respect for the manager is obvious, there is always a genuine affection for the man who seems likely to end his tenure as Chelsea boss in the summer.

Abramovich remains a mystery figure to most, but not to those who play football for him. The Russian sees the players after almost every game and his demeanour is rarely influenced by results.

"If we have won, he shakes your hand and if you've lost, he is the same," says Lampard. "He's always there and he has never shouted, bawled or complained that he has spent all of this money. He comes to the training ground and sits in on meetings with a translator. It's great for the lads to see that he is not just a figurehead who doesn't care about the players or the results.

"He speaks to you. For instance, if you have an injury or a gash, hew will come right up and see if you're OK and other times he will say "s★★★ result" and maybe that we should have done that a bit better. His English is very broken but he can say a few words. I have heard him say "s★★★ game" a few times."

Criticism is something Lampard has had his fair share of, and he's not shy owning up to his mistakes. Moving to Chelsea was possibly the best decision he has made, though he is indebted to his family for their help in his transformation from West Ham fledgeling to Premiership superstar.

"Moving away from home helped me mature," he says. "My whole West Ham life seems a million years ago and I don't mean that disrespectfully. Obviously, when I left there I wasn't happy about certain things, like giving up pie and chips for lunch. The time had come where I had to move on. I had been playing under my uncle (Harry Redknapp) and my dad. There's only so far you can go with that relationship and I knew I needed to go and play with better players, a bigger club and more pressure."

He and his father, the real one that is, remain extremely close, and having left West Ham himself, Frank senior now watches his son in virtually every game.

"To say he helps me is an understatement. He is always on at me – in a good way. When I was younger it was different because if I had a bad game, he would get the hump.

"We speak more as adults now. I ring him before and after training and we talk about things. He asks me if I had trained hard: "Did you do this, did you get some shots in?"

"He's mellowed a touch."

With two dads looking after him the situation should be ideal. It does have its comic moments, though, as he sometimes receives two different sets of instructions.

Perhaps he should listen to a third voice, his Spanish girlfriend Elen. The pair have been together for nearly two years, more than enough time to offer her opinion. "She likes to think she's helped improve me as a player. Sometimes she says good things and other times she hasn't a clue, but she's the first to criticise me."

And he takes it?

"She's from Barcelona," says Lampard with a smile. "She thinks she knows all about football."

'A WORD WITH DAD'

I must admit I enjoyed writing that piece and hearing of how much young Frank has matured, not really having to read it because I see it in his play. He has improved dramatically since coming over to Chelsea to make my old number eight shirt his very own. I had a very similar situation where my father was so instrumental in my making the grade, just as my old mate Frank Senior has his very talented son.

Once my father had led me through my first three seasons at Stamford Bridge – and many years before that – he passed me over to Mr Tony Waddington who I had a very similar relationship with, only mine in those days was social as well as professional and my manager improved me both as a player and a person, by giving me the kind of responsibility that I would have never have received under the management of Dave Sexton at Chelsea. One has to move on as Frank says and, to be quite honest, the West Ham support-ers were very unfair towards the two Lampards and one Harry Redknapp, because of them being family, when things went wrong I would sit in despair as they were the first targets for such abuse. So Frank was correct in his decision to leave so that he could go out and prove himself on his own merit with a complete stranger, and I hope one or two Hammers have forgiven these people for doing their utmost at Upton Park and finally showing just what a job they did keeping them just behind the Champions League contenders. My friendship with the three of them remains, although I don't see much of the two Franks but do my utmost to get to see Harry when my medical condition allows. So Frank now wears that great number eight shirt worn by Jimmy Greaves, something I was always aware of in my days at the Bridge.

I once got a little close to young Frank and remember being in a Bar over his way with his father and a couple of other friends, and pulled him to one side, telling him if he wanted any help through that coming summer, I would take him over Victoria Park and work with him. I had my ideas about this up and coming young player but to be quite honest he has simply amazed me with his rapid all round progress, something I was talking about to his father earlier today. But that summer I went to Bermuda and got married and from that day until my accident some six months later, my life was going downhill and that would not have been the best environment for him to be in, although once I get my head down into something I love doing I become a different person. Like all the great characters I enjoy writing about, we live and breathe the game of football. I believe I would have helped Frank loads and I know just how influential his father has been in his career so far. My son Anthony was signed by Harry as Apprentice so I had days there when the boys were training, and I would watch my boy over one side and keep a slight look out for young Frank who was finding his way through at that time with players like Hartson and Berkovic and then Ian Wright – be it a short while – then the great Di Canio.

So he had to make his mark around such fine players as these and that is not easy when your uncle and father are picking the team, but he was strong and it shows now that he has benefited from that experience. He is correct and Harry and Frank will agree that a still young Frank could only go so far with them at the helm. So it was no surprise really when I spoke to Frank senior – on the telephone – and he told me that Chelsea and Leeds United wanted his boy and asked for my opinion. I was flattered because Frank has handled Frank with kid gloves – not taking that the wrong way – in the way he was so focused on his son's progress – and knew that nothing less than a hundred and ten per cent would be good enough if he was to fulfil his dream of playing for his country. But how I wish young Jamie could have overcome his tremendously difficult times with horrific injuries – and could have made the perfect midfield duo in the middle of the England team. One day Frank senior bought his son a pair of spikes to help him with his five and ten yard bursts, which was correct because that would help him win knock-downs and latch onto balls outside of his opponents' goal and within shooting range. He has perfected the art of latching onto loose balls and hits the target with an incredible ratio of goal-bound shots and when he hits them they stay hit. Frank also gave my boy a pair of spikes, which was also correct, but young Anthony was never helped by his mother, who should have kept her nose out of the football side of his life. She began complaining that Joe Cole was getting more playing time than Anthony and I tried to explain that he should use that as 'motivation' to improve, just as Frank has done. When Frank left West Ham, supporters at Upton Park believed that Joe Cole would be further up the list of runners for an England shirt than Frank, so they must eat humble pie and for once applaud young Lampard for his brilliant progress, even when one Juan Sebastian Veron arrived for a hefty £18million. Frank's season to date has been remarkable, and I'll never forget whilst hospitalised in the Royal London Hospital a couple of close friends and one family member – who must remain anonymous for the love I have for them – were cursing the signing of Frank Lampard.

I explained on several occasions that Frank Lampard was being played in a way that was foreign to him and once he was slotted into that position, just inside of the right-sided player they would see an entirely different footballer. They certainly are not cussing him now!

As for Frank senior's telephone call, I simply said that going to Chelsea is Frank's opportunity of a lifetime and my old mate thanked me, although he already knew what my answer would be and now Frank wears that Chelsea number eight shirt that Greaves and I wore and let's not forget that the great Charlie Cooke didn't do too badly when first wearing it before I got into the team.

And speaking of Charlie, I heard that he had said on the radio after watching Chelsea play earlier this season that 'how much young Frank Lampard reminded him of a young Alan Hudson.'

And that was without us ever getting to work together over Victoria Park in the east end of London, in that summer at a time that changed the course of my life. I thought my life would change with my wedding coming up in Bermuda, my autobiography 'The Working Man's Ballet' being released, and my writing for a great boss and friend at the *Sporting Life* – Tom Clarke – going well in both the racing and football circles around the country. This, I thought, would be a new springboard into the future of the rest of my days here, but a 'nutty' foreign driver had other ideas and I spent eight and a half weeks in the Intensive Trauma Unit followed by being hospitalised for the near entirety of the year of 1998. I have never been a 'lucky' person – missing FA Cup Finals and World Cups through freak injuries – but this really took 'unlucky' onto a different plain!

'HERE WE GO AT LAST'

So here we go: It's 7.45pm and Stamford Bridge is throbbing with excitement and expectation as the two teams take to the field and I am seated in my usual seat at the Grosvenor Club amongst a house full of Bluenoses. This was the time for all the talking to stop and there was plenty of that pre-match!

The red hot atmosphere could be felt inside this drinking hole, as Chelsea once again stole the lead from a team they were finding it almost impossible to overcome, they got into the reds from the very beginning and it paid off when Eidur Gudjohnsen cashed in on a terrible mistake by German goalkeeper Jens Lehmann and that started the Gunners' machine rolling at a different rate of knots as they knew that an equaliser would be invaluable in the return in two weeks time. The headlines went like this: The *Express* saying that the game was WORTHY OF PAT ON THE BACK: and that CHELSEA FALL SHORT AGAIN: with Ranieri gets stirring display he demands but the

Blues lose initiative as Pires cancels out Gudjohnsen's super strike: The *Sun* went: BOB THE BUILDER: as PIRES FIXES IT AFTER JENS BLUNDER: with ENGLAND'S BATTLE OF EUROPE: and TINKY N PERKY: Also that Rom red with shame as fans salute Ranieri: In the *Sun* as well was a photograph of Marcel Desailly being sent off and saying that WE'VE BLOWN IT: The French international says that: BLUES FAILURE TO NAIL WOBBLING GUNNERS WILL COST US DEAR: A great big photograph on the back page of Pires heading his goal with John Terry just a step behind, in the *Daily Mail* was underneath DEADLOCKED and Titanic battle will go all the way after Pires header saves Arsenal: Inside was that PIRES PUNCTURES THE BLUE BALLOON and ADVANTAGE ARSENAL AS RANIERI HAS IT ALL TO DO.

At the bottom of the newspaper an exclusive by Mario Melchiot saying that WE CAN WIN DOUBLE: The *Mail* also said that WENGER FACES STARK CHOICES IN PURSUIT OF TREBLE DREAM: The *Standard* said simply that ARSENAL DRAW and PIRES HEADER GIVES WENGER ADVANTAGE AS BLUES LACK BELIEF: inside of the *Standard* Ian Chadband wrote this piece, after the headlines of BRIDGE OF SIGHS and RANIERI FANS NOW KNOW THAT ROCKY ROAD LIES IN FRONT OF THEM: They began singing their gladiator's name with gusto and ended by telling Mr Eriksson in the nicest possible way that he wasn't wanted. For six heady minutes, they even roared their belief that Arsenal's first command-ment − Chelsea shall not beat us − was about to be dismantled. Ultimately though, as the Blues' band trekked home up the Fulham Road, their voices of defiance seemed to have given way to the merest hint of resignation. Arsenal had once again turned their home into the Bridge of sighs. Which is probably as much as anything why it couldn't live up to it's billing. London's grandest footballing derby of all!

Well, it was engrossing enough fare at Stamford Bridge but one which, for the neutral, probably needed a stirring and unexpected outcome. Chelsea's triumph over a quite exceptional side to truly bring the event alive. The problem was that it felt as I we had been here before. The fourth meeting this season and yet another points win for Arsenal. Of course, the home fans could all console themselves at Fulham Broadway that the tie was still wide open, that Arsenal could be ruffled out of their stride, that Thierry Henry could be shackled.

So why did they all look as if they all missed the last tube then?

The main ingredient missing last night was the sudden death edge that great sporting occasions demand.

Dressing up an old fashioned London derby in fancy new European clothes made it no less frenetic, but the drama was somehow muted by the gradual realisation that two very competent defences were going to ensure the definite action would have to wait for Highbury.

For all the exotic overseas talent and technical excellence on view, this somehow felt a very British affair – sort of Champions League brought to you by Bovril.

When has there been a Champions League game quite as busy as this, with such hectic, congested midfield, battling, offering such little time and scope for real expression – although the splendid Edu succeeded best of all?

You knew it was going to be a bit different when Wayne Bridge powered into the box, got brushed by Kolo Toure and decided, disgracefully, not to fall theatrically to the floor.

Yet the only time when it felt as if we might be about to witness a game to match the hype came in those few minutes early in the second half after Jens Lehmann's wanderings – what is German for 'safe hands'? – allowed Eidur Gudjohnsen to cash in. I'd not seen the Bridge erupt so gleefully since they put five past Manchester United a few years back. Seconds later, Adrian Mutu was denied a tap-in by Toure's crucial interception. Then Lehmann spilled a Frank Lampard strike and Damien Duff nearly converted the subsequent rebound. As they kept pouring forward, the bloke next to me in the West Stand triumphantly trumpeted the fatal judgement "We've got them."

He should have known you've never got Arsenal these days. Last year's version, maybe, but the steel of this team is now every bit as striking as their artistry and cunning.

That they should survive six minutes seemed quite routine. Yes, but Robert Pires with a decisive header?

Hail a team who can simultaneously deal in predictability and surprises.

This equaliser quite knocked the wind out of the occasion just when it was getting interesting following yet another chorus of the evening's theme tune, "There's only one Ranieri."

How bizarre that this purely parochial affair should end up mainly as a vehicle to plea for an endangered Roman monument!

At one point, the songs of praise had been bellowed out so loud that you could have sworn the Arsenal contingent had even joined the Standard's campaign to keep Claudio Ranieri in London.

Indeed, it was tempting to pop down to Roman Abramovich's private box to see if he and his Russian pals might fancy one of our rosettes.

They say the man can't be persuaded by sentiment but, then, neither can Arsenal. Once they had equalised, they were at their most mean-spirited.

By the time Marcel Desailly had received his second yellow card – incidentally, was his first for slapping the ball out of Lehmann's hands the most pathetic ever witnessed in this competition? – they had already asserted a comfortable degree of control over proceedings without bothering to search for another gear.

If they are as good as we've come to fancy they are, they will doubtless find it in a fortnight's time. As for Chelsea, though, they will have to remove the impression left last night following Arsenal's clinical equaliser that their shoulders dropped.

Once again, they have to discover the special resilience that has marked their Champions League away-days this term. Then, eight miles up the road, perhaps we could still witness London club football's finest hour and a half.

DIFFERENT

Well that was a different view than I would usually take but it all makes for this book to work. As for Desailly knocking the ball out of Lehmann's hands he should know better because the goalkeeper seems to do that without any aid and looks Chelsea's best bet in the second leg where there are many equations as to how this match should be entered. Chelsea need to score we know, but if Arsenal score first I see that as Chelsea's biggest chance in this encounter. I only say that in a way that they would have to come out and push onto Arsenal rather than let them have the freedom of the attacking space, like they have so many times once Chelsea go in front, only this time if they go behind, that last throw of the dice could just be the one that the Gunners will not relish. The pitch at Highbury is tight and that is why over the years they have been a much better away side, especially since having the pace of Henry and the nimbleness of Pires, the two players who make ground into their opponents area so quickly, not giving them the time to get bodies back in numbers, whereas that is what their opponents can do at Highbury. The theories are many about the return and in my way of thinking the FA Cup semi-final against Manchester United could have a great bearing on this second leg!

So Arsenal have a massively difficult match at the weekend when they take on Manchester United in the FA Cup semi-final at Villa Park and this could be the most incredible turnaround before going back into Premiership action. The Blues take on Wolves home in a match I am sure Wenger would gave preferred for his team, but that's the price of success, sometimes it can work against you as the season end closes in and Easter has always been the time to find out just how much petrol is left in the tank or how the 'bottle' is holding up to the pressure from those who read your every prediction and want to prove you wrong. I have mentioned several times about players 'shouting' of what they are and are not going to do. It began at Newcastle with Solano warning Europe that Newcastle were better equipped for the Champions League than Chelsea: Result – A first round knockout for the Geordies whilst the Blues are keeping that flag flying high up there in the sky. Both John Terry and Frank Lampard have been guilty of this and even if they go on to win the Double, I still do not think it healthy to get into such situations. I do know that a lot of this is down to their agents fixing newspaper deals etc. But they should be low key figures and their manager and coach should protect their best interest otherwise you start promising your loyal fans this, that and t'other, and you'll only end up with a very bad tasting egg on your eyebrow.

Tony Banks of the *Express* was as good a piece in his summation of the first leg war at the Bridge, although at times it became stagnant rather like two chess players fearing that defeat would have their lives fall from underneath their once confident chess board. For Arsenal, phase one of the 20 days that will decide their destiny is over, negotiated safely. But Arsene Wenger's team are already looking ahead to the challenge with Edu, insisting that, 'they must not be bullied out of their stride by Manchester United.'

United's visit on Sunday will be the defending champion's last real chance to slow Arsenal's seemingly headlong dash toward the title.

As the Gunners dust themselves down after their tumultuous, but inconclusive, clash with Chelsea, they can expect a rough ride. Arsenal believe that United will try to exploit any tiredness after a draining 1-1 draw at Stamford Bridge, but there are also worries that the bad feeling from the club's meeting at Old Trafford which was to be called 'The war of Manchester' when it all kicked off after Dutch ace Ruud van Nistelrooy missed a late penalty and Keown and several of his team mates went 'taunting' and jumping around like 'chimps' all over the latest United scoring sensation. There is never any love lost in these matches and the 'war of words' from both managers – mainly Ferguson – does not help matters. Those words run start the players' tongues running loose, and they have many nasty things to say about each other, not really a recipe for a fight-free occasion. Arsenal began well and made the running when Thierry – who else – thundered a wickedly spinning shot that had the goalkeeper looking like he had just been hit by Cassius Clay. The Frenchman stood there arms raised like he had just floored both Sonny Liston and Floyd Patterson at the same time, one with a right uppercut and the other with a left twister where he rolled his wrists as contact was made. Sorry I forgot, this was a football match – so far anyway – and Arsenal were in front and looking dangerous when at last United pulled up their sleeves and showed some of the fight that made them treble winners in 1999.

Even though there was no Beckham here today. I had backed Arsenal but was never comfortable as first Scholes then Giggs got into the action, then finally a whipped low cross found new signing Louis Saha all alone at the far past after the Dutchman missed the first opportunity by a whisker. 1-1 and Manchester United were jubilant whilst Arsenal looked tired and dejected and with the big semi-final coming up between these two teams only next week, the heat was really on and three days later that second appointment with Chelsea at Highbury to decide which English side went into the semi-finals of this season's Champions League.

Chelsea face Wolves at home and Spurs at White Hart Lane before going back into the lions den with the Gunners, whiles Arsenal – in the meantime – face a much tougher couple of matches. But at this stage of the season, show me an easy match and I'll show you the winners – right now – of the second leg at Highbury. Wolves came to town and though knowing Dave Jones will attack the Blues for two different reasons, one they need the three points and secondly that is the way he approaches matches, and I can only respect him for such tactics. Chelsea began the match sloppily and that gave the visiting team hope, but have we not seen that far too often this season, but the fans were in for a few shocks, enough to take their minds off of the biggest game in the club's history in ten days time. The headlines read that: ROMAN CAN'T BUY DECENCY and that CHELSEA STILL PLAN A FOREIGN SOLUTION: Plus for a change KENYON'S CLANGER saying that after his failure to land the Swede he must now get it right and NEEDS TO LAND BECKS AFTER TAKING BLAME FOR SVEN FIASCO: Also that STAMFORD FRIDGE as ICE-COLD KENYON'S MADE CHELSEA CHILLY: The Tinkerman made his way to the centre-circle and like the true Roman he is turned to all points of the stadium to accept applause. To the majority of the home supporters it looked like Dead Man Walking saying his thanks and his goodbyes. The media tried their best to get him to explain such an act, but it seems once again the man is too decent to begin a War of words at such a crucial time. He remains humble. He remains in control of his feelings, but how he does so is quite astounding!

He is preparing for the biggest phase in Chelsea's history and is still unwounded by such talk of the season that has been like an avalanche of incredible lack of support by his superiors. The Roman doesn't wear bullet-proof vests as every Chelsea fan can witness and they cannot understand either why he has not taken the money and run. The game begun and David Jones said that; "We took the game to them but got too cavalier and lost our shape. It was not so much they won the match as we lost it." The Tinkerman had made five changes from the team who had almost beaten Arsenal three days earlier and every one failed to deliver. Not for the first time, were all of his changes wrong and this was not a good time to begin losing your way and your nerve, although I cannot imagine him doing such a thing. Only the Jimmy Floyd substitution paid off as the Dutchman took three pot shots and each one hit the back of the Wolves net. I am not one for consistently changing the team but the result turned out right but the performance did not deserve a five-two victory. But who can argue? Frank Lampard was quick to pat Jimmy Floyd on the back when saying that: "Jimmy has been on ninety-nine goals for quite some time now, so it was great to see him take the match ball home today. It was a great relief for him."

Chelsea looked a little jaded, although they made changes but that does not mean that much really, because tiredness and mental strain can come in different ways when playing in such huge matches. Then there was Wolves scrapping for their lives. Abramovich and Kenyon are slowly seeing the 'pressure plan' coming together, but deep down inside this other Roman is some kind of fighter. He is now in a wonderful position as if he is asked to leave the building he goes with 'loadsamoney' and will walk into another job as soon as he has walked his dog. He will have made many, many friends around the Stamford Bridge area and at this moment in time all around the rest of the country and Europe, if only for the way he has 'hung in there' against such adversity. Mario Melchiot got the first goal but he and Babarayo never looked comfortable in the full-back positions while Joe Cole once again missed a glorious opportunity to impress. If only I could spend some time with young Joe, I can promise you I would improve him overnight, if I couldn't then I don't think he'll ever be the player we once thought he would be at West Ham. He does not use his great strengths in the right areas of the playing field and prefers to run with the ball all of the time instead of varying his game. You don't see Paul Scholes getting hold of the ball and think he's at the circus, he plays the game as a midfield player should play it. Frank has learned since leaving the Hammers to mix his game, have a rest here and there, and time his forward runs to near perfection when the time is right. You become far too predictable for opponents and that is playing into their hands. You watch Teddy Sherringham and see the way he plays first-time balls into the right areas and with half the pace of a Joe Cole, arrives in the box at just the right time. Joe is old enough now to begin forwarding his football education!

Great players know the right decisions at an early age – I mean truly great players – and you cannot teach greatness!

If you had asked the West Ham fans who they would have preferred out of Joe Cole and Frank Lampard, three-quarters would have plumped for the youngster but Frank has gone forward rapidly whilst Joe has stood still in his short football career. As the old West Ham boss – Ron Greenwood – would say, 'simplicity is genius' and I am not one to argue with such a philosophy!

Maybe young Joe Cole should sit down and think about Mr Greenwood's words maybe once or twice a week, and if that does not work, then everyday!

BACK TO THE MATCH

While Crespo looked everything but a £16million player and in the engine room only Lampard once again looked the real deal, thank god for the Blues. And of course another crucial goal!

Chelsea 5 Jimmy Floyd 3, Melchiot and Lampard Wolves 2 Camara and Craddock. Att: nearly another full-house.

JIMMY JOINS THE PREMIERSHIP HUNDRED CLUB

Here is how that club looks:

	Games	Goals
Shearer	372	240
Andy Cole	327	161
Ferdinand, Les	333	148
Fowler	306	143
Sherringham	369	138
Yorke	330	120
Owen	208	113
Dublin	307	111
Henry	165	104
Jimmy Floyd	200	102

OSGOOD QUICK TO TOE THE LINE

It seems that Roman Abramovich minions have learned the script regarding Claudio Ranieri.

Chelsea legend – and my ex-roommate and teammate – Peter Osgood, famously banned from the Bridge by Ken Bates, has been re-instated by the new regime and entertained corporate hospitality guests during Wednesday evening's Champions League match with Arsenal.

Osgood told guests that Ranieri "does not know his best team" and that his sides played "boring" football. He also said that Damien Duff was being held back because he was played out of position too often. Now I was not present at this gathering and one of the reasons I do not like attending is because I never seem to give my views on what is going on. You can work the rest out for yourself!

Ossie – as I have mentioned several times – was better than all of Chelsea's recent recruits playing up front, rolled into one. And I can say that not just as a player who set goals up for him but sometimes stood back and watched his majestic finishing. His idol as a Windsor bricklayer was Jimmy Greaves and has arguably been the best striker since the great man. He is hell bent on returning to the new regime and it seems an eternity that he was Matthew Harding's man. Nevertheless Peter Osgood was – and still is with those who can still remember – the 'king' of the shed and that can never be taken away from the history of a club who continue to under achieve, unless they can pull off the Champions League this time around. But even if they did they will have to continue to do so to allow the Russian billionaire's money to count!

Chelsea's next Premiership stop was just a few kilometres from Highbury at one of my all-time favourite venues. White Hart Lane was a special ground for me. I played my unofficial debut there against the great Jimmy Greaves in a 1-1 draw, which was the beginning of my run in that wonderful 1969/70 season. Just being on the same field as the maestro was enough, but to come off unscathed was a 'jab in the arm' that I needed to begin my career. Since that I played in matches there where we won the FA Cup semi-final against Watford in the same season, returned to there and scored the winner in that fantastic League Cup semi-final just as the referee – in those days – had the whistle between his lips. Then with Stoke City, ran the game and scored in their first win on the ground in a hundred years. A few weeks later played in a practice match in the England set-up – under our great friend 'The Don' Revie – which led to my international debut. Played another match for the Potters in an FA Cup tie when we drew there which led to them coming to the Victoria Ground only to be postponed because of that roof in the Butler Stand – of our very old ground – being blown off. That led to my being transferred across town to Arsenal because the club were not insured for such simple things, but that was the lovely thing about the Potteries, they could keep up with Chelsea building that monstrosity of a new stand, which led to

Osgood and myself leaving the place. The things you do for building football grounds?

All in all, I loved playing at White Hart Lane, maybe because my father would put me on his shoulders when the likes of Jimmy, Dave Mackay, John White, Bobby Smith and Danny Blanchflower were wearing the white shirt with the cockerel outstanding. I was even on his shoulders on the evening that Spurs put thirteen past Crewe in the FA Cup, but never saw a goal as the crowd was so massive!

That was a funny story, because quite some years later, when attending a match at Gresty Road, the home of the Alex, an elderly fan told me that in the first match Spurs were very fortunate to leave Crewe with a two-all draw. In the last seconds of a pulsating cup tie a Crewe playing missed an open goal, which would and should have erased the memory of that 13-2 defeat. A match that would never have taken place, but as Jimmy said once again: 'Funny old game.'

IT'S JIMMY AGAIN

Four days before the second leg of the tie against Arsenal the Blues were at the place they call 'The Lane' and the day before Matt Hughes of the *Evening Standard* wrote about the Tinkerman taking over at this club after he was relieved of his duties at the Bridge, come the summer. I won't go into this because although it is new – it was becoming as if I am forever going over old ground. But with a picture of Ranieri kicking an invisible ball, the headline surrounding it read that: IS RANIERI MORE SUITED TO SPURS THAN CHELSEA?

I will just give you the first three paragraphs that set the tone of the story: Chelsea and Tottenham will spend the next few months looking for a new manager, but are unlikely to step on each others toes.

While both clubs are looking for someone to deliver trophies to their success-starved fans, they have very different candidates in mind.

Peter Kenyon and Daniel Levy are engaged in a manhunt on an unprecedented scale but it has not begun well. Chelsea suffered a very public setback earlier this week when their top candidate, Sven Goran Eriksson, rejected Peter Kenyon's advances and chose to extend his contract with England, while Spurs have attracted more runners and riders than tomorrow's Grand National.

Hughes goes on to throw around all the names you have already read about so I will knock it on the head right there. But in the *Express* John Dillon, their chief writer, wrote with the headline that DIGNITY AGAIN LEFT IN DUST: Just for a second, it seems that some magical figures are jogging out of the haze and the dust hanging over the burning highway of Zallaq. Here comes Muhammad Ali leading the way, and just behind are Zinedine Zidane and David Beckham. And then Michael Schumacher roars past in his red Ferrari.

It is a mirage, of course, inspired by the latest piece of dubious TV advert trickery, which shows Ali, Zidane and Beckham taking part in a training run together.

So extraordinary is the fantasy, that it is perfectly feasible while at the Bahrain Grand Prix to add Schumacher to the imaginary gathering.

When you first glimpse the racetrack, which has arisen from the bare desert, its minaret-topped grandstand roofs swirling like the canopies of Bedouin tents, you realise just how much fantasy can be turned into reality in sport these days. And how quickly.

It cost £100million to build in just eighteen months and the money was provided with a simple wave of a King's hand. Despite the grainy air, it shines with readiness for Sunday's race, the first grand prix in the Middle East.

Above it all is a circular, black glass tower, a beacon of the latest Manhattan design school, soaring out of the sand and the rock. Driving away from it last night in the early Gulf dark, it was a sight shimmering almost mythically in intense white spotlights.

This is impressive stuff. But the glittering jewel, which has been built here, is also a symbol of a threat.

It throbs with the potential for a whole lot more of sport to be wrenched in the 21st century from its traditional roots into the great rootless vacuum of the global marketplace. Into new settings, which mat gleam on the outside, but are hollow within. Into spaces where a game, whatever it is, will just be a part of an ever-broadening entertainment complex, sterile and removed from the glorious tangle of folklore and emotions, which are built up around them in proper homes. England playing against Cameroon in Japan in utter silence two years ago comes to mind. Much money will be made, but that does not guarantee that it will be a good thing.

The US baseball team season began on Tuesday with the opening competitive match between the New York Yankees and Tampa Bay.

In Tokyo.

If baseball, America's spiritual summer game, will tug itself from its roots for such a significant occasion in pursuit of 'new markets', others will be keen to follow. Manchester United, Real Madrid and UEFA have surely taken note.

Why is Peter Kenyon so keen for Beckham to join Chelsea?

Well, Kenyon sold countless Manchester United shirts in Japan with that famous name on the back, and made his name in the process. He wants an action replay at Stamford Bridge. This is the priority for many in sport these days. It is a world full of Peter Kenyons.

Bahrain is a place where the idea of modern sport as fleeting diversionary entertainment rather than passion, comes easily to mind. It is an international zone, a melting pot of ex-pat workers of which there are twice as many as the 640,000 natives. So there are Irish bars and American bars. Everyone is splashed with TV screens pouring out sporting footage merely as moving wallpaper.

At the Crowne Plaza hotel bar here the other night, Andre Agassi's defeat in the Nadaq-100 tournament in Florida was being shown by satellite on America's ESPN station.

Only it was Spanish. 'En Vivo', rather than live. Nobody noticed. Nobody was watching anyway. That may be commonplace, but that is precisely the pint. The action is devalued. One is not the most tribal sport to use as a test case in this debate, but it is pertinent because this weekend marks its most concerted charge so far into the new markets.

"In ten years time," the pugnacious F1 boss Bernie Ecclestone has said, "Europe will be Third World."

And to prove his point, next month's race at the famous Imola track in San Marino will be the last there.

Ecclestone, ferocious pragmatist that he is, knows that his sport must look elsewhere to find the £1.3billion it costs to run each year, hence the move to nations where they allow fag adverts. "We're going to Bahrain and China this year, and Turkey next year, too," he adds. "Then Russia and India, We've an agreement with South Korea for 2009."

Football got to South Korea first with the 2002 World Cup but really; Formula One is racing away in the hunt to cash in on globalisation.

Others will soon follow. Marketing men everywhere are casting eager eyes all over events in Bahrain this weekend.

They are the ones who dreamed up that TV advert featuring Ali, Beckham and Zidane. Surely it is clever, but it is harmful too. It blurs and cheapens Ali's achievement. It damages history.

The accompanying ad, which simulates a fight between Ali in his prime and his daughter Laila, is even more maddening.

Extraordinarily, a mirage becomes reality. And the reality behind it fades out of proper focus.

A similar threat to the old ideas of sport will come roaring out of the clouds of sand and dust here on Sunday.

BACK TO THE LANE

Now a lot of Chelsea fans, or fans all over, may ask what the hell is that to do with the Tinker and Talsiman?

I think it is something to keep an eye on, because wasn't it only a few short weeks ago Bernie Ecclestone was photographed through a window with Roman Abramovich at Stamford Bridge at one of the home matches?

Plus the Beckham situation is brewing up and Chelsea will surely be first in line, and with the relationship between David and Peter Kenyon, Chelsea have a head start. But Chelsea's minds were on Highbury on Wednesday evening, but firstly they had to play the team who have become quite incredibly obsessed with not being able to beat the Blues from across west London. So Chelsea it seemed did not have to be at their best, although a good perform-ance would put them in the right frame of mind for the biggest match in their history in three days time. The biggest headline after the match was Scott Parker shouting that ARSENAL ARE THERE FOR THE TAKING: Chelsea's latest signing did not just mean in the Champions League but the Premiership too, after yet another win against Spurs. This young man – who will be come a great partner for Frank Lampard – has a very positive attitude and after his Man-of-the-Match performance he said that: "They have a fantastic squad but after the defeat against Manchester United – in the FA Cup semi-final – that can only help us. Who knows just how it well affect them now?

"They might come back stronger or they might crack a little bit, and if they do, we are waiting to pounce. They haven't lost a lot of games, so who is to know just how they will react?

"That is the main test for them now. It's definitely put us right back in the picture. We know if we are to have a chance of winning the league, then we've got to keep winning and putting pressure on Arsenal. Beating Spurs was a massive result for us – a real confidence booster." There have been two Gulf wars and a change of government since Tottenham last beat Chelsea in a league match, way back in 1987. It seems almost as long since Chelsea have beaten Arsenal. Chelsea won this match in a canter and Parker was outstanding in the engine room that was in a different class than Spurs. Chelsea simply played possession football, which left their opposition chasing shadows for most of the game. It was in this department that started off a brilliant move that saw Wayne Bridge, Frank Lampard and Damien Duff combine to set up for Jimmy Floyd's 38th minute winner. I have seen this kind of goal taken with more ease but it was four goals in two matches for Jimmy Floyd and that is all that matters at this time of the season. The ball came across the six yard box and the Dutch striker seemed to 'scuff' the ball rather than take it with the ease of a top striker and I thought for a split second he had squandered the chance. To think that the story goes that Roman Abramovich was on his way to looking at Spurs as the club to take over, but changed his mind whilst flying over Stamford Bridge. But somehow I cannot see how he could have bought a club down the old Seven Sisters Road when the Kings Road was only a short helicopter ride away!

Tottenham 0 Chelsea 1 Jimmy Floyd Att: Not full house

Manchester United were now to face Millwall – are Dennis Wise and Ray Wilkins lucky people – in the FA Cup Final, but for Chelsea and Arsenal it was all systems go as a packed Highbury awaited a battle that would leave the last English team in the Champions League and I had taken my seat in the Grosvernor Club along with Steve August and my son Allen. The club was buzzing in anticipation and the action ready to take place, as the Tinkerman took his place alongside Wenger looking anything but a Dead Man Walking.

BRIDGE SHATTERS ARSENAL DREAM

The game began in great fashion as Vieira bossed the centre of the field in the early exchanges, releasing Robert Pires on the left in that little space where he is so difficult to pick up, and once in possession he makes ground with great pace although he takes tiny steps when running the ball into enemy territory. In the early stages, Arsenal were superior and carried the game to Chelsea, but Duff had a wonderful chance once jinking around a couple of defenders before being caught just as he was going to 'pull the trigger' by an low-flying Arsenal boot. The ball rolled into the side-netting as our club erupted with the roar 'goal' only for many disappointed 'Bluenoses' holding their heads in disbelief. That would have been against the run of play, but as I pointed out to my friend Jonathan Pearce, this was cup football and winning cup matches is not always about being the best team. Pires missed a header that was far simpler than the one he scored at the Bridge, rather reminiscent of the one he missed against Manchester United in the FA Cup, when he mistimed his jump, only this time it went wide rather than high. Reyes was looking more and more like the star he is going to be, with his lightning pace and his jinking in and out of blue shirts, a spectacle to be seen, yeah, I love what this player is going to become!

Henry was off-target and form and this surely was a good sign for Chelsea and could this be a case of BRIDGE OVER TROUBLED WATERS?

Could Robert Pires's header from a great run and cross from Ashley Cole, we were asking? Then a deep cross into Chelsea's far post right on the blow of the half-time whistle proved to be the answer as Henry headed the cross down, Freddie Lundberg missed his kick and the Spaniard was in the right place at the right time to put the reds into a first-half lead as the Grosvenor Club went into a very deep lull. Arsenal went crazy and entered that famous tunnel a goal in front, but was this a good or bad thing as Chelsea now had been given no alternative but to get out and at them in the second forty-five minutes, as the boys were trying to work out the tactics of the Tinkerman for sitting back and allowing the Premiership leaders the opportunity to bring the game onto them. I thought 'no' as the Tinkerman – who started with only four players from that £120million summer buying spree on the field – brought on Jesper Gronkjaer!

His starting line-up was the same as the one at White Hart Lane on Saturday, so the pointers were looking good for him not tinkering with a winning side for a change.

Arsenal came out a different team and in the first ten minutes there were screams across our club such as 'They are gone' and 'If we cannot take them now we'll never do it'. This was all well and good, but would Vieira restart his command of the middle or would Frank come more into the game. Chelsea had width, although I did not agree with his substitution, Parker should have still be involved in this one hell of a tie and just as I was thinking that, Makelele hit a shot from fully thirty-five yards that the German in the red net could only make a right 'pigs ear' of once again, and who was on hand? Chelsea's saviour in so many matches before, Frank 'The Inspirational' Lampard. Frank doesn't miss from there. 'Thank you Jens', Frank looked to say as he coolly ran to his large band of fans to kiss the badge!

The ball swerved and dipped but the keeper should have held onto it safely enough but could only parry it out to the oncoming Lampard, did he take his eye off the ball when seeing Frank, ask him, not me!

1-1 and this was really now game on!

Could Arsenal fight their way back into a match like they failed to do once Scholes hit them against United in the FA Cup semi-final, we would soon find out. Where was Henry I asked myself?

Pires was not getting the first-half supply down the left and Chelsea were growing in hope and stature as even the big French captain looked vulnerable and Chelsea took the game as if knowing this time Arsenal had too many players flagging at the same time. Tired legs looked on the Arsenal menu but there was no time to freshen them up and the Blues could taste a victory they have long awaited. And what a match to get it in!

The alarm bells were ringing around Highbury and they did not have anybody to stop them, only Ashley Cole showing that great attacking quality but his pals were missing especially the so-called complete player, Thierry Henry!

Master craftsman, master goal-maker, master goal-taker, was on walkabout!

Chelsea pushed and pushed with every man outfighting the Gunners invincible machine and after the closest of misses, when Joe Cole – a substitute for Duff – crossed for Eidur Gudjohnsen to smash towards the unguarded Arsenal net – where was the keeper again?

Then out from nowhere there was the 'always lively' Ashley Cole to somehow swoop the ball off of the line and keep his team in what had been an enthralling, if not great, cup-tie. But Arsenal still could not get off the ropes and it seemed they had become punchdrunk from a ninety-minute battle with Manchester United and now over an hour of Chelsea's persistence – and it looked that they were possibly ready to go down before the last bell when all of a sudden in the Grosvenor and all over Chelsea it was BLUE HEAVEN wrote the *Daily Mail*!

There were eighty-seven minutes on the Highbury clock, the one I had wanted to stop on many occasions in my playing days there, when Bridge made a bold run forward, played a cool one-two with Gudjohnsen and fired a low shot into Lehmann's bottom hand corner of the net, the ball flashing right across the big frame of this incapable German, he was down and out and so were his team. Chelsea had fired the killing blow and although the screams throughout our watering hole were for the 'Mug in the Middle' to blow his whistle, there was now a great belief – only because Arsenal were now legless – that Chelsea had at last slayed the slayer. Chelsea had now quite amazingly won all of their six away matches in their Champion's League campaign, but this was the sweetest of them all. Two weeks ago, Peter Kenyon was courting the Swede – left angry when he did an England u-turn – and the cry now was 'who needs him'. The Tinkerman is the King and long may it last!

A smiling, crying dancing Roman was never seen so emotional – even the *Mail* wrote that RANIERI'S IRON MASK SLIPS AS PASSION COMES TO FORE – and I can only say that it must have been as much a shock as expectation, for this tie was in the hands of the Gunners for the best part of two-thirds of the playing time but they had too much of the ball in the first half – if you can – without killing off the battling Blues. The *Sun's* headlines surrounding a photograph of Crespo chasing matchwinner Wayne Bridge was MR CRAZY-Ranieri goes bonkers and not even Rom dare sack him now: Mark Irwin wrote that – Claudio Ranieri went crazy after masterminding the greatest result of his Chelsea reign. Wayne Bridge's 87th minute winner sealed a sensational Champions League quarter-final win against arch rivals Arsenal. And the under fire Italian admitted that, "Tonight I am a crazy man and Roman Abramovich is also going mad like me!"

Now this stunning victory will have every Chelsea fan asking: How can Rom sack him?

The Blues boss was like a madman after Bridge struck. He said that, "I was delirious for 30 seconds after that goal went in. I wanted to join my players on the pitch. People have said I am a dead man walking. But I am not. I am still moving and I will continue to fight.

"What happens next season?

"I am focusing only on this season. That is my way. That's important for me, for the club, for everyone."

On the game he said: "In the first half we wanted to close down the space but were very nervous. When we went 1-0 down, I knew we had to do something more. But I told my players at half-time, we had to stay calm and after the break we played much better. In the second half we were fantastic."

Wenger said that: "We have hit the wall and it could take us time to recover. Chelsea are on the up, while we are on the way down. Tonight, we crossed each other. We have lost our belief and it is going to be difficult to bounce back. It will test our character and mental strength. The Premiership is far from being done for us."

The Tinkerman's headlines were becoming stronger in his case for his fight to keep the job he loves at the club he loves and the support that has become so strong from the Chelsea faithful. The *Mirror* went: CAN YOU STILL SACK HIM NOW in Claudio's finest hour. For Arsenal the same rag it spelt TROUBLE for IN JUST 82 HOURS ARSENAL HAVE BEEN DUMPED OUT OF THE FA CUP AND EUROPE…A SEASON IN CRISIS!

Also in the *Express* the tickertape read TRUE BLUE: REAL'S MOVE FOR CHELSEA COACH HAS BOOT ON THE OTHER FOOT AS ABRAMOVICH FINDS THE MAN HE WANTED TO SACK IS

INDESPENSIBLE: RANIERI CALLS THE SHOTS: NOW IT'S KEEP THE BOSS OR ELSE.

Running along the foot of the page read that; LAMPARD CARRIES ROMAN ARMY ALL THE WAY TO GATES OF GLORY.

Back to the Tinkerman and the *Mail* saying that RANIERI GLORY LEAVES KENYON IN FIRING LINE. There were quotes galore but I picked out Roman Abramovich's which made me smile a little: "Chelsea played great and I think tonight the team showed the Russian character to hold on, to fight to win. We are now waiting for Monaco." I found that strange as his manager seems to think that fighting spirit comes from his Gladiators, is there always going to be some kind of animosity between the two parties. I have never seen anything like this even between two opposition leaders. Claudio said that: "That was the best night of my career, and now we can win it all". Then it turned to the superb form of Frank Lampard with the headline that: LAMPARDS RUN PUTS PRESSURE ON SCHOLES – All action Frank has to start for England. John Terry – for the first time – was quick to play down talk of glory.

The back page of the *Standard* went Keep Ranieri as £12million NEW BOY IN PLEA TO CHELSEA: DON'T SACK CLAUDIO.

He followed up with I CAN'T WAIT TO JOIN CHELSKI AFTER THIS. LETS HOPE CLAUDIO IS THERE TO MEET ME.

The letters coming in said that RANIERI FOR ENGLAND, HE'D DO A BETTER JOB THAN ERIKSSON.

In the *Mirror* on a different page it was that: RANIERI'S REVENGE: TINKERMAN ON THE BRINK OF HIS OWN AMAZING TREBLE whilst tucked in the corner in small print: ITS CLAUDIO V KENYON FOR SACK.

With two contrasting photographs of the Tinkerman, it also said that WHY WE'RE ALL CRAZY ABOUT CRAZY MAN. On the same page, alongside a photograph of the Water Carrier it read: BLUES MAY GET A DIDI SHOCK. The back page had Ranieri sporting a huge Italian grin beside the headline that: RANIERI'S REVENGE – KENYON TO GO IF CLAUDIO STAYS ON AT CHELSEA.

In the *Sun* it was more dramatic as Joe Cole shouted: WE'LL BEAT THE LOT: BUBBLING BLUES CAN CLEAN UP SAYS COLE.

Also in the Sun it read that the CHELSEA SAGA GOES ON: RANIERI'S D-DAY-CLAUDIO IN CRUNCH TALKS.

The report read that: Claudio Ranieri wants his Chelsea future sorted out once and for all within the next forty-eight hours. He plans to end the club's stalling tactics in showdown talks with chief executive Peter Kenyon on Wednesday – the week before the Monaco match – for the Italian believes Kenyon and owner Roman Abramovich are trying to buy time after their bid to lure Sven Goran Eriksson was sensationally scuppered by the *Sun* two weeks ago. But the Stamford Bridge boss insists he cannot put up with any more distractions ahead of the Champions League semi-final against Monaco. He just goes on to say all what he has said in the past about his loving his job, the club and just wants all speculation to come to a halt.

Now for Monaco in the semi-final, after the French felled the Spanish giants Real Madrid, it was certainly a night and a quarter-final of complete shocks!

As happens after such a fantastic high it was back to the Premiership with a bump as the Blues hosted Middlesbrough, which ended in a deadly boring no-score draw. The newspapers soon changed their tune in their bid to keep Ranieri in his seat at the Bridge. Headlines went like this: TINKERED AND BLINKERED – Ranieri pays hefty price for resting Duff and Bridge; The *Mirror* went even further saying that: TINKER HAS A STINKER – Claudio messes about again and poor draw spells end to Chelsea title hopes. The *Express* were right to the point with: CHANGING WINNING SIDE COSTS CHELSEA BOSS TILT AT TITLE – RANIERI'S FALLEN HOOK FOR IT HOOK, LINE AND TINKER: *The Times* were just a very simple: NEW ROLE APPEALS TO RANIERI – and in tiny letters – Head coach concedes title before pivotal meeting: Mendietta and Junhinho brought a little sunshine to a dull match while only Frank Lampard – who missed a couple of chances he would usually put away with his eyes closed – working tirelessly once again and John Terry once again as steady as that Stamford Bridge 'rock' that has been formed since his rise to fame. John Terry forced a early tip over from Mark Schwarzer, but Chelsea's best chance came when a Eidur Gudjohnsen drive came back of a post and Frank Lampard – unlike him – somehow scopped the ball wide of an open goal. Veron added a little venom, curling two free kicks just over, but Chelsea were indebted to goalkeeper Marco Ambrosio for clawing away the influential Gaizka Mendietta's free-kick. It was finally summed up by *Sportsmail* who said that: ARSENAL LEFT LAUGHING AFTER CHELSEA GO ON EASTER STROLL – RANIERI IN TOP FORM AS HIS MEN SURRENGER.

Chelsea 0 Middlesbrough 0 Att: 40,873

Leading scorers in the Premiership list read like this: Henry 25, Shearer 21, Saha 19 (15 for Fulham), Foresell 16, Angel 15, Owen 14, Jimmy Floyd 12, Pires 12, Keane (Spurs) 12, Beattie 11, Ferdinand (Leicester City) 11: These were all the players over double figures after the thirty-one or thirty-two matches their clubs have played.

THE HEAT GOES ON

POWER BATTLE – Ranieri must accept he'll have no say in transfer matters. The Tinkerman was quoted as saying that: "I feel good at Chelsea and I would love to stay, but I don't know what's in Kenyon's mind."

The new kid on the block seemed to be Porto manager Jose Mourinho, as the *Express* headline read: RANIERI'S TIME IS UP:

Then picking up the Express I was shocked to find these headlines: ITALIAN IS SET FOR MORE TALKS WITH KENYON – and in bigger letters – FOUR MORE YEARS – with below it – HOT PROPERT RANIERI WANTS A NEW £10million DEAL SORTED OUT BEFORE CHAMPIONS LEAGUE SEMI-FINAL:

On Thursday the 15th of April the *Mail* headlined that is was: NO JOY FOR RANIERI AS CHELSEA KEEP HIM GUESSING – with inside saying that – RANIERI IS KEPT IN THE DARK WITH CHELSEA PLAYING THE FIELD.

My Friday *Sentinel* column was written from Cyprus and it was headlined that: 'FIND US KEEPERS' IS THE MANAGERS AGE-OLD REQUEST' and it read like this: I am writing from Cyprus this week and you'll have to forgive my overwhelming sense of nostalgia. No, not because I played my second and last International against the Cypriots back in 1975, but because this was the destination of an early Stoke trip under Tony Waddington. It brings a tear to my eye to think of my old mentor, sadly taken many years ago now, and recall the fun we had here on the island. This was a manager who knew his business, all right, but also knew his players must be allowed to enjoy themselves.

When it comes to the art of management, and getting the best from your best, this man wrote the first chapter.

A long, hard slog on the training field used to sober me up in those days, but out here in April 2004 it is the locals taking to prayer at half-five in the morning.

Waddo was a master of assembling a mixture of homegrown and imported talent and then moulding them into a great footballing unit.

Importing, in those days, of course, meant as far north of Scotland or as far south as the Smoke.

But nowadays they pour into our game from far and wide to sprinkle their glitter to our football.

Our manager thougfht he had found one of the last pieces of our jigsaw when he replaced the great Gordon Banks – via a more than adequate, in fact very good John Farmer – with the potentially great Peter Shilton.

But Shilts was never to live up to the hype – not with Stoke City anyway – and to this day we would have won the old first division championship had Gordon never had that tragic car accident when losing an eye.

No goalkeeper is going to cost Arsenal this Premiership, of course, but even Arsene Wenger's legendary teambuilding skills have yet to extend to the man standing between the goalposts. That German clown he has masquerading as a top-class keeper has cost them dearly in recent weeks and clearly isn't up to the job.

Wenger has tried and failed with him, Alex Maninger and Richard Wright, when it comes to finding a long-term replacement for David Seaman. The French Professor must make the right appointment this summer if Arsenal are to stand any chance of succeeding where they failed this. Until he has someone who has the same class as his outfield players, all their fine work threatens to be undermined by a keeper dropping a series of Bernard Langers between the sticks.

What a pity such a side is hampered by such an obvious Achilles heel. We, the footballing neutral, will be forever grateful for the skill and grace of Thierry Henry, a player who can charm the birds off the trees in north London.

Patrick Vieira is a giant of a player, Wenger's Lord Admiral, while Robert Pires is the third of his musketeers.

He runs the ball with nimble feet and his eye for space is something unique, the finest claret in Wenger's very expensive cellar.

They've well and truly conquered the Premiership this tear, but to conquer Europe next they will need a better sentinel standing guard behind such a crack fighting unit.

CHAMPIONS LEAGUE

CLAUDE CRUNCH: Makelele in race to show he is ready for Monaco.

I repeat I enjoy reading and sharing with you the writing of Mick Dennis of the *Express* and on this day there shows a photograph of Claudio Ranieri with a turned-up nose as if seeing one of his tinkerings fail once too often. It was headed DIARY OF A TINKERMAN: CLAUDIO RANIERI is putting down his thoughts on his season with the help of an Italian broadcast journalist. It will be published in the summer, but some of his entries could look like this:

Tuesday March 23 – A good day. But it started not good. In the *Daily Express*, someone called Mick Dennis is saying that I am a 'dead man walking' very poor English. It should be 'dead man, he is walking'.

But I put on a nice suit. On my way to the training ground I change my shoes, socks and tie. At the training ground now I recognise nearly all of the players. A good day.

Wednesday March 24: Look, a football team is like a meal. Sometimes you have a gnocci and sometimes you have oreccehiette. Always you have antipasta. Against Arsenal in the Champions League today, we play like Chicken Scarpariello and take the lead. But then we eat meatballs and the Arsenal equalise. Mr Arbramovich comes to see the team with a face like Botox injection, which has gone bad.

I don't have a friendship with Mr Abramovich. When I first met him he says to me: "I am Roman." I say to him: "I am Roman also!" He has not said anything to me since that day. CRESPO + HASSELBAINK written down then scribbled out.

Thursday March 25: My wife Rosanna and my daughter Claudia help me choose what to wear today and on the way to the training ground, only the cuff links need changing. And also the shoes. And I take off the tie and leave the neck of the shirt unbuttoned. I meet somebody called Winston Bogarde, but I do not know what it is he does.

Friday March 26: Here is something I do not understand. Hernan Crespo. We are paying many, many Euros. Why is he not able to see a barber?

Saturday March 27: When the sun is shining, always there are clouds as well. The newspaper pictures of my friend Sven Goran Eriksson at Mr Kenyon's apartment.

I know why we buy bad players like Joe Cole. It is for Mr Eriksson! I know also why my friend Mr Ken Bates says to me that Mr Kenyon is a dodgepot. This word is not in my dictionary but I think it is not nice.

The football is against Wolves who are very strong, very fast, very fit, very rubbish. I send on Jimmy Hasselbaink and he scores many goals. HASELBAINK + MUTU written down then scribbled out.

Sunday March 28: Mr Eriksson is on the television because today he tells the Football Association he will stay with them. This makes me laugh very many times.

Ha! I am laughing. Ha! I do not trust Mr Eriksson because he changes ladies like I change my players.

First he is with Mrs Eriksson, then he is with Nancy Dell'Olio – the lady wears dark sunglasses to our games at night – and then he is with that old blonde lady, then he is with Miss Dell'Olio again. I think at heart he is a Nancy Boy.

Saturday April 3: I am sorry to be writing this diary but I have been to many meetings with my agent, my friend, Jon Smith. At the football today we beat Tottenham. Of course. Some people say that if Chelsea sack me off, then I can manage Tottenham. But I am a stupid man.

Sunday April 4: Very big news. The newspaper, it says David Beckham is having an affair with a Loos woman. They say he has sent her many text messages, like this: "I want to **** your ****." I do not know where he finds the asterisk on his telephone. I think that it would take me a lot longer to send text than to make love. My wife Rosanna, says that I am right.

My daughter, Claudia, says that she can do text messages and that she would like to give one to David Beckham.

Monday April 5: They are saying that David Beckham will perhaps be divorcing his Posh wife or that he is coming to play for Chelsea. I think he will come and play for Chelsea because a divorce would not be possible. How could he lose the tattoo of his wife's name?

Tuesday April 6: My mother has telephoned to say I must pick Duff in the Champions League against Arsenal. My wife says that I must tell Joe Cole to play with the team and not play with himself. My daughter asked whether David has come to the team yet.

Look, a football team is like a Ferrari. Sometimes you have to change the tyres. Also the sparking plugs. And maybe the colour of the paint.

Wayne Bridge, one of Eriksson's signings, scores a very good goal. We beat

Arsenal. Everyone is very, very happy. I cry. Mr Kenyon is also crying. MUTU + CRESPO once again scribbled out.

Wednesday April 7: My agent, my friend, Mr Jon telephones. He says to me that if Chelsea sack me off, they have to give me 10 million pounds.

A newspaperman asks me how I would cope with pressure. He is a stupid newspaperman, I think.

GUDJOHNSEN +HASSELBAINK scribbled off one last time!

OH FOR HUMOUR

Once I had come down off those wonderful drugs that had kept me in some kind of different world, before facing up to my incredible amount of bodily injuries and face up to a runaway wife of six months, before that dreadful evening it was quite clear I had to get the path of my life back on the straight and narrow and my drive had to include one of our greatest assets, a sense of humour!

Mick Dennis has just brightened up a story that at times must have made the Tinkerman feel as if he had ran over his cat or changed his mind about just where he wants to go or what he wants to do, something only his Rosanna can help him with.

I thank Mick Dennis for his diary as we have to move on to more serious stuff.

Newcastle powered past PSV with yet another super Alan Shearer strike – this time a powering header and that takes them into the semi-final of the UEFA Cup. So wouldn't it be nice to see both our clubs go through to the finals, because there is one thing for certain, the Swede will not be bringing our boys back from Portugal with any such thing. His latest – seemingly outburst – as to the injury to the bang in form Jonathan Woodgate at Newcastle, could cost him a place on the aeroplane, is sheer lunacy for he must take players who have been in form at the latter end of the season and that looks good for Frank Lampard and John Terry!

'I'M OUT IN COLD'

ABROMOVICH GAVE RANIERI A VICTORY HUG BUT MANAGER THINKS IT WAS ONLY FOR SHOW

I have come across this piece and because of this man being one of the great all-time greatest players the world has seen, I am delighted to welcome him into my book. Michel Platini, need I say anymore!

The great man says that: "It's a philosophic mission. We must give football a framework so a club like Chelsea is not the archetype of the club of the future. There is cheating and an imbalance. We shall have to erect barriers not to cross. Otherwise, clubs will be out. We'll have to give them time. They have contracts, which bind them to players, and can't overturn everything in one go.

"We'll have to be a little patient and then the clubs that are not in order financially will be punished. Believe me, this is the right way to go. Otherwise I will leave. I won't stay."

Platini wants big-time football to be organised on the French model, making sure teams operate within budgetary controls, or face severe penalties like relegation.

He continued: "There is a good framework for French clubs and we are going to save them that way. It isn't right Spanish, Italian and English clubs obtain such advantages."

Michael Platini is now a part of the governing body of FIFA and if the world was in perfect order – that is forgetting the outside world war going on – then this man should be running FIFA. Sepp Blatter – the leader – is some kind of fool!

'IF'

RANIERI REVEALS HIS INSPIRATION

On April 17th, Andrew Dillon wrote about the Tinkerman with the heading above in three categories, the first being: If I get the bullet? Secondly: If we land the title?

Third and lastly: If we rule Europe?

This piece about the Chelsea boss followed: Claudio Ranieri has turned to one of England's best-loved poems for inspiration to stay cool during a turbulent season. Rudyard Kipling's 1910 ode "If" questions whether the reader can 'keep your head when all around you are losing theirs' and to treat victory and defeat the same.

It is more a question of WHEN rather than IF, when he loses his this summer and gets sacked as Chelsea boss.

But as he gears up for the biggest week of the club's history, the Italian insists he will not be rattled. Chelsea visit Monaco in the Champions League semi-final first leg on Tuesday evening. And Ranieri said that: "All Englishman know the poem by Rudyard Kipling. I read this poem when I was young and the words are so true. In England there is stress. But if you go out and give everything and don't win, the fans say, 'don't worry', next week we will do better. In Italy if you draw or lose they say; 'don't worry' and then they stone you. It is a different philosophy. I also understand about triumph and failure. I want to win all the time but I will not let these things change me. I am the kind of person who can go home every day and shut everything out." Ranieri's future at Stamford Bridge has still to be resolved – despite further talks with chief executive Peter Kenyon this week to clear the air. He is too shrewd to be strung along into believing there is a chance he can save his job by winning the Champions league. The fight to prevent Manchester United leapfrogging his Blues into second place in the Premiership is his overwhelming priority.

And the seemingly doomed boss rapped a defiant message to the executioners at Chelsea who want him out: They will NEVER end his love affair with English football. Ranieri added that: "The stress is of my making, because I want to win always. It could be I lose my job at the end of the season. When the ownership of a club changes, the owner has the right to change the coach. Roman Abramovich wanted to change last July, but he didn't find what he was looking for. Vicente Del Bosque was sacked by Real Madrid for winning the Spanish League but not the Champions League. But I am still in love with English football despite everything that has happened this year and it will always be that way. I want to stay in this country."

I have news for the Tinkerman: Every other foreigner – it seems – wants to stay in this country, and I'm not just talking about football. So we don't take that kind of talk as if you have a love affair with our country!

He carries on that: "When I say there isn't pressure here, it's because in my homeland it is worse. England has been my favourite place to work. There is another culture about football than in Italy."

YOUNG

When I was young I loved football. I went everywhere to try to play football. But when you start to play professionally, slowly, slowly, the boy in you disappears. You must work and there is stress. In Spain and in England the boy in me came back. And Gianfranco Zola told me England is better than Spain. He was right. "You come here and enjoy."

DIDIER IS RUNNING SCARED OF CLAUDIO

Didier Deschamps has pinpointed the Chelsea man, for he believes he is most likely to deny Monaco a Champions League final place – Claudio Ranieri.

Monaco boss, the French World Cup and European Championship winner Deschamps – as a player – is convinced his counterpart is Blues' most valuable weapon.

The former Chelsea midfielder takes on Ranieri's troops in Tuesday night's semi-final first-leg. And he said: "They have a well-tuned defensive system and it comes from the manager and his Italian culture. They are so well in place at the back that they leave you very little space. That is why they have conceded just five Champions League goals – and just one away."

TEMPO

Deschamps is baffled Ranieri is still fighting to save his Chelsea job. He said that: "Even if they have huge numbers of foreign players, Chelsea keep a fairly English style in their game – notably the commitment and tempo they impose and maintain throughout a game. It will be difficult for us because Chelsea have an important attacking potential as well. They can start with Hasselbaink and Gudjohnsen and finish with Crespo and Mutu."

Deschamps admits he struggled to adapt to English football when he joined Chelsea after five years in Serie A. He said that: "It was a very good experience but, yes, it was difficult after a more tactical Italian game. But it remains a good memory because of a very good squad and an extraordinary set of fans."

And he accepts that his cash-strapped Monaco side will start the match as underdogs.

Yet he warned that: "Chelsea are very competitive, but my players have seen that anything is possible over two matches."

I sense that the tiny Frenchman is quietly confident that his very lively and talented forward players will give Chelsea more to think about than the likes of Sparta Prague and a couple of pretty ordinary opponents in earlier rounds. Let's not forget that the Champions League is not the European Cup of old, where only the best from each nation gets a shot at the biggest club prize in world football. I walked out at half-time of the Chelsea and Sparta Prague match at Stamford Bridge because I felt that, if I were sitting at home watching, and a movie or any other programme that looked exciting viewing was on another channel, I could always turn it off if disappointed. I remember playing in matches like the Bruges match in the European Cup Winners Cup in 1971 and the place was simply rocking. This was a very talented Belgium team but they were also very difficult to break down, mainly because not only could they defend when they had possession, they could keep the ball for quite some time. It was no wonder – I remember – coming off of the field at Stamford Bridge, after more than a hundred and twenty minutes of non-stop running having lost ten pounds in weight and sat in the postmatch party completely drained. Losing such weight on an English Wednesday evening was quite extraordinary because I recall Peter Osgood telling me that whilst in Mexico in 1970 – the one I missed through injury – that players were losing that kind of weight in matches, but that was in the daylight and at least a hundred degrees, if you take into consideration the heavy load that a football match brings with it!

The match coming up will be one of great intensity, as the Blues have to be professional in their approach and as long as our friend the Tinkerman does not get overexcited about his tinkering, then they can come back to London with a huge advantage. But let's never forget this team is very dangerous, with Fernando Morientes the one player that John Terry must eliminate.

WELL DONE AITCH

It is no secret that Harry Redknapp is my best pal in football and my delight was quite clear in the company of some new friends in Cyprus, as Portsmouth beat the Premiership champions at Fratton Park, thanks to a scrappy Steve Stone winner ten minutes before the interval. This result will surely be their springboard to a fighting finish that will see them clear of the trap door. Wolves and Leicester look doomed and Leeds United are playing as if they are complete strangers to one another.

They look the three to leave the Premiership and of the three managers, Dave Jones is the only one I have any sorrow for. But my joy at Portsmouth staying alive in the top flight for another season is as great as it gets, for it is only if they had failed to stay the distance that the pain would have been quite unbearable around the Redknapp household.

Well done Aitch: **Portsmouth 1 Stone Manchester United 0**

After an enthralling match, my mate said that: "We defended for our lives at the end. It is not often you beat United, and I am delighted with my first-ever League victory over them – having knocked them out of the FA Cup twice with Bournemouth and West Ham – which was quite a feat. Before the match I thought a draw would be a bonus, just to keep us going, so three points are fantastic."

As I said Harry has got a good record against Manchester United in the FA Cup, after knocking them out twice whilst managing both West Ham and Bournemouth, which was one of the biggest upsets in FA Cup history.

Sir Alex Ferguson made comments about how hard his team worked and if I hear the silly term of someone 'working their socks off' one more time I'll go crazy. What the hell does that mean?

How can a man work his socks off?

I hear the likes of Ray Wilkins say "He has worked his socks off Marcus," and I cringe. Why cannot he simply say the player could not have worked any harder or given any more. I am one of great experience in this matter and can confirm that no matter however hard I have worked my socks have always stayed on, unless it was with a beautiful young lady, of course!

Whilst Portsmouth were turning Manchester United over, Chelsea were doing bookmakers a great favour by failing to overcome Everton at the Bridge. The *Sunday Express* headline was that: Spy trip wasted as Ranieri's men fall flat – and – CHELSEA KEEP DID GUESSING!

The *Sportsmail* called Chelsea: THE JOKE TEAM – WILL THE REAL CHELSEA TURN UP IN EUROPE?

Without going into the dreary details of this match, the newspaper verdict read like this: Chelsea dropped more points in the race for second place in the Premiership, after an insipid display against an unadventurous Everton team. Rooney should have put Everton ahead, then Lampard hit the woodwork twice, but neither side deserved more than the one point.

Frank Lampard was their best player again and was unlucky by hitting the woodwork on two occasions.

With one day to go before the match in Monaco it was headlined in the *Sun* that Chelsea players were on £580,000 A MAN TO WIN CHAMPIONS LEAGUE.

The David Beckham saga continues as the headlines in the *Daily Mail* showed a photograph of him embracing teammate Santiago Solari and Steve Curry touched on that: It is less than twelve months since a Presidential election at a leading Spanish football club gave Manchester United fans their first inkling that David Beckham might be leaving his Alma Mater.

Jose Laporta was elected President of Barcelona last June on the promise he would deliver Beckham to the Nou Camp. Now Real Madrid have a presidential candidate who will base his campaign on selling the England captain.

News that the Madrid millionaire, Enrique Sobrino, is to challenge Florentino Perez for president at the Bernabeu and use Beckham's absenteeism as a reason to be rid of him, is not a manifesto likely to produce election victory. What it will have done, however, is alert both Chelsea and Arsenal to the fact that Beckham's position at Real Madrid is being challenged and undermined in influential quarters.

Anyone who has seen Beckham at work will know that Senor Sobrino does not understand what drives him because the last thing he can be accused of is a poor work ethic. But he will get encouragement to pursue his platform for election from London, where the movers and shakers are planning what they can do to lure football's hottest property to England's capital.

It is understood there is a release clause in Beckham's contract that would necessitate an outlay of 138million euros – almost a £100million – which is definitely more than Arsenal could find but is unlikely to deter Chelsea owner Roman Abramovich, officially declared number one on Britain's Rich List. Abramovich, his Russian legion and hired hand Peter Kenyon, will be watching the situation in Madrid with diligence and anxiety, particularly since chief executive Kenyon has ground to make up in terms of his reputation. The messy saga of Claudio Ranieri's fixture – put on hold while he tries to deliver Chelsea into the Champions League final – has not left him with much of a credit rating, either with the fans or players. Kenyon was tempted from Manchester United on a schedule for development, a far-ranging syllabus that includes pushing the Chelsea brand around the globe. His blueprint involves not only going out to recruit the best players and the top coach, but also to ensure the club has a structure where it can promote from within, in much the same way United did under the manager Sir Alex Ferguson and Kenyon's predecessor, Martin Edwards.

Abramovich had indicated that, in addition to evolution, he wants revolution – and he will spare no expense.

Having plunged so much money into football, he has clearly enjoyed the profile it has given him, his commitment is to elevate Chelsea to the plateau where Manchester United and Real Madrid sit. The acquisition of Beckham would be a short cut to instant recognition and acceptance of the Chelsea brand around the world, most notably in the Far East, where the England captain has deity status whether he wears the red of United, the white of Real, or the royal blue of Chelsea.

The development of an overseas market was one of Kenyon's most notable achievements at Old Trafford. Yet he would be first to accept that having Beckham as a tool towards that end was a beneficial marketing advantage.

Beckham has said he is happy at the Bernabeu, but his domestic circumstances have changed hugely in the light of publicity about his private life, and if he has to come home to save his marriage, then Chelsea will welcome him with open arms.

LACK OF FIREPOWER

The Tinkerman shrugged off any fears his supporters have about the lack of firepower by saying that: "I hope that we are saving up our goals for that game. We have scored away from home in the Champions League and that is very important. I am not concerned about the last few results. Of course we respect Monaco, they are a fine team, but I know I have good players in good condition. There are no excuses for today's draw. I don't want excuses. But its okay and now we look forward. I hope to have all my players available."

Now I don't always think that is a good thing with the Tinkerman!

Sometimes you are better off having bare bones and know that these players will go out and give you everything, rather than wondering that they can be pulled off at any given time. For instance, the substituting of Scott Parker really wrangles me for, firstly, he plays him out of position then pulls him off, and for me that is 'Kamikaze' management and the kind of managing that can be fatal. In Europe you must use your very strongest team and have the best eleven players on the field at the same time. Of course, someone may get a knock or be off form, but that is when you use your head and change things accordingly, surely, plain and simple common sense!

But the Italian – it seems – loses touch with reality and goes into Gladiator mode instead of keeping his cool and seeing the game as it is.

The back page the following day was like this ROMAN PUTS HIS SHIRT ON BECKS: Plus: CLAUDIO'S GIVEN BAD NEW – and THE JOBS YOURS – with the words that – CHELSEA OFFER RANIERI ROLE TO PORTO BOSS – beside a picture of Jose Mourinho with thumbs up.

Harry Harris reports that: ROMAN GIVES CHELSEA JOB TO MOURINHO but went on to say that: A staggering 95 per cent of our readers voted for Claudio Ranieri to be allowed to stay and finish the job he started at Chelsea, but the job has already been offered to Porto boss Jose Mourinho.

I understand that Mourinho is ready to turn down Real Madrid, because he wants to coach in the Premiership and follow his mentor Sir Bobby Robson.

In addition, Roman Abramovich has outbid Real President Florentino Perez in the quest to land the coach, recently nominated number one in the world.

The midweek so-called showdown between chief executive Peter Kenyon and Ranieri was a complete farce, if not a sham.

The meeting was described as cordial as Kenyon outlined the club's five-year plan to go forward with a coach who would take a more global view of operations.

Ranieri agreed he would be willing to do that and Kenyon said he would get back to him after talks with Abramovich.

That has been seen as 'playing for time' while Chelsea review their options, notably advanced moves for Mourinho.

Ironically, Ranieri and Mourinho could clash in the final of the Champions League. Mourinho will be instantly elevated to one of the highest-paid coaches in the world, and Ranieri is poised for one of the biggest managerial payouts of all time to compensate him for all of the tribulations of Chelsea's quest to finds one of the best coaches for their new £200million team, with more big signings lined up for next season.

Ranieri is set for an £8million pay-off, £6million on the remaining three years' worth of potential bonuses, and a £1million loyalty payment wrapped up in a confidentiality clause.

He is also writing a diary of the season, but is loathe to spice it up at the request of the publishers, and would rather do a deal with Chelsea to retain his dignity, which prompted our readers to back the Italian to such an extent. But realistically it is Ranieri out, Mourinho in.

Alongside a rare article involving Jesper Gronkjaer was the massive headline that read: RISE AND RISE OF EUROPE'S MOST WANTED MANAGER.

Chelsea winger Gronkjaer believes the secret of Chelsea's Champions League success this season is the controversial rotation policy of Tinkerman manager Claudio Ranieri.

The Flying Dane admits it took time for players to adapt to the regime but reckons it was a major factor in the club reaching this week's semi-final against Monaco.

It was the introduction of Gronkjarer as a half-time substitute that helped Chelsea surge to victory in the quarter-final with Arsenal and he said that: "As a player it's natural you want to be involved in every match and there is some frustration at first when you don't get picked. But it becomes a way of life. You get used to it.

"You can see rotation can help with the amount of games we have to play in a season, especially if you progress in the Champions League. Then you see how it benefits the team. You still have your ups and downs as a player, and you have to learn to bounce back up. You cannot afford to feel sorry for yourself."

Gronkjaer's role against Arsenal was crucial and he added that: "I believe it was the best result the club has had for many years. You can't compare it even to the victory away to Lazio in the Champions League group stage. The Arsenal game was so important and it signifies what Chelsea can achieve. But it is only one game. There is a long way to go and we have to keep on proving ourselves."

Bookmakers – mainly with WilsonSports and Racing – have made Chelsea favourites to win the Champions League when holders AC Milan, Arsenal and Real Madrid were all surprisingly eliminated in the quarter-finals.

"Making us favourites only happened because of the media attention surrounding the club," said the 26-year-old Danish international. "Monaco must be a good team – they are always near the top of the French League and they have knocked out Real Madrid."

It is the morning of the semi-final in Monaco and, as my pal Den and I lunch on the beach in Famagusta, Hernan Crespo is shouting through the *Star* newspaper that: I'LL FIRE CHELSEA INTO FINAL – I'll prove I'm no £17million flop: Danny Fullbrook wrote a few lines saying that Romam Abramovich should be grateful he has Claudio Ranieri in charge of his Chelsea team tonight.

Red Rom has made it perfectly clear that he wants rid of the likeable Ranieri, as he builds a new Blue future at Stamford Bridge.

But it is Ranieri's tactical knowhow and defensive superiority, which has put Chelsea on the verge of their greatest ever triumph. Abramovich fell in love with the Champions League and decided to invest millions in Chelsea after watching Real Madrid and Manchester United knock six bells out of each other in last year's quarter-finals. He was at Old Trafford to see the spills and thrills of United winning 4-3 on the night, but crash out 6-5 on aggregate.

It was exciting stuff, but tellingly Madrid failed to make the final despite their high octane attacking play, and has since learned that not every football match is like that. Ronaldo, Raul, Zidane, David Beckham et al made the same mistake this year as Monaco overcame a 4-2 deficit to win their quarter-final 3-1 and book a last four berth against Chelsea as the Spanish giants again threw caution to the wind.

Chelsea, by contrast, have efficiently manoeuvred their way into the semi-finals under Ranieri's leadership with the type of away record every manager in Europe would be proud of.

In five matches on the continent before they faced Arsenal in the last round they had won every match without conceding a single goal. Arsenal's Jose Reyes is the only player to have scored a goal against Chelsea away from Stamford Bridge this season in Europe – but it was not enough. If Abramovich does get to celebrate Chelsea becoming European Champions, then he will have a lot to thank Ranieri and his brand of football for.

It was not by accident that AC Milan won last year playing with a cautious Italian style.

Fernando Morientes says that: "Frank Lampard is the player Monaco fear most and he said that: "Lampard is an extremely dangerous player and we will have to keep a close eye on him. Chelsea have pretty much a complete team, but of course it was pretty expensive to assemble."

He went on to be complimentary about the Blues but added also that, "We proved against Real Madrid that we can beat anyone and I'm sure we will find a way of beating Chelsea. The confidence that we now have after knocking out such a great side is amazing and we have real belief now. If we work hard and take the chances that come our way, we will make the final."

WAR ON TWO FRONTS
UNBREAKABLE BOND BORN OUT OF TRAGEDY

From the *Express*'s David Barnes in Monaco: Chelsea captain Marcel Desailly is heading for a poignant Champions League reunion with Monaco manager Didier Deschamps today.

Their semi-final first leg in Monte Carlo evokes the close friendship they have shared while acquiring football's greatest honours.

For both men – in addition to winning a World Cup with France – are dual European club champions already, together with Marseille and separately, Desailly with AC Milan and Deschamps with Juventus. Yet, inescapably and whoever goes on to contest the final, the setting for today's showdown will always be of tragic, if unspoken, significance to them.

For it was in Monaco exactly twenty years ago that Deschamps had the sad duty of telling Desailly his brother, Seth, had been killed in a car crash. Now they will be there on serious Champions League business. Then they were representing their country as teenagers on the lower slopes of football greatness. Desailly recalled: "Our life as inseparable friends had never been as fantastic as on that Sunday in November of 1984.

"We were staying in a Monaco hotel with the France junior team and had beaten Italy 2-0. What more could you ask for at sixteen?

"When Didier came into the room, I found him strange. He arranged his things in silence as if he were in a mood with me. He put his hand on my arm, a cold hand that gave me the shivers. He was trembling and had trouble speaking. I was afraid.

"I asked him what was the matter and he told me: "Marcel, Seth is dead…. a car accident at noon." Didier went down to the hotel dining room with me.

He didn't leave me for a second. I needed him, his presence and he had need of mine because I knew he was suffering. He was very fond of Beth. The rest of the squad were sat in silence at the table. They knew. Everyone knew. When the news fell, none of them had the courage to tell me.

"I don't hold that against them. A lot of strength is needed, even for an adult, to do such a thing. Didier did it. He told them: "It is for me to go and see Marcel." Not once have we ever spoken of this scene. But his hand on my arm will remain for me a supreme proof of friendship."

The bond between Desailly, who relates that moving passage in his book, Capitaine, and Deschamps, gives extra savour to a succulent, if unexpected semi.

Deschamps actually passed on his captain's armband to Desailly when he quit playing for France. Desailly, who played with Deschamps for a season at Chelsea, added that:

"Didier was already a lad of great maturity at fifteen. His presence alone reassured me. He always listened, brought me his strength, his wisdom. I offered him my extravagance, my laid-back attitude." The friendship blossomed in the happier, more carefree times they shared during their Nantes apprenticeship for big time football. Desailly explained that: "We lived our finest years, a rare period suspended between adolescence and adulthood. The time for competition to get a first team place or earn more than the boy in the next room had not yet come and we were obsessed by one thing: having a good time."

It was still all eyes on Monaco and I could not help feeling that the home side had the edge because of their attacking flair and looking back over the papers since returning home to Chelsea, came across a quote from my 'Man of the Match' Jerome Rothen, saying that: "A good team is one with great spirit and we've had that in our economic situation." So here was a match set up by two teams of vast background differences with Chelsea, the millionaires in the land of millionaires, which they call 'The Millionaires Playground' but the fighting spirit is not held in a pound coin, a euro or a peseta. The sight of Rothen and Morientes will bring shudders to the likes of Chelsea's full-backs as the ex-Real striker glides through down the channels in between the centre and full-backs whilst the trickery of Rothen is extremely exciting. Chelsea need to bolt down the hatches, unlike Real Madrid in the last round, and just hope that the playground is to their liking. This is not schoolboy stuff though and the Tinkerman must have his very best head on for tonight's big kick off otherwise you give a 'sniff' to the likes of Morientes and you pay the price, a price that money just cannot buy!

Crespo was now seen on the back page of the *Express* once again shouting that: 'THIS IS MY MOMENT'. In the *Mail* Jimmy Floyd was back page saying that: 'I CAN SHOOT CHELSEA TO THE FINAL'.

There is no doubt that the battle between John Terry – who was rested against Everton on Saturday – will need all of his strength and mental awareness to keep Morientes out of the firing line. I feel this is where the match will be won or lost, although the Tinkerman must get it right in his engine room with Frank Lampard and Scott Parker being my two in the middle of the pitch to combat any movement through the middle of the field and, of course, Mario Melchiot must have a big match if he is going to contain Rothen.

As the game came closer the story of Peter Kenyon having talks with Jose Mourinho were ripe but Porto president Pinto da Costa pledged that he will fight to keep his head coach from going anywhere and Chelsea in particular. But it seems the coach is hell-bent on Premiership football next season and that spells danger for the Tinkerman. In the *Daily Mail* today it read that David O'Leary had been sounded out by Peter Kenyon, but that looks to me like just another case of throwing certain people off the tracks that will lead to their eventual man in charge, and that will certainly not be the Tinkerman, even if he comes through this massive challenge.

CHAMPIONS LEAGUE SEMI-FINAL FIRST LEG
'ROTHEN RUNS RIOT'

It is the eve of my return journey from Famagusta – now Magusa – and I await the evening match in Monaco, which will be the most important match in the history of Chelsea Football Club, I say that because never before has there been so much importance – prestige and money to be earned – in such a competition and the Tinkerman saga goes on like the flying Scotski – and that is without my great pal Tommy Wisbey amongst the unwelcome passengers!

The big question now is can he overcome the power struggle and prepare his team after three very disappointing Premiership matches. Two draws at home against Everton and Middlesbrough and a defeat at Aston Villa, are simply not good enough when you have a squad of such size.

I will begin my feelings about their performance in my Friday column in the *Sentinel* and one which I wrote with horror – being explained in the first few lines: I have had my gambling head return whist on the island as my hotel – owned and run by great friends – has two betting shops and a casino. It's not Vegas but oh so tempting!

Last weekend I bet that Palace would draw at home to Wigan, Rotherham would do the same thing at home to Watford and the following day Sunderland would oblige by the same score against West Brom. Let me explain that I had three doubles and a treble and with the first two doing exactly as I said, I was two-thirds away from adding onto my new home here on this beautiful island. Once again the 'Mug in the Middle' messed up and as the two minute warning sign was held, up I was fifteen grand better off. Come two minutes and forty seconds, West Brom's best player Koumas – only on the field because their best defender pulled a hamstring – hit a hammerblow which kept my new home the same size. How unlucky can one get, now you know how I was the one hit by that runaway car many moons ago. My judgement is good in choosing the right results at the moment but my luck is simply incredible. Then I ponder before the Chelsea match wondering do I back Monaco – who I thought were a great bet, or just don't try to 'chase' that lost fifteen. I sat in horror as Monaco pulled back – with ten men – to overcome a Chelsea side who had dominated after losing an early goal and sat at half-time relieved that I was right to pull the oars in, and then the Tinkerman decides to put his neck further in the noose by changing a system that was working a treat. I have backed Claudio Ranieri but there are times I think the man is a stark raving lunatic. Why fix it if it is not broken, sprang to mind!

Then Morientes hit a wonderfully-struck volley that made the entire Chelsea purchases look a real waste of money. Why did Chelsea not buy him if they are so clever and hell bent on breaking the all-time spending spree. Again I am speechless, nearly!

I apologise for that, but it is all a part of the Alan Hudson column, the highs, the lows, the good, the bad and this last three days, the 'ugly'.

I have wrote several times about how dangerous it is playing against ten men, because when you are up against that situation you must – yourself – work even harder to make that 'spare' man work to your advantage.

Surely coaches of such experience must know such a thing!

After all, when you get £10million for being given your P45, at least show the supporters that you have a trick or two up your sleeve. Why did Ranieri bring Veron into the match? Why did he play Huth out of position as a substitute? And lastly, because of this his team became ragged – for the first time on their European 'Mission Impossible' and if I were in the seat of Peter Kenyon, I would take the opportunity that they have been looking for and called him into the office and gave him a hefty cheque and wished him well in his new job of creating jigsaw puzzles!

Ranieri, in my eyes, has just signed his own death warrant and his employers have missed the ceremony at 'Hangers Corner', if that indeed is what they have been trying to achieve?

The plot thickens!

FROM TINKER TO STINKER

At half-time I was close to calling my local bar where all the 'Bluenoses' would be screaming across the room to each other 'They got ten men and we the away goal' well isn't football a marvellous game, "Surely its in the bag, come on you Super Blues" shouts Brian. "Let's just hope they keep it as it is, he has no reason to change it," says Peter. Russ is peaceful in the corner dreaming of the final and thinking back to Wayne Bridge's goal at Highbury, what a moment that was!

The 'Water Carrier' who once played at the Bridge played his cards right, by telling his players to go test that water and in Jerome Rothen had the kind of player that made Damien Duff look like he was a newcomer to the wide game. "My goodness, who is this player" I asked my drinking companion big

Den, "Why is he not on Chelsea's list of summer bargains". With a man short they got the ball to him as much as humanly possible and it paid off, for it took Frank Lampard to lose his main role as navigating offence to aid poor old Mario Melchiot. Rothen put Chelsea well and truly on the back foot and with Veron playing as if he had just come off the moon that more than squared the match up as a ten-a-side, if not making it look as if Chelsea had now had a man short. Funny how one disruption can sink a smooth running ship, bad captaincy!

THE STINKERMAN

The *Daily Express* was the responsible for the above headline and it wore Claudio so well after such an appalling display of tinkering!

That headline was followed inside by: CLAUDIO GAMBLES AND BLOWS THE LOT – RANIERI SEES HIS DREAMS GO BUST IN MONTE CARLO: His comment here was that: 'THIS WAS EASILY THE WORST FORTY-FIVE MINUTES OF MY REIGN'.

In an amazing two-page interview with Spanish writer Juan Castro – the newspaper being called the *Marca* – the headlines read that: 'ABRAMOVICH KNOWS NOTHING ABOUT FOOTBALL. I ALREADY HAVE HIS SWORD STICKING INTO ME...AND EVEN IF WE WIN THE CHAMPIONS LEAGUE I'LL BE SACKED': 'He and his crew thought I'll sign him and we'll win.'

MARKS OUT OF TEN

We all have felt for Claudio Ranieri along this very rocky road of a season, and in his favour goes that he has stood form with great dignity, but a man of such great honour and dignity must see it through right to the bitter end. It seems right now that, as the pressure gets even more intense, one Roman is cracking. I have not changed my feelings about what has happened because for me, I think Chelsea got lucky against Arsenal, if only because of the circumstances that surrounded the match, but this is all about the end of the season pressure and fixture pile-up, call it what you will. Manchester United in the semi-final of the FA Cup beat Arsenal in that Champions League match at Highbury when Wayne Bridge wheeled across the Arsenal goalmouth with the German in the wrong position one more time – and oh god – Wenger was just quoted as saying he will wear that awful coloured yellow jersey next season. Don't back Arsenal to win in Europe!

I am never one to take such notice of the marks out of ten that newspaper writers give, but this was close by the *Mail*'s Ian McGarry as he gave Frank Lampard eight – for his first half performance I am certain – and the Tinkerman three, which for me was far too many for an awful display of management at such a delicate part of such an important ball game. This reminded me though, of Dave Sexton preparing for our European Cup Winners Cup Final replay against Real Madrid in Athens, way back in 1971.

We had been pegged back to a 1-1 draw in the dying minutes by a very useful
Spanish team, in the match I went through in the first half and as I was about
to put the ball into the keeper's left-hand corner, a big Spanish leg came across
my thighs and I hit the ground thinking that I had just been shot. No, I
promise I have never dived like today's players, mainly because with all the
running I did I would have looked an even bigger idiot than some of the
modern day actors – Makelele – the latest clown!

By taking this knock I received which we called in those days a 'dead leg'
which needed treatment but looked much worse than what it was. But I was
struggling and the FA Cup Final of the year before came shooting from the
back to the front of my mind. There was no way I was going to miss this replay,
especially with a badly-bruised leg. So I told Sexton my treatment was merely
precautionary as his mind was working like this crazy Italian around this time.
We had won the match once and he was probably thinking 'sod young
Hudson, he will be out with the hounds later while I am at church' but I was
having none of it, I was going to run this off in the most important match of
out lives in a Blue shirt. And, for me, very much still a very young life!

But back to the display of the French winger – which is not a criticism of
Chelsea's defending – just a mention of a player who – if this was not a one-
off display – is some kind of player. He had Chelsea chasing shadows and those
shadows gave Chelsea more daylight in other parts of their attacking plan. This
was a big step up for Chelsea and they failed to do the 'Italian Job' by giving
a second half performance so foreign to all those trips abroad so far this season.
But this was not down to the players, it seemed that the Tinkerman was having
some kind of personal crisis standing, on a very sedate first-half touchline.
After an inspiring first forty-five minutes, Frank looked out of sorts – a big
minus for Chelsea – after the interval which was more baffling when you
think his industrious nature gets more and more witnessed the longer the
match continues. One again we were witnessing the effect that a runaway train
can have on a player and the Italian now becomes that deadly and dangerous
steam engine. Oh, how they miss the Chelsea playmaker – and goal-taker –
when he is not at his best, but this is the big stage and your opponents a little
more than the Premiership and the two main players I have mentioned are
brilliant. Then again, we'll wait and see what goes on at the Bridge in a
fortnight. I believe the French team will score at least one goal!

I also felt that the Stinkerman's decision to pull off Scott Parker once again
was a massive mistake, because in matches where you have the spare player, you
must impose yourself even more so than before and Parker imposes himself on
the opposition alright. I add that I think he made this move because it paid off
at Highbury but this time it backfired big time he and – if he only knew it –
that was his biggest mistake – and most costly – since taking over at Stamford
Bridge. But after Monaco had gained full control of this match, I sat antici-
pating a strike from the French team and when it came, what a strike it was
from Fernando Morientes, the man Real Madrid allowed to leave, and that

came back to haunt them as this ultra-talented striker hit two of the goals that put an end of their champions League dreams. The ball was hit sweetly into the right hand side of the Chelsea box with Morientes being policed by John Terry, but before the Chelsea skipper could get his full body across Morientes, the Monaco striker hit an unstoppable volley into the near post of Marco Ambrosio and Chelsea were in tatters and about to concede yet again, how costly that third goal could turn out to be!

I am now back in England and looking over the response to such a woeful second half display and what is the most astounding thing is that Chelsea are still punting for a new manager before the second leg is even upon us. I say this through the newspapers and oh to be a 'fly on the wall' once more as to how much of this book is media fabrication – not on my side – and how much really has come from the wagging tongues in the offices at Stamford Bridge. Before I go into any more reports of this first Monaco match I'll just let you know before the French team come to town that the Blues face Southampton at the Bridge and it will be interesting to see just what kind of team the STINKERMAN – which he is now being called – is about to select.

The headlines on the back page of the *Sun* went like this: TINKBOMB with Ranieri saying that: WE LOST THE PLOT AND ITS ALL MY FAULT inside read that ITS JUAN FOOT IN THE GRAVE AS CLAUDIO FLOPS BIG TIME.

The sending-off of Makelele did not help and the *Sun* had this to say about that incident: CHEATING MAKELELE FIRES UP FRENCH AFTER SHAMEFUL PLAY-ACTING. This followed the headline of CONACO!

What I must add as I breeze through the papers that were waiting for me on my return from Cyprus, were the collection of photographs that were inside and outside of them. The two main characters of the book began with the title-holders but through a long, traumatic and never ending season it seems that two youngsters – Frank Lampard and John Terry – have stolen the show. And it was their faces more than all others that told the story of the Tinker and the Talisman, in other words – Tony Bennett again – they were hurting badly as they left the pitch in Monaco!

I am not going to write what these journalists had to say about the game because you will know, by now, it is becoming laughable, but I never thought I'd see and read the day where the headlines and pictures told the whole story: CRUELLEST OF ALL – BLUES COLLAPSE AFTER CLAUDIO BLAST was on the back of the *Express*, with a shot of Eidur Gudjohnsen leaving the field as if just being caught for a rape charge. Alongside him Frank stood closed eyes, looking like he had just won the lottery and could not remember whether he threw the ticket or not. The third character here was Makelele, who for me, quite an average performer and should never play in front of Scott Parker. At the bottom of the page it showed the Stinkerman looking like Tommy Cooper after one of his silliest tricks had had the audience in fits – only this time fits of madness!

The headlines just kept on coming as inside, above Morientes pulling his tongue out to both Chelsea and Real Madrid, said: RANIERI FALLS FOR THE OLD ONE-TWO – I AM TO BLAME BUT THIS ROMAN HAS BEEN STABBED IN THE BACK.

Other news baffled the Chelsea faithful – and me – when on the back of the *Sun* it showed a nightmare picture of Veron by the side of a headline I'M NOT FIT TO PLAY – VERON'S PLEA TO RANIERI AS HE SENT HIM ON THE PITCH TO PLAY: Inside he said that. "We all feel we have blown it." "WE FEEL LIKE SHIT"

In the *Express* it was back to Veron as the top of the page read that CHELSEA'S HORROR IN MONACO FOLLOWED A BLAZING HALF-TIME ROW – Don't put me on begged Veron – £15million man in furious bust-up with Ranieri. Inside it ran RANIERI'S STRING OF TACTICAL BLUNDERS IN MONTE CARLO SEEM TO HAVE VINDICATED ABRAMOVICH'S RUTHLESS SEARCH FOR A SUCCESSOR: THE PROOF THAT ROMAN NEEDED: Juan Sebastian Veron had been out for five months and came on against Middlesbrough just two weeks ago – after having treatment in Buenos Aires on a bad back injury – he then pulled out of the following match at Aston Villa claiming he had strained a back muscle in the warm-up. Now tell me does that sound like the kind of preparation for a match of this nature?

BLUES GIVEN A FEW LESSONS IN FOOTBALL
BY DESCHAMPS

John Dillon wrote that: Prince Albert of Monaco stood on a table amid the beautiful people as Café Sass twirled his red and white scarf above his head and whooped with delight. And they say Chelsea are the club with all the wealthy and powerful connections. Around the same time in the early hours yesterday, Roman Abramovich was presumably on his yacht in the nearby harbour, pondering yet another shortlist of managerial replacements for Claudio Ranieri and, perhaps, wondering why he ever got involved with football. Old money conquered new money here on Tuesday when Monaco tore apart Chelsea's carefully constructed barrier of resolve and moved one more, loaded roll of dice from the European Cup Final. Abramovich is scouring Europe for someone – anyone? – to replace Ranieri. Given his taste for buying expensive new players as soon as he hears about them, we can now guess he may now fancy Dider Deschamps, as his new coach along with apparent favourite Jose Mourinho of Porto.

Ranieri is supposed to have said Abramovich knows nothing about football. But in a week when the Champions League is dominated at its critical stage by the modest clubs of Europe, he ought now at least to understand the game does not allow success to be bought off a peg. Monaco represent the old money. Prince Albert's father, Prince Ranier, is club member number one and his family have ruled here since 1391. But with great irony given the opulent surroundings, Chelsea's former midfielder, Deschamps, has had to plaster together a team by the methods more familiar to managers at the cheap end of the Premiership.

Mourinho, whose team met Deportivo in the other semi-final last night, has fashioned an equally powerful attacking force in the same way, which must surely underline the point to Abramovich.

But it is Deschamps, 37, whose achievement is the most notable for two reasons. Need I go any further as the Stinkerman is showing signs of a split personality, for his tinkering is supposed to be all about playing players at the right time in a very long and hard season. The *Mail* said that A TINKER TOO FAR COSTS CLAUDIO HIS CREDIT: EVEN THE TEAM DOUBT MANAGER AFTER GAMBLES IN MONACO FAIL SPECTACU-LARLY.

On my return to London, I was reading through the numerous newspapers that my son Allen and Steve August had saved me and came across a piece written by Steve Howard of the *Sun* with the headline that I'LL FINISH MY BEST MATES DREAM: Didier Deschamps is ready to kill off the Champions League hopes of yet another great mate. The Monaco coach did it in the last round when Zinedine Zidane's mighty Real Madrid lost 3-1 at the Stade Louis II and crashed out on away goals. And the French World Cup-winning skipper will have no qualms either about ending 35-year-old Marcel Desailly's dreams of a last appearance in the Champions League Final. Deschamps also 35, has known Desailly since they were kids at Nantes. He also starred alongside him for Marseille and Chelsea. They won the 1998 World Cup and Euro 2000 together before Deschamps handed over the French captaincy to a man he acknowledges as his best friend in football.

Deschamps, a Champions League winner with Juventus and Marseille, said that: "I seem to have known Marcel all my life, he is like a brother to me. But there can be no sentiment in football. Once the teams walk out on the pitch, we will be in opposing corners – both wanting totally different results. Yes, it is difficult when you are close but you have to blank it out – just as I had to do with Azou in the last round. It will be lovely to see Marcel again and normally I would really want to get him to another Champions League Final. But this is a time when there is so much at stake. This is a time when friend-ship must be forgotten for ninety minutes. I respect Marcel enormously but don't fear him. And it will not concern me if Chelsea fall at the final hurdle." Roman Abramovich's billions do not worry him either.

MIXTURE

Monaco almost went out of business last summer with debts of £35million.

Deschamps added that: "Every coach wants as much help as he can get. And, yes, money is a key factor in success. But it still cannot guarantee success. You only get that through hard work and correct tactics."

It was a mixture of both that saw Monaco, seven times French champions, stun favourites Real Madrid in the quarter-final after losing 4-2 in the Bernabeu.

Yet striker Fernando Morientes, the Monaco ace on loan from Real, claimed that people should not have been that surprised. Morientes – already a triple Champions League winner – said: "We were disappointed with the 4-2 scoreline – we thought we deserved far more. And we carried that belief and spirit into the second-leg. And that is the spirit that has been created under Deschamps. We know we are the underdogs against Chelsea – just as we were against Real. We know we don't have many fans and we know that people look down on us. But we have each other, we have our pride and we know you don't win matches on reputation."

This had been a big setback and, on returning from France, they had to travel to St James's Park, where the opposition were desperate for a result themselves in that yearly race for the fourth Champions League spot for next season. The media were now doing a u-turn about the Stinkerman situation, having backed him recently along with the many, many thousands of fans that frequent the Bridge each and every home match.

Chelsea though had a great opportunity to get back some self- pride as the home side were without three very instrumental players in Craig Bellamy, Keiron Dyer and Jermaine Jenas but with Alan Shearer around and about 'never say never' and Newcastle know that they have a player who will die for the cause every time he pulls that black and white shirt over his head. Today was no different and after Joe Cole had put the Blues in front after only five minutes, and then should have scored again not long after, the Geordies slowly played their way back into a pulsating match. Jonathan Woodgate was looking more and more the player he was in his early days at Leeds United and is surely very much in the frame with Campbell and Terry for Portugal. Chelsea's first two attacks saw Joe Cole stroll through a wide open Newcastle defence to notch the first, then he should have done so again when a delightful Eidur Gudjohnsen pass saw him face Shay Given once more only when seeing the whites of arguably the best goalkeeper in the Premiership's eyes, Cole scuffed his great chance and the opportunity to put Newcastle under real pressure and a couple of goals down. I am so surprised today of the amount of one on one misses by players with so much ability, or am I?

The match came alive a minute before the break as United piled on the pressure knowing if Chelsea went in a goal up it would be just the tonic they needed after their midweek drubbing in France. There is no better time to score and the goal was a peach – if you were a Newcastle fan or a neutral that is – and it came after Shearer, Laurent Robert and Shola Ameobi all went close to pegging Chelsea back. Then, as I said, the equaliser came after Ameobi turned Desailly – what is he doing still playing – with far too much ease before firing a great right-footed strike into the Chelsea net. But the best was yet to come as the best striker in the Premiership hit a goal that will go down with any of the best he cares to remember and he needs some memory. Within just three minutes of the second half, a ball dropped for the ex-England captain after he too embarrassed the ex-French captain by turning him also and after changing his body swivelled and hit an almost unstoppable 'big dipper'" from fully thirty-five yards that left Ambrosia clutching at rice. Robson said afterwards that it was the best goal his skipper has scored for the club and there could not have been one person in a packed St James's Park who could have argued with such a statement. Chelsea had now picked up only two points since their Champions League win at Highbury, but they still were a point in front of champions Manchester United with a four-goal superior goal difference, but that just about tells you the story of the season had by the team who usually went into top gear after the Easter period. Ranieri said that he was: "very pleased with the players' reaction after Tuesday's defeat in Monaco. They reacted very well and I think we deserved a point, but if we had stayed out there for another two hours I do not think we would have scored. We have a few days to get together and we need a change of luck because without luck you cannot do a thing."

It still amazes me that the Stinkerman talks of such thing, when Chelsea Football Club have paid out so much money on so-called goal scorers, and that is on top of already having Jimmy Floyd and Eidur, not forgetting Mikael Forssell, who is banging them in right, left and centre at Birmingham!

The headline in the *Daily Mail* said it all: SHEARER CLASSIC!

PAY SHOCKER FOR LAMPARD
Chelsea reject Frank's demand for pay parity with overseas players

Exclusive by Ian McGarry of the *Mail*: Chelsea have refused Frank Lampard's demands to be paid the same as his celebrated overseas teammates. Contract negotiations aimed at tying outstanding England midfielder Lampard to Chelsea long-term were dramatically halted last night – April 23rd – after weeks of discussions failed to produce an agreement.

Steve Kutner, Lampard's agent, confirmed that: "Talks between Chelsea and ourselves have stopped because the club said that they could not agree to the terms which we were looking for."

Lampard, 25, and widely accepted as Chelsea's best player this season, is keen to stay, although it was chief executive Peter Kenyon who had intimated that the club wanted the player to sign a new five-year deal. It is understood that there have been four meetings between the parties, the last of which was in London yesterday afternoon.

Lampard is thought to be seeking financial parity with other players such as Frenchman Claude Makelele and Argentine Juan Veron, who earned in the region £80,000-a-week after joining Russian billionaires' Roman Abramovich's purchase of the club in July last year.

Kenyon has indicated that will not happen and unbelievably, Chelsea have now put themselves in a position where they risk alienating a player who is an overwhelming favourite of the fans and seen by them as the heart of the team.

Lampard – who signed from West Ham for £11million – and has two years left on his current contract, earns less than half the amount as the teammates with whom he seeks equality.

After the debacle of their 3-1 defeat in Monaco at Stade Louis II on Tuesday, and the continuing chaos surrounding who will be manager next season, a stalemate in contract extension talks with a valuable, high profile player was the last thing the unsettled club needed.

The situation could be exacerbated further by growing interest in Lampard from Inter Milan, who sent two of their most senior officials to assess him in Monaco.

Inter general manager Gabriele Oriali was accompanied by assistant director of sport Marco Branca, and they returned home convinced that an attempt should be made to purchase Lampard in the summer.

Inter have been tracking the player all season and Tuesday's examination was simply a final look before they set their recruiting targets for next season. The Italian club are willing to offer a choice of player – possibly Holland midfielder Andy van der Meyde or even powerful left-sided Brazil striker Adriano – to reduce the cash requirement in a valuation that is expected to be more than £15million.

As *Sportsmail* revealed last February, Inter have been tracking Lampard for months and scouts had already prepared a detailed dossier on his suitability for the Italian league.

Club president Massimo Moratti would have no trouble dealing with Lampard's representative as Steve Kutner's clients include Paul Ince, who was captain for Inter for two years.

The preferred option of the player is to sign a new contract and stay at Chelsea and he admitted as much in an interview with *Sportsmail* immediately before the Champions League match against Arsenal, in which he was to score a vital, second-leg goal.

"I wouldn't rule it out (playing abroad) but the way I feel just now is I'm very settled here. My family lives here and my girlfriend is living here and I'm very happy. If it remained that way then I would stay here – at Chelsea – for the rest of my career, for sure. Going abroad is something I might do, but not definitely."

If talks do not resume and a compromise cannot be found, Lampard could simply afford to sit tight, forcing the club into a situation in which they would have to offer a new deal or risk losing him for a considerably smaller fee than they could command at the end of this season.

As if the Lampard situation was not demoralising enough, Chelsea are also bracing themselves for some more bad news today with UEFA expected to hand Marcel Desailly a three match ban for elbowing Monaco striker Fernando Morientes during Tuesday's defeat.

The Spain forward added his voice to the criticism of the Chelsea captain last night when he taunted Desailly that his advancing years were the reason he resorted to foul play. Morientes said that: "Desailly was trying to upset me throughout the game constantly, but I never responded to his provocation." If UEFA do the right thing after watching the video his season in Europe would be over.

"The problem for Desailly is that he is no longer the player he was, and his age has caught up with him. I have lost respect for what he did."

Desailly's Chelsea position, meanwhile, may come under threat with the news that £17million-rated Argentine centre-half Walter Samuel wants to leave Roma and join the London club.

BATESY – MY PROGRAMME NOTES

Chelsea invested £45million in Juan Sebastian Veron when he signed from Manchester United lat August.

A £16million transfer fee, 5 per cent levy to the Premiership, £20million wages over four years, bonuses, 13 per cent National Insurance contributions plus £2million or so as Pini Zahavi's cut.

Something tells me there could be a few medical bills as well. And what have they got in return?

A player who has made just nine starts this season. From his attitude on the pitch against Monaco this week, you got the impression he wasn't interested.

So when is he going to be fit?

Rather, will he ever be fit?

I think it is perfectly reasonable to ask this question. It is also perfectly reasonable to ask how he passed his medical before joining Chelsea. If he indeed did!

Further, is it true that, at the time, doubts were voiced in the club about his fitness! And that they were overruled from above?

Most people who saw his second-half performance against Monaco could hardly believe it. Yet they should not have been surprised. For as soon as he arrived at Stamford Bridge, Veron claimed he was unfit.

This was all the more remarkable seeing that just a week earlier, there had been glowing reports of his form on United's pre-season tour of the USA.

How then did he only manage nine of Chelsea's first nineteen matches?

And out of them how many ninety-minute performances did he deliver?

Since then he has stumbled through a further 78 minutes in five months. You have to wonder how bad this back problem is.

DISASTER

What do Chelsea do with their £45million investment now?

If they wanted to offload him, who is going to buy him?

What is he going to offer any potential club?

I raised my own doubts when I heard he was coming to Chelsea. He was a bloody disaster at United and I firmly believe the club didn't need him. In fact, former chief executive Trevor Birch held the deal up as he tried to talk Roman Abramovich and his advisors out of it. Well, chickens came home to roost at Stade Louis II on Tuesday night. And turkeys.

Okay, Claudio Ranieri cocked up by playing Veron. But even if he weren't fully fit, he could have still pulled his finger out. There is no doubt the decision to send him on after the break cost us the game. He didn't make one tackle, he hardly completed a pass, he gave the ball away and he got caught in possession.

In Italy people sat back and allowed Veron to play. How unfair opponents in the Premiership don't. Not that it affected Gianfranco Zola.

There was one point in the match when he was tracking this guy and running alongside him as if he was out in the park for a jog.

I must come in here: I am amazed that the ex-Chelsea chairman would notice such an instant and it is pretty funny because years ago in the USA my son Anthony – who had never played soccer before – played in a small sided match at an indoor football centre my old pal Don Shanks was running. My wife then – Maureen – asked if he could join in to which the obvious reply was "of course he can, he'll enjoy it," and Anthony entered the arena as I sat not knowing what to expect. My son was a good athlete and could run from one side of the field to the other whilst the others boys stopped to take a well earned rest. But he never once touched the ball, when his team had possession he ran along enjoying watching but, to my compete amazement, he did exactly the same when the other team had the ball. Exactly what Bates has just said, and on the day following the Monaco match, I mentioned this to his elder brother Allen, who remembered it well. Maybe the gist of my story is that Anthony should have made it as a player after all on this latest experience involving the Argentine superstar come misfit!

Years later Anthony was signed at West Ham and became disillusioned about not having been given the 'god given' talent of Joe Cole who he had played with in the youth team, but as I said earlier, this should have been his biggest and best opportunity to work harder at his game and try to catch Cole up. Again I repeat myself, this is only what Frank Lampard has done after the club bringing so many players in – Veron included – and simply got it into his mind that he would work as hard as he possibly could, to make himself irreplaceable, and Frank has more than succeeded, I am delighted to write!

Ken Bates' programme notes are good but I have stopped right there because I am sure he would not have given me as much space in his book, and if he did it would be quite insulting, I am certain of that.

I remember the first time I spent some time with him – we were in his office – talking about me working in Drakes Bar, after which he offered to show me around the stand which was still being built. Then as we arrived back at the top near his office he showed me the outside surroundings and pointed over to the West Stand and said: "You know we have the bars here named after ex-Chelsea heroes and I am thinking of having one for you," and with that pointed finger said: "It would be over there and be called BRANDIES." I was not amused, but accepted that the man was who he was and got his little kicks his way, but at the end of the day I have performed admirably in front of many, many thousands of Chelsea fans in that stadium, and brandy or no brandy, I stick with a childish 'sticks and stones'. And oh, by the way, I have seen you fall out of a black cab on more than one occasion – at the gates of the Bridge – after a healthy and wealthy lunch. In fact it was quite funny once, Mr Bates got out of a black cab and half-stumbled under a crane whilst they were still building the entrance, and me and my friend Malcolm Molineux were in fits as we sat outside the pub opposite the main entrance to the ground.

He goes on by saying that: No wonder some of these foreign players are viewed as mercenaries. Yes – you can have one or two – especially if you have a solid home-grown base. But more than that you are inviting trouble.

Your programme notes are now closed down for a second time Mr Bates, but of course like me you have also left the building!

In the *Express* three days after Monaco, the headline read like this; DON'T SELL BECKS-REAL'S £20million 'BONUS' TO KEEP ENGLAND ACE: Harry Harris wrote that: Real Madrid have been handed a stunning incentive by Sportswear giants Adidas – keep David Beckham and there's an extra £20million in it for you.

In the *Mail* it read like this: CHELSEA'S BUY-TO-LET BECKS BID – Year-long loan back to Madrid could hole key to a Real deal: In the *Standard* David was front-page news with:

£40million BECKS FOR CHELSEA – I'll be playing in Premiership next year, friends told: Chelsea are poised to make a £40million bid to bring David Beckham back to the Premiership.

The Club has made little secret of its desire to capture the England captain from Real Madrid.

And the possibility of his return escalated today after it was revealed he has told members of his inner circle he will be playing in England next season.

Reliable sources says it is now a 'certainty' Beckham will leave Madrid in the next few months in a spectacular summer deal.

It has been a tumultuous year in Spain. Following speculations that Beckham had two affairs, and his wife Victoria's refusal to move from the Spanish capital, the player is ready to move for the sake of the family.

Already Britain's richest sportsman, it is believed Beckham will earn up to £100,000 a week at Stamford Bridge. He will continue to earn about £15million a year from personal associations with twelve companies and his commercial standing has not been affected by recent negative publicity.

His impending return is being discussed in the upper echelons of his business entourage.

The *Evening Standard* revealed two weeks ago that Chelsea were forging links with the Real Madrid midfielder. Even before his private life broke, Victoria was allegedly telling close friends that her husband would be coming back to play in England after Euro 2004. Beckham has since denied this, stating he is happy in Madrid and intends to see out his four-year deal at the Bernabeu. Yet there are continuing, but unconfirmed, reports that he met Chelsea's new owner, Russian billionaire Roman Abramovich, in a Madrid restaurant in the last week of February in a meeting organised by a close friend of Beckham.

That friend – former youth-team player Dave Gardner – has been regularly seen in Madrid in recent weeks and is said to be working towards a position where a deal could happen if all the parties are willing.

Beckham's new personal manager, Terry Byrne, was also on Chelsea's backroom staff under Gianluca Vialli and still has close links at the club.

It was reported today that several top companies with whom Beckham has lucrative deals are also being kept informed of events.

Vodafone, Marks and Spencer and Pepsi arrange long-term advertising promotions around the player.. Beckham features in a major campaign for Pepsi with other Real Madrid players.

There were also reports today that Chelsea may sign Beckham on a buy-to-let basis – buying him this summer but loaning the player back to the player to the Spanish champions next season.

A sign now, play later, deal would allow the Blues to prepare for an assault on foreign markets at the beginning of 2005/6 season.

The situation at Real is also volatile, with millionaire entrepreneur Enrique Sobrino challenging Florentino Perez   for presidency in this summer's club elections.

Part of his election pledge has been to sell Beckham.

The following day there was something of a turnaround in views as to where the London born Beckham will be heading, if he does indeed leave Madrid! The *Express* headlines read that: Homesick England captain to snub Chelsea for Arsenal – Huge bonus for Wenger as Beckham asks Real to set up move to Highbury – I WANT TO BE A GUNNER: says David, right out of the blue! In an *Express* exclusive David Hytner reports that: David Beckham is desperate to leave Madrid and has ordered his advisers to do a deal to take him to Arsenal. The England captain is ready to put the last few months of hell behind him to return to Britain – and Arsene Wenger is ready to welcome him at Highbury.

Beckham told Madrid president Florentino Perez he wanted to leave Spain the week after the news of his alleged affair broke out. As Beckham is rated at £40million, Chelsea, with their unlimited funds, had seemed most likely to secure his signature.

But *Express Sport* can reveal that Arsenal are plotting a player–plus–cash deal to bring the midfielder home. Beckham has told Madrid, Arsenal are the club he wants to sign for, believing there is less of a circus surrounding Highbury. And Real are likely to go with his demands as they view Chelsea's financial muscle more of a threat to their ambition than Arsenal's prowess on the field.

With all the media focus on Roman Abramovich's Chelsea, Beckham is also concerned he would simply become a brand image for the club. Wenger dropped a heavy hint yesterday that he wanted the ex-Manchester United star. "Beckham would interest me, of course he would. He's an interesting player for any manager because he's a great player. He does not live far from here either. He wouldn't need a helicopter to get here, he could come by bike!

"But we cannot afford him."

Arsenal do not have the cash to buy Beckham outright, but the prospect of bringing him in by offloading a few players is an appealing one to the Arsenal board. However, Real are certain to exact a heavy price to release Beckham. The Spanish giants have long coveted Patrick Vieira, while Freddie Lundberg is another player who is admired throughout Europe.

Robert Pires and Thierry Henry could also enter negotiations, although Arsenal would never part with their striker.

Wenger also warned United to hang on to star man Ruud van Nistelrooy in the face of overtures from Spain – or face the consequences.

"When you lose a striker who scores 25–30 goals a season you cannot say you are stronger. No matter how much money you have available, there are not so many strikers at Nistelrooy's level.

"You do not have to find a striker on the corner of every street who is as good as him. But I cannot imagine that Ferguson would allow him to go."

Well, there you have it, you could say 'what a difference a day makes' in the media here in England.

The evening after Chelsea's defeat at the hands of Monaco there was heartache for Newcastle United as well, as Marseille took them apart in France by two goals scored by the French Football of the Year, Didier Drogba. This is the first time I have seen this player and I can assure you it will not be the last, for he is so wonderfully gifted and the Geordies had nothing to stop him. In some ways he reminds me of Jay Jay Okocha of Bolton, but is obviously deadlier around the opponents' penalty area, because for all of his brilliance this season the Bolton player did not score a single Premiership goal, which if you had asked for odds at the beginning of the season they would have offered you any price you liked!

One headline in the *Daily Mail* simply said it all: DEADLY DROGBA.

It was still all Chelsea on the Friday before the Manchester United match at Old Trafford, one which Chelsea only needed a point to secure second place in the Premiership. The headlines on this Friday morning read: ROMAN WANTS NEW LEGION – SECOND BEST JUST NOT GOOD ENOUGH said John Terry – and then it was all about the new manager coming in: DO IT YOUR WAY JOSE – New Blues boss wants final say: In the *Star* it showed: MONEY CAN'T BUY YOU SUCCESS AS CHELSEA SKIPPER TERRY IS LEFT GUTTED BY EURO EXIT – SECOND IS SO HARD TO TAKE: This was on a full double page giving us an indication of the coming and goings once Mourinho has his Chelsea tracksuit on:

OUT: Juan Sebastian Veron, Marcel Desailly, Jimmy Floyd, Mario Melchiot, Emmanuel Petit, Jesper Gronkjaer and Hernan Crespo: While in the IN tray were: Frank Lampard, John Terry, Glen Johnson, William Gallas, Wayne Bridge, Damien Duff, Adrian Mutu, Scott Parker and MAYBE Joe Cole.

In the *Daily Mail* it was interesting to read such headlines: 'SO WHAT HAS ROMAN REALLY DONE FOR US?': Well, he's spent more per minute on Veron than Bill Gates earns: They did a breakdown of the cost of the new Revolution at Stamford Bridge and this what it showed with the heading:

WHAT THE CZAR GOT FOR HIS MILLIONS

	Transfer fee	Weekly wage	Per minute on field
Glen Johnson	£6million	£22,000	£3,068
Geremi	£7million	£35,000	£3,171
Wayne Bridge	£7million	£35,000	£2,239
Damien Duff	£17million	£40,000	£8,071
Hernan Crespo	£16.8million	£82,000	£11,700
Joe Cole	£6.6million	£38,000	£3,748
Claude Makelele	16.6million	£82,000	£6,000
Scott Parker	£10million	£85,000	£19,133
Adrian Mutu	£15.8million	£54,000	£8,211

Matt Lawton wrote that: Financial statistics can be misleading, but here is one that might trouble someone as rich as Roman Abramovich: during their season together at Stamford Bridge, Juan Sebastian Veron has cost the Russian more per-minute than he has earned.

If fact for the time that Veron has spent on the pitch for Chelsea, the Argentine international midfielder has challenged as prolific an accumulator of wealth as Bill Gates. Last year, Abramovich, currently the 25th richest man in the world, earned £13,689 per minute, while Gates – of Microsoft fame – leads Chelsea's owner by a few lengths on £17,000.

But Veron, Abramovich will be staggered to discover, had drained the Russian private fortune of £19,133 for every sixty seconds he has strutted his stuff.

If Chelsea's Russian owner was looking for value for money when he agreed to pay £15million for Veron last summer and then handed him a contract that, with bonuses, is worth the best part of £100,000 a week, he must be feeling rather disappointed.

Veron, like many of those who arrived in west London last summer, has amounted to little more than an extravagance this season, chief dilettante among a group of players who have merely dabbled with the idea of representing Chelsea.

At Stamford Bridge on Wednesday night, eight of the Chelsea players who started against Monaco were at the club before Abramovich arrived.

Of the three who made it into Claudio Ranieri's side, two of them – Joe

Cole and Wayne Bridge – were young Englishmen who still have something to prove, so much for blowing £120million on the big occasion. In fairness to Damien Duff, injury denied him the opportunity to help his colleagues pursue a place in the Champions League Final.

For the likes of Hernan Crespo, Veron, Adrian Mutu and Claude Makelele, such excuses simply will not wash.

Just how responsible Ranieri is for recruiting these players remains a mystery, but the feeling is that the Italian was emasculated as a manager the moment Sven Goran Eriksson was caught on camera outside Roman Abramovich's London home last July.

If your intention from the start is to sack your coach at the end of the season, it seems unlikely that you would then let him loose with the company chequebook

Many of those who were signed by Chelsea last summer, and indeed in January, appeared to come with Eriksson's blessing. They were players he had worked with in the past, as well as in his current role as England coach. From a distance, many suspected, he was building his team for when he arrived this summer.

The Swede, of course, will deny such suggestions, just as he continues to deny that the meeting with Abramovich was anything more than a social chat over a cup of tea.

A chance to discuss new players in the company of Pini Zahavi, the Israeli super agent, is somewhere closer to the truth.

Lucky for Eriksson, then, that he did eventually choose to reject Chelsea's advances and remain with the Football Association, because he might have been forced to admit to his mistakes and ask Abramovich if he could start again.

Rebuilding Chelsea is the task that now appears to face Jose Mourinho, the Porto coach who is expected to leave for Stamford Bridge the moment the European Cup in Gelsenkisrchen on May 26th has reached it's conclusion. Mourinho will be under enormous pressure to deliver the prizes that proved to be beyond Ranieri, and in such a situation he will need players who share his commitment and desire.

Winning the Premiership is the least Arbramovich will accept, and that will not be easy when a wonderful Arsenal team will be looking to defend their title and a wounded Manchester United will be hell-bent on gaining revenge. That probably means saying au revoir or whatever else the likes of Veron, Crespo, and Makelele, and then calling on Abramovich to support another major spending spree.

Arjen Robben is already on his way, and David Trezeguet and others are sure to follow. Mario Melchiot's failure to deal with Monaco's Jerome Rothen exposed the need for another right-back, while Jesper Gronkjaer's inconsistency pointed to the recruitment of David Beckham. Frank Lampard deserves world-class assistance and the failings of Mutu and Crespo call for new goal-scoring talent.

Mourinho looked perfectly at ease as he signed autographs for Chelsea supporters on Wednesday. That, however, was the calm before the storm.

GREAVSIE

Hands up for those who had heard of Jose Mourinho six months ago.

Go on, be honest. If I had said 'Mourinho' to you at the start of the year, would you really have a clue?

I'm not being patronising – because I didn't. In January, I could have said to you: "The boss of Porto, that's who he is."

And you would have replied: "Yeah, so what?"

I bet that would have been the reaction from the Premiership chairmen as well.

Yet victories over Manchester United, Lyon and Deportivo, have made him the most wanted man in Europe.

Little wonder English managers in the Premiership and further down the leagues are shaking their heads.

Let's take a pair of them for example.

Sam Allardyce and Alan Curbishley have been working miracles at Bolton and Charlton.

Yet when the Manchester United job comes up in a couple of years – or that at Arsenal if Arsene Wenger decides to move on – will they be in the running?

Would Steve Bruce make an emotional return to Old Trafford as boss given the amazing job he has done with Birmingham City?

What about Nigel Worthington, who has steered Norwich back to the promised land of the Premiership.

FEELING

And what about Gary Megson, who has managed to keep his team motivated enough to win promotion two times in three seasons.

When the Chelsea job comes up at the end of the season, and indeed any other big job such as that at Liverpool, they will be nowhere in the running.

The problem is that there is a modern day feeling that British is not the best. Despite the perfect example in Alex Ferguson, who was brought down from Scotland to revive an ailing giant.

Every time a top Premiership job comes up, it is immediately Sven Goran Eriksson, Fabien Capello, Giovanni Trapattoni and now Mourinho who are mentioned.

Yet I look at all the European Cup wins for British clubs and each time it has been a British manager who has achieved it. People tell me that game has moved on, that it is a more a European style now, and it is all more tactically astute.

Yet I have still not seen a new way to defend, score a goal or indeed create one from the time when I was a player.

We have all become completely bamboozled by the Continent. We watch a back-flick over there and a gasp in awe – one of our players does it and we all have a laugh.

There is also a patronising view of our good British managers. It is always said that: "Oh, he has done a great job on limited resources."

But how often are they given a chance with huge resources to show what they can do?

It is as if chairmen are thinking that they would not know the Continental market well enough to find the best players.

Yet Allardyce, for example, probably knows it better than anyone given the amount of travelling he has done assembling his all-stars.

It is time that the likes of Chelsea and Liverpool gave a man such a chance.

STANDARDS

It is wrong to think that you need a Continental coach to get Continental players playing.

Quite the opposite. You often need the steel of someone such as Allardyce to ensure that these highly-paid stars do not let their standards slip.

That is what he has done at Bolton and that is why they stand a more-than-respectable seventh in the Premiership.

Big Sam is right, if he was called 'Allardyce' things might be very different.

Unfortunately, the name 'Big Sam' just does not have the same ring about it.

'THEY ARE A VERY, VERY DANGEROUS TEAM'

Is what I told my two friends just before Chelsea scored their second goal.

There is a saying that you are at your most vulnerable after just scoring. And Chelsea scored a goal as close to the final whistle of the first half that would have taken them into the dressing room brimming. They could have sat down and relaxed and by the time the buzzer went they would have had fifteen minutes to take it all in and realise that the 'same again' was the key to the final. In the other dressing room ex-Chelsea player Didier Deschamps would have had quite a job on his hands to bring his team round, although he may have seen what I saw. Chelsea had thrown everything but the owner's yachts at the French champions and only two goals to show for their complete domination. That sounded great but before the 'Mug in Middle' blew for the walk down the tunnel, Monaco pulled a goal back with literally a couple of seconds on his watch. Now we had quite a different couple of dressing rooms as the pendulum swung in favour of Monaco and they had just shown us that they were exactly what I wrote last Sunday – in my *Sentinel* column – a very, very dangerous team!

Chelsea missed chances – Joe Cole in particular – who had enough time to bring the ball down to his feet before taking on the keeper, but he hit it first time and it nearly hit me, and I was in my club some half a mile down the Kings Road!

Gronkjaer scored what looked a fantastic effort, but having watched this player so many times I can only ask the question 'did he mean it', as he cut inside onto his left foot and hit a cross that sailed over the keeper's head and into the top corner of the net. Spectacular. Or fluke?

There was absolutely no fluke about the second as once again, Frank Lampard went on one of his tremendously powerful runs and found himself with the ball on his right side, but although surrounded by a sea of red and white shirts he kept his 'cool' and calmly placed it out of Flavio Roma's reach. 2-0, game-on, all square and with forty-five minutes to put the match out of Monaco's reach. Chelsea's delight lasted only ninety seconds. Fernando Morientes had already struck the Chelsea post as a reminder of just how dangerous he would become and he was involved in the goal that many thought was handball. The move began with one of the two players I mentioned to you about looking out for!

Jerome Rothen and Morientes himself, the blond wide man began the move. Morientes caused havoc with a header and before the Chelsea support-ers knew it their team had just thrown away half of a very important lead. A photograph in the next morning's *Mirror* showed that goal-scorer Hugo Ibarra had his hand on the post with the ball desperately close to it. Next to that was a raging Cudicini pointing to his arm hoping the 'Mug' – who actually refereed this match well – would do something about it. The goal stood and the match had a whole different complexion. Just before Chelsea scored their second goal, I told my friends that the longer this game went the more dangerous Monaco would become. They must have thought I had a crystal ball as I explained the more the game opened up, the more Chelsea would be in trouble. Monaco were just showing signs of 'coming out to play.'

The match was now on a knife-edge and I felt for my friends in our club knowing that the opposition would come out in a far better frame of mind than their Blue-shirted loved ones. Chelsea tried to begin the second half the way they did the first but spaces and gaps were opening up and the French team loved that situation, for they are quick on the break and played the ball at pace. The equaliser was inevitable, and the man who got it also, as he received the ball after a swift exchange of passes between Patrice Evra and Rothen, he played a great one-two with Lucas Bernardi and coolly and clinically levelled the scores on the night and put his team back where it all started, two goals to the good. Chelsea now looked like Arsenal did against them in the last round, heavy-legged, jaded, unsure and with a haunting look on their faces as the SKY cameras moved in on close-ups. Monaco played the clock out from twenty-five minutes from the end, but still found time to create another chance or two. The Stinkerman stood there on the line like a man waiting to be taken to the gallows as his eyes went from his watch to the scoreboard on numerous occasions. This looked like – as Chelsea's second goal went in – the night of all nights for Chelsea and all their fans, but what they did not understand is this team they were playing are a very, very useful outfit, and all what you have read over the last few pages is true. Monaco are a team fighting to stay alive financially but their players stuck to the task of the evening's match and by the final bell, Chelsea supporters knew that they had been beaten by a superior team although they will always look back to that first leg when the Stinkerman made some eerie substitutions when his team had the ten men of Monaco in pretty bad shape at the interval. One manager or referee's mistake can become very costly in big matches, something I write about often for you – the readers in the *Sentinel*!

There are many unanswered questions at Stamford Bridge and the biggest one is "Who really brought these summer signings into the club," for whoever it was, should be going to the gallows with the once-loved Tinkerman but now who is looked at as the Stinkerman?

I thought that Roman Abramovich had the best football advisers inside his Russian Empire, but after watching all those £millions worth of strike force – bought in the summer – I can only repeat myself by saying why spend all those roubles when your people could have gone to Real Madrid and got Morientes on loan with a clause in that loan deal to have first option-to-buy this wonderful front player. If it were the Swede who marked his card, he needs to go with the other two to the gallows!

What I have found out by writing this book 'The Tinker and Talisman' is that players do far too much talking off the field, for instance Crespo screamed that he would get Chelsea to the final and show that the £17million shelled out for him was going to be justified. On the morning of the match it was Joe Cole's turn to shout to the newspapers that, it would be him who would put the skids under the French, and what a golden opportunity to do so in that period when Chelsea were pressing.

Over all Chelsea have done very well to finish above Manchester United – or is that such a feat these days – and go further than both them and Arsenal in the Champions League.

They would have settled for that last August, but this was a painful knockout punch because they came so close, yet so very far away!

I'll remind you of the very painful headlines the next morning, with several in the *Express*: BLUE GLOOM: CHELSEA AGONY AS 'HANDBALL' GOAL SIGNALS THE BEGINNING OF THE END – CHELSEA SQUANDER TWO GOAL LEAD ON THE NIGHT AS MORIENTES DRIVES FINAL NAIL IN THE COFFIN OF BLUE BOSS TO SEND MONACO THROUGH – IT'S THE END OF THE ROAD FOR RANIERI – TINKER SIGNING OFF WITH HONOUR – MILLIONS SPENT BUT STILL NO TROPHIES FOR RICH KIDS: The *Daily Mirror* went like this: HAND OF GOD II – HEARTACHE FOR DEVASTATED RANIERI AS ARGENTINE'S DODGY GOAL KO'S CHELSEA – *MOURINHO ARRIVES AND CLAUDIO ERA GETS LOST IN TRANSLATION*: The *Daily Star* went: TEARO CLAUDIO: CHAMPIONS LEAGUE SEMI-FINAL SPECIAL BLUES LEFT BLUBBING AFTER BLOWING TWO-GOAL LEAD – *CHELSEA DREAMS ARE MONACO'D* RANIERI RIDE OUT OF LUCK: The *Sun* said that: GONACO: BLUES CRASH BUT RANIERI SAYS "I'M SO PROUD" – *RANIERI BRAVES NEARLY DID DIDI* – CHELSEA CRASH OUT OF EUROPE: The *Daily Mail*'s headlines were: MORIENTES SHOWS ROUTE TO GOAL – HEARTBROKEN: TEARS AND DRAMA AS BLUES BLOW THEIR BIG CHANCE TO LET RANIERI BOW OUT IN TRIUMPH – WASTEFUL CHELSEA THROW IT ALL AWAY – 'ARM OF GOD' TURNS TIE BUT BLAME LIES WITH BLUES: BLUES BLOW CHANCE TO GIVE RANIERI A GREAT SEND-OFF.

The *London Standard* has Chelsea captain John terry saying that: "WE'RE FAILURES": While inside pages say that: PLAYERS ARE TO BLAME THIS TIME.

UEFA Champions League semi-final: Chelsea 2 Gronkjaer and Lampard Monaco 2 Ibarra and Morientes Att: 37,132 (Monaco win 5-3 on aggregate)

From the very first minute, I was surprised how Monaco approached this match, as I expected they would play with more poise and composure from the back, trying to keep the ball away from their opponents because time was very much on their side. But that was not to be as they hit the ball long into Terry and Gallas with only Morientes playing in Chelsea's half. This was one of the first times I had seen a foreign team play rather like an 'English-style' game and they paid the price before Monaco scored that all important goal on the stroke of half-time. Lampard again led the way to the French goal, although it was rather a lucky goal that gave them the hope of cutting this lead down and then try to take it themselves. There is no doubt a goal on the whistle has a great psychological boost to the scorers and quite the opposite to the team on the receiving end. This proved to be the case as Chelsea began the second half well, but slowly, slowly, Monaco crept into their territory and the spaces on the field came at just the right time. It reminded me a little of Arsenal when Chelsea had them on the ropes at Highbury in the last round of this competition.

It was Morientes who put them in the driving seat in Monte Carlo against Real Madrid, and it was him who did the same here and with the game came a Blue-shirted team who now looked knackered after so many hard fought matches recently. The Stinkerman had run out of tinkers and could just stand – chin in hand – and watch the French champions play out time. Chelsea had done well and will learn some very important lessons along this rocky road to Monaco and with a more potent threat up-front – when dominating – will put the game out of the reach of such opponents. That first forty-five minutes was crucial and, apart from taking their chances, they did everything right but once again you must look at the money spent on strikers and again it took a winger and a midfield player to get them back in the game. Chelsea – like Arsenal and Manchester United in earlier rounds – left the field dejected, knowing that the season and their trophy cabinet was empty for this season. Now it was time to see what the future holds for Claudio Ranieri!

It is never easy lifting oneself after such a massive defeat but the Blues were playing for pride and several of them their Chelsea status. If what we have read is true then Jose Mourinho – sitting smug in the stand – was not just doing one scouting mission but two. Firstly, his team were playing the winners of this match in the final and secondly he was watching the team he is taking over, so the next match was at Old Trafford and all eyes were on just which players were fighting for their Chelsea lives as the speculation grew further after Wednesday evening's great disappointment. Whoever the next manager was, nobody was safe unless your shirt had the name of Terry, Lampard, Parker or Cudicini on the back of it.

On the Friday my column in the *Sentinel* read like this:

RANIERI HAS ONLY HIMSELF TO BLAME

The Chelsea boss is not the only one to swing from the nearest lamppost after this week's European exit. What about those people responsible for some of the signings which left Chelsea falling at the penultimate hurdle?

If it really was the Swedish fella advising on the likes of Hernan Crespo, then thank God for Chelsea that he's staying with England. I was led to believe that billionaire owner – Roman Abramovich – was surrounded by the best advisers roubles could buy? But you have to wonder about some of those whispering into his ear when they let someone such as Fernando Morientes slip through the net.

This player was going relatively cheaply when Real Madrid were farming him out on loan at the start of the season.

But we all know that there is only one man going to pay the ultimate price for Chelsea's European failure – and Claudio Ranieri can already hear them erecting the gallows. He was resigned to his fate long before Wednesday's mishap – and lets not feel too sorry for a man about to pocket a pay-off that you and I can only dream about.

And what's to bet against him popping up at somewhere like Spurs next season?

The tie wasn't lost on Wednesday – of course – it was lost in the match in Monte Carlo when the Stinkerman tinkered once too often.

As I have always said, one mistake by a manager or referee can be fatal to the final outcome. Mind you, all English football fans were joining the Chelsea supporters in dreaming of a Champions League final when they went two up just before the break. But you know what they say 'you are always at your most vulnerable when you've just scored'. And the French outfit proved it by immediately making it 2-1 and turning the tie on its head. Chelsea missed chances, chief amongst them Joe Cole, whose first time shot was closer to hitting me – and I was half a mile away. Just before Chelsea's second goal, I told my mates that Morientes would become the more dangerous the longer the match wore on. I explained that the more the game opened up the more Chelsea would be in trouble because Monaco were showing signs of 'coming out to play'.

Chelsea fans knew they had been beaten by the better team – over the two legs – but will always look back and wonder what might have been if the Stinkerman had not messed about with his team in the first match!

MOUR WANTS FOUR
NEW BOSS HANDS IN WISH LIST OF BIG NAMES WANTED

Jose Mourinho has told Chelsea to: "get me David Beckham and three of my Porto stars" – as well as his backroom staff from the club he has guided into the European Cup final. Chelsea owner Roman Abramovich has immediately agreed to sanction a £50million bid for three Porto players – winger Costinha, right back Paulo Ferreira and the brilliant Brazilian born playmaker Deco. All three are Portugal Internationals.

Mourinho shares Abramovich's desire to land the England captain Beckham from Real Madrid and the three Porto targets are on his summer shopping list discussed when he was in London this week for Chelsea's match with Monaco.

"At the moment Porto has got a large number of players who are at the absolute highest level," said Mourinho. "In football every player has his price."

Chelsea can afford to pay that price. Abramovich has already informed Mourinho that a 150million euros – £101 million is available to make signings for next season. Beckham has repeatedly insisted he wants to stay at Real for another year, but problems in his private life mean he will review his future at the end of the month. Mourinho has already made it clear that he wants the England captain – if Real will negotiate at a price Abramovich considers reasonable.

Whatever happens with Beckham, Mourinho is intent on bringing the heartbeat of the side that has reached the Champions League final with him to Stamford Bridge.

The indications from Porto are that the club are willing to do business on two or even three players on Mourinho's list. Porto already knew there was a £45million offer for all three of their stars and, as an alternative, Abramovich is offering £30million for Deco plus either Ferreira or Costinha.

Porto president Jorge Nuno Pinto is resigned to losing his coach but he is particularly keen to keep Ferreira. "Money is important," said Pinta da Costa. "But it can only buy players who are for sale."

As the *Express* revealed yesterday, Mourinho and his agent, Jorge Mendez, discussed his future at Les Ambassedeurs casino in London in midweek.

Abramovich and Chelsea chief executive Peter Kenyon got a full briefing from their chief Mr Fix It, agent, Pini Zahavi, who hosted the lunch. And as we reported yesterday, Mourinho also agreed to a salary that will make him one of the highest-paid coaches in the game, with a four-year deal worth £10million.

Mourinho, meantime, will bring three of his own staff with him to Chelsea – assistant Baltemar Brito, goalkeeping coach Silvino Louro and trainer Rui Faria.

COLD TRAFFORD

Was the headline in the *Sun* on Monday morning with the following words: UNITED FAITHFUL TURN THEIR BACK ON FERGUSON SPEECH

The *Mail* saw it this way: COLD COMFORT FOR DEFIANT RANIERI – It went on to say that: ABRAMOVICH SPENDS BUT PASSION BUYS SUCCESS FOR TINKERMAN.

On the morning of the match the *Daily Mail* had headlines saying that: IT'S DOWN TO PRIDE AND PREJUDICE – and that – FERGIE SALUTES DIGNIFIED RIVAL BUT KENYON IS THE REAL ENEMY: Alex Ferguson saluted Claudio Ranieri as he brought his Chelsea team to Old Trafford. If Chelsea get anything out of this match it will mean that Manchester United will be deprived of an automatic Champions League place.

The United boss said of Ranieri that: "I don't have to say anything specific to Claudio as I have so much respect for him, for he has handled himself very well. He has held his nerve, he's kept his dignity, and throughout it all he's kept his team playing very well. He's done a great job at Chelsea. I don't think anyone could argue against that." But Peter Kenyon, United's former chief executive, might not receive such a warm welcome when he returns for the first time since taking the same role at Chelsea. Ferguson blames Kenyon for wrecking his efforts to sign Ronaldinho and believes the Chelsea official, who has a strained relationship with Ranieri, is trying to second-guess United's transfer moves. He stopped short of criticising Kenyon, but privately he is scornful of Chelsea's treatment of their manager. In public, he restricted comments to the midweek Champions League exit after Monaco won 5-3 on aggregate. "I felt for Claudio desperately after that 2-2 draw on Wednesday," said Ferguson. "What happened is what happened to Manchester United before in Europe. If you make mistakes then you tend to get punished. Overall, they've had a successful season."

Ranieri would agree and, in outlining his blueprint for next season, he applied considerable pressure on Joe Mourinho, the man who will have to continue the job.

Ranieri said that: "When Roman Abramovich took over he did not ask me to win a trophy. Finishing second in the Premiership and getting to the semi-finals of the Champions League is a great achievement. The plan was to build the foundations, and that is now strong, as is the spirit in my players, it should be possible, with some small changes, to do even better next season."

The Stinkerman's words were coded but the message was quite clear: If Mourinho fails to win anything then he will have failed. Chelsea are four points clear of United and need one more today to ensure second place behind Arsenal and clinch an automatic Champions League slot.

Only once in the last decade have United finished outside the top two, and having to qualify for the Champions League would pose problems. At least eight players are destined for the European Championship and will return just in time for the Champions League qualifying fixtures in August. As a result, Ferguson will field his strongest team while Chelsea will be without Hernan Crespo and Juan Sebastian Veron. Jimmy Floyd or Joe Cole will partner Eidur Gudjohnsen in attack.

"We are not good like United yet, you cannot judge on one full season. We want to be like them and Arsenal, but we have to do even better next year."

Over to you Jose!

In the past Chelsea's visits to Old Trafford have been tense affairs and the Blues have a very decent record there. I'll always remember my first match there in the season when we won the FA Cup against Leeds United. I had just turned eighteen and can recall their home team dressing room door swing open, with the odour of Horse Liniment and the sound of those metal studs coming towards our team who were just going into the tunnel. I remember thinking 'George Best, Bobby Charlton, Denis Law, and Paddy Crerand', all players I had admired so much in my foot-balling education. There was some atmosphere in the ground and we kicked into the Stretford End in the first forty-five minutes and by half-time were two goals in front and I thought that if I can play against these kind of players – and win – then I might just have made it. With seconds on the clock I hit a half-volley, which Alex Stepney could not see, only for it be disallowed for offside. Peter 'Nobby' Houseman was the culprit right out on the touchline, a decision that would not have been given today for Peter not being involved in the play. I played against them twice this season and had another one disallowed at the Bridge in another fine win, but I felt I was jinxed, after yet another strange decision. I picked the ball up and got to the United goal line and carried the ball into the six-yard box where I tucked it neatly past Alex again. No goal!

But the following season it was quite a bizarre goal I scored against them, with Crerand in possession on the edge of his box – I was walking away – when he rolled the ball across the eighteen yard line and as I turned my head slightly realised that it was more in my favour than Alex's, so I flew onto the ball and side-footed it powerfully past the ex-Millwall and Chelsea goalkeeper. The Shed erupted but United came back and beat us 2-1 after a howler of a mistake in our defence let in the lanky figure of Alan Gowling to score the winner.

Back to this match though, one which Chelsea dominated from the start against a lacklustre home team. It was clear to see that United were out of sorts and Chelsea took full advantage of this as they played controlled football, almost looking like they were the home side themselves. After Jesper Gronkjaer had crashed Chelsea in front, cutting in from the right and hitting a 'beauty' out of the reach of Tim Howard, United looked to be back in the match when van Nistelrooy stepped up to blast a penalty to the right of Howard and the USA goalkeeper kept it out, which meant the Ducthman had missed his third penalty out of the last five he had taken. This was just what Chelsea needed for had the 'Red Devils' nicked an equaliser then, we might have seen a better and more exciting performance in the second half. Chelsea had Huth sent-off whilst Sir Alex pulled Scholes off before he saw red also. Scholes was booked for a blatant dive – really out of character – and then after a naughty tackle, the referee went for his yellow card and then realised that he had already shown him it, so immediately changed his mind and gave him nothing. Scholes got lucky for had he seen 'red' he would have missed the final through suspension. Then, with just thirteen minutes left it was 'Van the Man' who made amends by turning a mistake by Cudicini into the Italian's net. In all fairness this match was a little like watching paint dry and I can't help myself thinking just 'why' and 'how' on earth could Manchester United allow David Beckham to leave Old Trafford. The lack of service to front players has never been so evident and with van Nistelrooy brutally out of touch, Millwall just might fancy their chances in the FA Cup final.

Manchester United 1 van Nistelrooy Chelsea 1 Gronkjaer: Att: 67,609

With only one league match left the season now was over, apart from the decision, which would tell us just what was going on with the owner, manager, and chief executive. On the Tuesday it was revealed that Chelsea were chasing the signature of Roberto Carlos from Real Madrid with the headline in the *Standard* saying that:

ROBERTO CARLOS: 'CHELSEA WANT ME'

Written by Matt Hughes: Roberto Carlos today claimed he has had an offer from Chelsea – but still hopes to win a new deal with Real Madrid.

The World Cup winner, one of six 'Galacticos' on the books at the Bernabeu, insists his heart still lies with Madrid, who conceded their Spanish title to Valencia at the weekend.

The 31-year-old told the Onda Cero radio station, that his advisers had been contacted by Chelsea.

"I have not spoken to anyone directly but people from Chelsea spoke to my lawyers."

It is reported that a three-year deal, worth £4million annually was offered.

But the Brazilian, who has a history of making extravagant claims linking him with the Premiership when he is in negotiations, said he hoped to remain at Real Madrid.

"I am happy here and people know that. My aim is to keep playing until I am thirty-eight and I want to spend five of those years in Madrid and then the last two in Brazil with Santos. I want a four-year contract. The club have given me two options but I want to hold out for four years.

"I want to speak to Jorge Valdano, the director of football, and president Florentino Perez next week and sort out my future before going on holiday."

Meanwhile Gianfranco Zola has put a return to Chelsea on hold until the end of the season in order to concentrate on Cagliari's promotion push. One player, however, who seems certain to leave Stamford Bridge is Juan Veron.

Chelsea favourite Zola has the opportunity to return to Stamford Bridge in a possible coaching role next season, but could also complete a dream return to Serie A with his hometown club. Cagliari are second in the Serie B with five games remaining, one point behind leaders Palermo and, with five teams gaining automatic promotion this season, their return to topflight football is all but assured.

The return of the 37-year-old to Chelsea would be a huge hit with fans. Zola said that: "I am not sure what's going to happen but Chelsea still have a special place in my heart. It will be a difficult decision. On one hand I want to carry on with what I have been doing for the last fifteen years, but I might have the chance to do something new.

"When the promotion is complete I will decide. There are five games left and we can still win the league."

Veron's £16million transfer has been a disappointment and Chelsea have decided to cut their losses, with Internazionale said to be willing to pay up to £10million.

Ken Bates and Peter Kenyon filled the back two pages of the *Standard* with the chief executive repeating that: "We have failed at Chelsea this season for second is not good enough."

COOL PETER WILL STILL NOT RISE TO BATES

As for Bates, he was at Stamford Bridge for an evening with Peter Kenyon and Bruce Buck, the new chairman of Chelsea Village. Ken Dyer reported that: The chances of Peter Kenyon giving chapter and verse on Claudio Ranieri's future were about as strong as those of Ron Atkinson becoming lead singer of the Brixton Tabernacle gospel choir.

It just wasn't going to happen.

It was worth a try though, and plenty of Chelsea punters forked out £40 a head to eat a perfectly acceptable three-course dinner and then hear what the club's chief executive had to say about this and other contentious subjects. Kenyon and Bruce Buck, the chairman of Chelsea Village, held court in the Charles Kingsley suite at Stamford Bridge, answering questions which ranged from the future of Frank Lampard – 'he's going nowhere' – to the club badge.

For most Chelsea supporters up to now, Kenyon has been the man behind the apartment curtains, Roman Abramovich's emissary.

Last night a group of those Blues supporters had their first real chance to nail Kenyon and Buck, an amenable man with a nice line in dry humour, and tried their hardest.

Kenyon knew what was coming, though, the slow full tosses and even a few googlies.

To be fair to him, he answered some of the questions and played others back with a perpendicular bat of which Geoffrey Boycott, in his prime, would have been proud.

It was never going to be a particularly comfortable evening for Kenyon even before the former chairman Ken Bates turned up to add some spice to the proceedings.

Bates listened assiduously to some of the answers, looked bored by others and, at one stage, seemed to have nodded off.

Fortified by a glass or two of Pouilly Fume, however, he did become animated once or twice throughout the session, particularly when a question was asked about his current litigation with the club.

"I didn't ask that question, I promise you", shouted Bates. "But where's your cheque?"

Buck took it all with commendable good humour.

"I hope we can reach an amicable solution," he replied. "I was talking to Ken the other day and he said he was in the doctors office. "The doctor reckons I have another twenty-five years to live," he told me, "so I am increasing my claim."

Bates was palpably underwhelmed by some answers. "He's talking bollocks, " he muttered on one occasion. "And that's a technical term."

His sharpest riposte, and one which drew laughter and applause from the assembled audience, came when Buck, in jocular fashion, asked Bates if he could talk to him afterwards about "knocking down the hotel."

"No," bellowed Bates. "You can fuck off. Take that as a No."

Season ticket prices, plans for a new training ground and the possibility of Gianfranco Zola returning to the club were all covered, but it was the questions about the popular Ranieri that drew most reaction from the assembly.

Kenyon has gone on record as saying this season would be a failure if the trophy cabinet remained empty and he was consistent in that stance. "I have been around enough footballers who throw away their runners-up medals. We're second and we reached the semi-final of the Champions League. It's a very good achievement and thanks to everybody who have been involved."

He got no further: "What about the manager?" came an irritated voice from the floor. "Don't ignore that."

"I didn't ignore it," replied Kenyon. "We've had a good season, but we are not where anybody at Chelsea wants us to be and that is what we are all planning and working hard to achieve."

Cue the applause, then Buck recalled the line: "Of all the people who didn't win, we were first."

The next question, from table number nine, was the most predictable of the night.

"Is Claudio staying?"

The answer from Kenyon was no less foreseeable. "Claudio has a three-year contract," pause for sarcastic laughter. "There has been no new manager appointed."

"Hang on," said master of ceremonies, Neil Barnett. "There is a follow-up question."

"Why has the club treated Claudio Ranieri so appallingly?"

More applause.

"What happened on Roman's yacht?" someone yelled. "That's none of your business" snapped Kenyon.

"All through this process we've conducted discussions on an ongoing basis with Claudio. If you don't believe me that's unfortunate, but there's not been a decision taken on Claudio Ranieri. Those decisions will be taken over the forthcoming weeks and that is the fact of the matter."

As an answer it fell way short of satisfying most of those present, but what else did they expect Kenyon to say?

The real answers, I suspect, will be found behind the curtains.

KEEP HIM IN THE CAPITAL

I was very amused to read Ken Dyer – of the *London Evening Standard* – write the following:

A – Is for Abramovich – Chelsea's reclusive Russian always makes a point of popping into the dressing room after a match. Recently, while bonding with his players, he told Ranieri that it "will be better next season". Most Blues fans don't think it was all that bad this time around, Roman.

B – Is for Bogarde – the footballer, not the actor, although you've had as much chance of seeing Winston playing for Chelsea's first team as Humphrey. At last, however, the ludicrously expensive millstone around Chelsea's neck is about to be removed with the end of the Dutchman's contract in sight.

C – Is for Champions League – considering everything, Ranieri did brilliantly to guide his much-rotated team through the Group stages and into the semi-final. He never picked his team until the night before a match. A plate of pasta, a glass or two of chianti and everything seems more civilised somehow.

D – Is for Dead Man Walking – or, as Ken Bates put it earlier this week, death by a thousand cuts. Both describe Ranieri's predicament for much of the season, although the knowledge of a few million quid payout when the coup de grace finally comes does make the torment much easier to bear.

E – Is for Eriksson – the canny Swede was courted by Chelsea, even before the start of last season, and let there be no doubt, he really fancied the job. In the end, though, Sven decided to stay with England. However, a disappointing European Championships this summer and – who knows – he could be popping around Roman Arbramovich's place again for a cup of Darjeeling.

F – Is for Failure – if people doubted it before, that description of a trophy-less Chelsea season by new chief executive Peter Kenyon certainly upped the ante as far as Claudio was concerned. In almost four years in the job, the Italian never had the satisfaction of seeing his captain lift any sort of trophy.

G – Is for Gladiator – Ranieri, a Roman by birth, described his captain John Terry thus. The centre-half, for his part, was always publicly supportive of his coach although there must have been more times, particularly after the Monaco semi-final away leg, when he would have surely considered inviting a couple of lions to Harlington for lunch, or rather on, his Tinkerman coach.

H – Is for Half-time – this is when Ranieri used to shuffle his considerable pack. Sometimes it worked, occasionally it didn't, but the coach just went on rotating, whatever anyone thought.

I – Is for If – that incomparable poem by Rudyard Kipling, which Ranieri was prone to quote from time to time. Whatever else he did or did not do, it was the way Claudio behaved that endeared him to most people. There is no doubt that, for most of us, he is definitely 'a man, my son'.

J – Is for Jose Mourinho – the bookies favourite to take over the Ranieri rotavator this summer. He may indeed be more than the flavour of the month but the Porto coach will know if he is offered and accepts the Chelsea job, the Italian will be one hard act to follow.

K – Is for Kenyon – the Chelsea chief executive said this week that no decision has yet been taken on Ranieri's future. He couldn't realistically say anything else at this stage, but the hunch is that the axe will fall soon after the

Champions League Final between Porto and Monaco in a couple of weeks time.

L – Is for Lazio – surely apart from that victory at Highbury was Claudio's finest hour particularly the 4-0 away win in his home city. L could also stand for Lampard, who has been the one constant in Ranieri's team this season and Chelsea's outstanding player.

M – Is for Mum – Claudio invariably gets an earful when he telephones his mother back home in Italy. Like all mums, they want the best for their boy and momma Ranieri can't be happy with a certain Roman. "Get me his number," you can imagine her saying to her number one son. 'He can't treat my bambino like this. I will sink his yacht.'

N – Is for No chance – Ranieri has been careful not to write himself off. However, he must have known from last August when Sven Goran Eriksson decided to pop in for a cuppa with Abramovich, that he had two chances of keeping his job at Stamford Bridge beyond the end of the season – none and a dog's.

O – Is for On yer bike – which is what Ranieri will be told this summer. In many ways, though, perhaps it's not a bad time for him to quit the Kings Road. After all, his CV couldn't be more impressive, his star could not be any brighter, his stock any higher.

P – Is for Pin – which, some say, is the method he uses to pick his teams. Certainly some of his selections had everyone scratching their heads but what do we know?

Most of the time on a wing and a prayer, it all seemed to work.

Q – Is for quotable – because that is what he invariably was. Whether he was talking about aliens, ET or the Muskateers, Claudio was always good value. The fans will miss him if he goes but no more than the media. He was different, he was refreshing, he was dignified, he was good.

R – Is for Rotation – you can imagine Ranieri rotating everything, from toothpaste to teapots. He admitted in an interview that he was reading three books at once. "Yes" he roared, "you tell them Claudio even rotates books."

S – Is for Spurs – which some people think is a possible destination for Ranieri when he leaves Chelsea. The *Evening Standard's* 'Keep Claudio in London' campaign attracted a lot of response.

T – couldn't stand for anything else then Tinkerman – Ranieri introduced the word himself, he relished using it at every opportunity and it has since gone down in English folklore. Think of Ranieri and Tinkerman comes to mind as naturally as night follows day.

U – Is for Useless – a common description of one of Ranieri's signings, Juan Veron. Certainly the Argentine has talent, but Chelsea fans have not seen much of it this season. A mega-expensive misfit, or so it seems.

V – Is for V-sign – something that Ranieri must have been tempted to employ on numerous occasions this season. It is to his enormous credit that he has invariably kept his cool. The one time the pressure got to him was in

Monaco, with disastrous results.

W – Is for Weep – which is what this emotional Italian could well be doing when the Chelsea fans give him a deserved standing ovation tomorrow.

X – marks the spot on the contract, as yet unwritten according to the Chelsea hierarchy, where Ranieri's successor will sign upon the dotted line sometime within the next month.

Y – Is for Yacht – the place where Abramovich and his staff are said to have had meaningful discussions with so many people.

Z – Is for Zahavi – the Israeli agent seems to be at the centre of the important happenings at Chelsea this season or Gianfranco Zola, who will surely be back at Chelsea at some stage.

THE BIG MATCH UP

Ian Chadband – of the *Evening Standard* – examines the comparisons, which led the Chelsea hierarchy to ditch the Tinkerman in favour of the Thinkerman: From Tinkerman to Thinkerman, from self-deprecation to self-appreciation, from jokey affability to blazing intensity. All it has taken is Jose Mourinho's first cocksure strut into Stamford Bridge to give the unmistakable feel that a second revolution in the space of 12 months is about to erupt at Chelsea. In every area on and off the field, from man management to youth development, from dealing with his billionaire boss to playing happy families with his squad, the not so retiring wallflower that is Senor Mourinho could hardly have made it plainer that Claudio Ranieris building foundations were going to be torn apart.

Time will tell if it proves a revolution of style. Certainly, it's hard to recall any new manager ever bidding his predecessor with the pointed jibe that Mourinho offered yesterday when he observed, jokily but still cruelly and rather unnecessarily, that Ranieri had only won the Spanish Cup in twenty years. He is probably going to be easier to admire than love. Mourinho thinks he is special and asserts that he is a proven champion, yet, for the moment, the only thing that the Chelsea fans know for certain is that he's rather different than their dear old Claudio. Here, *Standard Sport* examines those comparisons between the old favourite and the new young master, which have convinced the Chelsea hierarchy that they have got the right man.

THE CHARMER V THE FIGHTER

Everyone liked Ranieri: he was dignified, affable, a genuine good guy, but he didn't win anything. Mourinho is combative, likes to get under the oppositions' skin and does not appear to care about winning popularity contests. Yet, as he likes to point out, perhaps a mite defensively, he does win football trophies. "I did not come here for fights, I came to work and win, but in a certain situation if my group, my players, my club needed my support, 'I WILL FIGHT,' he explained yesterday.

Recalling his celebrated spat with Sir Alex Ferguson. "It's like family, you help if you can."

Well, yes, but seasoned Mourinho watchers reckon he can rival Dennis Wise for starting an argument in an empty room if he thinks it will give him a psychological edge. At Sporting Lisbon, they are still gnashing their teeth about how Mourinho supposedly insulted their club a few months earlier. A few Premiership managers may feel the same this season if he dismisses them as coldly as he did Ranieri yesterday.

ALOOFNESS V APPROACHABILITY

Here's the odd thing. Ranieri's public image was always that of a loveable, clubbable figure yet some of his players did not find him the easiest to approach with their concerns. Conversely, Mourinho's arrogant streak in public conceals a passionate determination to be everyone's mate. His players rave about him. "I'm a very communicative person and will be very open with them. I like to see feedback about my work and love openness. It's very important to know how they feel working under me."

Speaking five languages in a multi-national squad helps, Er, but woe betide anyone who crosses him, in whatever language.

I must come in here because I am enjoying getting to know this man and like his style. The reason I step in is that what he has touched on, was one of the biggest problems our team of the late 60's and early 70's had with Dave Sexton. Okay, I am not foolish enough to ignore the fact that we were no band of angels and that the face of football has changed dramatically, but there is still the same understanding involved. One instance that springs to mind was whilst on an end of season trip and several of the boys went out on a fishing expedition, the usual relaxing on deck with a chilled drink or ten, and once we arrived back at the hotel we gave the fish to the kitchen to be cooked for our dinner. Then we organised a time to meet in the bar and went off to get changed. An hour had gone by when we were sitting around the table before entering the restaurant, we asked Dave's assistant Ron Suart to ask the manager down for a drink so that we could clear the air on both sides of that electric fence he had built around him. Ron returned and said "Dave would be down in half hour" and we sat sensibly discussing points to bring up and to listen to what he had to say. It was the perfect time, in the Caribbean, nice and relaxed, the season was over after a long hard season and all we wanted was to mend a few bridges caused by both parties. We felt that if we could finally get him to understand us a little more and if he could accept certain things would have a real 'live' chance of winning that elusive First Division Championship. But we had to clear the air, not in Dave's way, where it always became like he was managing a prizefighter, but in a way that we could at least be civil with one another and that we all wanted the same thing, a First Division Championship Medal, which is off course today the Premiership. Well, we waited for an hour and went in for dinner without a 'dickey bird' from the manager or his trusted sidekick. So it was still war and it was tiny things like that where he lost our respect, and at times we went over the top to have a dig back at him. I don't care who agrees or not here, all I know is that we were away representing our club and country, and after a lovely day out at sea, wanted to get something much more out of the trip – something very serious – rather than return for pre-season knowing that it was going to be like a battle of several wars with Dave, who should have been the main part of our team. My point is made and that is why Jose Mourinho gets the very best out of his players and from what I have seen they really do put it in for him – even the most talented Deco. I am sure the new boss would have relished having the likes of Bonetti, McCreadie, Hudson, Osgood, Cooke and of course those defenders who he would organise so magnificently. Our most under-rated player at the time was

John Dempsey, who made his debut with me in a 5-0 thrashing by Southampton at the Dell – the other being 'Suave' Marvin Hinton. Lou Hinton was a wonderful player who just lacked that extra height, stopping him from being a regular in front of David Webb. Having said that, Bobby Moore was no great shakes when it came to heading the ball and he was the world's best defender. I never played again in that season of 1968 and had to wait for the lads to have an iffy start to the next season and was shocked that I was selected against Tottenham Hotspurs at White Hart Lane, a venue which had become a lucky ground for me and where I gave many big performances. This also included a behind closed-doors game for England which led to my England debut.

LARGE SQUAD V SMALL SQUAD

Effectively, Chelsea's squad is 34 strong if you count their players out on loan and those about to join. Ranieri never complained but it is certainly too many for Mourinho. "A big squad cannot work well. I need small groups. I need everyone motivated. When you have a big box of oranges and one is sick, a month later you will have to throw ten in the garbage." For a bloke who sees himself as a father figure to his players, it's easier to keep close tabs on 24 rather than 34. A cull is inevitable.

I must come in here again, shortly, to say to Senor Mourinho, we do understand the fundamentals, and the reason why you like a smaller squad, so please don't start getting like Clouseau – I mean Ranieri – and start talking of oranges, champions and foundations plus all the rest of it, you should just get on with the job at hand. Do not worry about explaining anything to us for you will be judged by the way your team plays whether they eat pasta, oranges or good old pie and mash. And by going about it your way, taken on the brilliance of your Porto team, I am sure the Chelsea faithful are looking forward to this upcoming season. I certainly am!

COACH V COACH/MANAGER

This could prove a key difference. Ranieri appeared to see himself as just a coach whose duties stretched no further than matches and training. It's no accident that Mourinho's titles are coach and manager. He wants to be involved in everything, and, by all accounts in Portugal, has an amazing capacity to attend to the slightest of details. There's a hint of train spotter about Mourinho, evident from his schooldays where legend has it that he'd name dogs after footballers and try to line them up in a 4-4-2 formation. He's zealous about pursuing that extra edge for his side, anything from USA-style motivation techniques – "my philosophy is guidance and discovery" – to make players pore over home videos of their own displays.

POODLE V ROTTWEILLER

Mourinho smiled yesterday when he said, "I don't have to control Roman, he has to control me" and it is probably no joke. The impression during Ranieri's reign was of a manager having big signings hoisted upon him, weather he fancied them or not. You have to wonder whether Abramovich appreciates just how determined Mourinho will be to run his own show. There is a famous story of Mourinho at Uniao Leiria when he ordered the chairman to leave the training ground during a practice session and, despite a battle of wills, got his own way. There may come a point when he'll have to be just as single-minded and stubborn with Abramovich, and there's no guarantee he will win.

TINKER V MOTIVATOR

Both have built their sides on platforms of organisation and miserly defences, yet Mourinho's Porto mastered the art of stopping other teams playing more completely than Ranieri ever did. It was never pretty – don't expect thrills a minute with his Chelsea – but was always efficient. Mourinho also doesn't believe you need to rotate when in the modern game, the best way for players to keep in good shape is to play. Ultimately, though, the difference between a winning coach and a nearly man could be down to that rare ability to make them believe. "He really is special in this area," Porto keeper Vitor Baia was quoted as saying recently. We know Vitor. The man told us so himself.

Well, I really did enjoy reading and writing that piece and feel that there is a great deal of that will come true this upcoming season. He does love pressure, you can tell by the way he stands and is so intense in his watching his teams every move – as I said earlier – he is a perfectionist and looks for great performances from his team. And if it came down to a dogfight with the likes of – say Don Revie and his team of animals – he would love every minute of it. I am going to be a big Mourinho fan, I really can see that happening!

The last word must go to Claudio Ranieri – the undisputed TINKERMAN – who messed up in Monaco on a night when we needed a cool and clear head, when his team were performing more than satisfactory. The meaning of that word comes in many forms Claudio, like acceptable, competent, good enough, pleasing, and sufficient, and it is times like these that you must not talk of apples, oranges or foundations. These are the times you earn your stars and only you and you alone, can tell us where your stars were that evening of complete devastation. Our hearts go out to you for all you went through the past eleven months. I believe you made those mistakes in Monaco because you had done so the round before at Highbury and it worked in your favour.

Lastly, I am sure had Arsenal had gone through on that nerve-wrecking night they would had pushed Monaco aside before facing Porto in the Final, and that says so much about you and your team. You tinkered once too often and all at Stamford Bridge paid the price!

'AND NOW THE END IS NEAR, AND SO I FACE THE IRON CURTAIN'

The one and only Francis Albert Sinatra

Chelsea's season was finished and the end was closing in on the Tinkerman with the news of Jose Mourinho taking over the helm at Stamford Bridge, but first the Porto boss had some unfinished business with the Champions League Final. The Blues still had two matches left but were confirmed runners-up to their – now – biggest rivals, my other former club Arsenal. Southampton came to the Bridge on a bit of a run but Chelsea shrugged them aside as if they were from a different planet. Goals came from Johnson an own goal and two from the ever-improving Frank Lampard who was now the runner-up to Thierry Henry for Players Player of the Year and without a doubt Chelsea's.
Chelsea 4 Southampton 0: 40,000

Frank's contribution was monumental and deservedly ranks him along with all the great number eights of yesteryear. I must give a mention to another player of great ability who wore the eight shirt. I have mentioned my admiration for Micky Fillery and I now mention Micky Hazzard, a ballplaying old type inside forward who linked up brilliantly both the defence of Tottenham with Paul Miller and Steve Perryman – the king pins at the back – and the attack along with the tremendously influential Argie, Ossie Ardilles, and the wonderfully-gifted Glenn Hoddle, one of the greatest-ever players who have graced the many hundreds of football grounds around the globe. People overlook Glenn as a player at Chelsea, but not me, for as I explained earlier, he made his debut against our terrific Stoke City team at the Victoria Ground in the mid-seventies. I knew that day just how far he would go in our game!

The side with those three – who were the heartbeat – was playing brilliantly whilst I was doing my stint as the captain of a great Seattle Sounders team in the North American League. The book I am writing for you would not be complete without a mention to my former team-mates who broke the all-time record in such fantastic fashion. It was a an awesome achievement and one that people in this country take no notice of because of it not being like Serie A, La Liga or the old First Division, but I'll tell you one thing – and that is both the New York Cosmos – whose record we broke – and ourselves would have finished in the top five over here. Our head coach was ex-Derby winger Alan Hinton – a man I named Clouseau – who took over incredibly enough from Jimmy Gabriel and my mate Aitch at Pompey, who signed me.

I will be forever grateful to both men for introducing that wonderful part of the world to me. I am a great believer that there is always something good comes out of bad and it was that day bumping into Bobby Moore – at the Bridge – that brought the good into a life that was falling as flat as that man I told you earlier about, being put under the door by the ambulance men from the Royal London Hospital. Our team was one of 'Bassetts' with players from all over the country, but also included three Americans, who could have played at the highest level in the English top flight.

'GUNS OF NAVARONE'

Jack Brand was our German/American goalkeeper, a keeper as nutty as any other fruitcake you would come across between the white posts. Our back-up keeper was an American/Russian who must have had shares in the vodka that both he and I drank on such a regular basis. Mike Ivanho was his name and partying was his game, a six-foot-three, overweight, ex-bankers son, who had done six months 'porridge' for embellishing his own father's bank. This was how the story went, for I was to reach Seattle a year after; Mike pulls up for training at our Renton training ground which was right next to the incredibly noisy Boeing Aeroplane factory.

As he got out of his motor two more cars pulled up alongside him and out got ex-Saints winger Tommy Jenkins and ex-Colchester defender who was that good I can't remember his name. No sorry, Adrian Webster, the captain before I arrived. "Hi, big man what's going on?"

I can only imagine the big fella going to the trunk of his car and opening up to the sight of many thousands of dollars. "Do you fancy training or going to Vegas", said Mike, and the return was as quick as a John McEnroe return of service. Renton was only a quarter of an hour drive from Sea/Tac Airport as it was called then. And the three boys were there as quick this time as a McEnroe forehand passing shot.

They booked into the best hotel and never left the room for four complete days, ordering drinks and women by the bucketload, and never pulled the curtains open once. Ivanho was to become my great friend, as you can only imagine!

At the back of our team was possibly one of the greatest full-backs to have played the game, David Nish, a classy ballplayer who had the winger more worried about him than the other way around, sheer brilliance. In the middle of defence was a Canadian lad named Ian Bridge – who ended up with my wife Maureen once I left for pastures greener. I never did trust the Canadians, or my wife, come to that!

He was a very good player, my former wife tells me!

On the left-hand side was Bruce Rioch, another ex-Derby County cast-off and the man who broke my leg at the Baseball Ground with a crude tackle from behind, but it was my fault for my father always stressed the importance of never turning your back on such players. Rioch was the spine of our back four, a man who never liked me, because although he captained both Brian Clough's Derby County and the Scotland national side, he could not get the Seattle captaincy off of yours truly. Left-back was another Yank who could have made a name for himself across the pond. He was a fine left-back with a sweet left peg.

So much so that I can't remember his name either?

In the engine room was former Bolton right-half Roy Greaves, a player who was of great assistance to me, a whole-hearted performer who was very underrated, but not by me. On my left-hand side was a skinny little left footed genius who played at Ipswich before failing a medical which left him not only joining neighbours Norwich City but having to leave the country for him not being able to join any other club. He did not need a medical at Seattle such was the club in the early stages of joining the elite. Stevie Buttle was a knockkneed cripple with the 'football brain' that was right on my wavelength and he kept defying the odds with magnificent performances, one of the best when tearing the heart out of Dutch superstar Johan Neeskens, the sidekick of the incredible Johan Cruyff in the Giant Stadium, New York. Buttle was a player of wonderful vision and had a left foot that could have opened a can of peas, not the ones that Osgood said to Tommy Smith that Hutch said someone put on his face and not one fell off. That was in the middle of a brawl at Anfield when Tommy was partnering the ageing Ron Yeats. The outcome was a match-up to the Battle of Navarone. On the left wing in our Seattle team was the wonderful Tommy Hutchison, who left Coventry City to join us and what a bargain buy he turned out to be. The loping Hutch took on full-backs for a laugh and toyed with them. He was great both on and off the playing field, which is vital in the dressing room, with his wit as quick as his feet. I loved playing balls to Tommy and just stood and watched him take over the show. Tommy was the man who scored two goals in that FA Cup Final against Spurs at Wembley, the only problem, though, was that one was past his own goalkeeper with a flying header. The match was a 1-1 draw and Spurs went on to win the replay easily. Tommy was one hell of a player! Up front we had two other former Derby lads, Jeff Bourne, a goalscoring machine in training and when he came off of our bench. Roger Davies was the leader of the pack that one season scoring goals at a high rate of knots, outscoring even the great New York mafia man Georgio Chinaglia, a wonderful player, who was turned away by Swansea City some time before. Swansea's loss was the New York Cosmo's great gain for he was to become the best ever goal machine in the North American League. And one hell of a nice man, and I am not just saying that because of his stature amongst the New York and Italian groups who ran New York amok. Alongside Davies was a young Tacoma born lad, Mark Peterson, another boy who could have made the grade here with his intelligent running and sight for goal. I loved my time playing in the USA and living a life that suited me right down to the seedy bars that came with it. But along with those there was the class in a city that never sleeps, and today is one of the greatest and most popular in the world, even 'Frazier' is aired from there!

'IF ONLY'

Talking of popularity brings us to the very last match of Chelsea's season and the match that the Chelsea faithful wanted them needing a point to stay in the

Premiership, 'if only' was their wish. But they were doomed before coming through the gates of Roman Abramovich's new home. Leeds United lost in a match that was as boring compared to the encounters with these bitter rivals over the years. No Hunter, Bremner and Giles, biting every time we came to have possession, a 'mean machine' in every sense of the word and the FA Cup Final replay of 1970 was one of the most fiercely competed match as you'd ever wish to see. This day, however was a non-event and Chelsea won with a goal from Jesper Gronkjaer in the twentieth minute in front of another packed house.

Chelsea had finished in their highest position since winning the title way back in 1954/55 but this was not the end of a season that will be forever remembered for the love tangle between the Tinker and Talisman and the news to follow from the home of Porto was that Jose Mourinho would be joining the Premiership the following season and all that was needed now was the departure of the manager who had left a place in the hearts of every single Chelsea supporter, although by most, including myself, for the messing up of the match in Monte Carlo where he tinkered once too often and opened the door for a mighty fightback by Morientes and his Monaco teammates.

WISECRACKS

Chelsea have no interest in tomorrow's FA Cup Final. Or do they?

Dennis Wise has become something of a legendary figure at Stamford Bridge to the point of nearly getting enough votes in the all-time 'Chelsea Dream Team' the name of a new book written by my great friend Martin Knight and new one Paul Lilliard. I was delighted that my name appeared in a team that included Ron Harris, Peter Bonetti, Eddie McCreadie, Peter Osgood and Charlie Cooke. The last two players being the King and Prince of Stamford Bridge in those heady days of the late sixties and early seventies. Apart from 'The Cat' and 'Chopper' that's not bad for four drunkards!

Martin and Paul came up with great idea and the response has been terrific. Gianfranco Zola has also been a great favourite of the fans after his last season where he played magnificently. He, like all great players, makes the game look simple with his silky first touch and vision as wide as the M6 – that is if you are heading to Stoke-on-Trent, the place I had the greatest of pleasures being a big part of Tony Waddington's life, and he mine. Jimmy Greaves is arguably the greatest player to ever pull a royal blue shirt over his head for a club who remain the greatest underachievers in the history of the game we love so much. That is when you look over to the north side of London at Tottenham Hotspurs and Arsenal, having both won the 'Double' with the Gunners – another old club of mine – winning it more than once – in fact twice under Arsene Wenger alone. Then of course there is the great feat of last season, going the entire Premiership season undefeated. The FA Cup final tomorrow always brings back memories of one of the worst days of my life after that heartbreaking day at West Bromwich Albion, when going down the only hole in the

Hawthorns pitch, and with my luck possibly the entire Midlands. But seven years ago I underwent some pretty scary moments in the Intensive Trauma Unit after an accident that dwarfed all others throughout my life!

If there were six players from our team it just goes to show just how highly thought of by every one at Stamford Bridge, except Ken Bates the ex-Chairman of the Board!

Ron Harris was chosen at right back which I totally disagree with for 'Chopper' was the man who marked the most dangerous man in a different coloured shirt. My vote would go to Gary Locke, a terrific young player who was unfortunate to break into the team as Dave Sexton was dismantling it. Gary had all the attributes needed to become a Chelsea legend himself along with two other players who were vastly underrated. Colin Pates and Micky Fillery both had wonderful ability but – as has been said of me – if born on another day, life would have been more fruitful!

I have no hesitation in selecting Gary as Chelsea's best right-back in my years in the game. He also would have relished the role of wing-back – where do these stupid names come from – today? No wingers under Ramsey? No more inside forwards?

Simply midfielders! ·

Wise had declared himself fit to make a return to the Millwall starting line-up and how – after about forty minutes – he must have regretted that decision – as a ball was whipped across the face of the goal and without looking over his right shoulder, was found guilty of the cardinal sin of ballwatching. As 'Dennis the Menace' shaped to volley the ball out of Cardiff and into the old Kent Road, Ronaldo came from behind him to slam the ball into the net against a team who had done so well for forty minutes by keeping them at bay. A stalemate at half-time would have been no more than the underdogs deserved and that would have done wonders for their confidence coming out for the second half, instead they were facing an uphill struggle – a near impossible task – for such a mistake.

The result, the ball nestled into the back of the south Londoner's net by Portuguese international, Ronaldo. What was going to happen next was just as bad, as two such men with a wealth of experience – Wilkins and Wise – prepared their team for the second half more like Eric and Ernie.

By sitting back and giving the Premiership champions of last season all the time and space to cut them down without putting any pressure on themselves. Wise surely knew from his experience with Wimbledon beating red-hot favourites Liverpool in that incredible match won by a great Lawrie Sanchez header and the first ever penalty miss in a Cup Final by the usually deadly John Aldridge. But you only get those kind of breaks if you are prepared to venture into the other team's half, something Millwall failed to do. These two Chelsea legends should have apologised to their team and travelling fans for such instructions and even the Millwall faithful where I were – in the bar in the Dee European Hotel in Cyprus – were cursing such tactics as they roared their lions on without any response before United had picked them off with two goals by Ruud van Nisterooy, one being a penalty and the third a simple tap-in. At 0-0 they could have something to build on, at 0-1 they were facing a long second half. At 0-2 they were dead but the final goal buried them alive. United 3 Millwall 0. Another great friend Michael Bloomfield, better known as 'Millwall Mick' – who can be seen in the controversial movie The Football Factor – was not a happy bunny at the way his team went down like a night in the lanes of a bowling alley. But at last they made their way there and for the first third of the game didn't look too uncomfortable until that uncharacteristic mistake by their player/manager. Dennis has been around long enough to know that you can't take chances in and around your box when playing a team with so many dangerous and potent players around!

THE CHAMPIONS LEAGUE FINAL

As a Cup Final it was a little disappointing because of the one-way traffic in the second half, which left Sir Alex Ferguson beaming at the final whistle for up until they met Arsenal in the semi-final it looked as if – for the first time for so long – that their trophy cupboard at Old Trafford would look like Old Mother Hubbard's. Three days later there was the sacking of Gerard Houllier of Liverpool and one I feel was overdue for the red side of the Mersey were consistently a shadow of the Liverpool of old and I am not a lover of the French manager for two reasons, firstly not picking David Ginola when he was the French National team manager, and secondly the way Roy Evans was treated after the role of joint managers. So the big day was here, though no Liverpool, Manchester United, Arsenal and Chelsea. Jose Mourinho – Chelsea's likely new head coach – was at the party with Porto the team who put out Manchester United in the quarter-final and so was Didier Deschamps – the former Chelsea player and now boss of Monaco, the conquerors of Chelsea in the last round. The build-up for the final was terrific in a stadium that puts us to shame as we continue to build a new Wembley. All the big guns were out of the competition, Real Madrid, AC Milan and of course our representatives. This match really should have been the Tinkerman's final curtain, as Francis Albert Sinatra would sing. Chelsea had every right to feel they should have been there on the strength of two forty-five minute performances of complete dominance over the French side in Monte Carlo and Stamford Bridge and then of course United would feel the same way as they led Porto into the last minute of the second leg at Old Trafford. But this was the knock-out stages of the Champions League and it only takes a split second to throw the game away and end all of your dreams through one tiny mistake. Fernando Morientes – who scored four goals in the beating of both Chelsea and Real Madrid – was the main hope of Monaco while Deco was the player Porto pinned their hopes on with a little more magic. The first half-just like Saturday – looked heading for a stalemate – when the ball arrived at the feet of Carlos Alberto – no relation to the great Brazilian captain of the

'70 World Cup winning side – and in one swift move he tried to knock a ball through an eye of the needle to a teammate and as the ball ricocheted off a defender, he hit a stunning volley out of the outstretched arms of the unsighted Monaco keeper. 1-0 the same as Saturday. But the only difference being that Monaco – who were no strangers to falling behind – for they had come from behind in the last two matches leading up to this final in Germany. But the thing here was that Porto have shown that once they are in front they are comfortable to hit their opponents on the break. I have no doubt Deschamps words would have been "If we can do it against Real Madrid and Chelsea we can do it again tonight."

Whilst in the opposing dressing room Mourinho would have been telling his players "You have been magnificent at holding onto leads up until tonight, so let's keep our discipline and go and do it one last time."

The new Chelsea boss wrote the script as Monaco started to throw bodies forward in search of that all-important equaliser. That was the way it was and with the French outfit throwing numbers in and around the Porto box a move broke down and as quick as a flash Deco was in possession. The Portuguese international ran at the French defence before slipping the ball to his left and keeping his run going, feinting to rush into the six yard box, pulled out and made just enough space for a return pass. He controlled it delicately and after disguising to put his shot to the keeper's left he sent four of the opposition the wrong way with a delightful finish. 2-0 and the same as Saturday. A brilliantly executed finish, which made me laugh after reading the *Daily Times* as a journalist wrote that Deco was left with the simplest of chances. As I have said before it is true that teams are at their most vulnerable after scoring, but Mourinho's team were ultra-professional and stood firm to anything Morientes and co. could throw at them. All I have to say to the man from the *Times* is that "maybe it looked easier from your seat in the press box but with the player still having to get the ball past four of the opposition, you must have been drinking with George Best, Oliver Reed and yours truly on the afternoon of the game."The goal itself reminded me so much of the way Peter Osgood and I used to pull off such a move, for many times I had got to the by-line and right as I was to make contact with the ball, Ossie would put on the brakes and pull himself away from his marker. There is absolutely nothing the defender can do, especially some of the big lumps Ossie had to contend with. For you elder Chelsea statesmen, you may remember the evening at the Bridge when we came from a two-goal first leg deficit against Bruges and with the score level, I found myself on the left goal-line at the Shed End and between us we worked the oracle just the same way. Ossie pulled out and I rolled the ball into his path and joined the spectators from my vantage point to see the master at work. Many people say that was the greatest night ever at the Bridge, even to this day!

Back to Germany and Porto now making life easier for themselves by scoring a third, which killed off Monaco completely. 3-0 and once again, the same as Saturday.

But the difference here was that Porto did the job against a very good team who never lay down and died like Millwall who caved in like a bunch of dominoes. Porto were now the new Champions of Europe and Mourinho the most wanted man in European football, and it will only be days now before the 'Dead Man' will certainly be walking!

Chelsea and Roman Abramovich have their man!

Just how Chelsea will handle the funeral of the Tinkerman, only the men who pull the purse-strings know. But although it was planned months prior they did not take into account of the huge character of the Roman. He is a true Roman in every sense of the word, in fact he stood defiant until the end and I can only say that he reminded me of the character in one of my all-time favourite movies, Julius Ben Hur, a man proud of his heritage and can walk out the front of Stamford Bridge exactly the way he came in, but with a little difference of being quite a few million richer. I and thousands of Chelsea fans applaud him for that!

It is nothing to be ashamed about, for Chelsea wanted a different character and I can never blame them for that, after all it was Mr Abramovich's roubles that stopped Chelsea going into receivership last July and there are millions of football fans over the world who don't realise just how close that really was!

In today's football climate Claudio – the undisputed Tinkerman – is a gentleman who was in the right job at the wrong time. It is understandable these people want their own man, and it still remains a mystery who really bought all of those players last summer!

MUZZY IZZET

I had my reservations quite a while ago and my curiosity led me to be a little more convinced when a great friend of mine – Johnny Westwood – told me of a story regarding his good friend Muzzy Izzet. Muzzy was sold by Ruud Gullit for pittance and has done fantastically well for Leicester City since his move there, however Chelsea showed interest in having him return. And I have no doubt that he was, and still is, good enough to have got in any of Chelsea's teams since. Anyhow, he was interviewed – for the sake of a better word – by Colin Hutchison, Ken Bates's right hand and money man. Once they had talked about the financial side of the transfer the young Turk asked why he had not be seen by the manager Gianluca Vialli, and to his astonishment was told that "I would not worry too much about the manager for he will not be here too much longer."

Muzzy is a man of great principals and therefore the deal fell through, because of the way they operated at Chelsea Football Club. He has now become a Birmingham City player and I have no doubt he will do a blinding job for Steve Bruce. Both Muzzy and Matt Elliott have held Leicester City together for a long time and I was very surprised how Elliott never became a Chelsea player, as little did I know back in the seventies that I knew his father from around our neck of the woods. He has been as good a defender as any in this country over the years. The moral of the story is just how many other deals have been done without the manager knowing!

I am sure there will be no way in the world that Jose Mourinho would stand for such a thing. I write this piece on a British Airway flight from Famagusta and must thank Colin Burr – a staunch Blue from our days – for arranging my flights for me. I have had to cut my trip short for yet another operation at the Middlesex Hospital the day following my return. I have lost count of how many times I have been wheeled down to theatre and there was a time in those scary days – for my family – in the Intensive Trauma Unit when they literally had to bring the operating theatre to my bedside as they thought by being so weak it could have been fatal. Football kept me alive all through this, even my surgeons have told me that, for I had been working out to the very day of my accident. But a little down the road those great memories of playing against the likes of Best, Moore, Pele, Cruyff, Beckenbauer and Dave Mackay kept me from going out of my mind in those early days. I had always tasted the best things in life and wanted to taste them again, so I had to make a firm decision, that my work in the gymnasium came first from now on and that will stay that way for the rest of my days here on earth. I mention Bobby not only for his brilliance on a football field, but also because Betty Shine, the well known healer, had been contacted by both of us, and with myself I believe I left my body back in the December of 1997 whilst under the strongest of sedations. I look forward to putting the final touches to this manuscript and hope you are enjoying it as much as I have bringing it to you, whether a football lover or not. There are some nasty people in our lives but I believe the angels far outweigh the opposition and that counts from the very first until the very last whistle – in my case – blows. In life that is of course!

Call it the fat lady singing or whatever you will, for there is always an ending, only on this occasion I feel an angel has flown over Stamford Bridge just like Mr Abramovich did some twelve months ago.

MOURINHO

Fernando Morientes is the latest name to be linked with Chelsea as he told the French Sports L'Equipe that: "We are coming to an agreement and can say the deal is 90 per cent done. I really like the idea but the finalisation of the contract is taking longer than expected." Morientes adviser Joan Palencia said that: "Chelsea are in love with Fernando. The Russian is delighted and is very impressed with him. He thinks he is a wonderful player."

Morientes was the leading scorer in the Champions League this season with an impressive eleven goals and he says that: "People forget so easily that no one can force me to go to a team where I don't want to play. I play football to be happy."

It was also reported that the Blues were closing in on nineteen-year-old Peruvian striker Jefferson Farfan. But the Allanza Lima star has not made enough international appearances to qualify for a work permit in the

Premiership so Chelsea are planning to sign him and farm him out to PSV Eindhoven but the plan had hit a brick wall. A spokesman for the young star said that: "Chelsea have made a serious offer and we are analysing it."

It was also reported David Beckham had squashed all rumours of a move back to Chelsea by pledging his future to Real Madrid. The headline in the *Daily Mail* went like this: "I'M STAYING": And the words by the brilliant Jeff Powell: Forget The midfield diamond and the manager's platinum salary, nothing could be better calculated to give England lift-off for Euro 2004 than Golden Balls reaffirming his vows to Real Madrid. At the stroke of a pen, David Beckham's declaration of loyalty to his paymasters will end most of the freak show distraction, which his own celebrity presence was threatening to inflict on England's expedition. Maybe he has pledged himself to Real rather than Chelsea for all the right, patriotic reasons. Maybe not!

But whatever the motivation for yesterday's joint statement from Mr and Mrs Beckham, it has not come a minute too soon. Furthermore it represents a step back from the seductive, glamorous yet ultimately superficial world of global propaganda and commercial marketing – a partial return to the solid, working-class values of the east end of London from whence he rose to stardom. Here if I am sadly mistaken, is Beckham's realisation that he comes from a place where you take pride in your job and your willingness to see it through. Nor can there be any going back now for that would be unforgivable. David Beckham's duty, before he returns to salvaging his reputation in Madrid, is to apply every fibre of his being to his country's cause. He needs to repeat the sort of heroic performance with which he rescued 2002 World Cup qualification from the jaws of defeat against the Greeks at Old Trafford. Nothing less will suffice in Portugal. If David Beckham can reproduce that form, his public will have genuine cause to admire him – and thank his wife for sticking by him through those lurid allegations of infidelity. For Victoria Beckham is prepared to lie back and think of England in such trying circumstances, then the nation is in her debt too.

Jeff really is a master at work. I just love the last couple of lines, mate!

GEORGE RAYNOR

I was also interested in John Dillon's column for one simple reason for he mentions a man who my family came across at Butlins in Skegness so many years ago when my brother John and I were youngsters – we were at Primary School at the time. There were so many children around but my father, Bill, made sure that he let him know, in no uncertain terms, that his son was going to be a real player, it went like this: Steve McLaren is back in the England fold, but only offered as an emergency replacement for Brian Kidd. David Platt, who has just been sacked after failure with the England under 21's, was the last Englishman offered any serious sort of job in Continental football at Sampdoria three years ago. Humbling for his nation, it all fell though because he did not have the required coaching qualifications. What a contrast it made to the long past days when an Englishman, George Raynor, revolutionalised the game by creating the immortal Hungarian team that won at Wembley in 1953. Dillon of the Express went on to say that: Amongst the names touted as potential replacements for the Italian Claudio Ranieri at Chelsea, there have been no Englishmen. The bitter twist here is that Mourinho, a man who learned at Bobby Robson's knee, seems favourite for the job. Mourinho's achievements with the Champions League winners Porto – last year's UEFA Cup had been both impressive and rapid. His record outstrips anything young English guns have managed. But then the likes of Sam Allardyce and Alan Curbishley operate in a league that is more demanding, there is no opportunity for them to flex their strengths on the European stage. Porto, by contrast, win the championship every year whoever is in charge. This does not detract from Mourinho's success. And at least he is an Anglophile. He is eager to work in England as soon as he can. His current base in Porto has long been Europe's most Anglophile city too. It even has red telephone boxes and a famous bridge across the Douro that looks remarkably like the one spanning the Tyne in Robson's spiritual home town. The landmark sight of Portugal's little England was built by Frenchman, Gustav Eiffel.

That man at Butlins was George Raynor!

SKIPPER WARNS THE BLUES OFF TREZEGUET

Chelsea have been warned against signing striker David Trezeguet by French teammate Marcel Desailly. Chelsea owner Roman Abramovich wants to sign two strikers and the Juventus star is a top candidate along with Andrei Shevchenko of AC Milan and Fernando Morientes who is on loan to Monaco. But Trezeguet claims have been undermined by a damming report from Chelsea captain Desailly, who has seen him at close quarters on International duty. The defender does not doubt his ability, but believes he could be disruptive in the dressing room and he has advised the club not to buy him. In Trezeguet's favour however is that Juventus are keen to sell him now, 12 months before his contract runs out. Abramovich is believed to have made Shevchenko his number one target, but AC Milan would want a huge fee for the Ukranian. Chelsea are also proposing a £9million move for Morientes, who scored in both legs against them in the Champions League for the French club. Abramovich sent chief executive Peter Kenyon and his right hand man Eugene Tenenbaum to Monaco last week to negotiate a deal. And Morientes said that: "I'm getting close to resolving my future."

Chelsea will sell both Crespo and Jimmy Floyd Hasselbaink to make room for the new arrivals.

I myself think that Desailly is completely out of order for he was the one player who wanted out of Chelsea just before Mr Moneybags came in with all of his roubles and did a U-turn for financial reasons, no other reason at all!

That is not a sign of someone who wanted to play as long as he could for the club, it was strictly business and after the way he performed for the team this season he never earned his salary. He was the weakest link in a defence that played better with Billy Gallas alongside John Terry.

RANIERI'S SET
HE'LL TAKE A MILLION FOR NEW MOVE

As reported by Raoul Simons of the *Standard*: Claudio Ranieri will probably settle for no more than a £1million in his ongoing compensation row with Chelsea. The Italian had hoped for as much as £6million after being axed as coach at Stamford Bridge with three years left on his contract. Chelsea dispute this claim, arguing that any financial loss from his departure will be mitigated by the salary from his next coaching job, likely to be Valencia. The club's legal advisers say Ranieri would only be entitled to the full pay-out if he did not work for the next three years. That appears unlikely after it was revealed yesterday that he had agreed personal terms to return to the Spanish champions. Despite the aggressive public stance taken by his advisers towards Chelsea, *Standard Sport* understands behind the scenes that they have adopted a more realistic position over the settlement in light of the offer from Valencia. If Ranieri joins them – or any other club – payouts from Chelsea could be severely restricted and may depend on the club's goodwill. After unveiling new manager Jose Mourinho, Peter Kenyon outlined the club's stance saying that: "Ken Bates was responsible for Claudio's contract and we will honour it. Part of the contract is about him mitigating the cost, which is a standard clause. In layman's terms that means if he doesn't get a job in three years we will continue to pay him. If he walks into a job he's not due anything by the terms of his contract."

With the bitter row simmering, Ranieri's UK representative Phil Smith responded to Kenyon's comments by saying that: "I heard what Kenyon said. If that means payment of all monies and his season's bonuses that are due under the balance of the contract, without deductions, then there is no dispute."

ALL CHANGE AT CHELSEA FOR THE JOSE REVOLUTION

Inside of the *Standard* there is a wonderful photograph of the 'Three Wise Men', Peter Kenyon, Jose Mourinho and Roman Abramovich, standing in hysterics and it was one of those where the newspaper should have put a few quid down for the best caption. Once again the 'Fly on the wall' comes into play here, and just lately every photograph of Peter Kenyon I have seen has been one of sheer delight. Underneath this particular photo were the words: Happy Days – new boss Jose Mourinho in buoyant mood with Roman Abramovich and Peter Kenyon yesterday. I find it interesting how Mourinho, only a few short days ago won the Champions League with Porto and if you had been in the Intensive Trauma Unit – for my stint of eight and a half weeks – and woke up to this you would have thought that Chelsea just had, such was the glee on the faces of the three men who look like they are ready to take on the world. Chelsea, I am sure have made the right decision and if the 'Three Wise Men' are caught by a snapper at this time next year with a duplicate of this photo you will know they just have. There were several things that caught my eye after a piece coming up written by Ian Chadband – which I feel is perfect for the ending of the book for you. I could not resist including a short story in the *Sun* about one of the greatest talents this country has ever seen. Paul Gascoigne has taken being funny to a new level in a career where he has had several chances to prove himself and, as the European Championships loom, my mind flashes back to Euro '96' and his wonderful goal against the Scots. A long ball was hit into the opposition half and Gascoigne and Henry went in search for it, and just when the big centre-back thought he had it, Gascoigne flipped it over his head leaving him sprawling in no man's land, and the England midfield player went around his giant frame and coolly volleyed it past the helpless Andy Goram. What a goal! What a player! What a talent! What a waste!

COCAINE

As those of you who know me will tell you, I go off the rails every now and then for it is a questionable temperament that would sometimes lead me astray. Almost like that runaway car in the Mile End Road on that black evening some time ago, going wild with nothing anyone else could do. Before my return to Stoke City in the early eighties I was out of work once again after leaving Seattle through no fault of my own. It was simply a case of a new owner coming in who could not afford to pay my wages. He knocked me for over a hundred grand in my contract. With no job and no home I moved in with my great pal TD which was recipe for a right old knees-up. He lived in a high rise building estate in South London on the thirty-something floor named the 'Dungeon' and part of my training, apart from running the park opposite, was running up the stairs whilst he took the lift. I am a certainty to get into anything that is going, but as I say I'll try anything once!

Well this once was cocaine that I first came across in Tampa Bay, Florida, whilst out with a couple of pals, one old, Ken Adam, and one new his mate Bobby, who drove a Cadillac. This particular day we went down to Clearwater across the Causeway called the Howard Franklyn Bridge. Anyhow, Ken was in the front and all of a sudden he went into the glove department to get a tiny packet that he laid out on his armrest whilst I was wondering what was going on. He chopped it up and then he rolled up a twenty-dollar bill and began taking this stuff up his nose. Then Bobby leant across and did the same, then Ken asked me if I done coke. I said that I hadn't, but I'd give it a go. I leant forward and blew the lot all over the place. I cannot begin to tell you the kind of names they called me. Then I gathered it was very expensive. I was more careful the next time and took in this substance. Then after a good few hours out on the beach-front hotel drinking all kinds of concoctions we stopped on the way home at a friends for a Dinner Party, where I was sitting opposite a young lady I knew from our local bar, The Proud Lion. Next thing I knew they were handing round this silver tray with more of this stuff on it and it got to me and once again I snorted it – is the term they use, I believe. This girl opposite was not my type but after a couple more vodka and orange juices I was looking at a complete darling. I went into the bathroom to splash some cold water on my face but she still looked great. It would have been a case of going to make love to Sharon Stone and waking up with Steve Stone. No offence, Steve mate, but there is quite some difference, even you'd agree!

Then some ten years when out and about with TD I got involved again, this time in the Tin Pan Alley the afternoon joint owned by the Frazer's, and I got involved in a friendship with Mad Frankie's son Frank Junior. His stepbrother Jimmy ran the place and we spent many hours having fun amongst all the rascals that would socialise there. But young Frank and a girl I was seeing there were the main reasons we found ourselves in there most afternoons. Some time ago Jimmy died tragically after being hit by a car – in all places – the United States of America. As soon as I found out, I found it so hard to believe for nobody hardly walks across the road there for being 'nicked, for Jaywalking. I saw Jimmy at Tommy and Rene Wisbey's wedding Anniversary some five years ago and that was the last time I heard of both Jimmy and Frank junior. I remember having a very long day there and ended up in a house where I never knew I was there and this night lead into Friday morning and I had to train the day before the new season, but had to call in with a virus. Let's just say if I had been Rio Ferdinand I would have had good reason for missing a drug test. That was the last time I touched the stuff, for really I had never needed such a drug for I could be on a high on booze alone. My friend George Petros told me some days later that I looked like one of the KKK gang standing against a white door, he could only see the whites of my eyes and my clothing, the rest of me was completely like a glossy white paint.

I mention this because these are the problems facing the big money earners in today's game and I would not be giving away any secrets because it is rife here now in England. In our day we could just about afford a good meal at our favourite restaurant on a Saturday night and then expect a letter from the bank manager the following Thursday morning as regular as clockwork. I often wonder how we had such great times on so little money!

A funny thing happened after my first season as a first team player, going into Dave Sexton's office to renew my contract. When he asked me what I was looking for, I said that now that I was a regular first team player, I expected to be on no more and no less money than my teammates. His answer to that was "When you can come in here and put a dozen international caps on my table you can demand such a thing."

So I was on £75 a week, but the crazy thing is had I played for Sexton all of my career, I would have been on that same figure twenty years later, because I only ever got two caps.

As Greavesie would say, funny old game!

I was obviously missing something here because I was always led to believe that you got your weekly wage for playing for your club not your country. A cap alone should be your reward for representing them!

But Dave was never around by the time I won my first cap and had I stayed at Chelsea under his management I would never have got that because it was under Tony Waddington that my form took a different direction. I was reborn under his management. It was ironic that the only thing I had won – apart from the European Cup Winners Cup winner's medal is all I have to show for a career that needed no exaggeration when it came to the highs and the lows. And it wasn't until I got to Seattle that I enjoyed a longer stint of success where, although still being hampered with that chronic ankle injury, I managed to play consistently at the top of my game. In today's modern game caps are given away like confetti and that must disturb Robert Chelsea Moore who is no doubt looking down on us. As I come to the end of this book I received a telephone call from Neil Barnett asking if I'd do an interview for Chelsea TV for a run of programmes called 'Legends' to which I said it would be a pleasure. Whilst sitting there in between filming, he whispered that the Tinkerman was in the building sorting out his compensation, this was to be Claudio's final curtain. This was coincidental because of being nearly a year since that first call from SKY asking me to come to the ground and give my views on the Russian takeover. I thought this weird because that was the day I began writing this book, now I am called in again – although for a different reason – only the second time I had been invited to the ground. These were the only couple of times I had been able to enter the ground without being hassled about 'What I was doing there' and did I have a pass or ticket. Orders from above!

But this was different for Mr Bates had left the building!

This also brought back memories of the last conversation I had with Matthew Harding after lunch in Langans when after I asked him about the future at Chelsea he answered swiftly saying that "I am just having to wait for him to die" that only ten days before his helicopter went down under the strangest of circumstances. I felt at the time this was or could have been 'Foul play'. I am still not convinced to this day, that it wasn't!

Had Matthew been with us today, he would have loved the challenge of the Russians and I am certain he would have welcomed the entrance made by the new man, Jose Mourinho, coming to take his beloved Blues to a new level.

'THE LORD GIVETH THE LORD TAKETH AWAY'

I was just perusing through the Dailies when I came across a very funny story concerning one of the greatest talents have seen in my days on earth. Paul Gascoigne – out of his new book Gazza – told of a story where he once decided to end it all. A distraught Gascoigne wanted to commit suicide after the death of his pal David Cheek, aged 43, who died of alcoholic poisoning following the pair of them out on a bender in 1998. The troubled star – then a Middlesborough player – stood on a platform at Stevenage Railway Station waiting to throw himself under the next train.

After waiting and waiting.........He walked up to a Railway man and demanded to be told what time the next train was coming through, only to be told he had missed it. He said I asked the man "Where's the fucking train only to be told that it had been and gone. That's when I began crying. Even when killing myself, I couldn't get it right."

He then called his estranged wife Sheryl who collected him and took him to a hotel. Later manager Bryan Robson took him to the Priory Clinic in London. He opens his heart out in his new book – a best seller – and I began to understand this poor bloke a little more. I am enjoying his book and can see some parallels and am delighted that I read it before finishing mine because of my understanding the true genius that was totally wasted by foolish incidents both on and off the playing field. He was on the brink of becoming an English type Diego Maradona but his tackle on Gary Charles in that FA Cup final at Wembley against Nottingham Forest became his Achilles Heal, after trying to become the first player in such a final done for GBH. His ability was unquestionable and for a short while he was the best inside-forward in world football. Like Bobby Moore once said of me that "Alan Hudson could have conquered the world and for a short while he supposedly did." Paul has phobias about phobias all through no fault of his own. I believe 'not' for the first time that here on earth that we are asked certain questions by the man upstairs and Paul – like myself – only had the answers with a 'bag of wind' at his feet.

He could unlock defences like James Caan in the movie 'The Thief'.

He tells stories of a schoolboy that was not much different than most of us, mine being just a David Beckham free–kick from the front gates of Stamford Bridge. Or as you Chelsea fans might say, an Ian Hutchinson throw-in.

There are several parallels that have made me cringe but at the same time forgive him for his daftness, which brings me warmth at a time where the world is not a very nice place to live in most of the time. This is purely a case of 'The Lord Giveth and the Lord taketh away'.

Michael Parkinson would ask him gently "Now then Paul, what would you like to be remembered for." To which he would answer with that smile which is wider than the River Thames "As long as it has nothing to do with the dentists chair." Amen!

My very good friend Paul Miller once told me of a great night out in his company in Glasgow and spoke of the man in glowing terms. That's nice to know. Paul made his name in that great Spurs team with Perryman, Hoddle, Ardiles and Hazzard before cracking it in the city. I wish Paul Gasoigne well in all he takes on and wonder just how Jose Mourinho would have handled the two of us, no, not one, but two.

I also urge him not to go train-spotting anymore!

NOVEMBER L, UNKNOWN aged 99

I have touched here and there on my own personal hell where some seven years ago I was mowed down by a speeding car as I was stepping on to the pavement in the Mile End Road in east London. The driver – an Indian – was allowed to walk free as I lay dying in the Resuscitation Room at the Royal London Hospital and tagged – not quite John Doe – although the old bill were called out on a 'fatality'. The tag said simply name NOVEMBER L, UNKNOWN aged 99. So this gives me the opportunity to thanks those wonderful surgeons and doctors Mr Frank Cross, Mr David Goodier, Mr Otto Chan, Mr David Badenoch, Professors Mundy and Norman Williams. David Goodier was responsible for piecing up my pelvis and had the daunting job of amputating my legs had they not found a sample machine in the Operating Theatre that stopped the massive blood loss. Professor Williams had the job of testing his Gracilis Neosphincter Operation on me and I had every confidence in him doing so. I was warned by more than one person not to have this done for the amount of surgery I had done in the Intensive Trauma Unit but there was nothing going to stop me having my colostomy reversed. This was no normal operation as my sphincter – which holds your stomach together – had been sliced off by the splinters of my pelvis and this operation had to be performed in four stages. I had as much confidence with the Professor as I did with my manager at Stoke City and can pay him no higher compliment. The only thing we did not agree on was that he was a Leeds United supporter, poor man!

After the third visit to the Operating Theatre I can only say I knew nothing about pain before this. The following morning he and his team visited me and before he could get a word in I said in a low voice "What the hell were you doing to me down there" to which he smiled, saying, "Alan, you gave us some tussle down there yesterday."

Anyhow the news was good and on his way through the hallway he stopped where my mother was sitting and said "Mrs Hudson, can I tell you that you have one hell of a son in there" in which my mother replied "I know that Professor."

With my pelvis, David Goodier was minutes from removing my legs when someone suggested that they try a machine in the corner that had been brought in by a rep just three days before. They could not stop the blood and were worried about both Gangrene and sepsis setting in. Someone looked at this machine that did not even have a plug attached to it, and they had to telephone the manufacturers to ask if it was in working order. The voice on the other end of the phone was positive, thank the lord, and the rest is history. But my family told me some time later that David came out of the OR with his hands held high as if he had just scored the winning goal in an FA Cup Final. He had the pads in his hands!

The machine was called a C-Clamp and I thank that rep whoever and wherever he is. Had it gone wrong my first job when I came around fifty-nine days later was how to take my own life!

It was simple in my eyes; all I would have had to do was save as many sleepers, painkillers, anti-depressants and every other form of medication given me. Then once I had collected them, get my favourite 'tipple' and go out in style, it was that simple and calculated, no fuss or bother to anyone!

People I have told laugh at me but I don't joke about things like that and I would have seen that as my only way out!

This is something that drives me on in my quest to have a better life than in a wheelchair, which I would have possibly been in had I not faced up to my demons in the way that I did. My uncle George and I went through the barrier together, the sun, the rain, the icy blowing wind and all else they could throw at us. This made Leeds United look like a band of wimps, and I am not talking about today's version. My schedule in the gymnasium now is an hour and a half on the cycle, five hundred sit-ups carried out in the steam room, many upper leg and knee exercises and about another fifteen minutes working on any part of my anatomy that I feel I needed. If you ask any old professional footballer just how tough pre-season training was, they will tell you it was close to hell, well I have that every day of my life in that gymnasium.

SPECTACULAR

This is how David Goodier summed up in my medical report: The left side is recovering but may take another year before it does so completely and he is left with stiffness in his hips, knees, ankles and feet, that will require a lot of physiotherapy to overcome and also will probably not recover completely. He has ahead of him further surgery to his rectum and bladder but overall his recovery thus far is nothing short of 'spectacular' but in no small amount this is due to the dedicated team of Anaesthetists, and ITU Consultants, Registrars, Senior House Officers, Nurses, Physiotherapists, Speech Therapists, Dieticians, Urologists, General Surgeons, Microbiologists, Renal Physicians and many other specialists of all grades and qualifications who had an active part in his management.

My nights in the Treves Ward – named after the doctor who treated the Elephant Man Joseph Merrick – were sheer hell after coming out of the ITU. I was hallucinating, coming down off the morphine and other wonderful drugs they used. I once saw my father in the corner of my room but he turned out to be a coat hanging on a peg whilst I was complimentary to the nurses for the wonderful white wine, which was water from out of the tap. But it is now reality for both Jose Mourinho and myself, although I have more experience than him in holding my nerve before the big occasion. Before each and every operation, I prepared myself professionally leaving no stone unturned knowing as soon as they came to get me for theatre I could go in there in an extremely positive and determined mood. I am still undergoing surgery but none as life-threatening as my days in the ITU, where at one time they had to bring the theatre to me for I was much too weak to move from my bed. They thought that I could die if moved. I always looked on surgery as another step in the right direction and normality. I have lost none of my zest for life and look forward to the new season coming up under Jose Mourinho.

EUROPEAN CHAMPIONSHIPS

Before I go into the Big Match I will just run you through my thoughts of the Euro 2004 in Portugal. One thing is outstanding again and that is players shouting from the rooftops about what they are and what they aren't going to do this summer. Anyhow, not surprisingly once again it backfired. Nobody ever won a football match in the *Daily Express* or *Mirror*. England's first match was always going to be tough against the favourites France and that was what it turned out to be. We lost, but took enough out of defeat to carry us through to play the Swiss. This was a match we were fortunate to win for if the Swiss had of had a decent header of the ball, we would have gone into our third match pointless in more ways than one. Frank Lampard and Steve Gerrard went in to the tournament on the back of great seasons for their clubs but it was Wayne Rooney who stole the limelight with his rendition of Roy of the Rovers which Europe had never seen before. When you see him walk out you think he is a 'mugger' until he gets the ball between his feet. He then takes off like a spinning-top by running at the heart of defences causing them all sorts of problems. I thought the Swede made a woeful mistake not taking Jermain Defoe instead of Emille Heskey and Darius Vassell.

I said it might just rebound on him and I was right. With Michael Owen, Jermain Defoe and Wayne Rooney, we could have gone one step further I am convinced of that. Our defending against dead balls in the second match was pitiful and in David 'Calamity' James we have an overgrown midget from deadball situations. He never positions himself correctly for corners or free kicks that are whipped into our danger areas. He must start in between the goal line and six-yard line giving himself the option of just what way to go. But he remains glued to his line and that is a forward's dream and as I said we were lucky the Swiss could not roll us over after being given the initiative to do so. Frank was in good form throughout whilst the England captain was ineffective in everything he did and when it comes to missing dead ball efforts plus penalties he does not give us much more than an average Joe. When Rooney killed Croatia off, I had this feeling that we had the best opportunity since we were knocked out by the Germans in the '70' World Cup in Mexico. As for yet another howler from the 'Mug in the Middle' by disallowing Sol Campbell's header, I can only say that 'What goes around comes around' although in between that Geoff Hurst hat-trick in '66' which would not have happened if the final had been in Germany with that Russian linesman – we had the 'Hand of God' so were, it seems, still paying for that dramatic win over West Germany all those years ago. Overall I don't believe the Swede is totally clued-up on our best players in this country and wonder just what he learned from keep on playing different sides in each half leading up to the biggest competition outside of the World Cup itself. In a nutshell, we were not good enough once again, so it is back to the drawing board. Our positives were Frank Lampard, Wayne Rooney, Sol Campbell, Ledley King and let's not forget the tireless running of Michael Owen, a player who must surely be coming up to burn-out time. I expected more from Gerrard but don't want to be too critical of such a terrific player. In the end it is the end and my first job would be – if taking over the England job – to refrain my players from talking to the media, for they not only let themselves and the country down but are giving the average Joe false hopes of winning something at last!

THE WIT AND WISDOM OF JOSE MOURINHO

On not winning straight away: I'm not asking for time or limits. We shouldn't be afraid to say, 'I want to win', or defend ourselves from outside pressures by just saying we want success, but it can wait until the last year of my contract......I accept that if I don't win this year it will be a failure.

On his spat with Sir Alex Ferguson, who refused to shake his hand after the first leg of the Champions League tie because 'of all the diving': After the match in Porto he (Ferguson) had a reaction, which was nothing. As a football thing, I felt my players were not big enough to cope with such pressure, and so I had to show that I was not afraid of him, and the boss was ready for a fight.

At the end of the second leg he came into our dressing room to congratulate me and I have respect for such an important man.

And is he looking forward to renewing hostilities? I haven't come here for fights, I have come here to win, but at the right moment if I feel my players, my group and my club are in a situation where they need my help – it's like family, and they will get it.

On what he looks for in players: I love players who love to win. Those players don't only love to win in ninety minutes. They love to win every day, in every training session and in every moment in their lives. I love this type of player.

On being top: We have top players. I'm sorry I am a bit arrogant. I am a top manager. I want top things.

Is he the new Wenger: I'm not obsessive. I've loved football as long as I can remember. And I don't believe in the idea of old managers and new ones, the ones who have success and the ones who don't. I want to be one more manager but – and don't call me arrogant – it is true I am a European Champion. I'm not just one out of a bottle. I'm a special one.

On what is required by a modern manager: Somebody told me once that in modern football if a manager only knows about football he will never become a big one. We must try to understand the culture of many other areas. I'm speaking about different sciences, areas that can make a manager do better and I'm concerned about those things.

I have to be involved with the medical team, statistics, audio-visual. This is modern football.

On who'll he sign this summer: If all the names that have been written in the last few days were right I'd have a 50 player squad. Many of the names are not correct, especially in regard to the Porto players.

On the ideal size of his squad: I hate to work with a big squad. With my methodology, I need a small squad. I want 21 outfield players plus goalkeepers, no more. In top clubs, when every player is a top player, the biggest issue is about motivation.

With 30 players a third choice right-back knows that, for him to play, the first choice needs to be injured and the second suspended. If you have a big box of oranges and one is sick, one month later you have ten oranges to throw in the garbage.

On how he will work with Roman Abramovich: I don't think that I have to control Abramovich, I think he has to control me. We spent two days getting to know each other well and we were four together – with Peter Kenyon and Eugene Tenenbaum – on the boat looking to the sea, but speaking only about Chelsea and ourselves.

Abramovich knows what I am and what I want. He wants to win. He had last season where he could smell success, and I know that taste very well. He wants the same as me: to win.

On being second choice to Sven Goran Eriksson: It was natural. Mr Eriksson is a manager with a lot of prestige in England and the world. I don't mind because now I am the man. If you say to me that Mr Eriksson is going to be head coach and you are his number two then I wouldn't accept that.

On his emphasis on preparation: You must try to know every coach's style. I will study the coaches here as soon as I can. I have to try to know them well. I will have scouts during pre-season looking at all the English teams.

SIMPLICITY IS GENIUS

There is one thing for certain and that is Jose Mourinho knows exactly what he wants and won't be swayed by any other person in his quest for success at Chelsea Football Club. As regards a couple of his answers, I thought that the right full-back thing was a little strange because he didn't mention players being out of form being a first, second or third choice.

Maybe his players don't have bad matches, only joking Jose!

Also my father told me at a very early age that players are the same people on the field as they are off of it, so that was nothing new from the new head coach. The most intriguing thing right now is just who he sees good enough to take him to a second consecutive Champions League Final. He has added the right-back from Porto for over an estimated £13million so someone has to go in that position. Also he's looking at Mario Melchiot to be moving on and Jimmy Floyd and Crespo to follow. The is no doubt in my mind that the axe will be swinging as early as humanly possible for he will not want dead wood in his way when the players return for pre-season training. I look forward to this season very much and hope to bring you another book on the events of all of this. In the meantime we await news from the European Championships for I am sure he will have had his eagle eye on several players from outside of Chelsea and also looked very closely at Frank Lampard and John Terry's displays. Frank once again was impressive in a lopsided midfield and if the Swede does not do something about his decision to play Heskey then we will have to wait another four years where all the country's hopes were built up and once again let down, although they were cheated against the host nation, even if they were second best on the night.

Lastly, I must go on again about the human wall being scrubbed for it causes more problems to the defenders' team than any other problem in the game. I would have the keeper standing on the six-yard box with a player on each post and say to the player taking the kick "Come on beat us if you can." The player taking the kick would not even attempt to try such a thing. The only thing negative about this theory is that David Beckham would only be a quarter of the player he is today. The other point is about penalty shoot-outs. something I believe should take place before the two teams go into battle. What this would do is cut out any negativity by a side looking to play for such a thing and your team would all be on the field at the same time. No injuries or sending-offs to make your task harder than what it is. And with the fans knowing the outcome would be all the more nail biting and exciting. I truly believe this would make for a better game and be just as exciting before the match kicks off. I would bank on this being a success and it will take someone just to listen to my case and put this into motion. Crazy, I hear you scream, but just sit back and imagine the plusses as the game dwindles down to the last quarter of an hour. Am I a genius or a complete fool, that is entirely up to you the reader, which brings me back to what Ron Greenwood once said that "Simplicity is genius" and that gives me the edge.

THE LAST WORDS

After reading about Chelsea Football Club playing a match for Gianfranco Zola, I can only say I am bitterly disappointed by such a gesture. I – being the most local player ever – was at the club for over ten years, from a schoolboy to an England international, and never had a testimonial of any kind. Ron Harris had two of them. I am still disabled and need to visit the gymnasium every day otherwise I would be in a wheelchair. Okay, Zola is the modern day hero of Chelsea's new supporters' club, but after what happened to me I thought that the new regime might just take that into consideration. It looks to me that 'Bates or no Bates' Chelsea haven't really changed that much.